THE WESTERN HUMANITIES

THE WESTERN HUMANITIES

Roy T. Matthews & F. DeWitt Platt
MICHIGAN STATE UNIVERSITY

MAYFIELD PUBLISHING COMPANY

MOUNTAIN VIEW, CALIFORNIA
LONDON · TORONTO

Library of Congress Cataloging-in-Publication Data

Matthews, Roy T.
    The western humanities/Roy T. Matthews,
    F. DeWitt Platt
        p.   cm.
    Includes bibliographical references and index.
    ISBN 0-87484-785-0
    1. Civilization, Western—History   I. Platt,
    F. DeWitt
II. Title
CB245.M375   1991
909'.09812—dc20   91-3088
                                                    CIP

Manufactured in the United States of America

10 9 8 7 6 5 4 3 2

Mayfield Publishing Company
1240 Villa Street
Mountain View, California 94041

Sponsoring editor, C. Lansing Hays; developmental editor, Kathleen Engelberg; managing editor, Linda Toy;
production editor, Carol Zafiropoulos; art director,
Jeanne M. Schreiber; illustrators, Joan Carol, Judith
Ogus, Robin Mouat; photo researcher, Stephen Forsling;
text and cover designer Anna Post George; indexer,
Susan Coerr. The text was set in 9½/12 Palatino by
Waldman Graphics and printed on Sterling Litho Gloss
by R. R. Donnelley and Sons Company.

(Text and photo credits appear on the continuation of the copy-
right page following the index.)

To Lee Ann and Dixie

There is nothing nobler or more admirable than when two people who see eye to eye keep house as man and wife, confounding their enemies and delighting their friends, as they themselves know better than anyone.

—Homer, *The Odyssey*

PREFACE

Anyone teaching the Western humanities today faces an imposing challenge: overcoming the present-mindedness of the contemporary world. Most students, mirroring society at large, demonstrate little knowledge or even concern about the great artistic and literary monuments and movements of the Western tradition or about the political, economic, and social milestones of Western history. They seem caught up in the popular culture of the moment, forgetful of even the recent past. Very often, when they do recognize a work of art or literature, they still cannot relate it to a specific time or place or to other artistic works. In *The Western Humanities*, we address this problem by placing the cultural achievements of the Western tradition in their historical context. We discuss not only the works that were produced in successive periods but the prevailing historical and material conditions that so powerfully influenced their form and content. Our intention is to demystify the cultural record by showing that literature and the arts do not spring forth spontaneously and independently of each other but reflect a set of specific historical circumstances. By providing this substantial context, out of which both ideas and artifacts emerge, we hope to give students a deeper understanding of the meaning of cultural works and a broader basis for appreciating the humanities.

At the same time that we point out the linkages between cultural expression and historical conditions, we also emphasize the universal aspects of creativity and expression. People everywhere have the impulse to seek answers to the mysteries of human existence; to discover or invent order in the universe; to respond creatively to nature, both inner and outer; to delight the senses and the mind with beauty and truth; to communicate their thoughts and share their visions with others. Thus, another of our intentions is to demonstrate that the desire to express oneself and to create lasting monuments has been a compelling drive in human beings since before the dawn of civilized life. We believe that this emphasis will help students see that they, along with their ideas, questions, and aspirations, are not isolated from the past but belong to a tradition that began thousands of years ago.

Our third aim is to help young people prepare themselves for the uncertainties of the future. When students examine the past and learn how earlier generations confronted and overcame crises—and managed to leave enduring legacies—they will discover that the human spirit is irrepressible. In the humanities—in philosophy, religion, art, music, literature—human beings have found answers to their deepest needs and most perplexing questions. We hope that students will be encouraged by this record as they begin to shape the world of the twenty-first century.

The Western Humanities is an outgrowth of more than twenty-five years of university teaching for each of us. Instructing thousands of undergraduate students through the years left us dissatisfied with available textbooks. In our eyes the existing books failed in one of two ways: They either ignored material developments and focused exclusively on cultural artifacts without context or perspective, or they stressed political, social, and economic changes with too little or too disjointed a discussion of literature and the arts. Our goal in writing this book has been to balance and integrate these two elements—that is, to provide an analysis and an appreciation of cultural expression and artifacts within an interpretive historical framework. Our hope is that *The Western Humanities* will assist instructors in meeting today's teaching challenges as well as help the next generation of students to understand and claim their cultural heritage.

ORGANIZATION AND CONTENT

The Western Humanities is organized chronologically, in twenty-one chapters, around successive historical periods, from prehistory to the present. In our introduction for students we distinguish three sweeping historical periods—ancient, medieval, and modern—although we do not formally divide our study into parts. We explain that the first of these periods extends from about 3000 B.C. to A.D. 500 and includes the civilizations of Mesopotamia, Egypt, Greece, and Rome (covered in Chapters 1–7). The second period extends from about 500 to 1500, when Western civilization became centered in Europe and was largely dominated by the Christian church (Chapters 8–10). The third period, beginning in about 1400 and extending to the present, witnessed the gradual birth of the modern world (Chapters 11–21). Timelines are provided in the introduction to support these distinctions and to give students a basic framework for the study of the humanities.

In the body of the book, the first part of every chapter, approximately one-third by length, covers the material conditions of the era—the historical, political, economic, and social developments. From the mass of available historical information we have distilled what we consider the crucial points, always aiming to capture the essence of complex periods and to fashion a coherent narrative framework for the story of Western culture. In this discussion many of the major themes, issues, and problems of the period come into view. The remaining part of each chapter is devoted to cultural expression, both in the realm of attitude and idea—philosophy, history, religion, science—and in the realm of cultural artifact—art, music, drama, literature, and film. In this part we describe and analyze the significant cultural achievements of the age, focusing on pervasive themes, choices, and elements of style. We examine how intellectuals, artists, writers, and other creative individuals responded to the challenges presented to them by their society and how they chose values and forms by which to live. Included among these individuals are those whom the Western tradition has often neglected or discounted, namely, women and members of racial and ethnic minorities. Their experiences, roles, and rich contributions are given their rightful place alongside those of the more conventionally favored artists, thinkers, and writers.

As the integrated study of all forms of creative human expression, a survey of the humanities can be unwieldy and confusing for the beginning student. We believe that the clearest and most effective way to present this closely woven web of experience and expression is to untangle the various realms and discuss them separately in a straightforward way. Thus, our treatment of cultural achievements is broken down into sections on art, architecture, music, literature, and so on. These sections vary in length, order, and focus from chapter to chapter, just as preferred or more developed forms of expression vary from one period to another. This approach gives students an unobstructed view of each form and reveals the continuities—as well as the strains and disruptions—in that form from one period to the next.

At the same time, we work from a unified perspective and stress the integrated nature of the humanities. We emphasize that the creative works of a particular period represent a coherent response to the unique character and deepest urges of that period. By pointing out linkages and reverberations, we show that the various areas of expression are tied together by shared stylistic elements and by the themes and issues that inform and shape the era. Rather than weave our own synthesis so tightly into this discussion that instructors would have to spend their class time sorting out our point of view from the true subject of the book, we prefer to present the material in as direct a way as possible. We believe this approach gives instructors the flexibility to teach from their own strengths and perspectives, and we invite them to do so. Consistent with our desire to present the material in this book in a straightforward way, we have written *The Western Humanities* in a style we believe to be direct, succinct, and lively. We have paid special attention to sorting out and explaining complex ideas and sequences of events carefully and clearly, avoiding florid expression and its resulting obfuscation. We hope this style will succeed in making the study of the humanities accessible to a broad range of students.

Each chapter ends with a brief section describing the cultural legacy of that era. Here we show what achievements proved to be of lasting value and endured into succeeding periods, even to the present day. Students will find that some ideas, movements, or artistic methods with which they are familiar have a very long history indeed. They will also discover that the meaning and ascribed value of cultural objects and texts can change from one time and place to another. Our goal here is not only to help students establish a context for their culture but to show that the humanities have developed as a dynamic series of choices made by individuals in one era and transformed by individuals in other eras. We hope to convey both the richness and the energy of the Western tradition, to which so many have contributed and from which so many have drawn.

SPECIAL FEATURES AND LEARNING AIDS

In addition to the overall distinctive qualities of *The Western Humanities*—its interpretive context for the humanities, its balanced treatment of history and culture, its focus on the cultural legacy of each period—the book has several specific features that we believe contribute to its usefulness and appeal. Chapter 8 includes an extended discussion and analysis of Islamic history and culture, broadening the horizons of the Western tradition to cover this important area. Chapter 15, another unique chapter, presents a concise discussion of the seventeenth-century revolutions in science and political philosophy that laid the foundations for what we consider modern thinking. Chapter 21 brings us up to the present with an analysis of the events of the early 1990s and a discussion of the diverse artists and writers who express themselves in the global style known as Post-Modernism. Throughout the book we consider not just art, literature, and music but also less commonly covered topics like history, theology, and technology.

The Western Humanities is abundantly illustrated with high-quality photographs—more than 450 in all, over 300 of them in color. Accompanying the illustrations are extended captions that provide information not found in the text about the work, its meaning, its creator, or its linkages with other works. Each chapter opens with a full-page color photograph representative of the period. This photograph is reproduced again in the body of the chapter with an accompanying caption.

Several types of learning aids are incorporated in the text to help students grasp and remember information. Maps appear in every chapter, providing visual orientation, and numerous timelines graphically represent the progression of events and their relation to each other. The judicious use of color in both maps and timelines increases their usefulness.

Diagrams and line drawings are provided where careful visual explication is necessary, as in identifying the elements of an architectural style. Tables throughout the text organize historical and cultural information in a succinct and memorable way. The study of the humanities entails the use of many concepts and terms that may be unfamiliar to students. Key terms appear in bold type when they are introduced in the text; they are also defined in an extensive glossary at the end of the book. Pronunciation guidelines are given in the glossary where necessary. New terms are listed at the end of each chapter as a review and study aid.

The domains of the humanities are so vast that no book can pretend to hold them all. To extend the boundaries of the book we provide annotated lists of suggestions for further reading at the ends of all the chapters. Here we identify and briefly discuss not only recommended editions or translations of all the primary materials mentioned in the text but also a selection of secondary sources suitable for student reading and research. Beginning in Chapter 11 we also include annotated suggestions for listening. These sections direct students who are interested in broadening their musical experience to the major or representative works of the composers treated in the text.

A growing concern today is how to help college students become more skillful writers. In response to this need, we have included an appendix on writing research papers and examination essays in the humanities. Here we give general guidelines on writing and more specific suggestions about choosing and researching a topic in the humanities, writing an acceptable college paper, and preparing for exams.

The Western Humanities is also published in an alternative two-volume version. Chapters 1 to 12 are included in Volume I, *Beginnings Through the Renaissance*, and Chapters 11 to 21 are included in Volume II, *The Renaissance to the Present*. For instructors who teach only one part of the course, this version offers flexibility and convenience. Since some schools with two-term courses include the Renaissance in the first term and others in the second, we have included coverage of the Renaissance period in both volumes.

ANCILLARY PACKAGE

As instructors, we are keenly aware of the problems encountered in teaching the humanities, especially to large, diverse classes. We have therefore created an Instructor's Manual, as well as a comprehensive package of ancillary resource materials, designed to help solve those problems. We believe these supplementary materials will be particularly useful to instructors who must manage large classes. Our Instructor's Manual identifies both general teaching strategies and specific lecture suggestions that can be used to present the humanities and create a lively classroom environment. Each chapter of the manual opens with a section called Teaching Strategies and Suggestions, summarizing an approach we have found appropriate to the specific content of the chapter. A detailed lecture outline follows, accompanied by a listing of developments in other cultures that were occurring at the same time. This unique feature will help instructors increase the multicultural awareness and global orientation of their students. The manual also highlights learning objectives for each chapter and provides listings of additional resources, including films and musical selections suitable for classroom presentation and suggested further readings for the instructor. Sample test items are given at the end of each chapter, broken down into identification, discussion/essay, and multiple choice questions, with answers keyed to the appropriate pages in the text.

The Instructor's Manual concludes with a section containing forty-five Listening Guides written by Jack Boyd of Abilene Christian College. These guides offer students an introduction to the listening experience by discussing and interpreting specific musical selections, which are available on accompanying compact disks to instructors who have adopted the text. The Listening Guides may be photocopied and distributed to students.

Also available with *The Western Humanities* is a set of 100 slides of art and architecture, along with slides of the maps from the text. Instructors without access to extensive art and music libraries may find the slides, Listening Guides, and compact disks especially useful. All are designed to help instructors provide their students with as direct an experience as possible of Western art and music.

ACKNOWLEDGMENTS

Writing this text has been a challenging but rewarding experience for us. The task was made more enjoyable by the participation and support of many people, whom we want to single out and thank. First, we acknowledge and express gratitude for the help of former students. Their questions and insights have affected the way we address certain issues and frame particular arguments. Second, we offer our appreciation to colleagues in the former Humanities Depart-

ment at Michigan State University. In that combative but fostering environment we first learned to take a multidisciplinary approach to Western culture. We thank you for your pioneering spirit and the sense you engendered in us of being part of a great educational adventure. Third, we salute Henry Rehn, who, though an undergraduate at the time, supported the project in its infancy, and we thank Pat Thompson, head of the MSU Art Library, and her then assistant Edita Herbstova, both of whom responded to our requests usually with the desired information and always with a smile.

Beyond the confines of MSU, we have also been fortunate in the people who have worked closely with us at Mayfield Publishing Company over the course of almost six years. First and foremost we wish to thank Lansing Hays, the sponsoring editor, who believed in us from the first and has been a nurturing force on this project ever since. Kate Engelberg, the developmental editor, has shared our vision even when we had disagreements. Her patience, tact, and support have been matched by her quick grasp of complex material and her ability to show us how better to phrase a thought or idea. For all of this we are deeply grateful. Carol Zafiropoulos, Linda Toy, Martha Branch, and Jeanne Schreiber, the production team, have patiently and lovingly transformed our manuscript into this beautiful book; we thank you.

We also want to express appreciation to the academic reviewers, listed below. Their detailed comments, warnings, and suggestions have often saved us from errors. Though we never met any of them face to face, we sometimes felt as if they were part of the editorial team. We offer our thanks to the following reviewers for both their criticism and their encouragement:

Lawrence Bryant, *California State University, Chico*
Charles H. Cutter, *San Diego State University*
David H. Darst, *Florida State University*
Sterling Eisiminger, *Clemson University*
Ann W. Engar, *University of Utah*
Jon D. Green, *Brigham Young University*
Fred W. Hallberg, *University of Northern Iowa*
Stephen L. Harris, *California State University, Sacramento*
Mark Hawkins, *Foothill College*
Robert E. Lynch, *New Jersey Institute of Technology*
Frederic H. Miller, *California State University, Fullerton*
George E. Moore, *San Jose State University*
Christine Oravec, *University of Utah*
Don Porter, *College of San Mateo*
Irvin M. Roth, *Foothill College*
Stanley J. Underdal, *San Jose State University*
Audrey V. Wilson, *Florida State University*

CONTENTS

INTRODUCTION
Why Study Cultural History?

To be ignorant of what occurred before you were born is to remain always a child.
— CICERO, FIRST CENTURY B.C.

Anyone who cannot give an account to oneself of the past three thousand years remains in darkness, without experience, living from day to day.
— GOETHE, NINETEENTH CENTURY A.D.

The underlying premise of this book is that some basic knowledge of the Western cultural heritage is necessary for those who want to become educated human beings in charge of their own destinies. If people are not educated into their place in human history—five thousand years of relatively uninterrupted though sometimes topsy-turvy developments—then they are rendered powerless, subject to passing fads and outlandish beliefs. They become vulnerable to the flattery of demagogues who promise heaven on earth, or they fall prey to the misconception that present-day events are unique, without precedent in history, or superior to everything that has gone before.

Perhaps the worst that can happen is to exist in a limbo of ignorance—in Goethe's words, "living from day to day." Without knowledge of the past and the perspective it brings, people may come to believe that their contemporary world will last forever, when in reality much of it is doomed to be forgotten. In contrast to the instant obsolescence of popular culture, the study of Western culture offers an alternative that has passed the unforgiving test of time. Long after today's heroes and celebrities have fallen into obliv-

ion, the achievements of our artistic and literary ancestors—those who have forged the Western tradition—will remain. Their works echo down the ages and seem fresh in every period. The ancient Roman writer Seneca put it well when he wrote, in the first century A.D., "Life is short but art is long."

When people realize that the rich legacy of Western culture is their own, their view of themselves and the times they live in can expand beyond the present moment. They find that they need not be confined by the limits of today but can draw on the creative insights of people who lived hundreds and even thousands of years ago. They discover that their own culture has a history and a context that give it meaning and shape. Studying and experiencing their cultural legacy can help them understand their place in today's world.

THE BOUNDARIES OF THE WEST

The subject of this volume is Western culture, but what exactly do we mean, first, by "culture," and second, by the "West"? *Culture* is a term with several meanings, but we use it here to mean the artistic and intellectual expressions of a people, their creative achievements. By the *West* we mean that part of the globe that lies west of Asia and Asia Minor and north of Africa, especially Europe—the geographical framework for much of this study.

The Western tradition is not confined exclusively to Europe as defined today, however. The contributions of peoples who lived beyond the boundaries of present-day Europe are also included in Western culture, either because they were forerunners of the West, such as those who created the first civilizations in Mesopotamia and Egypt, or because they were part of the West for periods of time, such as those who lived in the North African and Near Eastern lands bordering the Mediterranean Sea during the Roman and early Christian eras. Regardless of geography, Western culture draws deeply from ideals forged in these lands.

When areas that had been part of the Western tradition at one time were absorbed into other cultural traditions, as happened in Mesopotamia, Egypt, and North Africa in the seventh century when the people embraced the Muslim faith, then they are generally no longer included in Western cultural history. Because of the enormous influence of Islamic civilization on Western civilization, however, we do include in this volume both an account of Islamic history and a description and appreciation of Islamic culture. Different in many ways from our own, the rich tradition of Islam has an important place in today's world.

After about 1500, with voyages and explorations reaching the farthest parts of the globe, the European focus of Western culture that had held for centuries began to dissolve. Starting from this time, the almost exclusive European mold was broken and Western values and ideals began to be exported throughout the world, largely through the efforts of missionaries, soldiers, colonists, and merchants. Coinciding with this development and further complicating the pattern of change were the actions of those who imported and enslaved countless numbers of black Africans to work on plantations in North and South America. The interplay of Western culture with many previously isolated cultures, whether desired or not, forever changed all who were touched by the process.

The Westernization of the globe that has been going on ever since 1500 is perhaps the dominant theme of the twentieth century. What human greed, missionary zeal, and dreams of empire failed to accomplish prior to 1900 has been achieved in this century by modern technology, the media, and popular culture. The world today is a global village, much of it dominated by Western values and styles of life. In our time, Westernization has become a two-way interchange. When artists and writers from other cultures adopt Western forms or ideas, they are not only Westernizing their own traditions but also injecting fresh sensibilities and habits of thought into the Western tradition. The globalization of culture means that a South American novel or a Japanese film can be as accessible to Western audiences as a European painting and yet carry with it an intriguingly new vocabulary of cultural symbols and meanings.

HISTORICAL PERIODS AND CULTURAL STYLES

In cultural history the past is often divided into historical periods and cultural styles. A historical period is an interval of time that has a certain unity because it is characterized by the prevalence of a unique culture, ideology, or technology or because it is bounded by defining historical events, such as the death of a military leader like Alexander the Great or a political upheaval like the fall of Rome. A cultural style is a combination of features of artistic or literary expression, execution, or performance that define a particular school or era. A historical period may have the identical time frame as a cultural style, or it may embrace more than one style simultaneously or two styles successively. Each chapter of this survey focuses on a historical period and includes significant aspects of culture—usually the arts, architecture, literature, religion, music, and philosophy—organized around a discussion of the relevant style or styles appropriate to that time.

The survey begins with prehistory, the era before writing was invented, setting forth the emergence of human beings from an obscure past. After the appearance of writing in about 3000 B.C., the Western cultural heritage is divided into three sweeping historical periods: ancient, medieval, and modern.

The ancient period dates from 3000 B.C. to A.D. 500 (Time Line 1). During these thirty-five hundred years the light of Western civilization begins to shine in Mesopotamia and Egypt, shines more brightly still in eighth-century B.C. Greece and Rome, loses some of its luster when Greece succumbs to Rome in 146 B.C., and finally is snuffed out when the Roman empire collapses in the fifth century A.D. Coinciding with these historical periods are the cultural styles of Mesopotamia; Egypt; Greece, including Archaic, Classical (or Hellenic), and Hellenistic styles; and Rome, including Republican and Imperial styles.

The medieval period, or the Middle Ages, covers events between A.D. 500 and 1500, a one-thousand-year span that is further divided into three subperiods (Time Line 2). The Early Middle Ages (500–1000) is typified by frequent barbarian invasions and political chaos so that civilization itself is threatened and barely survives. No single international style characterizes this turbulent period, though several regional styles flourish. The High Middle Ages (1000–1300) is

THE ANCIENT WORLD

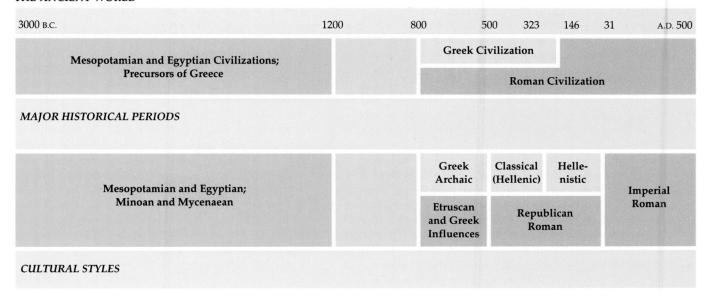

a period of stability and the zenith of medieval culture. Two successive styles appear, the Romanesque and the Gothic, with the latter dominating culture for the rest of the medieval period. The Late Middle Ages (1300–1500) is a transitional period in which the medieval age is dying and the modern age is struggling to be born.

The modern period begins in about 1400 (there is often overlap between historical periods) and continues today (Time Line 3). With the advent of the modern period a new way of defining historical changes starts to make more sense—the division of history into movements, the activities of large groups of people united to achieve a common goal. The modern period consists of waves of movements that aim to change the world in some specific way.

The first modern movement is the Renaissance (1400–1600), or "rebirth," which attempts to revive the cultural values of ancient Greece and Rome. It is accompanied by two successive styles, Renaissance style and Mannerism. The next significant movement is the Reformation (1500–1600), which is dedicated to restoring Christianity to the ideals of the early church set forth in the Bible. Although it does not spawn a specific style, this religious upheaval does have a profound impact on the subjects of the arts and literature and the way they are expressed, especially in the Mannerist style.

The Reformation is followed by the Scientific Revolution (1600–1700), a movement that results in the abandonment of ancient science and the birth of modern science. Radical in its conclusions, the Scientific

THE MEDIEVAL WORLD

500		1000	1150	1300	1500
Early Middle Ages			High Middle Ages		Late Middle Ages

MAJOR HISTORICAL PERIODS

| Regional Styles | | | Romanesque | Gothic | |

CULTURAL STYLES

THE MODERN WORLD

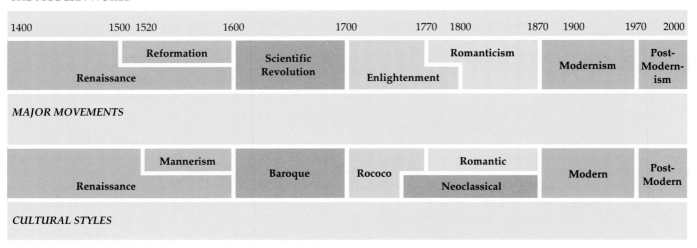

| 1400 | | 1500 | 1520 | | 1600 | | 1700 | | 1770 | 1800 | | 1870 | 1900 | | 1970 | 2000 |

MAJOR MOVEMENTS

Reformation

Renaissance

Scientific Revolution

Enlightenment

Romanticism

Modernism

Post-Modern-ism

CULTURAL STYLES

Renaissance

Mannerism

Baroque

Rococo

Romantic

Neoclassical

Modern

Post-Modern

Revolution is somewhat out of touch with the style of its age, which is known as the Baroque. This magnificent style is devoted to overwhelming the senses through theatrical and sensuous effects and is associated with the attempts of the Roman Catholic church to reassert its authority in the world.

The Scientific Revolution gives impetus to the Enlightenment (1700–1800), a movement that pledges to reform politics and society according to the principles of the new science. In stylistic terms the eighteenth century is schizophrenic, dominated first by the Rococo, an extravagant and fanciful style that represents the last phase of the Baroque, and then by the Neoclassical, a style inspired by the works of ancient Greece and Rome and reflective of the principles of the Scientific Revolution. Before the eighteenth century is over the Enlightenment calls forth its antithesis, Romanticism (1770–1870), a movement centered on feeling, fantasy, and everything that cannot be proven scientifically. The Romantic style, marked by a revived taste for the Gothic and a love of nature, is the perfect accompaniment to this movement.

Toward the end of the nineteenth century Modernism (1870–1970) arises, bent on destroying every vestige of both the Greco-Roman tradition and the Christian faith and on fashioning new ways of understanding that are independent of the past. Since 1970 Post-Modernism has emerged, a movement that tries to make peace with the past by embracing old forms of expression while at the same time adopting a global and multivoiced perspective.

Although every cultural period is marked by innovation and creativity, our treatment of them in this book varies somewhat, with more space and greater weight given to the achievements of certain times. We make these adjustments because some periods or styles are more significant than others, especially in the defining influence that their achievements have had on our own era. For example, some styles seem to tower over the rest, such as Classicism in fifth-century Greece, the High Renaissance of sixteenth-century Italy, and Modernism in the mid–twentieth century, as compared to other styles, such as that of the Early Middle Ages or the seventeenth-century Baroque.

AN INTEGRATED APPROACH TO CULTURAL HISTORY

Our approach to the Western heritage in this book is to root cultural achievements in their historical settings, showing how the material conditions—the political, social, and economic events of each period—influenced their creation. About one-third of each chapter is devoted to an interpretive discussion of material history, and the remaining two-thirds are devoted to the arts, architecture, philosophy, religion, literature, and music of the period. These two aspects of history do not occur separately, of course, and one of our aims is to show how they are intertwined.

As just one example of this integrated approach, consider the Gothic cathedral, that lofty, light-filled house of worship marked by pointed arches, towering spires, and radiant stained glass windows. Gothic cathedrals were erected during the High Middle Ages, following a bleak period when urban life had virtually ceased. Although religion was still the dominant force in European life, trade was starting to flourish once again, town life was reviving, and urban dwellers were beginning to prosper. In part as testimonials to their new wealth, cities and towns commissioned architects and hired workers to erect these soaring churches, which dominated the landscape for miles around and proclaimed the economic well-being of their makers.

We adopt an integrated approach to Western culture not just in considering how the arts are related to material conditions but also in looking for the common themes, aspirations, and ideas that permeate the artistic and literary expressions of every individual era. The creative accomplishments of an age tend to reflect a shared perspective, even when this perspective is not explicitly recognized at the time. Thus, each period possesses a unique outlook that can be analyzed in the cultural record. A good example of this phenomenon is Classical Greece in the fifth century B.C., when the ideal of moderation, or balance in all things, played a major role in sculpture, architecture, philosophy, religion, and tragic drama. The cultural record in other periods is not always as clear as that in ancient Greece, but shared qualities can often be uncovered that distinguish the varied aspects of culture in an era to form a unifying thread.

A corollary of this idea is that creative individuals and their works are very much influenced by the times in which they live. This is not to say that incomparable geniuses—like Shakespeare in Renaissance England—do not appear and rise above their own ages, speaking directly to the human mind and heart in every age that follows. Yet even Shakespeare reflected the political attitudes and social patterns of his time. Though a man for the ages, he still regarded monarchy as the correct form of government and women as the inferiors of men.

THE SELECTION OF CULTURAL WORKS

The Western cultural heritage is vast, and any selection of works for a survey text reflects choices made by the authors. All of the works we chose to include have had a significant impact on Western culture, but for different reasons. We chose some because they blazed a new trail, such as Picasso's *Demoiselles d'Avignon* (see Figure 19.20), which marked the advent of Cubism in painting, or Fielding's *Tom Jones*, one of the earliest novels. Other works were included because they seemed to embody a style to perfection, such as the regal statue called *Poseidon* (or *Zeus*) (see Figure 3.20), executed in the Classical style of fifth-century Athens, or Dante's *Divine Comedy*, which epitomized the ideals of the High Middle Ages. Still other works caught our attention because they served as links between successive styles, as is the case with Giotto's frescoes (see Figure 10.18), or because they represented the end of an age or an artistic style, as in the haunting sculpture called *The Last Pagan* (see Figure 7.15). Finally, we included some works, especially paintings, simply because of their great beauty, such as Chardin's *Little Girl Playing Shuttlecock* (see Figure 16.1) or Roberts' *The Conversation* (see Figure 21.25).

Through all the ages of Western cultural history, through all the shifting styles and tastes embodied in painting, sculpture, architecture, poetry, and song, there glows a creative spark that can be found in human beings in every period. This diversity is a hallmark of the Western experience, and we celebrate it in this book.

A CHALLENGE TO THE READER

The purpose of all education is and should be self-knowledge. This goal was first established by the ancient Greeks in their injunction to "Know thyself," the inscription carved above the entrance to Apollo's temple at Delphi. Self-knowledge means awareness of oneself and one's place in society and the world. Reaching this goal is not easy, because becoming an educated human being is a lifelong process, requiring time, energy, and commitment. But all journeys begin with a single step, and we intend this volume as a first step toward understanding and defining oneself in terms of one's historical and cultural heritage. Our challenge to the reader is to use this book to begin the long journey to self-knowledge.

PREHISTORY AND NEAR EASTERN CIVILIZATIONS

A man or woman born in the West in the earlier part of this century and still living today has seen more change in a lifetime than previous generations experienced for hundreds of years. Yet despite the rapid rate of change in modern times, Western civilization stands firmly on a foundation that is almost five thousand years old, and people in the West often turn back to this foundation to discover their heritage and to cast new light on their values. As the clock seems to speed up, the past becomes increasingly important as a guide to the future.

Before we begin to explore this heritage and what it means today, we need to discuss two important terms—*culture* and *civilization*. *Culture* usually refers to the sum of human endeavors: methods and practices for survival; political, economic, and social institutions; and values, beliefs, and the arts. *Civilization*, on the other hand, refers to the way people live in a complex political, economic, and social structure, usually in an urban setting and usually after making certain technological and artistic advances. Culture is passed from one generation to another by human behavior, speech, and artifacts; civilization is transmitted primarily by writing (Figure 1.1). The term *culture* can also be used to refer to the creative, artistic, and intellectual expressions of a civilization. We will use the term in both these senses. In the words of Matthew Arnold, the nineteenth-century English poet and critic, culture is "the best that has been thought and said." To this we would add, "and done."

FIGURE 1.1 Rosetta Stone. Ca. 197–196 B.C. British Museum. *Although scholars knew that Egypt had a writing system, they were unable to solve the mystery of hieroglyphics until the nineteenth century. The key was provided by the Rosetta Stone, discovered by members of Napoleon's expedition when he invaded Egypt in 1799. On the stone the same event is described in hieroglyphics, in Egyptian cursive script, and in Greek. By comparing the Greek text with the other two, scholars were able to decipher both Egyptian scripts. This discovery marks the origin of modern Egyptology.*

PREHISTORY AND EARLY CULTURES

Where and when does the story of human culture begin? The latest evidence from paleoanthropology, the study of early human life, indicates that human beings originated in the distant past in lands far from western Europe. Human development thus begins during prehistory, long before our predecessors compiled—or could compile—written records of their cultures. The first ancestors of human beings probably appeared about four to five million years ago. Although this seems ancient, it's recent compared to the appearance of life forms on earth, estimated at two to three billion years ago, and to the formation of the planet itself, believed to have occurred some four to six billion years ago.

The periods of time involved in these processes are so vast that only metaphors can make them comprehensible. If we take the seven-day week, made familiar by the biblical account of creation, and combine it with recent scientific estimates about when the earth and life began, then the following analogy may be made. The earth was created just after midnight on Monday morning, the first life appeared about Thursday noon, and the early ancestors of human beings didn't show up until about eleven o'clock on Sunday night. To complete the analogy, the birth of civilization occurred almost an hour later, in the last tenth of a second before midnight on the last day of the week.

Although the record of human evolution is incomplete and obscured by time, sufficient evidence exists to show that hominids, the earliest primate ancestors of modern humans, probably originated in eastern Africa. From among them, about two million years ago, the genus *Homo* evolved, a form marked by a larger brain and the ability to adapt somewhat to the environment. Hominids of the *Homo* genus made and used tools and developed rudimentary cultures. Anthropologists designate this earliest cultural period as the *Paleolithic*, or Old Stone Age. It corresponds to the geological period known as the Pleistocene epoch, or Ice Age, the time of extensive climate changes caused by the advance and retreat of massive glaciers (Time Line 1.1).

Stone Age culture spread widely over a vast area, but remains of hominid life are scarce and incomplete. Evidence indicates that they lived in packs, followed herds of wandering animals, and ate wild seasonal fruits and vegetables. Anthropologists believe that duties and work divided along sex lines as all-male teams hunted game for meat and fur while females and children gathered plant foods, prepared meals, and tended the young. During the night, all sought shelter together in caves for safety and refuge against the elements. This way of life hinged on cooperation and food sharing among small social groups.

In the early Old Stone Age, or Lower Paleolithic, hominids invented crude stone tools, used fire, and probably developed speech—a major breakthrough that allowed them to communicate in ways denied

TIME LINE 1.1 GEOLOGICAL TIME AND PREHISTORIC CULTURAL PERIODS   All dates approximate and B.C.

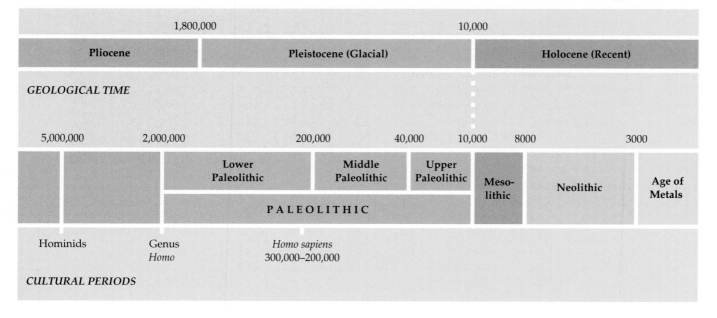

FIGURE 1.2   Bison Cave Painting. Ca. 14,000–12,000 B.C. Altamira, Spain. *This polychrome bison, one of several on the cave's ceiling, is outlined in black and colored in red. These bison varied in size from 4 to 6 feet long. Whether the animals were painted separately or as part of a total design is unknown, but the artist has succeeded in capturing the strength and power of the beasts.*

other animals. Their first tools were simple choppers and, somewhat later, hand axes. In the Middle Paleolithic, more advanced hominids developed pointed tools and scrapers, which they chiseled with precision and care. In the Upper Paleolithic, double-faced blades became common.

By about 200,000 B.C. the species *Homo sapiens* had evolved from earlier hominids, and between 50,000 and 30,000 B.C. this species apparently displaced other, less advanced hominids. More fully developed physically and mentally, they slowly spread throughout the Eastern Hemisphere and eventually migrated into the Western Hemisphere over the land bridge between Siberia and Alaska. Their tools were more sophisticated and included bows and arrows, fishhooks, and needles. By this time, they were burying their dead with rituals, and they had begun to paint

and sculpt. Clearly, these ancestors of ours were capable not only of cooperative living but of symbolic thought.

Paintings of reindeer, bisons, and horses in caves in Altamira, Spain, and Lascaux, France, dating from the Upper Paleolithic, are the earliest examples of human art. Many of these paintings, located deep in caves, were probably used as part of ceremonies and rituals prior to a hunting expedition. By painting numerous wild animals pierced with arrows, the artists were attempting to ensure a successful hunt that would supply the tribe with food (Figure 1.2). The ritual participants were, in effect, practicing magic.

Another type of Upper Paleolithic art was the carved female figurine, such as the "Venus" of Willendorf found in Austria (Figure 1.3). Made of limestone, the statue is faceless and rotund. The dis-

FIGURE 1.3   "Venus" of Willendorf. Ca. 25,000 B.C. Height 10.5 cm. Museum Naturhistorisches, Vienna. *Discovered around A.D. 1908, this female statuette measures just under 5 inches high. Carved from limestone, it still shows evidence of having been painted red. Many other statues like it have been discovered, but this one remains the most famous because of the unusual balance it strikes between symbolism and realism.*

tended stomach and full breasts suggest that the figurine was used as a fertility symbol and image of a mother goddess, representing the creative power of nature. As a mythological figure, the mother goddess appeared in many ancient cultures, beginning in Paleolithic times. This figurine may have been used in religious ceremonies to ensure the propagation of the tribe. But the statue also reveals the aesthetic interests of the sculptor, who took care to depict the figure's hands resting on her breasts and the rows of tightly knit hair.

As the last glaciers retreated from Europe, as tundra and steppes gave way to forests and herds of reindeer and elephants were replaced by elk and deer, human beings were forced to adapt to new liv-

ing conditions. Their stone tools became more advanced and included knives and hammers. Following a transitional period known as the Mesolithic (about 10,000–8000 B.C.), a transformation occurred that has been called the most important event in human history: Hunters and gatherers became farmers and herders. Thus began the *Neolithic* period, or New Stone Age (about 8000 B.C.). At various places all over the world—in southeast Asia, in Central America, in parts of South America, and in the Near East—human beings ceased their nomadic existence and learned to domesticate wild animals by herding them together, breeding them, and using them as beasts of burden and sources of food and hides. They learned to plow the earth and sow the seeds of wild grains and grasses, providing themselves with a much more reliable food supply. This in turn encouraged the development of permanent settlements and eventually the rise of urban centers. The agrarian pattern of life begun at this time dominated the West until about two hundred years ago.

Precisely why and how the agrarian revolution came at this time is a hotly debated topic among anthropologists. Nonetheless, most agree that with the retreat of the last glaciers from Europe, methods of food gathering changed dramatically, causing either surpluses or shortages. In some areas, grain surpluses allowed populations to grow, and this led to forced migrations as the number of humans outstripped the available food. In less productive lands, the people began to experiment with domesticating animals and planting grains. These innovations in marginal lands caused food production to rise, soon matching that found in more fertile areas, so that eventually a uniform agricultural economy spread to many parts of the globe. Thus, economic causes accounted for the transformation from food-gathering to food-producing cultures.

The agricultural revolution expanded across the Near East and probably into Europe and Africa. Between 6000 and 3000 B.C. human beings also learned to mine and use copper, ending the Neolithic Period and ushering in the Age of Metals. In about 3000 B.C., artisans combined copper and tin to produce bronze, a strong alloy, which they used in their tools, weapons, and jewelry.

The Bronze Age, which extended from about 3000 to about 1200 B.C., gave rise to two major civilizations in the Near East. The earlier developed in Mesopotamia, the land between the Tigris and Euphrates rivers (in present-day Iraq), and the other, probably emerging just slightly later, originated along the Nile River in Egypt. Mesopotamian and Egyptian civilizations shared certain characteristics: Both were ruled by kings who were in turn supported by a priestly caste; their economies were slave-based; their societies were stratified, with class privileges at the upper end; small, educated elites shared power with the rulers; and palaces and religious edifices were built for ceremonial and governmental purposes. These early civilizations made deep and lasting impressions on their neighbors and successors that helped shape life in the Western world.

THE CIVILIZATIONS OF THE TIGRIS AND EUPHRATES RIVER VALLEY: MESOPOTAMIA

The Tigris-Euphrates river valley forms part of what is known as the Fertile Crescent, which starts at the Persian Gulf, runs slightly northwestward through the Tigris-Euphrates valley, and then turns westerly to the Mediterranean Sea and curves south along the shoreline toward Egypt (Map 1.1). This arc of land contained some of the most arable soil in the Near East, many of the heavily traveled trade routes, and most of the early centers of civilization.

Mesopotamia is a Greek word meaning "land between the two rivers." The hill country and Zagros Mountains rise to the east of the Tigris-Euphrates valley, and the vast Arabian desert stretches to the west. The twin rivers course down to the Persian Gulf, draining an area approximately 600 miles long and 250 miles wide. Near the mouth of the gulf, on the river delta, human wanderers settled down in about 6000 B.C., founding villages and tilling the land. Despite the heat, the marshes, the unpredictable, violent floods that swept down the river valleys, and the invaders who came from both the mountains and the desert, some of these communities prospered and grew.

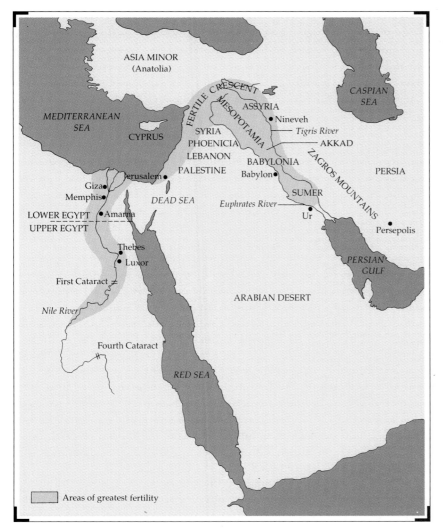

MAP 1.1

Mesopotamia and Ancient Egypt: The Fertile Crescent

TIME LINE 1.2   MESOPOTAMIAN CIVILIZATIONS   All dates approximate and B.C.

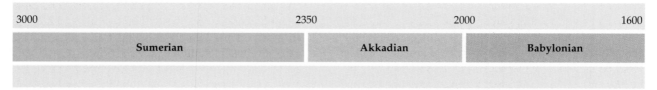

The Sumerian, Akkadian, and Babylonian Kingdoms

Three successive civilizations—Sumerian, Akkadian, and Babylonian—flourished in Mesopotamia over a period of nearly 1500 years (Time Line 1.2). The Sumerians established the first of these, and, indeed, as historian Samuel Kramer asserts, "History began at Sumer." The rulers of Sumer created an exalted image of a just and stable society with a rich cultural life, a standard that captured the imagination of their people and was adopted eventually by friend and foe alike.

Sumer's most inspirational king, Gilgamesh, ruled during the first Dynasty of Ur (about 2700 B.C.), a state centered between the rivers. Because of his adventures and exploits, this king was later immortalized as a hero in the poem, the *Epic of Gilgamesh*. A second ruler, Urukagina, reformed the law codes and sponsored public works projects near the end of the Sumerian period, about 2350 B.C. His reforms, following years of harsh and unfair rule, restored the rights of his subjects and revitalized the economy. Yet Urukagina's vision failed in its goal. The despotic policies and domestic squabbles of his successors weakened Sumer and made the cities an easy prey for the Akkadians of northern Mesopotamia.

The Akkadian dynasties, lasting from about 2350 to about 2000 B.C., incorporated the Sumerian way of life into their own society and carried this hybrid civilization far beyond the Tigris-Euphrates valley. According to legends—which are similar to the later story of the Hebrew leader, Moses—Sargon, the first and greatest Akkadian ruler, was born of lowly origins and abandoned at birth in the reed marshes; yet Sargon survived and rose to prominence at the Sumerian court. Excavated inscriptions reveal that Sargon conquered the Sumerians and founded a far-flung empire to the east and northeast. At its height, Sargon's power was felt from Egypt to India, but his successors, lacking his intelligence and skill, could not hold the Akkadian empire together. The incursions of the Guti tribes from the Zagros Mountains precipitated the final collapse of the weakened Akkadian empire and the division of southern Mesopotamia into petty kingdoms.

Babylonia was the third civilization in Mesopotamia. From northern Mesopotamia, their power base, the Babylonians governed the entire valley from about 2000 to 1600 B.C. Under their most successful military leader and renowned law giver, Hammurabi (1792–1750 B.C.), the Babylonians reached their political and cultural ascendancy. However, the ruler of the Old Hittite Kingdom, a state centered in Asia Minor, invaded Babylon in about 1600 B.C. and toppled the dynasty of Hammurabi.

Agriculture dominated the economy of Mesopotamia throughout its long history. Harsh living conditions and unpredictable floods forced the inhabitants to learn to control the rivers through irrigation systems and cooperative tilling of the soil. In the earlier years, the farmers planted small scattered holdings beside the river's banks, using crude tools to direct the sluggish water onto their crops through short channels. Later, they dug a complex canal system to irrigate their cultivated plots, which might lie some distance from the river. As production increased, prosperity allowed larger populations to thrive. Villages soon grew into small cities—with populations ranging from 10,000 to 50,000—surrounded by hamlets and tilled fields. Trade developed with nearby areas, and wheeled vehicles—perfected by the Sumerians—and sail boats carried goods up and down Mesopotamia and eventually throughout the Fertile Crescent.

By the beginning of the Bronze Age, the family had replaced the tribe or clan as the basic unit in society. Families now owned their lands outright. In cooperation with and under the general direction of the religious and secular authorities, families worked their fields and maintained the irrigation ditches. Marriages were arranged by parents, who always made economics an essential consideration in such matters. According to the law codes, women possessed some rights, such as holding property; but a wife was clearly under her husband's power. Divorce was easier for men than for women, and women were punished more severely than men for breaking moral and marital laws.

The political structure reflected the order and functions of the social system. At the top stood the ruler who, depending on the time and circumstances, might be a powerful king or merely a local lord. He was supported by an army, bureaucracy, judicial system, and priesthood. The king usually obtained advice from prominent leaders, meeting in council, who constituted the next layer of the social order: rich landowners, wealthy merchants, priests, and military chiefs. The next group consisted of artisans, craftspeople, and petty businesspeople and traders. Below them were small landowners and tenant farmers. At the bottom of the social scale were serfs and slaves, who had either been captured in war or had fallen into debt.

The Cradle of Civilization

The three Mesopotamian civilizations responded to the same geography, climate, and natural resources, and their cultures reflected this shared background. The Sumerians were probably the most influential: From Sumer came writing, the lunar calendar, a mathematical computation system, medical and scientific discoveries, and architectural innovations. However, each civilization, through its religion, literature, law, and art, deeply affected other Near Eastern people.

Writing Thousands of clay tablets inscribed with the wedge-shaped symbols of Sumerian script have been uncovered in Mesopotamia, indicating that the Sumerians had developed a form of writing by 3000 B.C. With the invention of writing, new roads opened up for human cultures. Now, people no longer had to rely on memory, speech, and person-to-person interactions to communicate and transmit information. In-

stead, they could create a permanent body of knowledge that could accumulate and be passed on from one generation to the next. With writing came the possibility of civilization.

At first, the Sumerians needed a simple way to keep agricultural and business records and to record the deeds and sayings of their rulers. Their earliest symbols are *pictograms*, or pictures, carefully drawn to represent particular objects. To these they added *ideograms*, pictures drawn to represent ideas or concepts. A simple drawing of a bowl, for example, could be used to mean "food." As these pictures became more and more stylized, meaning began to be transferred from the represented object to the sign itself; that is, the sign began to stand for a word rather than an object.

Later, Sumerian scribes and writers identified the syllabic sounds of spoken words and created *phonograms*, symbols for separate speech sounds, borrowing from and building on the earlier pictograms and ideograms. The written symbols now represented sounds rather than objects or ideas. These simplified and standardized symbols eventually resulted in a phonetic writing system of syllable-based sounds that, when combined, produced words (Figure 1.4). (It was left to later civilizations to separate out the vowel sounds from the syllables and thus create a true alphabet, based on individual speech sounds.)

The Sumerians could now express complex, abstract concepts, and their system could be used to write other languages. The Akkadians and Babylonians adopted and modified the Sumerian script to keep records and preserve their literature, including the *Epic of Gilgamesh* and the Code of Hammurabi. By the end of the Bronze Age (about 1200 B.C.), other

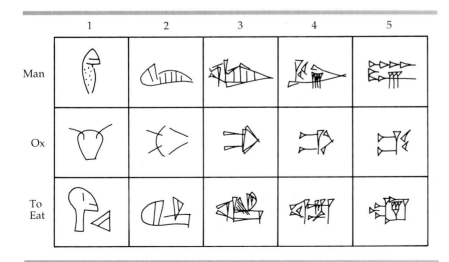

	1	2	3	4	5
Man					
Ox					
To Eat					

FIGURE 1.4 Sumerian Cuneiform Writing. Ca. 3000–1000 B.C. *The columns illustrate the evolution of Sumerian writing from pictograms to script. Column one shows the pictogram: a man, an ox, and the verb "to eat" (represented by the mouth and a bowl). In column two, the pictographic symbols have been turned 90 degrees, as the Sumerians did in their first writing. Columns three and four show how the script changed between 2500 and 1800 B.C. Column five is an Assyrian adaptation of the Sumerian cuneiform script.*

written languages existed, but Akkadian-Sumerian was the language of diplomacy and trade in the Near East.

The Sumerian writing system has been labeled *cuneiform*, a term derived from the Latin word *cuneus*, which means "wedge." Using wedge-shaped reeds or styluses, scribes pressed the symbols into wet clay tablets, and artists and craftspeople, wielding metal tools, incised the script into stone monuments or cylindrical pillars. Preserved for thousands of years in hardened clay and stone, cuneiform writing has provided invaluable insight into the life and culture of ancient Mesopotamia.

Religion   Sumerian, Akkadian, and Babylonian religions, despite individual differences, shared many basic attitudes and concepts that became the foundation for other Near Eastern belief systems. The underlying beliefs of Mesopotamian religion were that the gods had created human beings to serve them, that the gods were in complete control, and that powerless mortals had no choice but to obey and worship these deities. The hostile climate and unpredictable rivers made life precarious, and the gods appeared capricious. The Mesopotamians held a vague notion of a shadowy netherworld where the dead rested, but they did not believe in an afterlife as such or any rewards or punishments upon death. Happiness seldom was an earthly goal; pessimism ran as a constant theme throughout their religion and literature.

Mesopotamian religion had three important characteristics. It was *polytheistic*—many gods and goddesses existed and often competed with one another; it was *anthropomorphic*—the deities possessed human form and had their own personalities and unique traits; and it was *pantheistic*—hundreds of divinities were found everywhere, in nature and the universe. Since Mesopotamians thought of their gods in human form with all the strengths and weaknesses of mortals, they believed their deities lived in the same way as people, and they were pragmatic in approaching the supernatural powers. For example, they believed that their deities held council, made decisions, and ordered the forces of nature to wreak havoc or to bestow plenty on mortals.

Mesopotamians divided the deities into two basic groups, the sky gods and the earth gods. In these two categories were the four major deities: Anu, the heaven god; Enlil, the air god; Enki, the water god; and Ninhursag, the mother goddess. Enlil emerged as the most powerful god for the Sumerians. He gave mortals the plough and the pickaxe, and he brought forth for humanity all the productive forces of the universe, such as trees, grains, and "whatever was needful." Although Enlil had to carry out the orders of the other gods who often set off waves of destruction, he was not a god of misdeeds.

Rituals, ceremonies, and the priesthood were absolutely essential to Mesopotamian religion. Although the average Mesopotamian might participate in worship services, the priests played the central role in all religious functions. They also controlled and administered large parcels of land, which enhanced their power in religious as well as economic and political matters. Priests carefully formulated and consciously followed the procedures for rites and rituals, which were written down and stored in their temples. This cultic literature not only told the Mesopotamians how to worship but also informed them about their deities' origins, characteristics, and deeds. Religious myths and instructions constituted a major part of Mesopotamian literature and made writing an essential component of the culture.

Literature   Of the surviving epics, tales, and legends that offer glimpses into the Mesopotamian mind, the most famous is the *Epic of Gilgamesh*. King Gilgamesh, whose reign in about 2700 B.C. is well documented, became a larger-than-life hero in Sumerian folk tales (Figure 1.5). In all probability the Gilgamesh epic began as an oral poem and was not put in writing on clay tablets for hundreds of years. The most complete surviving version, from 600 B.C., was based on a Babylonian copy written in Akkadian and dating from about 1600 B.C. Although this poem influenced other Near Eastern writings with its characters, plot, and themes, the *Epic of Gilgamesh* stands on its own as a poetic utterance worthy of being favorably compared with the Greek and Roman epics of later times.

Through its royal hero, the *Epic of Gilgamesh* focuses on fundamental themes that concern warriors in an aristocratic society: the need to be brave in the face of danger, the choice of death before dishonor, the conflict between companionship and sexual pleasure, the power of the gods over weak mortals, and the finality of death. Above all, it deals with human beings' vain quest for immortality. As the tale begins, the extravagant and despotic policies of Gilgamesh have led his subjects to pray for relief. In response, a goddess creates from clay a "wild man" of tremendous physical strength and sends him to kill Gilgamesh. But Enkidu, as he is called, is instead tamed by the love of a prostitute, loses his innocence, wrestles Gilgamesh to a draw, and becomes his boon companion.

As the epic unfolds, Gilgamesh chooses friendship with Enkidu rather than the love offered by the goddess Ishtar. Gilgamesh is punished for this choice by being made to watch helplessly as Enkidu dies from an illness sent by the gods. Forced to confront the

FIGURE 1.5 Gilgamesh Fighting a Lion. Ca. 2500–2000 B.C. Impression of cylinder seal. British Museum. *Superhuman feats were attributed to the Sumerian king as he was transformed into a legendary figure. The scene depicted on this small agate seal is probably the earliest artistic representation of a literary scene in the Western tradition.*

fate awaiting all mortals, a grieving Gilgamesh begins a search for immortality.

The next section of the epic, which details Gilgamesh's search, includes the Sumerian tale of the great flood, which parallels the later Hebrew story of Noah and the ark. Although the Sumerian account of the flood was probably a later addition to the original story of Gilgamesh, the episode does fit into the narrative and reinforces one of the epic's major themes: the inescapable mortality of human beings. Gilgamesh hears the story of the flood from its sole survivor, Utnapishtim. Utnapishtim tells Gilgamesh how he built an ark and loaded it with animals and his family, how the waters rose, and how he released birds from the ark to discover if the waters were receding. The old man then explains how the gods, feeling sorry for the last remaining human, granted him immortality. Utnapishtim refuses to divulge the secret of eternal life to Gilgamesh, but the old man's wife blurts out where a plant may be found that will renew youth but not give immortality. Although Gilgamesh locates the plant, he loses it on his journey home. Gilgamesh, seeing the city of Uruk which he had built, realizes that the deeds humans do on earth are the measure of their immortality and that death is inevitable.

The *Epic of Gilgamesh* is essentially a secular morality tale. Gilgamesh's triumphs and failures mirror the lives of all mortals, and the Sumerians saw themselves in Gilgamesh's change from an overly confident and powerful hero to a doubting and fearful human being. Those who, like Gilgamesh, ignore the power of the deities have to pay a heavy price for their pride.

Law   The Mesopotamians produced the fairest and most humane law codes prior to the Hebrews. The central theme of Sumerian law, whose first extant records date from about 2050 B.C., was justice. From the earliest times, the Sumerian kings understood justice to mean "the straight thing," that is, dealing fairly with all of their subjects and prohibiting the exploitation of the weak by the strong. This concept of equity applied especially to economic matters, such as debts, contracts, and titles to land.

The most famous set of laws from Mesopotamian civilization is that of the Babylonian king Hammurabi. Dating from about 1700 B.C., the Code of Hammurabi has been found preserved on a seven-foot-high black stone *stele*, or pillar. At the top, Hammurabi is depicted standing in front of Shamash, the Babylonian and Sumerian god of justice. Like other ancient lawgivers (Moses, for example), Hammurabi receives the legal code from a deity. Below the two figures are carved the prologue, the collection of laws, and an epilogue (Figure 1.6).

FIGURE 1.6 Code of Hammurabi. Ca. 1790–1750 B.C. Louvre, Paris. *Hammurabi stands on the left while the god Shamash, with flames shooting out of his shoulders and holding the symbols of power in his hands, sits on the right. The relief, with its details and folds of cloth, is carved deep enough into the hard stone stele to suggest a three-dimensional sculpture.*

The prologue lists Hammurabi's accomplishments and sings his praises, while making it clear that the gods were the source of his power to establish "law and justice." The epilogue warns future rulers to carry out these laws or else be subject to defeat and ruin.

The laws concerning punishment for crimes are based on the judicial principle of *lex talionis,* or retaliation, which demands an "eye for an eye," although Hammurabi's code often substitutes payments in kind for damages done. Every major area of civil and criminal law was covered in the code, including property rights, sales, contracts, inheritance, adoption, prices and wages, and personal rights for women, children, and slaves. Hammurabi's code, like other Mesopotamian laws, was only one part of a complex judicial system that encompassed judges, courts, trials, legal proceedings, and contracts.

Art and Architecture The art of Mesopotamia, like the rest of its culture, evolved from Sumerian styles to the Akkadian and Babylonian schools. Artisans worked in many forms—small seals, pottery, jewelry, vases, reliefs, and statues—and in many media—clay, stone, precious gems, gold, silver, leather, and ivory. Artifacts and crafted works from all three civilizations recorded the changing techniques of the producers as well as the shifting tastes of the consumers, whether they were rich individuals decorating their homes or officials issuing commissions for statues to adorn their temples. The temples, usually the center of the city and set on high mounds above the other structures, were often splendidly ornamented and housed exquisitely carved statues of gods and goddesses.

A fine example of Sumerian artistry is a bull's head carved on the sound box of a lyre (Figure 1.7). Working in gold leaf and semiprecious gems, the unknown artist has captured the vigor and power of the animal in a bold and simple style. Such elegant musical instruments were played in homes and in palaces to accompany the poets and storytellers as they sang of the heroes' adventures and the deities' powers.

Mesopotamian artists carved thousands of figures, many on the walls of temples and palaces and others as free-standing statues. A notable early type of free-standing statue that became standard in Sumerian temples depicts a figure in a contemplative, worshiping pose, his hands folded and clasped in front of him. Many of these are likenesses of Gudea, a ruler who flourished in about 2250 B.C. (Figure 1.8).

In contrast to the finely crafted sculpture, Mesopotamian architecture often seems uninspired, particularly the domestic architecture. Most Mesopotamian houses were square or rectangular, showing little variety. Even though the Mesopotamians knew about the arch, the vault, and the column, they did not employ them widely; they used primarily the basic *post-and-lintel construction* of two vertical posts capped by a horizontal lintel, or beam, for entrance ways. The clay bricks used in construction limited the builders in styles and decorations, notably on the exterior. If private homes of clay bricks looked drab from the street, however, they were often attractive inside, built around an open courtyard with decorated rooms. The exteriors of temples and palthe ziggurat, approached by sets of steps. Below, a complex of shrines, storehouses, and administrative offices were constructed around the base or on the several levels of the massive hill. In the low plain of the Tigris-Euphrates valley, the ziggurat literally and figuratively dominated the landscape. The Tower of Babel, described in the Jewish scriptures as reaching to the sky, may have been suggested by the Sumerian ziggurats.

Of the numerous ziggurats and temples that have survived, the best preserved one is at Ur in southern Mesopotamia (modern Iraq) (Figure 1.9). Built around 2100 B.C., this ziggurat was laid out to the four points

FIGURE 1.7 Bull's Head on Lyre. Ca. 3000–1500 B.C. Baghdad Museum, Baghdad. *The lyre's sound box, on which the bull's head is carved, is a hollow chamber that increases the resonance of the sound. Music played an important role in Mesopotamian life, and patrons often commissioned the construction of elegant instruments. Thus, even at this early stage of civilization, those with wealth influenced the arts.*

FIGURE 1.8 *Gudea.* Ca. 2150 B.C. Louvre, Paris. *Little is known of Gudea, but over thirty small statues have been found of this Guti ruler. The body and head of this statuette, which measures 17¾ inches high, were discovered separately and later joined together.*

aces were sometimes adorned with colored glazed bricks, mosaics, and painted cones arranged in patterns, or, more rarely, imported stone and marble.

Archeologists have not yet determined exactly how Mesopotamian cities were laid out. Urban centers were protected by walls, whose imposing and elaborately decorated gates proclaimed the city's wealth and power to inhabitants and visitors alike. The most prominent structure in each Sumerian city was the ***ziggurat***, a terraced brick and mudbrick pyramid that served as the center of worship. The ziggurat resembled a hill or a stairway to the sky from which the deities could descend; or perhaps the structure was conceived as the gods' cosmic mountain. A temple of welcome for the gods stood on the top of

FIGURE 1.9 Ziggurat of Ur. Ca. 2100 B.C. Ur (Muqaiyir, Iraq). *A temple to Nanna, the moon god, stood on the top of the ziggurat, which was terraced on three different levels. On the first level was an entrance way approached by two sets of steps on each side and one in the front. The base measured 200 by 150 feet and stood 70 feet high.*

of the compass. A central stairway led up to the highest platform, on which the major temple rested. The citizens of Ur built this ziggurat to the moon god Nanna. Other cities constructed similar massive podiums in the hopes that they would please the gods and goddesses, that the rivers would be kind to them, and that life would continue. Thus the central themes of Mesopotamian civilization manifested themselves in the ziggurats.

THE CIVILIZATION OF THE NILE RIVER VALLEY: EGYPT

Another great river, the Nile, provided the setting for Egyptian civilization. Unlike the culture of the Mesopotamian valley, however, Nilotic culture evolved continuously, responding mainly to internal changes rather than to external influences. It thus achieved a unified character that lasted for about three thousand years. Isolated by deserts on either side, Egypt developed an introspective attitude that was little influenced by neighboring cultures and led to a sense of cultural superiority. Subjected to the annual floodings of the Nile and aware of the revolutions of the sun, Egypt saw itself as part of a cyclical pattern in a timeless world.

The periodic overflowings of the Nile made civilized life possible in Egypt. Red sandy deserts stretched east and west of the waterway. Beside the Nile's banks, however, the black alluvial soil of the narrow floodplain offered rich land for planting, although the river's gifts of water and arable land were limited. Irrigation canals and ditches plus patient, backbreaking labor were required to deliver the life-giving liquid into the desert.

Because the survival and prosperity of the people depended on the Nile, the river dominated and shaped the Egyptian experience. About 95 percent of the people lived on the less than 5 percent of Egyptian land that was arable. The resulting concentration of people led to the emergence of the agricultural village, the fundamental unit of Egyptian civilization. The reward for farm labor tended to be subsistence living, yet the perennial hope that next year's flood would bring a more bountiful harvest created an optimistic outlook that contrasted with the darker Mesopotamian view.

The Nile linked the "Two Lands," Upper and Lower Egypt, two regions whose differing geography made for two distinct ways of life. Since the Nile flows northward, Lower Egypt referred to the northern lands fed by the river's spreading delta, a region made wealthy by its fertile soil. In contrast, Upper Egypt, or the southern lands, was an area of near subsistence living due to the harsh topography and poor farming conditions. In addition, Lower Egypt, because of its proximity to both Mediterranean and Near Eastern cultures, tended to be more cosmopolitan than the provincial, isolated lands of Upper Egypt.

The earliest Neolithic settlers in the Nile valley probably arrived about 6000 B.C. These earliest Egyptians took up an agricultural life, wresting control of the surrounding lands, taming the river, and domesticating animals. In the rich alluvial soil they cultivated barley, wheat, and vegetables for themselves and fodder for their animals. They hunted with bows and arrows and fished with nets, thereby supplementing their simple fare. They also planted flax from which thread was woven into linen on primitive looms. Most tools and weapons were made of stone or flint, but copper, which had to be imported, became more important after 3500 B.C. The early Egyptians lived in simply furnished, flat-topped houses built of sun-dried bricks. These basic patterns characterized peasant life throughout much of Egypt's history.

Continuity and Change over Three Thousand Years

Egypt stepped from the shadows of its illiterate past in about 3100 B.C., when Menes proclaimed himself king and united the upper and lower lands. His power reached from the Mediterranean to the first cataract of the Nile, making Egypt a state to be reckoned with in the Near East. Egypt's lengthy, complex history is conventionally divided into twenty-six dynasties, which are in turn classified into groups. The three major groups of dynasties are known as the Old Kingdom, the Middle Kingdom, and the New Kingdom. They are preceded and followed, respectively, by two dynastic groups known as the Early Dynastic Period and the Late Dynastic Period. In addition, two intermediate dynastic groupings (the First and the Second) precede and follow the Middle Kingdom (see Time Line 1.3).

In the Early Dynastic Period (about 3100–2700 B.C.), the kings brought prosperity through their control of the economy and fostered political harmony through diplomacy and dynastic marriages. These rulers, claiming to be gods on earth, adopted the trappings of divinity and built royal tombs to ensure their immortality.

With the Old Kingdom (about 2700–2185 B.C.) Egypt entered a five-hundred-year period of peace and prosperity. Isolated from major civilizations, Egypt rose to greatness as its political institutions matured and its language was adapted to literary uses. The most enduring accomplishment of the Old Kingdom became the pyramid—the royal tomb devised by the Fourth Dynasty kings (Figure 1.10). Massive in size and awesome as the visible symbol of the kings' power, the pyramids served to link the rulers with the gods and the cosmos. Yet, although the kings could impress their people with divine claims, they could neither subdue the forces of nature nor make their power last forever. For reasons not fully understood, these rulers loosened their control over the state and thus ushered in an age of political fragmentation called the First Intermediate Period.

In the First Intermediate Period (about 2185–2050 B.C.), civil war raged sporadically and starvation wiped out much of the populace. Eventually, a family from Thebes in Upper Egypt reunited the state and initiated the Middle Kingdom (about 2050–1800 B.C.). The new dynasty, the twelfth, extended Egypt's southern boundary and helped bring about a cultural renaissance, especially in literature, but unity was short-lived.

The Second Intermediate Period (about 1800–1552 B.C.) was an age of chaos provoked both by repeated failures of the Nile to flood and by a resurgence of local warlords. A weakened Lower Egypt succumbed to the Hyksos, Semitic-speaking invaders from Palestine. Backed by warriors in horse-drawn chariots, the Hyksos with their bronze weapons easily defeated the copper-armed Egyptians. The Hyksos era constituted a watershed in Egypt's history because it ended the isolation that had fed the feelings of

TIME LINE 1.3   EGYPTIAN CIVILIZATION   All dates approximate and B.C.

6000	3100	2700	2185	2050	1800	1552	1079	525
Neolithic and Predynastic Periods	Early Dynastic Period	Old Kingdom	First Intermediate Period	Middle Kingdom	Second Intermediate Period	New Kingdom	Late Dynastic Period	Persian Conquest

FIGURE 1.10 The Pyramids at Giza. View from the Air, Looking North-east. Pyramid of Mykerinus (foreground), ca. 2525 B.C.; Pyramid of Kheops (center), ca. 2590 B.C.; Pyramid of Khephren (rear), ca. 2560 B.C. *The Fourth Dynasty was the Age of Pyramids, when this characteristic shape was standardized and became a symbol of Egyptian civilization. The Great Pyramid, in the center, was the first structure at Giza.*

cultural superiority. Egyptian nobility now joined aristocracies everywhere in employing the horse for war and sport, and Egyptian artisans fully entered the Bronze Age.

Ahmose I, a Theban King, drove out the Hyksos and inaugurated the New Kingdom (1552–1079 B.C.), the most cosmopolitan era in Egyptian history. Pursuing the Hyksos into Palestine, Ahmose conquered the foreign peoples along the way, creating the first Egyptian empire. To the northeast, Egypt's kings, now called pharaohs, pursued imperial ambitions against the cities in Palestine, Phoenicia, and Syria, a move that provoked deadly warfare with the Hittites of Anatolia. Egypt finally secured its possessions by peacefully dividing up the Near East with the Hittites and the Assyrians. To the south, the pharaohs pushed Egypt's frontiers to the Nile's fourth cataract. As the empire grew, Egypt's society underwent the greatest changes of its entire history, including religious innovation by a ruling family, widespread material affluence, extravagant temple building, and artistic and literary experimentation.

But imperial success gave way to decline after 1200 B.C., signaled by the pharaoh's growing dependence on unreliable foreign troops. Bands of homeless wanderers, called Sea Peoples by the Egyptians, began to disrupt trade and normal social life. Over the course of a century, the marauding invaders forced Egypt to withdraw behind its historic borders and thus brought the empire to an end. The success of the Sea People's challenge, despite their small numbers, lay in their new weapons, for these destructive migrants were the leading edge of the Age of Iron. Egypt's lack of iron ore probably contributed fatally to its military decline.

During the Late Period (about 1079–525 B.C.), Egypt slipped into senility. Ignoring their kingdom's weak condition, the pharaohs continued to meddle, albeit unsuccessfully, in the affairs of the Near East until Egypt fell to Assyria. When Assyrian power declined, a Libyan dynasty ruled Egypt until the Persians subdued them in 525 B.C. Egypt, now part of the Persian Empire, ceased to exist as an independent state.

Just as the pharaoh dominated the state, so the rulers controlled the predominantly agrarian economy. Although in theory all land belonged to the pharaoh, in practice departments of government or the priesthood of a temple exploited the land and the king's serfs. Upper Egypt provided the bulk of farm produce that Lower Egypt exported to Mediterranean neighbors. In prosperous years the pharaohs claimed up to half of the farm crops to support their building programs, especially funerary monuments. But in years of famine dynasties fell and the state splintered into separate units.

Foreign trade was also a royal monopoly. The government obtained cedar from Lebanon, olive oil from Palestine, and myrrh from Punt, probably on the Somali coast. Since Egypt never developed a coinage, the pharaohs bartered for these imports with papyrus rolls (for writing), linen, weapons, and furniture. The pharaohs also exported gold from the eastern desert and copper from the Sinai peninsula. In addition, Egypt served as the carrier of tropical African goods—ebony, ivory, and animal skins—to the eastern Mediterranean.

Egyptian society was hierarchical, and at the top stood the pharaoh—the king and god incarnate. Because divine blood coursed through the ruler's veins, he could marry only within his own family. Tradition decreed that the Chief Queen, who was identified with the goddess Hathor, the mother of the god Horus, would produce the royal heir. If she failed to produce offspring, the successor pharaoh was selected from sons of the ruler's other wives or royal cousins. On rare occasions, when there was no suitable heir, the Chief Queen became the pharaoh, as did Hatshepsut in the New Kingdom.

Ranked below the ruling family were the royal officials, nobles, large landowners, and priests. The pharaoh's word was law, but these groups were delegated powers for executing his will. Early in the Old Kingdom, many opportunities existed for commoners to rise in the royal service, but the priests and bureaucrats gradually closed off avenues for social mobility by making their offices hereditary. On a lower level, artists and artisans worked for the pharaonic court and the nobility. Although their status was low, those who headed their professions were accorded inflated titles and positions. At the bottom of the social pyramid peasants and a small number of slaves formed the bulk of Egypt's population. Personal liberty took second place to the general welfare, and peasants were pressed into forced labor during natural disasters such as floods and at harvest time.

A Quest for Eternal Cultural Values

Until the invasion of the Hyksos, Egypt, in its splendid isolation, forged a civilization whose serene values and timeless forms deeply mirrored the religious beliefs of the rulers and the stability of the state. But as contact with other cultures and civilizations grew, Egyptian culture changed to reflect new influences. Writers borrowed words from other languages, for example, and sculptors displayed the human figure in more natural settings and poses. Still, Egyptian culture retained its distinctive qualities, and innovations continued to express traditional ideals.

Religion   Egypt was a theocracy, or a state ruled by a god. Believing that the deities had planned their country's future from the beginning, the Egyptians thought of their society as sacred. From the time that Menes first united Egypt, religious dogma taught that the king, as god on earth, embodied the state. Egyptian rulers also identified themselves with the deities. For example, Menes claimed to be the "two ladies," the goddesses who stood for Upper and Lower Egypt. Other rulers identified themselves with Ra, the sun god, and with Ra's son, Horus, the sky god who was always depicted as having the head of a falcon. Because of the king's divinity, the resources of the state were concentrated on giving the ruler proper homage, as in the Old Kingdom's massive tombs, designed on a superhuman scale to ensure his safe passage to the next life.

Egyptian subjects worshiped the pharaoh, but the pharaoh could venerate any deity he pleased. Hence, the shifting fortunes of Egypt's many cults depended on the ruler's preference. For example, Ptah (who, like the Hebrew God in Genesis, created through speech) became the god of Memphis, which was the capital of the Old Kingdom. The kings of the Fifth Dynasty, on the other hand, called themselves sons of Ra, the sun god, and they honored this celestial deity by building him temples more impressive than their own royal tombs. Later, the Twelfth Dynasty brought Amen (a word meaning "hidden one") to the fore, and a series of rulers adopted his name, as in Amenemhat. Royal favor to a god generally increased the wealth and influence of the god's cult and priests.

Consequently, by the time of the New Kingdom, society had become top-heavy with priests and their privileged religious properties.

Egypt came close to having a national deity during the New Kingdom when Akhenaten (about 1369–1353 B.C.) reshaped the royal religion at his capital, Amarna. Elevating Aten, the god of the sun's disk, to supremacy above the other gods, Akhenaten systematically disavowed the older divinities—a heretical view in tolerant, polytheistic Egypt. This innovation aroused the opposition of conservative nobles who supported the powerful priests of the Theban god, Amen. Akhenaten ultimately failed, and later pharaohs tried to erase his name and memory from history. The Amarna revolution, however, like the religious choices of the pharaohs generally, had little effect on the ordinary Egyptian, who continued to believe that the pharaoh could intervene with the other gods for the benefit of all.

The foremost distinguishing mark of Egyptian religion was its promise of immortality—a belief that generated a more optimistic attitude toward human existence than that found in Mesopotamia. At first, in the Old Kingdom, only the kings were accorded this reward. Eventually, nobles and royal officials were buried in the vicinity of the rulers' tombs, thereby ensuring their immortality as assistants to the risen god in the afterlife. By the First Intermediate Period, the nobles had claimed their own right to immortality by erecting tombs on which the royal funerary texts were copied. Later, immortality apparently was opened to all Egyptians, although only the wealthy minority could afford the cost of a proper burial.

Writing and Literature   Late predynastic Egypt learned the idea of writing, but not foreign words, from Mesopotamia. The Egyptians initially drew pic-

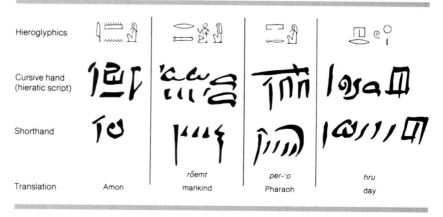

FIGURE 1.11   Egyptian Writing. *From the Old Kingdom onward, the hieroglyphs (in the top line) constituted the style of formal writing that appeared on tomb walls and in monuments. Religious and governmental scribes soon devised a cursive script for their daily work (in the bottom line) that was quicker and simpler to use.*

Hieroglyphics

Cursive hand (hieratic script)

Shorthand

Translation   Amon   rôemt   per-'o   hru
                                    mankind   Pharaoh   day

FIGURE 1.12 IMHOTEP. Step Pyramid of King Djoser. Ca. 2680 B.C. Sakkareh, Egypt.
Though isolated from its neighbors until about 1730 B.C., Egypt was influenced by
surrounding cultures, as the design for the step pyramid at Sakkareh shows. Resting on a
rectangular base and rising in six progressively smaller stages, this pyramid was modeled on
Mesopotamia's ziggurat. But unlike the ziggurats, which were made of dried clay bricks, it
was built of cut stone, the first building to be so constructed in the world.

tographs, called *hieroglyphs*, for such words as
"hoe," "arrowhead," and "plow." This early hiero-
glyphic script could also depict abstract words for
which no adequate picture was available, but because
such picture writing was time-consuming and clumsy
to execute, the scribes soon made the pictographs
function as signs, or clusters of consonants, for other
words (Figure 1.11).

Egyptian literature produced no single great work
that rivals *Gilgamesh*, but the Egyptian experience was
rich in its variety of literary genres. For example, Pyramid Texts, the writings inscribed in burial chambers,
formed the chief literary genre in the Old Kingdom.
As this era gave way to the First Intermediate Period,
new prose genres, like prophecies and pessimistic
writings, arose that addressed the prevalent political
disintegration and social upheaval. Such was the
tenor of the times that writers expressed views con-
tradicting Egypt's otherwise optimistic attitudes to
death and life. *An Argument between a Man Contem-
plating Suicide and His Soul* describes a desperate mortal finally choosing the emptiness of death rather than
life in a materialistic and violent world.

The prophecies, hymns, and prose narratives of
the Middle Kingdom constitute the classical period of
Egyptian letters. The most famous work of the Middle Kingdom, as well as of all Egyptian literature, is
the *Story of Sinuhe*, a prose tale that celebrates the
ruler Senusert I and his subject, the hero named in
the title. Fleeing Egypt, Sinuhe earns fame and fortune in Lebanon yet yearns for his beloved homeland. Sinuhe's exploits smack of the folk tale, for in
one episode he subdues a taunting giant of a man,
much as David defeated Goliath in the Old Testament
story. Eventually, a gracious Senusert writes Sinuhe,
forgiving his wandering subject's unnamed crime
and inviting him to return home. The travel yarn concludes with a homecoming scene in which a joyful
Sinuhe is reintegrated into Egyptian court society.

The richest period in Egyptian letters occurred
during the New Kingdom. In addition to songs prais-
ing the pharaoh, poets now composed lyrics telling
of the pain of parted lovers, and new genres included
model letters, wisdom literature, and fairy tales.
Akhenaten's revolution led to unique forms of literary expression, as in the *Hymn to Aten*, which praised
this universal god. While the hymn has similarities
to Psalm 104 of the Old Testament, Akhenaten's text,
unlike the Jewish scriptures, was not a declaration of
monotheism. Instead, the *Hymn to Aten* recognized a
special link between Akhenaten and his family and
the god of the solar disk but without keeping the
ruling dynasty from worshiping other deities.

Architecture   The classic Egyptian building was the
pyramid, whose shape seemed to embody a constant
and eternal order. During the Old Kingdom, the pyramid became the only building deemed suitable for a
ruler-god's resting place preparatory to the afterlife.
A modified version of the pyramid appeared first in
about 2680 B.C. in the step pyramid of King Djoser at
Sakkareh, opposite Memphis (Figure 1.12). Later

FIGURE 1.13 Hatshepsut's Temple. Ca. 1490 B.C. Deir el Bahri, across from Luxor, Egypt. *Hatshepsut's temple was planned for the same purpose as the pyramids—to serve as a shrine for the royal remains. In actuality an ascending series of three colonnaded courtyards, this temple provided a spectacular approach to a hidden sanctuary carved in the steep cliffs.*

Egyptian rulers preferred the true pyramid form, and this design did not develop further.

The true pyramid appeared in the Old Kingdom when the Fourth Dynasty ruler Kheops erected the Great Pyramid at Giza, across the Nile from Cairo (see Figure 1.10). The anonymous architect executed this largest stone building in the world—6.25 million tons—with mathematical precision. Many of the tomb's two million stones were quarried on the site, although most were obtained farther upstream and ferried to Giza during the flooding of the Nile. The infinitesimally small deviation between the two sets of opposing base sides of the pyramid showed the scientific spirit already at work in this early stage of

FIGURE 1.14 The Great Sphinx. Ca. 2560 B.C. Giza, Egypt. *Sphinxes, creatures part lion and part human, were often depicted in Egyptian art. The most famous sphinx was the one at Giza, carved from the rock on the site. The sphinx's colossal size prevented the anonymous sculptor from rendering it with any subtle facial expressions. More significant as a monument than as a great work of art, the Great Sphinx had a practical purpose—to guard the nearby pyramid tombs.*

Egypt's history. Later, two of Kheops's successors, Khephren and Mykerinus, added their pyramids to make the complex at Giza the symbol of the Old Kingdom and one of the wonders of the ancient world.

The fascination with majestic pyramids ended with the Old Kingdom, and the pyramids eventually gave way to funerary temples when the New Kingdom pharaohs began to construct splendid monuments for themselves that reflected Egypt's new imperial status. The temple of Queen Hatshepsut is perhaps the most beautiful example of this architectural development (Figure 1.13). Designed by the royal architect Senmut, the temple of Hatshepsut was carved into the face of the mountain at Deir el Bahri, across the Nile from Luxor. Senmut, adopting the post-and-lintel style of construction, gave the queen's temple two levels of pillared colonnades, each accessible by long sloping ramps. The most arresting features of Hatshepsut's temple are its round columns, which are used alongside rectangular pillars in the porticoes. These columns—with their plain tops and grooved surfaces—suggest the graceful columns of later Greek architecture, although some scholars dismiss this similarity as coincidental. Be that as it may, this Egyptian monument, like the later Greek temples, shows a harmonious sense of proportion throughout its impressive colonnades.

Sculpture, Painting, and Minor Arts   In the royal graveyard at Giza, artisans of the Old Kingdom carved from the living rock a mythical creature that stirred the imagination of most peoples in the ancient world—a sphinx, half-lion and half-man (Figure 1.14). Although this creature often inspired feelings of dread, in actuality there was little mystery to the sphinx, since its original purpose was to guard the royal tombs, perhaps to frighten away grave robbers. Indeed, this first sphinx's face was that of Khephren, the Fourth Dynasty king whose pyramid stood nearby. Today, this crumbling relic stands as a reminder of the claims to immortality of the Old Kingdom rulers.

The sheer size and mythical character of the Great Sphinx set it apart from Old Kingdom sculptures in the round, which favored human-scaled figures and realistic images. The life-size statue of King Mykerinus and his Chief Queen, found beneath the ruler's pyramid at Giza, showed this art's brilliant realism (Figure 1.15). The sculpture embodies the characteristics of what became the standard, or classical, Egyptian style: their left legs forward, the king's clenched fists, their headdresses (sacred regalia for him and wig for her), their rigid poses, their serene countenances, and the figures' angularity. Although sculpted in the round, the couple was intended to

FIGURE 1.15 *King Mykerinus and His Chief Queen.* Ca. 2525 B.C. Museum of Fine Arts, Boston. *This life-sized slate sculpture of Mykerinus, a Fourth Dynasty ruler, and his Chief Queen was removed from its resting place beneath the king's pyramid at Giza (see Figure 1.10). In addition to such sculptures, the royal tombs contained furniture, including beds, chairs, and tables, and funerary equipment, such as vessels, figurines of attendants, and ornaments.*

FIGURE 1.16 *Hatshepsut.* Ca. 1460 B.C. Metropolitan Museum of Art. *This sculpture is one of over two hundred statues of Hatshepsut intended to adorn her massive and elegant funeral temple at Deir el Bahri in the western hills of Thebes. Despite the authoritative pose and regalia that convey her Pharaonic status, she is subtly represented as a woman.*

be viewed from the front, so the work has a two-dimensional quality.

In contrast to practices in the Old Kingdom, the wives of rulers in the New Kingdom acquired claims to divinity in their own right. A statue of Hatshepsut represents her in the clothing and with the sacred pose of pharaoh (Figure 1.16). Having first been Chief Queen to Thutmose III in the New Kingdom, after his death she seized leadership, probably with the cooperation of the powerful Theban priesthood of Amen. Although more than a thousand years separated this sculpture from that of Mykerinus (see Figure 1.14), in its expression of dignity and authority the statue of Hatshepsut bears a strong resemblance to the earlier work, thus demonstrating the continuity of the Egyptian style.

A major challenge to Egypt's traditional, austere forms occurred in Akhenaten's revolutionary reign. A low-relief sculpture of the royal family exemplifies the naturalism and fluid lines that this artistic rebellion favored (Figure 1.17). Akhenaten nuzzles one of his daughters in an intimate pose, while his wife dandles another daughter on her knees and allows a third to stand on her right arm. The domesticity of this scene is quite unlike the sacred gestures of traditional Egyptian sculpture, but the religious subject of this relief remains true to that tradition, as the rays streaming from the disk of Aten onto the royal family indicate.

Just as Egypt's sculpture in the round developed a rigid *canon*, or set of rules, so did two-dimensional

FIGURE 1.17 *Family Scene: Pharaoh Akhenaten, Queen Neferititi, and Their Three Daughters.* Ca. 1350 B.C. Agyptisches Museum, Berlin. *The religious ideas associated with Akhenaten's reforms are expressed in the lines streaming from the sun's disk above the royal couple. Each ray of the sun ends in a tiny hand that offers a blessing to the royal family.*

FIGURE 1.18 Herdsmen and Cattle. Ca. 2563–2423 B.C. Tomb of Ptahhopep, Sakkareh, Egypt. *In this relief sculpture, the cattle as well as the human figures are depicted with feet sideways. Though failing to show perspective, the Egyptian artist nevertheless has created a realistic scene. The cattle move in the casual way of domesticated animals, with the odd one here and there turning away from the forward motion. Near the top two herdsmen lead the cattle while a third one prods them along with a rod.*

representations acquire a fixed formula, whether in relief sculptures or in wall paintings. The Egyptians never discovered the principles of perspective. On a flat surface, the human figures were depicted in profile, with both feet pointing sideways, as in the low-relief sculpture from an Old Kingdom tomb shown in Figure 1.18. However, the artistic canon required that the eye and the shoulders be shown frontally, and both arms had to be visible along with all of the fingers. The craftsman determined the human proportions exactly, by the use of a grid. Throughout most Egyptian art history, the human figure was conceived as being 19 squares high standing and 15 squares high seated, and anatomical parts were made accordingly proportional. The canon of proportions was established by the time of the Old Kingdom, and its continued use, with slight variations, helped Egyptian art retain its unmistakable style. Wall paintings, in contrast to relief sculptures, permitted a greater sense of space to be created, but the rules regarding the human figure still had to be observed

(Figure 1.19). Given these stringent conventions, the Egyptian artists who worked in two dimensions were amazingly successful in creating the image of a carefree society bubbling with life.

Besides their excellence in sculpture and painting, the Egyptians set an incomparable standard in the minor arts, examples of which have been found in royal tombs. Discovered in 1922, the burial chamber of the New Kingdom pharaoh Tutankhamen has yielded up the richest domestic treasures. Of the thirty-four excavated royal tombs, only that of King Tut—as he is popularly known—escaped relatively free from violation by thieves in ancient times. A decorated chair may be taken as representative of the elegant craftsmanship of the hundreds of objects found in Tutankhamen's tomb. His ceremonial cedar chair, faced with gold, ivory, and bronze, has exquisite carved figures in the back (Figure 1.20). These carvings include the god of eternity, with his arms outstretched, and hieroglyphs that honor and praise the dead ruler.

FIGURE 1.19 Banqueting Scene. Ca. 1567–1320 B.C. British Museum. *In a small space, the Egyptian painter has created a delightful banqueting scene, a favorite subject in tomb decoration. The scene depicts nearly nude dancers accompanied by extravagantly dressed musicians, whose braided hair cascades around their faces.*

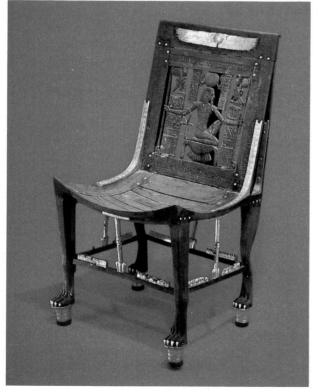

HEIRS TO THE MESOPOTAMIAN AND EGYPTIAN EMPIRES

With the decline of Mesopotamian and Egyptian empires after 1000 B.C., successor kingdoms arose in the eastern Mediterranean, notably those of the Hittites, the Assyrians, the Medes, and the Persians. If the length of their rule and the richness of their achieve-

FIGURE 1.20 Ceremonial Chair for King Tutankhamen. Ca. 1334–1323 B.C. Cairo Museum, Egypt. *This elegantly decorated chair was intended for the ruler's use in a religious ceremony, probably at his coronation. As such, it is the ancestor of all royal thrones in the West. Its lion-paw legs became a favorite motif in Western-style furniture.*

TIME LINE 1.4 HEIRS TO THE MESOPOTAMIAN AND EGYPTIAN CULTURES   All dates approximate and B.C.

3000		1450	1180
Hittites in Anatolia		Hittite Empire	

2000		850	612
Rise of Assyria		Assyrian Empire	

700	612	550	327
Rise of Medes	Medean Empire	Persian Empire	

ments failed to measure up to Mesopotamian and Egyptian civilizations, they nevertheless brought law and order to numerous peoples over vast territories and offered a convincing model of what civilized life ought to be.

The Hittites and Assyrians were rival empires whose fortunes ebbed and flowed, although Assyrian power lasted longer than Hittite (see Time Line 1.4). In 612 B.C., Nineveh, the Assyrian capital city, was sacked by the Medes, an Indo-European people from the southwest Iranian plateau, and the Assyrian empire passed under their control. Medean rule, however, was shortly supplanted when their empire fell to the Persians, another nomadic Indo-European tribe, in about 550 B.C. With masterly skill, successive Persian rulers forged the strongest and largest empire that the eastern Mediterranean had seen until this time. At its height, Persian rule extended from Egypt in the south to central Russia in the north, and from Cyprus in the west to the Indus River in the east. Only Greece eluded Persia's grasp. In 327 B.C. Alexander the Great defeated the last Persian king, thus allowing the Greeks to assimilate the Persian lands.

Persian culture followed in the footsteps of Assyria, but Persian art lacked the savagery associated with the Assyrian style. Instead, Persian art emphasized contemplative themes with less action (Figure 1.21). Persian culture's most original and enduring contribution was the religion of Zoroaster (or Zarathustra), a prophet who lived in about 600 B.C. Rejecting polytheism, Zoroaster taught a dualistic religion in which the god of light, Ahuramazda, engaged in a universal struggle with the god of darkness, Ahriman. According to Zoroaster, those who lead puritanical lives not only gain favorable treatment in the afterlife but also ensure the triumph of the forces of good. Key ideas of Zoroastrianism influenced other religions: Zoroaster's martyrdom, the prophet's life filled with miracles, the evil spirit as the Prince of Darkness, and the notion of a Last Judgment.

FIGURE 1.21 Nobles Marching up the Stairs. Ca. 512–494 B.C. Persepolis, Iran. *This charming relief sculpture, carved on the side of a stairway at the Persian capital, Persepolis, depicts aristocrats mounting the stairs to greet their king on New Year's Day, a sacred festival celebrated on the summer solstice. Each noble bears a flower offering to the monarch as a sign of his devotion.*

The Legacy of Early Near Eastern Civilizations

Mesopotamia and Egypt provided the earliest models of civilization in the West. In both, large numbers of people were organized into societies characterized by class stratification, a division of labor, complex political, economic, and religious forms, technological advances, and cultural achievements. They weren't the only ancient civilizations—others developed in China, India, South America, and elsewhere—but they are the ones to which Westerners most directly trace their cultural roots.

Mesopotamia's gifts to Western civilization are impressive. In addition to writing, they established urbanism as a way of life in contrast to agrarian or village existence. In more practical matters, they created a mathematical system based on 60 that gave the world the 60-minute hour and the 360-degree circle. They also divided the seasons and devised a lunar calendar to mark off periods of days to aid them in their planting. Trade and commerce forced them to come up with ways of counting, of measuring, and of weighing that became the standard procedures for other Near Eastern peoples for centuries. Mesopotamian myths, legends, and epics found their way into the folk tales and literature of other cultures.

Egypt made equally impressive contributions to the West. Egyptian bureaucrats, who wanted to predict the correct date for the rising of the Nile's waters, originated a solar calendar that is the basis of the Western calendar. The Egyptian model, which divided the year into twelve months of thirty days each with five days of holiday at the end, was conveyed to Western culture by the Romans. In architecture, Egyptian builders devised the column with a decorated capital, which later Greek architects probably adopted. The Greek builders also borrowed the Egyptian tradition of sound engineering principles rooted in mathematics. Similarly, Greek sculptors owed a debt to Egyptian forms and poses. Indeed, the Egyptian idea of an aesthetic canon influenced both sculptors and artists in Greece.

In literature, the Egyptians explored a variety of genres—such as wisdom writing—and folk tales that influenced the Hebrews and Greeks. In science, Egyptian physicians became renowned throughout the Near East for their medical learning and knowledge of drugs. Finally, with its priceless treasures, its mysterious pyramids, and its cult of the dead, Egypt inspired curiosity and excitement in foreigners from ancient times onward. One of the first Western tourists to visit Egypt was the Greek historian Herodotus, whose writings in the fifth century B.C. helped to create the Egyptian mystique. The world's fascination with the culture of ancient Egypt has not abated today.

KEY CULTURAL TERMS

culture	*polytheism*
civilization	*anthropomorphism*
Paleolithic	*pantheism*
Neolithic	*stele*
pictogram	*post-and-lintel construction*
ideogram	*ziggurat*
phonogram	*hieroglyphs*
cuneiform	*canon*

SUGGESTIONS FOR FURTHER READING

PRIMARY SOURCES

KASTER, J., ed. and trans. *The Literature and Mythology of Ancient Egypt.* London: Allen Lane, 1970. An up-to-date anthology that includes creation myths, rituals, stories, songs, proverbs, and prayers.

KRAMER, S. N. *History Begins at Sumer.* Philadelphia: University of Pennsylvania Press, 1981. A standard collection of original Sumerian sources by one of the most renowned modern Sumerian scholars.

PRITCHARD, J. B. *Ancient Near Eastern Texts Relating to the Old Testament.* Princeton: Princeton University Press, 1969. For the serious student, a collection of the most important non-biblical texts, including myths, histories, prayers, and other types of writing.

SANDARS, N. K., ed. *The Epic of Gilgamesh.* New York: Penguin, 1972. The editor's informative introduction sets the tone for this famous ancient epic.

SECONDARY SOURCES

Prehistory and Mesopotamia

DAHLBERG, F., ed. *Woman, the Gatherer.* New Haven: Yale University Press, 1981. Six essays in support of the thesis that women's social and economic role in early societies was more important than previously assumed.

FAGAN, B. M. *People of the Earth: An Introduction to World Prehistory.* Boston: Little, Brown, 1983. Balanced introduction to the study of human history up to the beginning of civilization; for the beginning student.

FRANKFORT, H. *The Art and Architecture of the Ancient Orient.* Rev. ed. New York: Penguin, 1969. A sweeping but detailed and well-illustrated survey of art from the Sumerians to the Syrians (800 B.C.).

———. *The Birth of Civilization in the Near East.* New York: Barnes and Noble, 1968. One of the best introductions to Mesopotamia and Egypt by a well-known scholar.

KRAMER, S. N. *The Sumerians: Their History, Culture and Character.* Chicago: University of Chicago Press, 1963. Best for beginning students, again, by an outstanding Sumerian scholar.

LEAKEY, R. E. *The Making of Mankind.* New York: Dutton, 1981. Written by the son of one of the most famous families in anthropology whose discoveries regarding the origins of humans have generated many debates.

MACQUEEN, J. G. *The Hittites and their Contemporaries in Asia Minor.* Rev. ed. London: Thames and Hudson, 1986. Uses textual and archeological sources to create historical narrative and analysis of the Hittites.

OLMSTEAD, A. T. *History of the Persian Empire.* Chicago: University of Chicago Press, 1948. Despite its age, this work is still a classic of Persian studies.

STROMMENGER, E., and HIRMER, M. *5000 Years of the Art of Mesopotamia.* New York: Abrams, 1964. A sweeping survey that includes magnificent photos of ancient ruins and sculptures along with useful notes and floor plans.

Egypt

EDWARDS, I. E. S. *Treasures of Tutankhamun.* New York: Ballantine Books, 1976. The catalog for the famous art exhibit; splendidly illustrated.

JAMES, T. G. H., and DAVIES, W. V. *Egyptian Sculpture.* Cambridge: Harvard University Press, 1983. A short guide to Egyptian sculpture in the British Museum, the home of one of the finest collections outside Egypt.

MERTZ, B. *Temples, Tombs, and Hieroglyphs: A Popular History of Ancient Egypt.* New York: Dodd, Mead, 1978. A lively, entertaining guide suitable for the beginning student.

MICHALOWSKI, K. *Great Sculpture of Ancient Egypt.* New York: Reynal, 1978. A beautifully illustrated work that discusses the defining role played by the idea of an artistic canon.

WILSON, J. A. *Culture of Ancient Egypt.* Chicago: University of Chicago Press, 1956. Still the best introduction.

2

AEGEAN CIVILIZATION

The Minoans, the Mycenaeans, and the Greeks of the Archaic Age

Although Mesopotamia and Egypt offer successful models of civilization, the tradition of Greece is often the first in which Westerners feel they can recognize themselves. What ties us moderns to ancient Greece is their vision of humanity, for they were the first to place human beings at the center of the universe. The Near Eastern cultures focused on deities and godlike rulers, paying little attention to the strivings of humanity. The Greeks, on the other hand, no longer saw mortals as the inconsequential objects of divine whim. Instead, men and women assumed some importance in the scheme of things; they were seen as having some control over their destinies and some moral responsibility for their actions. By the fifth century B.C., the Greek philosopher Protagoras could proclaim, "Man is the measure of all things."

With their new way of thinking, the Greeks surged forward in all areas of creativity, ultimately reaching heights that some think have never been equaled. Because of their grandeur and noble appeal, Greek poetry, sculpture, and architecture became the standard against which later works were frequently judged. From the Greeks the Western tradition has inherited many of its political forms and practices, its views on human behavior, its insistence on philosophical rigor, and its approach to scientific inquiry. In essence, through their human-centered consciousness and their cultural achievements, the Greeks laid the foundation of Western civilization.

Greek culture developed in the basin of the Aegean Sea (Map 2.1). On rocky coasts and rugged islands and peninsulas, the people coaxed a sub-sistence living from the thin, stony soil and turned to the sea for trade, conquest, and expansion. During the Bronze Age, the inhabitants of the island of Crete and the Greek peninsula traded with the Egyptians and the Hittites of Anatolia. The early Greeks borrowed and adapted a writing system from the Phoenicians. They were indebted to the Egyptians for sculptural techniques and to other Near Eastern civilizations for techniques in working with metal and clay, for music and mathematics, and for elements of their religious system.

The people we now know as the Greeks were not the first to thrive in the Aegean basin (Time Line 2.1). Before their story begins, in the period known as the Archaic Age and dating from about 800 B.C., two other distinctive civilizations—the Minoan and the Mycenaean—established centers of culture in the area and left their mark on those who followed.

PRELUDE: MINOAN CIVILIZATION, 3000–1300 B.C.

During the same time that civilizations were flourishing in Egypt and Mesopotamia, another culture was developing among the Neolithic settlements on the island of Crete. By about 2000 B.C. a prosperous and stable mercantile civilization had emerged, and between 1700 and 1400 B.C. it reached its high point in

MAP 2.1

The Aegean World

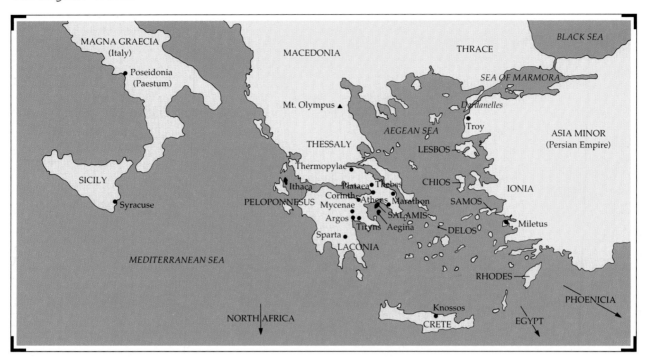

TIME LINE 2.1   MINOAN AND MYCENAEAN CIVILIZATIONS   All dates approximate and B.C.

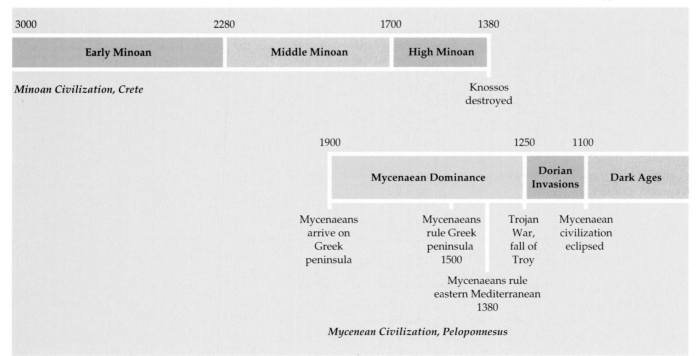

FIGURE 2.1 The Central Court at Knossos. Ca. 1750–1650 B.C. *The central court, measuring about 164 feet by 82 feet, was an open space surrounded by rooms and passageways to other parts of the palace. When British archeologist Sir Arthur Evans uncovered these ruins in 1902, he became convinced that he had discovered the palace of the legendary King Minos and labeled the civilization Minoan—a descriptive term used interchangeably with Cretan.*

wealth, power, and sophistication. This society, labeled Minoan after King Minos, a legendary Cretan ruler, apparently was organized into a complex class system that included nobles, merchants, artisans, bureaucrats, and laborers. Noble life was based in palaces, and twentieth-century archeological excavations of several palace sites indicate that communities were linked in a loose political federation, with the major center at Knossos on the north coast. Remarkably, no fortified walls protected the Minoan palaces, suggesting that the cities remained at peace with one another and that the island itself afforded adequate protection against invading sea raiders. Crete's tranquil image is further supported by the absence of weapons in excavated remains.

The palace at Knossos has revealed more about Cretan life than any other cultural artifact. The palace's central court, though no longer paved or walled, still provides a sense of the grandeur and expanse of this once-magnificent site (Figure 2.1). An impressive plumbing and drainage system brought running water to and from the palace, and a complex layout of rooms and passageways on several levels turned

the interior into a maze. Below ground, a storage area contained huge earthenware pots that held grains, oils, and wines, probably collected as taxes from the populace and serving as the basis of trade and wealth. Beautiful *friezes* (bands of designs and figures) decorated the walls of rooms and hallways. *Frescoes*—paint applied directly on wet plaster—of dolphins, octopuses, and other ocean creatures enlivened the palace walls.

Although archeologists have discovered two written Cretan scripts, which they have labeled Linear A and Linear B, neither of these scripts has revealed anything about Minoan political, social, or philosophical systems. Minoan religion appears to have been matriarchal, centering on the worship of a mother goddess, or great goddess, creator of the universe and source of all life. Statues of a bare-breasted goddess with snakes in her hands show how the deity was portrayed, but the precise purpose of these statues is unknown (Figure 2.2). Minoans also honored numerous minor household goddesses and venerated trees and stone pillars, to which they probably attributed supernatural powers. Near the end of their

FIGURE 2.2 Earth Goddess with Snakes. Ca. 1600–1580 B.C. Archaeological Museum, Heraklion, Crete. *This cult figure, about 11 inches high, was discovered in the Treasury of the Knossos Palace. Her triangular dress, with its apron and flounced skirt, is similar to those of Cretan youths in surviving frescoes.*

era, the Minoans began to bury their dead in underground tombs and chambers, but neither the reason for the new burial practice nor its ritualistic meaning has been discovered.

What has been uncovered on the palace walls, and which apparently had deep religious significance, is a fresco depicting bull leaping—a sport or ritual activity perhaps associated with a bull cult (Figure 2.3). Regardless of its meaning, this daring act is probably more fiction than fact: The maidens (painted white) stand at either end of the bull while a male athlete (painted red) somersaults over the beast's back, a feat that is virtually impossible to accomplish.

Minoan trade dominated the eastern Mediterranean until about 1380 B.C., when the island was dev-

FIGURE 2.3 *Bull Leaping.* Ca. 1500 B.C. Archaeological Museum, Heraklion, Crete. *This fresco (approximately 32 inches high) from the east wing of the palace at Knossos is one of the largest paintings recovered from Crete. The association of young men and women with bulls in this scene brings to mind the legend of the Minotaur, in which seven youths and seven maidens were periodically sacrificed to a monster, half man and half bull, who lived in an underground labyrinth, supposedly on Crete.*

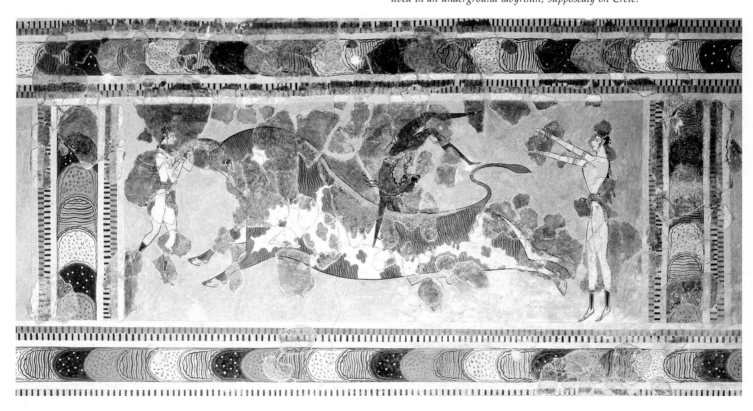

astated by a natural catastrophe—perhaps a volcanic eruption on a nearby island, an earthquake, a tidal wave, or a combination of these disasters. Weakened by Mycenaean incursions over the preceding centuries, Minoan civilization quickly fell to these raiders from the Greek mainland or to other invading seafarers. Whatever the whole story, the Minoans disappeared suddenly and mysteriously, leaving few remnants of their peaceful civilization.

The Greeks of the Archaic Age had no direct knowledge of Minoan civilization. What shaped the Greek attitude towards the Minoans was information conveyed through mythology. Myths are usually considered fiction, but buried within them are often actual folk memories or deep psychological truths.

For example, Crete is traditionally the birthplace of the god Zeus. The Minoans worshiped a Zeus who was born in a cave, grew to manhood, and died. They venerated the site of his birth and honored him as a child. The later Greeks, however, believed Zeus to be the immortal father and ruler of the Olympian deities, and they were incensed by the Minoan belief that the god died. The grain of truth in this story may be that although the Greeks eventually dominated Crete in physical terms, elements of Minoan religion found their way into later Greek beliefs; thus, in a sense, the Olympian gods *were* born in Crete.

Mythology created the image of Minoan civilization as sophisticated, materialistic, and pleasure-loving by later Greek standards. Significantly, modern excavations have borne out this impression. The Archaic Greeks, despite the allure of Crete, did not see the Minoan past as part of their heritage. Nonetheless, Cretan influences on Greece may be detected in language, religion, social organization, and economic pursuits.

BEGINNINGS:
MYCENAEAN CIVILIZATION,
1900–1100 B.C.

Unlike the Minoans, the Mycenaeans continued to live for the Greeks of the Archaic Age through the *Iliad* and the *Odyssey*. The events related in these two epic poems occur during the Mycenaean Age, and the stories furnished the Greeks with many of their heroes—Achilles, the doomed warrior, for example, and Odysseus, the tough and wily wandering sailor. Eventually, the Greeks traced their tradition to Mycenae, honoring its warriors as their ancestors and as models of ideal noble behavior and values.

Mycenaean civilization, named by archaeologists for Mycenae, one of its most prominent fortress cities,

developed on the rugged lower Greek peninsula known as the Peloponnesus. An aggressive, warrior people perhaps from the plains of southern Russia or from the Tigris-Euphrates valley, the Mycenaeans arrived on the peninsula in about 1900 B.C., and by about 1500 B.C., they ruled the entire Peloponnesus.

A feudal order similar to that found later in medieval Europe characterized the Mycenaean political system. Family ties and marriages, tentative alliances, and uneasy truces bound the local rulers in a confederation of petty kingdoms. The kings of these fortress states and their warriors controlled the surrounding countryside. A staunch loyalty developed between the kings and their noble allies, generating a rigid class structure that exploited those who were not warriors.

A royal tax system created a need for a large bureaucracy of collectors and civil employees who ranked just below the ruling elite. Paralleling the bureaucracy were the retainers, military providers, and servants who supported the kings and nobles. At the low end of the social scale stood the merchants, traders, artisans, small landowners, peasants, and slaves—the last, like the royal servants, probably captured in wars or raids.

The ruins of the Mycenaean fortress-palaces, with their massive double walls, narrow escape passages, and wide gateways, stand as mute testimony to the harshness of the militaristic life and the power of the local king. The best known palace ruin, at Mycenae, contains the famous Lion Gate, constructed from four massive hewn stones, or *ashlars* (Figure 2.4). On one of these stones two carved lions, separated by a column, face each other and stretch out their long, muscular bodies. Placed there to watch over the fortress and to remind the populace of the ruler's power, the beasts must have intimidated all visitors who entered or left the citadel.

Within the fortresses and across the eastern Mediterranean archaeologists have found jars, containers, vessels, and terra cotta figurines, revealing the high level of the Mycenaeans' artistic skill with clay and their wide-ranging trade and travel. The weapons and personal items crafted for the warriors show especially impressive artistic skills. A decorated sword blade of a lion hunt, inlaid in gold and silver, exemplifies the attention to delicate detail that the artisan brought to this art (Figure 2.5).

Mycenaean religion appears to have been a fusion of Minoan and local deities. Like the Minoans, the Mycenaeans venerated numerous household goddesses and worshiped aspects of nature in caves and natural shrines. Local deities seem to have been of two kinds: Some were predecessors of the Olympian gods and goddesses worshiped by the later Greeks

FIGURE 2.4 The Lion Gate at Mycenae. Ca. 1300 B.C. *The Lion Gate is a massive structure of four gigantic blocks—two posts and a beam forming the entrance and a triangular block on which are carved the two 9-foot-high lions and the central column. So impressive were the megalithic fortresses of the Mycenaeans to the later Greeks that they called them cyclopean, convinced that only a race of giants, the Cyclopes, could have built them.*

FIGURE 2.5 *Lion Hunt.* Ca. Sixteenth Century B.C. National Museum, Athens. *An anonymous craftsman has decorated every part of this 9-inch dagger. Whether or not the weapon was ever actually used in battle is not clear, but its fine details and realistic figures must have made it a prized possession of a Mycenaean warrior. This dagger survived because it was buried alongside its owner in a funeral mound.*

FIGURE 2.6 Mycenaean Shaft Grave Circle. Ca. 1600–1500 B.C. *About 92 feet in diameter, the circle contained six graves that, upon excavation, yielded well-preserved skeletons along with jewelry, ornaments, weapons, and vases. The positioning of the bodies in the graves is thought to indicate Egyptian influences.*

and had the same names; others were nature divinities and spirits. Two sets of **shaft graves** have been excavated at Mycenae, yielding fabulous gold treasures and indicating that the Mycenaeans buried their dead with honor (Figure 2.6). Perhaps influenced by the Egyptians, they wrapped the bodies and surrounded them with precious objects and pottery. From such practices and attitudes evolved the worship of heroes, a central aspect of Greek culture.

The Mycenaean feudal system flourished for several centuries, and after 1380 B.C., when Crete fell, the Mycenaeans extended their raiding and trading activities throughout the eastern Mediterranean. In about 1250 B.C. they attacked the wealthy and strategic city of Troy, on the western coast of present-day Turkey, near the Dardanelles (see Map 2.1). Although similar expeditions had brought booty to the Mycenaeans on earlier occasions, this long, exhausting foray weakened them, leaving them open to conquest by more vigorous tribes. Ironically, this siege

of the Trojan citadel probably inspired the *Iliad* and the *Odyssey*, Homer's enduring epics. Overwhelmed by the Dorians from the north, Mycenaean civilization faded, and by about 1100 B.C. the Age of the Mycenaeans closed. The three-century hiatus in Greek history that followed, when writing disappeared and cultural activities virtually ceased, served to heighten the fascinating image of the Mycenaeans for the Greeks of later times.

The Mycenaeans, as presented to them by Homer, gave the Greeks many of their ideals. Heir to three centuries of oral traditions about the Mycenaeans, Homer invented the Age of Heroes. He sang to the Greeks of a glittering past that both inspired and sobered them. In the *Iliad* and the *Odyssey* the Greeks found a universe with a basic moral order and a people with a distinct ethos, or ethical code. The pursuit of excellence that Homer attributed to his heroes became an ideal of historical Greece. Many aristocrats even traced their ancestry back to Homer's warriors and, through them, to the gods and goddesses. So rich was Homer's world that art and literature drew on it for subjects and incentive throughout Greek history. Through him the Mycenaeans gave the Greeks their myths, their religion, their ethics, their perception of the universe, and their insight into human character.

INTERLUDE: THE DARK AGES, 1100–800 B.C.

With the fall of the Mycenaean citadels, a period known as the Dark Ages began, and life reverted to simpler patterns. People now lived in isolated farming communities and produced only essential tools and domestic objects. Commercial and social interchange among communities, already made hazardous by the mountainous terrain, became even more dangerous, and communication with the eastern Mediterranean kingdoms nearly ceased.

Yet some fundamental changes were slowly occurring even during this era. Political power was gradually shifting from kings to the heads of powerful families, laying the foundation for a new form of government, and iron gradually replaced bronze in tools, weapons, and other crafted objects—thus ending the Bronze Age and beginning the Iron Age in Greece. Many Mycenaeans fled to the coast of Asia Minor, which later came to be called Ionia, thus paving the way for the formation of an extended Greek community around the Aegean and Mediterranean seas.

THE ARCHAIC AGE, 800–479 B.C.

In about 800 B.C. the Greeks emerged from their long years of stagnation and moved into an era of political innovation and cultural experimentation. Although scattered and isolated, they shared a sense of identity based on their common language, their heroic stories and folk tales, their myths and religious practices, and their commercial and trading interests. They claimed a common mythical parent, Hellen, who fathered three sons—the ancestors of the three major Greek tribes, the Ionians, the Aeolians, and the Dorians—and thus they called themselves Hellenes and their land Hellas. In the next three centuries the Greeks would reconstruct their political and social systems, develop new styles of art and architecture, invent new literary genres, and make the first formal philosophical inquiries into the nature of human behavior and the universe. By the end of this period, they would have laid the foundations for a new world.

Political, Economic, and Social Structures

By the beginning of the Archaic Age, the isolated farming community had evolved into the *polis* (plural, *poleis*), a small, well-defined city-state. Several hundred of these poleis lay scattered over the Greek mainland and abroad. Although each polis had its own separate history and unique traits, they all shared certain features. An *acropolis*, or fortified hilltop, served as a citadel where the rulers usually resided (Figure 2.7). Temples and holy shrines stood on the acropolis or below in an *agora*. The agora, an open area where political leaders held forth, citizens assembled, and the populace congregated to conduct business and socialize, was the center of a polis. The pursuit of both public and private matters in an agora served to bind the citizens of a polis together in their daily lives and to foster civic pride and loyalty. In effect, a polis, through its control of the religious, cultural, and psychological components of its relatively closed community, molded the citizenry into an organic body with a collective identity.

Simultaneously with the emergence of the polis in about 800 B.C., the political system underwent a basic change. The kings had been deposed by the leaders of noble families who owned most of the land and possessed the weapons and horses. These wealthy warriors established oligarchies, or government by the few. The kingships, once abolished, faded into memories and myths used by the nobles to inspire and guide future generations. Although the oligarchies worked to benefit the aristocrats, they were also characterized by exemplary leadership, civic idealism, and cultural and artistic patronage. However, most oligarchies eventually failed because of unforeseen and far-reaching military and economic changes.

New military tactics now made obsolete the aristocrats who had distinguished themselves in battle as sword-wielding warriors in horse-drawn chariots. Foot soldiers—armed with long spears, protected by shields and personal armor, and grouped in closed ranks called phalanxes—were proving more effective in battles than individual warriors. These foot soldiers, or hoplites, were recruited from among independent farmers, merchants, traders, and artisans, who were also profiting from an expanding economy. As their military value became evident, these commoners soon demanded a voice in political decisions.

FIGURE 2.7 Acropolis, Athens. View from the West. *The acropolis dominates Athens in the twentieth century just as it did in ancient times when it was the center of Athenian ceremonial and religious life. Today it is the towering symbol of Athens' cultural heritage as well as the center of the local tourist industry. A landmark in the history of town planning, the acropolis is the ancestor of all carefully laid out urban environments from ancient Rome to Renaissance Florence to modern Brasilia.*

At the same time, a growing population, beginning to strain the limited agricultural resources, led to an era of overseas expansion and colonization. The Hellenes sent citizens to join their earlier Ionian settlements and to establish new colonies along the coasts of Spain, North Africa, the Black Sea and southern Russia, and Sicily and southern Italy, which became known as *Magna Graecia,* or Greater Greece.

Foreign ventures and expanded trade increased the wealth of the new middle class and reinforced their desires for more economic opportunities and political influence, but the entrenched aristocracy blocked their way to power. Frustrated by the inability of reform efforts to solve deep-seated problems, in the sixth century B.C. many poleis turned to rulers whom they entrusted with extraordinary powers to make sweeping economic and political changes. Many of these tyrants, as the Greeks called them, restructured their societies to allow more citizens to benefit from the growing economy, to move up the social scale, and to participate in the political process. However, some tyrants perpetuated their rule through heirs or political alliances and governed

harshly for years, thus giving the word *tyrant* its modern meaning.

Regardless of the different results of the tyrants' reigns, by about 500 B.C. life in the poleis was similar in many ways. Citizens—freeborn males who could claim the right to enter into politics by virtue of family and wealth—voiced their opinions in a widening democratic process. They sat on juries, debated in the assemblies, and defended their polis in time of war. Civic responsibility, recognized as a central element in everyday life, was now passed on by the aristocrats to this new band of citizens.

Although horizons were expanding for the male citizens, other members of this predominantly middle-class society were severely restricted in political and economic matters. Women—except for priestesses and a rare literary figure like Sappho—were subservient to men. In Athens, for example, women possessed no legal or economic status, for they were by law under the control of the males in the household. Typically, women remained secluded at home, tending to the children and waiting on their husbands. Families often married off their daughters

sula. When the Persians landed near Athens at Mar-   the ensuing Golden Age.

FIGURE 2.9 EUPHRONIOS. *The Death of Sarpedon.* Ca. 520 B.C. Metropolitan Museum of Art. *This vase painting illustrates a famous scene from Book 16 of the* Iliad. *Following Homer, the painter has depicted the fallen warrior Sarpedon, the son of Zeus and a mortal woman, being carried to his rest by winged figures representing Death and Sleep. Euphronios uses bold colors to dramatize the scene, such as bright red for the gushing blood from Sarpedon's wounds and the device carried by Hermes, the bearded god with curly hair portrayed in the center. Though he is not mentioned in Homer, Hermes' presence is appropriate, since, among his other duties, he guided dead souls into the underworld.*

Epic Poetry The originator of the major traditions of *epic poetry* is traditionally believed to be Homer (about 800 B.C.), a *bard*, or poet who sang his verses while accompanying himself on a lyre-like instrument. In the *Iliad* and the *Odyssey*, Homer sang of the events before, during, and after the Trojan War, stories that had circulated among the Greeks since the fall of Mycenae. Homer entertained an aristocratic audience eager to claim kinship with the Mycenaean past. For many years his poems were transmitted orally by other bards and probably did not exist in written versions until the seventh century B.C. Homer's authorship and, indeed, even his very existence, are established solely by tradition; nothing is actually known about him. Nevertheless, by the end of the Archaic Age the appeal of Homer's poetry had embraced all social levels, and his authority approached that of a modern combination of television, Shakespeare, and the Bible.

The basic appeal of the Homeric epics lies in their well-crafted plots, filled with dramatic episodes and finely drawn characters. Set against the backdrop of the Trojan War, the *Iliad* describes the battle of Ilium, another name for Troy, and the *Odyssey* recounts events after the Greeks defeat the Trojans (Figure 2.9). The earlier of the epics, the *Iliad*, focuses on Achilles, the epitome of heroic Greek manhood. In contrast to the battlefield heroics of the *Iliad*, the *Odyssey* narrates the wanderings of the Greek warrior Odysseus after the fall of Troy. Moreover, the *Odyssey* celebrates marriage, for Odysseus, despite some amorous adventures, remains fixed on thoughts of his wife Penelope, who waits for him in Ithaca.

In both poems, the deities merrily intrude into the lives of mortals, changing and postponing the fate of friend and enemy alike. So great was Homer's authority that his works made him the theologian of Greek religion. His stories of the gods and goddesses, while not completely replacing other versions of their lives, became the standard that circulated wherever Greek was spoken. Homer presented Zeus, the nominal protector of the moral order, as forever under siege by other gods seeking help for their favorite mortals. Although some later Greeks deplored Homer's inattention to moral issues, his roguish portraits of the deities remained indelibly imprinted in the minds of the general populace.

Homer's poetic expression also gave texture to the Greek language. Similes, figures of speech in which two unlike things are compared, help bring the dramatic, exotic events of the stories down to earth. For example, Homer creates a vivid image of Odysseus as a ferocious killer when he compares him to a lion "covered with blood, all his chest and his flanks on either side bloody. . . ." In a less violent simile, Homer has Achilles compare his fellow Greeks to "unwinged" baby birds and himself to their nurturing mother. Homer's images also provide a rich repertory of ready phrases and metaphors, known as **Homeric epithets**, such as "the wily Odysseus," "the swift-footed Achilles," and "rosy-fingered dawn."

Besides shaping the language, Homer served as a guide to behavior for the Archaic Greeks. Because they became part of the Greek educational curriculum, his poems acquired an ethical function. A young man who took Achilles or Odysseus for a model would learn to maintain his physical well-being, to speak eloquently in company with other men, to give and receive hospitality, to shed tears in public over the death of his closest friend, to admire the beauty of women, to esteem the material wealth of other nobles, to appreciate songs of bravery, and, above all, to protect his reputation as a man and warrior. On the other hand, a young woman who imitated Penelope, the patient and faithful wife of Odysseus, would inhabit a more circumscribed world, as she learned to weave at the loom, to manage a household, to cultivate her physical beauty, and to resist the advances of other men.

Lyric Poetry   Verses sung to the music of the lyre, or *lyric poetry*, became the dominant literary expression in the late Archaic Age, and lyric verses have dominated Western poetry ever since. Lyric poetry, which originated later than the epic, expressed an author's personal, private thoughts, though the muse Euterpe was credited with the inspiration. The shift from epic to lyric poetry in the sixth century B.C. coincided with changes in the polis, where the rising democratic spirit encouraged a variety of voices to be heard.

Of the several types of lyric poetry, monody, or the solo lyric, became the most influential in Archaic Greece. Poets of monody achieved relative simplicity by using a single line of verse or by repeating a short stanza pattern. These solo lyricists did not hesitate to reveal their most intimate thoughts or details of their private lives.

Unlike the Homeric epics, which survive relatively whole, the solo lyrics are mutilated in the extreme. For example, the bulk of what remains of Sappho's verses consists of random lines and references gleaned from later commentators and only one or two entire lyrics. And of the music, the whole has been lost. The ancients, however, regarded Sappho (about 600 B.C.) as the greatest of the writers of solo lyrics. The philosopher Plato hailed her as the tenth muse in a short lyric he dedicated to her. A truly original writer, Sappho apparently owed no debt to Homer or any other poet. Her work is addressed to a small circle of aristocratic women friends on her native island of Lesbos in the Aegean. She was deeply personal in her interests, writing chiefly about herself, her friends, and their feelings for one another. In her elegant but restrained verses, Sappho sang mostly about moods of romantic passion: of longing, unrequited love, absence, regret, dead feelings, and fulfillment. Sappho's willing vulnerability and her love of truth made the solo lyric the perfect vehicle for confessional writing (Table 2.3).

FIGURE 2.10 Elements of Greek Architecture.

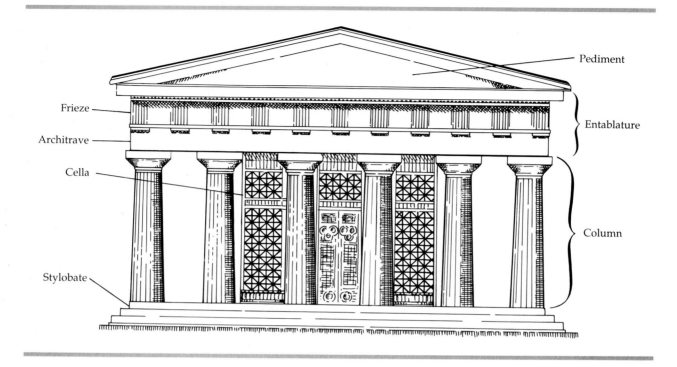

FIGURE 2.11 Greek Architecture of the Doric Order.

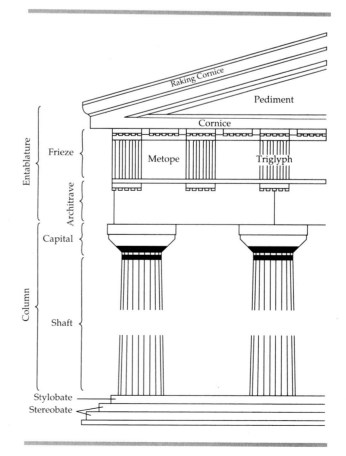

FIGURE 2.12 Temple of Hera at Paestum. Ca. 560–550 B.C.
*This temple stands not only as a model of Archaic Greek architecture
but as a reminder of Greek wealth and expansion. Colonists from
mainland Greece settled southern Italy, the land they thought of as
"greater Greece," in the seventh and sixth centuries B.C., bringing
with them the Olympian gods and goddesses and their ideas of how
to build temples in their honor.*

FIGURE 2.13 Temple of Aphaia, Aegina. View from the
Southeast. 510 B.C. *The Temple of Aphaia in Aegina became the
standard for the Doric Temple style from its creation until it was
superseded by the Athenian Parthenon in the 440s. Built of local
limestone and covered in stucco and painted, the Temple of Aphaia
gleamed like a jewel in its carefully planned site overlooking the
Saronic Gulf. Constructed and decorated with strict attention to
artistic refinements, such as the slender columns and the lifelike
sculptures, this temple represents the climax of Archaic architecture.*

Eventually, after much experimentation, Greek architects overcame the awkwardness of the early Doric
style by deciding that a temple's beauty was a function of mathematical proportions. The Temple of
Aphaia—erected in 510 B.C. by the citizens of Aegina,
Athens' neighbor and perennial enemy—seemed to
embody this principle (Figure 2.13). The architect of
this temple achieved its pleasing dimensions by using
the ratio 1:2, placing six columns on the ends and
twelve columns on the sides. The Temple of Aphaia,
with its harmonious proportions and graceful columns, became the widely imitated standard for the
Doric style over the next half century.

Sculpture   Like the art of Mesopotamia and Egypt,
Greek sculpture was rooted in religious practices and
beliefs. The Greek sculptors fashioned images of the
gods and goddesses to be used in temples either as
objects of worship or as decorations for the pediments and friezes. Of greater importance for the development of Greek sculpture were the *kouros* (plural, kourai) and the *kore* (plural, korai), free-standing

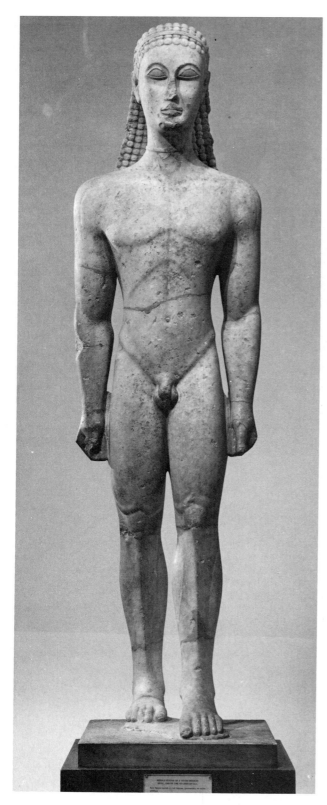

FIGURE 2.14 New York Kouros. Ca. 615–590 B.C. Metropolitan Museum of Art. *The New York Kouros is one of many similar statues dating from about the beginning of the sixth century B.C. During that century the male and female statues evolved from stiff and stereotyped models to natural and anatomically correct forms.*

statues of youths and maidens, respectively. Before 600 B.C. these sculptures had evolved from images of gods, to statues of dead heroes, and finally into memorials that might not even be directly related to the dead person to whom they were dedicated.

What made the *Archaic* statues of youths and maidens so different from Egyptian and Mesopotamian art was the Greek delight in the splendor of the human body. In their representations of the human form, the Greeks rejected the sacred approach of the Egyptians and Mesopotamians, which stressed conventional poses and formal gestures. Instead, Greek sculptors created athletic, muscular males and robust maidens filled with life. For the Greeks, the health and beauty of the subjects was as important as the statues' religious purpose.

The first Archaic statues of youths owed much to the Egyptian tradition, but gradually Greek sculpture broke free of its origins. An early example of the kourai type of sculpture is the New York Kouros (Figure 2.14), named for its present location in New York City's Metropolitan Museum of Art. Artistically, this marble statue of a youth with the left foot forward, the clenched fists, the arms held rigidly at the sides, the stylized hair, and the frontality, that is, the quality of being designed for viewing from the front, shows the Egyptian influence (see Figure 1.15). The Greek sculptor has moved beyond Egyptian techniques, however, by incorporating changes that make the figure more lifelike, such as by attempting to show the correct shape of the knees and suggesting an actual person's mouth. That the result is not a realistic or an idealized human figure is less important than that the sculptor has studied the human body with fresh eyes and endeavored to represent it accurately. With such ground-breaking works as the New York Kouros, the Greeks launched a dynamic tradition that later artists continually reshaped.

A generation after the New York Kouros, new sculptors expressed their changed notion of a beautiful living male body in such works as the Ptoon Kouros (Figure 2.15). This sculpture, which was probably a dedicatory offering to a god or goddess, still shows a powerful Egyptian influence, but it takes a giant step forward to a greater sense of life. The taut body and massive torso convincingly reproduce the athletic qualities of an Olympic competitor, and the curious facial expression, known as the "archaic smile," gives an enigmatic quality to the marble figure.

The korai sculptures, like the statues of youths, evolved from a frozen, lifeless style toward a greater realism, although women were never depicted in the nude at this stage in Greek sculpture. The earliest draped korai sculptures mixed Mesopotamian and

FIGURE 2.15 Ptoon Kouros. Ca.
540–520 B.C. National Museum, Athens.
*The Ptoon Kouros possesses the
distinguishing characteristics of all kourai:
frontality, attention to bodily details, and a
general formality. However, the subtle
innovations in the Ptoon Kouros foreshadow
the Hellenic sculpture style.*

FIGURE 2.16   Auxerre Kore. Ca. 675–600 B.C. Louvre, Paris. *The Auxerre Kore represents a fairly early stage in the development of this female form. The small size of the sculpture (about 29½ inches high) suggests that it may have been part of a burial rite.*

Egyptian traditions with Greek ideas, sometimes producing an interesting but awkward effect. Such an early work is the Auxerre Kore (Figure 2.16)—named for the museum in Auxerre, France—whose cylindrical shape is copied from Mesopotamian models and whose stiff pose, wiglike hair, and thin waist are bor-

rowed from Egypt. The Greek sculptor added the broad mouth and the Greek peplos (a loose-fitting outer robe) decorated with a meander pattern, but the Auxerre Kore, despite its charming details, is rigid and inert.

The Peplos Kore (Figure 2.17), dating about a century later, expresses beautifully the exciting changes that were taking place in late Archaic sculpture. The statue wears a chiton, or tunic, over her upper torso, and a belted peplos. The sculptor has replaced the rigidity of the Egyptian pose with a more graceful one, as shown, for example, by the way the figure holds her right arm. Traces of a painted necklace may be seen, for the Peplos Kore, like all Greek sculpture, was painted to make the figure as true to life as possible. The often awkward archaic smile is here rendered to perfection, giving this lovely maiden an aristocratic demeanor.

The Greek tradition of representing males nude and females clothed persisted throughout the Archaic Age and well into the succeeding Classical Age. The Greeks readily accepted male nudity, witnessing it in the army on campaigns, in the gymnasium during exercises, and in the games at Olympia and elsewhere, and this acceptance is reflected in their art. But they were much less comfortable with female nudity (except in Sparta, where women exercised in the nude), so women were usually depicted draped or robed.

The political turmoil brought on by the Persian Wars occurred simultaneously with the revolutionary changes in sculpture that were leading to a new style of art. The Temple of Aphaia at Aegina provides a laboratory setting for the transition from the Archaic to the Hellenic Style (480–323 B.C.) because of the different ages of the building's statues: The sculptures for the west pediment (about 500 B.C.) were made some fifteen years earlier than those on the east pediment (about 490–485 B.C.). Their stylistic differences demonstrate the changes that were underway.

An earlier statue (from the west pediment) depicts the Trojan hero Paris as a nude, somewhat sensual bowman, poised, ready to release an arrow (Figure 2.18). Paris, his body and face revealing very little tension, might have been posing, rather than preparing for action. A later sculpture (from the east pediment) portrays the legendary hero Herakles as a clothed archer, in a stance copied from the *Paris* figure (Figure 2.19). But what a contrast! Herakles' more muscular body is tensed and ready for action. While neither face registers emotion, Herakles' gaze and set jawline convey a more lifelike image of a warrior. The *Herakles* figure is a transitional work to the next style—the Hellenic.

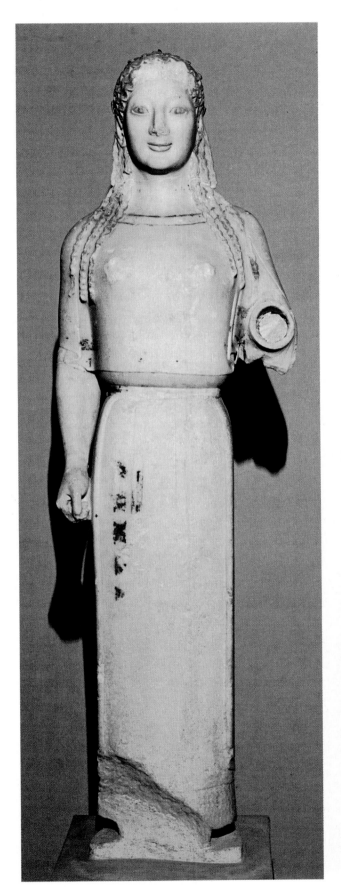

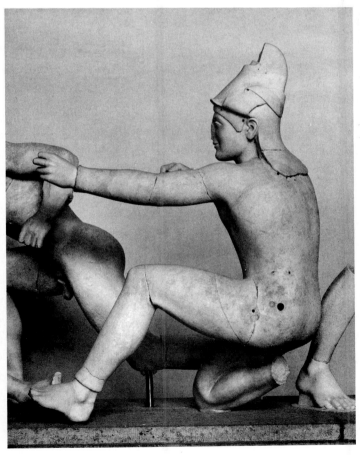

FIGURE 2.17   Peplos Kore. Ca. 535–530 B.C. Acropolis Museum, Athens. *The Peplos Kore represents the highest achievement in the art of the kore. The beauty of the face, the elegance of the dress, and the expectancy of the countenance—this maiden could have been one of those who inspired Sappho's love lyrics.*

FIGURE 2.18   *Paris.* West Pediment, Temple of Aphaia, Aegina. Ca. 500 B.C. Staatliche Antikensammlungen, Munich. *The pedimental sculptures on the Temple of Aphaia illustrate the rapid changes that were occurring in artistic ideals and techniques in the period just preceding the Golden Age of Athens. The sculpture of Paris from the earlier west pediment is formal and stylized in comparison with its counterpart on the east pediment.*

FIGURE 2.19 *Herakles.* East Pediment, Temple of Aphaia, Aegina. Ca. 490–485 B.C. Staatliche Antikensammlungen, Munich. *The statue of Herakles from the east pediment of the Temple of Aphaia shows the advances made in sculpture in the ten to fifteen years since the figure of Paris was crafted for the west pediment. More realistic, detailed, and lifelike than Paris, Herakles is emotionally charged and tense yet composed and restrained—a state admired and often depicted by Hellenic artists. Both archers were sculpted in marble.*

The Legacy of Archaic Greek Civilization

The Archaic Age in Greece was a precious moment in the story of the arts and humanities. Inheriting survival techniques from Neolithic cultures, continuing the urban ways of Mesopotamia and Egypt, and, more importantly, drawing spiritual and psychological sustenance from the Minoans and Mycenaeans, the Archaic Greeks developed a unique consciousness that expressed, through original artistic and literary forms, their views about the deities and themselves and how they both interacted. A mark of the creative power of the Archaic Greeks is that at the same time that they were inventing epic poetry, lyric poetry, the post-beam-triangle temple, the kore and kouros sculptures, and natural philosophy, they were involved in founding a new and better way to live in the polis.

The new way of life devised by the Archaic Greeks gave rise to what we call, in retrospect, the *humanities*—those original artistic and literary forms that made Greek civilization unique. But the cultural explosion of this brilliant age is inseparable from the Greeks' restless drive to experience life to the fullest and their deep regard for human powers. Having devised their cultural forms, the Archaic Greeks believed passionately that by simply employing these models, either through studying them or by creating new works, the individual became a better human being. In

this way, the Archaic Greeks' arts and humanities were imbued with an ethical content, thus suggesting for some—notably philosophers—an alternative way of life to that offered by religion.

Wherever we look in this age, we see creative energy, a trait that has characterized Western civilization through the ages. Even though the different cultural forms did not develop at the same pace during the Archaic Age—sculpture, for example, was not as expressive as lyric poetry—still, these early aesthetic efforts were fundamentally different from those of the earlier Near Eastern civilizations. The touchstone of the humanistic style developed by the Archaic Greeks was their belief in human powers, both intellectual and physical. Indeed, the most powerful literary voice of this age, Homer, was quoted over and over for his claim that mortals and divinities are part of the same family. Less confident people, hearing this assertion, might have reasoned that human beings are limited in their earthly hopes. But, for the Greeks of this period, Homer meant that humans are capable of godlike actions. The reverence that the Archaic Greeks expressed for all noteworthy deeds, whether in poetry, in warfare, or in the Olympic games, attested to their belief in the basic value of human achievement.

KEY CULTURAL TERMS

frieze	*pediment*
fresco	*entablature*
ashlar	*cornice*
shaft graves	*stylobate*
muse	*cella*
Olympian deities	*capital*
chthonian deities	*triglyph*
hubris	*metope*
epic poetry	*relief*
bard	*entasis*
Homeric epithet	*fluting*
lyric poetry	*kouros*
post-beam-triangle	*kore*
construction	*Archaic*
architrave	*humanities*

SUGGESTIONS FOR FURTHER READING

PRIMARY SOURCES

BARNSTONE, W., ed. and trans. *Greek Lyric Poetry*. New York: Bantam Books, 1962. Selections from literary fragments dating from the seventh century B.C. to the sixth century A.D.; includes helpful biographical notes.

HOMER. *Iliad*. Translated by R. Lattimore. Chicago: University of Chicago Press, 1962. An excellent modern translation of the story of the Trojan War.

————. *Odyssey*. Translated by R. Lattimore. New York: Harper & Row, 1968. The epic of Odysseus's adventures after the fall of Troy, again in Lattimore's lively translation.

WHEELWRIGHT, P., ed. *The Presocratics*. New York: Bobbs-Merrill, 1966. A nearly complete collection of quotations from early philosophers that captures the flavor of sixth-century Greek thought.

Of all the many translations of Greek literature, the Loeb Classical Library, published by Harvard University Press, is probably the best.

SECONDARY SOURCES

BEYE, C. R. *Ancient Greek Literature and Society*. Ithaca: Cornell University Press, 1987. Excellent treatment of early Greek writings with special emphasis on their public nature.

BOARDMAN, J., JASPER, G., and MURRAY, O., eds. *The Oxford History of the Classical World*. Oxford: Oxford University Press, 1986. An outstanding collection of essays on Greek and Roman history.

BRILLIANT, R. *Arts of the Ancient Greeks*. New York: McGraw-Hill, 1973. A comprehensive survey, lavishly illustrated with photos, drawings, and plans.

FINLEY, M. I. *Early Greece: The Bronze and Archaic Age*. New York: Norton, 1981. One of this well-known scholar's many studies of Greek life.

GRAVES, R. *The Greek Myths*. Garden City, N.Y.: Doubleday, 1981. Perhaps the most thorough treatment of the myths in modern times.

GUTHRIE, W. K. C. *The Greeks and Their Gods*. Boston: Beacon Press, 1954. A clearly written survey of the origins and evolution of Greek religion and its relationship to Greek philosophy.

————. *Greek Philosophers: From Thales to Aristotle*. New York: Harper & Row, 1960. A lucid explanation; one of the best introductions to a complex topic.

KITTO, H. D. F. *The Greeks*. New York: Penguin, 1957. A lively personal interpretation by an admirer of Greek civilization.

LAWRENCE, A. W. *Greek Architecture*. New York: Penguin, 1983. An up-to-date survey of Greek architecture from the Neolithic period to the Roman conquest.

NILSSON, M. *A History of Greek Religion*. Oxford: Clarendon Press, 1952. Traces the evolution of Greek religion from its Minoan roots to the development of the civic religion at the height of Greek civilization.

NORBERG-SCHULZ, C. *Meaning in Western Architecture*. London: Studio Vista, 1975. Analyzes a key architectural monument in each great age of the Western tradition, such as the Parthenon in fifth-century Greece.

POMEROY, S. *Goddesses, Whores, Wives, and Slaves: Women in Classical Antiquity*. New York: Schocken Books, 1975. An overview of the roles of women in public and private and their images in literature; from Homeric to Roman times.

RICHTER, G. A. *Korai*. London: Phaidon, 1968. *Kouroi*. Rev. ed. London: Phaidon, 1970. The definitive studies of Archaic Greek statuary; extensively illustrated.

3

CLASSICAL GREEK CIVILIZATION
The Hellenic Age

With the defeat of the Persians at Plataea in 479 B.C., the Greeks entered the *Hellenic* Age, a period that lasted until the death of Alexander the Great of Macedon in 323 B.C. During the more than 150 years of the Hellenic Age, the Greek world was buffeted by military explosions. The Greeks defeated the Persians for a second time and survived a century of destructive civil war, only to succumb ultimately to the Macedonians. But throughout these turbulent times the Greeks never wavered in their supreme confidence in the superiority of their way of life.

The Greek world consisted of several hundred poleis (city-states), located on the mainland, on the Aegean Islands and the coast of Asia Minor, and in the lands bordering the Mediterranean and Black Seas (Map 3.1). Athens was the cultural center of Greece, but many poleis contributed both materially and intellectually to Hellenic civilization. Corinth, for example, located on the isthmus between Athens and the Peloponnesus, dominated the economy of the Ionian Sea west of Greece, and the poleis of southern Italy *(Magna Graecia)* nurtured important schools of philosophy.

GENERAL CHARACTERISTICS OF HELLENIC CIVILIZATION

Despite diversity among the poleis, the Greeks of the Hellenic Age shared certain characteristics. Competitiveness and rivalry were certainly dominant fea-

tures, as was an increasingly urban style of life (Figure 3.1). Most Greeks still lived in the countryside, but the city now dominated politics, society, and the economy because, regardless of where citizens lived, they had to travel to the city to discharge their civic obligations.

Popular attitudes toward the Olympian deities were also changing, and public worship began to be assimilated into civic festivals. The great art of the age reflected this fusion in such works as the Parthenon, the temple to the goddess Athena, who was the protector of Athens (Figure 3.2). With gods and goddesses playing increasingly ceremonial rather than personal roles, religion became demystified and lost some of its value in the lives of the citizens. Religious dissatisfaction was also triggered by expanded political rights: The more democratic poleis raised the collective hopes of their citizens without being able to satisfy all of their personal longings.

Another feature of Hellenic civilization was a high regard for the balanced life and for moderation as the way to achieve it. In Athenian tragedy a recurrent theme is the danger of great wealth and high position. The playwrights preached that riches and status bred pride and led to envy by other citizens or, worse, envy by the gods. A modest life was the safest way to avoid personal calamity.

The Greeks also sought a balance between the opposite extremes that they recognized in human nature, symbolized by Apollo, god of moderation, and Dionysus, god of excess. As the god of light, Apollo embodied rational thought, ethical ideals, and aes-

MAP 3.1

The Athenian Empire, 431 *B.C.*

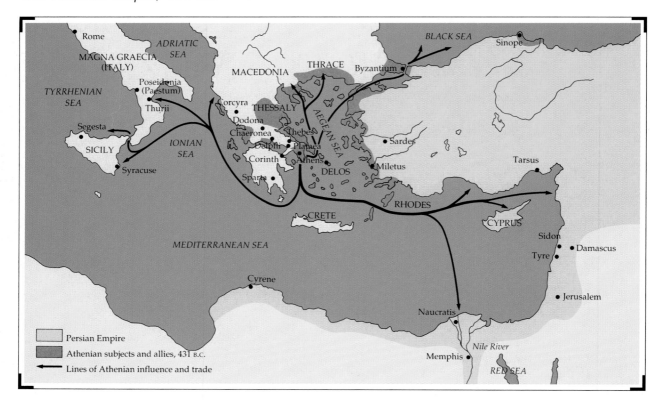

FIGURE 3.1 *Athletes Playing Ball.* Second Quarter of the Fifth Century B.C. National Museum, Athens. *From the dawn of the Archaic period in about 800 B.C., sports, especially competitive sports, were integral to Greek life. In the* Iliad, *which appeared at about that time, Homer describes the athletic games that were played at the funeral of the warrior Patroclus. Later, in Hellenic times, artists used sports contests as subjects, as in this low-relief sculpture depicting a ball game played with curved sticks. The athletes' superbly muscled bodies and the overall sense of calm seriousness are typical of the art of the Hellenic period.*

FIGURE 3.2 *Athena.* Roman Copy Based on Fifth-Century Statue by Phidias. Staatliche Museen, Berlin. *The stern features of Athena corresponded well with her function as a war goddess and the patron of Athens. Phidias's sculpture disappeared in ancient times, but numerous copies such as this one have survived. The original sculpture was larger than life and dominated the inner sanctum of the Parthenon.*

FIGURE 3.3 *Apollo.* West Pediment, Temple at Olympia. Ca. 460 B.C. Olympia Museum. *Apollo's serene countenance in this splendidly crafted head reflects his image as the god of moderation. As the deity who counseled "Nothing in excess," Apollo was a potent force in combating the destructive urges that assailed the Greeks.*

thetic balance. Apollo's temple with its oracle at Delphi was one of the holiest shrines in Greece, second only to the island of Delos, his birthplace (Figure 3.3).

Dionysus, on the other hand, was the god of wine, of drunken revelry, of sexual excess, and of madness. Women known as *maenads* followed and worshiped him, sometimes tearing apart beasts in their blind frenzy. By the Hellenic Age, these excesses were confined to rural areas, for the Dionysiac impulse was constantly being tamed by the Apollonian spirit and the urban way of life. In Athens, the drunken worship of Dionysus was transformed into a civic festival, the Dionysia, from which tragedy, perhaps the high-

est expression of the Greek ethical genius, was born (Figure 3.4).

Greek citizens of Hellenic times, then, were proud of their own polis and competitive in their approach to life. They typically lived in a city, where they participated in civic functions and religious rites. They were skeptical about the gods and goddesses, but they believed strongly in a life of moderation. However, despite the many basic things that they shared with their fellow Greek citizens in the other poleis—a common land, common language, common ancestry, common history, and Homer—they were never to be citizens of a politically united Greek world.

FIGURE 3.4 *Dionysus and His Followers.* Ca. 430 B.C. Staatliche Museum, Berlin. *Scrolling around a perfume vase, this painting depicts a bearded Dionysus seated on the right with his followers. Of his twelve devotees, eleven are maenads, young female revelers; the last is the bearded Silenus, the foster father and former schoolmaster of Dionysus. Silenus is depicted on the lower left in his usual drunken, disorderly state.*

DOMESTIC AND FOREIGN AFFAIRS: WAR, PEACE, AND THE TRIUMPH OF MACEDONIA

On the eve of the Hellenic Age, the Greeks, having defeated the Persians, were united in only two senses: in their continuing opposition to Persia and in their hostility to any polis that tried to control the others. Although they cooperated on short-term goals that served their common interests, good will among the poleis usually evaporated once specific ends were met.

Despite rivalries, the Greek economy expanded. A rising tide of middle-class citizens took advantage of the economic opportunities created by the vicissitudes of war and politics, causing manufacturing to grow and commerce to flourish. Speculators amassed huge fortunes by supplying ships or insuring cargoes, and entrepreneurs enriched themselves by buying and selling arms. Although the economic base

remained agricultural, people increasingly flocked to the polis to make their fortunes, to participate in government, and to discover a more stimulating life.

The Hellenic Age can be divided into four distinct phases: (1) the Delian League; (2) wars in Greece and with Persia and the Thirty Years' Peace; (3) the Peloponnesian War; (4) Spartan and Theban hegemony and the triumph of Macedonia (Time Line 3.1). While these conflicts raged, life within the polis went on; and in some poleis, notably Athens, extraordinary political, cultural, and intellectual changes were occurring.

After defeating the Persians, the Greeks realized that a mutual defense organization was the key to freedom from further Persian attack. In 478 B.C., a number of poleis met on Delos, Apollo's sacred island, and formed the Delian League, a defensive alliance, with Athens at its head. But within a short time, Athens began to transform the league into an instrument of imperialism. Flush with military successes and arrogant about the superiority of democ-

TIME LINE 3.1 PHASES OF HELLENIC HISTORY   All dates B.C.

479	460		431	404		323
Delian League	Wars in Greece and with Persia	Thirty Years' Peace	Peloponnesian War	Spartan and Theban Hegemony		Triumph of Macedonia

racy, Athens intervened in the domestic affairs of other poleis and imposed its form of government on them. When a league member refused to pay the tribute to the Delian treasury or tried to withdraw, for example, Athens sent soldiers to force the rebellious polis to submit. As the oppressive nature of Athenian policies emerged, Athens' independent neighbors became alarmed.

Athenian power, however, was restricted by strained relations with Sparta, by the continuing menace of Persia, and by the highly unstable Delian alliance. When a negotiated settlement finally resolved Persian claims, the Delian League fell apart, leaving Athens vulnerable to her enemies on the Greek mainland. Led first by Thebes and later by Sparta, the Greek poleis launched attacks on Athens. The war dragged on as both sides sparred for position and shifted their alliances. Then, in 445 B.C., when Sparta unexpectedly withdrew, Athens won a quick victory that forced her enemies to negotiate.

The ensuing period of time, known as the Thirty Years' Peace (which in fact lasted only fourteen years), brought the Golden Age of Athens to its zenith. Athenian democracy expanded so that even the poorest citizens were empowered with full rights. Artists and sculptors beautified the Acropolis, and the three great Athenian tragedians—Aeschylus, Sophocles, and Euripides—were active in the drama festivals. Drawing on the Delian treasury, Pericles, the popular leader and general, launched a glorious building program that was essentially a massive public works project (Figure 3.5).

The most eloquent summation of Athenian democracy was offered by Pericles in a speech over the Athenian war dead. Claiming that the soldiers had not died in vain, he defended Athens' open way of life, its tolerance of diverse beliefs, and the versatility of its citizens. With a glance toward hated Sparta, Pericles praised the Athenian ability to love beauty without sacrificing military strength. He concluded with the boast that Athens was the model for Greece.

Pericles' eloquence, however, looked like a cloak for imperialism to most of Greece, and those poleis who were not enamored of Athens became convinced that war was the only way to restrain Athenian aggression. Athens' foreign policy and its expansionism had given rise to an alliance system so delicately balanced that neither side could allow the other to gain the slightest advantage. When Athens' neighbor Corinth went to war with Corcyra (present-day Corfu) in western Greece over a disputed colony, Corcyra appealed to Athens for aid. The Athenians seized the opportunity to gain influence for the first time in the west and sent troops to Corcyra. Athens' initial victories, however, frightened Corinth, who

convinced the Spartans to join them and form the Peloponnesian League. The Peloponnesian War (431–404 B.C.) had begun.

Knowing the Peloponnesian League to be superior on land, Pericles abandoned offensive strategy and withdrew to a defensive position in Athens. He believed that the Athenians could hold out indefinitely within their own walls and win in a war of attrition. But like so many generals before and since, Pericles could not anticipate or control everything. A plague broke out in Athens in 430 B.C., killing off many citizens, including Pericles himself. The first phase of the war ended in 421 B.C., when a demoralized and repeatedly defeated Athens sued for peace.

The second half of the Peloponnesian War shifted from the Greek peninsula to distant Sicily and the west—a move that sealed Athens' fate. In 416 B.C.,

FIGURE 3.5 *Pericles.* Ca. 440 B.C. Vatican Museum. *Pericles possessed a vision of Athens as the political, economic, and cultural center of the Greek world. This portrait bust, even though it is a Roman copy of the Greek original, conveys his strong sense of leadership and determination.*

FIGURE 3.6 *Alexander the Great.* Ca. 200 B.C. Istanbul Museum. *Alexander's youth and fine features, idealized perhaps in this portrait bust, add to the legends that have accumulated around one of the most famous conquerors in history. Later rulers measured themselves against Alexander, whose dream of a united world was cut short by his early death.*

Segesta, a Sicilian polis, begged Athens for military assistance. After a long and heated debate, the Athenians decided to send help. The Sicilian expedition proved to be a disaster, because the Athenians, trying to conduct a war so far from home, were soundly defeated on land and sea and never recovered from their losses. Athens' enemies slowly destroyed what was left of the Athenian fleet, and the once-great polis, stripped of its last line of defense and under seige, capitulated. Athens never recovered its lost military and economic power.

In the early decades of the fourth century B.C., the various poleis scrambled for power. First Sparta and then Thebes emerged as the preeminent city-state, but the ultimate result of these power struggles was only to weaken further the poleis and make them easy prey for an invader.

At the northern edge of the civilized Greek world, that invader was gathering its forces. Macedonia was a primitive Greek state, governed by kings and pop-

ulated with a people speaking a rough dialect of the Greek language, unintelligible to Athenians. Their king, Philip, having been a hostage in Thebes when young, had become a *philhellene*—a lover of Greek civilization. A brilliant soldier, Philip subdued neighboring barbarians and warlords and expanded Macedonia to the east as far as the Black Sea. He then moved southward, conquering the poleis of central Greece. Reacting with alarm, Athens, Thebes, Corinth, and other poleis hastily raised an army, but Philip's well-disciplined troops crushed them at Chaeronea in 338 B.C. After establishing a league between Macedonia and the poleis, he granted the Greeks autonomy in everything except military affairs. Philip now announced an all-out war against Persia but was assassinated before he could launch his first campaign.

Philip's nineteen-year-old son, Alexander, succeeded to the throne. Tutored in philosophy by the famous thinker Aristotle, Alexander nevertheless had the heart of a warrior. When Thebes and other poleis attempted to take advantage of the unsettled situation at Philip's death, Alexander swiftly put down the uprising and burned Thebes to the ground, sparing only the house of the poet Pindar. Placing a general in command of Greece, Alexander turned his sights to the east (Figure 3.6).

Alexander dreamed of a world united under his name and a culture fused from Hellenic and Persian roots. His armies marched into Asia Minor, Egypt, and Mesopotamia, absorbing the great Persian Empire; then they swept through Asia all the way to the banks of the Indus River in India. Along the way, Alexander destroyed and looted the great centers of eastern civilization, but he also founded new cities and spread Greek culture everywhere he went.

Alexander's dream ended abruptly with his death in 323 B.C. at the age of thirty-two. Seizing the opportunity presented by his sudden death, the Greeks revolted against the Macedonian oppressors, but they were quickly overwhelmed. The Macedonians then occupied Athens and installed an aristocratic government. Thus ended democracy and Hellenic civilization—in Greece.

THE PERFECTION OF THE TRADITION: THE GLORY OF HELLENIC GREECE

Throughout this era of shifting political fortunes, artistic and intellectual life flourished. Athens—bursting with creative energy—was the jewel of the Greek world. Atop her Acropolis, perfectly proportioned

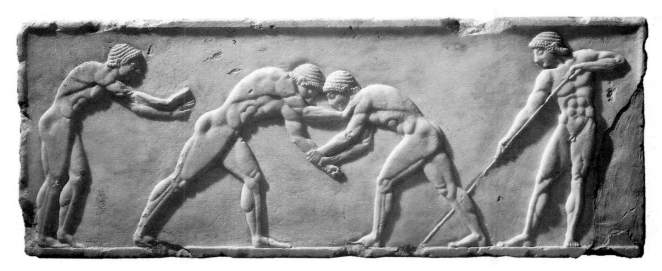

FIGURE 3.7 *Athletes in the Palaestra.* Second Quarter of the Fifth Century B.C. National Museum, Athens. *This low-relief sculpture depicts athletes warming up in the open-air exercise area where spectators would congregate to urge on their favorites. The youth on the left is preparing for a foot race, and the one on the right tests his javelin. The pair in the center has just begun to wrestle. This relief and the relief shown in Figure 3.1 were originally two sides of a sculptured base built into a wall that the Athenians constructed after the Persian Wars.*

marble temples gleamed in the brilliant Aegean sun. Below, in the agora, philosophers debated the most profound questions of human nature. Hundreds of citizens congregated outdoors daily to serve in the assembly, where they passed laws or sat on juries that made legal rulings. Other citizens who were at leisure cheered on the athletes exercising in the open-air gymnasium (Figure 3.7). During drama festivals, the whole city turned out to share the gripping tragedy or to laugh uproariously at the latest comedy.

The culture that flourished in Greece at this time is known as *Classic*, or *Classical*, a term with varied meanings. *Classic* means, first of all, "best" or "preeminent," and the judgment of the Western tradition is that Greek culture was in fact the highest moment in the entire history of the humanities. *Classic* also means having permanent and recognized significance; a classic work establishes a standard against which other efforts are measured. In this second sense, the aesthetic values and forms of Greek culture have been studied and imitated in all later stages of Western history. By extension, "the Classics" are the works that have survived from Greece and Rome.

Classic also refers to the body of specific aesthetic principles expressed through the art and literature of Greece and Rome, a system known as *Classicism*. The first stage of Classicism, which originated in the Hellenic Age, emphasized simplicity over complexity, balance, or symmetry, over asymmetry, and re-

straint over excess. At the heart of Classicism was the search for perfection, for the ideal form—whether expressed in the proportions of a temple constructed in marble or in the canon of the human anatomy molded in bronze or in a philosophical conclusion reached through logic. Hellenic Classicism found expression in many areas: theater, music, history, natural philosophy, architecture, and sculpture.

Theater: Tragedy

One of the most prominent institutions of Greek civilization was the theater, in which the dramatic form known as *tragedy* reached a state of perfection. Greek theater originally arose in connection with the worship of Dionysus. The word *tragedy* in Greek means "goat song," and this word may refer to a prehistoric religious ceremony in which competing male *choruses*—groups of singers—sang and danced, while intoxicated, in homage to the god of wine; the victory prize may have been a sacrificial goat. Whatever its precise origins, by the Archaic Age theater in Athens had taken the form of a series of competitive performances presented annually during the Great Dionysia, celebrated in March.

Features of the Tragic Theater At first, the chorus served as both the collective actor and the commentator on the events of the drama. Then, in the late

FIGURE 3.8 Theater at Epidauros. Ca. 300 B.C. *The best-preserved theater in Greece is the one at Epidauros. Although tragedy was created only in Athens, the popularity of the art form led to the construction of theaters all over Greece—a telling index of Athens' cultural imperialism. The acoustics in this ancient auditorium were remarkable. Performers' voices could clearly be heard throughout the theater even though it is in the open with fifty-four rows of seats accommodating 14,000 spectators.*

sixth century B.C., according to tradition, the poet Thespis—from whose name comes the word *thespian,* or "actor"—introduced an actor with whom the chorus could interact. The theater was born. Initially, the main function of the actor was simply to ask questions of the chorus. During the Hellenic Age the number of actors was increased to three, and occasionally, late in the fifth century B.C., a fourth was added. Any number of actors who did not speak might be on the stage, but only the three leading actors engaged in dialogue. In the fifth century B.C., the chorus achieved its classic function as mediator between actors and audience. As time went on, however, the role of the chorus declined, and the importance of the actors increased. By the fourth century B.C., the actor had become the focus of the drama.

Because the heart of tragedy was originally the chorus, the need for a space to accommodate their dancing and singing determined the theater's shape. The chorus performed in a circular area called an *orchestra,* or "dancing place," in the center of which was a functioning altar, serving as a reminder that tragedy was a religious rite. The audience sat around two-thirds of the orchestra on wooden bleachers or stone seats under the open sky. The other third of the orchestra was backed by a building called the *skene,* which could be painted to suggest a scene and through which entrances and exits could be made (Figure 3.8).

Such simple set decorations may have provided a slight realistic touch, but Greek theater was not concerned with either realism or the expressiveness of individual actors. Ideas and language were what counted. The actors—all men, even in the female roles—wore elaborate masks designed to project their voices, platform shoes, and long robes, which helped give the dramas a timeless, otherworldly quality.

Plays were performed in tetralogies (sets of four) on successive days of the Great Dionysia. Each competing playwright offered three tragedies, not necessarily related in theme or subject, that were performed during the day, and a satyr-play that was performed later. A *satyr-play* usually featured the indecent behavior and ribald speech of the satyrs—sexually insatiable half-men, half-goats—who followed Dionysus. That the Greeks liked to watch three deeply serious dramas followed by a play full of obscene high jinks demonstrates the breadth of their sensibility.

Tragic Drama   The essence of Greek tragedy is the deeply felt belief that mortals cannot escape pain and sorrow. The dramatists shared with Homer the insight that "we men are wretched things, and the gods . . . have woven sorrow into the very pattern of our lives." Although terrible things happened in the tragedies—murder, incest, suicide, rape, mutilation—the attitude of the play toward these events was deeply moral. Violence for its own sake was not the concern of the playwright, and violence was never depicted on stage.

The tragedies were primarily based on the legends of royal families—usually the dynasties of Thebes, Sparta, and Argos—dating from the Age of Heroes of which Homer sang in his epics (Figure 3.9). Since the audience already knew these stories, their interest focused on how the playwright treated a familiar tale, what his ideas were about its moral significance, and how his language shaped those ideas.

The plots dealt with fundamental human issues that did not admit of easy solutions, such as the decrees of the state versus the conscience of the individual or divine law versus human law, to name two recurring topics. Humans were forced to make hard choices without being able to foresee the consequences of their decisions. Nonetheless, the dramatists affirmed that a basic moral order existed underneath the shifting tide of human affairs. The political leaders of Athens recognized and accepted tragedy's ethical significance and educative function and thus made the plays a central part of their civic calendar.

According to the Greek philosopher Aristotle, whose immensely influential theory of tragedy, the *Poetics*, was based on his study of the dramas of the Hellenic Age, the purpose of tragedy was to work a cathartic, or purging, effect on the audience, to "arouse pity and terror" so that these negative emotions could be drained from the soul. The tragic heroes were warnings, not models; the spectators were instructed to seek modest lives and not aim too high. Many tragedians pursued these themes and competed in the Dionysia, but the works of only three still survive—Aeschylus, Sophocles, and Euripides.

Aeschylus Aeschylus (about 525–about 456 B.C.), the earliest of the three dramatists, won first prize in the Great Dionysia thirteen times. He composed about ninety plays, but only seven are extant. His masterpiece, the *Oresteia*, is the only trilogy that has come down intact, and even here the satyr-play is missing. The framing plot for the trilogy was the homecoming from Troy of the Greek king Agamemnon, who had sinned by sacrificing his daughter to gain military success; his murder by his vengeful and adulterous wife, Clytemnestra; and the dire consequences of this killing.

Aeschylus's treatment of these terrible events in the *Oresteia* embodies some of the principles of Classicism. In the first place, Aeschylus shows great simplicity by avoiding distracting subplots: The first play, *Agamemnon*, tells the story of the king's death and Clytemnestra's triumph; the second, the *Libation Bearers*, relates the vengeance murder of Clytemnestra by her son, Orestes; and the third, *Eumenides*, halts—with the help of the Olympians Athena and Apollo—the cycle of revenge by instituting an Athenian court to try such cases. The trilogy is symmetrical in that Agamemnon is killed in the first play as punishment for the murder of his daughter, Clytemnestra's death in the second avenges her slaying of Agamemnon, and the courtroom drama of the third absolves Orestes of the crime of matricide.

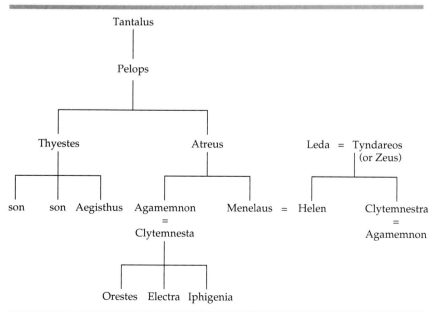

FIGURE 3.9 Genealogy of the House of Argos. *The tragic fate of the House of Argos (or the family of Atreus) was well under way before the opening scene of Aeschylus's tragedy* Agamemnon. *Thyestes seduced the wife of his brother Atreus; in retaliation, Atreus killed Thyestes' two sons and served them to him in a stew. Thyestes then cursed the line of Atreus, and dire consequences followed. Most importantly, Agamemnon, the son of Atreus, sacrificed his own daughter in order to gain favorable weather for his planned invasion of Troy. Besides the* Oresteia, *three more tragedies survive that have plots based on the House of Argos. Those other plays—which have no inner connection like Aeschylus's trilogy—are* Iphigenia in Taurus, Iphigenia in Aulis, *and* Electra, *all by Euripides.*

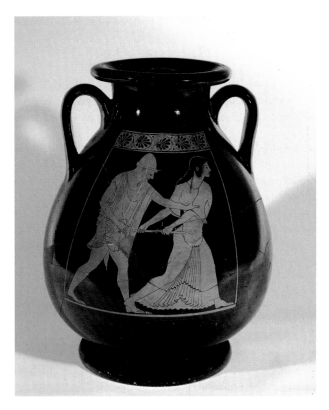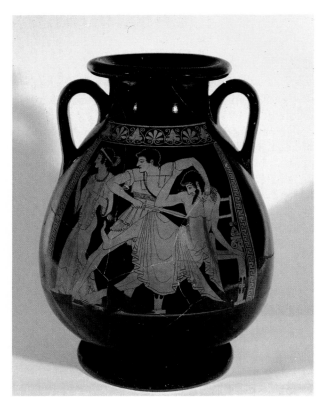

FIGURE 3.10 *Orestes Slaying Aegisthus.* Ca. Late Sixth Century B.C. Kunsthistorisches Museum, Vienna. *This vase painting presents a different version of events in Argos from those given by Aeschylus in the* Libation Bearers, *the second play of the* Oresteia. *The vase painter portrays Clytemnestra bearing an axe (left), a detail Aeschylus omitted, and the sister between Orestes and his mother is not named Electra as she is in the* Oresteia. *However, painter and playwright agree that Orestes killed Aegisthus, his mother's lover.*

Finally, Aeschylus shows great restraint inasmuch as all deaths occur offstage, and the chorus or messengers only describe them. However, for the Athenian audience, the *Oresteia* had moral significance as well as stylistic power. By transforming the Furies, the blind champions of vengeance killing, into the "Kindly Ones" (*Eumenides*), Aeschylus, in effect, affirmed the ethical superiority of the rational Olympians over the earthbound chthonian divinities (see Chapter 2). In the *Oresteia* Aeschylus confronts and resolves the opposition between several seemingly irreconcilable polarities—Olympian and chthonian gods, divine and human justice, religious cult and civic ritual, and fate and free will (Figure 3.10).

Sophocles Sophocles (about 496–406 B.C.), the most prolific of the great tragedians, wrote about 125 plays, but only seven survive. He was popular among the Athenians, who awarded him first prize twenty-four times. Sophocles' *Antigone* (442 B.C.) expresses beautifully the principles of Classical tragedy. The simple plot treats the conflicts between King Creon and his niece Antigone. The principal, although not the sole, philosophical issue explored by the play is whether human or divine law should take precedence. Antig-

one's two brothers have killed each other in a dispute over the Theban crown. Creon decrees that Eteocles, who died defending the city, be buried with honor but that the body of the rebel Polyneices be left as carrion for wild beasts. Antigone, whose name in Greek means "born to oppose," defies his order and buries her brother in compliance with religious teachings. Arrested and imprisoned, Antigone hangs herself, and Creon's son and wife kill themselves. Too late, King Creon sees the light; he gives up his throne saying, "There is no man can bear this guilt but I."

More tensions than that between state and divine law are at issue here. Creon represents the typical tyrant, concerned only with "law and order." His son, Haemon, is the voice of democracy, opposing the tyrannical will of his father. Creon believes in the superiority of public power over domestic life, in the necessity of the state to seek power for its own sake, in the priority of war over the commands of love, and in the right of men to control women. When the king tries to persuade his son to renounce his love for the disobedient Antigone, they argue about all four of these issues. Whether the Athenian citizens sided with Creon or Haemon is unknown, but *Antigone* has become the classic example of a tragic dilemma where two rights confront one another. In his desire for balance, Sophocles gives equally powerful arguments to the play's opposing characters.

Sophocles returned to the history of the Theban dynasty in later plays about Antigone's ill-fated father, Oedipus. In *Oedipus the King* he tells how the Theban ruler unwittingly kills his father and marries his mother and later blinds himself to atone for his guilt. Aristotle held up this play as a model in his analysis of Greek tragedy. In *Oedipus at Colonus,* his last play, Sophocles portrays the former king at peace with himself and his destiny.

Euripides By the time Euripides (about 480–406 B.C.) was writing for the stage, Athens was fighting for its existence in the Peloponnesian War, and with him, the creative phase of Classical theater came to an end. Euripides was in tune with the skeptical mood of the later years of this struggle, and by presenting unorthodox versions of myths and legends, he exposed the foolishness of some popular beliefs and, sometimes, the emptiness of contemporary values. When he staged *The Trojan Women* in 415 B.C., the Athenians could not have missed the parallel between the cruel enslavement of the women of Troy after the Greeks destroyed their city and the fate of the women of Melos, which Athens had just subjugated.

For his ninety or more tragedies (of which eighteen survive), the Athenians awarded the first prize to Euripides only five times, perhaps because his unorthodox plays angered the audience. But later ages, far removed from the stresses of Hellenic times, found his dramas more to their liking. Among the extant works, *The Bacchae* is his masterpiece, a gruesome tale about the introduction of the worship of Dionysus into Thebes. In this play the bacchae, or bacchantes (another name for the followers of Dionysus), blinded by religious frenzy, kill the king of Thebes under the delusion that he is a wild animal. Euripides' dark tragedy may have been a warning to the citizens of Athens about the dangers of both excess and repression in religion and politics.

Euripides followed Classical principles in *The Bacchae,* using a single plot, offstage violence, and well-defined conflict, but he also extended the range of Classical drama with his unorthodox, even romantic language, and his skeptical treatment of familiar themes. Moreover, Euripides pointed the way toward a different sort of theater by having the severed head of the hero brought on stage at the end of the tragedy.

With Euripides the creative phase of Classical theater came to an end. The playwrights who followed him seem to have read their works aloud rather than staging them with actors and choruses. The plays of all the Greek dramatists were presented frequently throughout Greece, however, as well as later in the Macedonian and Roman Empires.

Theater: Comedy

Comedies were performed in the Great Dionysia just as the tragedies were, and they were also entered in contests in another festival known as the Lesser Dionysia, celebrated in late winter. The comedies refused to take anyone or anything seriously. They featured burlesque actions, buffoonery, slapstick, obscenity, and horseplay, and actors wore grotesque costumes with padded bellies or rumps to give a ridiculous effect. Comic playwrights invented their own plots and focused on contemporary matters: politics, philosophies, the new social classes, and well-known personalities. Even the deities were ridiculed and portrayed in embarrassing situations.

The freedom of the comic playwrights could exist only in a democracy. And yet the freedom was limited to a highly ritualized setting—the drama festivals—that allowed, even encouraged, the overturning of rules and the burlesquing of traditions. This controlled expression of the unspeakable provided a catharsis that strengthened communal bonds in the polis. At the same time, the authors demonstrated their faith in the basic good sense of the average citizen.

The comedies of Aristophanes (about 445–about 388 B.C.) are the primary source for what is known as **Old Comedy,** comic Greek plays with a strong element of political criticism. Aristophanes composed forty-four works in all, of which eleven are extant. Like Euripides, he wrote his plays for war-torn Athens, and he satirized famous contemporaries such as the thinker Socrates, depicting him as a hopeless dreamer. Aristophanes must have stepped on many toes, for the Athenians awarded him first prize only four times.

In *Lysistrata,* Aristophanes transcended the limitations of the comedic form and approached the timeless quality of the tragedies. A sexually explicit and hilarious comedy, *Lysistrata* points out the absurdity of the prolonged Peloponnesian War, and, by implication, of all war. In the play, Lysistrata, an Athenian matron, persuades the women of Athens and Sparta to withhold sex from their husbands until they sign a peace treaty. Filled with sexual innuendos, obscenities, and ridiculous allusions to tragic dramas, the play ends with stirring reminders to the Greeks of their common ancestry, their joint victory over the Persians earlier in the century, and their reverence for the same gods. First staged in 411 B.C., seven years before Sparta won the Peloponnesian War, this

FIGURE 3.11 Detail, Scene from a Comedy. Mid–Fourth Century B.C. British Museum. *This scene, painted on a mixing bowl, portrays a situation from a Greek comedy. The actors on the right and left are outfitted in the grotesque costume of comedy with padded rumps and genitals. That these characters are on stage is indicated by the decorations at the bottom of the frame.*

play commented on but failed to derail Athens' headlong rush to disaster (Figure 3.11).

After the Peloponnesian War and the restoration of a harsher democracy in 403 B.C., free speech was severely repressed in Athens. Comedies still relied on burlesque and slapstick, but their political edge was blunted. For all practical purposes, the great creative age of Greek theater was now over.

Music

Like other peoples of the ancient Near East, the Greeks used music both in civic and religious events and in private entertainment. But the Greeks also gave music a new importance, making it one of the humanities along with art, literature, theater, and philosophy. Music became a form of expression subject to rules, styles, and rational analysis. One reason for this was that the Greeks believed music fulfilled an ethical function in the training of young citizens. They also believed that music had divine origins and was inspired by Euterpe, one of the nine muses (thus the word "music").

Nevertheless, the vast library of Greek music has vanished, scattered by time's indifferent wind. What knowledge there is of that lost heritage, which can only be partially reconstructed from surviving treatises on musical theory and references in other writings, shows a tradition which, despite some differences, became the foundation of Western music. Greek music apparently followed the diatonic system, which had been invented by Pythagoras, using a scale of eight notes, each of which was determined by its numerical ratio to the lowest tone. The Greek composers also devised a series of scales, called **modes,** which functioned roughly like major and minor keys in later Western music. The modes, however, were not interchangeable the way keys are, because the Greeks believed that each mode produced a different emotional and ethical effect on the listener. Modern research has been able to reproduce all of these modes, but otherwise this music remains a mystery.

Despite music's high ethical status in Greece, it had no independent role in Hellenic culture. Instead, music was integrated with verse, notably in epic and lyric poetry and in tragedy and comedy, with either the lyre (a stringed instrument) or the aulos (a wind instrument) providing accompaniment.

History

The study of history began in the fifth century B.C., when inquisitive and articulate Greeks started to analyze the meaning of their immediate past and to write down in prose the results of their research, or *historia*—the Greek word for inquiry. The Greeks before the Classical period had only a dim sense of their past; what they knew came from Homer, random artifacts, and the ruins of Mycenaean grandeur. Herodotus (about 484 B.C.–about 430 B.C.) was the first to approach history as a separate study and the first to practice historical writing in anything like the modern sense. He was motivated by the belief that the present had its causes in the past and could be a guide for the future. His *Histories* presented an account and an analysis of the Persian Wars, which Herodotus interpreted in terms of Europe versus Asia, or West versus East. In his desire to be fair to both sides, he traveled to Persia and recorded what he learned there.

The *Histories* have been criticized for implausible and inaccurate information, but Herodotus's clear prose style, his concern for research, his efforts to be impartial, his belief in historical cause and effect, and his desire to leave a record of the past as a legacy to future generations have justly earned him the title "Father of History."

Yet, for all his excellence, Herodotus pales in comparison with Thucydides (died about 401 B.C.). His subject was the Peloponnesian War, to some of whose events he was an eyewitness. Thucydides was much more skeptical and inquiring than Herodotus, and although he was an avid democrat and an admirer of Pericles, he strove to be completely fair in his account of Periclean Athens. He saw the weaknesses of his beloved polis and realized the baleful effects of imperialism. In his *History of the Peloponnesian War* he even wrote objectively of his own role as the losing admiral in a naval battle.

Thucydides was also able to use ordinary events to illuminate human motives and fundamental causes and effects in history. Like the dramatists writing at the same time, he showed that human weaknesses and flaws created the real-life tragedies he observed around him. His insight into human nature was penetrating as he chronicled how individuals shift loyalties and redefine their values to justify their actions.

This masterful writer rose above his narrative to give lessons to future generations, arguing that events that happened in the past would, at some time and in similar ways, recur. Yet he denied that history repeats itself simplistically, and he warned that his book must be read closely and thoughtfully if it were to be understood wisely.

Natural Philosophy

When the Hellenic Age opened, natural philosophy remained divided into two major camps: the materialists and the idealists (see Chapter 2). The materialists, who perpetuated the inquiries of Thales and the Milesian school, believed that the world was made of some basic physical thing. The idealists, in contrast, who stemmed from Pythagoras and the Sicilian school, were nonmaterialists, reasoning that the physical world was illusory and that behind it was a spiritual force or a metaphysical power.

By the mid–fifth century B.C., this simple pattern was being challenged by new philosophies, and by 400 B.C. a revolution in thought had occurred that overshadowed everything that had gone before. The first assault came from Elea in Sicily, where a new school of thinkers proposed to reconcile materialism and idealism. Then, in Athens the Sophists questioned philosophical inquiry itself and the notion of absolute truth. These corrosive figures provoked Socrates, the most revolutionary thinker of the entire ancient world, to respond to their claims. Socrates' life is regarded as a watershed in Greek thought. All Greek thinkers before him are now known as Pre-Socratics, and those who came after him—chiefly Plato and Aristotle in Hellenic Greece—followed his lead in studying the human experience.

The Pre-Socratics   The major pre-Socratic thinkers were concerned with determining the nature of the physical world. For Parmenides (about 515–? B.C.) and his followers in Elea, for example, the world was a single, unchanging, unmoving object whose order could be known through human reason. This attempt to reconcile materialism and idealism was modified by Parmenides' student Empedocles (about 484–about 424 B.C.), who claimed that everything, animate or inanimate, originated in the four elements of earth, water, fire, and air. These elements were unchanging, but the opposing forces of Love and Strife could combine them in different ways, to the detriment or benefit of humans. This essentially metaphysical explanation of change later influenced Aristotle.

Another school of pre-Socratic thinkers was the Atomists, who believed that everything was made up of atoms—eternal, invisible bodies of varying size

FIGURE 3.12 *Socrates.* Fourth Century B.C. British Museum. *This Roman marble copy of the original Greek statue supports the unflattering descriptions of Socrates by his contemporaries. By portraying the philosopher with a receding hair line and a dumpy body, the anonymous sculptor has made one of the world's most extraordinary human beings look very ordinary and human.*

that, by definition, could not be divided into smaller units—and the void, the empty space between the atoms. Atomic theory was developed most fully by Democritus of Thrace (about 460 B.C.–?). The movement and shape of the atoms were sufficient to explain not only physical objects but feelings, tastes, sight, ideas—in short, every aspect of the physical world.

Anaxagoras (about 500–428 B.C.), although not an Atomist, also explained the world in terms of small particles. His unique contribution was the idea that the combinations and divisions of these particles were controlled by a nonphysical agency he called *nous* (reason or mind). Socrates praised him for the originality of this conception, and then faulted him for seeing *nous* only as a mechanical force without religious significance.

The Sophists   The Sophists—from the Greek word *sophia,* or "wisdom"—scorned pre-Socratic speculation about atoms and elements as irrelevant and useless. These traveling teachers claimed to offer their students (for a fee) knowledge that guaranteed success in life. Their emphasis on the development of practical skills, such as effective public speaking, led their critics to accuse them of cynicism and a lack of interest in higher ethical values, but the Sophists were deeply serious and committed to humanistic values. Protagoras's dictum that "Man is the measure of all things" summed up their argument that each human being, as the center of the universe, has the power to make judgments about himself and his world. The Sophists helped free the human spirit to be critical and creative. If there was a danger in their teaching, it was a tendency toward unrestrained skepticism.

The Socratic Revolution   Socrates (about 470–399 B.C.), the thinker who launched a new era in philosophy, did not hesitate to condemn the Sophists. He claimed to oppose everything they stood for, especially their tendency to undermine values without offering new ones in their place. But Socrates shared certain traits with the Sophists, such as his rejection of philosophizing about nature, his focus on human problems, and his desire to empower individuals to make their own moral choices. What basically separated Socrates from the Sophists was his passionate conviction that an enduring moral and intellectual order existed in the universe.

Socrates' method for arriving at true moral and intellectual values was deceptively simple yet maddeningly elusive. At the heart of his thinking was the *psyche* (mind, or soul); being immortal, the psyche was deemed more important than the mortal and doomed body. Those who want wisdom must protect, nourish, and expand their psyches by giving their minds the maximum amount of knowledge, but not just any knowledge. The knowledge the psyche acquired had to be won through stimulating conversations and debates as well as by contemplation of abstract virtues and moral values. Only then could the psyche approach its highest potential.

"Virtue is Knowledge," claimed Socrates, by which he meant that a person who knows the truth, acquired through personal struggle to self-enlightenment, will not commit evil deeds. And this moral dictum may be reversed: Those who do wrong do so out of ignorance. If people used their psyches to think more deeply and clearly, they would lead virtuous lives. His belief in the essential goodness of human nature and the necessity of well-defined knowledge became a central tenet of Western thought.

After having pointed out the proper path to wisdom, Socrates left the rest up to his students. Bombarding inquiring youths with questions on such topics as the meaning of justice, he used rigorous logic to refute all of the squirming students' attempts at precise definition. Then—as shown by Plato's dialogues, the principal source for Socrates' life—the students, collapsing into confusion, admitted the serious gaps in their knowledge. Socrates' step-by-step questions, interspersed with gentle humor and ironic jabs, honed his students' logical skills and compelled them to begin a quest for knowledge in light of their self-confessed ignorance. The Socratic method was adopted by many teachers in Greece and Rome and remains an honored pedagogical device.

The Athenians of this era began to perceive Socrates as a threat to their way of life. This short, homely and rather insignificant looking man—as surviving statues reveal—aroused suspicion in the polis by his public arguments (Figure 3.12). When Athens fell to the Spartans in 404 B.C., opposition to Socrates began to swell. Many citizens now found subversion or even blasphemy in his words and in the behavior of his followers. Five years after the end of the Peloponnesian War, Socrates was accused of impiety and of corrupting the Athenian youth, and a jury declared him guilty and sentenced him to die. Plato, a former student, was so moved by Socrates' eloquent, though ineffective, defense and by the injustice of his death that the younger man dedicated the remainder of his life to righting the wrong and explaining the Socratic philosophy.

Plato   The spirit of Socrates hovers over the rest of Greek philosophy, especially in the accomplishments of his most famous student, Plato (about 427–347 B.C.). Plato's philosophy is the fountainhead of West-

ern *idealism,* a thought system that emphasizes spiritual values and makes ideas, rather than matter, the basis of everything that exists. *Platonism* arose out of certain premises that were Socratic in origin—the concept of the psyche and the theory of remembrance. Like Socrates, Plato emphasized the immortal and immutable psyche over the mortal and changeful body. But Plato advanced a new polarity, favoring the invisible world of the Forms, or Ideas, in opposition to the physical world. The psyche's true home was the world of the Forms, which it inhabited prior to birth and after death—the time when the psyche was lost in wonder among the eternal Ideas. In contrast, the body lived exclusively in the material world, completely absorbed by the life of the senses. Once trapped inside the body, the psyche could glimpse the higher reality, or Forms, only through remembrance.

Nonetheless, Plato thought that through a set of mental exercises the psyche would be able to recall the Ideas to which it had once been exposed. The best training for the psyche was the study of mathematics, since mathematics required signs and symbols to represent other things. After the mastery of mathematics, the student proceeded, with the help of logic, to higher stages of abstract learning, such as defining the Forms of Justice, Beauty, and Love. By showing that wisdom came only after an intellectual progression that culminated in an understanding of the absolute Ideas, Plato silenced the Sophists, who claimed that knowledge was relative.

A major implication of Plato's idealism is that the psyche and the body are constantly at war. The psyche's attempts to remember the lost Ideas met resistance from the body's pursuit of power, fame, and physical comforts. This dualism especially plagued the philosopher, the lover of wisdom; but the true philosopher took comfort in recognizing that at death the psyche would return freely to the world of the Forms.

Plato identified the Form of the Good, the ultimate Idea, with God. Yet the Platonic deity was neither the creator of the world nor the absolute and final power. Instead, Plato's deity was necessary for his idealism to function; in his thought, God was the source from which descended the imperfect objects of the natural world. In a related theological notion, he, like Socrates, attributed the presence of evil to ignorance; but Plato added the psyche's misdirected judgment and insatiable bodily appetites as other causes of evil.

Socrates' death provoked Plato to envision a perfect state where justice flourished. The book that resulted from Plato's speculations—the *Republic*—sets forth his model state and, incidentally, launched the study of political philosophy in the West. Plato thought that a just state could only be realized when all social classes worked together for the good of the whole, each class performing its assigned tasks. Because of the importance of the psyche, social status was determined by the ability to reason and not by wealth or inheritance. A tiny elite of philosopher kings and queens, who were the best qualified to run the state, reigned. Possessing wisdom as a result of their education in the Platonic system, they lived simply, shunning the creature comforts that corrupted weaker rulers.

The two lower ranks were similarly equipped for their roles in society by their intellects and their training: A middle group provided police and military protection, and the third and largest segment operated the economy. In Plato's dream world both the individual and the society aimed for virtue, and the laws and the institutions ensured that the ideal would be achieved.

Aristotle   Socrates may have been revolutionary; Plato was certainly poetic; but Aristotle (384–322 B.C.) had the most comprehensive mind of the ancient world. His curiosity and gargantuan intellect led him into every major field of inquiry of his time, except mathematics and music. Born in Macedonia, he was connected to some of the most glittering personalities of his day. He first studied philosophy under Plato in Athens, then tutored the future Alexander the Great back at Philip's court. After Philip's conquest of Greece, Aristotle settled in Athens and opened a school, the Lyceum, that quickly rivaled the Academy, the school Plato had established.

Although his philosophy owed much to Platonism, Aristotle emphasized the role of the human senses. To Aristotle, the natural world was the only world; no separate, invisible realm of Ideas existed. Nature could be studied and understood by observation, classification, and comparison of data from the physical world, that is, through the empirical method.

Aristotle rejected the world of the Forms because he believed that Form and Matter were inseparable, both rooted in nature. Each material object contained a predetermined Form that, with proper training or nourishment, would evolve into its final Form and ultimate purpose. This growth process, in his view, was potentiality evolving into actuality, as when an embryo becomes a human or a seed matures into a plant. Thus, the philosopher could conclude that everything had a purpose or end.

Aristotle's thought rested on the concept of God, which he equated with the First Cause. Aristotle's God was a philosopher's deity, purely rational, self-absorbed, and uncaring about the world or its inhabitants. Had this deity been anything else, Aristotle's God would not have been the supreme power or First Cause.

Rejecting Platonic dualism and its exclusive regard for the psyche, Aristotle devised a down-to-earth ethical goal—a sound mind in a healthy body—that he called happiness. To achieve happiness, he advised striking a mean, or a balance, between extremes of behavior. For example, courage is the mean between the excess of foolhardiness and the deficiency of cowardice. Noting that actions like murder and adultery are vicious by their very nature, he condemned them as being unable to be moderated. Although Aristotle disavowed many of Plato's ideas, he agreed with his former mentor that the cultivation of the higher intellect was more important than that of the body.

Aristotle's ethics are related to his politics, for he taught that happiness finally depended on the type of government under which an individual lived. Unlike Plato, who based his politics on speculative thinking, Aristotle reached his political views after careful research. First collecting over 150 state constitutions, Aristotle then classified and compared them, concluding that the best form of government was a constitutional regime ruled by the middle class. His preference for the middle class stemmed from his belief that they, exciting neither envy from the poor nor contempt from the wealthy, would honor and work for the good of all.

Aristotle's influence on Western civilization is immeasurable. His writings formed the core of knowledge that Christian scholars later studied as they struggled to keep the light of civilization burning after the collapse of the Roman Empire. Likewise, Jewish and Moslem thinkers ranked his books just below their own religious scriptures. Today, Aristotelianism is embedded in the official theology of the Roman Catholic Church, and Aristotle's logic continues to be taught in college philosophy courses.

Architecture

Of all the Greek art forms, architecture most powerfully embodied the Classical ideals of the Hellenic Age. The stone temple, the supreme expression of the Hellenic building genius, now received its definitive shape. Ironically, the *Doric* temple, which had originated in the Archaic Age, reached perfection in Ionian Athens. The versatile Athenians also perfected a new architectural order, the *Ionic,* which reflected more clearly their cultural tradition.

FIGURE 3.13 The Delphic Sanctuary. Aerial View. Late Sixth Century–Late Fourth Century B.C. *The ruins of Apollo's temple—this is an active earthquake zone—are in the center of the illustration, marked by a rectangular foundation and a few standing columns. A Sacred Way, or road, zigzagged up the mountain to the temple's entrance. During the fourth century B.C., a gymnasium for boys and a theater were established in the sanctuary, and a stadium was constructed for athletic contests.*

Sanctuaries Before there were temples, however, Greece had sanctuaries, places considered sacred to a god or goddess. Of these sacred places, Apollo's shrine at Delphi was the oldest and the most famous (Figure 3.13). Delphi, thought to be the center of the earth, was hallowed ground to the entire Greek world, and the major poleis supported the god's priesthood there. Apollo's temple was the most splendid building on the site. Inside was Apollo's oracle—the only woman permitted at Delphi—to whom people journeyed from all over Greece with their questions.

With the rise of the poleis, the concept of a holy place set aside from the business of everyday life was adapted to the religious needs of each community. By the Hellenic Age, each polis had its own sacred area, usually built on a hill or protected by walls, which contained buildings and altars. Although each polis worshiped the entire pantheon of deities, one god or goddess was gradually singled out as a patron, and a temple was erected to house the statue of this particular divinity.

The Temple: The Perfection of the Form By Hellenic times, the Greek world was polarized between eastern (the mainland and the Aegean Islands) and western (Magna Graecia) styles of temple design, although in both styles the temples were rectilinear and of post-beam-triangle construction. Influenced by the Pythagorean quest for harmony through mathematical rules, the eastern builders had standardized six as the perfect number of columns for the ends of temples and thirteen, or twice the number of end columns plus one, as the perfect number of columns for the sides. These balanced proportions, along with simple designs and restrained decorative schemes, made the eastern temples majestically expressive of Classical ideals.

Architects in western Greece, somewhat removed from the centers of Classical culture, were more experimental. Their buildings deviated from the eastern ideals, as can be seen in the Second Temple of Hera at Poseidonia, built of limestone in about 450 B.C. (Figure 3.14). The best-preserved of all Greek temples, this Doric structure does not have the harmo-

west

FIGURE 3.14   Second Temple of Hera at Poseidonia. Ca. 450 B.C. *This temple of Hera is among the best preserved structures from the ancient world. Since Hera may have been a chthonic goddess prior to becoming consort to Olympian Zeus, it is appropriate that this Doric temple, with its ground-hugging appearance, be her monument.*

east

FIGURE 3.16 MNESICLES. The Erechtheum. View from the West. Ca. 410 B.C. Athens. *The Erechtheum was probably built to quiet conservatives who rejected Athena's new temple, the Parthenon, as a symbol of Athenian imperialism. Reflecting its ties with the past, the Erechtheum housed the ancient wooden cult statue of Athena, which pious Athenians believed had fallen from the sky. Its Ionic porches set the standard for the graceful Ionic order.*

nious proportions of the eastern version of this style. Although the Second Temple of Hera owed much to eastern influences, including the six columns at the ends and the porches, it had too many (fourteen) columns on the sides, its columns were too thick, and the low-pitched roof made the building seem squat.

Between 447 and 438 B.C., the architects Ictinus and Callicrates perfected the eastern-style Doric temple in the Parthenon, a temple on Athens' Acropolis dedicated to Athena (Figure 3.15). When completed, this temple established a new standard of Classicism, with eight columns on the ends and seventeen on the sides and with the numerical ratio of 9:4 used throughout, expressed, for example, in the relation of a column's height to its diameter. Inside, the builders designed two chambers, an east room for a 40-foot-high statue of Athena and a smaller room housing the Delian League treasury. The rest of the Acropolis project, finally finished in 405 B.C., included the Propylaea, the gate leading to the sanctuary; the temple of Athena Nike, a gift to Athens' patron goddess thanking her for a military victory; and the Erechtheum, a temple dedicated to three deities.

◀ **FIGURE 3.15** ICTINUS AND CALLICRATES. The Parthenon. Close-up View from the East. Third Quarter of the Fifth Century B.C. Athens. *A great humanistic icon, the Parthenon has had a long history since its days as a Greek temple. It served successively as a Christian church, a mosque, and an ammunitions depot, until it was accidentally blown up at the end of the seventeenth century A.D. Today, concerned nations through UNESCO are cooperating with the Greek government to preserve this noble ruin.*

Ictinus and Callicrates introduced many subtle variations, called refinements, in their designs, so that no line is exactly straight, horizontal, or perpendicular. For example, the stepped base of the temple forms a gentle arc so that the ends are lower than the middles; the floor slopes slightly to the edges; and the columns tilt inward away from the ends. These and other refinements were no accidents but were intended to be corrections for real and imaginary optical illusions. The Parthenon's fame exerted such authority that these refinements, along with harmonious proportions, became standardized as the essence of Greek architecture.

The second order of Greek architecture, the Ionic, originated in the late Archaic Age and, like the Doric, came to flower in Hellenic times. The Ionic style, freer than the Doric and more graceful, reflected its origins in the Ionian world; traditionally, the Ionians contrasted their opulence with the simplicity of the Dorians. In place of the alternating metopes and triglyphs of Doric buildings, the Ionic temple had a running frieze to which sculpted figures might be added. More decorated than the plain Doric, the Ionic columns had elegant bases, and their tops were crowned with capitals that suggested either a scroll's ends or a ram's horns. What solidified the Ionic temple's impression of elegance were its slender and delicate columns.

The Athenians chose the Ionic style for the exquisite, though eccentric, Erechtheum, the last of the great buildings erected on the Acropolis (Figure 3.16). The artistic freedom associated with the Ionic style may have led the architect, Mnesicles, to make the

FIGURE 3.17 MNESICLES. The Erechtheum. View from the South. Ca. 410 B.C. Athens. *The Erechtheum presented a unique and charming exterior with each wall offering a different perspective. Two Ionic porches of differing dimensions faced the northern and eastern sides; this Porch of the Maidens, which was inaccessible from the outside, fronted the southern wall; and the western exposure was a blank wall.*

floor plan asymmetrical and to introduce so many design variations, but a more likely explanation was Mnesicles' need to integrate three existing shrines into a single building—those of the Olympians Athena and Poseidon and that of the legendary King Erechtheus, who introduced the horse to Athens. Mnesicles took the unusual step of stressing the site's unbalanced nature by adding two Ionic porches and the temple's crowning feature, the Porch of the Maidens (Figure 3.17). By his bold design, Mnesicles created a marvelous illusion of harmony that was in keeping with the age's Classical ideals.

Sculpture

Equally impressive is the Greek achievement in sculpture. Believing that the task of sculpture was to imitate nature, the Greeks created images of gods and goddesses as well as of men and women that have haunted the Western imagination ever since. They not only forged a canon of idealized human proportions that later sculptors followed, but also developed a repertoire of postures, gestures, and subjects that have become embedded in Western art.

During the Hellenic Age, Classical sculpture moved through three separate phases: The *Severe style*, which ushered in the period and lasted until 450 B.C., the *High Classical style*, which coincided with the zenith of Athenian imperial greatness, and the *Fourth Century style*, which concluded with the death of Alexander the Great in 323 B.C.

Sculpture in the Severe style, inspired perhaps by its association with funeral customs, was characterized by a feeling of dignified nobility. The *Kritios Boy*—showing a figure fully at rest—is an elegant expression of this first phase of Classicism (Figure 3.18). Kritios, the supposed sculptor, fixed the mouth severely and altered the frontality, a feature of the Archaic style, by tilting the head subtly to the right and slightly twisting the upper torso. The flat-footed stance of the Archaic kourai has given way to a posture that places the body's weight on one leg and uses the other leg as a support. This stance is called *contrapposto* (counterpoise), and its invention helped to make the Classical revolution; thereafter, sculptors were able to render the human figure in freer and more relaxed poses.

Mourning Athena, another sculpture from the same period, conveys an air of gentle sorrow (Figure 3.19).

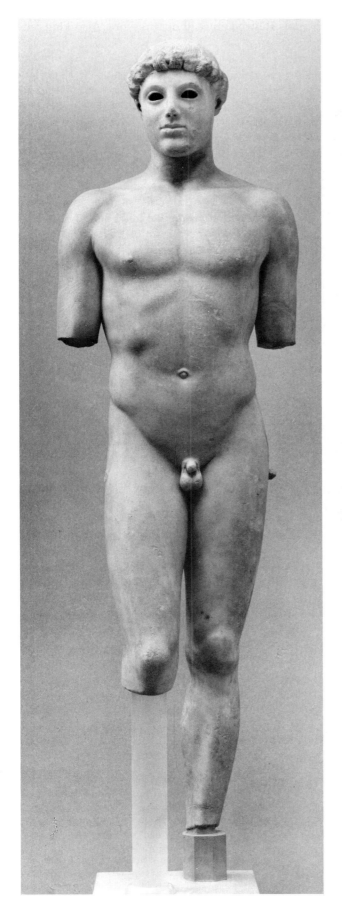

FIGURE 3.19 *Mourning Athena. Ca.* 460 B.C. *Acropolis Museum, Athens. This low-relief sculpture was carved into a stele, or standing stone, to serve as a votive offering to the goddess Athena. The work was found on the Athenian Acropolis, but the accompanying inscription has been lost. The sense of melancholy surrounding the attentive goddess makes this one of the most arresting sculptures in Greek art.*

FIGURE 3.18 *Kritios Boy. Ca.* 480 B.C. *Acropolis Museum, Athens. This statue is carved from marble probably mined at Mt. Pentelicus in Attica. Two features—the treatment of the eyes, which were originally set with semiprecious stones, and the roll of hair— show that the Kritios sculptor was accustomed to working in bronze. The figure's beautifully rendered muscles and sense of inner life announce the arrival of the Hellenic style.*

FIGURE 3.23 *Centaur versus Lapith.* Metope XXX, South Face of the Parthenon. Ca. 448–442 B.C. British Museum. *This struggling pair was designed to fit comfortably into the metope frame, and thus the proportions of the figures in relation to each other and to the small space were worked out with precision. The intertwined limbs of the warrior and the centaur visibly demonstrated the new freedom of High Classicism. The anguished countenance of the Lapith, however, is almost unique in High Classicism and is a portent of the more emotional faces of the Hellenistic style, the next major artistic development.*

FIGURE 3.24 *Poseidon, Apollo, and Artemis.* Parthenon frieze. Ca. 448–442 B.C. Acropolis Museum, Athens. *The Hellenic style always stressed the human dimension of the Greek gods and goddesses, embodying Homer's claim that gods and humans are of the same race. In this section of the Parthenon frieze, the Homeric deities spring to life, resplendent in their beautiful bodies and handsome faces.*

such as Amazons against men, Greeks against Trojans, and gods against giants. The south metopes portrayed the battle between the legendary Lapiths and the half-men, half-horse Centaurs (Figure 3.23). For the Greeks, the struggle between the human Lapiths and the bestial Centaurs symbolized the contest between civilization and barbarism, or, possibly, between the Greeks and the Persians.

Inside the columns, running around the perimeter of the upper *cella* walls in a continuous band, was a low-relief frieze. Borrowed from the Ionic order, this running frieze introduced greater liveliness into High Classicism. The 525-foot-long band is filled with hundreds of men and women, walking and riding horses, along with sacrificial animals for Athena and the rest of the Olympians. The subject of this vivid scene is the procession of the Great Panathenaea festival, Athens' most important civic and religious ritual, which was held every four years. This panoramic view of the thrilling procession concluded with a stunning group portrait of the twelve gods and goddesses, seated in casual majesty, awaiting their human worshipers. In one scene, a bearded Poseidon talks quietly with Apollo, while Artemis at the right absentmindedly adjusts her robe (Figure 3.24). Their tranquil faces, their sense of inner life, and the prevailing calm are the marks of mature Classicism. The entire Parthenon frieze was the most ambitious work of sculpture in the Greek tradition.

The transition to Fourth Century style coincided with the end of the creative phase of tragedy and the disintegration of the Greek world as it passed into the Macedonian political orbit. Sculpture remained innovative, since each generation seemed to produce a master who challenged the prevailing aesthetic rules, and free expression continued as a leading principle of Fourth Century style. But sculptors now expressed such new ideas as beauty for its own sake and a delight in sensuality. Earlier Classicism had stressed the notion that humans could become godlike, but the last phase concluded that gods and mortals alike reveled in human joys.

This new focus is apparent in Praxiteles' *Hermes with the Infant Dionysus*. This sculpture, perhaps the only original work by a known sculptor that survives from ancient Greece, portrays two gods blissfully at play (Figure 3.25). Hermes, lounging in a casual yet dignified pose, probably dangled grapes before the attentive baby god. The contrapposto posture, beautifully defined in Hermes' stance, became widely imitated as the "Praxitelean curve." Hermes' sensuous body, his intent gaze, and his delicate features are hallmarks of Fourth Century Classicism; by the next generation Praxiteles' treatment of the male figure had superseded the more rugged *Doryphoros* canon.

FIGURE 3.25 PRAXITELES. *Hermes with the Infant Dionysus.* Ca. 350–340 B.C. Olympia Museum. *In this statue of Hermes, Praxiteles changed the look of Classical art with his rendering of the god's body. For example, Hermes' small head and long legs contributed to the Praxitelean canon for the male figure. The sculptor has also created a dramatic contrast between Hermes' well-muscled body and his soft face. As a direct result of Praxiteles' new vision, sculptors in the Hellenistic Age became interested in more frankly sensual portrayals of the human figure, both male and female.*

The Legacy of Hellenic Civilization

Although Athens failed in its dream of political mastery of Greece, the Athenian miracle so impressed its contemporaries that Attic culture dominated the Hellenic Age. Tragic poets, comic playwrights, and natural philosophers made the Attic dialect the medium of expression for poetry and prose. The buildings on the Athenian Acropolis expressed visually the purity and restraint of the Attic style. And Athenian democracy, which served as the exciting teacher of its citizens, was the envy of most of the other Greek poleis. After the fall of Greece to Macedonia, however, the idea of democracy fell into disrepute. Almost 2000 years passed before some in Europe were ready to give democracy a second chance.

But *humanism,* the other great creation of Athens, survived as a guide to refined living for the cultivated classes in the West. Athenian culture became the heart of the educational curriculum that was followed in Hellenistic civilization; that model was adopted by Rome and transmitted in the humanistic tradition to Europe. In time, the study and the practice of humanistic learning—literature, philosophy, theater, music, and the arts and architecture—became the crowning glory of Western civilization, affecting private individuals and entire societies.

Moreover, Classicism—the style of humanistic achievements in the Hellenic Age—had three great effects on the Western tradition. First, the principles of Greek Classicism—balance, simplicity, and restraint—set the standard by which the styles of other times are often measured. Second, the actual works of Classicism became basic building blocks of Western culture. In the realm of thought, the works of Plato and Aristotle quickly acquired a luster of authority and retained it until the seventeenth century A.D. Aristotle's literary criticism created a new writing genre, and his analysis of tragedy made this type of play the ultimate challenge to ambitious writers. The Greek tragedies themselves—of Aeschylus, Sophocles, and Euripides—are thought by many to be unsurpassed.

The comic plays of Aristophanes are less well known today, but their spirit still lives in period comedies and contemporary political satire. The histories of Herodotus and Thucydides retain their vitality as important sources for their respective eras, although modern research has cast doubt on some of their conclusions. Architecture has had the most potent effect of Greece's accomplishments; the ruins on the Athenian Acropolis and elsewhere are eternal reminders of this Greek heritage. Finally, the idealized statues of men and women, such as the *Doryphoros*, have inspired Western artists with their vision of noble beings alert to the rich possibilities of human life.

The third and perhaps most important contribution of Classicism to the Western tradition was a skeptical spirit that was rooted in democracy. By asserting that the purpose of human life can best be realized in cities that are shaped by the citizens' needs, as Athenian humanism claimed, the humanists declared war on all tyrants, hierarchical societies, and divinely ordered states—in other words, the prevailing order of the ancient world. Because of this critical aspect of humanism, the Greek heritage has sometimes been called into question and, during repressive periods, been subjected to attack. On the contrary, however, the passion for questioning, for inquiry, which characterizes the skeptical spirit, is at the core of Western consciousness.

KEY CULTURAL TERMS

Hellenic	*idealism*
maenad	*Platonism*
Classic (Classical)	*Doric*
Classicism	*Ionic*
tragedy	*Severe style*
chorus	*High Classical style*
orchestra	*Fourth Century style*
skene	*contrapposto*
satyr-play	*Praxitelean curve*
Old Comedy	*humanism*
modes	

SUGGESTIONS FOR FURTHER READING

PRIMARY SOURCES

AESCHYLUS. *Oresteia.* Translated by R. Fagles. New York: Penguin, 1986. A good modern version of the only dramatic trilogy that survives from ancient Greece.

ARISTOPHANES. *Lysistrata.* Translated by J. Henderson. New York: Oxford University Press, 1987. This modern version captures the antiwar spirit and bawdy humor of the original comedy.

EURIPIDES. *The Bacchae and Other Plays.* Translated by P. Vellacott. New York: Penguin, 1972. An excellent collection of Euripides' dramas, in each of which strong-minded women play major roles.

HERODOTUS. *The Histories.* Translated by A. de Sélincourt. New York: Penguin, 1972. Prefaced with an informative introduction, this translation captures both the language and the narrative of the first history book in Western literature.

KAPLAN, J., ed. *The Pocket Aristotle.* New York: Washington Square Press, 1966. Edited selections from the *Physics,* the *Nicomachean Ethics, Politics,* and *Poetics* give a sense of Aristotle's method of inquiry.

ROUSE, W. H. D., trans. *Great Dialogues of Plato.* New York: New American Library, 1963. Includes the full text of the *Republic,* the *Apology, Phaedo,* and *Symposium.*

SOPHOCLES. *The Theban Plays.* Translated by E. F. Watling. New York: Penguin, 1974. The three plays about the misfortunes of King Oedipus and his family; includes *Oedipus Rex* and *Antigone.*

THUCYDIDES. *The Peloponnesian War.* Translated by R. Warner. New York: Penguin, 1970. An updated translation that captures the sweep and drama of the original.

SECONDARY SOURCES

ARNOTT, P. D. *An Introduction to the Greek Theater.* Bloomington: Indiana University Press, 1963. Perhaps the best of similar summaries on a fascinating and controversial topic.

BECATTI, G. *The Art of Ancient Greece and Rome.* New York: Abrams, 1967. An excellent survey of the major monuments of art and architecture from Archaic Greece to the fall of Rome.

BOARDMAN, J., and others. *Greek Art and Architecture.* New York: Abrams, 1967. Essays by distinguished scholars surveying the styles of Greek art; well illustrated.

BURN, A. R. *The Pelican History of Greece.* New York: Penguin, 1966. For the inquisitive student, this thoughtful treatment examines the Greeks from prehistoric to Roman times.

DAVIES, J. K. *Democracy and Classical Greece.* New York: Humanities Press, 1978. Based on current research; covers both Athens and Sparta.

FROST, F. J. *Greek Society.* Rev. ed. Lexington, Mass.: D. C. Heath, 1987. Explores Greek social and economic institutions, focusing on class structure and representative figures from each class.

JONES, A. H. M. *Athenian Democracy.* Oxford: Blackwell, 1969. Articles examining different aspects of Athenian government and politics.

KITTO, H. D. F. *Greek Tragedy.* London: Methuen, 1968. First published in 1939, this brilliant interpretation of the form and meaning of Greek tragedy, based on all the surviving plays, is for the advanced student.

LACEY, W. K. *The Family in Classical Greece.* Ithaca, N.Y.: Cornell University Press, 1984. This pioneering study focuses on the family in the Archaic and Classical periods, especially in Athens.

RIDGWAY, B. S. *Fifth Century Styles in Greek Sculpture.* Princeton: Princeton University Press, 1981. A well-documented treatment that focuses on shifting aspects of style; for the ambitious student.

4

CLASSICAL GREEK CIVILIZATION
The Hellenistic Age

The Hellenistic Age covers the relatively brief period from the death of Alexander the Great in 323 B.C. to the triumph of Rome over Macedonian Greece in 146 B.C. During this time a new urban civilization sprang up in the eastern Mediterranean basin across most of Alexander's old empire. In contrast to Hellenic civilization, this new civilization was dominated by large metropolitan centers tied together by trade and commerce. More racially mixed and ethnically varied than Hellenic Greece, this civilization has come to be called *Hellenistic* because of the preeminent role Greece played in its development. Greece, for example, furnished the Hellenistic world with its diplomatic and commercial language, its bureaucrats, and most of its cultural forms. And yet Hellenistic culture was eclectic, for the subjects of the various states made their presence known (Figure 4.1). From Oriental roots came such key motifs of Hellenistic society as the concept of a ruler who is also divine, the aesthetic ideal that identifies grandiosity with earthly majesty, and new religious cults that promised immortality.

FIGURE 4.1 Black Youth Singing. Second Century B.C. Bibliothèque Nationale, Paris. *Since the Archaic Age, Greek artists had occasionally depicted black Africans in their works. During the Hellenistic Age, with the migration of peoples and the increased use of slaves, sculptors frequently chose black figures as subjects. This small bronze statue of a young African is an illustration of the racial diversity of the Hellenistic Age. Originally, the figure held a small musical instrument—now lost—which accounts for its exaggerated pose.*

Because the accomplishments of Hellenic Greece loom so large in Western history, the Hellenistic Age is sometimes belittled or even ignored. This neglect is misguided, however. Alexander's dream of a peaceful world community united by a common leader and his role as the leader of such a world-state had an impact that has lasted into modern times. The multiracial states of the Hellenistic period are the first examples of a type whose modern versions include the United States and the Soviet Union. And, not least, Hellenistic achievements in philosophy, art, and architecture are considerable.

The fusion of Mediterranean civilizations that characterized Hellenistic society destroyed the Hellenic political order in which poleis were guided by their citizens. In its stead arose the large Hellenistic kingdoms, ruled by men who declared themselves deities. The Hellenistic economic order rested on specialized luxury crafts and professionalized occupations, international trade and banking, and an abundant and cheap supply of slaves. The large ports exported and imported basic agricultural commodities such as grain, olive oil, wine, and timber, exchanging them for expensive handmade consumer products like pottery, silks, and jewelry, as well as luxury items like spices. Shipping firms, insurance companies, and banks watched over the transfer of these goods and enriched themselves in the process.

Class divisions in Hellenistic society were pronounced. In the larger cities and port towns, especially, the discrepancies in the social order were strikingly apparent and clearly entrenched. For the rich, urban life was often luxurious and cosmopolitan, but the bulk of society remained provincial, untouched by the glamour of Hellenistic high life. Those in the middle social ranks, primarily small tradespeople and skilled artisans, struggled to keep ahead and hoped to improve their plight. However, for the poorest free classes—laborers, unskilled workers, and small landowners—life offered little hope on this earth. At the bottom of society, slaves, whose numbers mounted during the wars of this period, were expected to toil and bear the brunt of all backbreaking labor.

THE STAGES OF HELLENISTIC HISTORY

The shadow of Rome hung over the Hellenistic world, although the kingdoms were unaware that their fate depended on the rising western Mediterranean power. While Rome watched, the Hellenistic states quarreled and jockeyed for power. The events of this age fall into two stages: (1) the disintegration of Alexander's empire and the rise of the successor states; and (2) the arrival and triumph of Rome (Time Line 4.1).

The End of the Empire and the Rise of the States

The years from 323 to 307 B.C. saw the shattering of Alexander's dream of a united Greek and Persian civilization. Alexander left no designated successor. After his death, his chief generals divided his empire, carving out three dynastic kingdoms that, along with a few minor states and leagues of Greek city-states, survived until Rome began to move into the area. The era of the successor states (307 to 215 B.C.) was the zenith of Hellenistic culture. Politically, the states were hardly ever at peace, but culturally they were united. Greeks and barbarians mingled freely, and a civilization began to emerge that was not unlike what Alexander had imagined. This period saw the growth

TIME LINE 4.1   THE HELLENISTIC AGE

All dates B.C.

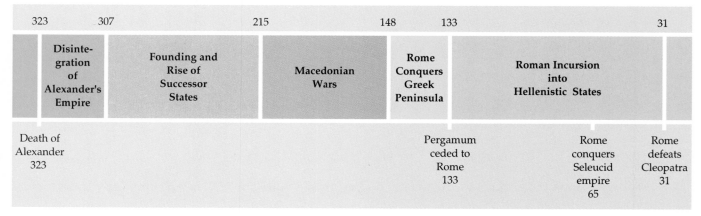

MAP 4.1

The Successor States and the Hellenistic World

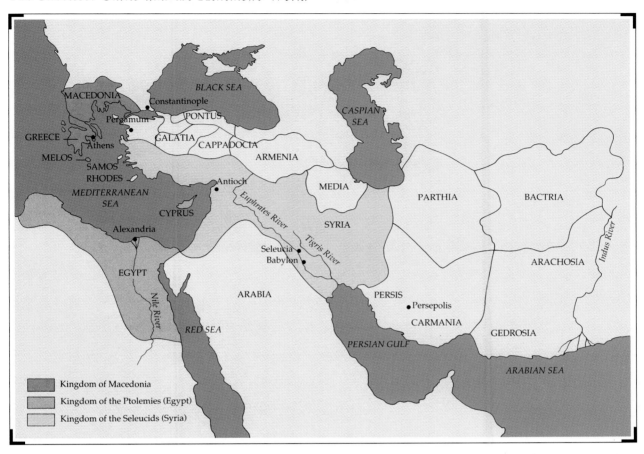

Kingdom of Macedonia

Kingdom of the Ptolemies (Egypt)

Kingdom of the Seleucids (Syria)

and spread of the *koine*, a form of colloquial Greek that was spoken throughout the Hellenistic world, from Gaul to Syria.

The three successor states were based in Macedonia, in the former Persian empire, and in Egypt. Alexander's general Antigonus founded the kingdom of Macedonia, which controlled Greece until two leagues of poleis challenged Macedonian hegemony. The ensuing warfare with the Greek leagues wore down Antigonus's heirs and ultimately weakened this state.

A second general, Seleucus, established a dynasty in Asia Minor, building his government on the ruins of the old Persian empire. At its height, Seleucid power extended as far east as present-day Iraq. In about the middle of the third century B.C., however, the eastern region of the Seleucid kingdom broke away and formed the two smaller states of Parthia and Bactria, who would later prove to be prickly adversaries of Rome. In time, the Seleucid rulers, distracted by the invading Gauls, a wandering tribe of Celtic peoples from central and eastern Europe, lost

control of their kingdom and had to relinquish their northwestern lands in Asia Minor to a new kingdom known as Pergamum, named after an old Greek city.

To a third general, Ptolemy, fell the richest prize of all, Egypt, the oldest civilization surviving in the ancient world. Although the Ptolemaic dynasty included weak and corrupt rulers, Egypt enjoyed a resurgence as a unified and independent state. The Ptolemies made Alexandria their capital, and eventually this city became the greatest urban center of the Hellenistic Age, enriched by the grains harvested in the Nile River valley and the goods and traffic that passed through its port (Map 4.1).

The Arrival and Triumph of Rome

The second phase of Hellenistic Civilization began in the late third century B.C. when Macedonia joined Carthage, a Phoenician state in North Africa opposite Sicily, in its struggle against Rome. Thereafter, the

FIGURE 4.2 Acropolis at Pergamum. Second Century B.C. Reconstruction by H. Schlief. Staatliche Museen, Berlin. *The architecture of Pergamum was in the Hellenic style, but the city's mixed population and economy made it the commercial and political hub of a Hellenistic kingdom. Under Eumenes II the capital and the country reached its height of power around 160 B.C.*

unforgiving Romans used every opportunity to humiliate their enemy on the Greek peninsula. Between 215 and 148 B.C., Rome fought four wars with Macedonia, thus becoming entangled in Greek political and military squabbles. Finally, in 146 B.C. Rome, after conquering and subduing northern Greece, brought the entire peninsula under its control. The other Hellenistic kingdoms soon submitted. In 133 B.C. the ruler of Pergamum willed his state to Rome, hoping thereby to give an advantage to his subjects, who now passed under Roman rule. The Seleucid kingdom was conquered by the Romans in 65 B.C., after three different wars in Asia Minor. Egypt maintained its freedom longer than any other Hellenistic state, until 31 B.C., when Cleopatra and her forces were defeated by Octavian and the Roman navy.

THE CITIES OF HELLENISTIC CIVILIZATION

Alexander's most enduring legacy to the Hellenistic world was his new image of the city. The city is as old as civilization itself, since urban life is by definition a component of civilized existence. But in the vision of Alexander the Great, cities became keystones holding together his diverse and vast empire and serving as centers of government, trade, and culture. Alexander thought that each metropolitan area would radiate Greco-Oriental civilization, bringing urban culture to the hinterland. During his conquests, Alexander is reputed to have founded over seventy cities, many of which were named for him.

Pergamum

During the Hellenistic era, Alexander's successors emulated him, establishing urban centers such as Antioch on the Orontes River in southern Asia Minor and Seleucia, the new capital of the Seleucid kingdom, near Babylon on the Tigris River. Antioch and Seleucia, however, were provincial capitals in comparison to the new city of Pergamum in western Asia Minor, which now emerged as a brilliant center of art and thought, bringing together Greek and Persian civilizations. The Attalids, the ruling dynasty of Pergamum, decorated their city's acropolis with a splendid palace, a library second in the number of volumes only to the one in Alexandria, and a marble temple to Athena. Scattered on the hillside beneath the acropolis were shrines, markets, and private dwellings of the more prosperous citizens. At the base of the hill the tradespeople, artisans, and slaves lived crowded together (Figure 4.2).

Alexandria in Egypt

For all its claims to grandeur, however, Pergamum could not surpass the size, wealth, beauty, or culture of the premier Hellenistic city, Alexandria in Egypt. Founded by Alexander, this Egyptian center was the most famous and enduring of the conqueror's namesake towns (Figure 4.3). Under the Ptolemies, Alex-

andria grew to be a world city that attracted both the ambitious who came seeking opportunities and the apathetic who wanted to be left alone. Every attraction known to human desires is said to have existed here, just as in the teeming cities of the twentieth century. By the end of the first century B.C., Alexandria's population had climbed to almost one million, and the city was divided into five sections, including one reserved for royalty and separate residential quarters for the Egyptians and the Jews.

Unlike a self-contained Hellenic Age polis with a relatively homogeneous population, Alexandria resembled a modern metropolis in which activity revolves around the pursuit of wealth. With busy harbors, bustling markets, and international banks, Alexandria became a hub of commercial and financial enterprises. Economic interests held together Alexandria's population of mixed racial and ethnic groups.

Alexandria's economic vitality was matched by the splendor of its cultural achievements. The world's first museum—a temple to the muses—was built here as a place for scholars to study and to exchange ideas. For the convenience of these thinkers, there was erected nearby the famed library, whose staff collected the classics of Greek civilization, including the works of Plato and Aristotle, the tragedies of Aeschylus, Sophocles, and Euripides, the comedies of Aristophanes, and the scientific treatises of many Hellenistic philosophers. At the time of the Roman

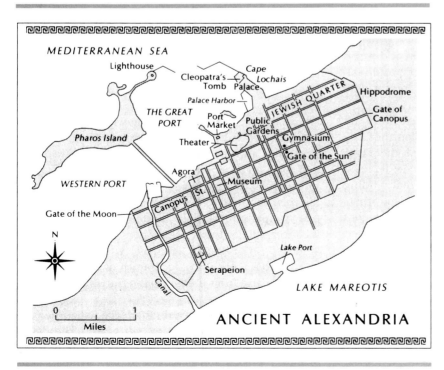

FIGURE 4.3 Plan of Ancient Alexandria. Third Century B.C. *Designed by Deinocrates of Rhodes, Alexander's personal architect, Alexandria was laid out in a grid formed by intersecting avenues and streets. The entire city was enclosed by a wall, accessible by four massive gates at the ends of the major avenues. To the north lay two harbors that made the city the most vital port in the Mediterranean. The harbors were protected by an outer island at the point of which stood the lighthouse of Pharos—now lost. Remarkable for its colossal size, the lighthouse was considered one of the wonders of the ancient world.*

FIGURE 4.8 The Olympieum. Various dates: Late Sixth Century B.C.; Second Quarter of Second Century B.C.; Completed, Second Quarter of Second Century A.D. Athens, Greece. *The thirteen standing Corinthian columns were part of the original plan of the Olympieum's architect. After the temporary cessation of building in 164 B.C., some of this temple's unfinished columns were transported to Rome and reused in a building there. Their use in Rome helped to popularize the Corinthian style among political leaders and wealthy tastemakers.*

FIGURE 4.9 Altar of Zeus at Pergamum. (Reconstruction.) Third and Second Quarters of the Second Century B.C. Pergamum Museum, Berlin. *This masterpiece of Hellenistic architecture was erected in the 170s B.C. by Eumenes II, the king of Pergamum, to commemorate his victories over various barbarian states in Asia Minor. Eumenes believed himself to be the savior and disseminator of Greek culture, and this altar with its giant frieze was meant to suggest Hellenic monuments, such as the Athenian Parthenon.*

transform Pergamum into another Athens. Thus, the idea of a "new" Athens—a recurrent motif in the humanistic tradition—had already been formulated by the Hellenistic Age.

Sculpture

Like Hellenistic architects, Hellenistic sculptors adapted many of the basic forms and ideas of the Hellenic style to meet the tastes of their day. The Hellenistic sculptors perpetuated such Hellenic principles as contrapposto and proportion as well as the Hellenic emphasis on religious and moral themes. But Hellenistic art increasingly expressed a secular, urban viewpoint, and Hellenic restraint often gave way to realism, eroticism, and violence, expressed and enjoyed for their own sake.

Between 230 and 220 B.C., King Attalos I of Pergamum dedicated in Athens a group of bronze sculptures that celebrated his recent victory over the barbaric Gauls. By donating these bronzes to Athens, which was outside of Pergamum's political orbit, the Attalid ruler hoped to establish his cultural credentials as a defender of Greek culture and thus further his claims to rule over the entire Hellenistic world.

One of these pieces, *Gaul and Wife* (which survives only in a Roman marble copy), shows a barbarian chief killing his spouse and fatally wounding himself rather than be enslaved (Figure 4.10). The sculptor demonstrates his keen eye for realistic details in the collapsed body of the woman and the man's open wound oozing with blood. The Hellenistic style's appreciation of the melodramatic is evident in the anguish of the defiant Gaul as his attention is divided between stabbing himself and supporting his fallen wife. But by treating a foreign enemy with such nobility, the anonymous sculptor perpetuates the deep moral sense that was central to Hellenic art.

A radically different subject is expressed in the *Old Market Woman*, which, like a stock character from New Comedy, depicted a well-known social type (Figure 4.11). The old woman, who might have strolled out of the market place of any Hellenistic city, represented a **genre subject**, or a scene taken from everyday life. The original third-century B.C. bronze portrayed a stooped figure, straining under the combined weight of her groceries and her advancing years. In this Roman marble copy, the left arm is missing, but she carries in her right a fowl and a brimming bucket. Her deeply lined and wrinkled face and her sagging breasts express the realism of Hellenistic style.

Among the masterpieces of Hellenistic art are the sculptures of the Pergamum altar frieze, which can

FIGURE 4.10 *Gaul and Wife*. Roman copy of a bronze original. Ca. 230–220 B.C. Terme Museum, Rome. *The rulers of the Hellenistic kingdom of Pergamum preferred art that was showy and overwrought, a taste that perhaps stemmed from their insecurity at being a new dynasty. A Pergamene style of sculpture developed under these kings in which gestures were theatrical and anatomical features were portrayed in exaggerated depth. Gaul and Wife is a superb example of this style.*

be seen in Figure 4.7, above. The subject here is a battle between the Olympian deities and the Giants, the monstrous race of pre-Greek gods and goddesses who were the offspring of Gaea (Earth) and Uranus (Sky, or the Heavens)—the first rulers of the universe. The Giants, having overturned their parents, are then defeated by *their* own children, the Olympian deities. To the Greeks, the final triumph of the Olympian gods and goddesses symbolized the coming of a just and moral order both in the universe and in their own society. Hence, when the Attalid rulers chose this subject for the altar frieze, they affirmed that they were continuing the values of Greek civilization. With the exception of the frieze on the Parthenon, the figures on this altar represent the most ambitious sculptural project in the ancient world.

FIGURE 4.11   Old Market Woman. Roman copy of a Hellenistic bronze. Third or Second Century B.C. Metropolitan Museum of Art. *Many Hellenistic sculptors depicted old women in pathetic situations, tired, drunk, or begging. Scholars are divided as to whether these statues were meant to be admired for their truthfulness or represented aristocratic contempt for an ugly social phenomenon.*

FIGURE 4.12   *Athena Battling with Alkyoneus.* From the Great Frieze of the Pergamum Altar, East Section. Second Quarter of Second Century B.C. Pergamum Museum, Berlin. *An unusual aspect of the sculptor's rendering of the Giants was the diversity of their bodily forms. In the illustration, Alkyoneus's outspread wings identify him as a Giant and an offspring of Gaea, the goddess of the Earth, who is shown on the bottom right.*

Filled with high-powered energy, the Pergamum frieze displays figures that threaten to explode from the space in which they are barely contained. In one celebrated panel, Athena grasps the dying Giant Alkyoneus while her sacred snake bites him on the chest (Figure 4.12). Her agitated draperies appear to be billowing in a strong wind, so that the folds hang expressively rather than simply disclosing her body, as in the Hellenic style. The expression of pain on Alkyoneus' face—deeply furrowed brow and bulging eyeballs—and the straining muscles with prominent veins reflect the Pergamum school's taste for exaggeration.

The sculpture of the Hellenistic Age is also characterized by a frank appreciation of female beauty, a famous example of which is the *Aphrodite of Melos*, perhaps better known as the Venus de Milo (Figure 4.13). This original sculpture, carved from Parian marble, shows many borrowings from the tradition of Praxiteles, as shown in his *Hermes with the Infant Dionysus* (see Figure 3.25). Both Aphrodite and Hermes exhibit exaggerated contrapposto, a sensuous, even erotic, modeling of the body, and a serene countenance with an unmistakable gaze. However, the Hellenistic sculptor, demonstrating a playful flair, teases the viewer with the rolled down draperies that call attention to Aphrodite's exposed lower torso.

The *Horse and Jockey*, original bronzes that were retrieved in this century from a sunken ship in the Aegean Sea off Artemision, show Hellenistic fluidity rather than the frozen style of Hellenic art (Figure 4.14). Whether the two figures are a true ensemble is a subject of scholarly debate. Arguing against their unity is the size disparity between the small jockey and the enormous horse. But the balance seems in favor of treating them as a group, especially when the jockey is seated on the horse. In this juxtaposition, the horse's forward motion seems to cause the jockey's cloak to blow behind him. The boy, contorting his face with the strain of the race, stretches out his left hand, as if to urge his mount on to victory. This sculpted pair shows other innovations in Hellenistic art. The boy athlete, who looks rather like a ragged street urchin, represents the new interest in children that arose in Hellenistic art. And the straining horse contrasts dramatically with the serene, well-proportioned horses on the Parthenon frieze.

FIGURE 4.13 *Aphrodite of Melos (Venus de Milo).* Ca. 160–150 B.C. Louvre, Paris. *This celebrated statue represents the classicizing tendency in Hellenistic art. The head is executed in the pure Hellenic style, as seen in the serene countenance, the exquisitely detailed hair, and the finely chiseled features. However, the body with its frank sensuality and its coy draperies is clearly in the Hellenistic Style.*

FIGURE 4.14 *Horse and Jockey of Artemision.* Mid–Second Century B.C. National Museum, Athens. *The jockey and horse may have been intended by an athlete as a votive offering to a deity for victory in a competition. Such statues had been erected in Greece from the Archaic Age onward.*

Rhodes: Late Hellenistic Style

Although much of the Hellenistic world, including Greece, fell into Roman hands in 146 B.C., the Aegean island of Rhodes remained free for over sixty more years (see Map 4.1). During this period, independent Rhodes became a cultural center that rivaled the older cities of Pergamum, Alexandria, and Athens in terms of concentration of scientists, artists, and humanists. The Rhodian style, which was influenced by the Pergamene school, was the final stage of Hellenistic art. This style alernated between lighthearted and gay on the one hand and colossal and theatrical on the other.

In response to their patrons, Rhodian sculptors developed the specialty of depicting scenes from the life of Aphrodite. Because the bath provided an opportunity for portraying her body nude at a realistic moment, this setting became the one preferred by these artists. The *Crouching Aphrodite* is an exquisite example of this Rhodian type (Figure 4.15). Fresh from her bath, Aphrodite casually fluffs her wet hair in order to dry it. Her crouching position provides a measure of modesty, but, otherwise, this is a sensual rendition of the goddess in all her nude glory.

Another popular representation of the goddess of love was the *Aphrodite of Cyrene,* a sculpture influenced by the Rhodian school (Figure 4.16). The sculptor has reworked certain Praxitelean influences—the "s-shaped" curve to the body and the explicit sensual appearance—in order to make her figure more erotic, as required by this last phase of the Hellenistic style.

The school of sculpture on Rhodes, even after the island's absorption into Rome, was still able to produce the sublime masterpiece of Rhodian and Hellenistic art, *The Laocoön Group* (Figure 4.17). The sculptors of this famous group, probably Hagesandros, Polydoros, and Athanadoros, were all members of a local dynasty of sculptors. Their sculpture depicts the priest Laocoön and his sons. According to Vergil's *Aeneid,* the Roman epic, the story recounts that Laocoön, a priest of Neptune, warned the Trojans not to bring the wooden horse—which, unknown to him, concealed a party of Greek warriors—into their city. (Laocoön's admonition to beware Greeks bearing gifts has become proverbial). As Laocoön finished his speech, sea serpents, sent by the gods, raced out of the sea and crushed him and his two sons to death. The Trojans interpreted Laocoön's speech as an impious act against the gods, and they hauled the horse into Troy.

FIGURE 4.15 *Crouching Aphrodite.* Ca. 100 B.C. Rhodes Museum. *This era frankly enjoyed wine, women, and song, and the many sculptures of Aphrodite, such as this famous one, are visual reminders of this aspect of Hellenistic life.*

In the *Laocoön* sculptural group, the snakes, which grasp and bite the priest and his sons, serve to integrate the three figures into an image of unrelieved horror: Laocoön's face is contorted in anguish as the serpent bites him, on the left, one of his sons is already dead, and the other son seems to be disentangling himself from the serpentine coils. This cele-brated work, with its technical virtuosity and its rhetorical violence, is a fitting climax to almost four hundred years of Hellenistic art. The *Laocoön* sculptural group vanished after the fall of Rome only to be rediscovered in the early sixteenth century A.D., when it influenced the sculptor Michelangelo and the subsequent rise of Baroque art.

FIGURE 4.16 *Aphrodite from Cyrene.* First Century B.C. Terme Museum, Rome. *That this statue represents Aphrodite may be inferred from the dolphin on her right, an allusion to her birth from the sea. Her exquisitely modeled body with its gentle curves and sleek surfaces appealed to the sensual tastes of Hellenistic patrons. But styles and preferences change, and modern viewers may regard this image as merely pretty.*

FIGURE 4.17 HAGESANDROS, POLYDOROS, AND ATHANADOROS *The Laocoön Group.*
Ca. A.D. 50. Vatican Museum. *Parallels are frequently made between the distorted features
of the dying Laocoön and the mortally wounded Alkyoneus from the Pergamum altar (see
Figure 4.12). This similarity points to some connection between the Rhodian and Pergamene
schools of sculpture, though the exact relationship is a matter of controversy.*

The Legacy of the Hellenistic World

In the Hellenistic Age, Athens and its culture achieved the status of an inspiring model to be honored and emulated. But the Hellenistic rulers had no interest in democracy; indeed, their larger political interests often conflicted with the needs of local subjects. Nor did these kings want to further humanism, which they regarded as either irrelevant to imperial goals or subversive of them. What appealed to the Hellenistic kings was a narrow, lifeless humanism, as exemplified by the dynasties of the Attalids in Pergamum and the Ptolemies in Egypt. The Hellenistic monarchs wanted to do no more than create new cultural centers that rivaled the fame of the old Athens. The great Hellenistic centers of Pergamum and Alexandria—with their libraries, poets, scientists, artists, schools of philosophy, marble buildings, and monuments—were perceived as politically useful to these ambitious rulers. In other words, they wanted to harness art to politics for propaganda purposes.

The Hellenistic world bequeathed the idea of a "new Athens" to Rome, which further diffused the Greek heritage to the major cities of the entire Mediterranean area. After the fall of Rome, the medieval rulers adopted this tradition, making their governments responsive to the religious and, to a lesser extent, the cultural needs of their citizens. With the rise of the secular state in the eighteenth century A.D., governments began to dissociate themselves from the religious lives of their people. But state support of the arts and humanities increased and remains today a legacy of the Hellenistic Age to the modern world.

KEY CULTURAL TERMS

Hellenistic	autarky
koine	*Skepticism*
New Comedy	*Epicureanism*
comedy of manners	ataraxia
Alexandrianism	*Stoicism*
pastoral	logos
idyll	*Corinthian*
Cynicism	*genre subject*

SUGGESTIONS FOR FURTHER READING

PRIMARY SOURCES

AUSTIN, M. M., ed. *The Hellenistic World from Alexander to the Roman Conquest: A Selection of Ancient Sources in Translation.* Cambridge: Cambridge University Press, 1981. Letters, decrees, and official pronouncements from the Hellenistic period; provides a real sense of the time.

SHAPIRO, H., and CURLEY, E., eds. *Hellenistic Philosophy: Selected Readings.* New York: Modern Library, 1965. Selections from writings on Epicureanism, Stoicism, Skepticism, and Neo-Platonism, with short introductions.

SECONDARY SOURCES

BIEBER, M. *The Sculpture of the Hellenistic Age.* New York: Columbia University Press, 1955. A thorough survey of Hellenistic sculpture showing major and minor style changes; over 800 illustrations.

BURKET, W. *Ancient Mystery Cults.* Cambridge: Harvard University Press, 1987. Four lectures on the structures, functions, and beliefs of the mystery cults; for the serious student.

CHARBONNEAUX, J., et al. *Hellenistic Art, 330–50 B.C.* New York: G. Braziller, 1973. An overview of Hellenistic architecture, painting, and sculpture; handsomely illustrated.

FERGUSON, J. *The Heritage of Hellenism: The Greek World from 323 to 31 B.C.* New York: Harcourt Brace Jovanovich, 1973. A different approach, with broad topics like "Learning" and "Humanity"; profusely illustrated.

GRANT, M. *From Alexander to Cleopatra: The Hellenistic World.* London: Weidenfeld and Nicolson, 1982. A useful introduction to this era with chapters on the arts, philosophy, and literature.

GREEN, P. *Alexander of Macedon, 356–323 B.C.* New York: Praeger, 1970. With many excellent photographs, this lively but critical biography offers a controversial view of Alexander.

LONG, A. A. *Hellenistic Philosophy: Stoics, Epicureans, Sceptics.* London: Duckworth, 1986. A general appraisal and analysis of these schools of thought.

POLLITT, J. J. *Art in the Hellenistic Age.* Cambridge: Cambridge University Press, 1986. An excellent recent survey by a leading authority; richly illustrated.

RIST, A. *The Poems of Theocritus.* Chapel Hill: University of North Carolina Press, 1978. One of the best studies of the finest poet of the Hellenistic Age.

TARN, W. W. *Alexander the Great.* Boston: Beacon Press, 1964. First published in 1948, this short biography still provides a useful introduction to Alexander's life and achievements.

———, and GRIFFITH, G. T. *Hellenistic Civilization.* Rev. ed. New York: New American Library, 1961. Still one of the best modern studies of the Hellenistic Age.

WEBSTER, T. B. L. *Hellenistic Poetry and Art.* London: Methuen, 1964. Focuses more on drama and poetry.

5

ROMAN CIVILIZATION
The Pre-Christian Centuries

Roman civilization is as ancient as the Greek civilization discussed in the preceding two chapters. From its legendary founding in 753 B.C., Rome grew steadily from a tiny city-state ruled by kings to a powerful republic, constantly adjusting to internal and external forces, and ultimately to a vast empire that controlled the known Western world. This chapter surveys the history and culture of Rome from its founding to the time when the empire teetered on the brink of collapse in A.D. 284. Chapter 7 picks up the story of Rome and follows it through its rejuvenated and Christian period to the last days of the empire. Before that, chapter 6 examines the Judeo-Christian tradition that wove itself inextricably into the Western heritage during the first centuries of imperial Rome.

THE COLOSSUS OF THE MEDITERRANEAN WORLD

In A.D. 248 the Romans celebrated the one-thousandth anniversary of the founding of their city. By this date, the Roman way of life had engulfed not only the peoples and cultures of the ancient Near East and the eastern Mediterranean but had also brought the light of civilized existence to the primitive tribes living in North Africa, in western Europe to the Rhine River, in central Europe to the Danube River, and in England (Map 5.1). So vast was Rome's dominion and so powerful its influence that until the eighteenth century Rome was the exemplar of power and wealth, one that the nations of Europe could only dream of equaling. Roman civilization had a profound and lasting impact on life in the West (Figure 5.1).

General Characteristics of Roman Civilization

Who were the Romans, and how did they create such a successful civilization? The Romans were and remained, above all, a practical people, interested chiefly in what was useful. Possessed of a virile moral sense, they were inclined to view intellectual brilliance with suspicion. Furthermore, Roman authority figures, such as political leaders and fathers, cultivated the virtue known in Latin as *gravitas*, or gravity, meaning a deep-seated seriousness (Figure 5.2). By Greek standards, the Romans were a dull lot, too self-controlled and afraid of the imagination. But the Romans made up for their absence of intellectual fire by their ingenious adaptations of borrowed cultural forms, and they compensated for their lack of originality through a gift for governing.

Early Rome was a minor city-state founded by herdsmen and farmers on seven low hills beside the Tiber River in central Italy. Over their long rise to world leadership, the Romans changed radically, but they never ceased to honor their agrarian roots. Roman morality and Roman law both echoed a rural ethic by stressing the need to submit to the order of nature and to live within one's means. Roman literary

MAP 5.1

The Roman Empire under Augustus

Roman Empire under Augustus

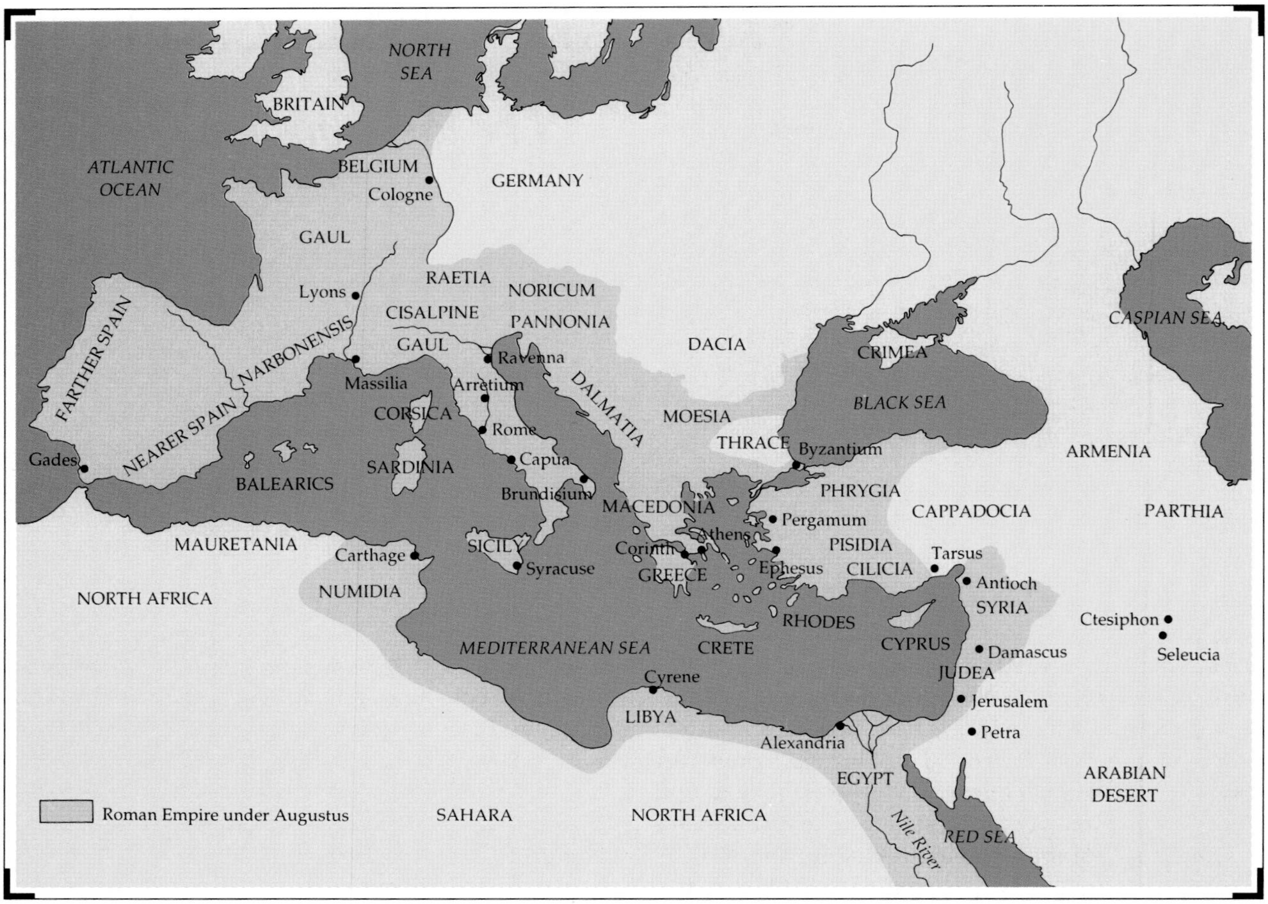

culture was also deeply imbued with a reverence for a rustic past. When Rome became prosperous and powerful, many writers bemoaned the corrupting power of luxury and appealed to the homespun values of Rome's founders. Rome's agrarian tradition also contributed the ideal of the patriotic farmer-soldier. Early leaders of the republican period who never strayed far from their farming heritage became national idols, celebrated in biographies and held up to school boys as models.

Another important Roman value was the sanctity of the family. Divorce was unheard of until the late republican era, and even then family values continued to be eulogized by moralists and honored by political leaders. Within the Roman family the roles of the father and the mother were strictly defined. The family was guided by the father, the *paterfamilias*, who exercised legal power of life and death over his entire household, including his spouse, children, and other relatives as well as servants and slaves (Figure 5.3). The paterfamilias wielded greater authority than

his Greek counterpart, but, in contrast, the Roman matron was freer and had more practical influence than the secluded wives of Greece. In general, the Roman matron was conspicuously present in society, attending and presiding at gatherings along with her mate and supervising the education of both her male and female offspring (Figure 5.4).

In Rome as elsewhere in the ancient world, religion permeated the life of the family. Each Roman household kept an undying fire burning on its hearth, symbolic of the goddess Vesta, to ensure the family's continuity. Above each hearth stood statuettes of Lares, the outdoor spirits guarding fields and buildings, and Penates, the interior protectors of cupboards and barns (Figure 5.5). Beyond the living, the family revered the deceased male ancestors, whose funeral masks adorned the walls and were regularly used in domestic rituals.

In sum, the Roman citizen was secure in the knowledge of both Rome's and his place in the world and in the cosmos. And the Roman matron, though

FIGURE 5.1 Porta Borsari at Verona. Mid–First Century A.D. Verona, Italy. *Roman architectural innovations strongly influenced the architecture of later periods. This structure was originally attached to a building that served as a gate to the Roman city of Verona. The building itself was razed during the Renaissance, but the facade was left standing and served as a model for palaces of that era. The wall, composed of stacked, rounded arches, is a typical Roman design. Most of the wall openings are beautifully framed with triangular pediments overhead and Corinthian columns or pilasters on the sides, resulting in a visual effect of ordered diversity.*

FIGURE 5.2 Statue of a Republican General. 75–50 B.C. Museo Nazionale, Rome. *This statue portrays an unknown military leader from the Late Republic. The deeply serious though realistic face is typical of the Roman style. By this time Roman generals were imitating the custom of Hellenistic leaders of having themselves depicted as nude or seminude figures. This fashion ended abruptly with the reign of Augustus, when rulers began to be represented wearing a cuirass, or breastplate (see Figure 5.23).*

FIGURE 5.3 Portrait Head of the Banker Lucius Caecilius Jucundus. Mid–First Century A.D. Museo Nazionale, Naples. *The stern gaze and sagging features of Lucius Caecilius Jucundus convey the quiet dignity and authority of a typical* paterfamilias. *This realistic portrait (note the large mole on his cheek) may have been based on a death mask.*

FIGURE 5.5 Statuettes of Lares. First Century B.C. Museo Nazionale, Naples. *These statuettes portray the Lares, the deities who guarded each Roman home. At first, images of the Lares were painted inside small family shrines, but wealthy citizens began to commission statuettes of these household deities. The posture of the bronze Lares—dancing on the balls of their feet and pouring wine from a drinking horn into a libation bowl—was also typical of the painted figures. The swinging skirts reflect a stylistic current that began in Hellenic art.*

FIGURE 5.4 *Eumachia.* Mid–First Century A.D. Museo Nazionale, Naples. *This statue of Eumachia, which was found at Pompeii, shows that Roman matrons were involved in public life. The inscription on the statue's base praises her for having donated a building in the town's forum for the use of the fullers—workers involved in the making of woolen cloth. Her statue was paid for by the fullers' association in gratitude for her gift. Her idealized face reflects the Hellenic ideal preferred during the reign of Augustus in the first century A.D.*

lacking the voting rights citizenship gave to her spouse, played many roles that society and tradition demanded of her. Like her husband, she understood the social rules and what her culture had called her to do.

The Etruscan and Greek Connections

Although the Romans took great pride in their native tradition, they were receptive to change and able to assimilate the contributions of superior cultures, as their experience with the Etruscans and Greeks demonstrates. In the late seventh century B.C., Rome, still a small city-state, was subjugated by the Etruscans, a sophisticated urban people of obscure origins in northern Italy. The Etruscans excelled at commerce and conducted a brisk maritime trade with the advanced cultures of the eastern Mediterranean (Figure 5.6). Under Etruscan domination, Rome prospered and became a hub of commerce and transportation. And under Etruscan tutelage the Romans began to put their spoken language into writing, using the Etruscan alphabet. Even what are called Roman numerals were invented by the Etruscans.

But despite the obvious advantages that contact with a higher culture had given them, the Romans rankled under Etruscan rule, and in 509 B.C. they expelled Tarquin the Proud, the last Etruscan king,

FIGURE 5.6 *Apollo of Veii.* Early Fifth Century B.C. Museo Nazionale di Villa Guilia, Rome. *This magnificent striding statue of Apollo shows strong influences from the art of Archaic Greece, such as the proportion of the torso to the limbs and the enigmatic smile. But the superb mastery of movement achieved by the Etruscan artist is well in advance of the Greek style.*

TABLE 5.2 THE CHIEF ROMAN GODS AND GODDESSES AND THEIR GREEK COUNTERPARTS

ROMAN	GREEK
Jupiter	Zeus
Juno	Hera
Neptune	Poseidon
Pluto	Hades
Apollo	Apollo
Diana	Artemis
Mars	Ares
Venus	Aphrodite
Vulcan	Hephaestus
Minerva	Athena
Mercury	Hermes
Vesta	Hestia

ing stories. And even after the fall of Rome, the Greco-Roman gods and goddesses continued to live in the art, music, and literature of Europe.

From the Punic Wars onward innovative cults sprang up in Rome. From Egypt came the worship of Isis, a religion that promised immortality, and from Asia Minor the cult of Cybele, a mother goddess. Army veterans returning from Persia brought back Mithra, the mortal son of the sun god, whose cult excluded women (Figure 5.8). Mithra's followers observed each seventh day as Sun Day and December 25 as the god's birthday; the faithful also underwent a baptism in the blood of a sacred bull.

Religious innovation was perpetuated in imperial Rome until Greek and oriental cults finally submerged the old Roman beliefs. Most of all, the emperor cult provided unity amid religious diversity. Emperor worship succeeded admirably, except among two groups of Roman subjects who refused to recognize the ruler's divinity—the Jews and the Christians, whose story of resistance and rebellion is told in Chapter 6.

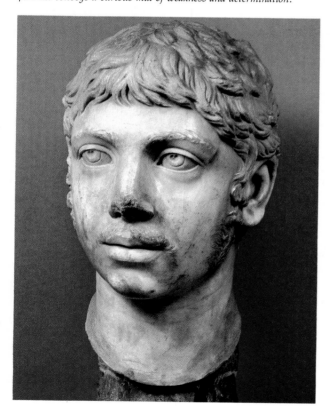

FIGURE 5.8 *Elagabalus.* (Marcus Aurelius Antoninus Heliogabalus). First Quarter of Third Century A.D. Museo Capitolino, Rome. *This youth ruled Rome from A.D. 218 until 222, when he was assassinated at the age of eighteen. A fanatic devotee of the sun god, he introduced the worship and the trappings of this Syrian cult into imperial circles. The face in this imperial portrait conveys a curious mix of weakness and determination.*

Language, Literature, and Drama

Latin, the Roman language, was at first an unimaginative, functional language, suited only to legal documents, financial records, and military commands. But with the growth of law and oratory in the Early Republic, grammar was standardized, vocabulary was increased, and word meanings were clarified. As the Romans conquered, they made Latin the language of state, except in the Greek-speaking East. By the late empire, Latin had spread throughout the civilized world and was the common tongue for the vast majority of Roman citizens.

Latin literature began to flourish in the Middle Republic (264–133 B.C.) with lyric and epic poetry, comedy, and tragedy, all in the Greek style, although writers were beginning to develop a distinctive Roman style. Over the centuries, Roman literature changed with the changing times, evolving through several quite distinct periods.

The First Literary Period, 250–31 B.C. The writing of the first literary period was noteworthy for its strongly Greek flavor and, in some writers, its grave moral tone. This period also saw the rise of a Roman theatrical tradition influenced both by roots reaching back to boisterous Etruscan religious celebrations and by contact with the Greek theater. Many educated Romans in this period could speak Greek, and many had seen performances of tragedies and comedies during their travels.

Plautus (about 254–184 B.C.), a plebeian from Italy, launched Rome's great age of comic theater with his almost 130 plays. His genius lay in breathing fresh life into the stale plots and stock characters borrowed from Menander and other Hellenistic, New Comedy playwrights. In his hands, the mistaken identities, verbal misunderstandings, and bungled schemes seemed brand new. Rome's other significant comic playwright was Terence (about 195–159 B.C.), a Carthaginian slave who was brought to Rome, educated, and set free. Although he wrote only six plays, he won the acclaim of Rome's educated elite, perhaps because of the pure Greek tone and themes of his works. Terence's highly polished style later inspired the magisterial Cicero. When the theater revived in Renaissance Europe, playwrights first turned to Plautus and Terence for characters and plots.

As Roman comedy began to decline, superseded by the vast spectacles that the masses demanded, two major poets with distinctively different personalities and talents appeared: Lucretius and Catullus. Both were heavily influenced by Greece. Lucretius (about 94–about 55 B.C.) stands in the long line of instructive literary figures dating from Homer. A gifted poet, Lucretius wrote *De Rerum Natura* (*On the Nature of Things*) to persuade the reader of the truth of Epicureanism, the philosophy based on scientific atomism that denied divine intervention in human affairs (see Chapter 4). As literature, *On the Nature of Things* ranks as one of the poetic masterpieces of the ancient world with its well-turned Latin phrases and its imaginative and vivid language.

In contrast to Lucretius's lengthy poem, the verses of Catullus (about 84–about 57 B.C.) are characterized by brevity, one of the hallmarks of the Alexandrian school of the Hellenistic Age. Catullus's "small" epics, epigrams, and love poems also closely imitate the scholarly and romantic qualities of Alexandrianism. Catullus is best remembered for his racy love poems, reflecting the lives of his highborn circle in Rome. These poems dwell on his long and often heartbreaking affair with his mistress, Clodia, whom he called Lesbia, in honor of the willful Sappho. Catullus's carefully honed lyrics express his innermost feelings of desire, disappointment, and jealousy.

The efforts of Lucretius and Catullus pale, however, when placed beside those of their contemporary Cicero (106–43 B.C.). An equestrian from Italy, he dominated Roman letters in his own day so much that his era is often labeled the Age of Cicero. By translating Greek treatises into Latin, he created a philosophical vocabulary for the Latin language where none had existed before. Between the fall of Rome and A.D. 1900, Cicero's fame among educated Europeans was such that he was regarded as an au-

FIGURE 5.9 *Cicero.* First Century B.C. Museo Capitolino, Rome. *The anonymous sculptor of this bust of Cicero has caught the character of the man as recalled in literary sources. Honored as one of Rome's finest intellectuals and a patriot devoted to rescuing the state from chaos, he is depicted deep in thought with stern and resolute features. This idealized portrait contributed to the mystique of Cicero as a hero of the Roman republic.*

thority on the order of Plato and Aristotle. For centuries his collected speeches served as models both of public oratory and of written argument. Similarly, his philosophical tracts set the agenda for generations of thinkers and reformers. Today's readers rank Cicero's personal letters as his masterpiece. These nearly eight hundred letters, frank in style and language, offer an honest, unique self-portrait of a major public figure in ancient times (Figure 5.9).

The Second Literary Period: The Golden Age, 31 B.C.– A.D. 14 The second period of Roman literature coincided with the personal reign of Augustus and is considered the Golden Age of Roman letters. This period's three greatest writers, Vergil, Horace, and Ovid, captured the age's euphoric mood as peace and stability once more returned to Rome. Of the three writers, Vergil best represented the times through his vision of Rome and his stirring verses.

The works of Vergil (70–19 B.C.), an Italian plebeian, were inspired by Greek literary forms—idylls (or vignettes), didactic (instructive) poems, and epics—yet his use of native themes and his focus on the best traits in the Roman people give an authentic Roman voice to his work. Deeply moved by Augustus's reforms, he put his art in the service of the state. Vergil's pastoral poetry, the *Eclogues* and *Georgics*, celebrated rural life and urged readers to seek harmony with nature in order to find peace—advice that became a significant moral theme of the Western heritage. But Vergil is best known for the *Aeneid*, an epic poem in twelve books that he wrote in imitation of the Homeric epics. In this work, infused with Roman values and ideals, Vergil gave full voice to his love of country, his respect for Augustus, and his faith in Rome's destiny.

The *Aeneid* tells of Aeneas, the legendary Trojan hero who wandered the Mediterranean before founding Rome. In the first six books, Vergil models his tale on the *Odyssey*, writing of travel and love. The second half is modeled on the *Iliad*, stressing fighting and intrigue. The *Aeneid* became Rome's bible and its literary masterpiece. Children were often required to memorize passages from the poem to instill in them the values that had made Rome great. Aeneas served as the prototype of the faithful leader who would not be diverted from his destined path. The work's rich language led later poets to mine the *Aeneid* for expressions and images. As Homer inspired Vergil, so Vergil became the model for Western poets when imaginative literature was revived in late medieval Europe.

The second major poet of the Golden Age was Horace (65–8 B.C.), another Italian plebeian who also welcomed Augustus as Rome's savior and offered patriotic sentiments in his verses. His poems, which were written to be read aloud, use Alexandrian forms such as odes and letters in verse. He helped to create a new poetic genre, the satire, which rebuked the manners of the age. Horace was at his best in addressing the heartbreaking brevity of life: ". . . what has been, has been, and I have had my hour."

Ovid (43 B.C.–about A.D. 17), the third voice of the Golden Age, was a wealthy Italian equestrian who did not devote his verses to patriotic themes or pay lip service to conventional morality. Ovid's love poems speak of the purely sensual and fleeting quality of sex and ignore the enduring value of committed love. His *Art of Love* offers advice, in a manner bordering on the scientific, on how to seduce women, whether willing or not. Such advice contrasted with Vergil's and Horace's attempts to raise the moral level of the Romans.

Ovid's masterpiece was the *Metamorphoses*, or *Transformations*. Somewhat irreverently, he breathed new life into more than two hundred Greek and Roman myths and legends that centered on the transformation of people into other forms. This work is the source of our knowledge of many Classical myths, and medieval and Renaissance poets turned to it continually for inspiration.

The Third Literary Period: The Silver Age, A.D. 14– 200 In the third literary period, the patriotic style of the previous era was replaced by the critical views of writers who often satirized the Roman society and state. Lacking the originality of the Golden Age, the writers of this era looked to their predecessors for models, while they polished their phrases and reworked earlier themes. This shift in literary taste reflected a new educational ideal that stressed skills in debate and oratory. As a result, moral considerations became secondary to aesthetic effects, with writers using rhetorical flourishes and exaggerated literary conceits.

One of Rome's outstanding Silver Age talents was Seneca (4 B.C.–A.D. 65). Born into a wealthy equestrian family in Spain, Seneca became a powerful senator and one of the age's chief thinkers. He is best remembered as a dramatist, though his works failed to measure up to the Greek heritage. His ten extant plays relied on emotionalism, rhetorical excess, and stage violence—the perennial traits of Roman tragedy. After his day the staging of tragedies ceased, not to be revived for more than fifteen hundred years.

The Silver Age produced Rome's last great Latin poet, Juvenal (about A.D. 60–about 140), who trained his censorious gaze on the follies of the empire. Juvenal expressed his outraged observations in sixteen satires, the literary form originated by Horace and others. The voice that speaks in Juvenal's satires is embittered, perhaps a reflection of his obscure social origins. But the carefully crafted language—obscene, bilious, and evocative but always just right—made him the master of this genre in Rome if not in world letters.

The leading historian of the Silver Age was Tacitus (A.D. 55?–117). He honored the Greek tradition of historical writing which dictated that history must be written according to literary rules, that the proper study of history is contemporary events, and that effects in history have human, not supernatural, causes.

Tacitus acquired his knowledge of statecraft as the governor of the province of Asia (modern southwest Turkey). Among his works are two that have earned him the front rank among Roman historians. The *Annals* focus on the rulers after the death of Augustus in A.D. 14 until the murder of Nero in 68. The *Histories* then pick up the story of Rome and carry it through 96, when the tyrannical Domitian was assassinated.

Tacitus was a master of the Latin language and had a flair for dramatic narrative. Like other Roman historians, he wrote history with a moral purpose, but his critical spirit set him apart from those who had nothing but glowing praise for Rome. Instead, Tacitus's perspective is that of a proud senator who cannot conceal his distaste for Rome's loss of political freedom. In his works he sought to uncover the origins of the misrule that had almost destroyed Rome in his day, and he ended by concluding that tyranny was an innate flaw in the imperial office.

Philosophy

The Romans adopted the ethical aspects of Greek thought, but they rejected systematic philosophy as dangerous, fearing that the study of philosophy would draw their young men away from the military to lives of dreamy speculation. As a result, Roman thought stressed rules of behavior with little regard for metaphysics.

In time, Roman versions of Epicureanism and Stoicism reached a wide audience, notably among influential aristocrats. Although Epicureanism had little impact, mainly because its focus on withdrawal from worldly cares contradicted the Roman sense of duty, Stoicism's effect was potent and lasting. Stoic values seemed to confirm the farmer-soldier ideal, suggesting that the early Romans were unintentional Stoics. In addition, Stoicism under the empire caused a few aristocrats to resist, if passively, the growing menace of autocracy; these hardy Stoics, some of whom, like Seneca, lost their lives for their ideas, believed that the natural law was superior to the earthbound justice of the rulers.

Stoicism   Although Stoicism was introduced to Rome in the Late Republic, its greatest influence was achieved in the empire through the writings and teaching of Seneca, Epictetus, and the emperor Marcus Aurelius.

Seneca's fame as a dramatist has been noted above. His fame as a philosopher rests on his *Letters on Morality*. These letters, which were usually written in response to pressing ethical problems, are filled with good advice, even though they break no new philosophical ground. Thus, for example, Seneca counseled a grieving acquaintance to maintain dignity and inner strength in the face of a loved one's death.

Seneca's *Letters* survived the fall of Rome, while the works of most other thinkers temporarily disappeared. Consequently, he became one of the great guides for Western thought when philosophy was revived in the Middle Ages. In the modern world, however, his reputation has suffered because of his closeness to Nero, an emperor of legendary cruelty. Despite Seneca's noble philosophy, doubt has been cast on his personal morality.

No such cloud hovers over Epictetus (about A.D. 55–115) who not only preached but lived his Stoic creed. According to tradition, Epictetus, though a slave in Rome, won his freedom because of his teachings. He subsequently founded a school in Asia Minor and attracted enthusiastic converts. He did not write anything, but Arrian, a pupil, composed the *Discourses* and the *Handbook*, both in Greek, which together preserved the essence of his master's ideas.

Epictetus's philosophy reflected his own victory over personal misfortune. He advised patience in the face of trouble, indifference to material things, and acceptance of one's destiny. While these ideas represented a rehash of basic Stoic beliefs, his moral wholeness gave them a special appeal.

Stoicism's finest hour arrived in A.D. 160 when Marcus Aurelius became emperor (Figure 5.10). Converted to Stoicism in his youth, the emperor wrote an account (in Greek) of his daily musings—called *Meditations*—while he was engaged in almost continual warfare against Germanic invaders along the Danube. His journal came to light after his death and was soon recognized as a masterpiece of Stoicism.

Like all Stoics, the emperor admonished himself to play with dignity the role that providence had assigned. If a divine plan guides the universe, then he must accept it; if, however, the world is ruled by chance, then a well-regulated mind is the best defense. Such reasoning enabled Marcus Aurelius to avoid moral confusion. Although the *Meditations* are Stoic in tone, a careful reading reveals their author to be a hard-headed Roman who was somewhat lacking in intellectual rigor. Marcus Aurelius's death in A.D. 180 signaled the end of Stoicism. The next century witnessed the swamping of all philosophies in the military anarchy and oriental cults of the times.

Neo-Platonism   Some Roman thinkers adopted Greek Stoicism; others were interested in blending the various Greek schools—Platonic, Aristotelean, Stoic, among others—into a philosophic synthesis. The outstanding example of this latter trend was

FIGURE 5.10 *Marcus Aurelius.* Ca. A.D. 173. Bronze, height 16'8". Piazza del Campidoglio, Rome. *The unknown artist has represented Marcus Aurelius as a warrior emperor, but the militaristic image is offset somewhat by the Stoic ruler's face. Here we see revealed a human being lost in thought and far removed from pomp and power. This magnificent equestrian statue marked the climax of sculpture in the Roman empire.*

Neo-Platonism, a school of thought founded primarily by Plotinus (A.D. 205–270) in the third century A.D. Neo-Platonism was the last major school of philosophy in the ancient world. The movement began as an attempt to correct the problem at the heart of Plato's system—the seemingly irreconcilable split between the absolute world of Ideas and the perishable material world. This Platonic dualism could and did lead to the notion that the everyday world has little purpose in the overall scheme of things. Plotinus now succeeded in bridging the two worlds with his theories, and his writings later influenced Christian thinkers in the Middle Ages and the Italian humanists of the Renaissance.

Plotinus resolved Platonic dualism not with logical analysis but with mystical insight, claiming that the union of the physical and spiritual worlds could be grasped only though an ecstatic vision. His retreat from philosophy into mysticism occurred during the turbulent era of the Barrack Emperors and the flight of many people from the cities to country villas and estates.

Law

The most original contribution of the Roman mind was law. Rome's law created a notion of justice founded on such ideals as fairness and equity for both citizens and subjects, as well as the presumption of innocence in criminal cases. These principles later became central to the Western legal tradition. But the most important facet of Roman law was born in Stoicism: the idea of *natural law,* or a higher justice than that made by human forces. This doctrine of natural law is the basis of the American Declaration of Independence.

Rome's law evolved over many centuries, starting in 450 B.C. with the first written code, the Twelve Tables. The Twelve Tables, which represented a plebeian victory over the patricians, treated basic aspects of civil life such as personal and property rights, religious practices, and moral behavior. But this milestone did not rid Rome of class distinctions; it merely recognized conflicting rights and thus necessitated a judge above both parties. In later times class divisions continued to affect the way the law was applied, since the dispensing of justice always favored the rich.

The branch of Roman law dealing with property rights was called civil law and developed through the office of the *praetor.* Each praetor, at the beginning of his term, issued an edict describing the legal procedures and precedents he would follow. The body of decisions handed down by the praetors eventually came to constitute Rome's system of civil law.

By the Late Republic, the development of law was enhanced by the advice of legal experts, called *jurisconsults* or *jurisprudentes.* They tended to broaden Roman justice with their Stoic views. The most creative phase of Roman law occurred in the second and third centuries A.D., when eminent jurisconsults helped to codify the law and extend its principles to cover all the citizens of the empire.

The Visual Arts

Architecture and sculpture dominated Rome's visual arts, but they were pressed into the service of practical needs. The Romans commissioned buildings and statues to serve the state, religion, or society, but they recognized that the practical did not have to forgo beauty, and many of Rome's engineering feats were beautiful in their functional elegance.

The early Romans learned lessons in architecture from the Etruscans, but after encountering the Greeks of Magna Graecia, they rebuilt Rome along Greek lines. By the second century B.C., wealthy Romans were collecting Greek statues in all styles—Archaic, Hellenic, and Hellenistic. Under Augustus, the Hellenic style in both sculpture and architecture became supreme, inching its way across the empire over the next two centuries. By the third century A.D. a new architectural style had arisen, blending Greek and Roman. This Greco-Roman blend is the style that passed into medieval civilization after the collapse of the Western Empire.

Architecture Over the years the Romans used many types of materials in their public and private buildings. The architects of the Early Republic built with sun-dried bricks and used terra cotta, a fired clay, for roofs and decorations. As Rome's wealth grew and new materials were imported, the bricks retained an important though less visible role in buildings, chiefly in foundations and walls. By the Late Republic two new products were adapted from the Greeks, mortar and ashlars (massive hewn stones), which, in time, revolutionized the face of Rome.

Much of the impetus for the building revolution sprang from the Romans' improvement of the recipe for mortar. They produced a moldable concrete by mixing lime, sand, small rocks, and rubble, but because the concrete was visually unappealing, the builders began to cover it with slabs of expensive and highly polished marble and granite imported from Greece or quarried in Italy.

The temple became one of Rome's chief architectural forms. The basic source for their temple was the Greek model with its post-beam-triangle construction, although Etruscan influence was also significant. The Romans adapted the Greek column as either support or decoration, preferring the ornamented Corinthian order to the plainer Doric and Ionic.

The Romans' most significant innovations in architecture were made with the rounded arch, which already had a long history by the time that they began to experiment with it. The Mesopotamians probably

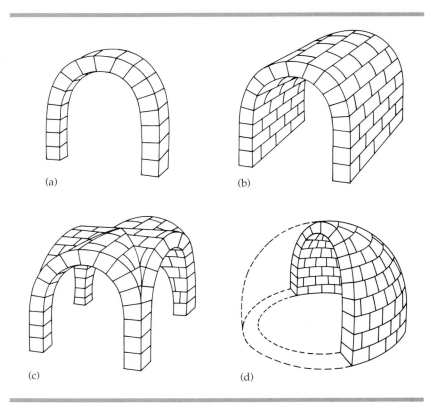

(a)

(b)

(c)

(d)

FIGURE 5.11 Structures Used in Roman Architecture. *Beginning with the basic arch (a), the Romans created the barrel vault (b) and the cross vault (c). These structural elements, along with the dome (d), which they formed by rotating a series of arches around a central axis, gave the Romans the architectural elements they needed to construct their innovative temples and monuments.*

FIGURE 5.12 Maison Carrée. Ca. 16 B.C. Nîmes, France. *This temple was probably modeled on temples in Rome, since buildings with Corinthian columns and similar overall designs were being constructed in the capital at this time. Reproducing architecture in the provincial cities was another way in which the Romans spread civilization throughout their conquered lands.*

invented this arch, the Greeks knew about it, and the Etruscans used it in their drainage systems. The arch's basic round form is created with wedge-shaped stones called *voussoirs*. A *keystone* at the center of the semicircle locks the arch in place. The installed arch is amazingly strong, diverting the weight of the upper walls both outward and downward onto columns or other supports (Figure 5.11).

The Romans demonstrated their inventive genius by creating ceilings, or *vaults*, from arches—by transforming the simple rounded arch into barrel vaults, groined vaults, and domes. They created the *barrel vault*—named because it looks like a barrel divided lengthwise—by building a series of contiguous arches. They intersected two barrel vaults at right angles in order to produce a *groined* or *cross vault*. Finally, the dome, the crown jewel of Rome's architectural vocabulary, was created by, in effect, turning an arch in a full circle (see Figure 5.11). The Romans were also able to build arches more safely after they discovered the correct mathematical ratio (1:2) between the height of an arch and the width of its base.

The prototype of imperial temples is the well-preserved Maison Carrée in Nîmes, France, a major provincial city under Augustus. Built about 16 B.C., the Maison Carrée incorporated Etruscan and Greek ideas (Figure 5.12). Raised on a platform in the Etruscan manner, this temple shows other Etruscan borrowings in the central stairway, the deep porch, and the engaged columns, that is, the columns built into the walls of the *cella*, the inner sanctum housing the cult statue. Greek influences are visible in the low gable—the triangular end of the building's roof—and the Corinthian columns. The Greek notion that beauty lies in mathematical harmony is also expressed in the predetermined ratio of the area of the cella to the area of the temple's porch. The aesthetic appeal of the Maison Carrée has made it one of the most famous buildings of Roman culture. In the eighteenth century Thomas Jefferson modeled the Statehouse in Richmond, Virginia, on this Roman temple.

Besides perfecting their version of the rectilinear temple, the Romans also invented the round temple, as seen in the Pantheon, a sanctuary dedicated to all of their deities. The Pantheon consists of three different units: the entrance porch, or portico, with its supporting columns; the huge drum, housing the sanctuary proper, which is attached to the porch; and the dome set on top of the drum (Figure 5.13). This design showed the Romans' reliance on a native heritage, because the rounded shape was probably inspired by the circular religious shrines of the pre-Romans, as modern archaeology has shown. The Pantheon also combined a religious with a secular image: The dome symbolized both the heaven of the deities and the vastness of the empire.

But the Pantheon did more than to reflect the deep longings of the Roman people; its rich interior illustrated the Roman genius for decoration (Figure 5.14). A polychrome marble floor and a dome with recessed panels created a dazzling interior, and statues, dec-

FIGURE 5.13 Pantheon Exterior. A.D. 126. Rome. *In modern Rome the Pantheon is crowded into a piazza where it faces a monument topped by an Egyptian obelisk. However, when built under the Emperor Hadrian, the Pantheon was part of a complex of structures that complemented each other, and the temple's façade faced a set of columns in an open forecourt. Its original setting reflected the Roman sense that urban space should be organized harmoniously.*

FIGURE 5.14 Pantheon Interior. A.D. 126. Rome. *The inner diameter of the dome is 144 feet. The height of the dome is 72 feet, or one half of the total height (144 feet) of the building. The sunlight sweeps around the interior and plays on the dome's decorations as the earth turns, creating constantly changing patterns of light and design.*

orative columns, triangular pediments, niches, and other architectural details alternated around the circular room. The most unusual effect of all was the round hole, thirty feet in diameter, called the *oculus*, or eye, which opened the dome to the sunlight and the elements. As the oldest standing domed structure in the world, the Pantheon is the direct ancestor of St. Peter's Basilica in Rome and St. Paul's Cathedral in London.

Rome's architecture consisted of more than beautiful temples. The city of Rome was the center of gov-

FIGURE 5.15 Roman Forum. Ca. 100 B.C. to ca. A.D. 400. *The forum was literally the center of the Roman world, for here the Romans erected the Golden Milestone from which all roads led out across the empire. The temples and public buildings, crowded together in a relatively small area, were rebuilt over several centuries as rulers added to Rome's architectural legacy.*

ernment for the Mediterranean world, the nucleus of the state's religious system, and the hub of an international economy. And at the heart of the city was its *forum*, which functioned like the agora of Greek city-states. In the forum citizens conducted business, ran the government, and socialized among the complex of public buildings, temples, sacred sites, and monuments (Figure 5.15). The high priest of Roman religion, the Pontifex Maximus, lived in the forum, and nearby stood the curia, or senate house. Under the empire the forum became a symbol of Roman power and civilization; the leading cities in each province had forums.

As part of his reforms, Augustus rebuilt and beautified much of the republican forum. Later emperors, like Trajan (A.D. 98–117), constructed their own forums, which not only served as new centers for trade and government but also perpetuated their names. Today, Trajan's forum, which originally included a library, law courts, and plazas for strolling, has vanished except for one of the most significant monuments of the Roman Empire, a column commemorating Trajan's conquest of Dacia (modern Romania) (Figure 5.16).

Another symbol of empire, the triumphal arch, originated in the republic in the second century B.C. The Romans used both single and triple arches to celebrate military victories and erected them across the empire. The style of these memorials varied until the Arch of Titus, constructed in A.D. 81, became the accepted model. This arch, which commemorated the capture of Jerusalem by the then general Titus in A.D. 70, stood at the entrance to the Via Sacra, the thoroughfare of the Roman Forum (Figure 5.17). Inscribed on the attic, or top story, of the arch is the dedication, and decorating the sides are composite columns, a Roman innovation that intertwined flowers in the capitals of Ionic columns. Inside the arch are reliefs of Titus's victorious march into Rome after subduing the Jews.

In addition to forums, columns, and arches, the emperors also commissioned amphitheaters as monuments to themselves and as gifts to the citizens. The amphitheaters were the sites of the gladiatorial contests and other blood sports that were the cornerstone of popular culture in the empire. The most famous of these structures was called the Colosseum, although it was actually named the Flavian amphitheater, in honor of the dynasty who built it (Figure 5.18). The name Colosseum, dating from a later time, referred to a large statue of the emperor Nero that stood nearby.

The exterior of the Colosseum was formed by stacking three tiers of rounded arches on top of one another; Greek columns were then inserted between

FIGURE 5.16 Trajan's Victory Column. A.D. 106–113. Rome. *Borrowing the idea of a victory column from Mesopotamia, the pragmatic Trajan used art to enhance his power in the eyes of the citizens. This work commemorated his conquest of Dacia—present-day Romania. The marble column, set on a foundation, enclosed a winding stairway that led to an observation platform and a statue of Trajan. Spiraling around the column's shaft was a stone relief sculpture that told the story of Trajan's victory in lively and painstaking detail.*

◀ **FIGURE 5.17** Arch of Titus. Ca. A.D. 81. Rome. *The Arch of Titus, like so many structures in Rome, was eventually incorporated into other buildings. Only in the early nineteenth century A.D. was the arch restored to its original splendor. Inspired by this arch, modern architects have designed similar structures throughout the Western world.*

the arches as decorations—Doric columns on the first level, Ionic on the second, and Corinthian on the third. A concrete and marble block foundation supported this immense amphitheater. The playing area, or arena (Latin for "sand"), was made of wood and usually covered with sand. A honeycomb of rooms, corridors, and cages ran underneath the wooden floor. The Colosseum's vast size and unusual features, like its retractable overhead awning, made it

one of the triumphs of Roman engineering, but the spectacular and brutal contests between men and wild beasts, in varied combinations, symbolized the sordid side of Rome.

Up and down the Italian peninsula and across the ancient world, the urban governments built forums, temples, and amphitheaters, laid roads, and engineered aqueducts in emulation of Rome. Sometimes old towns were made to conform to imperial standards. Pompeii, founded by the Greeks in southern Italy, was typical of the older provincial towns that the Romans remodeled to suit their needs. The Romans left Pompeii's temples and public buildings standing, but a new forum gave the old city a modern look, with municipal offices, a business center, temples to the emperors and to Apollo, and a shrine

FIGURE 5.18 Colosseum. Ca. A.D. 80–100. Rome. *Although the Flavians were a short-lived dynasty, starting with Vespasian in A.D. 69 and ending with Domitian in 96, they left Rome this structure, one of its most enduring landmarks. The Romans created the oval amphitheater (literally "theater on both sides") by joining two semicircular Greek theaters, another example of their ingenuity and practicality.*

FIGURE 5.19   The Forum at Pompeii. Ca. 150–120 B.C. Pompeii, Italy. *This forum served as the civic center of this provincial town of 15,000 to 20,000 inhabitants. Four streets, from the north, south, east, and west converged here, but no traffic was allowed in the central area.*

honoring the civic deities. On the edge of town were such amenities as a palaestra—an exercise yard with swimming pool—and several markets (Figure 5.19). But disaster abruptly ended the urban renewal of Pompeii. In A.D. 79 nearby Mount Vesuvius, an active volcano, erupted and buried the city and most of its people—a horrible fate for the city that produced a rich treasure for archeologists, who began excavations in the 1700s.

Like modern urban centers, Roman towns needed a continuous supply of water. In meeting the water demands of the cities, the Romans displayed their talent for organization and their preference for the practical by creating an elaborate network of aqueducts, sluices, and syphons that ran by gravity from a water source in nearby hills and culminated in a town's reservoirs and fountains.

The Romans started building underground aqueducts about 300 B.C. and constructed the first elevated aqueduct in 144 B.C. Under Augustus, they completed an aqueduct across the Gard River near Nîmes

FIGURE 5.20 Pont du Gard. Ca. Late First Century A.D. Gard River, near Nîmes, France. *This aqueduct spanning the river was only one segment of the thirty-one-mile system that supplied water to Nîmes. Between 8,000 and 12,000 gallons of water were delivered daily, or about 100 gallons per inhabitant.*

in southern France (Figure 5.20). Known as the Pont du Gard, this aqueduct had a beautiful functional design. Six large arches form the base, and above them are eleven smaller ones supporting a third tier of thirty-five even smaller arches. Atop the third tier is the sluice through which the water flowed, by gravity, to Nîmes. This graceful structure stands today as a reminder of how the Romans transformed an ordinary object into a work of art.

Sculpture Unlike Roman architecture, Roman sculpture was deeply affected by the tastes of artists and patrons as well as by class interests. For example, certain trends in the republic ran along class lines: The patricians gravitated to the Greek styles and the plebeians favored the local art, which is called Italo-Roman. Under the empire the same needs that gave rise to temples and amphitheaters were at work in changing the look of imperial sculpture.

Although Roman portrait sculpture never broke through to a distinct style during this period, it never-

FIGURE 5.21 *Head of Brutus.* Ca. 350–50 B.C. Palazzo dei Conservatori, Rome. *The finely detailed hair, beard, and facial lines are the work of a skilled sculptor, perhaps a Greek from southern Italy. The broad range of possible dates for this bronze head (ca. 350–50 B.C.) indicates that scholars still disagree over when it was cast.*

FIGURE 5.22 *Anonymous Youth.* 40–30 B.C. Cleveland Museum of Art, Cleveland, Ohio. *This bronze head measures 15 inches and is scaled closely to human dimensions. It is unknown whether the head was to be attached to a body or to be placed on a herm, a square stone pillar.*

theless passed through three definite phases. The first phase, lasting from the third to the first centuries B.C., can be seen in the *Head of Brutus* (Figure 5.21). Brutus, one of the great heroes who helped to turn out the last Etruscan king, is shown as a stern and resolute leader. In contrast, the artist who cast the *Anonymous Youth* (Figure 5.22) captured the characteristic realism of sculpture in the Late Republic. The *Anonymous Youth,* clearly worried and uncertain, was intended as a warning rather than as an inspiration to the viewer. This type of realistic sculpture, with its sense of unease, represents the second phase of Roman sculpture.

The third phase was shaped by the reign of Augustus. According to his biographer Suetonius, the emperor boasted that he found Rome a city of brick and left it a city of marble, and Augustus certainly did influence the direction of sculpture and architecture. Under his rule imperial portraiture reverted to the idealism of Hellenic Greece, displacing the realistic art of the Late Republic. But Augustus's pure idealism did not prevail for long, for under his suc-

cessors sculpture became more propagandistic, that is, more symbolic of imperial power. This move to symbolic idealism reflected the later emperors' need to find a highly visible way in which to overawe, and thus draw together, Rome's increasingly diversified masses.

Two major sculptural works associated with Augustus, the Prima Porta portrait and the Ara Pacis, or the Altar of Peace, helped to popularize the idealistic style. Augustus's statue, commissioned after his death, stood in a garden on his widow's estate, Prima Porta, just outside Rome (Figure 5.23). The pure Hellenic style is evident in Augustus's relaxed stance and idealized face, both of which were modeled on the

FIGURE 5.23 *Augustus,* from Prima Porta. Ca. A.D. 14. ▶
Marble, height 6'7½". Vatican Collection. *This larger than life statue still bears traces of bright colors. Found in Prima Porta, the villa of Augustus's wife, Livia, the statue resembled Augustus closely yet presented him as godlike. Augustus' successors commissioned similar sculptures to convey a sense of their dignity and power.*

MVNIP PI IX. P. M.
AN. XVIII

◀ **FIGURE 5.24** Ara Pacis. 9 B.C. Rome. *Like the Prima Porta statue, the Ara Pacis became a model for later emperors, who emulated its decorations, symbols, and size. The altar was rediscovered in the sixteenth century, excavated in the nineteenth and early twentieth centuries, and restored in 1938.*

Doryphorus by Polykleitos (see Figure 3.21). However, the accompanying symbols reveal the propagandistic intent of the sculpture and are portents of the path that imperial portraits will take. For example, the cupid represents Venus, who was the mother of Aeneas, and thus Augustus is symbolically connected to the legendary origins of Rome.

The second idealistic sculpture, the marble Ara Pacis, was funded by the Senate as an offering of thanks to Augustus for his peacekeeping missions. The entire structure was set on a platform and enclosed by three walls. On the fourth side, an entrance with steps led up to the altar (Figure 5.24). Relief sculptures decorated the exterior walls, some in an idealized style and others in a realistic style (Figure 5.25). The resulting tension between realism and idealism marked this altar as an early work in the imperial style.

This type of sculpture reached its highest potential as a propaganda tool on triumphal arches and victory columns, such as those on the Arch of Titus and Trajan's Column. One of the reliefs from the Arch of Titus, the *March of the Legions*, portrayed the army's victory march into Rome after the destruction of the Temple in Jerusalem in A.D. 70 (Figure 5.26).

The continuous frieze from Trajan's Victory Column is one of the sculptural marvels of the Roman world (Figure 5.27). This low-relief sculpture winds around the column like a long comic strip, telling the story of Trajan's campaign against Dacia. The emperor, always made slightly larger than his soldiers, looms over them in several scenes, thereby serving as a visual connection and as a reminder of his power. Scholars still study the carvings of campsites and fortifications on this relief, finding them a rich source for Roman military history.

The last great sculpture from this period is the equestrian statue of Marcus Aurelius (see Figure 5.10). This work reveals a falling away from Augustan idealism to a rugged, individualized style, although one that was still highly propagandistic in its use of symbols. In the Prima Porta statue Augustus had

◀ **FIGURE 5.25** *Family of Augustus,* Ara Pacis Relief. 9 B.C. Rome. *The figures in low relief, moving from right to left, are separated yet linked by their placement and clothing. The child to the right of center is given great prominence: He faces right while all the adults in the foreground are looking left and a man places his hand on the child's head. This singling out of the child may be an act of endearment or of recognition that he is to be the emperor.*

FIGURE 5.26 *March of the Legions,* from the Arch of Titus. Ca. A.D. 80. Marble relief, approx. 6′ × 12½′. Rome. *This rectangular marble relief occupies the south side of the Arch of Titus. It commemorates the Roman victory in the Jewish War of A.D. 66–70, when the Romans put down a rebellion by the Jews in Judea and subsequently dispersed them across the Roman world. In the relief, the Roman soldiers hold aloft the Jewish holy relics from the Temple as they seem to press forward and pass under the arch on the right.*

◄ **FIGURE 5.27** Detail of Trajan's Victory Column. A.D. 113. Rome. *Wrapped around the 100-foot-high column is the 645-foot relief carving with 2,500 figures depicting Trajan's two campaigns against the Dacians. Color was applied to heighten the realistic effect of the work which, in its original setting, could be viewed from nearby buildings.*

been portrayed as a military leader; his gesture showed that he was addressing his troops. But the rest of the symbols surrounding Augustus suggested that he ruled from his capital in Rome. The symbols in the Marcus Aurelius statue, on the other hand, stress that he was a warrior emperor, even though the gesturing motion of Augustus is repeated.

Painting and Mosaics **Murals**, or wall paintings, the most popular type of painting in Rome, have been found in private dwellings, public buildings, and

FIGURE 5.28 *Flagellation Scene.* Villa of Mysteries. Ca. 60–40 B.C. Pompeii, Italy. *The figures in this brilliantly colored wall frieze seem almost to be present in the room, partly because they are just under full life size and partly because the artist has placed them on a narrow painted ledge as if on a stage. The lack of depth in the mysterious scene adds to the illusion.*

temples. Surviving works hint at a highly decorative and brightly colored art. Originally the Romans applied tempera or paint set in a binding solution directly on to a dry wall. However, this quick and easy method produced a painting that soon faded and peeled. Later they adapted fresco painting as the most practical and lasting technique. Paints were mixed and worked into a freshly plastered wall. The colors dried into the wall, resulting in a nearly indestructible painting. The Romans were inspired by many subjects: landscapes, Greek and Roman myths, architectural vistas, religious scenes, and genre scenes, or "slices of life."

Of the many paintings scattered around the Roman world, the murals in the Villa of the Mysteries at Pompeii are the most famous. These intriguing and controversial scenes, which fill the walls in several rooms, portray twenty-nine nearly life-sized figures engaged in some mystery cult rite (Figure 5.28). The grouped figures—well balanced and separated—create tension among the participants, and the varied

FIGURE 5.30 *The Street Musicians.* Ca. 100 B.C. Museo Nazionale, Naples. *This mosaic may portray a scene from a comic play. Two masked figures dance and play the tambourine and the finger cymbals while a masked female figure plays the tibia, or double flute. This mosaic was found in the so-called Villa of Cicero at Pompeii.*

FIGURE 5.29 *Scene from an Amphitheater.* Third Century A.D. Villa at Nenning, Trier, Germany. *This detail from a large, complex mosaic depicts a gladiatorial contest. The rendering of the athletes—the muscular bodies and the shadows they cast on the ground—was part of the artistic tradition that went back to Greek mosaics. This pavement mosaic from a villa in Trier, a city in Gaul, shows that the popular tastes in the provinces were the same as those in Rome.*

expressions on the faces of the women, which are impossible to decipher, heighten the sense of theater.

The Romans learned to make *mosaics* from the Hellenistic Greeks in the third century B.C. But by the third century A.D. several local Roman mosaic styles had sprung up across the empire. Although subjects varied, certain ones seemed always to be in vogue, such as still lifes, landscapes, Greek and Roman myths, philosophers and orators, and scenes from the circus and amphitheaters. A pavement mosaic from the third century A.D. shows the intricacy of design and variety of color that artisans achieved even in the Roman provinces (Figure 5.29).

Music

The absorption of the Greek tradition in music was so complete that later Roman music, in effect, simply perpetuated Greek forms and ideas. And yet the Romans used music only for practical purposes and rejected the Greek notion that music played an ethical role in educating the soul or mind.

Not until imperial times did music come to play an important role in Roman life. Under the emperors music became wildly popular, as all classes succumbed to its seductive charms. *Pantomimes*—dramatic productions with instrumental music and dances—became the spectacle favored by the Roman masses. In the long run the pantomimes became a symbol of music's decadent trend under the empire. The largest of these productions featured 3,000 instrumentalists and 3,000 dancers, but the more common size was 300 performers in each category. A more serious sort of music was kept alive by the wealthy classes, who maintained household orchestras and choruses for their private amusement. An even more cultivated audience encouraged poets like Horace to set their verses to music, thus continuing the Greek tradition of lyric poetry.

Although what Roman music actually sounded like remains a subject of conjecture, their musical instruments, borrowed from across the Mediterranean world, can be identified with some certainty. From Greece came the stringed instruments, the lyre and the kithara, along with such woodwinds as the single aulos, or flute, and the double aulos—called by the Romans the tibia (Figure 5.30). From the Etruscans came the brasses. The Romans delighted in the harsh sounds made by these instruments, incorporating them into their military music just as the Etruscans did. The hydraulic organ, or water organ, was probably perfected in Hellenistic Alexandria, but in imperial Rome it became a crowd pleaser, adding deep, voluminous sounds to the pantomimes. The taste of the imperial Roman audience is evident in the water organ, which was impressive not for its musical qualities but as a feat of engineering expertise.

The Legacy of Pre-Christian Rome

Western civilization is built on the ruins of Rome. While no pre-Christian institutions survived to form a basis of European organization, other tangibles persisted in abundance, so that the mark of Rome may still be seen and heard in countless ways. The very languages of western Europe bear the stamp of Rome, and Roman law forms the basis of the legal codes of many Western countries. Until the beginning of the twentieth century, the European educational ideal was based on the Roman curriculum, in which students studied the *trivium*—the three arts of grammar, logic, and rhetoric—and the *quadrivium*—the four sciences of arithmetic, geometry, music, and astronomy. Even today, this ideal persists at the heart of Western education.

Rome's greatest legacy to the Western world was its shining image of a healthy civilization: a just and well-regulated society of multiethnic, multiracial citizens. The Idea of Rome, as we may call this achievement, was adapted from the Hellenistic rulers. However, the Hellenistic cities lacked the cohesiveness and longevity—and, most important, the vision—of the Roman creation. When the ancient world was swept away, the Idea of Rome remained a beacon in the darkness that descended over Europe.

KEY CULTURAL TERMS

syncretism

Neo-Platonism

natural law

voussoirs

keystone

vault

barrel vault

groined vault (cross vault)

oculus

forum

mural

mosaic

pantomime

SUGGESTIONS FOR FURTHER READING

PRIMARY SOURCES

APULEIUS. *The Golden Ass*. Translated by R. Graves. New York: Farrar, Straus & Giroux, 1951. A sound translation of one of the most lively and entertaining tales in ancient literature.

HORACE. *The Complete Works of Horace*. Introduction by C. Kraemer. New York: Modern Library, 1936. Masterly translations of the works that made Horace Rome's outstanding lyric poet.

JUVENAL. *The Sixteen Satires*. Translated by P. Green. New York: Penguin, 1970. Superb vernacular versions of Juvenal's bitter works.

VERGIL. *The Aeneid*. Translated by W. F. J. Knight. New York: Penguin, 1964. A sound English prose version of Vergil's poetic epic about Aeneas, the Trojan warrior whose conquests made possible the future supremacy of Rome.

SECONDARY SOURCES

ANDREAE, B. *The Art of Rome*. Translated by R. W. Wolf. London: Macmillan, 1978. A chronological survey of art and architecture that includes the monuments in the empire's chief cities; the photographs are unsurpassed in quality.

BALSDON, J. P. V. D. *Rome: The Story of an Empire*. New York: McGraw-Hill, 1970. Excellent discussion of Rome's ethnic minorities.

BARROW, R. H. *The Romans*. New York: Penguin, 1964. A short and sympathetic work that includes Roman values and ideas.

BOREN, H. C. *Roman Society: A Social, Economic, and Cultural History*. Lexington, Mass.: D. C. Heath, 1977. Discussion of cultural developments is integrated with discussion of social and economic changes.

BRILLIANT, R. *Roman Art from the Republic to Constantine*. London: Phaidon, 1974. A brief and solid presentation of Roman art in its most dynamic period; for the beginning student.

COWELL, F. R. *Cicero and the Roman Republic*. New York: Penguin, 1948. The life and ideas of Cicero, woven into a wider study of the rise and decline of the republic.

GRANT, M. *History of Rome*. London: Weidenfeld and Nicolson, 1978. Primarily a historical narrative but also touches on economic, social, and cultural aspects of Roman civilization; provides a solid background.

————. *Roman Literature*. New York: Penguin, 1964. A well-written account for the beginning student; includes history, poetry, and an assessment of such writers as Vergil and Ovid.

HADAS, M. *A History of Latin Literature*. New York: Columbia University Press, 1952. A chronological approach covering literature from the third century B.C. to the fifth century A.D.

HANFMANN, G. M. A. *Roman Art*. Greenwich, Conn.: New York Graphic Society Publishers, Ltd., 1964. A standard survey distinguished by a learned commentary.

WARD-PERKINS, J. B. *Roman Imperial Architecture*. 2d ed. New York: Penguin, 1981. A systematic survey supported by numerous photos, drawings, and plans.

WHEELER, R. E. M. *Roman Art and Architecture*. New York: Praeger, 1964. A succinct treatment, ideal for the beginning student.

JUDAISM AND THE RISE OF CHRISTIANITY

The great civilizations discussed so far—Mesopotamian, Egyptian, Greek, and Roman—were all wealthy, powerful, and culturally dynamic, and they contributed enormously to the Western heritage. Yet an even greater contribution, one that cannot be measured in terms of buildings, governments, or monuments, came from a politically insignificant people who lived in a tiny corner of the eastern Mediterranean during ancient times—the Jews. This people created a religion that helped to shape the character of the civilizations of the Western world. Through the Hebrew Bible—the Old Testament to Christians—Judaic beliefs were passed on into both Christianity and Islam and were spread around the world. In addition, the fruitful interaction of the Judeo-Christian heritage with the Greco-Roman Classical ideals enriched and transformed the Western humanities.

JUDAISM

Judaism is one of the oldest living religions in the world. It originated in the third millennium B.C. among a tribal Middle Eastern people who placed themselves at the center of world history and created sacred texts for passing on their heritage. Unlike the history and religion of other ancient peoples, the history and religion of the Jews are so inextricably connected that they cannot be separated.

The People and Their Religion

In about 2000 B.C. many tribes were wandering throughout the Middle East. They had been displaced from their homeland in the Mesopotamian river basin by the political upheavals that accompanied the collapse of the Akkadian kingdom and the coming of the Babylonians. Some of these nomads eventually settled in the stretch of arable land along the eastern coast of the Mediterranean Sea that is part of the Fertile Crescent. Sometimes forcefully, sometimes peacefully, these patriarchal tribes, under the guidance of the oldest and most respected male members, founded communities united by blood lines, economic interests, and folk traditions. One of these tribes, led by the patriarch Abraham, occupied territory called Canaan (Time Line 6.1). The Hebrews, as Abraham's tribe was known, settled not among the Canaanites in the thriving towns along the coast and trade routes but in the hill country to the east, where they tended their flocks and practiced their crafts (Map 6.1).

Although they had many similarities with other Middle Eastern tribal peoples, the Hebrews considered themselves unique. This belief was based on the relationship between Abraham and a great supernatural being who spoke to him and whom he obeyed. This deity made a *covenant,* or solemn agreement, with Abraham to protect his family and bring prosperity to his offspring if they agreed to obey his divine commands. The outward sign of this contract

TIME LINE 6.1   JEWISH CIVILIZATION

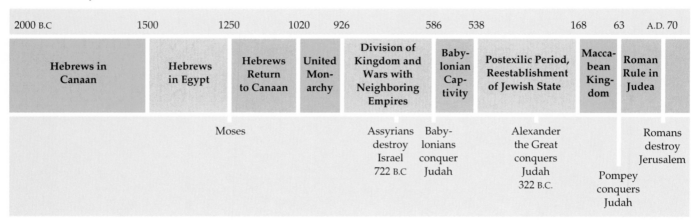

was the circumcision of all male children. Although he was associated with nature and conceived of as the source of all natural goods, the Hebrew deity differed from other Mesopotamian deities in his commitment to justice and righteousness. He was an ethical god and sought to impose ethical principles on humans.

Egypt, Exodus, and Moses   The Hebrews enjoyed many prosperous decades in Canaan, but then something disrupted their life—perhaps a drought, a changed economy, or the attraction of a better life elsewhere. Whatever the reasons, in about 1500 B.C. a group of Hebrews migrated south into Egypt, which had recently been overrun by the Hyksos, a Semitic people with whom the Hebrews shared language and cultural traits. Over the next few centuries the Hebrews thrived and came to exercise some degree of political power in Egypt until the Egyptians reconquered their land and enslaved both the Hyksos and the Hebrews. In about 1250 B.C. the extraordinary leader Moses arose among the Hebrews and tried to negotiate their release from the Pharaoh. Thwarted in his efforts, Moses rallied the Hebrews in defiance of the Pharaoh and led them on the exodus from Egypt—one of the most significant events in Jewish history. Hebrew scriptures describe Moses as a savior sent by God.

For many years the Hebrews wandered in the desert on the Sinai peninsula between Egypt and Canaan. During this time Moses molded his followers into a unified people under a set of ethical and societal laws. Like other ancient peoples, the Hebrews believed that the laws Moses received were given to them by God. What made the laws of Moses unique was their grounding in the covenant between the Hebrews and God. Also unique was the fact that no

distinction was made between religious and secular offenses. All crimes were seen as sins and all sins as crimes. Those who committed crimes could not simply make reparations to their victims; they also had to seek forgiveness from God. There were some crimes, such as murder, that were so offensive to God that they could not be forgiven by human beings alone. Furthermore, human life was seen as sacred, because it was given by God, who created and owned all things, and individual humans were precious because they were made in God's image.

The core of Mosaic law was the Ten Commandments, which set forth in summary form the proper behavior of human beings toward God and other human beings (Table 6.1). The commandments became the basis of a renewed covenant, which was now extended beyond Abraham and his descendants to include the entire people. The Hebrew God was a jealous god who tolerated no rivals; he was seen as the sole, omnipotent creator and ruler of the universe. If individuals followed his laws and worshiped him alone, they would be rewarded, and if they strayed, they would be punished. Likewise, if the tribe followed the divine commands, they would prosper, and if they disobeyed, they would meet adversity. As the mediator of the covenant between God and the Hebrew people, Moses played a crucial role in shaping Judaism into a comprehensive system of ethical monotheism.

While they were in the Sinai desert, the deity revealed a new name for himself—YHWH, a name so sacred that pious Jews never speak or write it. In the late Middle Ages, European scholars rendered YHWH as Jehovah, but today this term is generally considered a false reading of the sacred letters. In modern English, YHWH is usually rendered as Yahweh. In biblical times, Jewish priests called the deity Adonai, the Semitic term for Lord.

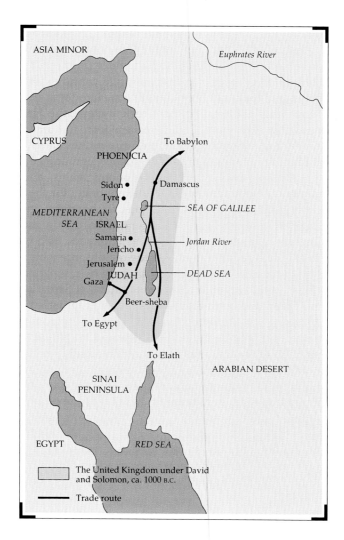

MAP 6.1

Ancient Israel

TABLE 6.1   THE TEN COMMANDMENTS

1. You shall have no other gods before me.

2. You shall not make for yourself a graven image, or any likeness of any thing that is in heaven above, or that is on the earth beneath, or that is in the water under the earth. . . .

3. You shall not take the name of the Lord your God in vain. . . .

4. Observe the sabbath day, to keep it holy, as the Lord your God commanded you. . . .

5. Honor your father and your mother. . . .

6. You shall not kill.

7. Neither shall you commit adultery.

8. Neither shall you steal.

9. Neither shall you bear false witness against your neighbor.

10. Neither shall you covet your neighbor's wife . . . or anything that is your neighbor's.

Source: The Bible, Revised Standard Version, Deuteronomy 5:6–21.

The Hebrews carried with them the stone tablets on which the Ten Commandments were carved as they wandered in the desert. The tablets were kept in a sacred decorated box called the Ark of the Covenant. Details of how to craft the Ark and all the other sacred objects used in worship were dictated to Moses by Yahweh (Figure 6.1). Yahweh also revealed hundreds of precepts, statutes, and laws to Moses during this time, covering every aspect of Hebrew life from the appointment of judges and the proper conduct toward slaves to diet, hygiene, and sexual relations.

After forty years of wandering, followed by Moses' death, the Hebrews finally found their way back to Canaan, the Promised Land pledged by Yahweh to their forefathers. Over the next two centuries, the Hebrews won Canaan, sometimes in war but primarily by infiltration and peaceful occupation. As they extended their control over the entire Promised Land, they came to be known as Israelites, a term derived from an early patriarch, Jacob, who had taken on the name Israel.

FIGURE 6.12 *Calf Bearer.* Ca. 570 B.C. Marble, height, 65".
Acropolis Museum, Athens. *This sixth-century B.C. Greek statue
shows a young man carrying a calf probably intended for a ritual
sacrifice. The statue is executed in the kouros style, popular in the
Archaic Age, as indicated by the frontality, stiffness, and stylized
beard. The shepherd image became associated with Jesus in the early
Christian period.*

FIGURE 6.13 *Christian Good Shepherd.* Second Century.
Marble. Vatican Museum. *This graceful statue blends Greek
influences with a Christian subject. The casual pose of the shepherd
with his easy contrapposto and dreamy gaze shows that the influence
of Praxiteles, the fourth-century B.C. Greek sculptor, was still active
after more than five centuries. The short cloak worn by the figure
was a typical costume of shepherds in the art of the times.*

FIGURE 6.14 Panel from Sarcophagus of Baebia Hertofila. Late Third Century A.D. Museo delle Terme, Rome. *Other panels on this sarcophagus, including images of the Good Shepherd and Jonah, helped to establish the subject of this relief: the communion meal. The diners seem inappropriately boisterous, and in fact a passage in one of Paul's letters (I Corinthians 11:20–22) chastised those who behaved this way during the sacrament. This relief shows that attitudes more appropriate to Greek or Roman revels persisted among early Christian converts.*

that identified such diverse figures as the philosopher Pythagoras and the Orphic cult leader Orpheus with shepherds. The pose of the youth carrying an animal on his shoulders appeared in Archaic Greek sculpture as early as the sixth century B.C. (Figure 6.12). The painter of the good shepherd fresco portrays the shepherd as a beardless youth without distinctive, godlike traits. A statue of a shepherd from the second century attests to the widespread use of this image (Figure 6.13). By such representations as these, the artists in effect declared the limits of their art in penetrating behind the mystery of Jesus as both God and man.

A relief panel sculpted on the marble sarcophagus of Baebia Hertofila, dating from the third century, also expresses a disguised Christian message (Figure 6.14). The panel portrays a communion meal, sym-

bolized by the round loaves of bread below the table and in the basket. The seven figures are partaking of a Christian meal instead of a Roman funeral feast, although the rowdiness of the scene does not suggest a Christian rite. The figures' crude features, especially the open-mouthed man on the right, demonstrate the sculptor's feeble technique. Yet the emotional impact of this simplified cartoon is quite effective.

The Legacy of Biblical Judaism and Early Christianity

The entire Jewish tradition has evolved from the early history of the Hebrews—their wandering without a homeland, their role as outsiders in other cultures, their brief period in control of the promised land of Canaan, and, above all, their deep and abiding sense of being the chosen people of the almighty God, Yahweh. Under the Romans, the Jews were punished for their religious views, a portent of the anti-Semitism and violent attacks that have dogged their existence down through the twentieth century. Despite adversity, the Jews have survived and today have the longest continuous history of any group of people in Western civilization.

Unlike the Greco-Roman deities, who were seen as encouraging and supporting human achievement and excellence in many areas of life, the God of the Hebrews was primarily concerned with the ethical conduct of human beings and their obedience to his laws. Yahweh's jealousy extended to all forms of human expression insofar as they detracted from his worship. As a consequence, the arts and humanities, when allowed in Judaism, tended to be subordinated to religious concerns. Ultimately, Jewish culture found its voice in the ideals of the Bible, among the highest moral standards of any ancient people. The Jewish ethical vision, which still drives Western reformers and revolutionaries today, demanded social justice for every person, no matter how poor or powerless, within the human community.

Inheriting this conception of God and culture, the Christians reinterpreted it and gave it their distinctive stamp. After the fall of Rome, when Christianity emerged as the religion of the West, the Judeo-Christian tradition merged with the Greco-Roman heritage to form the basis of Western civilization. Following the teaching of Jesus, the early Christians perpetuated the Jewish emphasis on God's unity and omnipotence as well as the demands for stringently ethical behavior. Accordingly, Jesus' golden rule—to treat others as one would like to be treated—became the goal of devout Christians. The first Christians also laid great emphasis on taking care of the sick, the impoverished, and the homeless—a tradition that has given rise in Western civilization to a wide variety of private and public social relief programs.

The early Christians, rejecting the relatively closed nature of Judaism, turned their religion into a missionary faith; in the first generation of missionaries, Paul and other church leaders took Jesus' message to all people, addressing them as individuals regardless of their racial and ethnic backgrounds. Today, after two thousand years, nearly one-third of the world's population subscribes—at least nominally—to Christian beliefs.

Under the early Roman Empire, Christian thought also became a transnational, or international, belief system that expressed uncompromising hostility to Greco-Roman culture and to the Roman state. Those Christian writers who, like the author of the Book of Revelation, described Rome as "the great whore" and forecast that city's destruction simply expressed the collective yearnings of the faithful in the early church. Under the onslaught of the Roman persecutions, the Christians anticipated a new order ruled by God's values. Thus, early Christians adopted Greco-Roman ideas not for their own sake but only for their usefulness to the Christian religion.

The hostility of the early church to humanism and secular thought was but the opening assault in a running battle between two ways of looking at the world. For the moment, in imperial Rome humanism was triumphant among the people who counted—the aristocrats, the intellectuals, and the ruling class. But by the end of the fourth century the balance had swung over in favor of Christianity, and the non-Christian intellectuals were rapidly disappearing. This state of affairs prevailed until the Italian Renaissance; then, artists, writers, and intellectuals challenged the reigning Christian world view by reviving humanistic learning and the Greco-Roman past. As the modern world has taken shape, Christianity has found itself assaulted from many sides and has never regained the preeminence that it held from the time of the fall of Rome to the coming of the Renaissance.

KEY CULTURAL TERMS

covenant	*canon*
Diaspora	*Gospels*
eschatology	*evangelists*
apocalypse	*theology*
Messiah	*liturgy*
scripture	*sarcophagus*

SUGGESTIONS FOR FURTHER READING

PRIMARY SOURCES

EUSEBIUS. *The History of the Church from Christ to Constantine.* Translated by G. A. Williamson. New York: Penguin, 1965. Though a partisan account written by a credulous observer, this work is the major source of early Christian history.

JOSEPHUS. *The Jewish War.* Translated by G. A. Williamson. New York: Penguin, 1974. Josephus, a Jew who served Rome, wrote one of the few surviving accounts of this period.

Holy Bible, New Testament, Old Testament. There are many translations of these sacred books, ranging from the King James version of the early seventeenth century to various twentieth-century translations based on recent scholarship. The Douay edition is the official Bible of the Roman Catholic church.

SECONDARY SOURCES

ALBRIGHT, W. F. *The Biblical Period from Abraham to Ezra: An Historical Review.* New York: Harper & Row, 1963. This brief book offers a historical perspective on the Hebrew people; useful for the beginning student.

ANDERSON, B. *Understanding the Old Testament.* 3d ed. Englewood Cliffs, N.J.: Prentice-Hall, 1975. Narrates in a clear style the phases of Hebrew history while analyzing the books of the Bible associated with each phase; one of the best studies on this topic.

ANDERSON, G. W. *The History and Religion of Israel.* London: Oxford University Press, 1966. A brief account that effectively weaves together the chronology of events and the debates over the ancient sources.

BROWN, P. *The World of Late Antiquity: A.D. 150–750.* New York: Harcourt Brace Jovanovich, 1971. By an outstanding scholar of this period, a thoughtful account of the changes that accompanied the end of the Classical period.

CHADWICK, H. *The Early Church.* New York: Penguin, 1967. A brief work on the events, controversies, and personalities of the Christian church up to the collapse of the Roman Empire.

EPSTEIN, I. *Judaism: A Historical Presentation.* New York: Penguin, 1960. Examines Judaism as a religion and a way of life, from its beginnings to modern times.

GASTER, T. H., ed. and trans. *The Dead Sea Scriptures.* 3d ed. Garden City, N.Y.: Anchor Press, 1976. Superb English versions of some of the Dead Sea Scrolls by a leading expert in the field.

HARRIS, S. *The New Testament: A Student's Introduction.* Mountain View, Ca.: Mayfield, 1988. A well-written introduction based on up-to-date research; includes color illustrations of paintings of biblical stories and events by Raphael, Tintoretto, and other great artists.

————. *Understanding the Bible: A Reader's Introduction.* 2d ed. Mountain View, Ca.: Mayfield, 1985. A clear, easy-to-read survey of the Bible within its cultural, historical, and geographical contexts.

HUMPHRIES, W. L. *Crisis and Story: Introduction to the Old Testament.* Mountain View, Ca.: Mayfield, 1990. A brief, nontechnical introduction that emphasizes the importance of narrative in the development of Jewish religious traditions and places them in their political and social context.

JOHNSON, P. *History of the Jews.* New York: Harper & Row, 1987. A sound recent study that makes the Jewish story come alive for the general reader.

KANIEL, M. *Judaism: The Art of World Religions.* Poole, England: Blandford Press, 1979. Focuses on artistic objects used in religious services.

LANDSBERGER, F. *A History of Jewish Art.* Cincinnati, Ohio: Union of American Hebrew Congregations, 1946. A broad survey covering ancient temples and sacred artifacts as well as works by modern Jewish artists.

LOWRIE, W. *Art in the Early Church.* Rev. ed. New York: Harper & Row, 1965. The ground-breaking work that first established early Christian art as a subject worthy of scholarly study.

MACMULLEN, R. *Christianizing the Roman Empire (A.D. 100–400).* New Haven: Yale University Press, 1984. A judicious work of scholarship that documents the shift to Christianity.

ORLINSKY, H. M. *Ancient Israel.* Ithaca, N.Y.: Cornell University Press, 1966. A brief historical overview integrating the development of Hebrew social and economic institutions with the evolution of the biblical tradition.

ROTH, C. *Jewish Art: An Illustrated History.* Greenwich, Conn.: New York Graphic Society Publishers, Ltd., 1961. Perhaps the best general survey available on Jewish art and architecture; incorporates recent archeological findings and scholarship.

WIGODER, G., ed. *Jewish Art and Civilization.* New York: Walker, 1972. Essays by leading scholars who discuss Jewish art by regions and countries; fully illustrated.

LATE ROMAN CIVILIZATION

What were the forces that brought the Roman Empire to an end? This chapter focuses on Rome's final era, from 284 to 476, when political, social, and economic crises seemed increasingly beyond human control and spiritual and cultural changes indicated growing disillusionment with the old Roman ways. The chapter suggests some causes for Rome's fall after more than twelve hundred years, during the last seven hundred of which it dominated the Mediterranean basin. Since the fate of Rome was inextricably tied up with the development of Christianity, the chapter also traces the growth of the church and offers reasons for its triumph (Figure 7.1). From the interweaving of Christianity and Classical humanism—the legacy of Greece and Rome—a new Western cultural ideal emerged.

THE LAST DAYS OF THE ROMAN EMPIRE

When the Roman general Diocletian seized power as emperor in 284, the empire appeared to be ungovernable. Twenty-seven rulers had preceded Diocletian in the previous fifty years, and most of them were killed by the army, either at the hands of rival factions or by their own troops. The office of emperor now depended on the army's approval, for the autocratic imperial regime had successfully stifled all other forms of political life.

Although Diocletian faced other dangers as great as having to pacify a fickle army, Rome's military problems seemed to touch on and to intensify most of the problems that were threatening to bring down the state. Throughout the third century, more and more soldiers were required to police the frontiers to turn back the Germanic invaders in the north and the Persians in the east. Military pay for these larger armies drained the imperial treasury, which was caught between increasing inflation and a declining economy. Unpaid and ill-equipped troops forced civilians to supply them with food and goods that the state could no longer provide. Population in the urban areas fell as thousands fled into the countryside to avoid military duty and burdensome taxes. Of those who remained in the towns and cities, most still clamored for the amenities of Roman life, including bread and circuses. They seemed oblivious that their demands, when they were able to be met, were a drain on precious state resources.

That segment of the populace finding hope and consolation in the Christian religion presented yet another problem to Rome: Christian converts often refused to enroll in the military on the grounds that killing someone in battle was murder, an act forbidden by the Fifth Commandment. With the pool of young men available for the army reduced, the government recruited soldiers from among barbarians who had been allowed to remain inside Roman territory—a course of action that further weakened the loyalty of the military.

FIGURE 7.1 *Young Christ.* Third Century. Museo delle Terme, Rome. *Early Christian art focused on biblical scenes and especially images of Jesus Christ. Lacking a clearcut tradition for portraying Jesus, church leaders simply borrowed from Classical art, making its tradition their own, as in this portrait of a young Christ. Like the gods on the Parthenon's frieze (see Figure 3.24), Christ is portrayed as a beardless youth, dressed in a Greek garment and seated in repose, his left foot resting against a chair leg. The image of Christ as a beardless youth persisted in the church until the fall of Rome, when it was supplanted by the image of an older, bearded man.*

Faced with this situation, Diocletian began a series of reforms that virtually refounded the Roman state and gave the empire a new lease on life. The almost two-hundred–year period of late Roman civilization may be divided into two phases: (1) Diocletian's reforms and the triumph of Christianity, lasting from 284 until 395 and (2) Christian Rome and the end of the empire in the West, extending from 395 until 476 (Time Line 7.1). In these years, basic social and cultural changes were set in motion that became integral to European civilization for centuries to come.

Diocletian's Reforms and the Triumph of Christianity, 284–395

Diocletian (284–305) stands as the creator of late Rome just as Augustus does of the early empire. Unlike Augustus, however, Diocletian insisted on divine status, building on the sun god cult that dated from the Severan dynasty (193–235). Isolating himself behind walls of curtains when with his subjects and bestowing grand titles on his representatives, he inflated the image of emperor to enhance the political power of the office.

Diocletian ruled as a god, but when he turned to the problems facing Rome, he showed that he had the soul of a bureaucrat. Possessed of an iron will, he inaugurated reforms that reined in the rebellious army, contained barbarian incursions, restored calm to Rome, restructured the empire, and returned modest prosperity to the economy for most of the fourth century. His efforts to restructure the governing apparatus met with mixed success. His greatest triumph was in dividing the empire into two separate areas. In the West, Rome still served as the ceremonial cap-

TIME LINE 7.1   LATE ROME, 284–476

284		303	311	313		361	363		395			476
Numbers of Christians Growing			Christian Toleration				Christian Toleration			Christian Rome		
		The Great Persecution 303-311	Edict of Milan	Founding of Constantinople 330		**Reign of Julian 361–363**			Sack of Rome by Visigoths 410		Sack of Rome by Vandals 455	Romulus Augustulus deposed
		Reign of Diocletian 284–305		Reign of Constantine 306–337				Christianity proclaimed official religion of Rome				

MAP 7.1

The Roman Empire in the Fourth Century

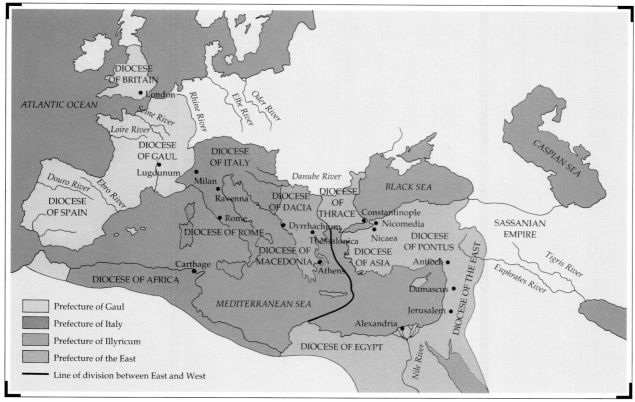

DIOCESE OF BRITAIN
• London
ATLANTIC OCEAN
Rhine River
Oder River
Elbe River
Seine River
Loire River
DIOCESE OF GAUL
• Lugdunum
DIOCESE OF ITALY
• Milan
Douro River
Ebro River
DIOCESE OF SPAIN
Ravenna
• Rome
DIOCESE OF ROME
• Carthage
DIOCESE OF AFRICA
MEDITERRANEAN SEA
Danube River
DIOCESE OF DACIA
DIOCESE OF THRACE
DIOCESE OF MACEDONIA
Dyrrhachium
Thessalonica
• Athens
BLACK SEA
Constantinople
Nicomedia
Nicaea
DIOCESE OF ASIA
DIOCESE OF PONTUS
Antioch •
Damascus •
Jerusalem •
DIOCESE OF THE EAST
Alexandria
DIOCESE OF EGYPT
Nile River
CASPIAN SEA
SASSANIAN EMPIRE
Tigris River
Euphrates River

Prefecture of Gaul
Prefecture of Italy
Prefecture of Illyricum
Prefecture of the East
—— Line of division between East and West

ital, though the actual capital depended on the emperor's movements. For example, Ravenna, on the Italian Adriatic coast, became the imperial residence for several decades. The Eastern Empire was centered first in Nicomedia in Asia Minor, but the capital was later shifted to Byzantium (now Istanbul, Turkey) and renamed Constantinople by Diocletian's successor, Constantine (Map 7.1).

Diocletian's plan for administering the vast empire under a tetrarchy, or a rule by four, proved unworkable, however. His reform called for each half of the empire to be governed by two tetrarchs, an Augustus supported by a Caesar, but the civil war that often broke out among rival tetrarchs only made an already confused situation worse (Figure 7.2). A third reform

FIGURE 7.2 *Diocletian's Tetrarchy. Ca. 300. Height, ca. 51".* St. Mark's Cathedral, Venice. *In this group portrait of the tetrarchs, the four rulers—two Augusti, or leaders, joined by their two Caesars, or successors—stand clasping shoulders to signify their unity and loyalty. By this time, the political leaders were no longer wearing imperial togas, as can be seen in the figures' cloaks, tunics, and hats, but the eagle-headed swords and decorated scabbards show that fine workmanship in armor was still practiced in late Rome. Despite the solidarity suggested by the sculpture, the tetrarchy was not a successful reform of the imperial administration.*

FIGURE 7.3 Colossal Statue of Constantine. Ca. 313. Marble, height, 8′. Palazzo dei Conservatori, Rome. *Like Diocletian, Constantine consciously nurtured the image of the emperor as a larger-than-life figure. To enhance this image, he commissioned a huge statue of himself, perhaps ten times life size, to stand in the gigantic basilica (which he had also built) in the Roman forum. All that remains of the statue today are the head, which measures over 8 feet tall, a hand, and some pieces of the limbs. The monument signaled the climax of the emperor cult and the beginning of its decline. With the spread of Christianity, rulers were no longer viewed as gods.*

bility on sons who inherited their fathers' tax burdens as well as their careers. This new tax code sped the process by which rural laborers attached themselves to landed estates and caused the final disappearance of the small independent farmer—the class that had made republican Rome great. Diocletian also recognized that money had virtually passed out of circulation, and his tax reforms moved the economy along toward barter, or exchange of goods. Thus, citizens now paid taxes in meat, leather, or wool; in bricks or building stone; in labor; or in army recruits.

The Great Persecution and Christian Toleration One area of Roman life remained untouched by Diocletian for most of his reign: the problem posed to a polytheistic state by the growing number of monotheistic Christian citizens. But in 303, for reasons that are not quite clear, he began what the Christians called the Great Persecution. For eight years—though Diocletian himself retired in 305—the imperial policy was to stamp out Christianity. In a series of six edicts the emperors forbade Christians to worship and ordered their churches and books destroyed and their bishops arrested. Christian leaders and suspected church members were forced to sacrifice to the ruler under penalty of death. Roman cities were ordered to rebuild pagan temples and to impose a religious test on all citizens. Then in 311 the assault was called off as suddenly as it had begun. How many Christians perished in the Great Persecution cannot be reliably determined, and certain areas, such as Britain and Gaul, were untouched. Whatever the number, the government's policy failed in its purpose, for the killings strengthened rather than weakened the church, and the courage of Christian martyrs won many new converts.

The Great Persecution had barely ceased when the Christians gained a stunning victory. In 313 toleration was restored to Christians by the Edict of Milan, also known as the Peace of the Church, at the order of the emperor Constantine (Figure 7.3). His reason for this action has been a source of wide speculation—was he a genuinely devout convert to Christianity, as has been claimed, or a politically acute opportunist who foresaw how powerful Christians would become, or perhaps a mixture of both? Regardless of his motives, the Christian community welcomed this opportunity to advance their interests in the state. Priests joined soldiers in army units, and bishops attended the imperial court. Constantine undertook a campaign throughout the empire to expand the restored faith, returning confiscated property to the church, building new churches, and giving tax exemptions to bishops.

of Diocletian's—grouping the provinces into dioceses—achieved his goal of making the state more centralized and hierarchical. But a side effect of this step was reduced efficiency since the empire became more bureaucratized as officials multiplied at all levels.

In addition, Diocletian could never hold in check the catastrophic inflation. He tried to freeze wages and prices, a policy that failed from the start. Moreover, the old tax system simply could not pay the costs of supporting the enlarged army and an expanded state bureaucracy. His plan for filling the empty treasury was to chain citizens to their private occupations and public offices, forcing social immo-

The greatest indication of Christianity's new power was that Constantine, who after 324 ruled in both the East and the West, built his eastern capital, Constantinople, as a fully Christian city. Dedicated in 330 on the site of ancient Byzantium, Constantinople was endowed with churches and other religious monuments along with a Senate house and mansions for its senators. These magnificent buildings were surrounded on three sides—the fourth side overlooked the water—by thick walls that turned the city into an almost impregnable fortress. But Constantine's new capital was more than a Christian city; the choice of its site showed Constantine's recognition of the superior vitality and wealth of the East when compared with the Western empire.

The successors to Constantine, all of them Christians except Julian, supported the spread of the church. By 395 most of the population was nominally Christian, including senators and other aristocrats. Christianity adapted to Rome's values, promising victory to Roman armies and a bountiful life to believers. But more importantly, the Christian religion attracted followers who responded to its ideal of charity and its belief in the spiritual worth of the poor.

Early Christian Controversies As Christians became a majority within the empire, their success generated problems stemming from the deep divisions within the faith. Unlike other cults, Christianity developed a creed, or set of authorized doctrines, which church leaders imposed on believers. Those who differed from the creed were excommunicated as heretics. Moreover, since the emperors were now Christians, the state became entangled in the new religion's problems. Distressed by church squabbles, Constantine tried to end a major controversy over the relationship of Jesus to God. The followers of the priest Arius (about 250–about 336) maintained that Jesus' nature was similar to the divine, a belief that came to be known as Arianism. Those who supported the priest Athanasius (about 296–373) believed that the natures of Jesus and God were identical. Although non-Christians found the quarrel over "similar" and "identical" natures ridiculous, fundamental issues were at stake, such as whether Jesus was eternal and whether God had made the ultimate sacrifice for humanity. To bring about harmony among the competing factions, Constantine, in 325, called a church council at Nicaea in Asia Minor. Under his guidance, the council issued the Nicene Creed, which proclaimed in favor of Athanasius.

Arianism, though condemned, divided the church for decades and remained strong in the church's ruling hierarchy. Arianism also triggered a crisis among new believers because most of the Germanic tribes who were moving into the empire became Christians through the efforts of Ulfilas, a fellow barbarian and an Arian bishop. Ulfilas's converts were treated as enemies of the true faith, for orthodox Christians, ever intolerant, recognized no difference between pagans and Christian heretics.

Despite these difficulties, Christianity continued to gain converts and grow in prestige. At the same time, an ascetic Christian movement was sweeping across the empire. Inspired by the sterner ideas of Jesus and Paul, this asceticism had two forms, both of which first arose in Roman Egypt during the early fourth century. Both groups of ascetics believed that the world was evil and must be shunned, but they differed over the best way to achieve salvation. Pachomius founded an isolated community in which a band of followers pursued perfection through a life of self-denial and moral rigor. His contemporary Antony chose the life of a hermit, seeking union with God through his individual efforts. The harsh messages of both Pachomius and Antony aroused favorable responses among the Romans, but ultimately the community style rather than the solitary style became the dominant form of Christian asceticism, evolving into monasticism in succeeding decades.

The end of paganism came with the reign of the emperor Theodosius I, called the Great (379–395). The emperor and the law courts now ignored the rights of non-Christians and enforced Christian conformity. After Theodosius, little remained to complete the Christian triumph. In 407 the destruction of non-Christian images and temples was ordered, thus placing paganism outside the law and making Christianity the state religion. Although paganism was eradicated in the urban areas, it survived in the countryside, kept alive by oral traditions, protected by an engrained conservatism, and hidden behind a Christian veneer.

Christian Rome and the End of the Western Empire, 395–476

Despite the success of Diocletian's reforms, Rome faced basic problems that ultimately proved insoluble: the progressive barbarization of the army, the growing bureaucratization of the state, and a constantly shrinking tax base. When fresh waves of Germans began to sweep through the Western Empire in the fifth century, the Roman rulers were without plans for assimilating the intruders. The Visigoths menaced Rome in 410, demanding tribute. When the Senate refused, Rome was sacked for the first time since 390 B.C., and a chagrined Senate paid a hefty ransom to the barbarians. This Germanic tribe moved on to France and eventually settled in Spain to found a kingdom.

While Visigoths attacked Rome, Saxons, Angles, and Jutes invaded Britain and ended that island's ties to the empire. Vandals raged through France and Spain, finally creating a North African kingdom in 442. From there they managed to launch an attack on Rome and sacked the city in 455. Burgundians settled in France in the middle Rhone Valley after 430. Elsewhere, minor tribes exploited Roman weakness.

Western society radically changed. Town life had all but disappeared earlier, leaving only noisy metropolises and the silent countryside. After the barbarians seized so much land and further disrupted the economy and tax structure, city life, even with its public dole and entertainments, became as untenable as life in the towns. Powerful landowners assumed many of the functions of local government officials, while their isolated and relatively secure estates attracted desperate city people fleeing to these rural refuges. The beginning of the economic and social institutions of the Middle Ages may be seen in these developments.

The Roman Senate and the church responded to the disintegrating conditions in quite different ways. The Senate had long ago ceased to be a factor in imperial affairs, and when, in the fourth century, Ravenna became the working capital of the Western Empire and the home of the official bureaucracy, it was reduced to the status of a ceremonial body. Yet the senators could still collect rents on their estates, doubling the fees where possible. The church's response was more praiseworthy than the Senate's. Some church leaders used the crisis to stamp out troublesome heresies, but, more positively, others offered shelter for the homeless, food for the hungry, and comfort to the grieving.

The end of the empire in the West came swiftly when Odoacer, the leader of a troop of Germans, defeated a Roman army in 476 and sent the young ruler, Romulus Augustulus, into exile. Instead of taking the imperial title, as was usual in such an event, Odoacer dispatched the symbols of office to the Eastern emperor in Constantinople, thereby signaling that centralized rule had ended in the West. Like other Germanic leaders in the western states, Odoacer prepared to rule not as a Roman emperor but as a barbarian king in northern Italy. The empire in the West was in ruins, leaving barbarian kingdoms in its place.

THE TRANSITION FROM CLASSICAL HUMANISM TO CHRISTIAN CIVILIZATION

Between 284 and 476 Roman civilization moved through two stages, both of which bristled with bitter pagan and Christian tensions. The first phase, which coincided with Diocletian's reforms, was paganism's last flowering, and the second phase, which began when the empire started to break apart after Constantine's reign, was a dynamic Christian age.

Literature, Theology, and History

During Rome's last two centuries, secular writers and Christian writers competed for the hearts and minds of educated Romans through poems, treatises, letters, and essays. The secular authors, who felt threatened by Christian activity and thought, preserved Classical forms and values in their writings. They turned to the humanistic tradition for inspiration and guidance because they believed that their morals and culture were undergirded by Rome's old religion and the farmer-soldier values. Nonetheless, these writers' views of the past were distorted by their romantic imaginations into nostalgia for a Rome that either was no more or had never been (Figure 7.4).

Secular literature in the late empire paled in comparison to that of earlier periods. Secular writers never experimented with new styles or attempted to modify established forms. No one wrote plays, novels, or epics. As a group the secular Roman authors reflected a growing sense of a lost age, convinced as they were that a civilized life was possible by studying and venerating the past. With the exception of a few poets, they never seemed able to define or to analyze the profound changes occurring in their own lifetime.

The other group of writers, the Christians, looked to the future and a new world to come. They were convinced that Rome was not only dying but was not worth saving. After Constantine decreed toleration for Christians in 313, these authors moved into the mainstream and slowly began to overshadow their pagan rivals. The bitter differences of opinion between them and the pagans, which characterized the late fourth century, faded away in the early fifth century. By then Christian literature had triumphed, though it remained deeply indebted to Greco-Roman thought and letters.

FIGURE 7.4 The House of Amor and Psyche (Replacement Copy of Statuary). Fourth Century. Ostia, Italy. *The non-Christian elite of late Rome still revered their Classical past, as shown by this sculpture of Amor and Psyche, the famed lovers from Greek legend, found in the private residence of a wealthy Roman. The erotic pair stood in one of four elegantly decorated, intimate bedrooms, which were dimly lit by small windows and lined in white marble. The tale still caught the fancy of sophisticated Romans living in isolated splendor, perhaps reminding them of the glories of a former age.*

The Fathers of the Church By about 300 Christian writers began to find a large, well-bred audience as their religion continued to win converts among the educated. Although they extolled the virtues and benefits of the new faith, they did not necessarily abandon Classical philosophy and literature; they believed that some of these writings conveyed God's veiled truth prior to the coming of Christ, and thus they combined Classical with biblical learning. No longer persecuted, these Christian writers lived either as interpreters of God's word or as bishops. Revered by later ages as the Fathers of the church, they set examples in their personal lives and public deeds. The three most famous church fathers were Ambrose, Jerome, and Augustine. Because of their superior talents, resolute convictions, and commanding personalities, the Fathers were not only powerful figures within the church but often intervened in secular matters, instructing the local authorities and even the emperors. More importantly, their writings laid the foundation of medieval Christian doctrine and philosophy.

The first of these men, Ambrose (about 340–397), devoted his life to affairs of the church (Figure 7.5). Born into a well-established Christian family (his sister was a nun), he was trained in the Greco-Roman classics, from which he drew material for sermons, tracts, and letters. Ambrose vigorously opposed the Arian heresy, and as Bishop of Milan he aided the urban poor and the victims of barbarian assaults. In scholarly sermons, he took the emperors to task, condemning them for the social injustices of their reigns. His letters shed light on problems of church government, and his treatises analyzed controversies dividing the church. Ambrose's hymns, perhaps his most memorable contribution, introduced to the Western church another way for Christians to praise their God and enrich their ceremonies.

The second major church father, Jerome (about 340–420), wrote extensively on religious issues, but

Figure 7.11 Constantine's Basilica in Trier. 310. Trier, Germany. *This basilica served first as an audience hall for Roman officials, then as a medieval castle, and today it is a Lutheran church. Although it is an impressive 220 feet long, 91 feet wide, and 100 feet high, its plan is simple: a narrow hall without aisles and an apse at the eastern end. Around the exterior of the apse, two stories of round arched windows give a graceful appearance by creating the impression of an arcade. That such a monumental basilica was erected so far from the Roman capital showed the impact of imperial art in the distant provinces.*

Figure 7.12 Sta. Maria Maggiore. 432–440. Rome. *This early church shows the way that builders adapted Greco-Roman forms. The Ionic columns and mosaics are Greek in origin, and the basilica is a Roman structure. In this way Christians not only satisfied their own religious needs but kept alive the Greco-Roman architectural tradition.*

Figure 7.13 Church of Sta. Costanza. Fourth Century. Rome. *The twelve pairs of columns were carved specifically for the rotunda, the circular area beneath the dome, rather than taken from other buildings, as was often the case in late Rome. The columns support the arches, above which are windows placed in the drum. The niches, or recessed openings, in the walls and the ceiling above the columns are decorated with mosaics with religious themes.*

only had Christians taken over Classical learning as a tool for studying God's word, but they had also Christianized the pagan basilica.

A second important design in Christian architecture was the round or polygonal structure topped by a dome. One of the earliest circular buildings (according to tradition, erected by Constantine as a tomb for his daughter) still stands in Rome. Now known as the Church of Sta. Costanza, the round edifice is a drum with a covering dome (Figure 7.13). As these structures evolved, they came to serve primarily as *baptisteries*, that is, a place set aside for baptism. The baptistery was usually separated from the basilica because Christians believed that the unbaptized were unworthy to enter the sanctuary and mingle with the members. This design, whose origins go back to the domed rooms of public baths and to funerary architecture and whose most impressive realization was the Pantheon (see Figure 5.13), became standardized as an octagon with a domed roof (Figure 7.14).

Sculpture During Diocletian's reign and before Christianity's conquest of the Roman arts, the late empire produced some unique and monumental works, such as the group portrait of Diocletian's tetrarchy, carved in red porphyry (see Figure 7.2) and the colossal statue of Constantine, a composite of marble and metal (see Figure 7.3). The generalized features of these figures show the trend to symbolic representation characteristic of the art of the late empire and the movement away from the idealized or realistic faces of Classical sculpture. These public

Figure 7.14 Baptistery at Frèjus. Fifth Century. Frèjus, France. *The Baptistery at Frèjus is one of the earliest surviving examples of the octagonal building. The eight-sided structure has a central dome resting on a solidly constructed drum pierced with windows. At one time it was believed that this style was imported from the east, but now evidence indicates it originated in the west, probably in France.*

FIGURE 7.15 *The Last Pagan.* Ca. 380–400. Museo Ostiense, Ostia, Italy. *Evidently this Roman, clad in the toga of an earlier era, has academic interests since a set of bound books rests beside his right foot. The drapery is cut at severe angles, which increases the overall effect of this care-laden man. The statue is of Greek marble and stands just over 6 feet tall.*

works are clearly forms of propaganda art. But Roman artists also continued to sculpt statues for private citizens, whose changing tastes were typified in a statue of a bedraggled scholar (Figure 7.15). Here the artist has fashioned a realistic work that delves into the psychology of his subject. The man's lined features, worried look, and weary slouch convey resignation and defeat. Symmachus, one of the last learned non-Christians, often visited Ostia, where this statue was found, and the sculptor may have been depicting this Roman intellectual.

In addition to free-standing sculptures, relief sculptures continued to be popular in late Roman art. In the Western Empire the best of these surviving reliefs are the original carvings on the Arch of Constantine. The carvings, coarse and yet stylized, reflect the impact of provincial art on Rome and signify a marked change in the long tradition of secular sculpture in the West. In one of the reliefs, Constantine and those around him are portrayed as distributing the fruits of the empire—a typical theme in Roman art (Figure 7.16). But the figures are depicted more as stereotypes than as real individuals.

Christian sculpture was undergoing aesthetic changes similar to those taking place in secular art. By the end of the third century, Christian art was symbolic in content and *impressionistic* in style (see Chapter 6). Simple representations of Jesus and the apostles had become common in the underground church. In 313, when the Peace of the Church brought Christian art literally above ground, artists began to receive the support of the Roman state.

Christian Rome's reshaping of the humanistic tradition can be seen in the carvings on sarcophagi. The Roman anxiety about life after death and the pursuit of intellectual matters easily evolved into Christian images and themes. The growing acceptance of inhumation, or burial, rather than cremation and the resultant increased demand for sarcophagi afforded many artists new opportunities to express themselves. After about the second century, rich Roman families commissioned artists to decorate the sides of these marble boxes with images of Classical heroes and heroines, gods and goddesses, military and political leaders, and scenes of famous events and battles. The Christians borrowed many of these subjects and transformed them into religious symbols pertaining to salvation and life after death. Thus, although the content of sarcophagus art became Christian after the Peace of the Church, the style remained Classical for some time.

Roman sarcophagi also depicted abstract concepts. For example, a carving of a seated philosopher, surrounded by attentive men and women, represents the life of the mind, its attention directed toward

FIGURE 7.16 *The Imperial Bounty*, from the Arch of Constantine. 312–315. Rome. *The style for this relief derived from Trier in Gaul. Unlike Classicism, this provincial style conveyed its message with cartoon-like directness. Constantine, enthroned in the center, divides the panel in two, as officials above dispense coins to the citizens below. Some of the crowd show their eagerness through their upturned heads and reaching hands.*

more important matters than earthly delights (Figure 7.17). The carvings, finely executed and well-balanced, capture this philosophical idea through superbly realized human characters. Meanwhile, biblical scenes, in particular those detailing the life and miracles of Jesus, began to appear on sarcophagi throughout the empire, illustrating the complex themes and messages of the new faith. One relief, probably from a Roman sarcophagus, weaves together events from the Old and New Testaments (Figure 7.18). On the left, Adam and Eve are expelled from the Garden of Eden; on the right Peter baptizes

FIGURE 7.17 The Plotinus Sarcophagus. Late Third Century. Lateran Museum, Rome. *This relief may depict Plotinus, a founder of Neo-Platonism, and his admirers. If so, then the scene is ironic, for Neo-Platonist philosophy rejected realistic art, claiming that art should be viewed with the inner eye. This Neo-Platonist belief influenced Christian mysticism, which, in turn, helped to create the symbolic art of the Middle Ages, an art that used traditional images to express religious faith.*

FIGURE 7.18   Relief from Christ–Peter Sarcophagus. 320–330. Lateran Museum, Rome. *This panel, crowded with biblical scenes and figures, reflects the primacy of religious values in Christian art. Nonetheless, the anonymous artisan knew Roman sarcophagus art, as shown by the depiction of Jesus as Apollo (center) and the deep, stylized folds of the draped clothing.*

FIGURE 7.19   Illumination from Vergil's *Aeneid*. Fifth Century. Vatican Library, the Vatican. *This page from an illustrated manuscript of Vergil's* Aeneid *shows Dido, the Queen of Carthage (center), flanked by Aeneas (left), and a guest. The scene depicts the banquet, described at the end of Book I, that Dido gave in honor of the newly arrived Trojans. After the meal Aeneas recounted his escape from Troy and seven subsequent years of wandering. Faithful to the Aeneid's description, the painting represents Aeneas speaking to Dido while she appears to be calling for the attendant, in the lower right corner, to wash the hands of the diners. That such works were being commissioned in fifth-century Christian Rome showed that not everyone was partaking of the new religion and its symbols. After the fall of Rome, however, decorated manuscripts became a favorite form of art for Christians.*

two soldiers. A beardless Christ—the typical image of Jesus in ancient art—stands in the center. In this relief the emphasis on Christ and Peter conveys the theme of Christ's message and deeds being spread by his most trusted disciple. Although there is a striking resemblance between this relief and the relief from the Arch of Constantine (see Figure 7.16), the similarity is only in style and composition; the purpose and content of the two sculptures are quite different.

Painting and Mosaics   Unlike architecture and sculpture, painting exhibited no changes directly caused by the Peace of the Church. In the fourth century, Christian frescoes flourished in the Roman catacombs and continued the symbolic, impressionist style of the previous era (see Chapter 6). Non-Christian paintings are extremely scarce from the fifth century, except for a few works such as a collection of illustrations for Vergil's *Aeneid*, probably painted for a wealthy patron. This extensive picture cycle, numbering over 225 scenes, recalls the style of earlier paintings (Figure 7.19), but it is also an early example of a new medium, the illustrated book. Books were now written on vellum, a parchment made from animal skins, and bound in pages rather than written on scrolls. In the Middle Ages, this type of decorated, or illuminated, book became a major art form. In the late empire, however, the form was in its infancy.

A more vital art form was the mosaic, which, as in other art forms, Christians ultimately turned to their own ends. Pagans continued to place mosaics on both floors and walls, but Christians more often put them on the walls. Christian artists also replaced the stone chips with bits of glass that reflected light, thus adding a glittering, ethereal quality to the basilicas and other buildings.

FIGURE 7.20 *Female Athletes.* Detail from Mosaic. 350–400. Villa at Piazza Armerina, Sicily. *This scene may show a female version of games that continued to be conducted in the Christian empire. The mosaic conveys a grace and lightheartedness somewhat at odds with this troubled age and with the changing artistic ideals of Christian art.*

In the late Roman mosaics, pagan and Christian subjects stand in sharp contrast. Among the many pagan mosaics that survive, one depicting young female athletes from a country villa in Sicily indicates the continued interest of the Romans in the body as the temple of the mind and as an object of admiration (Figure 7.20). The artist has captured the energy and playfulness of these (probably professional) performers in a variety of feats: dancing, running, and exercising. Their movements are realistic, graceful, and strikingly modern. In contrast to these worldly women, the mosaic of the church father Ambrose emphasizes his spiritual, other-worldly qualities (see Figure 7.5). Where their movements are fluid, his pose is static, and where their bodies are celebrated, the shape of his body is completely concealed under his clothing, in accordance with the church teaching that the body is sinful and should be hidden from view.

Mosaics became one of the dominant art forms in the Eastern Empire and those areas influenced by the Eastern rulers beginning late in the fifth century. In Ravenna, the small cruciform tomb of Galla Placidia, daughter of Theodosius the Great, contained some splendid mosaics that prefigured the Byzantine style of the next century. In succeeding centuries the Byzantine style dominated Christian art in the Eastern Empire. In the mosaics in the tomb of Galla Placidia, scrolls of vines and leaves wind around the ceiling, large flowers, or rosettes, decorate other sections, and animals and saints adorn parts of the curved walls. Over the entranceway stands the youthful shepherd watching over his flock (Figure 7.21). By the fifth century the rich and the powerful, such as the relatives of Galla Placidia, now honored the Good Shepherd in their sanctuaries as the giver of eternal life. The mosaics in the tomb of Galla Placidia clearly show the adaptation of Classical models to Christian purposes.

Music

The music of late Rome was in decline, but Christian music was just beginning to take shape. The Christians took the principles of Greco-Roman music and united them with the Jewish tradition of singing the psalms and the liturgy to make music an integral and dynamic part of their church rituals. In later times this Christian practice gave birth to a rich body of sacred music which included both singers and instrumentalists.

In late Rome, however, sacred music was limited to chanting and unaccompanied singing. The Antioch church, inspired by the singing in Jewish synagogues, developed a new musical genre, the hymn, a song of praise to God. From Antioch the practice of hymn singing spread to Constantinople and Milan and eventually was integrated into the Christian liturgy everywhere. A few hymns survive from the period before Constantine, but only a fragment of musical notation has come to light. As with other ancient music, how it actually sounded can only be a matter of speculation.

Ambrose, bishop of Milan, stands out among the earliest hymn writers as one of the founders of the Western sacred song. His hymns, which were written in Latin, coincided with a new era in the church; up until the fourth century the liturgy of the early church was in Greek. Ambrose's Latin hymns were probably meant to be sung antiphonally, that is, with lines sung alternately between a leader and chorus.

FIGURE 7.21 *The Good Shepherd.* Ca. 450. Mausoleum of Galla Placidia, Ravenna, Italy. *The young, beardless Christ, which was still the accepted image of the Christian savior in the fifth century, supports himself with the cross and feeds the sheep, the symbol of the church, with his left hand. Foliage and plants in the background tie in with similar decorations on the mausoleum's ceilings and walls. Upon entering the small tomb, worshipers would immediately be confronted with this large figure of Christ.*

WHY DID ROME FALL?

When the Western Empire collapsed in 476, many forces had been at work in undermining Rome since the end of the second century. During these three centuries the mounting pressures from the barbarians, the incompetence of the bureaucracy, the politically inert masses, the rampant inflation, the crushing and inequitable tax system, and, above all, the problems associated with a heterogeneous and uncontrollable army had together brought havoc on the state and society. Taking all of these difficulties into consideration, the wonder is that the empire was able to be propped up by Diocletian after 284 and to last as long as it did.

Nevertheless, all of the above forces, while playing an important role, were not as paramount a cause of Rome's decline and fall as was the change in the Roman constitution from a republic to an empire. This theory—which was first advanced by the French philosopher and historian Montesquieu in the eighteenth century—blamed Rome's fall on the moral consequences of the constitutional shift. According to Montesquieu, under the healthy republic, with its separation of political powers, the citizens actively decided their own future. But pressed down by a diseased empire, with power centered in one man in one city, the citizens became pawns of the ruling autocrat. Consequently, toward the end of the empire corruption engulfed all elements of society, from megalomaniacal emperors, to aristocrats wallowing in wealth and luxury, to the masses clamoring for handouts, to the aliens selling their votes for favors.

What effect did the triumph of Christianity have on the fall of Rome? This issue was first raised in the eighteenth century by English historian Edward Gibbon in his *Decline and Fall of the Roman Empire.* Gibbon's thesis was that the coming of Christianity was a major contributing factor in Rome's fall. Gibbon blamed the Christians for focusing on life in heaven rather than on earth and for sapping the military will of the Roman people. A careful review of Rome's last years reveals that Gibbon oversimplified events. Some Christians did avoid military service because of their pacifist ideas, and few Christians felt loyalty to the forms of pagan life. But by the time Christianity was firmly fixed as the official religion, in 395, the empire was already tottering on the brink of annihilation. Thus, there was very little that the Christians, or for that matter any other group, could do to prevent the fall of Rome.

The Legacy of Late Roman Civilization

Late Roman civilization, as we have described it, constituted the legacy of the ancient world to the next era, the Middle Ages. That legacy was neither the unadulterated humanism of Greece nor the Idea of Rome as formulated in the pre-Christian centuries. Rather, late Roman culture reflected a synthesis of Christian and Greco-Roman values achieved in a changing world. The intellectual voices of Christianity saw the wisdom of Greco-Roman thought as important for the support it lent to the spiritual values that were now considered primary. Late Roman art and architecture also reflected this synthesis of traditions.

Besides the amalgam of Christianity and humanism, the late Roman period also contributed much of the structure of everyday life to the medieval world. From late Rome came the sharp division of society into aristocratic landowners and dependent agricultural laborers, the emergence of the church in society as a state within the state, the rise of a barter economy, and the development of the military power of large-scale landed proprietors. In effect, the late Classical world was the womb from which would emerge the next incarnation of Western institutions as well as the Western humanities.

KEY CULTURAL TERMS

symbolic realism
peristyle
medallion
attic
basilica
apse
nave

aisles
clerestory windows
atrium
transept
cruciform
baptistery
impressionistic

SUGGESTIONS FOR FURTHER READING

Primary Sources

St. Augustine. *Confessions.* Translated by R. S. Pine-Coffin. New York: Penguin, 1966. One of the enduring books of Western literature; reveals the anguish and achievements of this influential thinker.

———. *The City of God.* Edited by D. Knowles. New York: Penguin, 1972. A monumental work that illustrates Augustine's blending of Classical and Christian thought.

Staniforth, M., Trans. *Early Christian Writings: The Apostolic Fathers.* New York: Penguin, 1968. Useful introduction to the issues and personalities of the early Christian church.

Secondary Sources

Brown, P. *Augustine of Hippo.* London: Faber, 1967. A careful study of the life and thought of this early church father.

———. *Society and the Holy in Late Antiquity.* Berkeley, Calif.: University of California Press, 1982. A collection of articles and reviews that treat some major topics of late Roman history.

Gough, M. *Origins of Christian Art.* London: Thames and Hudson, 1973. Excellent study of the evolution of Christian symbols in Christian art.

Grabar, A. *Early Christian Art.* New York: Odyssey Press, 1968. A handsomely illustrated study that includes photos of paintings and sacred objects rarely reproduced elsewhere.

Lane Fox, R. *Pagans and Christians.* New York: Knopf, 1986. A scholarly examination of how and why Christianity began its ascendancy over paganism in the third century.

Markus, R. A. *Christianity in the Roman World.* London: Thames and Hudson, 1974. A brief historical account, from the obscure roots of Christianity to the separation of the church into eastern and western branches.

L'Orange, H. P. *Art Forms and Civic Life in the Late Roman Empire.* Princeton, N.J.: Princeton University Press, 1965. An imaginative analysis of the way political and economic changes affect the arts.

Vogt, J. *The Decline of Rome: The Metamorphosis of Ancient Civilization.* New York: Praeger, 1965. By emphasizing the conflict between the forces for preservation and the forces for change, this book shows how a new cultural unity—western medieval Europe—emerged from Mediterranean civilization.

8

THE SUCCESSORS OF ROME

Byzantium, Islam, and the Early Medieval West

When Rome fell in 476, a power vacuum developed in the western Roman lands. Gradually, three new civilizations—Byzantium, Islam, and the Early Medieval West—emerged to compete for control of the Mediterranean basin. Although none succeeded in reviving Roman grandeur or uniting the Mediterranean world, these three contrasting civilizations developed religious and cultural values that today dominate half the globe.

Of the three, the Byzantine Empire (the former Eastern Roman Empire) seemed in 476 to have the greatest prospects for dominance and longevity, with its autocratic government, stable farm economy, Greek intellectual heritage, and what came to be called Orthodox Christianity. (The Eastern Empire is called "Byzantine" because Constantinople was founded on the site of the ancient Greek city of Byzantium.) In contrast, Islam did not appear until the seventh century, when it began a meteoric rise and quickly spread across the Mediterranean world. Building on Arabic roots and the new faith propounded by Muhammad, Islamic civilization borrowed freely from the Greco-Roman and Persian heritages to attain a brilliant culture superior in many respects to those of Byzantium and Western Europe.

At the same time, civilization in the West was all but eclipsed, its political and economic systems in disarray and its people huddled in wooden huts beside armed fortresses. In the midst of this chaos, however, a new world was being born, built on Classical ruins, spurred by Germanic energies, and ani-

mated by the new Christian ethos. This chapter traces the development of these three varied civilizations (Map 8.1).

THE EASTERN ROMAN EMPIRE AND BYZANTINE CIVILIZATION, 476–1453

The end of centralized rule in Rome's western lands in 476 had little effect on the Eastern Roman Empire. Diocletian's division of the empire into two administrative halves in the third century had already set the eastern region on a different path. During its one-thousand–year existence, the empire took its Roman heritage and became an autocratic, static entity in a world of great upheaval and movement of populations. The changing boundaries of the Byzantine world tell the story of an empire under continual siege. Byzantium's borders reached their farthest western limits in the sixth century and then contracted more or less steadily for the next eight hundred years. The empire lost territory to the Arabs in the east and to the Bulgars and other groups in the west. Finally, no longer able to defend even the city of Constantinople itself, the empire fell to the Ottoman Turks in 1453.

Although Byzantium was buffeted by rapid and sometimes catastrophic upheavals, great wealth and economic resources gave the state the means to sur-

MAP 8.1

The Byzantine, Carolingian, and Islamic Empires, ca. 814

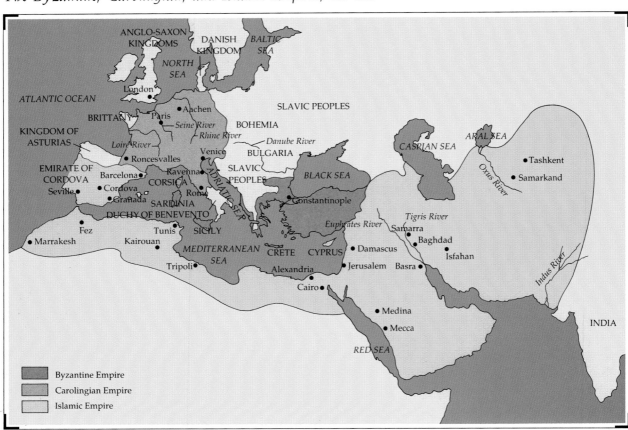

Byzantine Empire
Carolingian Empire
Islamic Empire

vive. The rulers, like those of the late Western Empire, kept a tight rein on their subjects' economic affairs, a policy that ensured that state interests were placed above individual gains. A rich and varied urban life developed, centered especially in Constantinople, the empire's capital and preeminent city, made virtually impregnable by its fortresslike site (Figure 8.1).

Beyond Constantinople the countryside was dotted with walled towns and vast farming estates owned by aristocrats and tilled by *coloni,* or serfs. Agriculture remained Byzantium's basic source of wealth, with grains, fruits, livestock, and timber the chief crops. Wine made from fermented grapes in Cappadocia in Asia Minor was prized across the empire.

Even though the frontiers of the empire expanded and contracted over the centuries, its heartland in Greece and Asia Minor remained basically stable. Here, a relatively uniform culture evolved that differed markedly from late Rome and from the West. The Byzantine world gave up its pagan and Latin roots to become a Christian, Greek civilization. The Orthodox church, led by the patriarch of Constantinople, emerged as a powerful force in society, but without the independence from secular rulers enjoyed by the Western church and the pope. Greek became the language of church, state, and scholarship in Byzantium, just as Latin served these functions in the West. But, like late Rome and unlike the West, Byzantium remained a state characterized by ethnic and racial diversity for most of its history; new peoples, such as the Serbs and the Bulgarians, helped to ensure this diversity as they were slowly assimilated into the Byzantine way of life.

History of the Byzantine Empire

The history of Byzantium reflects the fluctuating fortunes of the empire in relation to its hostile neighbors. In the first major period of Byzantine history, 476 to 641, the emperors, motivated by dreams of the Roman past and inspired by a sense of Christian mission (Time Line 8.1), made a valiant but ultimately futile effort to recover the lost western provinces.

The most memorable early emperor was Justinian (527–565), who conquered several of the Germanic

kingdoms that had sprung up in the former Western empire (Figure 8.2). He extended the borders of the empire to encompass Italy, southern Spain, and North Africa. Justinian's wars stretched the empire to its limit and exhausted the state treasury, leaving his successors unable to maintain the empire they inherited.

Between 641 and 867, the second period of Byzantine history, the empire was ill served by a series of weak rulers who lost all of the western lands that Justinian had recovered. The emperors were also

FIGURE 8.1 ISIDORE OF MILETUS AND ANTHEMIUS OF TRALLES. Hagia Sophia, Exterior. 532–537. Istanbul. *The Byzantine emperors transformed their capital into a glittering metropolis that easily outshone ravaged Rome. The most magnificent building in the city was Hagia Sophia ("Holy Wisdom"), originally built by Justinian as a church. The building's 101-foot-diameter makes it the largest domical structure in the world. Two half-domes at either end double the interior length to more than 200 feet. The beauty of Hagia Sophia made the domed church the ideal of Byzantine architecture.*

TIME LINE 8.1. **THE BYZANTINE EMPIRE**

476	641	867	1081	1261	1453
Revival of Empire	Withdrawal and Renewal	The Golden Age	The Challenge from the West	The Paleologian Emperors	

The fall of Rome

The fall of Constantinople

FIGURE 8.2 *Justinian and His Courtiers. Sixth Century. Ravenna, Italy. This mosaic represents a contemporary portrait of Justinian with his courtiers, including the Patriarch of Constantinople, who is holding the bejeweled cross. The luxurious trappings of office—purple robes, jeweled crown, and golden scepter—were calculated to enhance the emperor's earthly dignity. The Byzantine Empire's union of church and state is symbolized by the juxtaposition of the soldiers on the emperor's right with the ecclesiastical officials on his left.*

forced to yield much of Asia Minor to their Arab foes, and in 687 a Bulgarian kingdom was carved out of Byzantine territory in the Balkans.

Byzantium now became more militarized as a way of fending off enemy assaults. In the provinces, generals were given vast military and civil powers, and they began to replace the aristocrats as landowners. In time a style of feudalism—vast estates protected by private armies—arose, similar to the feudal developments in the West. Despite the changes in the social fabric, however, important cultural developments occurred, including a major revision of the law code and the establishment of a second university in Constantinople.

With the reign of Basil I (867–886), a new dynasty of capable rulers—called Macedonian because of their geographic origins—led Byzantium into its golden age (867–1081), the third major period in Byzantine history. Once again expanding the borders of the empire, these rulers restored the state to economic health as taxes from newly conquered, prosperous subjects filled the treasuries. The Bulgarian state, whose populace had earlier been converted to Orthodox Christianity, became a part of the empire. Orthodox missionaries, working among other Slavic tribes like the Serbs and the Croats, eventually tied the peo-

ples of eastern Europe to the religion and civilization of Byzantium, and in the late tenth century Byzantine missionaries introduced Christianity to Russia. As a result, medieval Russia became a spiritual and cultural client of Byzantium; after the fall of Constantinople, the Russian state claimed to be the principal heir to Byzantine civilization.

In 1081 an extraordinarily able feudal general, Alexios Comnenus (1081–1118), seized the throne and launched a new phase in Byzantine history, a period characterized by increasing pressure from the West (1081–1261). Despite the energy of the new dynasty, the empire was living on borrowed time, and Comnenus and his successors were unable to solve the social problems that now plagued the state. Under this dynasty, Byzantium became fully militarized and feudalized. The free peasantry disappeared, having been transformed into a vast population of serfs forced to labor on the landlords' estates.

The Comneni rulers, surrounded by enemies—Normans, Seljuk Turks, Hungarians, Serbs, Bulgars, and, after 1095, the European Crusaders who made Constantinople their first destination on their way to the Holy Land—tried to win allies, but in vain. In 1204 the soldiers of the Fourth Crusade conquered Constantinople and parceled out the remaining lands

among themselves. The empire appeared to be finished except for scattered holdings in Asia Minor. But, in 1261, Michael Paleologus (1261–1282), the ruler of one of these states, regained Constantinople and breathed some new life into the feeble empire. His dynasty ruled over the Byzantine world during the fifth and last phase of its history (1261–1453).

Michael Paleologus extended his power into the Greek peninsula and stabilized relations with the Bulgars and Serbs in the Balkans. Although Michael's successors continued to search for ways to strengthen the empire, they were forced to recognize that the empire was little but a diminished and ramshackle Greek state. From 1302 onward the Ottoman Turks—named for their leader Osman—built an empire on the ruins of the Byzantine empire. By 1330 this new state had absorbed Asia Minor, and by 1390 Serbia and Bulgaria were Turkish provinces. In 1453, when the Turks finally took Constantinople, they ravaged the city for three days, searching for booty and destroying priceless art treasures. Thus ended the last living vestige of ancient Rome. From the ashes of Byzantium rose the Ottoman Empire, which anchored the southeastern corner of Europe for nearly five hundred years until 1912, when revolutions and wars destroyed it.

Byzantine Culture: Christianity and Classicism

Byzantium inherited from Rome a legacy of unresolved conflict between Christian and Classical ideals that, in the wider Byzantine culture, revealed itself in the division between secular and religious forms of expression. The secular forms sometimes showed a playful or humorous side of Byzantine life, whereas the religious forms were always deeply serious. However, Byzantine culture, whether secular or religious, tended to follow Classical values by stressing serenity, dignity, and restraint. This timeless and even majestic quality was cultivated, perhaps, in compensation for the beleaguered nature of the Byzantine state.

The Orthodox Religion   At the same time that the bishop of Rome was becoming the head of the Christian church in the West, the bishop of Constantinople was rising to power over the Eastern (Orthodox) church in Byzantium. As patriarch (the title taken by eastern bishops) he functioned as the Orthodox faith's spiritual and doctrinal head. Many differences existed between the two Christian churches. Besides disagreeing over whether the pope or a patriarch should lead the church, they differed in language (Latin in the West, Greek in the East), religious practices (Roman priests were celibate, Orthodox priests could marry), and fine points of religious doctrine. In 1054 the patriarch of Constantinople refused to yield to the Roman church's demand for submission, and a final, permanent schism, or split, ended all ties between the two faiths (Time Line 8.2).

The patriarch of Constantinople had to deal with challenges from the pope, from rival patriarchs in other eastern cities, such as Antioch and Alexandria, and from the Byzantine emperors themselves, who viewed the church as an arm of the government. Although they made great claims for themselves and for the Orthodox church, the patriarchs never had the kind of power enjoyed by the popes. The Eastern church was also plagued by internal dissension and a variety of heresies that even persecution by the emperors, who desired a unified state with a common creed, did not always eliminate.

The most serious issue to confront the Orthodox church was the Iconoclastic Controversy (726–843),

TIME LINE 8.2   RELIGIOUS DEVELOPMENTS IN THE ORTHODOX CHURCH

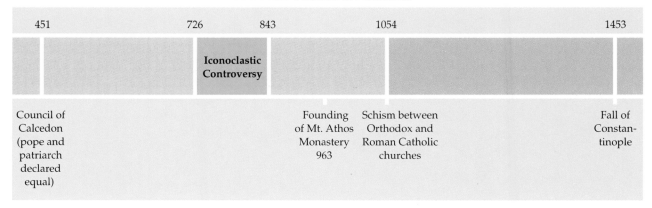

451	726	843	1054	1453
	Iconoclastic Controversy			
Council of Calcedon (pope and patriarch declared equal)		Founding of Mt. Athos Monastery 963	Schism between Orthodox and Roman Catholic churches	Fall of Constantinople

FIGURE 8.3 An Iconoclast Whitewashing an Image. Miniature from the Chludov Psalter. Ninth Century. Public Library, Moscow. *This miniature painting from the period of the Iconoclastic Controversy is historically inaccurate. It portrays an iconoclast attired as a monk, wearing a flowing robe and sporting a beard. In reality, however, the monks favored icons and protested their destruction. That the artist has depicted a monk desecrating a religious picture may indicate that the manuscript it appeared in was commissioned by a patron from the imperial circle, where images were despised.*

FIGURE 8.4 Mount Athos, Greece. *Since the tenth century, Mount Athos, located on a forty-mile-long peninsula in northern Greece, has been the site of a thriving monastic community. During that interval, the monks have enforced a strict code that excludes females, whether human or animal. Within the Mt. Athos complex each monastery was a self-governing unit that maintained order over its inmates, houses, and lands.*

which erupted when the emperor Leo III commanded the removal and destruction of all religious images (Figure 8.3). The iconoclasts, or image-breakers, believed that the devotion paid to sacred pictures was blasphemous and idolatrous. This belief may have been inspired by contacts in the Middle East with Judaism or Islam, for both religions strongly condemned the use of religious images. Siding with the iconoclastic emperors were the bishops, the army, and the civil service; opposed were the monks. Many monks lost their lives in the civil unrest that seized the empire. In the West the papacy refused to join the iconoclastic frenzy and broke relations with Byzantium during most of this period. The controversy lasted for over a hundred years, and, by the time the Byzantine rulers restored the veneration of icons, nearly all religious pictures had been destroyed by zealous reformers.

Monasticism, which furnished the chief foes of the iconoclastic emperors, was a basic expression of Orthodox piety. Monastic practices began in late Roman Egypt and quickly spread across the Roman world, adapting to local conditions (see Chapter 7). Like western ascetic practices, Byzantine monasticism took two forms, hermitic (or isolated) and communal. Communal monasticism in Byzantium was similar to monastic life in the West. The monastic communities were basically places where people retreated from the world to lead strictly disciplined lives. For centuries the monasteries received immense gifts of land and wealth from rulers, merchants, and peasants alike, and eventually they achieved a powerful economic position in Byzantine society.

The most important monastic complex in Byzantium was the one at Mount Athos, founded in 963 (Figure 8.4). Early in its history this mountain retreat in northern Greece, which during its heyday in the thirteenth century included over one hundred houses and about eight thousand monks, achieved relative independence from the secular authorities, which may explain how it survived into the twentieth century. The style of Mount Athos—self-governing, self-contained, and committed to study and prayer—influenced monastic development in the Orthodox world.

Law From the viewpoint of Western culture, Byzantium's greatest accomplishment was the codification of the Roman law made under the emperor Justinian in the sixth century. The Justinian Code, which summarized a thousand years of Roman legal developments, not only laid the foundation of Byzantine law but also furnished the starting point for the revival of Roman law in the West in the eleventh century. This law code preserved such legal principles as requiring court proceedings to settle disputes, protecting the individual against unreasonable demands of society, and setting limits to the legitimate power of the sovereign. Through the Justinian Code, these ideals permeated Byzantine society and served as a restraint on the autocratic emperors. When the West revived the study of the Roman law in the Middle Ages, these principles were adopted by the infant European states. Today, in virtually all of the Western states outside of the Soviet Union, these principles continue to be honored.

Architecture and Mosaics Besides law, the other great achievement of the Byzantine world was in architecture. Byzantine architecture was committed to

glorifying the state and the emperors along with spreading the Christian message. Most of the secular Byzantine structures, whether palaces or state buildings, were either destroyed in the fifteenth century or have since fallen into ruins, but many Byzantine churches still survive and attest to the lost grandeur of this civilization.

By the seventh century the **Byzantine style** had been born, a style that drew from Greek, Roman, and Oriental sources. From the Greco-Roman tradition came the basic elements of Byzantine architecture: columns, arches, vaults, and domes. Oriental taste contributed a love of rich ornamentation and riotous color. Christianity fused these ingredients, provided wealthy patrons, and suggested subjects for the interior decorations. The **Greek cross**, which has arms of equal length, came to be the preferred floor plan for most later Byzantine churches.

Despite their borrowings, the Byzantines made one significant innovation that became fundamental in their architecture: They invented **pendentives**—supports in the shape of inverted concave triangles—that allowed a dome to be suspended over a square base. As a result of this invention, the domed building soon became synonymous with the Byzantine style, notably in churches.

The Byzantine obsession with the dome probably stemmed from its central role in the magnificent church Hagia Sophia, or Holy Wisdom, in Constantinople (Figure 8.5). The dome had been employed in early Christian architecture (see Figure 7.14), and Romans had used the dome in important temples like the Pantheon (see Figure 5.13). Erected by Justinian,

Hagia Sophia was intended to awe the worshiper with the twin majesties of God and the emperor. The central dome measures more than 101 feet in diameter and rests on four pendentives that channel the weight to four huge pillars. Half-domes cover the east and west ends of the aisles.

In the vast interior, the architects showed that they were divided about the Classical legacy. On the one hand, they used such Classical features as vaulted aisles, well-proportioned columns, and rounded arches. But they ignored the basic rules of Classical symmetry; for example, they failed to harmonize the floor columns with the columns in the second story gallery. Their goal was not to produce a unified effect but rather to create an illusion of celestial light. Glittering walls covered with polychrome marbles and brilliant mosaics, which have since disappeared or been covered with whitewash, suggested shimmering cloth to early viewers and contributed to the breathtaking effect of this magnificent church.

Although many later Byzantine architects adopted Hagia Sophia as their model—a floor plan that unites the early Christian longitudinal basilica with a central square surmounted by a dome or domes set upon drums—they also built churches that did not make use of the dome, particularly in Ravenna in Italy. Ravenna, a seaport on the northeast Adriatic coast, enjoyed the best of both Roman worlds. The Western emperors began to rule from there in 404 and to turn their new capital into an artistic jewel. In the late fifth century Ravenna fell into the hands of Germanic invaders, who continued to add to the city's splendor.

FIGURE 8.5 ISIDORE OF MILETUS AND ANTHEMIUS OF TRALLES. *Hagia Sophia, Interior. 532–537. Istanbul. Hagia Sophia was the mother church of the Orthodox faith. After the Ottoman conquest, the church became an Islamic mosque, and some of the trappings, such as the calligraphic writings, still survive from this stage of the building's life. Today, Hagia Sophia is a museum, and its striking mixture of Byzantine and Islamic elements makes it a vivid symbol of the meeting of West and East.*

When the city became a Byzantine outpost under Justinian, two new churches were built there, San Vitale and Sant' Apollinare in Classe (Ravenna's port). San Vitale was domed (Figure 8.6), but Sant' Apollinare in Classe imitated late Roman styles with its basilica shape and its symbolic mosaics (Figure 8.7). The Western Classical ideal was visible in the harmonious nave of this church, where twenty-four perfectly proportioned columns were echoed above by precious marbles, which no longer exist. But the architect turned to Oriental sources for his imaginative treatment of the columnar capitals in the nave. Instead of using stylized Corinthian capitals, he twisted and curled the acanthus leaves into fanciful shapes, as if blown by a stiff wind. The overall result

FIGURE 8.6 San Vitale, Exterior. 526–547. Ravenna, Italy. *Ravenna's church of San Vitale, with its octagonal plan and domed central core, is the prototype of the domed church that became standard in Byzantine civilization. From the outside, San Vitale's dome is not visible because it is covered by a timber and tile roof. This church inspired Charlemagne's Royal Chapel in Aachen (see Figure 8.21).*

FIGURE 8.7   Sant' Apollinare in Classe, Nave. Ca. 549. Classe, near Ravenna, Italy.
Dedicated in 549 by the Bishop of Ravenna, the church of Apollinare was built about three
miles outside the walled city of Ravenna at the local port of Classe. Today, the harbor has
long since silted up and the church presides like a sentinel over the surrounding farmlands.
Sant' Apollinare's glittering interior mosaics and splendid marble columns remind the visitor
that this country church was once at the center of the Byzantine world.

was an artful blending of the Western and Eastern traditions.

Mosaic making had experienced a lively flowering in late Rome, and in Byzantium it became a major form of artistic expression. Unlike the Roman mosaics, which were of stone and laid in the floor, the Byzantine mosaics were usually of glass and set into the walls. Of the Byzantine mosaics, the most beautiful and the most perfectly preserved are those in the churches of Ravenna.

The church of San Vitale is home to a pair of impressive mosaics, one depicting Justinian and his courtiers (see Figure 8.2), the other depicting Justinian's empress, Theodora, and her retinue (Figure 8.8). In both these mosaics, debts to late Roman art may be seen in the full frontal presentation of each figure, their large and staring eyes, and their long gowns. But the two-dimensional rendering of the figures reveals the new Byzantine aesthetic; the rulers and their companions seem to float in space, their

feet pointing downward and not touching any surface. In various ways, the mosaics make a comparison between Justinian and Theodora and Christ and the Virgin Mary. For example, Justinian is surrounded by twelve companions, and the lower portion of Theodora's robe shows the three Wise Men bearing gifts to the Christ Child.

During the Iconoclastic Controversy, the emperors destroyed virtually all figurative religious art that was under their control. After the conclusion of the controversy, a formalized repertory of church decoration evolved that characterized Byzantine art for the rest of its history. The aim of this religious art was strictly theological. For instance, Christ Pantocrator (Ruler of All) dominated each church's dome (Figure 8.9). In these portraits Christ was presented as the emperor of the universe and the judge of the world. Accordingly, he came to be pictured with a stern and forceful countenance, in contrast to Western portrayals, which increasingly focused on his suffering.

FIGURE 8.8 *Theodora and Her Attendants. Ca. 547. San Vitale, Ravenna. This mosaic depicting the Empress Theodora and her attendants from the church of San Vitale faces the panel of her husband, Justinian, with his courtiers (see Figure 8.2). Together these mosaics communicate the pageantry and the luxury of this age. The man on Theodora's right draws back a curtain, inviting the imperial party into some unseen interior. His gesture may mean that this scene was part of a religious procession.*

FIGURE 8.9 *Christ Pantocrator. Central Dome, Church of Dafni. 1100. Dafni, near Athens. In early Christian art Christ had been portrayed as a beardless youth, often in the guise of the Good Shepherd or Orpheus. In Byzantine art, starting in the seventh century, Christ began to be depicted as a mature man with a full beard, as in this mosaic. Part of the change was a result of a fashion for full beards at this time, but, more important, the bearded figure reflected Orthodox theology's focus on Christ as the stern judge of the world.*

THE ISLAMIC WORLD, 600–1517

Islamic civilization, another successor to the territories once controlled by Rome, was born at approximately the same time as Byzantine culture and in the same part of the world, the eastern Mediterranean. In Arabic, the word "islam" means submission (to God); a "muslim" is one who has submitted. Arabic religion and culture are known collectively as Islam, and those who practice the faith are known as Muslims. At its height, Islamic civilization extended over an enormous area that included southern Spain, Sicily, North Africa, Syria, Palestine, Mesopotamia, Persia, and the Arabian peninsula. The peoples living in these areas retained many elements of their native traditions but adopted the Islamic religion in a complex, two-way process of cultural assimilation. All of these territories have remained Islamic up to the present day, with the exceptions of southern Italy and Sicily, which fell to the Normans in the eleventh century; Spain, which the Christians won in the fifteenth century; and Palestine, which became the Jewish state of Israel after World War II.

The pre-Islamic Arabs inhabited the Arabian peninsula, a harsh land of treeless steppes and waterless deserts wedged between the Red Sea and the Persian Gulf. Their tradition traces their ancestry to Abraham and the Hebrew patriarchs, and their Semitic tongue, Arabic, is related to Hebrew as well as to Syriac and Coptic, the chief languages of Syria and Egypt, respectively, at this time.

Geography accounted for the differences between the two major groups of pre-Islamic Arabs on the Arabian peninsula. In the north, nomadic Bedouins lived in the desert, herding sheep and goats. Tribal membership provided identity and social cohesion. In contrast, the southern Arabs lived in cities and made their living through trade with their neighbors. Age-old caravan routes crossed Arabia, connecting India and the Roman world; local Arab merchants made the most of the opportunities created by the passing traffic, sometimes accumulating great fortunes.

Jews and Christians settled in southern Arabia as farmers and artisans and served as major sources for cultural interchange. From them the Arabs acquired knowledge of weaponry, textiles, food and wine, and writing. The Arabs also learned that their polytheism conflicted with Jewish and Christian monotheism. A meeting place for all these peoples was Mecca, the leading commercial city of southern Arabia. Because of its central location on the rich overland route between the Indian Ocean and the Mediterranean, Mecca flourished as the chief marketplace for the exchange of goods between travelers and the local populace.

History of Islam

At the beginning of the seventh century, political and social life in Mecca was dominated by a wealthy merchant aristocracy of the Quraish tribe (Time Line 8.3). Into this society in about 570 was born Muhammad, the founder of Islam and one of the most commanding figures in all of history. Descended from an obscure, albeit respectable, branch of the Quraish, he became a wealthy merchant. At the age of 40 he had a vision in which he felt himself called by God to be a prophet to the Arab people, just as Moses and Jesus had been prophets before him. Declaring that there was but one God (Allah), Muhammad attacked the polytheistic beliefs of his fellow Arabs and condemned the Kaaba, a local pagan shrine that housed a sacred black stone, perhaps a meteorite.

Since the Kaaba was a source of revenue from the business generated by the thousands of pilgrims who visited it every year, the Quraish leaders reacted to Muhammad's message with mounting suspicion and alarm. When he began converting others to his views,

TIME LINE 8.3   THE WORLD OF ISLAM, 600–1517

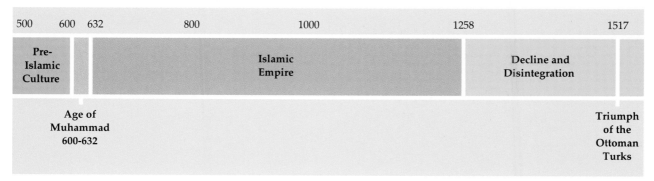

notably the poorer Arabs, Quraish hostility was translated into persecution. Under these threats Muhammad and his followers accepted an invitation to travel to Yathrib, a neighboring city in southwestern Arabia. This flight, or Hegira, transformed Muhammad's message of reform into a call for a new religion. This historic event in 622 marks the beginning of the Arab calendar, just as the birth of Christ marks the beginning of the Christian era in the West. Yathrib was later renamed Medina, "the city of the Prophet."

In Yathrib Muhammad's followers began to record the religious messages he received from Allah, and these writings became the Koran, the sacred book of Islam. Prominent among the divine words given to Muhammad was the *jihad,* the command to "holy war." Armed with this sacred order, Muhammad launched a religious and military movement that quickly conquered Arabia as both urban Arabs and desert Bedouins submitted to his authority. In 630 his forces defeated the Quraish, and a triumphant Muhammad reentered Mecca, making it his capital. The Kaaba shrine, now purified of pagan and other religious images, kept its sacred rock and thus remained an object of veneration for Muslims; this action ensured the willing cooperation of the newly converted business community who had at first bitterly opposed him. When Muhammad died in 632, he left an Arab state united around his prophecies.

In the century or so after the death of Muhammad, from 632 to 750, the energies awakened by his mission were unleashed in a series of military campaigns. Motivated by the lure of plundered wealth, the pressures of overpopulation, and the command to make holy war, the Arabs built a world state whose extent rivaled that of the Roman Empire. By 650 the Arabs ruled Syria, Mesopotamia, Egypt, and Persia, and by 740 North Africa had been added along with most of Spain. Only the militant kingdom of the Franks in the west and impregnable Constantinople in the east were able to withstand this Arab fury. At its height, the Arab empire stretched from the Indus River and the borders of China in the east to the Atlantic in the west and from the Taurus Mountains in the north to the Sahara in the south (see Map 8.1).

During the Abbasid dynasty (754–1258) Islamic civilization attained its golden age. A fusion gradually occurred between conquerors and conquered as the Arabs adapted other cultures to their own needs, and Arabic became the common cultural language throughout the empire. Millions converted to Islam, although Jews and Christians were allowed to retain their beliefs because they, like Muslims, were "people of the book." Trade with Europe, China, Russia, and Scandinavia generated great wealth for merchants and aristocrats, though the mainstay of the economy was agriculture, which, as always, depended on the backbreaking labor of an army of peasants working on small farms. This vast Islamic empire was a theocracy, autocratically ruled by a Caliph, or deputy, of the prophet Muhammad.

After the Abbasid era the Islamic world declined economically and politically as feudal agriculture replaced the commercial economy. In place of a unified caliphate, mutually hostile Islamic states confronted one another, and after 1453 the eastern Mediterranean area was clearly ruled by the Ottoman Turks from Constantinople. Eventually, in 1517, the Turks added Egypt and Syria to their holdings.

Islamic Religious and Cultural Developments

The Islamic civilization that flowered from the ninth to the twelfth century was more brilliant than that of either the West or Byzantium. Original learning flourished in science, mathematics, and law. Arab medicine was recognized in the West and in Byzantium as superior, and Islamic scholars made their civilization a successor to the Hellenic tradition by translating Greek philosophy, mathematics, and science into Arabic.

Nevertheless, religion, then as now, dominated Islamic life. Not only did the Koran serve as a guide for public and private morality, but the interpretation of koranic scriptures influenced the creation of such major cultural forms as jurisprudence and history. To the fundamentalist Muslim, religion, science, history, law, and theology were all different aspects of the same thing: God's divine word (Figure 8.10).

Islamic Religion   The two central beliefs of Islam are that there is but one God and that Muhammad is his prophet. Muslims worship the same God as Jews and Christians, but the Muslims alone recognize Muhammad as the *final* prophet of a tradition that goes back to Abraham and Moses in Judaism and also includes Jesus Christ as the giver of the Christian message. For the devout Muslim, Muhammad's voice is the culminating revelation from God that continues and perfects his earlier messages to Jews and Christians.

Muhammad's prophecies were recorded in the Koran during the generation after his death. Following no chronological pattern, this sacred book divides his revelations into chapters and verses beginning with the longest chapters and ending with the shortest. Muhammad's utterances reveal the prophet as a master of literary expression and of rhetorical skills. Within a century of Muhammad's death, a collection of his sayings and practices appeared that had been

FIGURE 8.10 The Great Mosque of Kairouan, Tunisia. Ninth Century. *As in the other civilizations of this period, the dominant building type in Islam was the house of worship. The Great Mosque of Kairouan in Tunisia, with its plain walls and square tower for calling the faithful to prayer, reflects the puritanical style of early Islam. Inside the walls a large unadorned courtyard serves as a praying area.*

preserved by the faithful and that came to be known as the Hadith, or the Tradition. Together, the Tradition and the Koran became the infallible guide to God's will on earth for Muslims.

The core of Muslim religious life rests on the five Pillars of the Faith, which include one basic statement and four required devotional practices. The affirmation of faith states: "There is but one God, Allah, and Muhammad is his Prophet." The four acts of devotion are to pray five times a day facing Mecca, to fast during the lunar month of Ramadan, to give alms to the poor, and to make the pilgrimage to Mecca. Islam, like Christianity, promises salvation in heaven for the good and damnation in hell for the wicked. Besides the five Pillars of the Faith, the Muslim who desires God's favor has to meet many other religious, ethical, legal, and social obligations which form the basis of the *Shari'a*, or holy law, which is rooted in the Koran and the Tradition.

History Because of Muhammad's supreme significance to Islam, lives of the Prophet and histories of his era appeared soon after his death. In time the Islamic world developed a great demand for historical writings, and diverse historical genres appeared, including accounts of territorial conquest, family genealogies, and town histories. Of the Islamic historians the greatest was Ibn Khaldun (1332–1406). His fame rests on the three-volume *Muqaddima*, or Prolegomena, which sets forth his scientific theory of history. In this work he reasoned that the best history should downplay the role of divine forces and instead focus on the role of human activity. He believed that historians who probed beneath the surface explanations would discover that human beings are motivated not by religious or idealistic impulses but by status concerns and desires to identify with certain groups. One of the founders of modern scientific history, Ibn Khaldun deserves wider recognition.

FIGURE 8.14 Ibn Tulun Mosque, Cairo. 876–879. *Ibn Tulun, a governor who founded a short-lived Egyptian dynasty independent of the caliphate in Baghdad, built this mosque in the congregational style created by Muhammad. The view is from inside the courtyard, with a domed fountain, used for ritual washing, standing in the foreground. Outside the walls rises the spire of the minaret with its encircling staircase. The finest surviving example of this style, the Ibn Tulun Mosque was imitated throughout the Muslim world.*

In the eleventh century the mosque evolved from a place for group prayer to a place for teaching, but the basic rectangular shape remained the same. In the teaching mosque, four large enclosed teaching halls with vaulted ceilings replaced the covered arcades on the perimeter of the courtyard, each opening into the central space.

Islamic artisans also excelled in palace architecture, and no more beautiful example exists than the Alhambra in Granada, the residence of the last Muslim rulers of Spain. Its exterior of plain red brick contrasted dramatically with its interior of restless splendor. The palace's asymmetrical plan included ornately decorated rooms, splendid courts, and formal gardens. The decoration of the Alhambra—variegated marbles, lustrous tiles, and painted stucco—

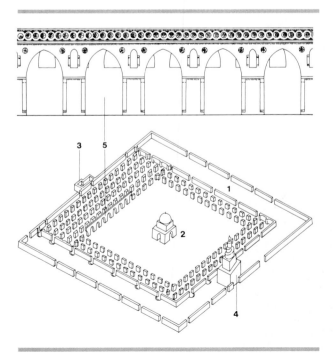

FIGURE 8.15 Floor Plan of Ibn Tulun Mosque. *This diagram shows the main features of the Ibn Tulun Mosque, a prototype of the congregational mosque that flourished in Islamic civilization in its early history. Constructed basically as an open rectangular area, the mosque has passageways (1) on three sides that lead through an arcaded area (5) into a central courtyard dominated by a domed fountain (2). In the middle of the eastern wall is the mihrab (3), a decorated niche indicating the direction of Mecca. Opposite the mihrab, on the western side, stands a minaret (4), a tower used by an official for calling the faithful to prayer.*

created a fantastic illusion of airiness. The Court of the Lions illustrates vividly the meaning of the term *arabesque*, with its calligraphic carvings, slender columns, geometric and floral shapes, and lacey decoration (Figure 8.16). The fountain surrounded by stone lions is a rare example of Islamic representational sculpture.

Notwithstanding the koranic prohibition, one branch of Islamic art, Persian *miniatures*, usually depicted realistic scenes. After the thirteenth century, illustrated manuscripts were produced in Persia under the patronage of the Mongol sultans, who had replaced the caliphs as rulers. Although the Mongols brought Chinese influences to the Persian miniatures, the Muslim artists rejected the openness of Chinese space and created their own ordered reality, as shown in a superb example from the fifteenth century (Figure 8.17). The painter records each object with painstaking naturalistic detail. The painting's high horizon and its rectangular format placed the two figures into a precise setting. Like all Persian miniatures, this exquisite work is characterized by fine detail, naturalistic figures and landscape, and subtle colors.

FIGURE 8.17 Scene from the *Khamsah* (Five Poems) of Amir-I Khusrau. 1485. Chester Beatty Library, Dublin. *During the fifteenth century, the age of the Mongol rulers in Persia, the art of Persian miniatures achieved its classic expression in paintings such as this. These small works are immediately recognizable by their rectangular designs, their representation of the human figure as being about one-fifth the height of the painting, and their use of extremely refined detail.*

FIGURE 8.16 Court of the Lions. The Alhambra. Thirteenth and Fourteenth Centuries. Granada, Spain. *The Alhambra is the only Muslim palace surviving from the medieval period. Because of its location in the West, this fairy-tale palace has made Granada a popular destination for tourists. As a result, the ornate Alhambra has played a pivotal role in developing a taste for the arabesque among many Westerners.*

THE EARLY MEDIEVAL WEST

Since the Italian Renaissance, it has been customary to describe the fall of Rome as marking the end of the ancient world and inaugurating the thousand-year era known as the medieval period, or the Middle Ages. Although Renaissance intellectuals used the word *medieval* as a negative term, today's scholars believe the civilization of the Middle Ages to be as worthy of study as the ancient and modern worlds. The rest of this chapter is devoted to the first phase of this era, the Early Medieval period, dating from about 500 to about 1000.

The Early Middle Ages: A Romano-Germanic Christianized World

In the first years after the fall of Rome, life in the West was precarious for most people. There was a return to an essentially agrarian form of existence, accompanied by a decline in trade and commerce and a lowering of the standard of living. Villages operated at the simplest economic level, and barter became the primary medium of exchange. What little security there was in this world was provided by the Christian church, with its bishops and priests, its increasingly powerful pope in Rome, and its spreading network of monasteries and convents.

By about 500 Western life stabilized to some slight degree. Three Germanic tribes occupied and ruled vast parts of the old Western Roman Empire: the Visigoths in Spain, the Ostrogoths in Italy and southern Germany, and the Franks in France and western Germany. Meanwhile, the Angles and Saxons made themselves dominant in England, the Vandals in North Africa, and the Burgundians in southern

France; other Germanic tribes claimed land in central Europe, the Scandinavian peninsula, and along the Baltic Sea. In what is present-day France, especially, life was being redefined in ways that would have a profound impact on the course of Western civilization.

At the same time that a Germanic tribe known as the Lombards was gaining control of the Italian peninsula, another Germanic tribe, the Franks, was achieving a semblance of centralized rule in Roman Gaul (modern-day France) under Clovis, the first important ruler of the Merovingian dynasty. An early convert to Latin Christianity, Clovis supported missionaries in newly conquered territories and thus strengthened political ties between Gaul and the pope (Time Line 8.4).

During these years of political expansion in the Frankish kingdom, some sense of security and order gradually developed, especially in and around the rulers' fortress-palaces. As the barbarian invasions subsided in the late sixth century, manorialism developed as a new economic system. Most of the Germanic invaders settled down as farmers on the manors, or landed estates, of the Frankish warrior class. There they became serfs, indentured servants who were bound to the land. Their value as workers earned them the protection of the lord of the manor in time of war.

The Frankish political and economic systems reflected a society composed of three well-defined ranks: those who fought, those who prayed, and those who worked. Each social rank was divided into a rigidly defined hierarchy of subgroups. The warrior class, headed by the king, consisted of the lords of the great manors and their families and, under them, their courtiers and bureaucrats, the less wealthy knights, and the lords of small manors. The upper clergy, who shared the high social status of the warriors, consisted of the archbishops, bishops, and abbots; the lower clergy comprised priests, monks, and

TIME LINE 8.4   THE KINGDOM OF THE FRANKS

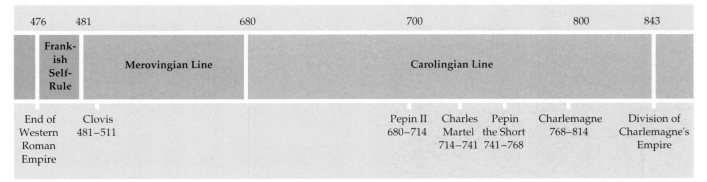

476	481	680	700	800	843
Frankish Self-Rule	Merovingian Line		Carolingian Line		
End of Western Roman Empire	Clovis 481–511		Pepin II 680–714 Charles Martel 714–741 Pepin the Short 741–768	Charlemagne 768–814	Division of Charlemagne's Empire

nuns and the clerical scribes and secretaries. Socially lower than either the warriors or the clergy were the workers, consisting of free farmers, artisans, and a few merchants, and the vast population of peasants, serfs, and a few slaves at the bottom.

In Frankish society the status of women declined sharply from what it had been in the Roman world. On the manors, noblewomen enjoyed few personal or property rights since, under Frankish law, land was passed through the male line. The noblewoman's primary function became the bearing of sons, and the peasant woman was simply another laborer. The only outlet for women who wanted a leadership role in this society was in the nunneries, for women traditionally ruled themselves in these religious institutions.

After 700 the Merovingians gradually lost control of the Frankish kingdom to the Carolingians, a family of ambitious landowners who served as court advisors to the Merovingians. Under Charles Martel ("Charles the Hammer"), Carolingian troops halted the advance of the Muslims at the Battle of Tours in southern France in 732, thereby ensuring the future of Europe as a Christian land.

The Carolingian dynasty triumphed over all its rivals in the reign of Pepin the Short (741–768), the son of Charles Martel. In 751, Pepin, with the approval of the pope and with the votes of the Frankish nobles, was declared King of the Franks. Three years later a new pope traveled to St. Denis, near Paris, crowned Pepin, and anointed him as defender of the church. This ceremony, cementing an alliance between the popes and the Franks, set the course for church-state relationships in the West.

In exchange for papal recognition of his royal title, Pepin crushed the Lombards who ruled most of Italy and gave the newly conquered lands in central Italy to the pope. These territories, which later became known as the Papal States, were conveyed in one of the most famous documents of the Early Middle Ages, the Donation of Pepin. The alliance symbolized by the Donation of Pepin benefited both parties: The pope's authority was enhanced, and the church was given a stronger economic foundation; the Frankish kings gained legitimacy and a claim to be the hereditary protectors of Rome. Of more lasting effect, this union redirected the church's interests away from the Eastern Empire and linked Rome's destiny with western Europe.

Besides the Donation of Pepin, another famous papal document dates from this period, the Donation of Constantine. Unlike the Donation of Pepin, which was genuine, the Donation of Constantine was a forgery, probably devised at the papal court. It claimed that Constantine, the fourth-century Roman emperor, had granted the church extensive territories in Italy. During the early Renaissance, this document was proven fraudulent (see Chapter 11).

Charlemagne ("Charles the Great") (768–814), the son of Pepin the Short, established the first real empire in medieval Europe and challenged the Byzantine rulers' claims to the western Roman lands. A man of imposing stature and personality, Charlemagne was, without question, the most powerful ruler in the Early Middle Ages. Historians have named a dynasty and an age for him—Carolingian, from Carolus, Latin for Charles. Charlemagne conquered vast expanses of land, fighting the Lombards in Italy, the Saxons in Germany, and the Muslims in Spain. He followed up his victories by colonizing most of these areas, converting the populace to Christianity, and installing his own representatives as a link with the local authorities.

As a reward for his military and religious activities, Pope Leo III (795–816) crowned Charlemagne as "Charles Augustus, Emperor of the Romans" on Christmas Day, 800. With this act, Leo may have hoped to assert the authority of the church over the state, but Charlemagne continued to believe in the supremacy of the state. The coronation widened the rift between Byzantium and the West while reinforcing Charlemagne's reputation as a "new Constantine" who would set Western civilization on a new path.

Charlemagne created the most efficient and centralized state the West had seen since the Roman Empire. He built up a capable bureaucracy, instituted a fair judicial system, and brought learned people to his court as part of a revival of the arts and humanities. He granted large tracts of land to local warriors and then held them responsible for maintaining law and order in their domains. This administrative system represented a fusion of the Roman approach to governing an empire with the Germanic warrior tradition, and it worked as long as Charlemagne lived.

The end of the Carolingian era began in 843 when Charlemagne's grandsons divided the empire into three parts, a move that also hastened the splintering of western Europe into smaller kingdoms. In the ninth and tenth centuries, the divided Frankish kingdoms could not hold back the rampaging Vikings from Scandinavia and the Magyars from the Hungarian plains, the final wave of barbarian invasions into western Europe. By the end of the tenth century, however, two new kingdoms—the germs of modern France and Germany—were emerging out of the political chaos.

The first of these kingdoms was France, which developed from the ambitions of Hugh Capet (987–996), a noble landowner who was crowned king of the

FIGURE 8.18   Church of St. Pantaleon. 966–980, Restored 1890–1892. Cologne, Germany. *Otto the Great founded this church for a Benedictine monastery in Cologne where his brother was Archbishop. As a builder of churches, Otto was following in Charlemagne's footsteps, identifying himself as God's chosen instrument intent on expanding both the Christian faith and his own empire. Of the original fortresslike church, only the westworks with three towers survive. Like so many other churches of the tenth century, St. Pantaleon was flanked by two tall towers and an enclosed entrance. The rest of the church was restored at the end of the nineteenth century.*

lies and forced the pope, in return, to recognize him as emperor. In founding his empire and seeking papal sanctions, Otto was clearly following the dream of Charlemagne—to restore the lost Roman world (Figure 8.18).

Religion and Culture in the Early Middle Ages

During the Early Middle Ages literature, art, and architecture degenerated from the already low standards of late Rome. There was a brief, bright moment in the early ninth century under Charlemagne when literature, learning, and the arts flourished, but by the mid–ninth century this renaissance faded in the wake of political disintegration and foreign invasions. Later, Otto the Great encouraged the cultivation of letters within his empire. Notwithstanding their sporadic nature, these intellectual and artistic developments helped to blend the Germanic and Greco-Roman worlds into an emerging Christian Europe.

Christianity: Leadership and Organization   Regardless of internal dissension and external foes in the period between 500 and 1000, Christianity strengthened itself and its hold on society. The early popes faced heresy, disorganization, and a vast world of unbaptized men and women. The energetic and dedicated Pope Gregory the Great (590–604) was the most successful of the early medieval pontiffs. He reformed the clergy, whose poor training and lax habits, in particular their sexual behavior, worked against the church's efforts to set high moral standards. He standardized the use of music in the service of worship, so that the Gregorian chants became synonymous with the medieval church. He encouraged the founding of new monasteries among the Germanic peoples. Abroad, he sent missionaries to England, thus ensuring the triumph of Christianity among the Anglo-Saxons. Despite the successes and reforms of Gregory and the later popes, however, they could not break the grip of secular power over church affairs, a thorny problem that awaited solution in the High Middle Ages.

The church found a new source of strength in monasticism. Western monks followed the guidelines that were laid down by St. Benedict (480–543) and observed in the Benedictine order's first monastery at Monte Cassino, south of Rome. The Benedictines, after a period of rigorous intellectual training and self-denial, vowed to lead lives of chastity, obedience, and poverty. They divided their days into alternating periods of work, prayer, and study. The monks were

western Franks with the approval of the local bishops and counts. From their power base in Paris, the Capetian kings slowly spread their authority and enlarged their domains by consolidating their grip over the other feudal lords.

The second emerging state in western Europe was that of Otto the Great (936–973), who was elected king of the Germans and Saxons. A superb military leader and dedicated church reformer, Otto halted the Magyar advance in the east and extended his kingdom into Italy in the south. There he released the papacy from the control of corrupt Roman fami-

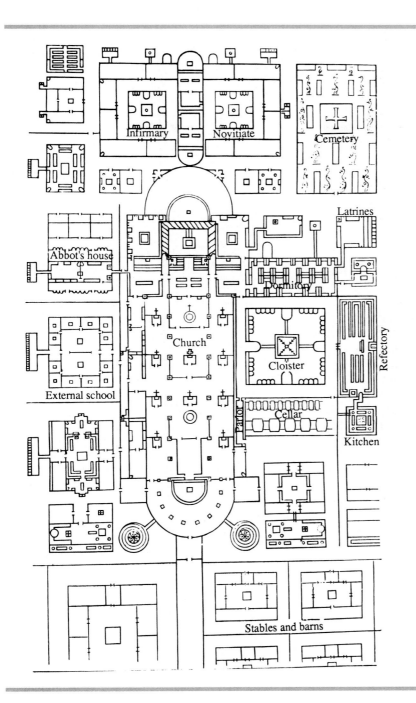

FIGURE 8.19 Plan of St. Gall Monastery. Ca. 820. *One of the most prominent monasteries of the ninth century was the Benedictine House at St. Gall in Switzerland. Although the monastery no longer exists, its original plan, perhaps by Linhard, has been preserved. The plan reveals the self-sufficient system of the monastery, with its school, hospital, dormitories, poor house, and various buildings and plots of land.*

known as the regular clergy, because they followed a *regula*, or rule.

The monasteries that spread across Europe served many purposes. They were havens for the populace during times of invasion. They were centers for copying ancient literary and philosophical texts, which were then studied in their libraries. The monks often established schools for the local young men. Finally, the self-sufficient monasteries were often models of agricultural productivity and economic resourcefulness (Figure 8.19).

Literature, History, and Learning   Writers during this period were more interested in conserving the past than in composing original works. Consequently, literature—all of it written in Latin—was eclectic, blending Christian ideas with Classical thought and often mixing genres, such as history, biography, science, philosophy, and theology.

The most highly educated scholar of the Early Middle Ages was Boethius (about 480–524), a Roman aristocrat and a courtier of Theodoric, the Ostrogoth king in Italy. That rarity in this age, an intellectual who knew Greek, Boethius translated much of Aristotle's vast writings into Latin. In the later Middle Ages, from the sixth through the eleventh centuries, all that Latin scholars knew of Aristotle was through Boethius's translations.

Boethius rose to prominence in Theodoric's court but then fell from favor and was eventually executed. While in prison he wrote the *Consolation of Philosophy*, a work widely read throughout the Middle Ages and beyond. In it he described his mental struggle with despair at life's cruel turn of events. He personified Philosophy as a learned woman with whom he argued many issues in search of the meaning of happiness. In the face of imminent death, Boethius finally concluded that true contentment was reserved for those who combined intellectual inquiry with Christian beliefs.

Although several scholars wrote historical chronicles, only Gregory of Tours and Bede can be classified as historians. Both consulted written documents and other sources and in general strove for (but did not always achieve) objectivity and historical accuracy. Gregory of Tours (about 538–593) left the single surviving record of the sixth-century Merovingian kingdom in his *History of the Franks*. Gregory's account lacks historical cohesion and shows stylistic confusion, but he manages to capture the flavor of his times in his lively and humane character sketches of the Frankish rulers. In Anglo-Saxon England, Bede (673–735), an English monk and scholar, composed the *Ecclesiastical History of the English People*, which described the missionary activities that led to the founding of the English church. Written in a pure Latin style, his *History* is a major source for the chronology of this troubled age.

When Charlemagne came to power, cultural life revived and enjoyed its greatest flowering in the Early Middle Ages. The Carolingian Renaissance, which represented Europe's first genuine rebirth of Classical studies within the context of Christian beliefs, had its roots in educational reform. Recognizing that ignorance posed a threat to his regime, Charlemagne founded a palace school at his residence at Aachen, in present-day western Germany. To this school he invited the most learned men of the day to train his own staff and to teach the sons of the nobility. Leading scholars from England, Ireland, and Italy answered this call, settling down in Aachen, where they pursued their scholarship. Foremost among them was Alcuin of York (735–804), who led the palace school, giving instruction in Latin, composing his own textbooks, and overseeing the copying of manuscripts.

Another important scholar at Aachen was Einhard (about 770–840), who came from Gaul and served

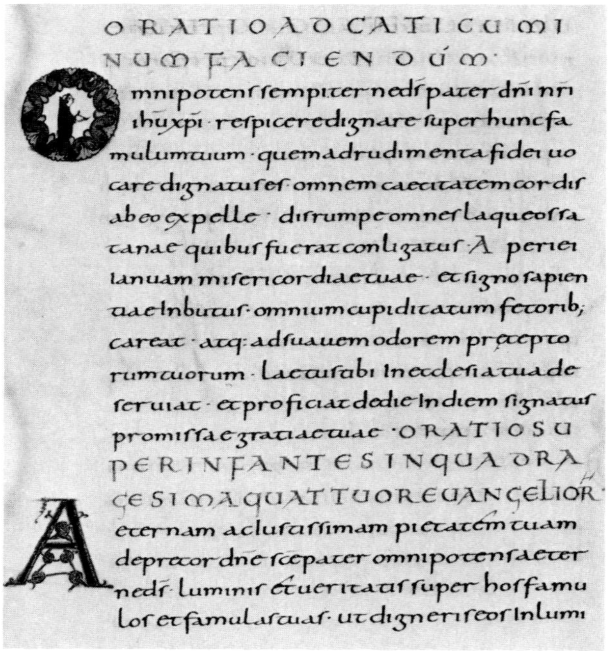

FIGURE 8.20 Carolingian Minuscule. Ninth Century. Bibliothèque Nationale, Paris. *Because Christianity relied heavily on written works, legible texts were important, but the prevailing style of writing, which used separately formed lower-case letters, was almost impossible to read. To overcome this difficulty, scribes during Charlemagne's reign perfected a new style of writing—the Carolingian minuscule—which was characterized by clearly formed letters linked into words, spaces between words, and capital letters at the beginning of sentences, as shown in this manuscript. All subsequent Western handwriting styles follow from this tradition.*

Charlemagne in many ways. His lasting contribution was his brief and simple biography of the famed ruler, the *Vita Caroli* (the *Life of Charles*). Modeled on the lives of the Caesars by the Roman historian Suetonius, this work is a major literary achievement of the Early Middle Ages and still gives today's readers a vivid portrait of Charlemagne and his times.

One of the important achievements of the palace school was a significant innovation in handwriting. Trained scribes developed a flowing style consisting primarily of rounded lower-case letters that became the standard form for all later handwriting styles in the West. With the development of this legible and uniform Latin script, known as Carolingian minuscule, educated men and women gained access to written material, and monks, in transcribing books, were liable to fewer errors (Figure 8.20).

Music Music became an integral part of the church liturgy during the Early Middle Ages and kept alive the Greek heritage of music as an art form. From this religious nursery ultimately arose all of the sacred and secular music of the modern West. The name of

Pope Gregory the Great is preserved in the most famous early medieval musical form, the *Gregorian chant*, which became the official liturgical music of the early church—that is, used in the Mass (the celebration of the eucharist) and other services of the yearly cycle of public worship. The chants consisted of a single melodic line sung in unison, without instrumental accompaniment, by male voices. They had an impersonal, nonemotional quality and served religious rather than aesthetic or emotional purposes. Notwithstanding this aim, the chants cast a spell over their listeners, evoking in them feelings of otherworldliness, peace, and purity.

In the ninth century, one of the most important advancements in music history occurred, the rise of polyphony—two lines of melody which are sounded at the same time. Polyphony, unlike the monophonic Gregorian chants, gave music a vertical as well as a horizontal quality. But further musical developments would have to await more settled social and political conditions.

Architecture   The overall decline of living conditions in western Europe took its toll in architecture and art as patronage evaporated, skills fell into disuse, and artistic talents were necessarily directed to more pragmatic ends. The few artisans and builders who were still in business traveled across western Europe constructing churches and chapels in protected places.

Charlemagne gave full support to the construction of impressive churches and palaces, especially his own royal residence. Today, most of the original apartments and offices of his palace are restored rather than original, but the Palace Chapel remains largely as it was first built (Figure 8.21). Inspired by the design of San Vitale in Ravenna, this magnificent room reflects the architect's reinterpretation of the graceful Byzantine style to incorporate the massive solidity of Roman monuments and the vigor of Germanic taste. Octagonal in shape, the chapel stands two stories tall. Heavy square pillars support the second level, where galleries are framed by graceful arches and columns brought from Italy. The bronze

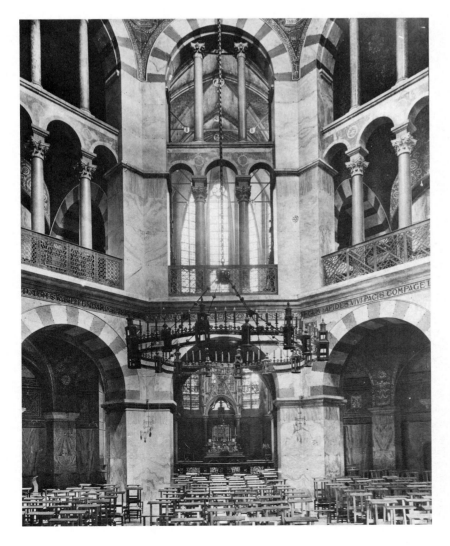

FIGURE 8.21   Charlemagne's Palace Chapel. Ca. 792–805. Aachen, Germany. *Odo of Metz designed the Royal Chapel for Charlemagne, and Pope Leo III probably dedicated it in 805. Although the chapel is inspired by Byzantine architecture, the decorative scheme and the roof design make it a Roman rather than a Byzantine building. From the tenth to the sixteenth centuries the Germans crowned their kings in this chapel.*

gratings and mosaic floor were also brought to Aachen from Italy. An *ambulatory*, or passageway for walking, extends around the circumference of the central space behind the pillars. Spiral steps lead up to the upper floor, where the tribune, or emperor's throne, was located. From here, Charlemagne observed and participated in the services and ceremonies of the church and was in turn observed by his subjects, enthroned as Christ's representative on earth.

Painting: Illuminated Manuscripts Although nearly all of the murals, frescoes, and mosaics from this period have vanished, the surviving *illuminated manuscripts* offer an excellent view of the early medieval painting ideal. The art of manuscript illumination was influenced by the barbarian practice of decorating small objects and the Classical tradition of fine metal work that had been maintained in Italy. During the Early Middle Ages, gifted artists and dedicated monks joined these disparate artistic elements to produce richly illustrated books and bejeweled book covers. Most of these decorated books were used in the liturgy of the Mass, such as the psalters, the collections of the psalms, and the gospel books, which were the texts of the first four books of the New Testament. For three centuries, in monasteries and abbeys from Ireland to Germany, scribes copied the Bible and their fellow artists adorned the pages with geometric and foliage designs, mythical animals, Christian symbols, and portraits of biblical characters and saints.

Manuscript illumination became both more symbolic and more realistic in the Carolingian Renaissance, partly because Italian artists were now influencing Frankish tastes. For example, the gospel of St. Medard of Soissons follows Italian practice in being filled with Christian symbols and religious icons as well as making visual references to Classical architecture. In a portrait of St. Mark, the painter decorates the page with the lion, St. Mark's symbol, and frames the saint with a rounded arch, Corinthian columns, and folded curtains (Figure 8.22). In this small work the figure of St. Mark exhibits a dynamic sense of life in his energetic body and tilted head.

At the end of the Early Middle Ages, the style of manuscript illumination became even more elaborate and richer in tone, as in the Gospel Book of Otto III, a product of the German Reichnau school. The miniaturist who painted this manuscript represents the figure of St. Luke in a state of religious ecstacy. Enthroned, St. Luke supports a host of Jewish prophets and heavenly messengers; books from the Old Testament are stacked in his lap. Hovering above the saint's head is his symbol, the ox (Figure 8.23).

FIGURE 8.23 *St. Luke,* from the Gospel Book of Otto III. Ca. 1000. Bayerische Staatsbibliothek, Munich. *In this illumination from a gospel book, the biblical symbols and images above St. Luke dominate the earthly and human forms. The unnatural colors and placement of the figures suggest a mystical meaning. This portrait of St. Luke measures about 8 inches by 10 inches.*

FIGURE 8.22 *St. Mark,* from the Gospel Book of St. Medard of Soissons. Early Ninth Century. Bibliothèque Nationale, Paris. *The so-called Italo-Alpine style of painting is evident in this portrait of St. Mark because it includes Roman decorations, in particular the columns derived from the Corinthian order. Although this gospel book was made for Charlemagne, it ended up in the abbey of St. Medard by 827 as a gift to the monks from Louis the Pious, Charlemagne's heir. Painted on vellum, it measures 14 by 10 inches.*

9

THE HIGH MIDDLE AGES
The Christian Centuries

Although the ambitious hopes of Charlemagne for Europe were blasted by the barbarian invasions of the ninth and tenth centuries, society had grown more settled by the early eleventh century, and a brighter era began to unfold in the West. Between 1000 and 1300—the period called the High Middle Ages—a new foundation was laid that would support the future development of Western civilized life.

During this time the Christian church grew in influence to become the dominant institution of the medieval world. At the same time, feudalism was established as the principal military, economic, and political system, and feudal monarchies in France, England, and central Europe began to form the germs of future European states. Despite the prevalence of the feudal system, town life revived to an extent unseen in the West since the declining years of the Roman Empire, and a new urban class was born. Midway between the feudal aristocrats and the peasants, this middle class included merchants, moneylenders, and skilled artisans, among others—virtually any free persons associated with town life.

These momentous changes in the political, social, and economic realms were reflected in the cultural interests of the time. Theologians, writers, and architects worked to harmonize the opposing trends of the time, the secular and the spiritual. Their achievement was a stunning but short-lived synthesis that seemed to resolve many contradictions. Moving from rugged warrior values, dominant between 1000 and 1150, Western culture became more refined, learned, and increasingly secular between 1150 and 1300. The

earlier 150-year-period is associated with monastic and feudal themes in literature and the Romanesque style in architecture. The later period saw a growing trend toward urban and courtly themes in literature and the rise of the Gothic style in architecture, the most spectacular realization of which was the Gothic cathedral.

FEUDALISM

Out of feudalism—a military and political system based on personal loyalty and kinship—arose a new social order, a code of conduct, and an artistic and literary tradition. In the beginning, feudalism restored law and order to western Europe, even though local lords often exploited those under them. But the nature of feudalism changed during the High Middle Ages; the feudal nobility slowly lost power to the feudal kings, who laid the foundations of the early modern national monarchies. As a result, by the early 1300s feudalism no longer served its original function and was being superseded in many areas by different political, social, and economic forms.

The Feudal System and Feudal Society

With origins in both Roman and German practices, feudalism evolved in the Early Middle Ages under the Franks and expanded under Charlemagne. As a military system it offered some protection from barbarian invaders but at the cost of fragmenting society into rival states. As the feudal chiefs began to pass their lands on to their eldest sons, Europe became dominated by a military aristocracy (see Chapter 8).

Feudal wealth was reckoned in terms of land—the feudal estate included lands, manor houses, and the serfs who worked the land. The feudal lords attracted warriors, called vassals, to their private armies by offering them landed estates, and thus feudalism depended on the manorial economy. The feudal estate, called a fief, enabled the warrior to outfit himself with the proper military equipment, including horses and attendants, and to live in a style worthy of an aristocrat.

Mature feudalism was a complex web of agreements, obligations, and rituals. A written agreement spelled out the mutual duties and obligations of the lord and the vassal. Typically, the lord gave military protection to his vassal and settled quarrels among his supporters through his court. The vassal in turn offered his lord "aid and counsel" by furnishing military or, occasionally, financial aid and sitting as counsel in the lord's court. Despite guarantees and safeguards, conflicts often arose between a lord and his vassal. Sometimes differences were settled by peers before the lord in his court; more often they resulted in civil wars that inflicted loss of life and goods on innocent parties as well as on the belligerents.

Throughout Europe the vassal-lord relationship was the heart of feudalism, but the specific form of the institution varied geographically. Feudalism's prototype was that of northern France, around Paris; from there it spread westward into Normandy and eastward into Champagne. From France feudalism radiated out across Europe, from Normandy over the English Channel to the British Isles, southward into Sicily, eastward into central Germany and Poland, and across the Alps into northern Italy. Each area modified the French form to suit its local needs. Those who profited from feudalism held on to the institution as long as possible, so that well into the twentieth century its vestiges were evident in central Europe and Russia and were eliminated only by revolution.

The hierarchical social order spawned by feudalism was defined and elaborated in the unwritten rules of conduct known as the *chivalric code*. In the early eleventh century, chivalry (from the French word *cheval*, meaning "horse") was largely a warrior code, although one rooted in Christian values. More an ideal than a reality, it nevertheless inspired the vassal to honor his lord and to respect his peers. He was also expected to protect the weak from danger and to practice his ideals—bravery, strength, and honesty—with all members of society.

In the early eleventh century, under the growing power of the church, chivalry evolved into a more refined code. The French clergy initiated the Peace of God, a call for an end to fighting at certain specified times, and other clerics were encouraging the knights to show more humane treatment to certain people, especially women, clergy, and peasants. By the twelfth century both the Peace of God and the notion of protected classes—notably women—were incorporated into the warrior code. Especially influential

FIGURE 9.1 *Count Eckhart and Uta.* Naumburg Cathedral. Ca. 1245. Naumburg, Germany. *In this representation of a feudal lord and lady, the most striking features are the woman's chaste beauty, reflecting her role as the queen of chivalry and linking her to the Virgin Mary, and the man's great heraldic shield and sword, symbolizing his position as an aristocratic warrior and defender of honor. These two figures are among several that stand in Naumburg Cathedral, representing noble men and women associated with the founding of the cathedral. The Naumburg statues are considered among the most beautiful sculptures from this period.*

FIGURE 9.2 *Labors of the Months.* Amiens Cathedral. Ca. 1220–1230. Amiens, France. *These carefully observed depictions of peasant life from the western portals of Amiens Cathedral show peasants engaged in their daily rounds. These three quatrefoils—four-leafed shapes—represent the summer months and the tasks of harvesting, threshing, and pruning.*

in altering the status of women was the rise of courtly love, a movement at first centered in the aristocratic courts of southern France and later spreading to courts across Europe. Perhaps the greatest contribution of medieval civilization, courtly love encouraged the intermingling of the sexes in social settings where dancing, music, and conversation were enjoyed in accordance with the rules of courtesy. Thus, after 1200 the protection of women was enshrined at the heart of a more courtly version of the chivalric code. Much of the secular literature, art, and music of the High Middle Ages was inspired by these values. Because they were identified with the Virgin Mary, women were idealized and venerated with an almost holy respect (Figure 9.1). A contradictory and equally unrealistic trend was the association of women with evil because of their descent from Eve, who tempted Adam to eat the forbidden fruit and brought the burden of original sin to humanity.

Whatever the image of woman in medieval society, however, on a practical level her position was determined by the social status of her husband or father. A few women—such as Eleanor of Aquitaine, wife of King Henry II of England in the twelfth century—sometimes influenced a spouse's decisions or wielded power on behalf of a son. But their rarity as rulers in their own right testifies to how little power women really had in the Middle Ages, despite their glorified image.

Peasant Life

Feudalism and chivalry were designed to serve the best interests of the relatively few members of the noble classes. Life was very different in the timeless world of the peasants, who made up the vast majority of the population. Some of them were free, but many were bound in service. The two most common forms

of servitude, slavery and serfdom, were legacies from Rome. Slavery was a dying institution because the church's teachings had convinced the feudal lords of its inhumanity. But serfdom, which bound peasants to their lord's service by inheritance, was firmly entrenched by the twelfth century and restricted the movements of those caught up in it. Law and tradition allowed each lord to control completely the world of the peasants on his manor.

The routine of the serfs and the free peasants was laid down by custom and regulated by daily and seasonal events (Figure 9.2). Living in wooden huts, they eked out a bare subsistence from their tiny plots of land, raised their children, and found relief in the frequent Holy Days and feast days set by the church calendar. In time, as farming innovations were introduced (such as three-field crop rotation, which allowed the land to replenish itself), the plight of the serfs improved. Increasing the productivity of the soil brought economic benefits to the lord of the manor, and he in turn could undertake such measures as paying the peasants in coin and selling them tracts of land.

As serfs gained a few legal rights, they could become economically independent and win their freedom from the manorial system. These trends, however, were confined to western Europe, notably England and France. In central and eastern Europe, serfs continued to be exploited, in some areas for centuries to come.

The Rise of Towns

Despite the dominance of the feudal system, a new trend was beginning that ran counter to all the principles of feudalism: the rise of urban areas where free individuals pursued their own economic goals.

FIGURE 9.3 *Street Scene in a Medieval Town.* Bibliothèque Nationale, Paris. *Four businesses are crowded together into this narrow street. In the background, three furriers await customers. Other merchants have hung out signs to advertise their trades, such as the barber who displays four "barber bowls"—a device placed over the head during a haircut. In the left foreground, tailors stitch clothing, and, on the right, a grocer arranges pies in front of his shop. Most tradesmen lived above their stores, which meant that the town was filled with people both day and night.*

Although the rural manors provided work and security for approximately 90 percent of the population, town life was beginning to flourish. Triggered in part by changes in agriculture, the population of Europe nearly doubled between 1000 and 1300, from thirty-five million to almost seventy million, and many people sought economic opportunities in the new and revitalized urban areas. These centers sprang up in various locations: at the sites of old Roman towns, near the castles of local feudal lords, around regional markets or the seats of bishops, or simply along rivers or roads where trade routes crossed (Figure 9.3). From this point on, the future of the West lay with the town dwellers, who expanded in steadily increasing numbers regardless of the uncertainties of the economy and the turmoil of urban living.

As town populations increased and urban life became more competitive, the residents formed associations, called guilds, to protect their special interests. The artisan and craft guilds, for example,

regulated working conditions, created apprenticeship programs, and set wages, and the merchant and banking guilds approved new businesses and supervised trade contracts. The artisan and the merchant guilds often quarreled over issues inside the town walls, but they joined hands against the intrusions of the church and the local nobility.

Because this kind of economic life was so at odds with the feudal system, urban dwellers, led by the guilds, founded self-governing towns, called communes, often with written documents (charters) that specified their political and economic rights in relation to the feudal lords. A serf, for example, could become a freeman if he lived in a chartered town for a year and a day. By about 1200, many towns in northern and western Europe had charters, and their political independence spurred economic growth. Moreover, these charters symbolized the fact that town life was protected and to some degree independent of the feudal world.

Artisans who crafted goods and merchants who sold them needed buyers, secure trade routes, and markets for their products if they were to prosper. The earliest trade routes were the rivers and old Roman roads. As demand increased in the West for luxury items from the Orient, new trade routes opened between Europe and the East. Italian cities—Venice, Pisa, and Genoa—took the lead in this international commerce, trading the luxurious woolen cloth of Flanders for the silks of China and the spices of the Middle East (Map 9.1). Along the overland leg of this route in Europe, local lords promised to give traders safe passage through their territory for a fee. Some nobles as well as a few strategically located towns in central France sponsored fairs as a lure for this rich international trade.

The role of women in this urban world was still subordinate to that of men, as it was on the feudal manor. Indeed, in this hierarchical society sex roles became hardened through custom and legislation. As a consequence, females could neither hold governmental office nor have any public voice in politics. The few women with economic power—such as those directly involved in manufacturing and trade or the occasional rich widow who kept her husband's business afloat—were exceptions to this general exclusionary rule.

The Feudal Monarchy

Politically, feudalism was leading to a new form of rule. By about 1100 some powerful feudal lords began to expand their holdings into larger and larger kingdoms. As these ambitious rulers subdued weaker lords, they often sealed their victories through marriages with the conquered families. Over the ensuing generations, the heirs extended and consolidated their lands, always trying to win the loyalty of their new subjects.

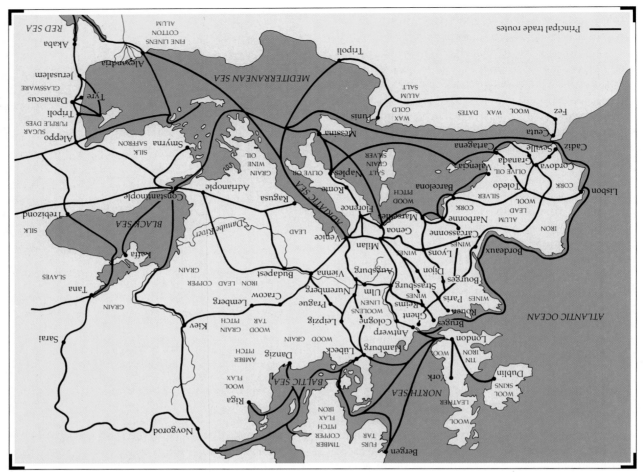

MAP 9.1
Principal Trading Routes and Towns of Europe, 1300

TIME LINE 9.1　The French Feudal Monarchy in the High Middle Ages

1000	1100	1200	1300
		Capetian Line	
	Louis VI (the Fat) 1108–1137	Philip Augustus 1180–1223	Louis IX (St. Louis) 1226–1270	Philip IV (the Fair) 1285–1314

TIME LINE 9.1　The French Feudal Monarchy in the High Middle Ages

Unlike modern states, these feudal monarchies were simply clusters of feudal lands that the monarchs were constantly trying to control. The major domestic problem faced by a feudal monarch was building a centralized rule while keeping his (or in some instances, her) kingdom from disintegrating into a set of separate, warring states. During the High Middle Ages, four feudal monarchies dominated the West: the French monarchy, the English monarchy, the Holy Roman Empire, and the papal monarchy, which in its political aspect closely resembled the three secular monarchies.

The French Monarchy　The origins of modern France stem from the late tenth-century reign of Hugh Capet, who exercised power over a part of the old

FIGURE 9.4　*Harold's Oath of Allegiance*. Panel from the Bayeux Tapestry. Third Quarter of the Eleventh Century. Wool embroidery on linen, height 20". Bayeux, France. Probably stitched by English women and today housed in the Cathedral of Bayeux, this famous embroidery provides an important historic record of the events leading up to the Battle of Hastings. In its emphasis on the disastrous consequences of betrayed loyalties, it clearly reflects the feudal world view. Harold is cast as a villain who breaks his oath of allegiance to William and loses the English crown as a result of this treachery. In the panel, a seated William points to Harold, who is taking an oath while touching two shrines holding relics. The tapestry thus presents a justification for the Norman conquest of England.

Frankish kingdom (see Chapter 8). From him arose the Capetian dynasty, a line of resolute successors each of whom stubbornly continued to call himself King of the Franks. By the early eleventh century, the Capetians, having fought off their rivals, had founded a feudal monarchy in central France, with Paris as its center.

During the twelfth and thirteenth centuries, a series of able monarchs managed to consolidate and expand the Capetian power base and control the great vassals by forming alliances, at different times and in different ways, with the lesser nobles, the middle class, the clergy, and the papacy. The establishment of central authority in France was a slow and difficult process, but by the time of the reign of Philip IV (called "the Fair") in 1285, France was the most powerful feudal kingdom in Europe and the French tradition of royal absolutism was well established (Time Line 9.1).

The English Monarchy　Like the French kings, the English monarchs methodically amassed power at the expense of the feudal landowners, but otherwise the two kingdoms evolved quite differently. The English rulers never controlled their kingdom in the same manner or to the same degree as did their counterparts in Paris. Moreover, because some of the English kings made grievous mistakes, England's feudal barons won pivotal battles against the crown. In addition, judicial reforms and the growth of advisory councils tended to limit, not to expand, the English kings' power.

Three major events determined the course of English history during this period. The first was the French invasion of England. For five centuries England had been ruled by an Anglo-Saxon monarchy. When Edward the Confessor died in 1066 without a clear successor, Duke William, the ruler of the duchy of Normandy in northern France, invaded England to claim the throne. At the battle of Hastings in 1066, William conquered the Anglo-Saxon contender, Harold, and became King of England (Figure 9.4). For the rest of the High Middle Ages England

was ruled by Norman kings and their French succes-sors. During this time the conquerors and the con-quered were blended into one nation and one culture (Time Line 9.2).

The second event occurred in 1215 when the English feudal barons forced King John (1199-1216) to sign the Magna Carta ("great charter"), a docu-ment that limited royal authority by guaranteeing that the king would not do certain things and that the barons had certain financial and governmental control over the crown. The signing of the Magna Carta was primarily a victory for the barons, but in the long run all freemen gained, for the document promised them certain judicial rights, such as trial by jury.

The third event occurred during the reign of John's son, Henry III (1216-1272), when Parliament, today Great Britain's national legislative body, made its first appearance. Faced by renewed hostility from his English barons, Henry agreed to convene the Great Council, an ancient but little-used body. Two repre-sentatives from each county and two from each town were summoned together to talk, and thus Parlia-ment (from the French word *parler*, "to talk") began to advise the king. At first, Parliament was part of the royal government, but, in time, it came to speak for the people against the crown, and England moved further along the road to a limited feudal monarchy.

The Holy Roman Empire   While France and England grew into unified feudal monarchies, the Holy Ro-man Empire struggled and failed to achieve a cen-tralized state. The Holy Roman Empire began as the Ottonian empire in the late tenth century. From the early eleventh to the early twelfth centuries, the em-pire prospered and trade expanded. During these same years, however, a conflict with the papacy arose that would undermine the empire. The conflict con-cerned the European-wide practice of lay invest-ture—the appointment of priests, bishops, and arch-bishops by local lords and nobles, not infrequently

for money. By making such appointments, the secu-lar rulers were able to some extent to control the wealth and influence of the church within their own territories. The conflict was prolonged and compli-cated, but the central issue was this: Are the bishops and archbishops the servants of the pope or of the secular ruler?

The specific issue of lay investiture was settled by the Concordat of Worms in 1122, which allowed the pope to confer spiritual authority on the clergy and the emperor to invest them with land and secular authority. But the rivalry between the Holy Roman rulers and the papacy would not die. Under the em-pire's next dynasty, the Hohenstaufens, a new issue emerged. Were the popes or the emperors to control central Europe? The Hohenstaufens produced two able rulers, Frederick Barbarossa and Frederick II, but neither was able to achieve the German dream of an empire reaching from the Baltic Ocean in the north to Sicily in the south. Under their incompetent suc-cessors, the papacy resumed its sway over Italian pol-itics, and the Holy Roman Emperors ceased to play a major role in European affairs for many years (Time Line 9.3).

The Papal Monarchy   The papacy during the High Middle Ages closely resembled the feudal monarchies in Europe, with the exception that it was guided by the ideal of Christendom—a universal state ruled by the popes under God's law. The church's most pow-erful claim to authority was that only through the clergy—those trained and ordained to administer the sacraments—could a Christian hope to reach ever-lasting life. The church defined and upheld society's moral standards by both teaching and example at the same time that it participated in the politics of the period.

The key to the church's power during the High Middle Ages was a reform movement that had origi-nated in the monastery at Cluny, France, and swept through Europe in the 900s. Prior to this movement

Time Line 9.2   The English Feudal Monarchy in the High Middle Ages

1000	1066	1100	1154	1200	1300
Anglo-Saxon Kingdom	Normans Rule England		Angevin Line		
	William of Normandy 1066-1087		Henry II 1154-1189		Edward I 1272-1307
			Richard I (the Lion-Hearted) 1189-1199		
			John (1199-1216)	Henry III 1216-1272	

Time Line 9.3 The Holy Roman Empire in the High Middle Ages

1000	1039	1100	1125	1152	1200	1250	1273	1300
	Salian Line			Hohenstaufen Line			Habsburg Line	

Salian Line: Henry III 1039–1056 · Henry IV 1056–1106 · Henry V 1106–1125
Hohenstaufen Line: Frederick Barbarossa 1152–1190 · Frederick II 1212–1250
Habsburg Line: Rudolph 1273–1291

the church had been riddled with scandal and corruption. Many clergy were poorly trained—some barely literate—and lived less than exemplary lives. Bishops often acted as if they were the vassals of local feudal lords rather than agents of the church, a reflection of the entrenched nature of lay investiture. The buying and selling of church offices, a practice known as simony, meant that positions often went to the highest bidder. Worst of all, many clergymen expressed blatant disregard for the sacraments.

The monastery at Cluny was founded in 910 by the Benedictine order of monks. Free of feudal obligations and loyal only to the pope, the monastery inaugurated reforms that raised the moral level of the clergy and rid the church of scandal. Little by little, these Cluniacs impressed Europe with their superior spirituality. Encouraged by their success, the Cluny monks quickly established new monasteries and reformed others.

As their reforms spread, the church began to be revivified. Campaigns were undertaken within the church to eliminate corrupt practices and to reimpose celibacy on the clergy. A landmark occurred in 1059 when the College of Cardinals was founded with sole responsibility for electing the popes, thus freeing the papacy from German and Italian politics. By late in the eleventh century the reformed popes had arrived at a point where their political power rivaled that of the feudal monarchs.

Of the great medieval popes, the two most powerful were Gregory VII and Innocent III (Time Line 9.4). Gregory VII (1073–1085) was brought to St. Peter's chair by the Cluniac revival. Once enthroned, he purified the wayward clergy, demanding full obedience to canon law. Although he was less effective in freeing the church from feudalism, he was able to liberate many church offices from local lay influence. Innocent III (1198–1216), the second of these medieval popes, was probably the most powerful pontiff in the history of the church. He excommunicated kings, intervened at will in the secular affairs of England, France, and the Holy Roman Empire, and preached crusades against the Muslims abroad and heretics at home (Figure 9.5). Motivated by the ideal of Christendom, his aim was to unite Europe under the papal banner.

Pope Boniface VIII (1294–1303) unwittingly undid the three centuries' work of his predecessors. By his extravagant papal claims, he made a mockery of his office. In 1302, he issued the papal bull (from the Latin for *bolla*, or seal) known as *Unam sanctam*, a proclamation of papal superiority over all secular rulers. The French crown's answer to this papal challenge was swift: Philip IV (the Fair) sent an army to arrest the pope. In the melee that followed, an unnerved Boniface VIII had to flee for his life and died soon thereafter. This episode revealed that the popes were no match for the feudal kings. Boniface VIII's

Time Line 9.4 The Papal Monarchy in the High Middle Ages

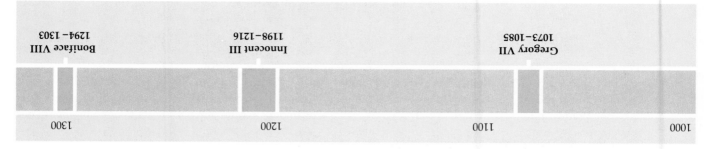

1000	1100	1200	1300

Gregory VII 1073–1085
Innocent III 1198–1216
Boniface VIII 1294–1303

humiliation precipitated a decline in papal prestige from which the papacy did not fully recover until the sixteenth century.

FIGURE 9.5 *Pope Innocent III. Thirteenth Century. This handsome mosaic portrays Innocent III in his crown and vestments—the rich trappings of papal monarchical power. The artist, influenced by the Byzantine style, has depicted him with large staring eyes—a sign of piety. In actuality, however, Innocent III was a realistic and somewhat ruthless ruler when it came to dealing with his adversaries.*

MEDIEVAL CHRISTIANITY AND THE CHURCH

In addition to its political significance, the institution of the church had incalculable influence in the High Middle Ages, bringing Christian values to bear on virtually every facet of medieval life. The church owed its influence not only to the maneuverings of the popes but to the tireless work of the clergy and the powerful effect of the Christian belief system.

By this time in its history the church had evolved an elaborate organization to carry out its work. The pope, as the spiritual leader of Christianity, stood at the head of a strict hierarchy. Supporting him was the papal curia—a staff of administrators, financial experts, secretaries, clerics, and legal advisors. A system of ecclesiastical courts handled the church's judicial functions and interpreted canon law, the church's law code based on the Bible. These courts were technically restricted to cases involving clerical personnel, but in actuality their jurisdiction was broader because of the huge number of people enmeshed in the workings of the church. The church's judicial branch rivaled the feudal courts in jurisdiction, and canon law sometimes challenged the authority of feudal law.

Tithes, taxes, and special collections provided the funds needed by the church to carry on its daily operations as well as to meet its charitable obligations. Given the absence of modern financial methods, the system was relatively efficient, and as long as the church spent the funds wisely, the populace kept up its generous contributions.

Christian Beliefs and Practices

A great part of the immense authority of the church sprang from the belief shared by the overwhelming majority of the medieval population that the church held the keys to the kingdom of heaven and provided the only way to salvation. By attempting to adhere to the Christian moral code and by participating in the rituals and ceremonies prescribed by the church, Christians hoped for redemption and eternal life after death.

These rituals and ceremonies were basically inseparable from the doctrines of the religion. They had been derived from the teachings of Jesus and Paul, clarified by the church fathers, particularly Augustine, and further defined by medieval theologians. Finally, the Fourth Lateran Council of 1215 under Pope Innocent III had officially proclaimed the sacraments as the outward signs of God's grace and the only way to heaven.

As established by the council, the sacraments numbered seven: baptism, confirmation, the Eucharist (Holy Communion), penance, marriage, last rites, and ordination for the priesthood. Baptism, the Eucharist, and penance were deemed of primary importance. In baptism the parents were assured that the infant had been rescued from original sin. In the Eucharist, the central part of the Mass, the church taught that a miracle occurred whereby the priest turned the bread and wine into the body and blood of Jesus. Known as the doctrine of transubstantiation, this miracle gave the priest additional prestige. That

the outer appearance of the bread and wine remained the same while their inner nature changed was explained by medieval philosophers. For the uneducated congregation, however, the Mass and the miracle were simply another sign of the church's spiritual power.

The third of these primary sacraments, penance, evolved into a rather complicated practice. First, sinners confessed their sins individually to a priest; the priest conveyed God's forgiveness for the mortal penalties of sin, so that hell could be avoided; the priest then directed that an earthly punishment—the penance—be carried out in an effort to erase the effects of the sin. Depending on the severity of the sin, penance could range from saying a few prayers to going on a pilgrimage or a crusade. This sacrament was made even more complex by its association with purgatory.

The doctrine of purgatory was formulated by Pope Gregory the Great in the sixth century. Neither hell nor heaven, purgatory was reserved for those souls whose sins were such that they could avoid damnation but whose good deeds were insufficient to merit immediate salvation. All souls in purgatory were ultimately destined for Heaven; penance was a means of reducing time in purgatory. Thus the living could do penance on earth in hope of spending less time in purgatory.

Confession and penance became widespread practices of the eleventh-century church. By 1300 both were integral parts of Christian rituals and beliefs. In political terms, penance, along with the Mass, became effective means for controlling the moral behavior of church members.

Religious Orders and Lay Piety

Crucial to the workings of the church were the clergy, who were the most visible signs of the church's presence in everyday life. The ''secular'' clergy (from *saeculum*, Latin for ''world.'') moved freely in society, and the ''regular'' clergy lived apart from the world in monasteries under a special rule (*regula* in Latin). The monasteries served as refuges from the world, as schools, and as places of study where manuscripts could be copied and traditional learning maintained. They also gave rise to the reform movements that periodically cleansed the church of corruption.

As noted earlier, the Benedictines at Cluny originated the reform movement that helped to establish the moral and political authority of the medieval church. After Cluny other waves of reform followed, the most important of which was represented by the

FIGURE 9.6 *St. Francis of Assisi. Ca. 1274. Attributed to School of Berlinghieri. Tempera on panel, 81 × 51 cm. Accademia, Florence. Many miraculous events were reported to have occurred in the life of Francis, the founder of the Franciscan order. In this painting, completed some fifty years after the saint's death, he is portrayed as receiving the stigmata, or the wounds of Christ—a sign to Christians that Francis was a man marked in a special way by God.*

founding of the Cistercian order in the twelfth century. Bernard of Clairvaux, a mystic, a saint, and one of the most forceful personalities of the period, personally founded over 160 Cistercian abbeys. Unlike the moderate Benedictines, the Cistercians observed a severe rule, living usually in isolated monasteries where the brothers worked with the local peasants. The Cistercians also simplified their worship services, stripping them of elaborate ceremonies.

For women, the religious impulse found an outlet in convents and nunneries. Here, women could devote themselves to Christ and follow ascetic lives filled with prayer, contemplation, and service. Con-

vents had existed since the time of Charlemagne, although seldom with the large endowments monasteries enjoyed or with as much influence in local affairs.

Another type of religious order appeared in the thirteenth century with the rise of two major mendicant, or begging, orders, the Franciscans and the Dominicans. These new churchmen, called *friars*, were originally dedicated to working among the urban poor, but their mission changed, and by 1250 they were dominating higher education. For example, Thomas Aquinas, the age's leading scholar, was a Dominican friar. In the fourteenth century the two orders became notorious for their association with the Inquisition, the church court charged with stamping out heresy.

While both orders of friars made important contributions, the Franciscans had a greater impact on medieval society, largely because of the gentle nature of its sainted founder, Francis (1182–1226). Many people still find Francis's piety, selflessness, and legendary humility the personification of a sublime Christian (Figure 9.6).

As monastic reform slowed in the late twelfth century, a wave of lay piety swelled up from the lower social ranks. These unorthodox movements, usually rooted in social and economic causes, quickly ran into trouble with the church. At first, the clergy tried to direct this new populist energy along established lines, but church officials condemned the new groups as heretics when they appeared to be growing uncontrollable.

The most powerful of these heretical sects was the Albigensian, which was centered at Albi in southern France. The Albigensians were also known as the Cathari, from the Greek word for ''pure.'' Their unorthodox beliefs were derived partly from Zoroastrianism, the source of their concept of a universal struggle between a good God and an evil deity, and partly from Manicheism, the source of their notion that the flesh is evil. The Albigensians stressed that Jesus was divine and not human, that the wealth of the church was a sign of its depravity, and that the goal of Christian living was to achieve the status of Cathari, or perfection.

These unorthodox beliefs spread rapidly across much of southern France, permeating the church and the secular society at all levels. In 1214 Pope Innocent III called for the destruction of the hated beliefs. His message found eager hearers among the feudal nobles who were greedy for the heretics' lands. The repression of the Albigensians was carried out with incredible ferocity and cruelty. Many Cathari were slaughtered and their property confiscated, while others were tried by the Inquisition and burned at the stake. Actions like these reflected the less benign face of the medieval church and gave one more measure of its immense power.

THE AGE OF SYNTHESIS: EQUILIBRIUM BETWEEN THE SPIRITUAL AND THE SECULAR

Between 1000 and 1300 Christian values permeated all aspects of European cultural life. The Christian faith was a unifying agent that brought together and reconciled the opposing realms of the spiritual and the secular, the immaterial and the material—as symbolized in many cities and towns by the soaring spires of the *cathedral* (Figure 9.7). Medieval culture drew from the arts and humanities of the Classical world, the heritage of the various European peoples, and, to a lesser extent, the traditions of Byzantium and Islam. Because of these diverse influences, the culture of the High Middle Ages was by no means uniform. What many writers, thinkers, and artists shared was a set of common concerns and interests, most notably the quest for forms that could transcend and bring together the contradictions of the age.

A historical watershed occurred in the mid-twelfth century that was reflected in architecture, sculpture, music, learning, and literature. Before 1150, Western culture tended to express the rugged virtues of the feudal castle and the cloistered monastery; the militant warrior and the ascetic monk were the social ideals; and women were treated as chattel, or property. After 1150, the urban values of the new towns became paramount along with a more courtly attitude toward women. The church indirectly encouraged this trend with the rise of the cult of the Virgin Mary; Mary's status became so great that she was revered almost as much as Christ.

Learning and Theology

From about 1000 onward, scholars revived the school system that had flourished briefly under Charlemagne in the Early Middle Ages. These few monastic schools—along with many new cathedral schools—appealed to an age that was hungry for learning and set Europe's intellectual tone until about 1200. During these two centuries, the only serious rival to the schools were the handful of independent scholars who drew crowds of students to their lectures in Paris and elsewhere. By 1200, new educational institutions arose—the universities—that soon surpassed the

monastic and cathedral schools and forced the independent masters out of business. Since then, the universities have dominated intellectual life in the West.

Cathedral Schools and the Development of Scholasticism During the twelfth century the new cathedral schools reached the height of their power, with Chartres and Paris leading the way. Schooling, with rare exceptions, was the exclusive province of men who were preparing for careers in either the church or the dynastic states. For the next three hundred years the curriculum stayed the same as that codified by Boethius in the sixth century: the trivium (grammar, logic, and rhetoric) and the quadrivium (arithmetic, astronomy, geometry, and music)—the seven liberal arts—which, in turn, were based on the works of the Classical authors and those of the early church fathers. Teachers and pupils communicated in Latin, and students read the Christian works in the original Latin. In contrast, Classical writings were known only from misleading Latin summaries until they were replaced in the twelfth century with more accurate Latin versions made from Arabic translations.

The introduction of the new versions of the Classical texts, notably those of Aristotle, caused a revolution in education and elevated the Greek thinker to the status of an authority whose word could not be questioned. By 1300 Aristotle's writings virtually monopolized the curriculum at every educational level.

The revival of Aristotle contributed to the development of a body of thought known as *scholasticism.* In general, the aim of a scholastic thinker was to bring Aristotle's thought into harmony with the Christian faith. Scholasticism was also a system of reasoning that had been perfected in oral debates in the schools. In the scholastic method, a scholar divided each problem into three parts. First, a question was set forth for intellectual analysis; next, a discussion thoroughly summarized the arguments for and against the question, usually citing the Bible, the church fathers, Aristotle, and other ancient authors; finally, a solution was offered, reinforced with support from religious and secular sources.

The scholastic method was not meant to discover new knowledge; rather, it used deductive logic to clarify existing issues and to explore the intellectual ramifications of a topic. This aspect of scholasticism, which tended to uphold rather than to question religious beliefs, was discarded in favor of an inductive, mathematically based style of reasoning in the seventeenth century.

Peter Abelard The primacy of the cathedral schools of Chartres and Paris in the twelfth century was challenged by a few independent masters who pitted their own intellects against the authority of the faculty of these institutions. Of this daring breed of scholars, Peter Abelard (in French, Pierre Abelard)

FIGURE 9.7 Chartres Cathedral. Aerial View. Ca. 1220–1225. Chartres, France. *Looming over the town and dominating the countryside for miles around, the Gothic cathedral symbolized the preeminent role of the Christian Church in medieval life. No other building could soar past its spires, either literally or figuratively. People worshiped inside the building right up to its walls, and conducted their business affairs within the shadows of its towers. Thus, the cathedral also symbolized the integration of the secular and the sacred in medieval life.*

(1079–1142) was the most brilliant and controversial. More important, he was one of the first medieval thinkers to proclaim a clear distinction between reason and faith. Unhindered by his vows as a monk, Abelard attended the lectures of William of Champeaux (about 1070–1121), the most revered teacher in the cathedral school of Paris. Dissatisfied with what he was hearing, Abelard began his own lecture series before William's course was completed. Overnight, Abelard became the sensation of Paris and his words found eager listeners. A master logician, Abelard demolished William's arguments and drove his rival into a monastery.

What divided Abelard and William of Champeaux was the problem of universals, the supreme intellectual issue between 1050 and 1150. This controversy revolved around the question of whether or not universal terms, or generalities, like "human being" and "church" truly existed. At stake in this dispute between the two schools of thought, known as *Realism* and *Nominalism*, were basic Christian ideas, such as whether Jesus' sacrifice had removed the stain of original sin from each individual. The Realists, following Plato, reasoned that universal terms did exist and were more "real" than separate entities. Hence, "humanity," for example, was constantly present in each and every individual. In opposition, the Nominalists denied the existence of universals and claimed that only separate things and individual persons were actual. Hence, "church" and "human being" existed only in particular instances.

In these debates, Abelard showed that William's extreme Realism denied human individuality and was thus inconsistent with church teachings. For his part, Abelard taught a moderate Realism that held that the universals existed, but only as mental words, and hence could be used as an intellectual convenience. Later in the century, when new translations of Aristotle became available, thinkers discovered that Abelard and the Greek genius agreed on universals, a discovery that further enhanced Abelard's fame. In the next century, Abelard's moderate Realism was adopted by Thomas Aquinas, the greatest mind of the High Middle Ages.

The Rise of the Universities   After 1100 a period of cultural ferment erupted that a modern historian has called the twelfth-century renaissance. Even though this term is exaggerated, the century spawned some of the finest achievements of medieval times, including the founding of the universities. By 1200, conditions were ripe for the rise of universities at Bologna, at Paris, and at Oxford, the first Western schools of higher education since the sixth century. Unlike the ancient universities in Athens and Alexandria, these

medieval institutions were organized into self-governing corporations with charters. A century later, similar centers of learning were springing up elsewhere in Italy, France, and England, as well as in Spain, Portugal, and Germany. The University of Paris was the most celebrated institution of advanced learning during the High Middle Ages. Divided into faculties by specialization, it awarded degrees in both civil law and canon law, medicine, theology, and the liberal arts. The liberal arts degree was basically devoted to mastering the new translations of Aristotle. Other universities taught a similar curriculum, but their faculties lacked the international renown of the Parisian professors.

Intellectual Controversy and Thomas Aquinas   More and more of Aristotle's works became available in the late twelfth and early thirteenth centuries. Between 1150 and 1200 a few hardy Christian scholars traveled to centers of learning off the main track, such as Muslim Sicily and Toledo, Spain—freed from Muslim control only in 1085—to meet Islamic and Jewish scholars and study Aristotle's writings. There they learned Arabic and translated the Greek and Arabic philosophical and scientific works into Latin, the form in which they entered the mainstream of European medieval thought.

At the University of Paris, the introduction of these improved and more complete versions split the intellectual community into two camps. On one side was the theological faculty, who welcomed the Arabic writings but wanted to reconcile them to Christian thinking. Arrayed against them were the members of the arts faculty, who advocated that reason be fully divorced from faith, or, in other words, that philosophy be separated from theology. The leaders of the arts faculty were called Latin Averroists because they claimed inspiration from the Arabic philosopher Ibn Rushd, known in the West as Averroes.

Faced with the skeptical Latin Averroists, the Parisian theologians devised two ways to relate the new learning to orthodox beliefs. The more traditional view was set forth by Bonaventure (1221–1274), who was later made a saint. Denying that knowledge was possible apart from God's grace, Bonaventure, following Augustine's mode of reasoning, argued that truth had to begin in the supernatural world and thus could not arise in the senses, as Aristotle had argued. A new and brilliant theological view, and the one that carried the day, was set forth by Thomas Aquinas (1226–1274), a Dominican friar who taught at Paris from 1252 to 1259 and again from 1269 to 1272. Within a generation of his death, he was made a saint, and six hundred years later, in 1874, the papacy declared his thought to be the official basis of Roman Catholic

two centuries. Its supreme expression was the can-**zone**, or love poem, the ancestor of all later Western love poetry. At the educated feudal courts of southern France, professional minstrels sang the songs before the assembled court; the poems' composers—called *troubadors*—were often local nobles. Addressed to court ladies whose identities were thinly disguised in the poem, these troubador songs made devotion to a highborn woman the passionate ideal of the chivalrous knight. In the mature Provençal lyrics, adulterous passion was the central theme, and women were idolized and made the masters over men. Where previously adoration had been reserved for God, the troubadour lyrics now celebrated the worship of women.

As the influence of Provençal poetry spread, the status of women in Western literature was revolutionized, a development paralleled in the church, where the cult of the Virgin Mary was beginning to flourish. For the moment, most real-life medieval women were unaffected by these literary and religious changes; their happiness depended on submitting to the limited roles that the masculine society allowed them to fill. After 1400, though, these cultural changes encouraged upper-class women to play a more prominent role in society, as hostesses and as arbiters of social decorum.

After 1150 courtly *romances* quickly replaced the feudal *chansons de geste* in popularity. The romances were long narratives of the chivalric and sentimental adventures of knights and ladies. The name *romance* arose from the mistaken belief that the medieval authors were imitating a Roman literary form. Their subjects derived from stories of ancient Troy and Celtic legends from the British Isles, the most enduring of which proved to be the Celtic stories of King Arthur and his knights of the Round Table.

The first poet to make Arthur and his court subject was Chrétien de Troyes, whose versions set the standard for later romances. Chrétien (about 1148–about 1190) wrote his romances for the feudal courts of northern France. His treatment of the adulterous love of the knight Lancelot and Arthur's queen, Guinevere, is characteristic of the way romances combined aristocratic, courtly, and religious themes. In this version, Lancelot rescues Queen Guinevere after experiencing many adventures and personal humiliations for her sake; this humbling of Lancelot is necessary to teach him to love Guinevere with unquestioning obedience.

A curiosity for modern readers is that Chrétien identifies Lancelot with Christ, so that many episodes echo scenes of Jesus' suffering and death. While the work avoids sacrilege, the net effect is unsettling in its mixing of the sacred with the profane. Chrétien describes Lancelot and Guinevere's passion without judging their behavior. Such moral neutrality was unacceptable to other Christian writers, who believed adultery to be a deadly sin. In an English prose version of this tale—Thomas Malory's *Le Morte d'Arthur*, published in 1485—the lovers were blamed for the collapse of Arthur's court. Perhaps because today's world tends to agree with Malory's more judgmental view, his story of Lancelot is the one better known by modern readers.

Dante   Vernacular writing appeared late in Italy; not until the thirteenth century did Italian poetry begin to emerge. But, despite its later start, Italy brought forth by 1300 the greatest literary figure of the High Middle Ages, Dante Alighieri (1265–1321). A native of Florence in the province of Tuscany, Dante was the first of a proud tradition that soon made the Tuscan dialect the standard literary speech of Italy.

Born into a minor aristocratic family, Dante was given an excellent education with a thorough grounding in both Greco-Roman and Christian classics. Attracted to the values of ancient Rome, he combined a career in public office with the life of an intellectual—a tradition of civic duty inherited from the ancient Roman republic. When Dante's political allies fell from office in 1301, he was exiled from Florence for the rest of his life. During these years, when he suffered from poverty and wandered about Italy, he composed the *Commedia*, or *Comedy*, which stands as the culmination of the literature of the Middle Ages.

The *Comedy*'s sublime qualities were immediately recognized, and soon its admirers attached the epithet "divine" to Dante's masterpiece.

Divided into three book-length parts, the *Divine Comedy* narrates Dante's fictional travels through three realms of the Christian afterlife. Led first by the ghost of Vergil, the ancient Roman poet, Dante descends into hell, where he hears from the damned the nature of their various crimes against God and the moral law. Vergil next leads Dante into purgatory, where the lesser sinners expiate their guilt while awaiting the joys of heaven. At a fixed spot in purgatory, Vergil is forced to relinquish his role to Beatrice, a young Florentine woman and Dante's symbol of the eternal female. With Beatrice's guidance, Dante enters paradise and even has a vision of the almighty God.

The majestic complexity of Dante's monumental poem, however, can scarcely be conveyed by this simple synopsis. Written as an allegory, the *Divine Comedy* was meant to be understood on several levels at the same time. Read literally, the poem bears witness to the author's personal fears as a moral sinner yet affirms his hope for eternal salvation. Read alle-

gorically, the poem represents a comprehensive synthesis of the opposing tendencies that characterized medieval culture, such as balancing the Classical with the Christian, Aristotle with Aquinas, the ancient with the new, the proud with the humble, and the secular with the spiritual.

Of the great cultural symbols that abound in the *Divine Comedy*, the richest in meaning are the central figures of Vergil and Beatrice, who represent human reason and divine revelation, respectively. In the poem Vergil is made inferior to Beatrice, thus revealing Dante's acceptance of a basic idea of Thomas Aquinas—reason can lead only to awareness of sin; revelation is necessary to reach God's ultimate truth. Besides this fundamental Christian belief, the two figures convey other meanings. Vergil stands for Classical civilization and the secular literary life; Beatrice (Italian for "blessing") symbolizes spiritualized love and Christianized culture. By turning Beatrice into an image of God's grace, Dante revealed that the High Middle Ages were open to new symbols of Christian truth. (By the time of the Catholic Counter-Reformation in the sixteenth century, however, Dante's image was considered blasphemous and was censured by religious critics.)

Dante's spiritual odyssey is set during the season of Easter. The poet's journey through hell coincided with Jesus' descent into hell on Good Friday, and Dante's ascent up the Mount of Purgatory happens at Eastern dawn—the time of Jesus' resurrection. Thus Dante's allegory has the religious aim of forcing his readers to meditate on the fate of their own immortal souls.

Dante's vision of the afterlife underscored his belief that humans have free will. Predestination had no place in his system, as his picture of hell shows. With one exception, all of the damned earned their fate by their deeds on earth. Excepted were the people consigned to Limbo—the pious pagans—who lived prior to Jesus and thus were denied his message of hope. Moreover, those in Limbo, such as Aristotle and Plato, were not subjected to any punishment other than being removed from God's presence.

The intricate structure of Dante's massive poem owes much to numerology, a pseudoscience of numbers that absorbed the medieval mind. The numbers three and nine, for example, occur prominently in the *Divine Comedy*. Three is a common symbol of the Christian Trinity (the union of the Father, the Son, and the Holy Ghost in one God), and the poem is written in a three-line verse form called **terza rima** (an interlocking rhyme scheme in three-line stanzas, as *aba, bcb, cdc,* and so on, ending in a rhyming couplet), which was Dante's invention. The other number, nine, symbolizes the Trinity squared. More

important, Dante identified the number nine with the dead Beatrice, whose soul lived on in the ninth heaven, the one nearest to God. He also divides hell, purgatory, and paradise into nine sections each.

Despite its allegorical and theological features, the *Divine Comedy* is a deeply personal poem. Dante rewards and punishes his Florentine friends and foes by the location that he assigns each in the afterlife. He also reveals his private feelings as he enters into discussions with various saints and sinners along the way. Beyond his desire for salvation, his most cherished idea is to bring about a harmony between the church and the secular state on earth.

Architecture and Art

Just as scholars and writers devoted their efforts to exploring and elaborating on religious concerns and Christian values, artists, artisans, and architects channeled their talents into glorifying the Christian house of worship. Because the dominating physical presence of the church made it a ubiquitous symbol in both the countryside and the towns, architecture ranked higher than the other arts in medieval life. Indeed, the arts lacked an independent status, for they were regarded as mere auxiliary sources of church decoration—statues, stained glass windows, and wall paintings, most of which portrayed saints and biblical heroes. In this respect, these art forms conformed to the church's teachings that the purpose of art was to represent Christian truth.

Even though the church dominated art and architecture, it did not prevent architects and artists from experimenting. In about 1000 an international style emerged called the **Romanesque** that was the first in a succession of uniform styles to sweep over Europe. The Romanesque, carried along by the monastic revival, was favored until about 1200. But by 1150, the *Gothic* style was already being born in Paris; it was to become the reigning style of the towns for the remainder of the Middle Ages, succumbing finally to Renaissance fashion in about 1500.

Romanesque Churches and Related Arts The Romanesque earned its name from the ancient Roman buildings that had characterized the churches of the Early Middle Ages. These Roman features, along with Christian influences, had flourished briefly in some churches built during the Carolingian era (see Figure 8.21). The Romanesque church architects revived such basic Roman elements as the basilica plan and employed rounded arches, vaulted ceilings, and columns for both support and decoration (see Figure 7.10). They also perpetuated early Christian ideas by

Pointing each basilica toward Jerusalem in the east and curving the building's eastern end into an apse to house the altar. A transept, or crossing arm, was added at the church's eastern end in order to convert the floor plan into a cruciform shape to symbolize the cross (Figure 9.9). Other Christian beliefs dictated such practices as having three doorways in the western facade, which symbolized the Trinity, and building the baptistery apart from the church to keep the unbaptized out of sacred space.

In its origins, the Romanesque is associated with the Cluniac monastic order because the headquarters church at Cluny in eastern France was built in this style. The extravagant success of the Cluniac movement in the eleventh century led to the spread of the Romanesque style over the map of Europe. In appearance, the Romanesque style reflected both the needs of the monastic communities and the physical demands created by the unsettled conditions of the day. These churches were sturdy and earth hugging, with massive walls and very few windows. They looked like the spiritual fortresses that they indeed were (Figure 9.10).

Many Romanesque churches were pilgrimage churches—destinations for pilgrims traveling vast distances to see and venerate holy relics, very often

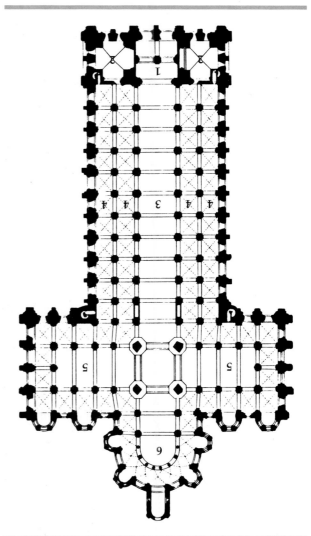

FIGURE 9.9 Floor Plan of a Typical Romanesque Church. *This floor plan identifies the characteristic features of a Romanesque church with its cruciform floor plan: (1) narthex, (2) towers, (3) nave, (4) side aisles, (5) transept, and (6) apse.*

FIGURE 9.10 Church of Sainte-Marie-Madeleine, Vézelay, France. View from the West. Ca. 1089–1206. *This church conveys the fortress-like quality of life that was typical of Romanesque architecture and reflects the harsh style of life of twelfth-century Europe. The church's facade is massive, pierced only by doorways at ground level and arched openings above. Highlighting its impressively stark exterior is a simple plan of decoration consisting largely of sculptures over the three portals and on pillars and in niches in the central upper section.*

the supposed bones of saints. The foremost pilgrimage churches had to be built to accommodate the hordes of religious tourists, and this was usually done by building ambulatories, semicircular or polygonal aisles behind the apse.

A celebrated pilgrimage church in the Romanesque style is Sainte-Marie-Madeleine in Vézelay, France. Attached to a Cluniac convent, this church attracted penitents eager to view the bones of Mary Magdalene. Vézelay's builders followed a basilica design with a cruciform floor plan. Inside, the most striking feature is the nearly 200-foot-long nave, which could hold a large number of pilgrims as well as allow religious processions (Figure 9.11). Typical of the Romanesque style, the nave is divided into sections called *bays*. Each bay is framed by a pair of rounded arches constructed from blocks of local pink and grey stones. These colors alternate in the overhead arches and create a dazzling effect for which this

church is famous. The ceiling of each bay is a groin vault—a Roman building technique. The support system for the tall nave walls was also taken from Roman architecture—a series of arches resting on clusters of columns.

Vézelay's Romanesque builders used sculpture to provide "sermons in stone" for illiterate visitors. Symbolic rather than idealistic or realistic, the Romanesque figures were designed to convey religious meanings. For example, instead of copying the ancient Greco-Roman columns, the artisans created their own style of decorated column. The capitals, or tops, of the interior columns are sculpted with religious scenes and motifs, such as one that shows an angel subduing a demon (Figure 9.12). Both figures have wings, suggesting that the demon is a fallen angel. Because people in the High Middle Ages feared devils of all kinds, the art often depicted such triumphs of divine, or magical, power over evil.

FIGURE 9.11 View of Nave, Looking East. Church of Sainte-Marie-Madeleine, Vézelay, France. Ca. 1089–1206. *Vézelay's nave was made unusually long so that religious pilgrims might make solemn processions along its length. A reliquary, or an area for displaying holy relics, was later set aside in the choir. Within the choir, the ambulatory allowed masses of pilgrims to view the relics at one time.*

Other carvings in this church, however, show a more mature art. The stone *tympanum* over the central doorway in the *narthex* depicts Jesus' ascension into heaven and a symbolic rendering of his mission to the Apostles (Figure 9.13). Jesus' lively draperies and pose reflected the dynamism and stress on mystical truth that were typical of Romanesque art. Each Apostle, gesticulating wildly, holds a gospel, showing that he accepts his missionary role. On the lintel below are depicted various real and legendary peoples, the recipients of the Christian message. Above the semicircular panel in framed units are portrayed biblical events, zodiac signs, and peasant scenes—a visual symbol of the integration of sacred and profane learning.

Beside church building and church decoration, the Romanesque style was also used in manuscript illumination. Originated in late Rome and developed in the Early Middle Ages, this art remained a cloistered activity in this age of monasticism (see Chapter 8). Perhaps only cloistered painters had the leisure to follow this painstaking skill. During the High Middle Ages, new local styles arose inspired by regional tastes and by a knowledge of Byzantine painting brought from the East by Crusaders. The English monks probably developed the finest of these local styles.

The Bury Bible, painted at Bury St. Edmunds monastery, reflects an English taste that is calmer and less exuberant than continental styles. Two panels from the Bury manuscript, set off by a border of highly colored foliage, show an episode in Moses' life (Figure 9.14). Borrowings from Byzantine art may be detected in the elongated figures, the large eyes, the flowing hair, and the hanging draperies. The naturalness of these scenes presented a vivid contrast with the spirited agitation of French Romanesque art.

Gothic Churches and Related Arts The word *Gothic* was invented by Renaissance scholars who preferred Greco-Roman styles. They despised medieval architecture, labelling it *Goth-ic*—meaning a barbaric creation of the Goths, or the Germanic peoples. Modern research, however, has shown that this Renaissance view is false. In fact, the Gothic grew out of the Romanesque and was not a German art. Nevertheless,

FIGURE 9.12 *Angel Subduing Demon.* Decorated Column Capital. Church of Sainte-Marie-Madeleine, Vézelay, France. Ca. 1089–1206. *The Vézelay capitals survive in near-immaculate condition. Late medieval moralists considered their vivacity and gaiety inappropriate in God's house, and the offending sculptures were plastered over. When they were uncovered during a nineteenth-century restoration of the church's interior, the capitals were revealed in their charming originality.*

FIGURE 9.13 *The Ascension and the Mission to the Apostles.* Tympanum over Central Portal. Church of Sainte-Marie-Madeleine. Vézelay, France. 1125–1135. *The subject of this tympanum, Jesus' missionary charge to his disciples, was especially appropriate for Sainte-Marie-Madeleine. Two crusades against the Muslims who occupied the holy places in the Middle East were preached and begun from this church.*

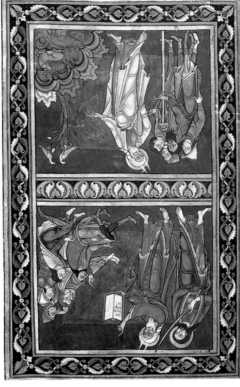

FIGURE 9.14 *Moses Expounding the Law of the Unclean Beasts.*
The Bury Bible. 1130–1140. Bury St. Edmunds, England.
Master and Fellows of Corpus Christi College, Cambridge.
These panels depict Moses delivering the dietary laws to the ancient Hebrews. The responses of his audience reveal the sure hand of the artist, known only as Master Hugo. For example, in the upper panel one figure pulls at his nose, while a nearby companion looks skeptical. Moses' head is depicted with horns, which reflected a biblical mistranslation of the term for the radiance that surrounded him after receiving God's law.

the term *Gothic* is still used today, although its negative connotation has long since been discarded.

Gothic architecture sprang from the religious revival of the twelfth century, when the clergy wanted to bring God's presence more tangibly to their urban congregations. As a result, clerics began to demand taller churches with more windows than were available in the relatively dark Romanesque churches. To the medieval mind, height and light were symbols of the divine. Another impetus behind the Gothic was the rise of the middle class, who wanted churches that reflected their growing economic power. Thus

spiritual and economic forces were united in pushing architects to seek a new kind of architecture.

Two problems with the Romanesque stood in the way: The groin vaults were so heavy that the nearly windowless walls had to be extremely thick in order to support their great weight, and the rounded arches limited the building's height to less than 100 feet.

During the early twelfth century, builders constantly sought solutions to these problems.

Eventually, in about 1145, the Gothic style was created by Suger (about 1081–1151), the Abbot of the royal Abbey Church of St. Denis, near Paris, and an advisor to the French kings. Suger's approach to architecture grew out of his religious faith, as in his

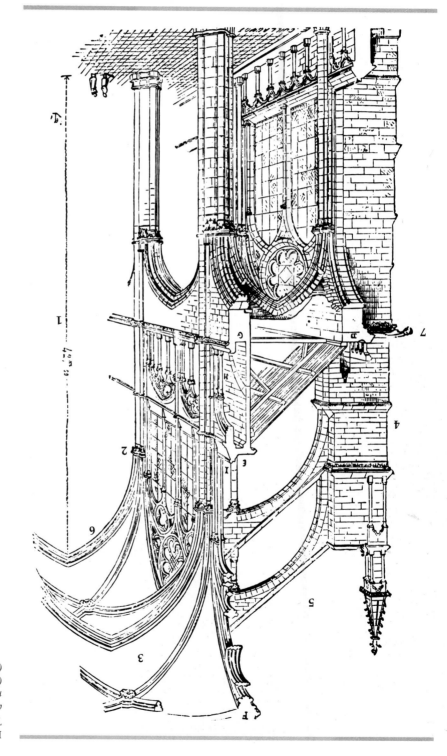

FIGURE 9.15 Principal Features of a Typical Gothic Church. In this schematic drawing, the features are numbered from the nave outward: (1) nave arcade, (2) clerestory, (3) vault, (4) buttress, (5) flying buttress, (6) pointed arch, and (7) gargoyle.

words, "Through the beauty of material things we come to understand God." The brilliant innovation employed by Suger and the architects and artisans he hired was to change the vaulting problem from one of weight to one of stress. First, they replaced the groin vault with a *ribbed vault*; this step allowed lighter materials to be placed between the stone ribs, thus reducing the weight. Next, they abandoned the rounded arch in favor of the Muslim pointed arch. The combination of pointed arch and ribbed vault permitted an increase in the building's height as well as a rechanneling of the ceiling's stresses downward and outward to huge *piers* internally and, in later buildings, to *flying buttresses* externally that formed a bridge between the upper nave walls and the nearby tall pillars (Figure 9.15). With the support skeleton transferred to the building's exterior, the builders could easily insert stained glass windows into the non-weight-bearing walls.

The glory of the Gothic church—the *choir*—was all that remained to be built. The plan and inspiration for the choir (the part of the church where the service was sung) were the pilgrimage churches, like Vézelay, that had enlarged their apses to accommodate religious tourists. In Suger's skillful hands, the east end of St. Denis was now elaborated into an oval-shaped area—the choir—ringed with several small chapels (Figure 9.16). At the heart of the choir was the apse, now arcaded; a spacious ambulatory area divided the apse from the chapels (Figure 9.17).

St. Denis gave only a foretaste of the triumphant art that was called the Gothic. Between 1145 and 1500 the Gothic style presented an overwhelming image of God's majesty and the power of the church. A Gothic exterior carried the eye heavenward by impressive vertical spires. A Gothic interior surrounded the daytime worshiper with colored, celestial light; the soaring nave ceiling, sometimes rising to more than 150 feet, was calculated to stir the soul. In its total physicality the Gothic church stood as a towering symbol of the medieval obsession with the divine.

During the High Middle Ages, the Gothic style went through two stages, the Early and the High. The Early Gothic style lasted until 1194 and was best represented by Notre Dame cathedral in Paris. The High Gothic style flourished until 1300 and reached perfection in the cathedral at Amiens, France.

EARLY GOTHIC STYLE, 1145–1194   The cathedral of Notre Dame ("Our Lady," the Virgin Mary) in Paris popularized the Early Gothic style, making it a fashion for other cities and towns. Begun in 1163, the cathedral was the most monumental work erected in the West to this time. Its floor plan was cruciform, but

FIGURE 9.16   Ambulatory. Church of St. Denis, Paris. Ca. 1145. *This interior view of the choir of St. Denis shows a portion of the ambulatory, the passageway that allowed pilgrims to walk around and view the chapels in the apse. The evenly spaced support columns and the pointed arches enabled the builders to construct this flowing, curved space. The ribbed arches in the ceiling are also central to the Gothic skeletal construction.*

FIGURE 9.17   Floor Plan, Ambulatory. Church of St. Denis, Paris. Ca. 1145. *This floor plan, based on a similar design used in the pilgrimage churches, became the basis for the reordering of interior space in the Gothic choirs. The features include (1) choir, (2) apse, (3) ambulatory, (4) transept, and (5) chapel.*

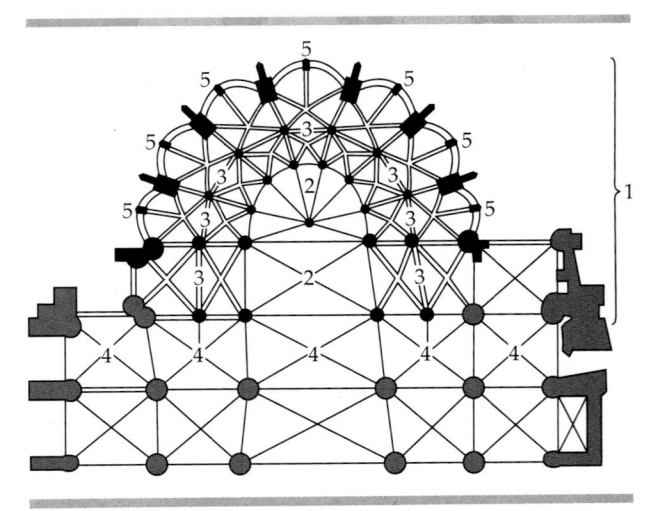

FIGURE 9.19 Western Facade, Notre Dame, Paris. 1220–1250. *In the gallery above the western portals are twenty-eight images of the kings of Judah, including David and Solomon. These sculptures, which are typical of Gothic churches, are more than decorations: They are reminders that Mary and Jesus were descended from royalty. In the medieval mind, this religious idea was meant to buttress the monarchical style of government.*

the length of the transept barely exceeded the width of the aisle walls (Figure 9.18).

Part of Notre Dame's beauty stems from the rational principles applied by the builders, notably the ideal of harmony, best expressed in the integration of sculpture and decorative details with building units. For instance, the west facade is divided into three equal horizontal bands: the three doorways, the *rose window* and *blind arcades*, and the two towers (Figure 9.19). Within each subdivision of this facade, figurative sculpture or architectural details play a harmonizing role, from the rows of saints flanking each of the portals to the *gargoyles*, or grotesque demons, peering down from the towers.

Inside Notre Dame, the spectacular nave reveals the awe-inspiring effects of Early Gothic art at its best (Figure 9.20). The strong vertical lines and the airy atmosphere represent the essence of this taste. With its ribbed vaults and pointed arches, the nave rises to a height of 110 feet from the pavement to the ceiling. Like the harmonious west facade, the nave is

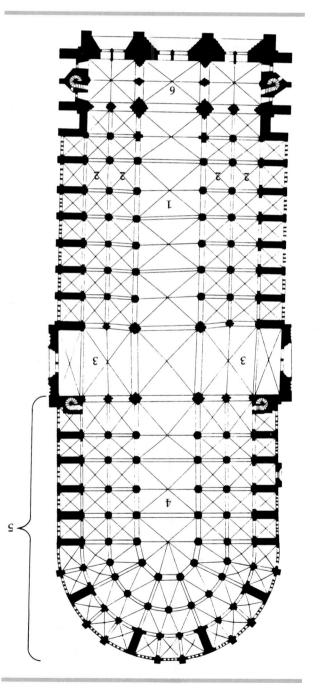

FIGURE 9.18 Floor Plan of Notre Dame, Paris. 1163–ca. 1250. *This drawing shows the principal features of Notre Dame Cathedral: (1) nave, (2) aisle, (3) transept, (4) apse, (5) choir, and (6) narthex.*

divided into three equal tiers: the nave and double aisles, the open spectator *gallery* above the aisles, and, at the top, the clerestory, as the window area is called.

Notre Dame reveals that the choir was coming to dominate the entire Early Gothic church. Notre Dame's choir is almost as long as the nave, so that the transept virtually divides the church into two halves. At first, the choir's walls had no special external supports, but as cracks began to appear in the choir's walls during the thirteenth century, flying buttresses were added to ensure greater stability—a feature that would later characterize High Gothic churches (Figure 9.21).

The down-to-earth Gothic sculptures that decorate Notre Dame differ from the exuberant Romanesque style. The Romanesque's animated images of Jesus have given way to the Gothic's more sober figures. In addition, the Gothic figures are modeled in three dimensions, and their draperies fall in natural folds. At the same time, the rise of the cult of the Virgin

FIGURE 9.21 Choir, Notre Dame, Paris. View from the East. 1163–1182. *Notre Dame's choir was originally built without chapels and flying buttresses—a sign of its Early Gothic origins. Paris's greatest church caught up with the High Gothic style in the fourteenth century, when these architectural features were added.*

FIGURE 9.20 Nave, Notre Dame, Paris. View from the Height of the Western Rose Window. 1180–1250. *The nave is clearly not aligned properly. The choir bends perceptibly to the north, which probably reflected the different building times for various parts of the cathedral. The transept and the choir were finished first, after which the nave and the double aisles were added. The western façade was completed last.*

FIGURE 9.22 *The Last Judgment.* Central Portal, West Facade. Notre Dame, Paris. Ca. 1210. *This tympanum represents Jesus enthroned and presiding over the Last Judgment. Surrounding him are the Apostles, the prophets, the church fathers, and the saints — arranged in descending order of their importance in relation to Jesus himself. Like all of the sculptures of Notre Dame's first story, the entire scene was gilded with gold paint until the mid–fifteenth century.*

esque art.

Despite these visual differences, however, the Gothic Dame" itself testifies to the appeal of the Virgin cult. as of female saints (Figure 9.22). The name "Notre meant an increased number of images of Mary as well remained true to the symbolic purposes of Roman-

frame.

glass, encased in iron settings, were then placed inside the stone *removed sections of the existing wall. The bits of predominantly blue* *43 feet in diameter, the window was installed after workers first* *restoration genius Viollet-le-Duc recreated the other two. Measuring* *of Notre Dame's three rose windows. The nineteenth-century* *Ca. 1255. This masterwork by Jehan de Chelles is the only original*

FIGURE 9.23 North Rose Window, Notre Dame, Paris.

Before Notre Dame was finished, its architects began to move in new directions, refining the traditional features into a new style, called **Rayonnant**, or Radiant. In the *Rayonnant* style, the solid walls gave way to sheets of stained glass framed by elegant *trac-eries,* or rich ornamentation, of stone. This radiant effect was especially evident in the north transept facade, which was rebuilt in this new style (Figure 9.23). With the addition of the transept's imposing rose window, organized so as to suggest the rays of the sun, the cathedral's interior was bathed in constantly shifting colors, giving it a mystical atmosphere.

FIGURE 9.24 Amiens Cathedral. Aerial View. Amiens, France. Ca. 1220–1270. *This aerial photograph shows the brilliantly articulated exterior skeleton of Amiens Cathedral. The cathedral churches openly displayed the exterior support system that made their interior spaces possible. In the Renaissance, this type of Gothicism was disliked for its "barbarism." Renaissance architects preferred classical structures that hid their structural supports.*

FIGURE 9.25 Nave. Amiens Cathedral. View from the West. Amiens, France. Ca. 1220–1236. *Gothic architecture was built to appeal to the emotions. The overwhelming height and the celestial light were intended to create a spiritual environment. Even in a photograph of the nave of Amiens Cathedral this spiritual feeling may be sensed. The dramatic contrast between the human elements—the chairs—and the voluminous space is a reminder of the frailty of mortals.*

HIGH GOTHIC STYLE, 1194–1300 The High Gothic style is a tribute to the growing confidence of the builders of the thirteenth century. These builders took the Gothic ingredients and refined them, creating grander churches than had been erected earlier. In comparison with Early Gothic architecture, High Gothic churches were taller and had greater volumes; artistic values now stressed wholeness rather than the division of space into harmonious units. Rejecting the restrained decorative ideal used in the Early Gothic style, the High Gothic architects covered the entire surface of their churches' western facades with sculptural and architectural designs.

The cathedral in Amiens is a perfect embodiment of the High Gothic style. Amiens was planned so that flying buttresses would surround its choir and march along its nave walls (Figure 9.24). Instead of trying to disguise these supports, the architect made the exterior skeleton central to his overall plan. As a result, more spacious window openings could be made in the nave and the choir walls than had been the case in Notre Dame. Furthermore, the design of Amiens' nave was also changed so that the entire space was perceived as a homogeneous volume. The division of the nave walls into three equal horizontal bands was eliminated, and the system of arches and bays overhead became less emphatic (Figure 9.25). Amiens' overall floor plan was conservative, however, for it resembled that of Notre Dame; for example, its transept bisected a choir and nave of equal length (Figure 9.26).

The western facade of Amiens shows how decoration changed in the High Gothic style (Figure 9.27). Amiens' western wall and towers are pierced with rich and intricate openings. The elegant tracery has the effect of dissolving the wall's apparent solidity. What surface remains intact is covered with an elaborate tapestry of architectural devices and sculptural figures (Figure 9.28).

The finest stained glass from the High Gothic era is from the cathedral in Chartres, a bishopric in Hugh Capet's old lands. Indeed, Chartres' windows are often recognized as the most exquisite of all Gothic stained glass. Chartres contains 176 windows, and most are the thirteenth-century originals. Outstanding examples of this art are the Charlemagne panels depicting scenes from the Song of Roland, illustrated earlier in this chapter (see Figure 9.8). Each figure is precisely rendered, though many are cropped off at the edge of the pictorial space. The glass itself is brilliant, notably in the dominant blue tones.

High Gothic painting survives best in the manuscript illuminations of the late thirteenth century. By this time, these small paintings were being influenced by developments elsewhere in Gothic art. Under this

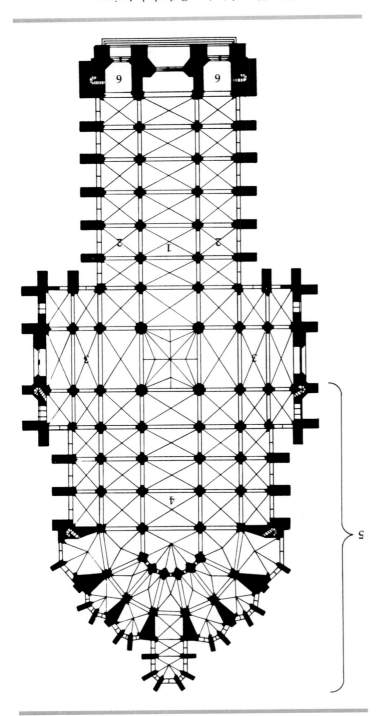

FIGURE 9.26 Floor Plan of Amiens Cathedral, Amiens, France. Ca. 1220–1236. *This drawing shows the principal features of Amiens Cathedral: (1) nave, (2) aisle, (3) transept, (4) apse, (5) choir, and (6) narthex.*

FIGURE 9.27 Western Facade. Amiens Cathedral. Amiens, France. Ca. 1220–1236. *Comparison of Amiens' facade with that of Notre Dame in Paris shows how the High Gothic differs from the Early Gothic. The basic form remains the same, but Amiens' surface is richer in detail and more splendid overall. The pointed features, as in the arches over the portals and in the peaked openings in the towers, are the most characteristic visual element in the High Gothic style.*

influence, the Gothic illuminators abandoned the lively draperies of the Romanesque and instead showed gowns hanging in a natural manner. More important, they sometimes allowed the architectural frame to dominate the painting, as in the Psalter of St. Louis IX of France. Commissioned by the sainted French king, this volume contains seventy-eight full-page paintings of scenes from the Old Testament. Of these paintings, "Balaam and his Ass" is a typical representation of the anonymous painter's style (Figure 9.29). The scene unfolds before a High Gothic church; two gables with rose windows are symmetrically balanced on the page. Although this painting owes much to changes in Gothic sculpture, the animated figures of the men, the angel, and the ass are reminiscent of the exuberant Romanesque Style.

FIGURE 9.28 *Golden Virgin.* Amiens Cathedral. Amiens, France. Ca. 1260. *The Golden Virgin of Amiens, so-called because it was originally covered with a thin layer of gold, is one of the most admired works of Gothic art. The artist has depicted Mary as a loving earthly mother with fine features, a high forehead, and a shy smile. This sculpture shows the new tenderness that was creeping into art during the High Middle Ages as part of the rise of the cult of the Virgin.*

Music

As with the other arts, the purpose of music during the High Middle Ages was understood to be the glorification of God. At the beginning of this period the monophonic (single-line) Gregorian chants were still the main form of musical expression, but two innovations—the introduction of tropes and the development of polyphony—pointed the way to a different sound in the future.

The *tropes*, or turns, were new texts and melodies that were inserted into the existing Gregorian chants. Added for both poetic and doctrinal reasons, these musical embellishments slowly changed the plain chants into more elaborate songs. Culminating in about 1150, this musical development coincided with the appearance of the richly articulated Gothic style churches.

The tropes also gave a powerful impetus to Western drama. From the practice of troping grew a new musical genre, the *liturgical drama*, which at first was sung and performed in the church but gradually moved outdoors. From the twelfth century onward these works were staged in the area in front of the church as sacred dramas or mystery plays ("mystery" is derived from the Latin for "action"). As their popularity increased, they began to be sung in the vernacular instead of Latin. Ultimately, the liturgical drama supplied one of the threads that led to the revival of the secular theater.

Gregorian chants were also being modified by the development of *polyphony*, in which two or more lines of melody are sung or played at the same time. In the early eleventh century polyphony was extremely simple and was known as *organum*. It consisted of a main melody, called the *cantus firmus*, accompanied by an identical melody sung four or five tones higher or lower. By about 1150, the second line began to have its own independent melody rather than duplicating the first. During the thirteenth century, two-voiced organum gave way to multivoiced songs called *motets*, which employed more complex melodies. In the motets, the main singer used the liturgy as a text while up to five other voices sang either commentaries or vernacular translations of the text. The result was a complex web of separate voices woven into a harmonious tapestry. By about 1250 the motet composers had laid the foundations of modern musical composition.

Notwithstanding these developments in sacred music, the church could not stop the rise of secular music any more than it could prevent the spread of courtly love. Indeed, the first secular music was associated with the same feudal courts where the *chansons de geste* and the troubadour songs flourished in

the twelfth century. At first, France was the center of this musical movement, but in the early thirteenth century, German poets took the lead. At the same time, music began to be practiced not just by aristocratic poets but by middle-class minstrels, and new musical instruments—some, such as the lute and the bagpipe, banned by the church—started to find their way into secular music (Figure 9.30).

The High Middle Ages also gave rise to some innovations which made modern music possible. The great reformer in this area was Guido of Arezzo (about 995–about 1050), an Italian monk, who modernized musical notation by his invention of the music staff, the set of five horizontal lines and four intermediate spaces on which notes may be drawn. Guido also began the practice of naming the musical tones by the syllables *ut* (or *do*), *re*, *mi*, *fa*, *sol*, and *la*, a step which greatly simplified the teaching of music. The music composed according to Guido's system can be reproduced by today's music historians; thus, Western music may be said to descend in an unbroken line from the music of this period.

FIGURE 9.29 *Balaam and His Ass.* Psalter of St. Louis IX, 1252–1270. Bibliothèque Nationale, Paris. *The architectural details in this miniature painting show a correspondence with the Rayonnant architectural style: the two gabled roofs, the two rose windows with exterior traceries, the pointed arches, and the pinnacles. Just as Gothic style architects emphasized the decorative aspects of their buildings, so did this anonymous miniature painter. The story of Balaam and his ass (from Numbers 22: 22–35 in the Old Testament) was a beast fable—a popular literary genre in the Middle Ages. In the biblical story, the ass could speak and see things of which his master, Balaam, was ignorant. In the painting, the ass turns his head and opens his mouth as if to speak.*

The Legacy of the Christian Centuries

cultural legacies. First and foremost was the birth of the courtly love movement that glorified individual romantic affection—the idea that *this* man loves *this* woman. Vernacular literature finally found its voice during this time in the first European poetry. Of special note, the vernacular writers created one of the richest literary traditions in the West through the stories of King Arthur and the knights of the Round Table. The basic theoretical system for composing music was developed during this period under the auspices of the church. Outside the church, the ancestor of all Western love songs was invented by the Provençal poets. In Gothic sculpture, artists began to move away from symbolic representation to a more realistic art.

Notwithstanding these innovations, the Christian centuries transmitted many of the legacies that had been received from ancient and other sources. The liberal arts, the Christian religion, the rationalist tradition, Muslim science, and the entire Greco-Roman heritage are only the major ingredients of this invaluable legacy to later ages.

The grandeur of this age of synthesis declined after 1300, when the secular and the spiritual began to go their separate ways. But the legacy of the Christian centuries survives, particularly in the writings of Dante, the theology of Thomas Aquinas, and the Gothic cathedrals. Of Dante's works, the *Divine Comedy* is his most enduring gift to world literature; his poetic style and literary forms influenced Italian writers for centuries. Furthermore, Dante's love for Beatrice has deeply influenced Western literature by encouraging poets to seek inspiration from a living woman.

The Roman Catholic world is the most significant beneficiary of the philosophy of Thomas Aquinas. Since the late nineteenth century Thomism has been regarded as the basis of orthodox beliefs. As for the Gothic style, it ceased to be practiced after about 1500, although it was revived in the nineteenth century as part of the Romantic movement, and even today universities often adopt Gothic elements in their official architecture.

Besides these great gifts, the Christian centuries have left the modern world other significant

FIGURE 9.30   Embellished Letter "B." Psalter from Würzburg-Ebrach. Early Thirteenth Century. Universitäts Bibliothek, Munich. In illuminated manuscripts the initial letter of a sentence was often embellished with intricate details, drawn from the artist's imagination and experience. In this particular example from a thirteenth-century German psalter, the letter "B" is interwoven with a band of musicians playing instruments typical of the era: organ (with bellows), bells, ivory horn, flute, stringed instruments, and an instrument for bows. The artist who painted this miniature scene has captured the liveliness of a musical performance, depicting several players in the act of singing.

KEY CULTURAL TERMS

chivalric code	*tympanum*
friars	*narthex*
cathedral	*ribbed vault*
scholasticism	*pier*
Realism	*flying buttress*
Nominalism	*choir*
via media	*rose window*
goliard	*blind arcade*
chanson de geste	*gargoyle*
vernacular language	*gallery*
canzone	Rayonnant
troubador	*tracery*
romance	*trope*
terza rima	*liturgical drama*
Romanesque style	*polyphony*
Gothic style	*organum*
bay	*motet*

SUGGESTIONS FOR FURTHER READING

PRIMARY SOURCES

CHRÉTIEN DE TROYES. *Arthurian Romances*. Translated by W. W. Comfort. New York: Everyman's Library Edition, 1955. A good prose version of Chrétien's romances, including *Lancelot*.

DANTE. *The Divine Comedy. The Inferno. The Purgatorio. The Paradiso.* Translated by John Ciardi. New York: New American Library, 1982. The best contemporary English translation; lively and with good footnotes.

ST. THOMAS AQUINAS. *Summa Theologica*. 3 vols. Translated by Fathers of the English Dominican Province. New York: Benziger, 1947. A good English version of St. Thomas's monumental work, which underlies Roman Catholic theology today.

The Song of Roland. Translated by P. Terry. Indianapolis, Ind.: Bobbs-Merrill, 1965. A recent translation that is readable and modern but still captures some of the language and drama of the original.

TIERNEY, B. *The Crisis of Church and State, 1050–1300*. Englewood Cliffs, N.J.: Prentice-Hall, 1964. Primary documents linked together by sound interpretations and explanations.

SECONDARY SOURCES

ARIÈS, P., and DUBY, G., eds. *A History of Private Life*. Vol. II, *Revelations of the Medieval World*. Translated by A. Goldhammer. Cambridge: Harvard University Press, 1988. Groundbreaking work that deals with ordinary life, particularly that of often neglected groups, such as women and homosexuals.

BARRACLOUGH, G. *The Medieval Papacy*. New York: Harcourt, Brace, & World, 1968. A fine text with many well-chosen illustrations.

BLOCH, M. *Feudal Society*. Translated by L. A. Morgan. London: Routledge and Kegan Paul, 1965. A monumental and influential work that focuses on the social aspects of feudalism.

CANTOR, N. F. *The Meaning of the Middle Ages: A Social and Cultural History*. Boston: Allyn and Bacon, 1973. A vigorously argued work that assumes some knowledge of the Middle Ages; shows how social changes affected medieval thought.

DUBY, G. *The Three Orders: Feudal Society Imagined*. Translated by A. Goldhammer. Chicago: University of Chicago Press, 1980. A learned study by one of France's leading scholars.

HUYGHE, R. *Larousse Encyclopedia of Byzantine and Medieval Art*. New York: Prometheus Press, 1968. Covers medieval Europe, Byzantium, Islam, Persia, India, China, Korea and Japan; helpful summaries and over 1000 illustrations.

JACKSON, W. T. H. *Medieval Literature: A History and a Guide*. New York: Collier Books, 1966. An excellent survey of both Latin and vernacular works.

KNOWLES, D. *The Evolution of Medieval Thought*. New York: Vintage, 1962. Links scholasticism with Greek thought and shows how it evolved as it was challenged by other schools of thought in the Late Middle Ages.

LABARGE, M. W. *Women in Medieval Life: A Small Sound of the Trumpet*. London: Hamish Hamilton, 1986. A survey of the activities of several women from various social groups.

MÂLE, E. *The Gothic Image: Religious Art in France of the Thirteenth Century*. New York: Harper & Row, 1958. A re-issue of the classic treatment of symbolism in medieval art; indispensable.

RORIG, F. *The Medieval Town*. Translated by D. J. A. Matthew. Berkeley: University of California Press, 1969. A brief but penetrating analysis of the rise and fall of medieval towns.

ROSENSTIEL, L., ed. *Schirmer History of Music*. New York: Schirmer Books, 1982. The finest guide for those who can read music; comprehensive.

SOUTHERN, R. W. *The Making of the Middle Ages*. New Haven: Yale University Press, 1963. A challenging work for the more serious student by an outstanding scholar.

STOKSTAD, M. *Medieval Art*. New York: Harper & Row, 1986. A readable guide based on the latest scholarship.

WHITE, L. *Medieval Technology and Social Change*. New York: Oxford University Press, 1986. The standard study of the interrelationships between inventions and society.

10

THE LATE MIDDLE AGES

1300—1500

People living during what a modern historian has termed the "calamitous" fourteenth century were thrown into confusion and despair. Many believed that the biblical apocalypse had arrived, attended by plague, famine, and war, for these were among the calamities that rained down on them. Amid the turbulence of this century, the unique culture of the High Middle Ages, which had blended the spiritual with the secular, began to come undone. In the Late Middle Ages, significant changes were affecting the achievements of the previous era. The church had to give up its dream of Christendom—a united Christian commonwealth—when faced with the reality of rival European states at war with each other. New military tactics and weapons rendered chivalry obsolete, and the chivalric code began to take on the colors of romantic fiction. In the universities, new intellectual currents drove a wedge between philosophy and theology, which had been so carefully integrated by Thomas Aquinas. And the balanced High Gothic style in art and architecture gave way to the florid Late Gothic style.

This chapter examines the third and final phase of medieval civilization during the period between 1300 and 1500. It also explores the explosion of secular interests that was occurring in this contradictory age and the technological and artistic innovations that were beginning to point the Western world in a new direction. Chapter 11 returns to the fifteenth century to focus on the specific developments that ushered in the Renaissance and the modern era.

HARD TIMES COME TO EUROPE

Shortly after the opening of the fourteenth century, Europe entered a disastrous period of economic depression, accompanied by soaring prices and widespread famine. Against the backdrop of the Hundred Years' War, social unrest increased, with urban riots and peasant revolts, and renegade feudal armies ravaged much of western Europe for decades. The church, in disgrace and disarray for much of this period, was unable to provide moral or political leadership. As old certainties evaporated, the optimistic mood of the High Middle Ages gave way to a sense of impending doom.

Ordeal by Plague, Famine, and War

Of all the calamities that now befell Europe, the worst was the plague, which first appeared in northern Italy in 1347. Imported from the East along newly opened trade routes, the plague bacillus was carried over sea and land by fleas, which in turn were transported by rats (Map 10.1). From Italy, the disease spread rapidly over most of Europe, halted only by the frost line in the north. Amazingly, a few cities and areas—like Milan and central Germany—were free of plague. But in other places the plague raged from 1348 until 1351,

MAP 10.1

Progress of the Black Death across Europe in the Fourteenth Century

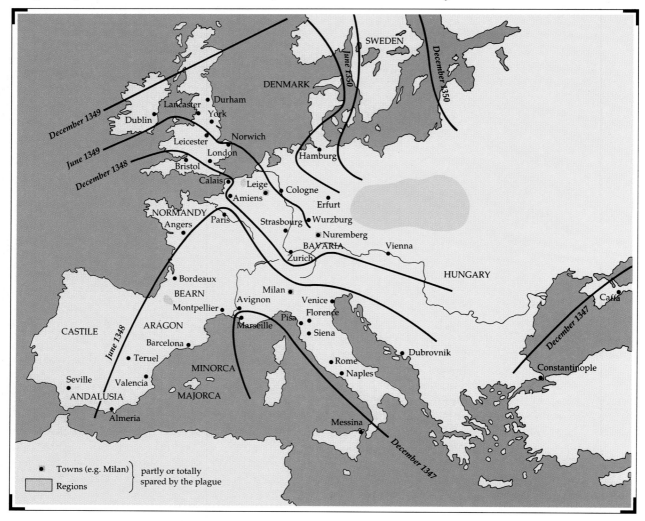

FIGURE 10.1 *Burial of Plague Victims. Mid–Fourteenth Century. The devastating plague of the mid–fourteenth century caused an air of melancholy to hover over the waning years of the Late Middle Ages. This small painting shows the gruesome burial rites, including interment in mass graves, that were a familiar sight in the regions hardest hit by the disease.*

and further onslaughts occurred at random throughout the century and into the next. So deadly was the disease that more than a third of Europe's 70 million people died in the first epidemic alone (Figure 10.1). The later outbreaks were less severe, but the West did not regain a population of 70 million until 1470.

The mechanism of disease transmission was not fully understood, and the medieval plague created panic and hysteria. Using medieval accounts of the disease, modern researchers have detected three different forms of plague: bubonic, pneumonic, and septicemic. The diseases were all extremely painful, and death could come within a matter of hours or a few days. People in the Late Middle Ages referred to these disease types collectively as "the plague," and in the sixteenth century historians began to label this medieval epidemic the "Black Death," which has become the generally accepted term.

The Black Death cast a long shadow over the Late Middle Ages. Many writers and artists reflected the melancholy times, occasionally brightening their dark works with an end-of-the-world gaiety. The age's leading image became the Dance of Death. In literature and in art, death was portrayed as a skeleton, democratically joining hands with kings, queens, popes, merchants, peasants, and prostitutes as they danced their way to destruction. In the direct manner of medieval thinking, this symbol forcefully showed the folly of human ambition and the transitoriness of life (Figure 10.2).

The crisis atmosphere surrounding the plague was compounded by growing famine conditions across the European continent. Starting in 1315, agricultural harvests failed with some regularity for more than a century. Besides raising the death rate, these famines weakened the populace and made them more susceptible to diseases.

Climatic changes or cyclic shifts in ocean currents may have occasioned the bad harvests, but the food shortages were probably triggered by the economic adjustments that had to be made because of the previous era's overproduction and too-rapid expansion. The new farm lands that had been opened after 1250 were now abandoned. Increased demand for meat caused farmers to turn to raising cattle rather than growing cereal and grain crops. Besides, cheap imported cereals from Italy and Germany severely depressed grain prices in other areas. Lower prices led farmers to specialize—in wines, fruit, or flax—rather than to invest in multiple crops. The Italian hinterland and the German lands along the Baltic became Europe's bread basket, and when plague disturbed these areas, famine spread across the continent.

In addition to plague and famine, war also disrupted the pattern of social and economic life. By 1450

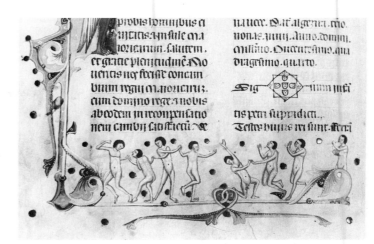

FIGURE 10.2 *The Dance of Death. Fifteenth Century. In the wake of the Black Plague, art and literature became filled with themes affirming the biblical message that life is short and death certain. One of the most vivid images of this theme was the* Danse Macabre, *or Dance of Death, which took many artistic and literary forms. In this example, a miniature painting taken from a Spanish manuscript of the fifteenth century, the corpses are shown nude, stripped of their human dignity, and dancing with wild abandon.*

the kings of Aragon in eastern Spain had defeated and replaced the French rulers of Naples, Sicily, and Sardinia. The increasingly powerful northern Italian cities waged war among themselves for commercial and political advantage. Farther east, from 1347 on, the Ottoman Turks were on the move, occupying Greece and the Balkan peninsula and finally conquering Constantinople in 1453. As the century ended, the Turks were marching westward, menacing Bohemia and Hungary. In the west, England and France fought the seemingly endless Hundred Years' War intermittently from 1337 to 1453. The Dukes of Burgundy were frequently parties to this struggle, as they attempted, but failed, to carve out a "middle kingdom" between France and the German empire.

One of the side effects of this almost constant warfare was a growing number of soldiers loose in the land from undispersed mercenary armies. The countryside was filled with bands of roving knights—nobles, younger sons or bastards of aristocratic families, and outlaws—who blackmailed landowners and peasants alike in Aragon, France, and Italy. All over Europe these dangerous circumstances in the countryside compelled town dwellers to retreat behind their city walls.

Depopulation, Rebellion, and Industrialization

The major consequence of the plagues, famines, and wars was depopulation, which caused the commercial map of Europe to be redrawn. In general, the regions hardest hit economically were those that had benefited most in the earlier boom, particularly

France. New centers now rose to economic importance, including Bohemia, Poland, Hungary, Scandinavia, and Portugal. The northern Italian cities, the largest cities in Europe—Florence, Genoa, and Venice—rallied from the plague's devastating losses in the fifteenth century to make a remarkable economic recovery.

Population decline also caused dramatic social dislocations. Plague-free regions lost settlers as healthy people flocked to plague-stricken areas, where laborers were in great demand. Europe experienced a sharp decrease in the density of the rural population. Thousands of villages simply disappeared as peasants abandoned their farms and settled in the towns, causing a rise in the number of urban dwellers. A short-term effect of depopulation and the shifts in population was to widen the gap between rich and poor and to foster deep class hatred. As class cohesion declined, the established social order broke down, and society now experienced warfare between peasants and landowners, guildsmen and merchants, and town laborers and middle-class elites. These social uprisings often had an anticlerical element, with the rebels attacking church property and denouncing the collection of tithes.

Starting in Flanders in 1296, social unrest mounted across Europe. In 1356 conditions in France reached a critical juncture when the *Jacquerie,* or rural renegades, made common cause with Parisian malcontents and killed many nobles. Across the English Channel in 1381, during the brief Peasants' Revolt, insurgents seized and occupied London. Among their demands was that the English king abolish the nobility. In the end, these uprisings failed to make any lasting impact on the social order. Fighting on foot and using farm tools as weapons, the poorly organized and ill-equipped rebels were no match for troops of armored knights on horseback.

While the immediate consequence of the demographic crisis was to intensify social unrest, the long-term effect was to produce a higher standard of living for the survivors. Peasants in western Europe found their labor more in demand and their bargaining positions with the landowners improved. Many were able to break out of servitude and become rent-paying farmers. Others, less fortunate, moved from the status of serf to sharecropper. As a result, by 1500 manorialism was dying out in western Europe except for minor obligations. But in central and eastern Europe—Poland, Bohemia, and Hungary, where the plague was less devastating and the landlords could hold firm—the peasants were not so lucky. On the contrary, estate owners there, and in Germany and Russia, bound the serfs ever more tightly to their farm labors.

As farming changed, so did Europe's fledgling industrial life. Textile manufacture, performed on hand looms, remained the leading industry, but its production and distribution centers shifted. Cut off by war from their former wool supplies and their retail markets, the Flemish and French weavers were challenged by woolen manufacturers from northern Italy, the Rhineland, and Poland. The greatest change in textile manufacturing, however, was ultimately precipitated by England's shift from the export of raw wool to the export of finished cloth, a change that disrupted the traditional rural way of life. Entrepreneurs wishing to escape the confining regulations of the town guilds devised the "putting out system," whereby raw wool was consigned to peasant families who wove it into cloth within their own cottages. As the new system prospered, the demand increased for raw wool, and many landowners turned English farmland into pasture for sheep in order to accommodate this need.

New industries also grew up around the production of rag paper, a Chinese invention perfected by the Arabs and manufactured widely in Spain after 1300; of salt, distributed by Venice and Lisbon and used in tanning leather and preserving food; and of iron, in demand for weapons, armor, and horseshoes. The development of movable type in the mid–fifteenth century was the most significant of these technological innovations; it gave rise to the printing and publishing industries and had enormous repercussions for education and literature. Additional breakthroughs occurred elsewhere. The suction pump helped increase productivity in the mines, the spinning wheel radically improved the turning of wool into thread, and new casting methods led to a superior bronze for cannons. Older inventions, such as eyeglasses, clocks, and gunpowder, were now perfected in this age of rapid change.

The Secular Monarchies

France and England maintained their positions as the leading states of Europe, but they exhausted their economies with wasteful wars. The Hundred Years' War, as the group of conflicts between the mid–fourteenth and the mid–fifteenth century is called, arose over feudal entanglements, dynastic rivalries, and military alliances dating from the High Middle Ages. The war was fought entirely on French soil. The French crown under the Valois dynasty had to contend not only with England, but with the Dukes of Burgundy, who threatened to break away from their French ties and set up an independent kingdom. The Burgundian Dukes aimed for a royal crown,

TIME LINE 10.1   ROYAL DYNASTIES IN LATE MEDIEVAL FRANCE

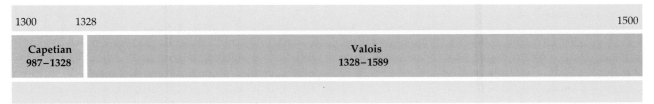

1300	1328	1500
Capetian **987–1328**	**Valois** **1328–1589**	

either that of France or one authorized by the Holy Roman Emperor. Whatever may have been its final political goal, the Duchy of Burgundy by the 1400s encompassed vast territories on the northeast border of France. Like the French kings, these dukes adopted a centralized state structure that included a treasury, a judiciary, and a standing army. The Burgundian court at Dijon was the most brilliant in northern Europe, attracting the leading artists and humanists of the age.

Despite the ravages of the Hundred Years' War, the Valois kings emerged from the conflict with more territory than when the hostilities began. Except for the port of Calais, England was forced to cede her overseas lands to the French crown. Burgundy remained a threat somewhat longer, until King Louis XI (1461–1483) brought the dukes under his control. The last major territory that had escaped the French crown was gained by Charles VIII (1483–1498) when he married the heiress to the County of Brittany. With the acquisition of Brittany, the contour of modern France was now complete (Time Line 10.1).

While the Hundred Years' War raged on the continent, life in England was disrupted by feudal rebellion, peasant unrest, and urban strife. Like France, England was also emerging from the feudal system but moving in a different direction from her rival across the channel. The English Parliament gained power at the expense of the king, meeting frequently when summoned and representing the interests of the nobles, the towns, and the rural counties. Parliament also expressed popular feelings when laws curbing papal power in England were passed.

When Henry VII (1485–1509) became king, it soon was apparent that part of the reason for the domi-nance of Parliament during this period was the weakness of the kings. This founder of England's brilliant Tudor dynasty abandoned foreign wars, lived off his own estates, and relied on his own advisers—all issues that had led to violent quarrels between his predecessors and Parliament. Henry VII's policies deflated parliamentary power, keeping the representative body subservient to the crown and making Henry as potent as his contemporaries in France (Time Line 10.2).

The success of the French and English kings in centralizing their states attracted many imitators. Their ruling style—with royal secretaries, efficient treasuries, national judiciaries, and representative assemblies—was adopted in part by other states. Spain was the most successful in achieving unity. Dynastic politics and civil war kept the states of central Europe and Scandinavia from becoming strong and centralized. The Holy Roman Empire was the least successful of these political entities, and Germany remained divided into combating states with weak centralized rule.

The Papal Monarchy

From its pinnacle of power and prestige in 1200 under Pope Innocent III, the church entered a period of decline in about 1300. In 1303, Pope Boniface VIII's reign ended in abject failure (see Chapter 9). For most of the next century or more, the church was beset with dislocation, schism, and heresy.

Papal dislocation occurred in 1309 when Pope Clement V abandoned Rome. For almost seventy years the seat of the papacy was in Avignon, a papal

TIME LINE 10.2   ROYAL DYNASTIES IN LATE MEDIEVAL ENGLAND

1300	1399	1461	1485	1500
Angevin **1154–1399**	**Lancastrian**	**Yorkist**	**Tudor** **1485–1603**	

fief on the Rhone River. This step, unique in the almost two-thousand-year history of the church, was taken because the papacy sought relief from Rome's factional politics. The Avignon popes found the Rhone valley a safer, more hospitable place from which to rule the church than the banks of the Tiber. The relocation provoked voices, which soon became legion, speaking against these popes for being in the pocket of the French crown.

The chief success of the Avignonese popes was to centralize the papacy, an accomplishment comparable to what was happening in the secular kingdoms. These popes reorganized the church's financial system and changed payments from kind to money. At the same time, unfortunately, they rarely made moral reforms. Their reigns lapsed into worldliness and greed, which made the papacy more vulnerable to criticism.

The Avignonese papacy had barely ended in 1378 when a new calamity, the Great Schism, threw the church into even more confusion. Under Pope Gregory XI, the papacy had returned to Rome in 1377, and the cardinals had elected an Italian pope when Gregory died. The French cardinals did not approve of this pope, and they withdrew and elected another pontiff to rule from Avignon. This scandalous situation divided western Christendom into two obediences with two popes, two Colleges of Cardinals, two curias, and two church tax systems. The rising power of the secular states became evident as rulers cast their support along political lines. France, Sicily, Scotland, Castile, Aragon, and Portugal rallied behind the Avignon pope; England, Flanders, Poland, Hungary, Germany, and the rest of Italy stayed loyal to the Roman pope. During these political shenanigans, the papal office was the real loser; the pope's authority diminished as pious Christians became bewildered and disgusted.

The worst was yet to come. In 1409 both sets of cardinals summoned a church council in Pisa to heal the fissure. The Pisan Council elected a new pope and called on the other two to resign. When they both refused, the church was faced with *three* rulers claiming papal authority. The Great Schism was finally resolved at the Council of Constance (1414–1418), convened by the Holy Roman Emperor. This council elected Martin V as Pope, deposed the Avignon ruler, accepted the resignation of the Roman claimant, and ignored the earlier conciliar choice.

With the success of the Council of Constance, the supporters of conciliar rule (that is, rule by councils) as a way of curbing the power of the popes seemed to be gaining ground in the church. But Martin V (1417–1431) quickly rejected this idea as soon as he was elected to the papal throne. Nevertheless, the conciliar movement remained alive until the mid–fifteenth century, when strong popes once again reasserted the monarchical power of their office.

Having surmounted their earlier crises by the restoration of the papal monarchy, the popes in the mid–fifteenth century turned their interest to the arts and humanities rather than to pressing moral and spiritual issues. Moreover, they were vitally concerned with the trappings of political power. They plunged into Italian politics more deeply than ever, ruling as secular princes in their papal lands. Their worldly interests and blatant political maneuvers only intensified the mounting disapproval of the papacy and provided the church's critics with more examples of the institution's corruption and decline.

THE CULTURAL FLOWERING OF THE LATE MIDDLE AGES

The calamitous political, social, and economic events of the Late Middle Ages were echoed in the cultural sphere by the breakdown of the medieval synthesis in religion, in theology, in literature, and in art. New secular voices began to be heard, challenging traditional views, and the interests of the bourgeoisie started to have an impact on art and architecture. Although the church remained the major financial supporter of the arts, rich town dwellers, notably bankers and merchants, were emerging as the new patrons of art (Figure 10.3). Their conspicuous art patronage was a way of establishing their cultural credentials in society.

Religion

Monastic reform had been a major force within the church in the High Middle Ages, but such collective acts of devotion were largely unknown in the Late Middle Ages. Dedicated and virtuous monks and nuns were increasingly rare, and their influence was waning. Innovative forms of religious expression did not come from members of religious orders but from lay people, inspired perhaps to protest and react against what they perceived as the increasing worldliness of the church and the declining commitment of many clergy.

Lay piety was thus one of the most significant developments in the religious landscape. The beguine movement, which encouraged lives devoted to helping the needy, had begun in the thirteenth century among lay women in northern France. Now, the beguines, along with male lay brethren called beghards, spread to Germany and the Netherlands, usually in proximity to Dominican monasteries. Medieval Germany's finest devotional writer, Meister Eckhart (about 1260–1328), composed tracts and sermons to guide these lay people's religious impulses into orthodox ways. A subtle thinker, Meister Eckhart's prose works reveal him to be one of the great mystics of the Christian tradition.

By 1400 other groups, such as the Brethren and Sisters of the Common Life and the Friends of God, were rising in the Rhineland, the Low Countries, and Flanders. This lay movement constituted the **devotio moderna**, or the "new devotion," with its ideal of a pious lay society. Disappointed with traditionally trained priests, members of these groups often rejected higher education and practiced the strict discipline of the earlier monastic orders, but without withdrawing into a monastery. Among the most important expressions of this new devotion was *The Imitation of Christ* by Thomas à Kempis (1380–1471). His manual, with its stern asceticism, reflected the harsh ideals of the Brethren of the Common life, the group of which Kempis was a member.

Within the pietistic movement, extreme ascetic practices that verged on heresy mounted in these turbulent years. The bizarre behavior of the flagellants, for example, was triggered by the plague. They regarded this disease as God's judgment on an evil society, and they engaged in ritual whippings in an attempt to divert divine wrath away from others (Figure 10.4).

The flagellants managed to escape official censure, but those more openly critical of the church did not. The leaders who attempted to reform the church in England and Bohemia met stout resistance from the popes. The English reform movement sprang from the teachings of John Wycliffe (about 1320–1384), an Oxford teacher whose message attracted the nobility as well as the common folk. Wishing to purify the church of worldliness, Wycliffe urged the abolition of ecclesiastical property, the subservience of the church to the state, and the denial of papal authority. The most lasting achievement of Wycliffe's movement was the introduction of the first complete English-language Bible, produced by scholars inspired by his teaching. After his followers (known as Lollards)

FIGURE 10.3 Jacques Coeur's House. 1443–1451. Bourges, France. *Coeur was an immensely successful entrepreneur who at one point was bankrolling the French kings. His magnificent mansion at Bourges spawned many imitations among wealthy businessmen across Europe. The building's high, spikey turrets, fanciful balconies, and highly decorated windows are all secular adaptations of the Late Gothic style more commonly seen in church architecture. Coeur conducted his continent-wide financial and commercial dealings from this house, sending messages by carrier pigeons released through the holes on the roof.*

FIGURE 10.4 *Flagellation Scene. Annales of Gilles Le Muisit.* Bibliothèque Royale Albert Ier, Brussels. *This miniature painting represents a scene that became a familiar sight across Europe during the plague years. The penitents, depicted with bare backs and feet, marched through the towns scourging themselves with whips. By this self-punishment, they hoped to atone for their own and society's sins and thus bring the plague to an end.*

were condemned as heretical, the secular officials launched savage persecutions that resulted in the murder of those supporters who did not recant.

The Bohemian reformers in the Holy Roman Empire were indebted to Wycliffe, whom some had met at Oxford, but, more importantly, their strength was rooted in the popular piety and evangelical preachers of mid-fourteenth-century Prague. The heresy became identified with Jan Hus (about 1369–1415), a Czech theologian who accepted Wycliffe's political views but rejected some of his religious teachings. Hus was invited to the Council of Constance in 1415, where his ideas were condemned, and he was burned at the stake by state authorities. His death outraged his fellow Czechs, many of whom, including the powerful and wealthy, now adopted his views. Hussite beliefs became a vehicle for Czech nationalism, as his ethnic comrades fought against German overlords and attacked church property. Because of the backing of powerful lay leaders, the Hussites survived into the next century. They gained more followers during the Protestant Reformation and exist today as the Moravian Brethren.

Although the secular authorities, instigated by the church, could usually be counted on to put down the heresies, the church had a more powerful internal weapon at its disposal: the Inquisition (from the Latin *inquisitio*, meaning "inquiry"). Born in the aftermath of the Albigensian heresy in the twelfth century (see Chapter 9), the Inquisition was a religious court for identifying and condemning heretics. The Inquisition reached its cruel height during the Late Middle Ages, particularly in Italy and Spain.

Because of its procedures, the Inquisition became the most notorious instrument ever created by the Christian church. Ignoring the basic ideals of Roman law, this church court allowed suspects to be condemned without ever facing their accusers. Confessions made under torture were also allowed to serve as evidence against other persons. Forbidden by the Bible to shed blood, the leaders of the Inquisition turned convicted heretics over to the state authorities, who then executed them by burning. By modern estimates, thousands of men and women perished in this way.

The Inquisition was also used to rid society of women—and to a lesser extent of men—who were suspected of being in league with the devil. The belief in witchcraft, an occult legacy of the ancient world, was next to universal during the Middle Ages. Many educated people sincerely believed that certain women were witches and that magical devices could protect the faithful from their spells. Consequently, hundreds of suspected individuals were killed by the Inquisition or by unruly mobs. Fear of witchcraft persisted as a dangerous part of popular lore into the eighteenth century.

Theology, Philosophy, and Science

Although the popes betrayed their spiritual mission in these years, the church was not without dedicated followers who cared deeply about theological issues. Many of these clerical thinkers were affiliated with the universities, principally in Paris and at Oxford. Their major disputes were over Thomism, the theological system of Thomas Aquinas, which in the Late Middle Ages was losing supporters and coming increasingly under attack. At the same time, the ongoing philosophical struggle between Realism and Nominalism finally ended with a Nominalist victory. In the long run, those who questioned Thomism and those who accepted Nominalism set philosophy and theology on separate paths and thus paved the way to the Renaissance and the Scientific Revolution.

The Via Antiqua *versus the* Via Moderna   The opening round in the theological war against Thomism began soon after the death of Thomas Aquinas in 1274 and before the High Middle Ages was over. In 1277, church officials in Paris condemned the Latin Averroists at the local university for their rationalist ideas. As part of their attack on extreme rationalism, the church authorities also rejected some of Aquinas's arguments. The censure of Thomism led to a heated controversy that raged for much of the Late Middle Ages among university scholars. In particular, Thomas's fellow Dominican friars waged an acrimonious battle with the Franciscan masters, their great rivals in theological studies.

During these theological debates, new labels were invented and assumed by the opposing sides. Aquinas's *via media* came to be termed by his opponents the **via antiqua**, or the old-fashioned way. Broadly speaking, the *via antiqua* followed Thomism in urging that faith and reason be combined as the correct approach to divine truth. In contrast, the **via moderna**, or the modern way, made a complete separation of biblical beliefs and rationalism. In time the *via moderna* prevailed, driving the *via antiqua* underground until it was rescued from oblivion in the modern period.

Duns Scotus and William of Ockham   The conflict between the *via antiqua* and the *via moderna* was best exemplified in the writings of John Duns Scotus and William of Ockham, respectively. The first of these commentators was sympathetic to the theology of Thomas Aquinas, but the second scholar was unmistakably hostile and tried to discredit Thomism.

Duns Scotus (about 1265–1308), the most persuasive voice of the *via antiqua*, was a Scottish thinker who was trained as a Franciscan and lectured at the universities in Oxford, Paris, and Cologne. Even though he was a supporter of Thomism, Duns Scotus unwittingly undermined Aquinas's synthesis by stressing that faith was superior to reason, a shift in focus that arose from his belief in God's absolute and limitless power. Pointing out that God's existence could not be proven either through the senses or by reason, he asserted that faith was the only way to explain the divine mystery. Furthermore, Duns Scotus concluded that because the theologian and the philosopher have different intellectual tasks, theology and science (that is, the study of nature) should be independent fields of inquiry.

What Duns Scotus unintentionally began, William of Ockham (about 1300–about 1349) purposely completed. Under the assaults of Ockham's keen intellect, the Thomist theological edifice collapsed. An Oxford-trained theologian, he recognized the importance of both reason and faith, but, like Scotus, he did not see how reason could prove God's existence. Both thinkers believed that only personal feelings and mystical experiences could reveal God and the divine moral order. Yet Ockham went further than Scotus by asserting that reason, the senses, and empirical evidence could enable human beings to discover and hence understand the natural world. To Ockham, faith and reason were both valid approaches to truth, but they should be kept apart so that each could achieve its respective end.

In the seemingly endless medieval debate between the Realists and the Nominalists, Ockham's reasoning swept Nominalism to its final victory. Like the Nominalists of the twelfth century, Ockham denied the existence of universals and claimed that only individual objects existed. He concluded that human beings can have clear and distinct knowledge only of specific things in the physical world; no useful knowledge can be gained through reason or the senses about the spiritual realm. Ockham's conclusion did not mean that human beings were cast adrift without access to the world of God. A corollary of his approach was that understanding of the spiritual realm rested solely on the truths of faith and theology.

In his reasoning, William of Ockham asserted a principle of economy that stripped away all that was irrelevant: Arguments should be drawn from a minimum of data and founded on closely constructed logic. "It is vain to do with more what can be done with fewer," he says in one of his works. Ockham's "razor" of logic eliminated superfluous information that could not be verified, thus enabling a student to cut to the core of a philosophical problem. The Ockhamites, following their mentor's logic and empiricism, challenged the Realists and dominated the intellectual life of the universities for the next two hundred years.

Developments in Science   Ockham's ideas broadened the path to modern science that had been opened by two thirteenth-century thinkers. In that earlier time, Robert Grosseteste (about 1175–1253), a Franciscan at Oxford University, had devised a scientific method for investigating natural phenomena; using step-by-step procedures, he employed mathematics and tested hypotheses until he reached satisfactory conclusions. Roger Bacon (about 1220–1292), another Franciscan and a follower of Grosseteste, advocated the use of the experimental method, which he demonstrated in his studies of optics, solar eclipses, and rainbows and in his treatises on mathematics, physics, and philosophy. From the modern standpoint, Bacon was perhaps the most original mind of this otherwise barren period in the history of science.

In the fourteenth century, other thinkers, with Grosseteste and Bacon as guides and Ockham's logic as a weapon, made further contributions to the advance of science. Outstanding among these men was one bold Parisian scholar who took advantage of the growing interest in the experimental method, Nicholas Oresme (about 1330–1382). Oresme answered all of Aristotle's objections to the idea that the earth moved. Using pure reason and applying theoretical arguments, he concluded that it was as plausible that the earth moved around the sun as that it was fixed. Having used reason to show that the earth may move, however, Oresme then chose to accept church doctrine, denying what he had demonstrated. Nevertheless, Oresme's arguments, along with Ockham's separation of natural philosophy from theology and Bacon's formulation of the experimental method, foreshadowed the end of the medieval conception of the physical and celestial worlds.

Literature

The powerful forces that were reshaping the wider culture—the rising new monarchies, the growing national consciousness among diverse peoples, the emerging secularism, and the developing urban environment—were also transforming literature in the Late Middle Ages. The rise of literacy produced a

FIGURE 10.5 FRANCESCO TRAINI. *Triumph of Death.* Detail. Ca. 1350. Pisa, Italy. *Like the storytellers in* The Decameron, *these well-dressed travelers have left their plague-stricken city, perhaps in search of safety or hoping for a day's pleasant diversion in the countryside. Instead, they come on three corpses rotting in coffins—even the dogs are afraid—and a hermit who points out the lesson: Death triumphs over all. This detail is from a huge fresco painted on the wall of the cemetery next to the Pisa Cathedral.*

growing educated class who learned to read and write the local languages rather than Latin, and a shift to vernacular literature began to occur. Two new groups—the monarchs and their courts and the urban middle class—started to supplant the nobility and the church as patrons and audiences. And, ultimately most important of all, in the mid–fifteenth century Johann Gutenberg developed a practicable method of using movable type to print books. This invention helped to seal the doom of medieval civilization and signaled the commencement of the modern world.

Northern Italian Literature: Petrarch and Boccaccio
New literary forms emerged in the areas where the chivalric and feudal modes were weakest—northern Italy and England. Petrarch and Boccaccio, both Florentines, like Dante, grew up in a Christian world that was rapidly being secularized. These two writers captured the mood of this transition era as Florence and the other Italian city-states shed their medieval outlook. Both authors looked back to the Classical world for inspiration, and yet both found in the bustling world of the nearby towns the materials and characters for their stories. Of the two, Petrarch was the more dedicated Classicist and often used ancient themes in his writings.

Francesco Petrarch ("Petrarca" in Italian) (1304–1374), though Florentine by birth and in spirit, flourished in Avignon amid the splendor and learning of the papal court. As a diplomat for popes and Italian princes, he won fame and wealth, but his reputation arose from his career as a professional man of letters. Rejecting the age's trend toward the vernacular, he dedicated his life to Latin writing and to the recovery of ancient manuscripts, although the work for which he is most famous today, a collection of love lyrics and sonnets, is written in Italian. His devotion struck a responsive chord among his fellow Italians, who in 1341 proclaimed him poet laureate for his lyrics, sonnets, treatises, and epics. In many ways, Petrarch, despite taking minor religious orders, shows the typical secular interests of his times. A conventional Christian, he only occasionally addressed religious issues in his works.

A religious theme is touched on in *Secretum,* or *My Secret,* in which Petrarch deals with the state of his soul. In this dialogue, "Augustinus," or St. Augustine, hounds "Franciscus," or Petrarch, about his innermost thoughts and desires, charging him with all the deadly sins. Freely admitting his moral lapses, Franciscus pleads that he is the same as any other man—driven by a love of learning, a weakness for fleshly attractions, and an appetite for personal comforts. Despite this confession, the dialogue shows that Petrarch could not liberate himself fully from medieval values.

Even more than his lifelong friend Petrarch, Giovanni Boccaccio (1313–1375) was a man of the world.

The son of a banker, Boccaccio began his literary career by penning prose romances along with poetic pastorals and sonnets, many of which were dedicated to Fiammetta, a young woman who was both his consuming passion and his literary muse. His early efforts, however, were overshadowed by his Italian prose masterpiece, *The Decameron*. Written in about 1351, this work reflects the grim conditions of the Black Death, which had just swept through Florence (Figure 10.5). In *The Decameron* (from the Greek for "ten"), Boccaccio describes how ten young men and women, in their efforts to escape the plague, flee the city to a country villa, where they pass the time, each telling a story a day for ten days. Most of their one hundred tales were based on folk stories and popular legends. While some tales deal lightly with social mores and a few contain moral messages, the majority simply entertain the listener. Boccaccio, speaking though a cross section of urban voices and relying on well-known stories, helped develop a form of literature that eventually led to the modern short story.

English Literature: Geoffrey Chaucer   Like its Italian counterpart, English literature rapidly matured into its own forms during the Late Middle Ages. The development of an English literary style was aided immensely by the evolution of a common language. Until this time most educated English people read and spoke French, but a rising sense of national consciousness, triggered by the Hundred Years' War and by an emerging educated urban class, hastened the spread of a native tongue. England's kings came to see themselves as different from their French ancestors and purposely began to speak English instead of French; they also made English the official language of government.

By 1300 important works in English were beginning to appear, such as *The Vision of Piers Plowman*, a moral allegory probably written by William Langland (about 1332–1400) that graphically exposes the plight of the poor and calls for a return to Christian virtues. This work provides insight into England's social and economic system and, through the author's anguish, reveals the social tension around the time of the Peasant's Revolt in 1381.

English literature was still establishing its own identity and a common language was slowly emerging when Geoffrey Chaucer (about 1340–1400) appeared on the scene. He wrote in an East Midland dialect of English that became the standard form for his generation as well as the foundation of modern English. The son of a wealthy London merchant, Chaucer spent his professional life as a courtier, a diplomat, and a public servant for the English crown. The profession of "writer" or "poet" was unknown in Chaucer's day. But his poetry brought him renown, and when he died he was the first commoner to be buried in Westminster Abbey, a favored burial spot for English royalty.

Chaucer began composing his most famous work, *The Canterbury Tales,* in 1385. He set the tales in the context of a pilgrimage to the tomb of Thomas à Becket, the twelfth-century martyr. Even though the journey has a religious purpose, Chaucer makes it plain that the travelers intend to have a good time along the way. To make the journey from London to Canterbury more interesting, the thirty-one pilgrims (including Chaucer himself) agree to tell tales—two each going and returning—and to award a prize for the best story told.

Chaucer completed only twenty-three tales and the general Prologue, in which he introduces the pilgrims. Each person on the pilgrimage not only represents an English social type but is also a unique and believable human being. In this poetic narrative about a group of ordinary people, the spiritual is mixed with the temporal and the serious with the comic.

Chaucer drew his pilgrims from nearly all walks of medieval society. The Knight, in this late stage of feudalism, personified much that was noble and honorable in the chivalric code; his bravery could not be questioned, but he was also a mercenary and cruel to his enemies. Certain representatives of the church are also somewhat skeptically treated. The Prioress, the head of a convent and from the upper class, is more concerned about her refined manners and polished language than the state of her soul. Similarly, the Monk lives a life of the flesh and enjoys good food, fine wines, and expensive clothing. The Friar seems the very opposite of his sworn ideals; he is eager to hear a confession for a fee, and he never goes among the poor or aids the sick. Yet, in the country Parson Chaucer portrays a true servant of God who preaches to his parish, looks after the infirm and dying, and never takes more than his share from his religious flock.

Among the secular travelers the most famous is the Wife of Bath. A widow five times over, this jolly woman is full of life and loves to talk. She has been on many pilgrimages and not only knows about foreign places but has a keen insight into people (Figure 10.6).

As for the tales they tell, the pilgrims' choices often reflect their own moral values. The worthy Knight tells a chivalric love story, but the Miller, a coarse, rough man well versed in lying and cheating, relates how a young wife took on a lover and deceived her husband—an example of the popular medieval tale known as a *fabliau.* Thus the pilgrims' stories, based on folk and fairy tales, romances, classical stories,

FIGURE 10.9 South Cloister of Gloucester Cathedral. Ca. 1370. Gloucester, England. *Fan vaulting, an intricate pattern in which ribs arch out from a single point in the ceiling, first appeared at Gloucester Cathedral and inspired many imitations. Although the ribs may appear to be structurally necessary, they are really a richly decorative device carved from stone. In Gloucester's south cloister, the tracery fans out from the top of each column and then merges in the center of the ceiling, giving the impression of a delicate screen.*

FIGURE 10.10 Siena Cathedral. 1250–1400. Siena, Italy. *Extant records and floor plans show that the Sienese changed their minds several times before deciding on the cathedral's final shape. At one time, about 1322, a commission of architects advised that the existing cathedral be demolished because the foundations and walls were not strong enough to support new additions. Nonetheless, construction went forward, and the cathedral is still standing after more than six hundred years.*

FIGURE 10.11 GIOTTO. Campanile of the Florentine Cathedral. Ca. 1334–1350. Florence, Italy. *Giotto's Tower, as this campanile is known in Florence, is one of the city's most cherished landmarks. Today, its bells still toll the time. The two sets of windows in the central section and the taller openings at the top give the campanile a strong sense of balanced proportion. Thus, despite being built in the fourteenth century, the tower anticipates the Classical ideal that was revived in the Renaissance.*

facade, for the first time in Italy, incorporated nearly life-sized figures into the total design, thus heightening its resemblance to the French Gothic. However, many features distinguish Siena from the French taste. For example, the decorative statues on Siena's facade were placed above the gables and not set in niches. Furthermore, the Sienese builders put mosaics into the spaces in the gables and above the central rose window.

Florence, Siena's greatest military and trade rival, refused to be outdone by its nearby competitor. The Florentine city fathers asked Giotto, the city's most renowned painter, to design a campanile for their own cathedral. Today, the first story of the bell tower—with its carvings, interlaced patterns of pink and white marble, and hexagonal inlays—still stands as conceived by Giotto (Figure 10.11). Giotto's plan, as left in a drawing, called for an open tower with a spire on top, as in a French Gothic tower. But later architects constructed a rectangular top instead and

decorated it with marble—making it distinctively Italian rather than reminiscent of the French.

Late Gothic Sculpture During the Late Middle Ages, sculpture, like architecture, continued to undergo stylistic changes, among which two general trends may be identified. One trend centered in Italy, notably in Siena, where the Pisano family began to experiment with sculptural forms that foreshadowed Renaissance art, with its return to Classical themes and values (see Chapter 11). Outstanding among the members of the gifted Pisano family was Giovanni Pisano (1245–1314), who designed the intricate Late Gothic facade of the Siena Cathedral (see Figure 10.10). Giovanni's great artistic reputation is largely based on the massive marble pulpit that he carved for the cathedral at Pisa. Using Classical themes derived from Roman art (as Renaissance artists were to do), he designed the pulpit to rest on acanthus leaves at the top of eight Corinthian columns (Figure 10.12).

◄ **FIGURE 10.12** GIOVANNI PISANO. *Pulpit in the Pisa Cathedral. Ca. 1302–1310. Pisa, Italy. Pisano built and carved this massive (17-foot-high) pulpit late in his life but at the height of his reputation. A superb artist but a quarrelsome man, Pisano recorded his frustrations in the lengthy inscription around the pulpit's base. In this message to posterity, he claimed that he had achieved much, had been condemned by many, and took full responsibility for this work of art. Pisano's advance from the shadows of anonymity to a position of great artistic repute was typical of a new breed of artist appearing in Italy in the fourteenth century.*

The lions that support two of the columns were modeled on those on an ancient Roman sarcophagus. Just as late Roman art blended Christian and Classical symbols, so Giovanni's treatment of the pulpit's base mixed images of the cardinal virtues, such as Justice and Temperance, with the figure of the Greek hero Herakles.

Pisano's octagonal pulpit includes eight panels in high relief that depict scenes from the lives of either John the Baptist or Christ. Of these panels, the scene depicting the Nativity ranks as his finest work. In this scene, he portrays a natural vitality through the care-

FIGURE 10.13 GIOVANNI PISANO. *Nativity Scene. Pulpit in the Pisa Cathedral. Ca. 1302–1310. Pisa, Italy. In this Late Gothic sculpture, Pisano cut deeply into the marble's surface to give a nearly three-dimensional effect. His many figures all seem involved in their own tasks but are nevertheless linked with one another around the Madonna and Child. For example, the two shepherds in the upper right-hand corner are tending their sheep but are turned so they face Mary and Jesus. Such balanced placements are evidence of Pisano's classicizing tendencies.*

◀ **FIGURE 10.14** CLAUS SLUTER. Moses, from *The Well of Moses.* Ca. 1395–1406. Chartreuse de Champmol, Dijon, France. *Sluter followed the allegorical tradition of medieval art in this portrait of the Hebrew prophet Moses. The book in Moses' right hand and the scroll over his left shoulder symbolize the Word of God. Sluter also depicted Moses with "horns" growing out of his forehead as was characteristic in medieval representations.*

ful balance and orderly spacing of the animals and people (Figure 10.13). The placement and the calm actions of the surrounding figures frame the Virgin and Child so that the viewer's attention is focused on these two central figures. Giovanni's swaying figures with their smooth draperies were rooted in Late Gothic art, but their quiet serenity attested to his classicizing manner.

The other trend in sculpture during this time centered in Burgundy, where Philip the Bold (1364–1404) supported scholars and artists at his ducal court in Dijon. Preeminent among these was Claus Sluter (about 1350–1406), a sculptor of Netherlandish origin who helped to define this last phase of Gothic art. Sluter's masterly sculptures are still housed in a monastery near Dijon, and his most famous work, *The Well of Moses*, was commissioned for the cloister of this monastic retreat.

The Well of Moses, which was designed as a decorative cover for an actual well in a courtyard, is surrounded at its base with Old Testament prophets symbolizing the sacraments of communion and baptism. The most beautifully rendered of the surviving life-sized statues is Moses, encased in a flowing robe and standing erect with a finely chiseled head (Figure 10.14). Sluter's sense of the dramatic moment, of the prophet's personal emotions, and of the individual features make the statue nearly an individual portrait. Sluter rendered Moses' beard and the unfurled scroll in precise detail and carved the figure to twist and bend in the pronounced, swaying manner of the Late Gothic style.

Late Gothic Painting and the Rise of New Trends Of all the arts, painting underwent the most radical changes in the Late Middle Ages. Illuminated manuscripts maintained their popularity, but their themes became more secular under the patronage of titled aristocrats and wealthy merchants. At the same time, painters of frescoes and wooden panels introduced new techniques for applying paint and mixing colors. Stylistically, painters preferred to work in the extravagant Late Gothic manner with its elegant refinement and its undulating figures. Nevertheless, as mentioned earlier, Giotto and other Italian painters discovered fresh ways of depicting human figures that started to revolutionize art.

ILLUMINATED MANUSCRIPTS The Burgundian court played a pivotal role in the production of one of the outstanding illuminated manuscripts of the medieval period, the *Très Riches Heures du Duc de Berry*. This famous collection of miniatures was painted by the three Limbourg brothers for the Duke of Berry, brother of Philip the Bold of Burgundy. These illustrations stand above the rest of their time for their exquisite detail, general liveliness, and well-managed crowd scenes—some of the marks of the Late Gothic style.

The *Très Riches Heures*, or the Very Rich Hours, represents a type of small prayer book that was a favorite of nobles and businessmen. These personal books of worship, with their litanies and prayers, were often handsomely hand-illustrated to enhance their value. The Duke of Berry's prayer book contained some 130 miniature paintings, including scenes from the life of Christ and the calendar cycle. In the calendar series each tiny painting, finely detailed and colored in jewel-like tones, notes a seasonal activity appropriate for each month. Some paintings represent the brilliant court life of the duke, and others depict the drudgery of peasant life, sharply differentiated from the court scenes by their action and color. The illustration for the month of January shows the Duke of Berry surrounded by his well-dressed courtiers enjoying a sumptuous feast (Figure 10.15).

NEW TRENDS IN ITALY: GIOTTO Regardless of the lasting appeal of the illuminated miniatures, this type of art was overshadowed by what was occurring in Italy. The paintings of Giotto (about 1276–1337) are generally recognized as having established a new direction in Western art, one that led into the Renaissance. In Giotto's own day, Dante praised him and the citizens of Florence honored him. Later, Vasari, the famous sixteenth-century painter and biographer, declared that Giotto had "rescued and restored" painting.

Giotto's revolution in painting was directed against the prevailing *Italo-Byzantine style*, which blended Late Gothic with Byzantine influences. He turned this painting style, with its two-dimensional, lifeless quality, into a three-dimensional art characterized by naturalism and the full expression of human emotions. Partly through the innovative use of light and shade, Giotto was able to create realistic-looking figures, rather than the flat, ornamental de-

◄ **FIGURE 10.15** LIMBOURG BROTHERS. Month of January, from the *Très Riches Heures du Duc de Berry*. 1413–1416. Ca. 8½ × 5½". Musée Condé, Chantilly, France. *This miniature painting provides insightful social history in its exquisite details. The duke, seated in the right center, is dressed in a blue patterned cloak and is greeting his guests for what was probably a New Year's celebration. Behind the duke stands a servant. Over the servant's head are written the words "aproche, aproche," a welcome that is the equivalent of "Come in, come in." Above this festive scene the zodiac signs of Capricorn and Aquarius identify the month as January.*

FIGURE 10.16 CIMABUE. *Madonna Enthroned*. Ca. 1280. Tempera on panel, 12'7½" × 7'4". Uffizi Gallery, Florence. *Although Cimabue was experiencing the same desire for freedom in art as the sculptor Giovanni Pisano, this painting of the Madonna shows that he still was strongly under the spell of the Italo-Byzantine tradition. Rather than showing the intense feeling of Giotto's portraits, Cimabue's Virgin and Child remain medieval and mystical.*

◀ FIGURE 10.17   GIOTTO. *Madonna Enthroned.* Ca. 1310.
Tempera on panel, 10′8″ × 6′8″. Uffizi Gallery, Florence.
Giotto's Madonna Enthroned, *so revolutionary in its composition
and spatial dimensions, has been called the most influential painting
of the fourteenth century. Especially innovative in this altarpiece is
the realistic treatment of the Virgin's eyes. They are shaped like
ordinary eyes and peer out at the viewer rather than gazing into the
distance, as in the Italo-Byzantine style.*

pictions found in most illuminated manuscripts or the
Italian altar paintings.

A painting by one of Giotto's contemporaries,
Cimabue (about 1240–1302), the *Madonna Enthroned,*
reveals the state of Italian painting at this time (Figure
10.16). The angels on the side are rendered stiffly,
aligned vertically without any sense of space between
them, and placed flat on the wood panel without any
precise relationship with the four prophets below
them. Although Cimabue's angels were balanced in
their placement and the depiction of the figures of
the Madonna and Christ child offered some sense of
rounded form, the overall effect of the work confirms
its debt to the two-dimensional tradition of Italo-
Byzantine art.

In contrast, Giotto's *Madonna Enthroned,* painted
about twenty years after Cimabue's, shows how
Giotto was transforming Florentine art (Figure 10.17).
Giotto's Madonna seems to be actually sitting on her
throne, and the angels around her chair are placed to
give a sense of space and volume. The angels' gazes
are highly expressive, suggesting feelings of wonder
and respect. The Virgin resembles an individual
woman and Christ a believable baby, not a shrunken
adult. Although Giotto uses Gothic touches—the arch
and the applied gold leaf—the natural rendering of
the figures points toward the great changes coming
in art.

Giotto was a prolific artist whose paintings
adorned churches in Florence and cities all over Italy.
At the Arena Chapel in Padua Giotto painted his masterpiece, two sets of frescoes, one of the life of the
Virgin and the other of the life of Christ. These thirty-
eight scenes show Giotto at the height of his powers,
rendering space with a sense of depth and organizing
figures so as to create dramatic tension. An outstanding scene from the Padua frescoes is the *Pietà,* or *Lamentation* (Figure 10.18). This scene, which portrays the
grief for the dead Christ, expresses total despair
through the mourners' faces and gestures, from Mary
who cradles the body of Jesus, to John who stands
with arms outstretched, to the hovering angels. In
the fresco's stark and rugged landscape, even nature

seems to mourn, notably in the barren tree that symbolizes the wood of the cross on which Jesus died.
When Giotto passed from the scene in 1337, no
painter for the rest of the century was able to achieve
his remarkable depiction of nature and human
emotions.

FLEMISH PAINTING: JAN VAN EYCK   When Philip the Good
(1419–1467) became Duke of Burgundy, he expanded
his territories to include the wealthy counties of Holland, Zeeland, and Luxembourg. Philip was the
greatest secular patron of the arts of his day. Of the
artists encouraged by his patronage, the brothers Jan
and Hubert van Eyck are the most famous, and their
religious works and portraits established the Flemish
style of art. Little is known of Hubert, but Jan van
Eyck (about 1370–about 1440) is considered the founder of the Flemish school.

As a general principle, Flemish art sought reality
through an accumulation of precise and often symbolic details, in contrast to Italian art which tended
to be more concerned with psychological truth as in
Giotto's frescoes in the Arena Chapel. This national
style, primarily expressed through painting with oils
on wood panels, turned each artwork into a brilliant
and precise reproduction of the original scene. The
finest detail in a patterned carpet, the reflected light
on a copper vase, or the wrinkled features of an el-
derly patron were laboriously and meticulously recorded. The Flemish style, with its close attention to
detail, was widely appreciated and quickly spread to
Italy and England.

Jan van Eyck, probably with his brother's help,
painted the *Altarpiece of the Lamb* for the cathedral at
Ghent, Belgium. This large work—originally commissioned to beautify the high altar—still remains in its
original place. The twenty panels are hinged together
so that when opened twelve are visible. These twelve
panels are divided into two levels—heavenly figures
and symbols on the upper level and earthly figures
on the lower level. On the ends of the upper level
are nude portraits of Adam and Eve, next to angels
singing and playing musical instruments. Mary on
the left and John the Baptist on the right flank a portrayal of God the Father, resplendent in a jewel-
encrusted robe and triple crown. Below, on the lower
level, are human figures who are depicted as moving
toward the center panel. Those on the left are knights
and judges, riding on horseback, while, on the
right, pilgrims and hermits approach on foot (Figure 10.19).

The focus of the *Ghent Altarpiece,* when opened, is
the lower center panel, the *Adoration of the Lamb.* In
this work, the sacrificial death of Jesus is symbolized
by the cross, the baptismal font in the foreground,

FIGURE 10.19 HUBERT AND JAN VAN EYCK. *Ghent Altarpiece.*
Ca. 1432. Oil on panel, 11′3″ × 14′5″. St. Bavo Cathedral,
Ghent, Belgium. *This large altarpiece, measuring 15 by 11 feet,
may seem to be a collection of separate paintings, but the work is
united in themes and symbolism. What links the panels is their
portrayal of Christ's redemption of humanity. From the sin of Adam
and Eve to the mystic Adoration of the Lamb, all of the paintings
touch in some manner on Christ's sacrifice.*

◄ **FIGURE 10.18** GIOTTO. *Lamentation.* Ca. 1305–1310. Arena
Chapel, Padua, Italy. *Works like this won for Giotto his
reputation as the modern reviver of realistic art—a tradition that
had been lost with the fall of ancient Rome. In this fresco he created
three-dimensional space in ways that even the Greeks and Romans
had not used. Giotto's illusion of depth was conveyed by
surrounding the dead Christ with numerous figures and, in
particular, by placing two mourners in the foreground with their
backs to the viewer. Although this was achieved without
mathematical precision, Giotto's perspective was convincing to his
generation.*

FIGURE 10.20 HUBERT AND JAN VAN EYCK. *Adoration of the Lamb*, Detail of the *Ghent Altarpiece*. Ca. 1432. St. Bavo Cathedral, Ghent, Belgium. *This lower center section of the opened altarpiece dramatically shows how the Flemish school could use religious symbolism to evoke a mystical effect. The exquisitely refined details, which derived from the tradition of manuscript painting, make this scene both credible and otherworldly at the same time.*

and the blood issuing from the lamb into the communion chalice. The surrounding worshipers include holy virgins, martyrs, and prophets, plus the four Evangelists and the twelve Apostles, who stand and kneel in groups amid unusual plants and trees (Figure 10.20).

In contrast to this mystical work, Jan van Eyck painted a decidedly secular but still symbolic work in his *Arnolfini Wedding Portrait* (Figure 10.21). In this painting, nearly every object—the lighted candle, the shoes, the fruit, the dog—refers to a wedding custom or belief. Yet, the details—for example, the mirror on the rear wall reflecting the couple's backs, the artist, and a fourth person—create a worldly setting. Van Eyck's painting is not an imaginary scene but a recording of an actual event, for Arnolfini was an Italian businessman who lived in Bruges. Thus, the commerce and wealth of Burgundy and the Italian cities are symbolically united by van Eyck in this wedding portrait.

FIGURE 10.21 JAN VAN EYCK. *Arnolfini Wedding Portrait*. 1434. Panel painting, 33 × 22½". National Gallery, London. *This work is a perfect expression of the symbolic realism that dominated northern European painting in the Late Middle Ages. The wedding is celebrated in a room filled with religious symbols of the marriage rite. For example, the bride and groom stand barefooted, indicating that they are in holy space, and above them is a chandelier with a single lighted candle, a sign of God's presence.*

The Legacy of the Late Middle Ages

All historical eras are periods of transition, but the changes of the Late Middle Ages were especially momentous. The medieval world was dying, and the modern era was struggling to be born. Dating from this turbulent period were many of the cultural tensions that defined the history of Europe for the next four hundred years.

The most revolutionary happening in the Late Middle Ages was the release of a powerful secular spirit that began to make its presence felt everywhere. The upsurge of vernacular literature and the divergence of philosophy and theology are two examples of this new development. But the greatest impact of the rise of secularism on cultural life was that painting and sculpture began to be liberated from the service of architecture. The first stirrings of this change were expressed in the works of Giotto and other Italian and Flemish artists. By the next century, painting in Italy had freed itself from the tutelage of architecture and become the most important artistic genre in the West.

This period also saw the emergence of a new breed of secular ruler who was prepared to mount a sustained drive against the church's combined political and spiritual powers. The victories of the English and the French kings over the papacy—each ruler was able to secure control over his national church—were signs of the breakup of Christendom.

Another important legacy of these years is that the towns, led by their bourgeois citizens, began to exercise their influence over the countryside. From today's perspective, the growth of the middle class as a dominant force in society was perhaps the single most critical development of this age. Finally, this period witnessed the unusual spectacle of the common people revolting against the aristocratic control of the culture and society. Their sporadic efforts failed, but the seeds of future revolution were planted.

KEY CULTURAL TERMS

devotio moderna
via antiqua
via moderna
Late Gothic style

Flamboyant style
Perpendicular style
fan vault
Italo-Byzantine style

SUGGESTIONS FOR FURTHER READING

PRIMARY SOURCES

BOCCACCIO, G. *The Decameron.* Translated by M. Musa and P. E. Bondanella. New York: Norton, 1977. An updated translation of the hundred stories—some learned, some coarse, but all humorous—that make up this work; first published about 1351.

CHAUCER, G. *The Canterbury Tales.* Edited by N. Coghill. New York: Penguin, 1978. Of many versions of these bawdy and lighthearted tales, Coghill's is one of the most readable and enjoyable; the original work dates from 1385.

LANGLAND, W. *The Vision of Piers Plowman.* Translated by H. W. Wells. New York: Sheed and Ward, 1959. A good modern version of Langland's work criticizing the religious establishment of his day and calling for a new order; written between 1362 and 1394.

SECONDARY SOURCES

ASTON, M. *The Fifteenth Century: The Prospect of Europe.* New York: Harcourt, Brace & World, 1968. A brief work with many illustrations of artistic and social life; excellent for the beginning student.

BISHOP, M. *Petrarch and His World.* Bloomington: Indiana University Press, 1963. A biography of the great Florentine poet interwoven with long passages from his writings; the author and translator is a distinguished scholar.

DUBY, G. *The Age of the Cathedrals: Art and Society, 980–1420.* Translated by E. Levieux and B. Thompson. Chicago: University of Chicago Press, 1981. A work devoted to three medieval worlds—the monastery, the cathedral, and the palace—by the foremost medieval historian active today.

HAY, D. *Europe in the Fourteenth and Fifteenth Centuries.* London: Longman, 1980. The standard, longer introduction to this period.

HOFSTATTER, H. H. *Art of the Late Middle Ages.* Translated by R. E. Wolf. New York: Abrams, 1968. An excellent guide to Late Medieval painting, sculpture, and architecture with abundant illustrations, more than half in color.

HOLMES, G. A. *Europe, Hierarchy and Revolt, 1320–1450.* New York: Harper & Row, 1975. Excellent study of the interrelationship of political upheavals and economic change.

———, ed. *The Oxford Illustrated History of Medieval Europe.* Oxford: Oxford University Press, 1988. In separate essays, several scholars trace the evolution of Europe from the fall of Rome to the emergence of monarchies; richly illustrated.

HUIZINGA, J. *The Waning of the Middle Ages.* New York: St. Martin's Press, 1924. Written nearly seventy years ago, but still challenges many conventional ways of viewing the Late Middle Ages.

LAMBERT, C. *Medieval Heresy: Popular Movements from Bogomil to Hus.* New York: Holmes & Meier Publishers, 1976. A scholarly survey summarizing the latest research on heretical movements between 900 and 1450.

MEISS, M. *Painting in Florence and Siena After the Black Death.* Princeton, N.J.: Princeton University Press, 1951. One of the first studies relating art to social movements.

OERTEL, P. *Early Italian Painting to 1400.* London: Thames and Hudson, 1966. A study primarily of thirteenth-century Italian painting focusing on Giotto and his stylistic influence on other artists.

TUCHMAN, B. *A Distant Mirror: The Calamitous 14th Century.* New York: Knopf, 1979. An eloquently written study that concentrates on the life of a French noble while analyzing the fundamental causes of change in the fourteenth century.

ZIEGLER, P. *The Black Death.* New York: John Day Company, 1969. The first general treatment in almost a century of the plague and its origins and spread across Europe; for the beginning student.

11

THE EARLY RENAISSANCE: RETURN TO CLASSICAL ROOTS

1400–1494

Believing they were living in a period that had broken radically with the past, Italian artists and intellectuals in the fifteenth century began to speak of a rebirth of civilization. Since the nineteenth century, the term *Renaissance* (meaning "rebirth") has been used by historians and others to describe the cultural and artistic activities of the fourteenth and fifteenth centuries that began in Italy and eventually spread to other European countries.

The Renaissance profoundly altered the course of Western culture, and, since the mid–nineteenth century, scholars have made a specialty of the Renaissance, studying and analyzing its culture. They have not always agreed on their findings, however, and several schools of thought have arisen concerning the definition and significance of this first modern period.

THE RENAISSANCE: SCHOOLS OF INTERPRETATION

In the middle of the nineteenth century, Swiss historian Jacob Burckhardt laid the foundation for Renaissance studies. Agreeing with the fifteenth-century Italians, he asserted that an actual rebirth of ideas began in their time after centuries of cultural stagnation. He maintained that a new way of understanding the world emerged during this period when the Italians began to look back to ancient Greece and Rome for inspiration and declared themselves part of a revitalized civilization that was distinctive and superior to the immediate past.

By the middle of the twentieth century, Burckhardt's view began to be reexamined. Pronouncing it too simplistic, some historians pointed out that the break with the past was not as dramatic as Burckhardt claimed; what changes did take place simply modified trends and attitudes that had been prevalent in Italian culture for centuries. These scholars claimed that the Italians, after the fall of Rome, never lost sight of their Classical roots and that the revival of learning in the fifteenth century was more a shift in educational and cultural emphasis than a rediscovery of antiquity. They also noted that the Renaissance passed through at least two phases, the Early and the High, and that each phase was distinct in its nature and contributions. Furthermore, these scholars insisted that the world of the Renaissance must be broadened geographically to include other states in Italy besides Florence, notably the Republic of Venice, and other regions outside of Italy, especially the Duchy of Burgundy.

Since 1960 a third school of interpretation has come to dominate Renaissance studies. This latest view contends that the word *Renaissance* should be used exclusively to describe what was happening in learning and the arts and should not be applied to politics and society. Moreover, this interpretation holds that the label should be used with extreme caution, because only now are historians beginning to comprehend the events of this complex age.

FIGURE 11.1 DOMENICO GHIRLANDAIO. *Old Man with a Child.* Ca. 1480. Panel, 24½ × 18″. Louvre. *This double portrait by the Florentine artist Ghirlandaio summarizes many of the new secular values of the Early Renaissance, such as its human-centeredness and its preference for simple scenes. Further, the work's subject, possibly a man with his grandchild, indicates the important role that the family played in the life of the times. In addition, the age's commitment to direct observation of the physical world is evident in the treatment of the man's diseased nose and the landscape glimpsed through the open window. Finally, the painter has made the exterior scene realistic by using linear and atmospheric perspective—two new techniques invented during the period.*

We tend to agree with the third group of scholars who say that the fifteenth-century Italians were misguided in the belief that they had made a profound break with the Middle Ages. In terms of politics, economics, and society, Italy in the 1400s was roughly like Italy in the 1300s. In *cultural* terms, however, the Italians of the 1400s did start down a new path (Figure 11.1).

This chapter examines the first phase of this new cultural style, the Early Renaissance (1400–1494). Chapter 12 is devoted to the brief High Renaissance (1494–1520) and to Early Mannerism (1520–1564), an anti-Classical phase of the Renaissance. Finally, Chapter 13 considers a number of developments including the religious reformations of the early sixteenth century and Late Mannerism (1564–1603), when Renaissance style was slowly undermined by new trends (Time Line 11.1).

EARLY RENAISSANCE HISTORY AND INSTITUTIONS

For most of the fifteenth century, the Italian peninsula was freed from threats of foreign invasion and intrusion into its domestic affairs. The major central European powers were distracted by their own problems, and southeastern Europe became Muslim as the Ottoman Turks solidified their conquests with the capture of Constantinople in 1453. The Muslim presence was to have important long-range repercussions for eastern and southern Europe as well as for the Italian interests in the Mediterranean. But overall these events had little impact on Italian affairs until 1494, when a French army led by Charles VIII entered Italy in the hope of furthering French monarchic ambitions.

Italian City-States during the Early Renaissance

During the Early Renaissance five Italian states competed for political mastery: in the north, the Republic of Venice, the Duchy of Milan, and the Republic of Florence; in the center, the Papal States, led by a rejuvenated post-Schism papacy; and, in the south, the Kingdom of Naples, including the island of Sicily. Besides these five powers, some smaller states like Ferrara and Modena were important artistic and intellectual centers that played minor but crucial roles in Italian affairs (Map 11.1).

In the first half of the fifteenth century the Italian states waged incessant wars among themselves, shifting sides when it was to their advantage, and no single principality could rule over the rest. Eventually, the Peace of Lodi, signed in 1454, established a delicate balance of power among Milan, Florence, and Venice, drawn together by their common fear that Italy might be invaded by foreigners. The Peace of Lodi coincided with the end of the Hundred Years' War and the fall of Constantinople—three pivotal events in European history. The decision of the Kingdom of Naples to join the northern Italians in this defensive pact ensured that Italy was tranquil for forty years, until the French invasion.

TIME LINE 11.1 **STAGES OF THE ITALIAN RENAISSANCE**

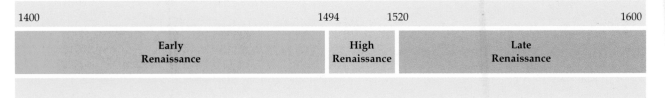

1400		1494	1520		1600
Early Renaissance		**High Renaissance**	**Late Renaissance**		

The impact of the internecine wars of the first half of the century, coupled with a changing economy, led to the emergence of autocratic rulers, or despots, across the map of Italy. The age of despots spelled the end of the great medieval legacy of republicanism in Venice, Milan, and Florence and the rise to power of either ruling families or elitist factions in these territories as well as in the Papal States and the Kingdom of Naples. What influence guilds, business leaders, and middle-class cliques had wielded in the fourteenth century now gave way to the despots, also called *signori*. Taking advantage of economic and class tensions, these autocrats pledged to solve local problems and in so doing proceeded to accumulate power in their own hands.

Under the despots, military tactics were rapidly changing because technological developments in weaponry affected the ways that wars were waged, troops were recruited, and generals were chosen. Campaigns were now fought with mercenary troops led by soldiers of fortune, called *condottieri*, who sold their military expertise to the highest bidder. Since professional warriors were loyal only to themselves, they often changed sides in the heat of battle and thus affected the final military outcome. In addition, a state's victory was sometimes jeopardized by the rivalries between local factions and families—the curse of every Italian city-state.

The most significant change in Renaissance warfare was the emergence of diplomacy as a peaceful

MAP 11.1

The States of Italy During the Renaissance, ca. 1494

alternative to armed struggle. The Italian regimes began to send representatives abroad to serve state interests. As a result, it became customary for diplomats, during a pause in the fighting, to set about making a peace settlement, although these negotiated arrangements seldom lasted very long—with the notable exception of the Peace of Lodi. The Italian method of establishing diplomatic ties slowly spread over the continent and became the standard of the European states in the following century.

A major factor in Italy's politics in this period was the shifting fortunes of the once-thriving economy. Emerging from the High Middle Ages in 1300 as Europe's leading commercial center and top manufacturer of finished woolens (see Chapter 9), the northern Italian city-states lost the economic race to the north Europeans by 1500. During these two hundred years, however, Italy's economy did not move in a downward spiral. In fact, the worst years were in the 1300s, when the peninsula suffered terrible population losses and a sharp decline in productivity due to the Black Death and the birth of the English woolen industry.

After this low point, the Italians made a remarkable, though limited, recovery in the 1400s. Venice, the most powerful of these mercantile states, renewed control of Mediterranean trade, and Florence, after subduing Pisa in 1405, gained a seaport. Other states made a niche for themselves in the luxury market by producing such items as ceramics, glassware, and lace. But the flow of history was moving against the north Italian cities. The woolen trade was lost forever to England and Flanders; although Florence countered this loss with a highly successful local silk industry, it was forced to give up its leadership in textiles. Even the Italian domination of international banking was being challenged by German businessmen. What finally sealed the Italians' economic doom were three events over which they had no control: the fall of Constantinople, Portugal's opening of the trade routes around Africa to India, and the discovery of the New World.

As more powerful secular rulers emerged in Europe, some used their powers to advance their political and economic interests beyond the geographical limits of continental Europe. Portugal led the way in the late fifteenth century as its ships opened the sea route to India around Africa's Cape of Good Hope. Spain was not far behind as the crown supported the Genoese sailor Christopher Columbus in his voyage to the West Indies in 1492. These explorations launched a maritime revolution that resulted, in the sixteenth century, in the shifting of the focus of international trade from the Mediterranean to the Atlantic.

The long-range prospect for Italy's economy may

FIGURE 11.2 ROGIER VAN DER WEYDEN. *Portrait of Francesco d'Este.* Ca. 1455–1460. Tempera and oil on wood, 11¾ × 8″. Metropolitan Museum of Art. Bequest of Michael Friedsam, 1931. The Friedsam Collection. *Ferrara, situated between Bologna and Venice, was home to the Este family, who dominated the city's political and cultural life. Through generous patronage, this family founded a public library and attracted leading Renaissance artists and scholars to their splendid court. This portrait was painted by the Flemish artist Rogier Van Der Weyden, who helped to introduce the Italians to the use of oil paints.*

have been bleak, but in the short run unprecedented levels of wealth were enjoyed by the upper-class families of the fifteenth century. Led by this elite, the city-states followed an urban way of life that had first appeared along with the revival of commerce as early as 1100. The culture of the Early Renaissance was substantially determined by the patronage of these families, who used their money to cultivate their tastes in literature and art (Figure 11.2). The courts of local rulers, or *grandi*, served as the centers of this way of life where educated men, and, on occasion, women, gathered to exchange ideas and to discuss philosophical issues.

Another prominent characteristic of Italy's urban way of life was the reverence paid to the family by both the noble elite and the wealthy merchant class. On a practical level, middle-class parents had to make sure that sons were properly educated to carry on the family businesses and that daughters were prepared to be loyal wives. In the average family, the condition

TIME LINE 11.2   PHASES OF FLORENTINE POLITICS

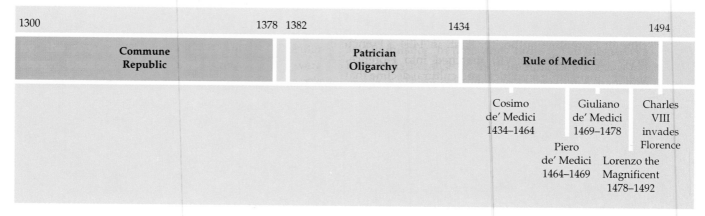

1300		1378 1382	1434	1494
Commune Republic		**Patrician Oligarchy**	**Rule of Medici**	

Cosimo de' Medici 1434–1464

Piero de' Medici 1464–1469

Giuliano de' Medici 1469–1478

Lorenzo the Magnificent 1478–1492

Charles VIII invades Florence

---

of women did not improve appreciably, but many more females were educated now than in earlier times. The marriages of both daughters and sons were arranged by the parents, and a costly dowry usually accompanied the prospective bride. Brides wed in their teens, but grooms waited until their mid-thirties. Because of this age discrepancy among the well-to-do, many women became rich and fairly young widows with substantial social power.

A few outstanding women at the ducal courts exhibited some degree of independence and exercised a certain amount of political influence. For example, Lucrezia Borgia (1480–1519), who held court in Ferrara and was the illegitimate daughter of Pope Alexander VI, married three times, supported writers and artists, and in her late years devoted herself to charitable causes. But most women did not have the opportunity to be independent.

Florence, the Center of the Renaissance

Amid the artistic and intellectual activity occurring throughout the Italian peninsula, Florence, the capital of the Tuscan region, stands head and shoulders above the other city-states. Florence's political system evolved through several stages after 1300—from republic to oligarchy to family rule. Simultaneously with these turbulent political activities, Florentine artists and writers made their city-state the center of the Early Renaissance to 1450.

The first phase of Florence's political evolution was the republic, which was born in the fourteenth century. But no sooner was the republic set up with its hopes for political equality than it fell into the hands of a wealthy oligarchy. This oligarchy, composed of the rich bankers and merchants as well as the more

successful guildsmen and craftsmen, ruled until the early fifteenth century, when the Medici family gained control of the state. The Medici dominated Florentine politics and cultural life from 1434 to 1494. The Medici period, which sometimes amounted to a mild despotism, constituted the third phase of Florentine political life during this time (Time Line 11.2).

The Medici arose from modest circumstances, lending money to poor Florentines and supplementing their income with profits from the woolen trade. Giovanni di Bicci de' Medici (1360–1429) amassed the family's first large fortune by setting up branch banks in major Italian cities and forming close financial ties with the papacy. His son Cosimo (1389–1464) added to the Medici's wealth and outmaneuvered his political enemies, becoming the unacknowledged ruler of Florence. As a matter of policy, he persuaded others through appeals to their self-interest and spent his money on those things that pleased him—books, paintings, sculptures, and palaces. This astute Florentine, who always claimed to be the common man's friend, was eventually awarded the title *Pater patriae,* Father of his Country—an ancient Roman title revived during the exuberance of the Renaissance.

Piero, Cosimo's son, ruled for only a short time. He was succeeded by his son, Lorenzo (1449–1492), called the Magnificent because of his grand style of living. Lorenzo, well-educated, vigorous, and accomplished, lived a full life. He controlled Florence with his brother Giuliano until Giuliano was assassinated in 1478 by the Pazzi family, the long-standing rivals of the Medici. Lorenzo, barely escaping death, brutally executed the conspirators and then governed alone in an autocratic manner for the next fourteen years. In foreign affairs, he used diplomacy to inaugurate an era of peace but at a high cost, since taxes were raised, thereby draining the city's resources and piling up debts owed to rich families.

12

THE HIGH RENAISSANCE AND EARLY MANNERISM

1494—1564

Between 1494 and 1564, one of the most brilliantly creative periods in Western history occurred in Italy. During this span of seventy years there flourished three artists—Leonardo da Vinci, Raphael, and Michelangelo—and a writer—Machiavelli—whose achievements became legendary in their own time and whose names today spark instant recognition among educated people everywhere. The works of these geniuses, along with the works of a small group of other talented but less well-known artists and intellectuals, affected the basic Western concept of art and fundamentally influenced the way we understand ourselves and the world.

The first phase of this seventy-year period is called the *High Renaissance*; lasting from 1494 to 1520, it represents the zenith of the cultural renewal known as the Renaissance. During the High Renaissance the Classical principles that had begun to be revived in Italy in the early fifteenth century—beauty, balance, order, serenity, harmony, rational design—reached a state of perfection. At the same time, the center of culture shifted from Florence, the heart of the Early Renaissance, to Rome, where the popes became the leading patrons of the new style. Florence had begun to decline in 1494, when the French invaded and took control of northern Italy. While Florence languished, a papal campaign to make Rome the world's most beautiful city gained momentum, and the popes used their wealth and prestige to attract the age's most talented artists into their service. Florence even had to yield the services of Michelangelo, its favorite son, to the Roman pontiffs (Figure 12.1).

After 1520, however, the Renaissance veered away from the humanistic values of Classicism toward an antihumanistic vision of the world. This new phase is labeled *Mannerism* because of the self-conscious, or "mannered," style adopted by its artists and intellectuals. Mannerist art and culture endured from 1520 until the end of the century, although this chapter covers the story of this style only until the end of its first phase in 1564, with the death of Michelangelo. Chapter 13 traces the path of the Renaissance in northern Europe and also picks up the thread of later changes in Mannerism, particularly focusing on the impact of religious controversy on Mannerism until its demise at the end of the sixteenth century.

THE RISE OF THE MODERN SOVEREIGN STATE

The most important political development in the first half of the sixteenth century was the emergence of powerful sovereign states in the newly unified and stabilized kingdoms of France, England, and Spain. This process was already underway in the last part of the fifteenth century (see Chapter 10), but it now began to have a profound effect on the course of international affairs. The ongoing rivalries of these aggressive national powers brought into existence the concept of the balance of power—a principle that has dominated politics ever since.

FIGURE 12.1 MICHELANGELO. *"Dying Slave."* 1513–1516. *Marble, ca. 7'5". Louvre. Michelangelo's so-called Dying Slave embodies the conflicting artistic tendencies at work between 1494 and 1564. The statue's idealized traits—the perfectly proportioned figure, the restrained facial expression, and the body's gentle S-curve shape—are hallmarks of the High Renaissance style. But the figure's overall sleekness and exaggerated arm movements—probably based on one of the figures in the first-century A.D. Laocoön Group, which had only recently been rediscovered—were portents of Early Mannerism.*

TABLE 12.1 FRENCH AND SPANISH RULERS, 1494–1564

FRANCE	SPAIN
Charles VIII, 1483–1498	Ferdinand V, 1479–1516 and Isabella, 1474–1504
Louis XII, 1498–1515	
Francis I, 1515–1547	Charles I, 1516–1556 (also Holy Roman Emperor, 1519–1556)
Henry II, 1547–1559	
Francis II, 1559–1560	Philip II, 1556–1598
Charles IX, 1560–1574	

During this seventy-year period Europe's international political life was controlled, either directly or indirectly, by France and Spain. France's central role was the result of the policies of a series of strong Valois kings, the dynasty that had governed France since the early fourteenth century. Spain's fortunes soared during this period, first under the joint rule of Ferdinand V and Isabella and then, after 1516, under Charles I. In 1519 Charles I was also elected Holy Roman Emperor as Charles V, thus joining the interests of Spain and the Holy Roman Empire until his abdication in 1556 (Table 12.1). England, the other emerging strong sovereign state, kept virtually aloof from continental affairs during this time.

After 1519 especially, the French and Spanish rulers dispatched their armies and allies into the weaker states, where they fought and claimed new lands as their own. As these sovereign monarchs gained power at home and abroad, the medieval dream of a united Christendom—pursued by Charlemagne, preached by the popes, and cherished by the Holy Roman Emperors—slowly faded away.

The source of the strength of these new states was that they were united around a ruler who exercised more and more central control. Within these new monarchies the kings devised varied techniques for increasing and centralizing their power. Although most claimed to rule by divine right, their practical policies were actually more important in increasing their power than any divine claims. They surrounded themselves with ministers and consultative councils, both of which depended on the crown. The royal ministers were often chosen from the bourgeois class, who were more trustworthy than the independent-minded feudal nobility. These ministers, many of whom grew rich and powerful, advised the rulers on such weighty matters as religion and war and ran the developing bureaucracies. The bureaucracies in turn strengthened centralized rule by extending the king's jurisdiction into areas formerly reserved to the feudal nobility, such as the justice system.

The crown further eroded the status of the feudal nobles by completing a process begun in the Late Middle Ages: The king's armies no longer relied on the warrior class but depended on standing mercenary armies. In order to pay the mercenary troops, the kings were forced to consult with representative bodies, such as Parliament in England, and to make them a part of their regular administration.

Rivalry between France and Spain—under Spanish and, later, Hapsburg rulers—plunged the European continent into wars for much of the sixteenth century. Between 1494 and 1529, Italy was a battleground where foreign armies acted out the dreams of ambitious rulers, ravaging the peninsula in the process. The conflict over Italy ended in 1529 with the triumph of the Holy Roman Emperor, Charles V, over the French king. But no sooner was Charles V victorious in Italy than he extended his war to Europe north of the Alps in the name of uniting Christendom. Between 1530 and 1559 central Europe was the stage for another series of exhausting dynastic wars. In the last forty years of the sixteenth century, from 1560 on, any hope for a united Europe was swept away by a rising tide of national consciousness, intensified dynastic rivalries, and bloody religious and civil wars (see Chapter 13).

The Struggle for Italy, 1494–1529

Italy's relative tranquility, established by the Peace of Lodi in 1454, was shattered by the French invasion in 1494. For the next thirty-five years, France, Spain, and the Holy Roman Empire fought among themselves, as well as with the papacy and most of the Italian states, for control of portions of this wealthy peninsula. The struggle began when a newly unified France, anxious to reassert a hereditary claim to Naples and southern Italy, gladly accepted Milan's call for aid in a controversy involving Naples, Florence, and the pope. The French king, Charles VIII (1483–1498), took Florence in 1494, then advanced to Rome and finally to Naples, wreaking havoc as he went.

But the Italians did not back down. Joined by Venice and the pope and supported by the Holy Roman Emperor and the Spanish monarch, they drove the French from Italian soil. The aid of these two foreign rulers was not simply altruistic, however; each had his own goals in Italy. The Spanish king wanted to keep his Sicilian lands intact, and the Holy Roman Emperor was determined to protect his long-standing political interests in Italy.

After the French ruler died, his successor, Louis XII (1498–1515), returned to Italy in 1499 to activate a hereditary claim to Milan. Once again the Spanish and the Germans joined with the Italians to drive the French from Italy. The inability of either side to resolve these conflicts with finality led to intermittent, but inconclusive, invasions of Italy over the next decades under both Louis XII and, after 1515, France's new king, Francis I (1515–1547). In the course of their campaigns, the French rulers, who were enamored of the Italian Renaissance, brought the new artistic and intellectual ideals to northern Europe (Figure 12.2).

In 1522 full-scale hostilities broke out between France and the Holy Roman Empire over Italy's fu-

FIGURE 12.2 JEAN CLOUET. *Francis I.* Ca. 1525. Oil on panel, 37¾ × 29⅛″. Louvre. *During his thirty-two-year-long reign, Francis I was a major force in sixteenth-century European affairs. He also embarked on a massive artistic program, inspired by the Italian Renaissance, to make his court the most splendid in Europe. Under his personal direction, Italian artworks and artists, including Leonardo da Vinci, were imported into France. Unfortunately, this rather stylized portrait by Jean Clouet, Francis's chief court artist, fails to do justice to this connoisseur of Italian culture. Indeed, the likeness owes more to the conventionalized portraits of the Gothic style than it does to the realistic works of the Italian Renaissance.*

ture. This struggle, the first of several wars fought in different locations, pitted the old Europe against the new. The Holy Roman Empire, ruled by Charles V (1519–1556) of the royal house of Hapsburg, was a ramshackle, decentralized relic from the feudal age. France, under the leadership of the bold and intellectual Francis I of the royal house of Valois, was the epitome of the new sovereign state.

The first Hapsburg-Valois war was the only one to be fought in Italy. Its most notorious moment occurred in 1527 when the troops of Charles V ran riot in Rome, raping, looting, and killing. The sack of Rome had two major consequences. First, it cast doubt on Rome's ability to control Italy—long a goal of the popes—for it showed that the secular rulers no longer respected the temporal power of the papacy. Second, it ended papal patronage of the arts for almost a decade and thus weakened Rome's role as a cultural leader. It also had a chilling effect on artistic ideals and contributed to the rise of Mannerism.

In 1529 the Treaty of Cambrai brought to a close this first phase of the Hapsburg-Valois rivalry. Twenty-five years of invasions and wars left most of Italy divided and exhausted. Some cities, like Florence and Rome, suffered nearly irreparable harm.

Florence, because it had so much to lose, fared the worst. The city never regained its former power and prestige after opening its gates to the French in 1494. By the 1530s the Medici rulers had resumed power as the Dukes of Florence, but in the power politics of the mid–sixteenth century, they were little more than puppets of the foreigners who controlled much of the peninsula.

In the aftermath of the Treaty of Cambrai, the only important Italian state to keep its political independence was Venice. Because it eluded the ravages of war and because of its stable government and exten-

MAP 12.1

European Empire of Charles V

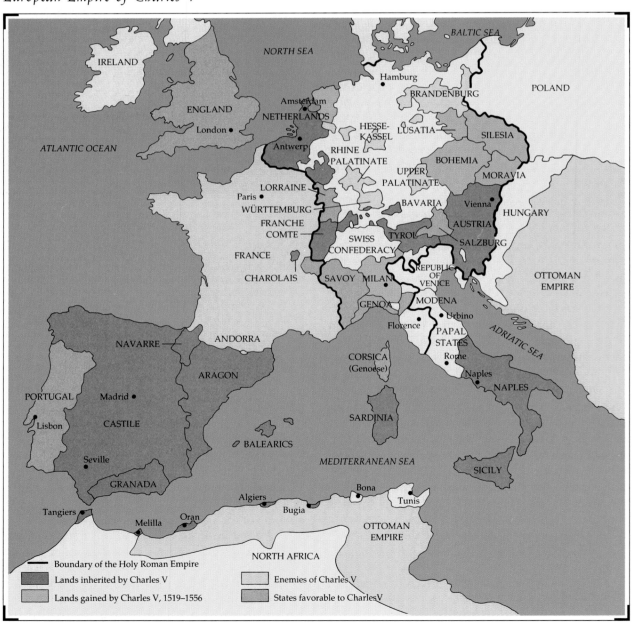

sive commercial activity in the Mediterranean, this state became the one remaining haven for artists and intellectuals in Italy for the rest of the sixteenth century.

Charles V and the Hapsburg Empire

By 1530 the struggle between the Valois and the Hapsburgs over the balance of power shifted to central Europe. The French felt themselves to be hemmed in by the Spanish in the south, the Germans to the east, and the Dutch to the north—peoples all ruled by the Hapsburg Emperor Charles V. In French eyes Charles had an insatiable appetite for power that expressed itself through his determination to surround France and to control the Continent through wars and alliances. In contrast, the Hapsburg ruler considered the French king a land-hungry upstart who stood in his way of a Europe united under a Christian prince—in other words, the dream of Christendom. These opposing perceptions prevailed until 1559 when, after a number of exhausting wars and a series of French military victories, the belligerents signed the Treaty of Cateau-Cambrésis. This treaty, recognizing that neither side could prevail, had the happy effect of ushering in a brief period of peace (Map 12.1).

The man who stood in the center of most of these events, Charles V, lived a life filled with paradoxes and ironies (Figure 12.3). Because of the size of his empire, he was in theory one of the most powerful rulers ever to live; but in actuality, again because of the vastness of his lands, he never quite succeeded in gaining complete control of his empire. In some ways, he was the last of medieval kings, for around him were gathered those who wanted a united Christian Europe; on the other hand, he foreshadowed a new age driven by sovereign kings, standing armies, diplomatic agreements, and strong religious differences.

Charles V's unique position at the center of Europe's political storm was the result of a series of timely deaths, propitious births, and politically astute arranged marriages. These circumstances, even before Charles came on the scene, had already permitted the Hapsburg line of rulers, which had existed since the thirteenth century, to accumulate more and more power, wealth, and land. Now, at the opening of the sixteenth century, Charles came into possession of an enormous empire. Born in 1500 to a German father and a Spanish mother, he was the grandson of both the Holy Roman Emperor Maximilian I and the Spanish King Ferdinand V. At the age of six

FIGURE 12.3 TITIAN. *Charles V with a Dog.* Ca. 1533. Oil on canvas, 6'3" × 3'8". Prado. *Titian's full-length, standing portrait of Charles V was painted when the Hapsburg emperor was at the height of his power. By rendering the "ruler of the world" in* contrapposto, *his fingers casually holding the collar of his dog, Titian endows the emperor with a natural grace. The lighting that illuminates Charles from the dark background and the breathless hush that seems to envelope the man and dog are trademarks of Titian's style.*

he inherited Burgundy and the Low Countries from his father; at sixteen he received Spain and the Spanish Hapsburg territories in Italy, along with the unimaginable riches of the recently acquired lands in the New World, from his maternal grandfather; and at nineteen he acquired Germany and Austria from his paternal grandfather, which set the stage for his successful bid to become the Holy Roman Emperor. By 1519, Charles V—simultaneously Charles I of Spain—ruled the largest empire the world has ever known. He was referred to by many of his subjects as "ruler of the world."

For most of his life, Charles traveled from one of his possessions to another, fighting battles, arranging peace treaties, and attempting to unify his empire by personal control and compromise. He frequently found that his attention was divided, for he might have to confront the French to the west and at the same time counter a threat from the Ottoman Turks in the east. Thus Charles would find himself caught between two powerful foes who drained both his personal energies and his imperial resources.

Within the Holy Roman Empire, the princes of the German principalities often took advantage of his prolonged absences and his preoccupation with the French and the Turks. They were especially able to gain political power at the emperor's expense after Martin Luther's revolt and the beginning of the Protestant Reformation (see Chapter 13). Charles made matters even worse by his contradictory policies, which often depended on the military pressures he was experiencing: At times he angered the disaffected German princes by meddling in their affairs and condemning Lutheran doctrines, and at other times he angered the popes by making concessions to the Protestants.

Exhausted and disillusioned by his inability to prevail in Europe, Charles abdicated in 1555 and retired to a monastery, leaving his possessions to be divided between his heirs. His brother Ferdinand took control of the German-Austrian inheritance and was soon elected Holy Roman Emperor. His son Philip assumed control of the Spanish Hapsburg holdings, including Spain, the New World territories, and the Netherlands. He became Philip II of Spain. Thus ended Charles's vision of a united Europe and Christendom, which, because of forces beyond his control, had turned into a nightmare of endless meetings, gory battles, and false hopes of peace and unity.

ECONOMIC EXPANSION AND SOCIAL DEVELOPMENTS

By the late fifteenth century Europe was well on the way to full recovery from the impact of the plague (see Chapter 10). The sixteenth century continued to be a time of growing population and increasing prosperity. The center of commerce now shifted from the Mediterranean to the Atlantic coast, making cities like London and Antwerp financial and merchandising centers. Skilled craftspeople turned out quality products, and enterprising merchants distributed these finished goods in increasing quantities across much of western Europe north of the Alps. At the same time, the first steps toward a worldwide market were taken, following the daring sailing expeditions and discoveries of the late fifteenth and early sixteenth centuries. New raw materials from America and innovative ways of manufacturing spurred economic growth.

Although the data are scattered and often unreliable, enough evidence is available to show that the population of Europe increased from about 45 million in 1400 to 69 million in 1500 and to about 89 million by 1600. In a few regions, the population grew at an accelerated pace, as in the Holy Roman Empire, where it rose from about 12 to 20 million. There was also a major population shift from rural to urban areas. This shift was reflected in the rise in the number of cities with populations of over 100,000 from five to eight between 1500 and 1600. Rome, for example, grew from about 50,000 in 1526—the year before the sack—to 100,000 by the end of the century.

Prosperity brought a higher standard of living to most of the urban middle class, but the expanding economy also created some serious problems. The basic problem was that throughout much of the century prices rose faster than wages. Those who were not profiting from increased economic growth, such as poor peasants and impecunious nobles living on unproductive farms, individuals with fixed incomes, and persons in outmoded jobs, suffered the most. In those areas of Europe hardest hit by inflation or agricultural and commercial stagnation, economic crises often became intertwined with social and religious matters that intensified long-standing regional and local differences.

Yet the boom offered economic opportunities to many people. Merchants who were engaged in a variety of businesses and financial arrangements made fortunes for themselves and provided employment for others. These merchants and the bankers who offered loans were also accumulating capital, which they then invested in other types of commercial activity. The campaigns of Charles V were financed by wealthy bankers operating in a well-organized money market. The amassing of surplus capital and its reinvestment ushered in the opening phase of commercial capitalism that laid the foundation for Europe's future economic expansion.

During the first half of the sixteenth century the full impact brought on by the abundance of raw materials and the vast market potential of the New World had only just begun to affect Europe's economy. South American gold and silver played an important role in the upward price revolution—a development that would go on for decades. Only later, after 1650, would New World agricultural products, such as tobacco, cotton, and cocoa, lead to the production of new manufactured goods and profoundly alter consumer habits.

In one area, however, a major economic change now occurred. Some Europeans, taking advantage of the institution of slavery and the existing slave trade in western Africa, mercilessly exploited the local Africans by buying and shipping them to European colonies in the New World. The slaves were put to work in the gold and silver mines of Central and South America and on the cotton and sugar cane plantations in the West Indies, where they became a major factor in the production of these newly discovered forms of wealth.

FROM HIGH RENAISSANCE TO EARLY MANNERISM

The characteristics of High Renaissance style were largely derived from the visual arts. Led by painters, sculptors, and architects who worshiped ancient Classical ideals, notably those of late-fifth-century B.C. Greece, the High Renaissance was filled with images of repose, harmony, and heroism. Under the spell of Classicism and the values of simplicity and restraint, artists sought to conquer unruly physical reality by subjecting it to the principle of a seemingly effortless order.

Although the visual arts dominated the High Renaissance, literary figures also contributed to this era. From Classicism the High Renaissance authors appropriated two of their chief aesthetic aims, secularism and idealism. Like their ancient predecessors, historians showed that contemporary events arose from human causes rather than from divine action—

TABLE 12.2 POPES OF THE HIGH RENAISSANCE

Alexander VI	1492–1503
Julius II	1503–1513
Leo X	1513–1521

unmistakable evidence of a mounting secular spirit. Actually, secularism more deeply affected the writing of history than the arts and architecture, where church patronage and religious subjects still held sway. A rising secular consciousness can also be seen in the popular manuals on manners that offered advice on how to become a perfect gentleman or lady. Although they have no counterpart in ancient literature, these books nevertheless have the Classical quality of treating their subject in idealized terms.

What distinguished the High Renaissance preoccupation with the Classical past from the Early Renaissance's renewed interest in ancient matters was largely a shift in creative sensibility. The Early Renaissance artists, in the course of growing away from the Late Gothic style, had invented new ways of recapturing the harmonious spirit of ancient art and architecture. The geniuses of the next generation, benefiting from the experiments of the Early Renaissance, succeeded in creating masterpieces of disciplined form and idealized beauty. The High Renaissance masters' superb confidence allowed them to produce works that were in harmony with themselves and the physical world—a hallmark of Classical art.

Regardless of its brilliance, the High Renaissance existed for only a fleeting moment in the history of Western culture—from the French invasion of Italy in 1494 until the death of Raphael in 1520 (preceded by the death of Leonardo in 1519) (Time Line 12.1). In this era, the Renaissance popes spared no expense in their patronage of the arts and letters (Table 12.2).

TIME LINE 12.1 ITALIAN CULTURAL STYLES BETWEEN 1494 AND 1564

1494		1520			1564
	High Renaissance		Early Mannerism		
French Invasion of Northern Italy 1494	Sistine Chapel ceiling frescoes by Michelangelo 1508–1512	Death of Raphael 1520 / Death of Leonardo da Vinci 1519	Publication of Machiavelli's *Prince* 1532	*Last Judgment* fresco in Sistine Chapel by Michelangelo 1536–1541	Death of Michelangelo 1564

FIGURE 12.6 LEONARDO DA VINCI. *Mona Lisa*. 1503. Oil on panel, 30¼ × 21". Louvre. *Leonardo's* Mona Lisa, *a likeness of the wife of the merchant Giocondo, illustrates the new status of Italy's urban middle class. This class was beginning to take its social cues from the fashionable world of the courts, the milieu described by Castiglione. Leonardo treats his middle-class subject as a model court lady, imbuing her presence with calm seriousness and quiet dignity.*

FIGURE 12.7 MICHELANGELO. Sistine Chapel Ceiling. ▶ 1508–1512. The Vatican. *Michelangelo's knowledge of architecture prompted him to paint illusionistic niches to hold the Hebrew prophets and the pagan sibyls on either side and low pedestals as seats for the nude youths that frame the nine central panels. Neo-Platonism inspired his use of triangles, circles, and squares, for these geometric shapes were believed to hold the key to the mystery of the universe. These various framing devices enabled him to give visual order to the more than three hundred figures in his monumental scheme.*

Louvre collection, Leonardo was elevated to membership among the immortals of Western art.

Michelangelo While Leonardo was working in Milan during most of the 1490s, Michelangelo Buonarroti (1475–1564) was beginning a career that would propel him to the forefront of first the Florentine and later the Roman Renaissance as well as make him the most formidable artist of the sixteenth century. Michelangelo's initial fame rested on his sculptural genius, which manifested itself at the age of thirteen when he was apprenticed to the Early Renaissance master Ghirlandaio and then, one year later, taken into the household of Lorenzo the Magnificent, the Medici ruler of Florence. In time Michelangelo achieved greatness in painting and architecture as well as in sculpture, but he always remained a sculptor at heart.

Michelangelo's artistic credo was formed early, and he remained faithful to it over his long life. Sculpture, he believed, was the art form whereby human figures were liberated from the lifeless prison of their surrounding material. In this sense, he compared the sculptor's creativity with the activity of God—a notion that would have been judged blasphemous in prior Christian ages. Michelangelo himself, unlike the skeptical Leonardo, was a deeply pious man given to bouts of spiritual anxiety. His art constituted a form of divine worship.

Central to Michelangelo's artistic vision was his most celebrated image, the heroic nude male. Like the ancient Greek and Roman sculptors whose works he studied and admired, Michelangelo viewed the nude male form as a symbol of human dignity. In the High Renaissance Michelangelo's nudes were based on Classical models, with robust bodies and serene faces. But in the 1530s, with the onset of Mannerism, the growing spiritual crisis in the church, and his own failing health, Michelangelo's depiction of the human figure changed. His later nudes were distorted in their bodily proportions and had unusually expressive faces.

In 1508 Michelangelo was asked to decorate the Sistine Chapel ceiling by Pope Julius II. Michelangelo tried to avoid this commission, claiming that he was a sculptor and without expertise in frescoes, but the

Lisa's mystery by enveloping her in the smoky atmosphere called *sfumato*—made possible by the oil medium—that softens her delicate features and the landscape in the background.

During the High Renaissance, Leonardo's great works contributed to the cult of genius—the high regard, even reverence, that the age accorded to a few select artists, poets, and intellectuals. *The Last Supper* earned him great fame while he was alive. The history of the *Mona Lisa* was more complicated since it was unseen while he lived and found among his effects when he died in 1519. After his death, as the *Mona Lisa* became widely known, first as a possession of the King of France and later as a jewel in the

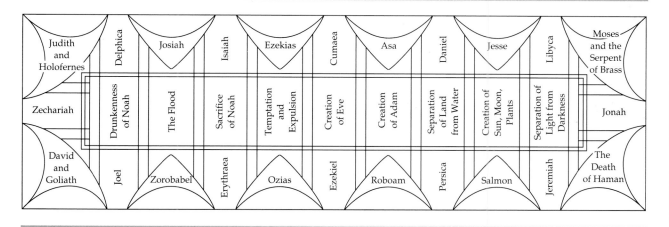

Judith and Holofernes	Delphica	Josiah	Isaiah	Ezekias	Cumaea	Asa	Daniel	Jesse	Libyca	Moses and the Serpent of Brass
Zechariah	Drunkenness of Noah	The Flood	Sacrifice of Noah	Temptation and Expulsion	Creation of Eve	Creation of Adam	Separation of Land from Water	Creation of Sun, Moon, Plants	Separation of Light from Darkness	Jonah
David and Goliath	Joel	Zorobabel	Erythraea	Ozias	Ezekiel	Roboam	Persica	Salmon	Jeremiah	The Death of Haman

FIGURE 12.8 Plan of Ceiling Frescoes, Sistine Chapel. 1508–1512. *The paintings on the Sistine Chapel ceiling may be grouped as follows: (1) the central section, which presents the history of the world from the creation (called "The Separation of Light from the Darkness") through the "Drunkenness of Noah"; (2) the gallery of portraits on both sides and at either end, which depict biblical prophets and pagan oracles; and (3) the four corner panels depicting Jewish heroes and heroines who overcame difficulties to help their people survive.*

pope was unyielding in his insistence. The chapel had been built by Julius II's uncle, Pope Sixtus IV, in the late 1400s as a private chapel, and most of the walls had already been covered with frescoes. Michelangelo's frescoes were intended to bring the chapel's decorative plan closer to completion.

The task presented to Michelangelo by the Sistine Chapel ceiling was enormous, for it was almost 70 feet from the floor, its sides were curved downward, necessitating numerous perspective changes, and its area covered some 5,800 square feet. Michelangelo overcame all of these difficulties, teaching himself fresco technique and working for four years on scaffolding, to create one of the glories of the High Renaissance and unquestionably the greatest cycle of paintings in Western art (Figure 12.7).

Michelangelo, probably with the support of a papal advisor, designed a complex layout (Figure 12.8) for the ceiling frescoes that combined biblical narrative, theology, Neo-Platonist philosophy, and

FIGURE 12.9 MICHELANGELO. *The Creation of Adam*, Detail of the Sistine Chapel Ceiling. 1511. The Vatican. *One of the most celebrated details of this fresco is the outstretched fingers of God and Adam that approach but do not touch. By means of this vivid symbol, Michelangelo suggests that a divine spark is about to pass from God into the body of Adam, electrifying it into the fullness of life. The image demonstrates the restraint that was characteristic of the High Renaissance style. The Vatican's ongoing restoration of the Sistine Chapel frescoes has revealed the brilliant colors of the original, apparent in this detail.*

Classical allusions. In the ceiling's long center, running from the altar to the rear of the chapel, he painted nine panels that illustrate the early history of the world, encompassing the creation, fall, and salvation of the human race. Framing each of these biblical scenes were nude youths, whose presence show Michelangelo's belief that the male form is an expression of divine power. The recent cleaning of the ceiling frescoes, although controversial, has brought out the original color harmonies that had faded over time.

On the long sides he depicted Hebrew prophets and pagan sibyls, or oracles—all foretelling the coming of Christ. The pagan sibyls represent the Neo-Platonist idea that God's word was revealed in the prophecies of pre-Christian seers. At either end of the ceiling he placed four Old Testament scenes of violence and death that had been allegorized as foreshadowing the coming of Christ. Michelangelo unified this complex of human and divine figures with an illusionistic architectural frame, and he painted a plain background to make the figures stand out simply and boldly to the viewer.

The most famous image from this vast work is a large panel from the central section, *The Creation of Adam* (Figure 12.9). In the treatment of this episode from the book of Genesis, Michelangelo reduces the scene to the fewest details, in accordance with the High Renaissance love of simplicity. Adam, stretched

out on a barely sketched bit of ground, seems to exist in some timeless space. Michelangelo depicts Adam as a pulsing, breathing human being. Such wondrous vitality in human flesh had not been seen in Western art since the vigorous nudes of ancient Greek art. In a bold move, Michelangelo ignored the Genesis story that told of God's molding Adam from dust. Instead, the artist paints Adam as half-awakened and reaching to God, who will implant a soul with his divine touch—an illustration of the Neo-Platonic idea of flesh yearning toward the spiritual.

By the 1530s Michelangelo's Mannerist style was in full bloom, triggered by his disappointment with Florence's loss of freedom and his own spiritual torment. In this new style he replaced his heroic vision with a fearful view of the world. A compelling example of this transformation is *The Last Judgment*, a fresco painted on the wall behind the Sistine Chapel's altar. *The Last Judgment* conveys both his own sense of sinfulness as well as humanity's future doom (Figure 12.10). Executed twenty-five years after the ceil-

FIGURE 12.10 MICHELANGELO. *The Last Judgment*. 1536–1541. 48 × 44'. Sistine Chapel, the Vatican. *This* Last Judgment *summarizes the anti-Classicism that was sweeping through the visual arts. Other painters studied this fresco for inspiration, borrowing its seemingly chaotic composition, its focus on large numbers of male nudes, and its use of bizarre perspective and odd postures as expressions of the Mannerist sensibility.*

13

THE RELIGIOUS REFORMATIONS, NORTHERN HUMANISM, AND LATE MANNERISM

1500—1603

While Italy was experiencing the High Renaissance, Germany became the epicenter of the spiritual earthquake called the *Reformation*, a movement that forever shattered the religious unity of the West. Like the Renaissance, the Reformation looked to the past for inspiration and ideals. But unlike the artists and intellectuals of the Renaissance, who found models in the Classical world of Greece and Rome, the religious leaders of the Reformation looked to the early Christian church before it became hierarchical and bureaucratic to clarify their beliefs and to purify ecclesiastical practices. Almost immediately they met with unbending resistance from the contemporary church and its officials. From the ongoing confrontations between these hostile groups emerged the labels the two sides still wear today: the Protestants, who wanted a complete renovation of the church, and the Roman Catholics, who were largely satisfied with things as they were.

The Catholics did not oppose all change. In the second half of the sixteenth century they conducted their own reforms, known as the *Counter-Reformation*, purifying the church and setting it on the path that it followed until the 1960s. In contrast, the Protestants disagreed over basic Christian doctrines and soon split into rival sects that went their separate ways. This sectarian tendency has remained an element in Protestantism until the present day.

This chapter brings to conclusion the story of the Renaissance, which first began in Italy in about 1400. The Renaissance, now in its Mannerist phase, moved north and to Spain in the early sixteenth century. The early stages of the Northern Renaissance and the Protestant Reformation unfolded within the broader political context examined in the last chapter. As the reforming zeal spread from Germany to France, Switzerland, the Low Countries, Scandinavia, England, and Scotland, the movement became bound up with local and international politics. Soon both the Protestants and the Catholics were swept into the dynastic and religious wars that dominated foreign affairs during this period.

This chapter picks up the thread of these events with the beginning of the reign of Charles V's son, Philip II, in Spain in 1556. For the rest of the century Europe's quarreling royal houses were polarized into two religious camps, with both sides looking for help from their coreligionists. Generally, the Catholics were led by Philip II, while the Protestants rallied around German princes or the English monarch Elizabeth I. The forces supporting the popes and the church managed to stop the expansion of Protestantism and win back many adherents, though not without widespread religious wars. By 1603 the religious map of Europe had settled into the Protestant and Catholic pattern that still exists today.

TIME LINE 13.1   THE RELIGIOUS REFORMATIONS OF THE SIXTEENTH CENTURY

1500		1545	1563		1600
	The Reformation and Founding of the Protestant Order		Council of Trent		The Counter-Reformation

Founding of independent Lutheran churches 1521

Luther's Ninety-five Theses 1517

Founding of Church of England 1533

Founding of Jesuit Order 1540

Founding of independent Calvinist churches 1541

MAP 13.1

The Religious Situation in Europe in 1560

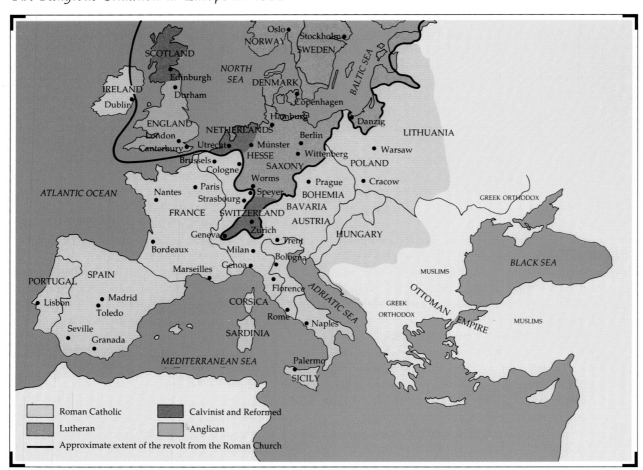

	Roman Catholic		Calvinist and Reformed
	Lutheran		Anglican

—— Approximate extent of the revolt from the Roman Church

THE BREAKUP OF CHRISTENDOM: CAUSES OF THE RELIGIOUS REFORMATIONS

Although the reasons for the breakup of Europe's religious unity are complicated and the ensuing events of the sixteenth century often confusing, two basic causes for this change are nevertheless clear: the radical reshaping of Western society and culture that began in about 1350 and the timeless spiritual yearnings of human beings. After 1500 these two forces came together in Germany to make conditions ripe for a religious explosion.

What made some modification in religion seem unavoidable were the historical trends that had become entrenched features of Europe during the Late Middle Ages. Especially contributing to the growing need for change were the presence of unrelieved corruption and abuses inside the church, the rise of sovereign states, the decay of medieval thought, and the revival of humanism.

The church had been plagued with problems since the Avignon papacy and the Great Schism of the fourteenth century and the challenges to its time-honored practices posed by the growth of heretical groups like the Hussites (see Chapter 10). Without firm guidance from the popes, many clergy led less than exemplary lives, particularly those inside the monasteries. Lay writers, now unafraid of the church, delighted in describing clerical scandals, and the populace gossiped about their priests' latest sins. Everywhere anticlericalism seemed on the rise.

Perhaps the church could have reformed the clergy and stemmed the tide of anticlericalism if the papacy had been morally and politically strong, but such was not the case. By 1500 the popes were deeply distracted by Italian politics and fully committed to worldly interests. Another factor leading to the church's decline was its loss of power to secular rulers who were determined to bring all of their subjects under state control. By 1500 the English and French kings, to the envy of other rulers, had made their national churches free of papal control in major ways. In England the crown regulated clerical assignments and forbade judicial appeals to Rome. France was even more independent, for the kings gained control of priestly appointments, along with the ecclesiastical courts and taxes.

In Germany, however, where no unified nation-state developed, the local political leaders did not have the power to dictate terms to the church, a fact that only intensified anticlericalism and hatred of Rome. The German princes, perceiving the popes and their Italian representatives as power hungry and greedy for gain, made church reform a rallying cry. Rebuffed by ecclesiastical officials, these German rulers, who already were struggling to be free from the control of Holy Roman Emperor Charles V, now turned against Rome and made the first rupture with the church. As events unfolded, the popes proved incapable of preventing these princes from converting their lands into independent states outside of papal jurisdiction (Map 13.1).

The Protestant Order

Rooted in the problems confronting the church and spurred on by theological issues, Protestantism erupted in Germany, where Martin Luther led a first generation to found a new religious sect in the 1520s. In the 1530s a second generation acted on the opportunity created by Luther. John Calvin, a French scholar, formed an independent church in Geneva, Switzerland, and King Henry VIII removed the English church from Roman rule (Time Line 13.1).

Luther's Revolt   One of the church's most glaring abuses, dating from the High Middles Ages, was the buying and selling of indulgences, which were pardons that reduced part or all of the time that Christians had to spend doing penance in atonement for their sins. The practice was based on the idea of a Treasury of Merit that held the inexhaustible surplus grace of Jesus and the saints. Through the sacraments of confession and penance, people could be forgiven for their sins during their lifetime, but after they died they still had to spend time in purgatory. To limit the time spent doing penance either on earth or in purgatory and thus speed up admission to heaven, the popes established indulgences, drawn on the Treasury of Merit. Indulgences were given to those who performed good deeds, such as going on crusades, and to those who gave money to the church.

THE NINETY-FIVE THESES   In 1517 the Archbishop of Mainz offered indulgences for sale to raise money, and Martin Luther (1483–1546), a monk teaching at nearby Wittenberg University, responded by compiling his famous Ninety-five Theses (Figure 13.1). These were questions and arguments about the legitimacy of indulgences, and they implicitly challenged the sacraments of confession and penance and the authority of the pope. Luther had simply hoped to arouse a debate in the university, but instead he ignited a firestorm of criticism against the church and

FIGURE 13.1   LUCAS CRANACH THE ELDER. *Martin Luther.* 1520. Copper engraving, 138 × 97 mm. The Metropolitan Museum of Art, Gift of Felix Warburg, 1920. *This portrait of Martin Luther, with its vivid rendering of his steel jaw and piercing eyes, shows some of the qualities that made him such a force to be reckoned with during the Reformation. The admiring likeness was done by the German artist Lucas Cranach, a supporter of the new faith and a close friend of Luther's. At the time of this engraving, the Reformation was barely underway; the thirty-seven-year-old Luther was still in communion with the church in Rome and a member of a monastic order.*

placed himself in the vanguard of a reform movement.

The church's response to Luther was initially hesitant, but in 1520 Pope Leo X excommunicated him. When Luther burned the papal document of excommunication in public, the church branded him a heretic and an outlaw. During this trouble and later, Luther survived because he was under the protection of his patron, Elector Frederick the Wise of Saxony. Frederick's support was based on mixed motives, since he also led the German princes who opposed the Holy Roman Emperor (Figure 13.2).

Luther's attack on indulgences arose from a spiritual quest that he had begun many years earlier. Obsessed by his sins, Luther had become a monk but had failed to find peace of mind. Through study, however, he reached the understanding that salvation came not because of good works but from God's unmerited love, or grace. "The just shall live by faith" (Romans 1:17) were the words that finally calmed Luther's soul; salvation would be achieved only by faith in Jesus' sacrificial death. Luther's belief led him to conclude that buying indulgences was trying to buy salvation—a direct contradiction of the biblical truth he had experienced in his theological studies.

LUTHER'S BELIEFS   In his theology, which came to be known as *Lutheranism,* Luther tried to revive primitive Christianity—practices and beliefs based on biblical precedents and reminiscent of the early church. He believed that the sole source of religious authority was the Bible, not the pope or church councils. He also thought that people could lead simple lives of piety and repentence without the benefit of priests to mediate with God. Since he viewed good works as unnecessary for salvation, he rejected such age-old practices as viewing relics, fasting, making pilgrimages, and abstaining from meat on Fridays. Along with indulgences, he repudiated the mystical definition of the sacraments, the notion of purgatory, the adoration of the saints, and Masses for the dead. In his pared-down sacramental system he retained only baptism and the Lord's Supper, as he called the Eucharist. Preaching in German became the heart of the liturgy, replacing the Latin Mass in importance.

SOCIAL AND POLITICAL IMPLICATIONS OF LUTHER'S REVOLT
The Ninety-five Theses circulated widely throughout Germany, and in 1521 Lutheran churches sprang up in Wittenberg and in most other German towns. Simultaneously, radical followers fomented new prob-

FIGURE 13.2   ALBRECHT DÜRER. *Elector Frederick the Wise.* 1524. Copper engraving. Print collection, Miriam and Ira D. Wallach Division of Art, Prints, and Photographs, The New York Public Library, Astor, Lenox, and Tilden Foundations. *Dürer's portrait captures the princely bearing of Frederick the Wise, the ruler of Electoral Saxony and Luther's great patron. Ironically, Frederick owned one of the largest collections of relics in Christendom. It has been estimated that the 17,443 artifacts in the Elector's collection in 1518 could reduce the time in purgatory by 127,799 years and 116 days.*

FIGURE 13.3 HANS BROSAMER. *Katherine von Bora.* Second Quarter of the Sixteenth Century. Woodcut, 37.1 × 28.9 cm. The British Museum, London. *Katherine von Bora was one of a dozen nuns liberated from a convent near Wittenberg in the heady days of 1523. She joined the mixed collection who lived with Luther in the Black Cloisters, his old monastery given him by Frederick the Wise. Despite Luther's protests, she determined to become his wife, and she did. He treated her with great deference, calling her "My lord Kate," though he poked fun at her supposed greed for property.*

lems, causing riots, driving priests from their homes, closing down monasteries, and destroying religious images. In his sermons Luther made it clear that he rejected this violence and advocated moderation. He did accept the abolition of monasticism, however, dropping the monk's habit in 1523 and two years later marrying Katherine von Bora, a former nun (Figure 13.3). When he and his wife had children, he created a familial tradition for Lutheran clergy.

Luther distanced himself not just from violence but from the political and social reforms espoused by some of his followers. In 1523 a brief Peasants' War erupted under the banner of Luther's faith, but Luther responded with a diatribe urging suppression of the workers by any means, thereby clearly showing his preference for the status quo. His reliance on Saxony's rulers for protection set the model for his religion; in the Lutheran faith, the church acted as an arm of the state, and the clergy's salaries were paid from public funds. Luther's revolt did not embrace individualism in the political or social arena; indeed, the Protestant princes were more powerful than their predecessors, since their powers were not limited by Rome.

LUTHER'S BIBLE Luther's voluminous writings constitute the largest legacy of any German author. Luther's German Bible holds first place, in terms of its enduring influence, among his vast output of tracts, essays, and letters. Although nineteen German Bibles were in print by 1518, Luther's version quickly drove the others from the field and gradually left its stamp on the German language. The secret of Luther's approach was his pithy style, which engaged the reader's emotions with everyday images and idiomatic speech.

The Reforms of John Calvin The first generation of Protestant reformers now gave way to a second generation, active in the 1530s. The most influential reformer among this second generation was John Calvin (1509–1564) (Figure 13.4). After earning a law degree in Paris, he experienced a religious conversion and cast his lot with the cause of the Reformation. Coming under the suspicion of the French authori-

FIGURE 13.4 ANONYMOUS. *John Calvin.* 1550s. Bibliothèque Publique et Universitaire de Geneva. *This anonymous portrait of Calvin shows the way that he probably wanted to be viewed rather than a natural likeness. Still, the angular features, the intense gaze, and set mouth suggest that the reputation Calvin had for strict discipline was justified. The florid beard and fur collar, although typical of middle-class fashion of the era, create an ironic contradiction in this otherwise austere portrait.*

FIGURE 13.10   ALBRECHT DÜRER. *Knight, Death, and the Devil.* 1513. Engraving, 250 × 192 mm. The Fogg Art Museum, Harvard University. Gift of William Gray from the Collection of Francis Calley Gray. *Dürer's plan for this work probably derived from a manual by Erasmus that advised a Christian prince on the best way to rule. In his version, Dürer portrays the Christian layman who has put on the armor of faith and rides steadfastly, oblivious to the various pitfalls that lie in his path. The knight is sometimes identified with Erasmus, whom Dürer venerated.*

Grünewald's supreme achievement is the altarpiece painted for the church of St. Anthony in Isenheim, Germany. The *Isenheim Altarpiece*, as this work is known, includes nine painted panels that can be displayed in three different positions, depending on the church calendar.

When the *Isenheim Altarpiece* is closed, the large central panel depicts the Crucifixion (Figure 13.11). By crowding the five figures and the symbolic lamb into the foreground and making Christ's body larger than the rest, Grünewald followed the Late Gothic

FIGURE 13.11   MATTHIAS GRÜNEWALD. *The Crucifixion,* from the *Isenheim Altarpiece.* 1515. 9'9½" × 10'9". Musée d'Unterlinden, Colmar, France. *Jesus' suffering and death were a central theme in North European piety, particularly after the plague of the fourteenth century. Northern artists typically rendered Christ's death in vivid and gory detail. Grünewald's Crucifixion comes out of this tradition; Christ's broken body symbolizes both his sacrificial death and the mortality of all human beings.*

FIGURE 13.12 PIETER BRUEGEL THE ELDER. *Peasant Wedding Feast*. Ca. 1567–1568. Oil on panel, 44⅞ × 64". Kunsthistorisches Museum, Vienna. *Bruegel had personally witnessed the details of peasant life that he painted. A member of the upper middle class, Bruegel enjoyed making outings into the countryside in disguise and participating in local celebrations and drinking parties. The attentiveness with which he records the behavior of the peasants reduces the otherwise somewhat negative tone of his scenes.*

style. This style is similarly apparent in every detail of Christ's tortured, twisted body: the gaping mouth, the exposed teeth, the slumped head, and the torso raked by thorns. And Grünewald's Late Gothic emotionalism is evident in his treatment of the secondary figures in this crucifixion panel. On the right, John the Baptist points toward Jesus, stressing the meaning of his sacrificial death. John the Baptist's calmness stands in stark contrast to the grieving tableau on the left, including Mary Magdalene, who kneels at Jesus' feet, and the Apostle John, who supports a swooning Mary. The swaying bodies of these three figures reinforce their anguished faces.

Pieter Bruegel the Elder The life and work of Pieter Bruegel the Elder (about 1525–1569) indicate that new winds were blowing through northern European art in the mid–sixteenth century. The great German artists Dürer and Grünewald were now dead, and German art, which dominated northern Europe in the early sixteenth century, had gone into decline. Protestant iconcoclasm had taken its toll, and the demand for religious art had markedly diminished. Within

this milieu, Bruegel chose a novel set of artistic subjects—landscapes, country life scenes, and folk narratives—and in the process became the first truly modern painter in northern Europe. Bruegel's subjects, rooted in the Flemish tradition, were often devoid of overt religious content and presented simply as secular art, although he also painted a number of pictures on standard religious themes such as the adoration of the Magi.

Bruegel's most memorable paintings are his scenes of peasant life. The peasants are always depicted in natural settings, neither romanticized nor patronized. Rather, Bruegel represents the common folk as types, never as individuals, and often as expressions of the blind forces of nature. For some viewers, these scenes also convey a pessimism tinged with grudging admiration about human nature as reflected in the peasants' simple, lusty behavior—an ambiguous perspective typical of the Mannerist style.

A painting that illustrates Bruegel's attitude toward country folk is his *Peasant Wedding Feast* (Figure 13.12). This banquet scene is set in a barn converted to a dining hall for the occasion. Bruegel's Mannerist

FIGURE 13.13 PIETER BRUEGEL THE ELDER. *Wedding Dance.* 1566. Oil on panel, 47 × 62″. Detroit Institute of Arts. *Bruegel has made a sensuous arrangement out of the dancers and bystanders at this country wedding. The line of dancers winds from the foreground back through the trees, where it reverses itself and returns to its original starting point. The sense of lively movement is reinforced by the vivid red colors in the hats and vests and by the stomping feet and flailing arms.*

values lead him to take the focus off the bride and groom and make the gathering itself the subject of the painting. He accomplishes this by placing the banqueting table along a diagonal, thrusting several figures into the foreground: the server pouring beer into jugs, the rustics carrying new dishes on a barn door, the child licking the plate clean with his fingers, and beyond them, the bagpipers standing beside the diners. Against the side wall under a makeshift banner, the quietly smiling bride sits with eyes half-closed and hands clasped before her.

Another of Bruegel's scenes of peasant life is his lively *Wedding Dance* (Figure 13.13). The painting records the exuberant revels of the lusty men and the kerchief-wearing women. The bride and groom cannot be distinguished from the other dancers. In a typical touch, Bruegel uses a high horizon and a high point of view, so that we look at the scene from above. This effect, along with the crude faces of the peasants, serves to underscore the impression that these are types and not individuals. The painting's composition reinforces the sense of peasant types in the way that the swirling figures in the foreground are repeated in the background in ever-diminishing size.

Mannerist Painting in Spain: El Greco

The strongest impact of the Counter-Reformation on the arts did not begin until after the close of the Council of Trent in 1563. Nowhere was Trent's influence greater than in Spain, and no Catholic artist expressed the spirit of Trent more than El Greco (1541–1614) in his Spanish paintings after 1576. These works, with their visionary style, also symbolize the spirit of Late Mannerism. El Greco's real name was

Domenikos Theotokopoulos. A native of Crete, he had lived in Venice, where he had absorbed the colorful styles of the painters of the Venetian school. Unsuccessful as a painter in Venice, he also failed to find rich patrons in Rome, though he learned from the works of Michelangelo and the Mannerists. He arrived in Toledo, Spain, in about 1576, and there he found an appreciative public among the wealthy nobility, but much to El Greco's despair, he never became a favorite of the Spanish ruler, Philip II, who found the Greek painter's works too bizarre.

For his select audience of aristocrats and Roman Catholic clergy, however, El Greco could do no wrong. They believed that his paintings of saints, martyrs, and other religious figures caught the essence of Spanish emotionalism and religious zeal—the same qualities that had led Loyola to found the Jesuits. In effect, El Greco's extravagant images gave visible form to his patrons' spiritual yearnings. In his paintings, he rejected a naturalistic world with conventional perspective, especially when a divine dimension was present or implied; his spiritualized vision came to be distinguished by elongated bodies, sharp lines in the folds of cloth, and luminous colors.

El Greco's masterpiece is *The Burial of Count Orgaz,* which was painted to honor the founder of the church of Santo Tomé in Toledo (Figure 13.14). This

FIGURE 13.14 EL GRECO. *The Burial of Count Orgaz.* 1586. Oil on canvas, 16′ × 11′10″. Church of Santo Tomé, Toledo, Spain. *A Manneristic invention in* The Burial of Count Orgaz *was the rich treatment of the robe of St. Stephen, the first Christian martyr and, in this painting, the beardless figure supporting the body of the dead count. Embroidered onto Stephen's garment is a picture of the stoning of St. Stephen, an episode narrated in the New Testament. By depicting one event inside another, El Greco created an illusionistic device—a typical notion of Mannerist painters, who were skeptical about conventional reality.*

FIGURE 13.15 EL GRECO. *Cardinal Guevara.* 1596–1600. Oil on canvas, 67¼ × 42½". The Metropolitan Museum of Art, New York. Bequest of Mrs. H. O. Havemeyer, 1929. The H. O. Havemeyer Collection. *El Greco's painting of Cardinal Guevara illustrates his mastery of Mannerist portraiture. Disturbing details are visible everywhere. Guevara's head is almost too small for his large body, made even grander by the red cardinal's robe, and the divided background—half wooden panel, half rich tapestry—sets up a dissonant effect. Even the chair the cardinal sits in contributes to the air of disjointedness, for its one visible leg seems barely to touch the floor.*

painting was designed to fit into a special place beside the church's high altar. Its subject is the miraculous scene that, according to legend, occurred during the count's burial when two saints, Augustine and Stephen, appeared and assisted with the last rites.

From this legend, El Greco has fashioned an arresting painting. The large canvas is divided into two halves, with the lower section devoted to the count's actual burial and the upper section focused on the reception of his soul in heaven. Except for two men who tilt their faces upward, the town dignitaries seem unaware of what is happening just above their heads. El Greco has devised two distinct styles to deal with these different planes of reality. The dignitaries below are rendered in realistic terms, down to the precise fashions of El Greco's era, such as the neck ruffs and the mustaches and goatees. The heavenly spectacle is depicted in the spiritualized manner that he increasingly used in his later works.

El Greco also painted several portraits of church officials, of which the best known is that of *Cardinal Guevara* (Figure 13.15). This painting portrays the Chief Inquisitor, dressed in his splendid red robes. El Greco has captured the personality of this austere and iron-willed churchman who vigorously pursued heretics and sentenced them to die in an *auto-da-fé*, Portuguese for "act of faith"—that is, a public ceremony in which heretics were executed, usually by being burned at the stake. El Greco's likeness suggests much about the inner man: Cardinal Guevara seems to have an uneasy conscience, as betrayed by the shifty expression of the eyes, the left hand clutching the chair arm, and the general sense that the subject is restraining himself. Through these means El Greco created another model for Mannerist portraiture.

Italian Culture, 1564–1603

The Council of Trent had more impact on the arts, architecture, and music in Italy than in any other Roman Catholic area because of the historic tradition of papal intrusion into Italian affairs. The council decreed that the arts and music should be easily accessible to the uneducated. In sacred music, for example, the intelligibility of the words should take precedence over the melody, and in architecture the building should create a worshipful environment. The church council envisioned paintings and sculptures that were simple and direct as well as unobjectionable and decent in appearance. Guided by this principle, the Counter-Reformation popes declared that some of the male nudes in Michelangelo's *Last Judgment* were obscene and ordered loincloths to be painted over them.

Figure 13.16 Tintoretto. *The Last Supper*. 1592–1594. Oil on canvas, 12′ × 18′8″. San Giorgio Maggiore, Venice. *Nothing better illustrates the distance between the High Renaissance and Mannerism than a comparison of Leonardo's* Last Supper *with that of Tintoretto. Everything about Tintoretto's spiritualized scene contradicts the quiet Classicism of Leonardo's work. Leonardo's painting is meant to appeal to the viewer's reason; Tintoretto's shadowy scene is calculated to stir the feelings.*

General church policy now returned to the medieval ideal of an art and music whose sole aim was to serve and clarify the Christian faith.

Since the Roman Catholic Church after Trent wanted a simplified art that spoke to the masses, its artistic policy tended to clash with Mannerism, which was elitist and deliberately complex. Only with the rise of the Baroque after 1600 was there a style that could conform to the church's need for art with a mass appeal. In the meantime, the general influence of Trent on the last stage of Mannerism was to intensify its spiritual values.

Late Mannerist Painting in Italy: Tintoretto With the death of Michelangelo in 1564, Venice displaced Rome as the dominant artistic center in Italy. From then until the end of the century, Venetian painters carried the banner of the Italian Renaissance, bringing Mannerism to a brilliant sunset. The leading exponent of **Late Mannerism** in Italy is Tintoretto (1518–1594). This Venetian artist created a feverish, emotional style that reflected impetuosity in its execution. With his haste, Tintoretto was reacting against his famous Venetian predecessor Titian, who had been noted for extraordinary discipline in the way he painted. But in other respects, he learned from Titian, adopting his love of color and his use of theatrical lighting. The special quality of Tintoretto's art, which he reached in his earliest paintings, was to place his human figures into arrangements that suggest a sculptural frieze.

Tintoretto's rendition of the familiar biblical account of *The Last Supper* shows his feverish style (Figure 13.16). Unlike the serene, classically balanced scene that Leonardo had painted (see Figure 12.5),

Tintoretto portrays an ethereal gathering, illuminated by eery light and filled with swooping angels. The diagonal table divides the pictorial space into two halves; on the left is the spiritual world of Jesus and his disciples, and on the right is the earthly realm of the servants. Tintoretto's depiction of these two different levels of reality is reminiscent of a similar division in El Greco's *The Burial of Count Orgaz* (see Figure 13.14). Especially notable is Jesus' body, including the feet, which positively glows. *The Last Supper*, finished in Tintoretto's final year, is a fitting climax to Mannerist painting.

Late Sixteenth-Century Music in Italy Unlike painting, Italian music remained under the sway of High Renaissance ideals, keeping to the path pioneered by Josquin des Prez (see Chapter 12). Nevertheless, the Council of Trent, along with other forces, led to the breakup of the High Renaissance style and created the conditions for the rise of the Baroque. For one thing, the council ruled that the Gregorian chant was preferable to polyphony for church liturgy and that the traditional chants should be simplified to ensure that the words could be easily understood. Most composers, considering the chants to be barbarous, continued to use polyphony but pruned its extravagant effects. The best of these composers and the chief representative of Counter-Reformation music was Giovanni Pierluigi da Palestrina (about 1525–1594). His controlled style established the Roman Catholic ideal for the next few centuries—polyphonic masses sung by choirs and with clearly enunciated and enormously expressive texts.

Nevertheless, the future of Italian music lay outside the church. Ironically, secular vocal music was also moving toward an ideal in which the words took precedence over the sound, but secular composers, unlike those in the church, rejected polyphony because it did not allow the text to be fully understood. The move to make the words primary in secular music was triggered by Renaissance humanists who were convinced that ancient music's power stemmed from the expressive way that the setting suited the clearly articulated words of the text. The most evident signs of this humanistic belief were in the works of the Florentine *Camerata*, a group of musical amateurs. Rejecting polyphony, the Florentine musicians composed pieces for a text with a single line of melody accompanied by simple chords and sung in a declamatory style.

The trend to expressive secular music in Italy was reflected most completely in the *madrigal*, a song for four or five voices composed with great care for the words of the poetic text. The focus of this vocal music was the mood and meaning of the words, rather than the structure of the music. Madrigals began to be written in the 1520s, but their heyday was the second half of the sixteenth century. Late in the century they were imported to England and quickly became the height of fashion there. By 1600 madrigals were the dominant form of secular music throughout Europe.

The Legacy of the Religious Reformations, Northern Humanism, and Late Mannerism

The period from 1520 until 1603 brings to a close the third and final phase of the Renaissance. This eighty-three-year-period, framed by the deaths of Raphael and Queen Elizabeth I, saw the foundations of early modern Europe move firmly into place. A world culture and economy, in embryo, begins during this period. This momentous development was foreshadowed in the shift of Europe's commercial axis from the Mediterranean to the Atlantic, as well as in the start of Europe's exportation of peoples, technology, religions, and ideas to colonies in Asia, Africa, and the Americas.

Probably the most important material change during this era was the rise of a system of sovereign and mutually hostile states. No single state was able to assert its authority over the others; the pattern set by their struggles would govern Western affairs until the emergence of global politics in the twentieth century. The European state system also spelled the doom of a united Christendom.

The reformations further split Christian Europe, dividing it into Protestant and Catholic armed camps. As a result, religious wars afflicted this century and the next, only fading away by about 1700. On a local level, religious differences led to intolerance and persecution. Although Europe's religious boundaries today remain roughly the same as they were in 1600, it took over three hundred years for Protestants and Catholics to accept that they could live together in harmony.

The reformations also left different cultural legacies to their respective Christian denominations. From Protestantism came a glorification of the work ethic, Puritanism, and a justification for capitalism. At the heart of the Protestant revolution, despite its insistence on the doctrine of original sin, was the notion that human beings can commune directly with God without church mediation. While Protestantism tended to view human beings as adrift in the universe, the Catholic church tried to control the spiritual and moral lives of its members and to insulate them from the surrounding world. This policy eventually placed the church on a collision course with the forces of modernity, but it nevertheless was followed by most of the popes until after World War II.

In the upheavals spawned by the religious crisis, the legacy of Northern humanism—rational morals allied to a simple faith—went unheeded by Protestants and Catholics alike. Not until the eighteenth century and the rationalist program of the Enlightenment did Christian humanist ideas find a willing audience.

In the arts and humanities, however, the legacy was clear: The Mannerist period left a rich and varied inheritance, including the work of Shakespeare, the most gifted and influential individual writer in the history of Western civilization.

KEY CULTURAL TERMS

Reformation	*Jesuits*
Counter-Reformation	*Christian humanism*
Lutheranism	*revenge tragedy*
Calvinism	*Late Mannerism*
Puritanism	*madrigal*
Anglicanism	

SUGGESTIONS FOR FURTHER READING

PRIMARY SOURCES

CALVIN, J. *Institutes of the Christian Religion.* Translated by F. L. Battles. Philadelphia: Westminster Press, 1960. A recent translation of Calvin's theological masterpiece.

ERASMUS, D. *Praise of Folly.* Translated by B. Radice. New York: Penguin, 1971. A lively translation of Erasmus's satire that ridiculed the hypocrisy of the age, especially in the church; originally published in 1516.

LUTHER, M. *Three Treatises.* Translations by various authors. Philadelphia: Fortress Press, 1960. Good versions of the short works that helped to make Luther an outstanding and controversial public figure in his day.

MONTAIGNE, M. *Essays and Selected Writings.* Translated and edited by D. Frame. New York: St. Martin's Press, 1963. The *Essays* reveal Montaigne as one of the founders of French skepticism.

RABELAIS, F. *The Histories of Gargantua* and *Pantagruel.* Translated by J. M. Cohen. Franklin Center, Pa.: Franklin Library, 1982. An excellent modern version of this lusty masterpiece.

SHAKESPEARE. *Hamlet. Othello. King Lear. Romeo and Juliet. Antony and Cleopatra. Macbeth.* One of the best editions available of Shakespeare's tragedies is published by Washington Square Press. This series is inexpensive and profusely illustrated, and it offers the text with a facing page of editorial notes.

SECONDARY SOURCES

BAINTON, R. *Here I Stand: A Life of Martin Luther.* New York: New American Library, 1955. Sympathetic older treatment of this controversial and influential historical figure.

BAKHTIN, M. *Rabelais and His World.* Cambridge: Harvard University Press, 1971. A ground-breaking analysis using the techniques of new literary criticism.

CHADWICK, O. *The Reformation.* New York: Penguin, 1976. This balanced survey of the Reformation era continues to be an outstanding introduction for beginning students; a reprint of the 1964 edition with revisions.

CUTTLER, C. D. *Northern Painting from Pucelle to Bruegel.* New York: Holt, Rinehart, and Winston, 1968. Contains an excellent discussion of Mannerism.

DICKENS, A. G. *The Counter Reformation.* New York: Harcourt, Brace & World, 1969. A standard treatment of how the Catholic church responded to the Protestant revolt.

ELTON, G. R. *Reform and Reformation: England, 1509–1558.* Cambridge: Harvard University Press, 1977. Superb narrative history written by one of the foremost scholars of Tudor England.

ERICKSON, E. H. *Young Man Luther: A Study in Psychoanalysis and History.* New York: Norton, 1962. Luther's personality and motives are analyzed by one of the most influential psychoanalysts of our times; one of the landmarks of psychohistory.

HAILE, H. G. *Luther: An Experiment in Biography.* Garden City, N.Y.: Doubleday, 1980. A humane biography that reveals the actual man behind the reformer.

OZMENT, S. *The Age of Reform, 1250–1550: An Intellectual and Religious History of Late Medieval and Reformation Europe.* New Haven: Yale University Press, 1980. Taking a broader view of the Reformation than most scholars, Ozment argues that the origins of the religious transformation of Europe are found in the attitudes of the populace and their leaders.

SNYDER, J. *Northern Renaissance Art.* Englewood Cliffs, N.J.: Prentice-Hall, 1985. Combines good illustrations with the latest scholarship.

SYPHER, W. *Four Stages of Renaissance Style.* Garden City, N.Y.: Doubleday, 1955. A controversial and uneven work that remains a brilliant attempt to rethink the Renaissance period.

TAWNEY, R. H. *Religion and the Rise of Captialism.* New York: Harcourt, Brace, 1952. A response to the thesis of Max Weber; forces the reader to reconsider the relationship between religion and economics.

WEBER, M. *The Protestant Ethic and the Spirit of Capitalism.* Translated by T. Parsons. New York: Scribner, 1958. A recent translation of the early twentieth-century work that is probably the most influential modern interpretation of the Protestant Reformation.

WELLS, S., ed. *The Cambridge Companion to Shakespeare Studies.* Cambridge: Cambridge University Press, 1986. A useful and authoritative guide for students of Shakespeare.

WENDEL, F. *Calvin: The Origins and Development of His Religious Thought.* Translated by P. Mairet. New York: Harper & Row, 1963. A historical treatment of Calvin's theology based on a new examination of the original texts; for the serious student.

SUGGESTIONS FOR LISTENING

GIOVANNI PIERLUIGI DA PALESTRINA (ABOUT 1525–1594). A prolific composer of Masses, Palestrina is the major musical figure of the Counter-Reformation. Unlike the highly emotional style of Josquin, Palestrina's music is noted for its tightly controlled quality and its perfection of detail, as illustrated in such Masses as *Hodie Christus Natus Est, Assumpta Est Maria,* and *Ave Maria.*

14

THE BAROQUE AGE

Glamour and Grandiosity

1600—1715

As the Roman Catholic church feverishly pursued its goal of turning back Protestantism, and as the political system of powerful sovereign secular states took hold in Europe, a new age dawned in the early seventeenth century. Known as the *Baroque*, it was a period characterized by a love of grandeur, opulence, and vast, expanding horizons. For the church, Baroque art and architecture provided spectacular and compelling images with which to reassert its presence in the world and to dazzle and indoctrinate the faithful. For the secular rulers, the Baroque offered a magnificence that enhanced their political power and control. Art during the Baroque period became a propagandistic tool in a way that the Mannerist art of the previous period—with its focus on the personal, the distorted, and the eccentric—could never be.

The term "baroque" was coined in the eighteenth century by artists and scholars whose taste was attuned to the Classical ideals of the Renaissance. To them, much of the culture of the seventeenth century was imperfect, or "baroque," a term probably derived from the Portuguese word "barroco," meaning an irregular pearl. Not until the mid–nineteenth century did the word acquire a positive value. Since then, "Baroque" has gained currency as a label for the seventeenth century and its prevailing cultural style.

The Baroque period was an era of constant turmoil and momentous change. Hardly a year passed free from warfare. Until the middle of the century, Europe was plagued by religious warfare, a legacy of the Reformation. In the second half of the century, the struggles had secular causes, notably territorial expansion and the extension of national boundaries. Further upheavals were caused by the continuing movement of peoples to the New World and by a growing race among the most powerful European states for overseas empires.

The seventeenth century was also a period of great scientific discoveries and intellectual change. Breakthroughs occurred that overturned age-old beliefs, and Western thought was freed from the errors of Greek science that had prevailed for more than two thousand years. Scholars revised their basic understanding of how the body functioned and how the universe was arranged. Because the Scientific Revolution, as this intellectual movement is called, had such an important influence on the making of the modern world, it is covered separately in Chapter 15, along with related philosophical ideas. This chapter focuses on the art, literature, and music of the Baroque age and their historical, political, and social context.

ABSOLUTISM, MONARCHY, AND THE BALANCE OF POWER

Although the Baroque style in art originated in Rome and from there spread across the continent, neither the Italian city-states nor the popes were any longer at the center of European political life. By the time Europe had recovered from the first wave of religious wars in 1600, a new system of sovereign states had

FIGURE 14.5 GIANLORENZO BERNINI. The Baldacchino. 1624–1633. Ht., ca. 100′. St. Peter's, Rome. *This magnificent canopy, a masterpiece of the Florid Baroque, reflects the grandiose ambitions of its patron, Pope Urban VIII, a member of the Barberini family. The Barberini crest was the source for the huge stylized bees displayed on the flaps of the bronze canopy. In his desire for worldly immortality, this pope shared a common outlook with the secular rulers of the Baroque age.*

FIGURE 14.6 GIANLORENZO BERNINI. *The Ecstasy of St. Teresa.* 1645–1652. Marble, Lifesize. Cornaro Chapel, Santa Maria della Vittoria, Rome. *Even though the subject of this sculpture is an ecstatic vision, its portrayal reflects the naturalism that was central to the Baroque style. Bernini based this work on the saint's personal account in which she described how an angel pierced her heart with a golden spear—a mystical moment the tableau faithfully reproduces.* ▶

Florid Baroque structures with their highly decorated walls.

The most famous sculptures by Bernini are the decorations that he made for the interior of St. Peter's, including altars, tombs, reliefs, statues, and liturgical furniture. For fifty years, commencing in 1629, the popes kept him employed on St. Peter's, executing sumptuous interior decorations. His masterpiece among these ornate works is the ***baldacchino***, the canopy, mainly bronze and partly gilt, that covers the spot where the bones of St. Peter are believed to lie—directly under Michelangelo's dome. Combining architectural and sculptural features, the baldacchino is supported by four 14-foot-high columns whose convoluted surfaces are covered with climbing vines (Figure 14.5). Bernini crowned this colossal work with a magnificent display of four large angels at the corners, four groups of cherubs with linked arms in the centers of the sides, and between these figures four scrolls that rise to support a ball and cross at the top.

The baldacchino's corkscrew-like columns were modeled on the type that by tradition supported Solomon's temple in Jerusalem and had been used in the old St. Peter's basilica. Thus these columns symbolized the church's claim to be the true successor to the Jewish faith. So popular was Bernini's Solomonic canopy that in southern Germany it inspired many imitators and became the standard covering for altars for the next two centuries.

The sculpture that marks the highest expression of Bernini's art is *The Ecstasy of St. Teresa* (Figure 14.6). Using stone, metal, and glass, he portrays the divine moment when the saint receives the vision of the Holy Spirit—symbolized here by the arrow with which the angel pierces her heart. In his conception, Bernini imagines the pair floating on a cloud and bathed by light from a hidden source; the light rays seem to turn into golden rods that cascade onto the angel and the saint. The intensity of the saint's expression, the agitation of the draperies, and the billowing clouds all work to create the illusion that the pair are sensuously real. By depicting St. Teresa's supernatural experience in physical terms, Bernini intended to force the viewer to suspend belief and accept the religious truth of the scene.

most outstanding was Bernini, the architect of St. Peter's.

Bernini brought the Florid Baroque to a dazzling climax in his sculptural works. His pieces, executed for such diverse projects as churches, fountains, and piazzas, or squares, often combined architecture with sculpture. His sculptural ideal was a dynamic composition that used undulating forms to delight the eye. His sensuous sculptures with their implicit movement were the perfect accompaniments to

FIGURE 14.7 CARAVAGGIO. *The Martyrdom of St. Matthew.* 1602. Oil on canvas, 323 × 343 cm. Contarelli Chapel, San Luigi dei Francesi, Rome. *Caravaggio's paintings made monumentality an important feature of the Florid Baroque style. By presenting the human figures in close-up and giving full weight to their bodies, as in this painting, the artist made their presence an inescapable fact to the viewer. This approach gave his paintings a dramatic immediacy.*

Painting In the Baroque period painting once again became an integral part of church decoration. In pursuit of church ideals, the painters of this tradition tended to use rich color and unusual lighting effects to depict spectacular or dramatic moments. They represented nature and the human form realistically in order to make art intelligible and meaningful to the ordinary viewer.

The earliest great Florid Baroque painter was Michelangelo Merisi (1573–1610), better known as Caravaggio. Caravaggio rejected the antinaturalism of Mannerism in favor of a dramatic realism. His concern with realism led him to pick his models directly from the streets, and he refused to idealize his subjects. To make his works more dramatic and emotionally stirring, he experimented with light and the placement of figures. His paintings offer startling contrasts of light and dark—the technique known as chiaroscuro—and he banished landscape from his canvases, often focusing on human figures grouped tightly in the foreground.

A superb example of Caravaggio's work is *The Martyrdom of St. Matthew,* one of a series of works he painted on the life of this early Christian saint (Figure 14.7). His revolutionary use of chiaroscuro, whereby the light drenches the foreground figures and the darkness renders the background indistinct, makes the agony of the saint more dramatically vivid. The tension in the scene is intensified by the thrusting limbs of the various figures. Caravaggio had an enormous influence on other painters, notably in France, Spain, and the Netherlands.

At about the same time that Caravaggio was creating his dramatic works, a new form caught the imagination of painters in the Florid Baroque tradition—the illusionistic ceiling fresco. In these paintings, artists constructed imaginary continuations of the architectural features already present in the room, expanding up through layers of carefully foreshortened, sculpted figures and culminating in patches of sky. Looking up as if at the heavens above, the viewer is overawed by the superhuman spectacle that seems to begin just overhead.

The superb example of this *illusionism* is the nave ceiling of the church of Sant' Ignazio (St. Ignatius) in Rome, painted by Andrea Pozzo (1642–1709). In this fresco, entitled *Allegory of the Missionary Work of the Jesuits,* Pozzo reveals a firm mastery of the technique of architectural perspective (Figure 14.8). The great nave ceiling is painted to appear as if the viewer were looking up through an immense open colonnade. Figures stand and cling to the encircling architectural supports and, in the center, an expansive vista opens to reveal Ignatius, the founder of the Jesuit order, being received by an open-armed Christ. The clusters of columns on either side are labeled for the four continents—Europe, Asia, America, and Africa— symbolizing the missionary zeal of the Jesuits around the globe. Illusionism, infinite space, and spectacular effects make this a masterpiece of the Florid Baroque.

Outside Italy, the principal centers of Florid Baroque painting were the studio of Velázquez in Spain and the workshop of Rubens in Flanders (present-day Belgium). While Velázquez softened the Florid Baroque to his country's taste, Rubens fully embraced this sensual style to become its most representative painter.

The work of Diego Velázquez (1599–1660) owes much to the tradition of Caravaggio, but without the

FIGURE 14.8 ANDREA POZZO. *Allegory of the Missionary Work of the Jesuits.* Ca. 1621–1625. Ceiling fresco. Sant' Ignazio, Rome. *Pozzo was motivated by spiritual concerns when he painted this supernatural vision. He believed that the illusion of infinite space could evoke feelings of spiritual exaltation in the viewer. The observer, overwhelmed by the sight of St. Ignatius Loyola's ascent into heaven, could thus be transported into a religious rapture.*

FIGURE 14.9   VELÁZQUEZ. *Las Meninas (The Maids of Honor).*
1656. Oil on canvas, 10′5″ × 9′. Prado, Madrid. *Velázquez uses
the mirror on the back wall, reflecting the Spanish king and queen,
to enhance the dynamic feeling of the scene. This illusionistic device
explodes the pictorial space by calling up presences within and
outside the painting.*

intense drama of the Italian's painting. Velázquez also used chiaroscuro, but he avoided the extreme contrasts that made Caravaggio's paintings controversial. Velázquez's works have a somber quietude that sometimes suggests that the subjects have been interrupted in what they are doing.

Velázquez's greatest work is *Las Meninas,* or *The Maids of Honor* (Figure 14.9). In his role as official artist to the Spanish court, Velázquez painted this group portrait of the Infanta, or princess, surrounded by her maids of honor (one of whom is a dwarf). What makes this painting so haunting is the artful play of soft light over the various figures. In the background, a man is illuminated by the light streaming through the open door, and even more abundant sunshine falls on the princess from the window on the right.

Velázquez also plays with space and illusion in this painting. On the left side he depicts himself, standing before a huge canvas with brush and palette in hand. The artist gazes directly at the viewer—or is he greeting the king and queen, who have just entered the room and are reflected in the mirror on the rear wall? The princess and two of her maids also look attentively out of the picture, but whether at the artist painting their portrait, at the royal couple, or at the viewer is left unclear. This fascination with illusion and with the effects of light and shade reveals Velázquez's links with Caravaggio and the art of the Florid Baroque.

In contrast to Velázquez's devotion to the ideal of grave beauty, the work of Peter Paul Rubens (1577–1640) is known for its ripe sensuality and for his portrayal of voluptuous female nudes. Rubens had already forged a sensuous style before he visited Italy, but his encounters with Caravaggio's tradition impressed him deeply, causing him to intensify his use of explosive forms and chiaroscuro. From the Venetian painters, especially Titian, he derived his love and mastery of gorgeous color. In his mature works, he placed human figures in a shallow foreground, bathed them in golden light with dark contours, and painted their clothes and flesh in sensuous tones.

As the most sought after artist of his day, Rubens was often given commissions by the kings of the great states, and he produced works for royalty, for the church, and for wealthy private patrons. As official painter to the French court, he was commissioned to paint a cycle of works glamorizing the life of Queen Marie de' Medici, widow of Henry IV and powerful regent for her son, Louis XIII. One of the typical works from this series was *The Landing of Marie de' Medici at Marseilles* (Figure 14.10). In this huge canvas,

FIGURE 14.10   PETER PAUL RUBENS. *The Landing of Marie de' Medici at Marseilles.* Ca. 1625. Oil on canvas, 12'11" × 9'8¼". Louvre. *The Medici cycle, of which this work is a superb example, not only established Rubens's European-wide reputation but defined historical narrative—the combining of a historical event with mythological motifs—as one of the great themes of Baroque art. By 1715 the French Academy had created a ranked set of painting subjects, of which historical narrative occupied the highest level.*

Rubens transforms a relatively insignificant event in the life of a queen into a splendid pageant of the French monarchy. The scene depicts the moment at which the young Medici heiress first sets foot on French soil on her way to meet her bridegroom. Rubens flatters his subject by showing her accompanied by the ancient god Neptune with his retinue while Fame soars above her head. All action in the painting is centered around the regal presence of the queen, as flags and clouds billow overhead and fleshy sea nymphs rise from the waters below. Rubens's mastery of both spiritual and secular subjects and the turbulent drama of his works made him the finest artist of the Florid Baroque.

The French Baroque

Although the Baroque originated in Rome, the pronouncements of the church had little effect on the art and architecture of France. Here, the royal court was the guiding force in the artistic life of the nation. The rulers and the royal ministers provided rich commissions that helped to shape the *French Baroque*, giving this style a secular focus and identifying it with absolutism. A second powerful influence on the French Baroque was the pervasiveness in French culture of the Classical values of simplicity and grave dignity. Accordingly, French artists and architects found the Florid Baroque alien and even offensive; their adaptation of this style was more impersonal, controlled, and restrained.

Architecture   The palace of Versailles was the consummate architectural expression of the French Baroque. A hunting lodge under Louis XIII, Versailles was transformed by Louis XIV into a magnificent royal residence that became the prototype of princely courts in the West. At Versailles, where all power was concentrated in the royal court, were collected the best architects, sculptors, painters, and landscape architects as well as the finest writers, composers, and musicians that France could produce. The duty of this talented assemblage was to use their gifts to surround Louis XIV with the splendor appropriate to the Sun King.

The redesign of Versailles gave Louis XIV the most splendid palace that has ever been seen in Europe. The chief architects of this revamped palace were Louis Le Vau (1612–1670) and Jules Hardouin-Mansart (1646–1708), but the guiding spirit was the Sun King himself. When finished, the palace consisted of a huge central structure with two immense wings (see Figure 14.2). The architecture is basically in the style of the Renaissance, with rounded arches, Classical columns, and porticoes inspired by Roman temples, but the overall effect is of restrained Baroque.

The most striking aspect of Versailles is its monumentality: The palace is only the most imposing building of an elaborate complex that includes a royal chapel and various support structures, all of which are set in an elaborate park over two miles long. Versailles' park, designed by André Le Nôtre (1613–1700), is studded with a rich display of fountains, reflecting pools, geometric flower beds, manicured woods, exotic trees, statues, urns, and graveled walks—a gorgeous outdoor setting for royal receptions and entertainments (Figure 14.11).

The most famous room in Versailles Palace is the Hall of Mirrors, a central chamber with a tunnel-vaulted ceiling (Figure 14.12). The grandiose design of this hallway reflects its original function as the throne room of Louis XIV. Named for its most prominent feature, this long hall is decorated with Baroque profusion, including, in addition to the mirrors, wood parquetry floors of intricate design, multicolored marbles, ceiling paintings depicting military victories and other deeds of Louis XIV, and gilded statues at the base of the paintings. In modern times, major political events have taken place in the Hall of Mirrors: The Germans proclaimed their empire from here in 1871 after having vanquished the French, and the peace treaty that ended World War I was signed here in 1919.

FIGURE 14.11   ANDRÉ LE NÔTRE, LANDSCAPE ARCHITECT, and VARIOUS SCULPTORS. Versailles Gardens. The Pool of Latona with Adjacent Parterres. 1660s. Versailles, France. *This fountain, composed of four concentric marble basins, is named for its crowning statue of Latona, the mother of the sun god Apollo, who was the inspiration for Louis XIV's reign. On either side of the fountain may be glimpsed parterres, or flower gardens with beds and paths arranged into patterns. Beyond the fountain stretches an avenue flanked by wooded areas that culminates in the grand canal, which extends the view into infinity. The rich profusion of this scene is a hallmark of Baroque design.*

FIGURE 14.12 CHARLES LEBRUN AND JULES HARDOUIN-MANSART. Hall of Mirrors, Versailles Palace. 1678–1684. Versailles, France. *Lebrun and Mansart designed this enormous hall to overlook the vast park at Versailles. Viewed through the floor-to-ceiling windows, which are placed along the width of the room, the majestic park becomes an extension of the interior space. The inside space, in turn, is enlarged by the tall mirrors that match the windows, echoing the outside view.*

Painting Classical values dominated Baroque painting in France even more completely than architecture. In pursuit of ancient Roman ideals (for Greek values were virtually unknown), French Baroque artists painted mythological subjects, stressed idealized human bodies, and cultivated a restrained style. The outstanding French Baroque artist was Nicolas Poussin (1594–1665), the finest Classical painter of the seventeenth century. Ironically, except for two disappointing years in Paris, Poussin spent his professional life in Rome, the home of the Florid Baroque. Although he was inspired by Caravaggio's use of

light and dark, the style that Poussin forged was uniquely his own, a detached, almost cold approach to his subject matter and a feeling for the unity of human beings with nature.

A beautiful example of Poussin's detached style is *Et in Arcadia Ego*, a painting in which the human figures are integrated into a quiet landscape (Figure 14.13). In ancient mythology, Arcadia was a land of pastures and flocks. In Poussin's painting, four shepherds, modeled on ancient statuary and dressed to suggest Roman times, are portrayed standing around a tomb, evidently absorbed in a discussion provoked

FIGURE 14.15 REMBRANDT VAN RIJN. *The Night Watch (The Militia Company of Captain Frans Banning Cocq)*. 1642. Oil on canvas, 12'2" × 14'7". Rijksmuseum, Amsterdam. *Because of its murky appearance, this painting acquired its nickname,* The Night Watch, *in the nineteenth century. But a cleaning of the painting's deteriorated surface showed that it was actually set in daylight. Restored to its original conception, this work now reveals Rembrandt's spectacular use of light and dark.*

FIGURE 14.16 REMBRANDT VAN RIJN. *Self-Portrait*. 1669. Oil on canvas, 23¼ × 20". Mauritshuis, The Hague. *In this last self-portrait, Rembrandt's eyes reveal the personal anguish of a man who has outlived wife, beloved mistress, and children. By this means, Rembrandt expresses one of the most popular themes of Baroque art, that of pathos—the quality that arouses feelings of pity and sorrow.*

FIGURE 14.17 JAN VERMEER. *The Lacemaker.* Ca. 1664. Oil on canvas, 9⅝ × 8¼". Louvre, Paris. *Unlike Rembrandt, Vermeer was not concerned with human personality as such. Rather, his aim was to create scenes that registered his deep pleasure in bourgeois order and comfort. In* The Lacemaker *he gives his female subject generalized features, turning her into a social type, but renders her sewing in exquisite detail, giving it a monumental presence. The painting thus becomes a visual metaphor of a virtuous household.*

Another great Dutch artist was Jan Vermeer (1632–1675), who specialized in domestic genre scenes. His works reveal a calm world where ordinary objects possess a timeless gravity. Color was important for establishing the domesticity and peacefulness of this closed-off world; Vermeer's favorites were yellow and blue. These serene works evoked the fabled cleanliness of Delft, the city where he lived and worked.

One of the most beautiful of his domestic scenes is *The Lacemaker* (Figure 14.17). Like most of his thirty-five extant paintings, *The Lacemaker* depicts an interior room where a single figure is encircled by everyday things. She is lit by a clear light falling on her from the side, another characteristic of Vermeer's paintings. The composition (the woman at the table and the rear wall parallel to the picture frame), the basic colors (yellow and blue), and the subject's absorption in her task typified Vermeer's works. *The Lacemaker* also has a moral message, for a woman engaged in household tasks symbolized the virtue of domesticity for Vermeer.

England also contributed to the creation of the Protestant Baroque, but conditions there led to a style markedly different from that of the Dutch school. Unlike the Netherlands, England had no art market, was dominated by an aristocracy, and, most importantly, had as yet no native-born painters of note. Painting in England was controlled by aristocratic patrons who preferred portraits to all other subjects and whose taste was courtly but restrained. The painter whose style suited these aristocratic demands was a Flemish artist, Anthony van Dyck (1599–1641). A pupil of Rubens, van Dyck eventually settled in England and became court painter to Charles I.

Van Dyck's elegant style captured the courtly qualities prized by his aristocratic patrons. He depicted his subjects' splendid costumes in all their radiant glory, using vibrant colors to reproduce their textures. He invented a repertory of poses for individual and group portraits that showed his subjects to their greatest advantage. Within a generation, his designs had become the standard for English portraiture. But van Dyck did more than cater to the vanity of his

explored other types of love in his plays, such as mother love and even political passion, it was in his study of sex as a powerful motive for action that Racine was most original.

The Baroque period in French drama also produced one of the comic geniuses of the Western theatre, Jean Baptiste Poquelin, better known as Molière (1622–1673). Molière analyzed the foibles of French life in twelve penetrating satirical comedies that had the lasting impact of tragedy. He peopled his plays with social types—the idler, the miser, the pedant, the seducer, the hypochondriac, the medical quack, the would-be gentleman, the pretentiously cultured lady—exposing the follies of the entire society. To create his comedic effects, Molière used not only topical humor and social satire but all the trappings of farce, including pratfalls, mistaken identities, sight gags, puns, and slapstick.

Molière was appointed official entertainer to Louis XIV in 1658; even so, he made many enemies among those who felt they were the butt of his jokes. When he died, for example, the French clergy refused to give him an official burial because they believed some of his plays to be attacks on the church. The testament to Molière's enduring brilliance is that many of his comedies are still performed today, including *Tartuffe*, *The Miser*, *The Bourgeois Gentleman*, and *The Misanthrope*, and that when they are, they are still enormously entertaining.

The English Baroque The outstanding contribution in English to the literature of the Baroque period was provided by John Milton (1608–1674), a stern Puritan who held high office in Cromwell's Commonwealth. The deeply learned Milton had a grand moral vision that led him to see the universe as locked in a struggle between the forces of darkness and the forces of light. Only an epic was capable of expressing such a monumental conception.

His supreme literary accomplishment was to Christianize the epic in his long poem *Paradise Lost*. Inspired by Homer's and Vergil's ancient works, but also intended as a Protestant response to Dante's *Comedy*, Milton's poem became an immediate classic. His grandiose themes in *Paradise Lost* were the rebellion of the angels led by Lucifer, the fall of Adam and Eve in the Garden of Eden, and Christ's redemption of humanity.

An astonishing aspect of *Paradise Lost* is Milton's portrait of Lucifer, which some readers have seen as a Baroque glamorization of evil. Lucifer is characterized as a creature of titanic ambition and deceitful charm. Despite his powerful presence, however, this epic story has moral balance. At the end, Adam, the author of original sin, is saved instead of being con-

demned to Hell. Adam's redemption occurs when he accepts Jesus as Lord. Adam's choice reflected Milton's belief in free will and the necessity of taking responsibility for one's actions.

In addition to its grand theme, *Paradise Lost* is Baroque in other ways. The mixing of Christian legend and ancient epic, for example, is typical of Baroque taste. Milton's convoluted style is Baroque with its occasionally odd word order, Latinisms, and complex metaphors. Most of all, Milton's epic is Baroque in its lofty tone and exaggerated rhetoric—literary equivalents, perhaps, of Rubens or Rembrandt.

Music

Unlike the Renaissance, when a single musical sound prevailed (see Chapter 12), the Baroque had no single musical ideal. Nonetheless, four trends during the Baroque period give it distinctive qualities. First, the development of major and minor tonality, which had been prefigured in Josquin des Prez's music in the early 1500s, was a central feature of the works of this time, making it the first stage in the rise of modern music. Second, the mixing of genres, which has been noted in literature and the arts, also occurred in Baroque music. Third, the expressiveness that had entered music in the late 1500s now became even more exaggerated, being used to stress meanings and emotions in the musical texts that otherwise might not have been heard. And last, this was an age of *virtuosos*, master musicians, especially singers, who performed with great technical skill and vivid personal style, and of a growing variety of musical instruments (Figure 14.20). The musical form that drew these trends together was *opera*, making it the quintessential symbol of the age.

Opera originated in Italy in the late sixteenth century among a group of Florentine musicians and poets with aristocratic ties. The first great composer of opera was Claudio Monteverdi (1567–1643), whose earliest opera, *Orfeo* (1607), was based on the legend of the ancient Greek poet-musician Orpheus. *Orfeo* united drama, dance, elaborate stage mechanisms, and painted scenery with music. Monteverdi wrote melodic arias, or songs, for the individual singers, and he increased the opera's dramatic appeal by concluding each of its five acts with a powerful chorus. His setting truly mirrored the text, using musical phrases to serve as aural symbols and thus to enhance the unfolding of events.

By the 1630s opera began to shed its aristocratic origins and become a popular entertainment. This change did not affect opera's focus on ancient myths and histories about noble men and women, nor did

FIGURE 14.20 JAN BRUEGEL. *Hearing.* Ca. 1620. Oil on canvas, ca. 2'3" × 3'6". Prado, Madrid. *One of a series of allegorical paintings representing the five senses, this work by Jan Bruegel depicts the sense of hearing. Set in a Renaissance interior framed by three rounded arches, it shows a variety of sources that make sounds pleasing to the human ear. Most prominent are the musical instruments, which collectively constitute an anthology of the instruments used in Baroque music.*

it halt the trend to brilliant singing called **bel canto**, literally "beautiful song." However, in order to appeal to a wider audience, operatic composers added elements from Italy's popular comic theater, such as farcical scenes and stock characters, notably humorous servants. By the end of this age, the operatic form was stylized into a recipe, including improbable plots, inadequate motivations for the characters, and magical transformations—signs of its Baroque nature.

Opera became immensely popular in Europe, especially in Italy, where it remains so today. By 1750 opera houses had been built in many major cities, with Venice leading the way with more than a dozen separate establishments. The rise of opera in Italy during the 1600s, like the founding of a commercial theater in London in the 1500s, presaged the downfall of the aristocratic patronage system and the emergence of entertainments with mass appeal.

The winding down of the Thirty Years' War allowed Italian opera to be exported to the rest of Europe. Only in France were composers able to defy the overpowering Italian influence and create an independent type of opera. This development was made possible by the grandeur of Louis XIV's court and French taste, which was more restrained than the opulent Italian. Nevertheless, French opera was founded by an Italian, Jean-Baptiste Lully (1632–1687), who later became a French citizen and Louis's court composer. Under Lully's direction, French opera developed its identifying features: dignified music, the full use of choruses, the inclusion of a ballet, and, most importantly, a French text. Lully's patron, the Sun King, sometimes performed in the opera's ballet sequences himself, dancing side by side with the composer. Lully's works, which dominated French music until 1750, ensured a powerful role for French music in the Western tradition.

Baroque music reached its climax after 1715 in Protestant northern Europe. Two German composers were responsible for this development—Bach in his homeland and Handel in England.

The greater of these late Baroque masters was Johann Sebastian Bach (1685–1750). A devout Lutheran who worked for German courts and municipalities far from the major cities, Bach created a body of sacred music that transcends all religious creeds and nationalities. Employing all of the Baroque musical genres, his works are distinguished by their inventiveness and complete mastery of major and minor tonality. His most memorable achievements are the Passions, the musical settings of the liturgy to be performed on Good Friday—the most tragic day in the Christian calendar. Composed around 1727, the *St. Matthew Passion* expresses the collective grief of the Christian community for the death of Jesus. Bach used a German text with arias and choruses, making the music bring out all of the emotional implications of the words. Thus the *St. Matthew Passion* is more dramatic than most operas and a sublime religious experience in itself.

The other great late Baroque master was George Frederic Handel (1685–1759) who was renowned for his Italian-style operas. More cosmopolitan than

Bach, Handel eventually settled in London, where he composed thirty-six operatic works. His operas succeeded in their day because of the brilliant way in which the music allows the singers to show their virtuosity, but they are generally not to the taste of modern audiences and have not found a place in the standard operatic repertory. In contrast, his mastery of sacred music has made his name immortal, particularly the *oratorio*—an opera-like form but without any stage action—which he perfected. Of the oratorios, the *Messiah*, based on biblical texts and sung in English, holds first place. Its popularity stems from its Baroque qualities: the emotionally stirring choruses and the delightful embellishments the soloists are permitted in their arias. As a result, the *Messiah* is probably the best known work of sacred music in the English-speaking world.

The Legacy of the Baroque Age

The Baroque period left a potent legacy to the modern world in politics, economics, and religion. The system of great states governed by a balance of power dominated European affairs until 1945. From the Baroque period date the roles of France and England as Europe's trendsetters, both politically and culturally. The concept and practice of "world war" also dates from this period. The economic system known as mercantilism originated during the Baroque period and prevailed in Europe into the nineteenth century. The religious orientation of the European states became well established in the seventeenth century, along with the division of the vast majority of Westerners into Protestant and Catholic camps.

Culturally, the Baroque is still with us, despite the fact that much about this style seems excessive to modern taste. Although Baroque operas are not often performed, the idea of opera originated in this age of spectacle. Other Baroque musical works, notably the majestic oratorios of Handel and the powerful compositions of Bach for church and court, are part of the regular concert repertoire in the West today. Some of the most admired and enduring artworks in Western history were created during this time, including Bernini's *Ecstasy of St. Teresa* and the paintings of Rembrandt. Many cities of Europe are still showcases of Baroque splendor. The church of St. Peter's in Rome, St. Paul's Cathedral in London, and the palace and gardens at Versailles are but three of the living monuments of this period, reminding us of the grand religious and political ideals of a very different age.

KEY CULTURAL TERMS

Baroque
Florid Baroque style
baldacchino
illusionism
French Baroque style
Protestant Baroque style
virtuoso

opera
bel canto
oratorio

SUGGESTIONS FOR FURTHER READING

PRIMARY SOURCES

CORNEILLE, P. *The Cid.* Translated by V. J. Cheng. Newark: University of Delaware Press, 1987. An up-to-date version of Corneille's drama, recounting the story of a hero torn between honor and love; imitates the poetic form of the original, first staged in 1636.

MILTON, J. *Paradise Lost.* New York: Norton, 1975. Milton's Baroque epic about rebellion—Lucifer's revolt in heaven and Adam and Eve's defiance on earth; Scott Elledge provides a useful introduction and notes to the text, which was first published in 1667.

MOLIÈRE (POQUELIN, J. B.). *The Misanthrope.* Translated by R. Wilbur. London: Methuen, 1967. A good version by a leading American poet. Useful English versions by various translators of Molière's other frequently performed comedies are also available, including *The Miser* (New York: Applause Theatre Book Publishers, 1987), *Tartuffe* (London: Faber and Faber, 1984), and *The Bourgeois Gentleman* (New York: Applause Theatre Book Publishers, 1987).

RACINE, J. B. *Phaedra.* Translated by R. Wilbur. New York: Harcourt Brace Jovanovich, 1986. A solid translation of this French tragic drama.

SECONDARY SOURCES

ADAM, A. *Grandeur and Illusion: French Literature and Society 1606–1715.* Translated by H. Tint. New York: Basic Books, 1972. A history of seventeenth-century French literature, showing how writing both reflected and transcended its social setting.

FRIEDRICH, C. J. *The Age of the Baroque: 1610–1660.* New York: Harper Torchbooks, 1962. A volume in the Rise of Modern Europe series; the chapters on culture still provide a stimulating introduction to developments during this period.

———. *The Age of Power.* Ithaca, N.Y.: Cornell University Press, 1964. A brief introduction for the student who wants an overview of the Baroque period.

HALEY, K. H. D. *The Dutch in the Seventeenth Century.* London: Thames and Hudson, 1972. A well-illustrated survey of the Dutch at the zenith of their civilization.

HILL, C. *Puritanism and Revolution: The English Revolution of the Seventeenth Century.* New York: Schocken, 1964. Collected essays by a highly respected scholar on the ideas current at the time of the English Civil War, a turning point in England's history.

HUBALA, E. *Baroque and Rococo Art.* New York: Universe Books, 1976. A splendid work with a succinct text and beautiful illustrations; for the serious student.

KAHR, M. M. *Dutch Painting in the Seventeenth Century.* Rev. ed. New York: Harper & Row, 1982. An innovative treatment of the Dutch school, showing its links with the international Baroque; contains many black-and-white illustrations.

LEWIS, W. H. *The Splendid Century: Life in the France of Louis XIV.* Garden City, N.Y.: Doubleday, 1957. A highly readable account of French society and politics that places Louis XIV's power and personality at the center of events.

MARTIN, J. R. *Baroque.* New York: Harper & Row, 1977. A refreshing approach to Baroque art, organized by topics such as "Space," "Time," and "Light."

OGG, D. *Europe in the Seventeenth Century.* New York: Collier Books, 1968. A solid overview by a scholar who has written widely on this period.

SCHAMA, S. *The Embarrassment of Riches: An Interpretation of Dutch Culture in the Golden Age.* New York: Knopf, 1987. A brilliant analysis of the Dutch way of life that weaves together society and the arts.

WEDGWOOD, C. V. *The Thirty Years' War.* New York: Methuen, 1981. A standard interpretation that first appeared in the late 1930s but is still worth reading.

WOLF, J. B. *Louis XIV.* New York: Norton, 1968. Perhaps the most thorough study of the Sun King in English.

———. *The Emergence of the Great Powers, 1685–1715.* New York: Harper & Row, 1951. In the Rise of Modern Europe series, this is a scholarly but clear account of a complex period; despite its age, Wolf's treatment is still fundamentally sound.

SUGGESTIONS FOR LISTENING

JOHANN SEBASTIAN BACH (1685–1750).

The greatest composer of the Baroque era, Bach is best known for his sacred music, which has tremendous emotional power. His church music for voices includes more than two hundred cantatas, or musical settings of biblical and chorale texts, such as *Jesu der du meine Seele* (Jesus, Thou Hast My Soul), *Wachet Auf* (Wake Up), and *O Haupt voll Blut und Wunden* (O Sacred Head Now Wounded); six motets, such as *Jesu meine Freude* (Jesus, My Joy); two passions, or musical settings of biblical passages and commentaries on the Easter season, such as the *St. Matthew Passion*; and a Mass, the *Mass in B Minor*. He also composed instrumental church music, notably about 170 organ chorales required by the liturgy for the church year. Besides sacred music Bach wrote secular music, including the *"Little" Fugue in G minor*, the *Brandenburg Concertos*, and *The Well-Tempered Clavier* (1722; 1740), a collection of works for clavier, or keyboard, that consisted of one prelude and fugue for each of the twelve major and minor keys.

GEORGE FREDERIC HANDEL (1685–1759).

The German-born Handel, who lived and worked mainly in England, made eighteenth-century England a center of Baroque music. Of the thirty-six Italian-style operas that he composed and produced in London, three of the best known are *Rinaldo* (1711), *Giulio Cesare* (1724), and *Serse* (1738). His oratorios—including the *Messiah*—were performed in public theaters rather than churches and especially appealed to the rising middle classes. Handel also produced a body of instrumental music of which the most significant are the two suites known as the *Fireworks Music* (1749) and the *Water Music* (about 1717) and six concertos for woodwinds and strings.

JEAN-BAPTISTE LULLY (1632–1687).

Lully's eleven operas helped to define the operatic genre in France, giving it an opening overture and a ballet movement. Of his operas, the best known are probably *Theseus* (1675) and *Amadis* (1684). Especially appealing to modern ears are the massed choruses and rhythmic dances of his operas.

CLAUDIO MONTEVERDI (1567–1643).

A prodigious composer of madrigals and sacred music, Monteverdi is best remembered as one of the pioneers of opera. He composed his operas in a highly expressive style that matched the spirit of music to the meaning of words in the text, as in *Orfeo* (1607) and *The Coronation of Poppea* (1642).

15

THE BAROQUE AGE II

*Revolutions in Scientific
and Political Thought, 1600—1715*

The Baroque age was more than a time of political upheaval and artistic spectacle. It was also the period when the event known as the Scientific Revolution took place. As centuries-old beliefs were challenged by discoveries in astronomy and physics, a whole new way of viewing the universe—and the position of humanity in it—emerged. At the same time, in England, a revolution in political philosophy was going on, leading to the notion that states ought to be governed by the people rather than by paternalistic rulers. These momentous changes in the way people thought added to the pervasive restlessness of the times.

The climax of this revolutionary age occurred between 1685 and 1715, a period that witnessed what one twentieth-century historian has called "the crisis of the European conscience." For a handful of scholars, the balance swung away from traditional ideas to modern views. These early modern scientists and philosophers opposed faith with reason, dogma with skepticism, and divine intervention with natural law. They made mathematics their guiding star in the search for truth, accepting as true those things that could be proven mathematically and rejecting as untrue those that could not. Their new philosophy eventually concluded that the universe was like a great clock that operated according to universal laws. Although we today tend to discount this clockwork image, we still owe a debt to these thinkers, who set Western culture on its present course and brought modernity into being.

THE BACKGROUND OF THE SCIENTIFIC REVOLUTION

The Scientific Revolution was both an outgrowth and a rejection of the Aristotelian cosmology that had held Western thinkers in thrall for two thousand years. The Aristotelian system, named for the fourth-century B.C. philosopher, was developed by the ancient Greeks and transmitted to the West through Roman and Islamic culture and the medieval scholastic tradition. The fundamental principle of this cosmology is *geocentrism*, the notion that the universe is earth-centered. Around the earth, according to the theory, revolved the five known planets (Mercury, Venus, Mars, Jupiter, and Saturn) and the sun and moon, each held aloft by a crystalline sphere. The earth, which did not move, was not considered a planet. Nearest the earth was the moon, and there was a complete division between the supralunar world, the region beyond the moon, and the sublunar world, the region beneath the moon (Figure 15.1). In the supralunar world, the planets moved in circular orbits and were made of an incorruptible element, aether; in the sublunar world, change was constant, motion was rectilinear, and matter was composed of the four elements, earth, air, fire, and water. This system had an absolute up and down: Up referred to the area beyond the spheres inhabited by the Unmoved Mover—Aristotle's name for the source of all

FIGURE 15.1 PETER APIAN. Geocentric Diagram of the Universe, from the *Cosmographia*. 1539. The Bancroft Library, University of California, Berkeley. *This schematic diagram illustrates the geocentric universe in the pre-Copernican era. The unmoving earth is placed at the center and is surrounded by nine moving spheres, containing, in sequential order, the moon, Mercury, Venus, the sun, Mars, Jupiter, Saturn, the fixed stars, and the empty sphere called the* primum mobile. *The ninth sphere, the* primum mobile, *was logically necessary in Aristotle's theory because it moved first and brought the other eight into motion. Beyond the ninth circle was the Empyrean, home of the Unmoved Mover in philosophy or of God in theology.*

celestial motion—and down referred to the center of the earth.

In the second century A.D., the Egyptian scholar Ptolemy brought Aristotle's geocentric theory up to date with new astronomical data and improved mathematical calculations, and the system is now called the Ptolemaic system. During the golden age of Muslim culture (800–1000 A.D.), Arab intellectuals preserved this legacy, improving and refining it to reflect new planetary sightings. In the High Middle Ages (1000–1300), Western scholars recovered the Ptolemaic heritage—with its Muslim additions—and gave it a Christian interpretation: Medieval Christian scientists began to identify the Unmoved Mover as God and the space beyond the spheres as heaven. More importantly, the church became attached to the geocentric theory because the doctrine of original sin seemed validated by it. In other words, the corrupt earth inhabited by fallen mortals corresponded to the sublunar world of decay and constant change.

Up to this point in the transmission of ancient knowledge, scientists simply made minor adjustments to Aristotle's original picture. But at the University of Paris in the 1300s a more self-assured and skeptical outlook arose among a few thinkers. Unconvinced by Aristotle's solution to the problem of motion (which was to attribute the forward motion of a projectile to air movement), the Parisian scholars offered an alternative explanation. They asserted that a projectile acquired "impetus," a propulsive quality that gradually diminished as the projectile moved through space. The theory of "impetus" commanded scholars' attention for centuries, leading them to consider a new range of scientific problems.

From the modern perspective, it matters little that the theory of "impetus" was untrue. As a first step away from the Aristotelian tradition, it made Western scientists aware that the great Greek thinker was not always right. And scholars at Paris and other universities began to advocate the application of mathematics to practical problems as well as the direct observation of nature, that is, collecting data (*empiricism*) and framing hypotheses from observable facts (*inductive reasoning*).

Aristotle had also used empirical data and inductive logic, but his writings had become so authoritative that for generations scholars did not examine his methodology and were afraid to tamper with his conclusions. Indeed, his followers relied on *deductive reasoning*; in other words, they only explored the ramifications of accepted truths. But with the new critical spirit that appeared in the Late Middle Ages, scholars looked at the world with new eyes. In time, this spirit led to the greatest achievement of Baroque science, the Scientific Revolution that overturned the Ptolemaic system and enthroned *heliocentrism*, the notion that the universe is centered around the sun.

THE SCIENTIFIC REVOLUTION: DISCOVERIES AND THEORIES

The term *Scientific Revolution* applies chiefly to astronomy and physics, the fields of study in which dramatic breakthroughs occurred in the Baroque age, although major advances were also made in medical science and lesser though still important gains occurred in chemistry, biology, and embryology. In addition, the Scientific Revolution gave rise to a type of literature that treated the impact of the new science on secular and religious thought. Armed with the new learning and impelled by a need to make a clean break with the past, a few scholars and publicists

TIME LINE 15.1   REVOLUTIONS IN SCIENTIFIC AND POLITICAL THOUGHT

1543	1600	1700	1715

The Scientific Revolution and Early Modern Political Philosophy

Contributions of Copernicus and Tycho Brahe	Jamestown founded 1607	Plymouth Colony 1620	Descartes's *Discourse on Method* 1637	Hobbes's *Leviathan* 1651	Pennsyl-vania Charter 1681	Locke's *Second Treatise* and *Essay Concerning Human Understanding* 1690
	Galileo sights four moons of Jupiter 1610	Grotius's *The Law of War and Peace* 1625		Bahamas Colony 1648		Newton's *Mathematical Principles* 1687

composed literary works that redefined the place of human beings in the cosmos and the purpose of human life. The chief result was to bring to a climax the separation of philosophy from theology, a gap that had been widening since the 1300s (see Chapter 10). From this point, philosophy begins to address secular concerns, and theology is relegated to a minor cultural role (Time Line 15.1).

THE MAGICAL AND THE PRACTICAL IN THE SCIENTIFIC REVOLUTION

The Scientific Revolution is notable for the paradoxes and ironies that the movement gave rise to, some of which will be discussed in a later section of this chapter. A paradox that should be noted at the outset, however, is that this revolution in human thought, which ushered in modern science, was rooted in both magical beliefs and practical technological achievements. With one or two exceptions, the makers of the Scientific Revolution were motivated by two divergent and rather contradictory sets of beliefs. On the one hand, they followed the lead of late medieval science by collecting empirical data, reasoning inductively, and using mathematics to verify results. Significantly, the most startling changes evolved in those areas where mathematics was applied to long-existing intellectual problems, namely in astronomy, physics, and biology.

On the other hand, these thinkers were entranced by Neo-Platonism, the ancient Greek philosophy that

was revived in the Early Renaissance (see Chapter 11). Like late medieval science, Neo-Platonism stressed the role of mathematics in problem solving, but Neo-Platonism also had a mystical streak—a legacy from Pythagoras—that led its devotees to seek harmony through numbers (see Chapter 2). Thinkers who followed Neo-Platonism believed that simplicity was superior to complexity in mathematical figuring because simplicity was the supreme sign that a solution was correct. This belief has become a guiding ideal of modern science, although other aspects of Neo-Platonism would be rejected today, such as the attribution of mysterious powers to the sun. One effect of Neo-Platonism's occult side was to tighten the link between astronomy and astrology, a connection as old as Greek science. Most of those who made the revolution in science supported this linkage, and a few even cast horoscopes for wealthy clients.

As for the role of technology in the Scientific Revolution, many of its achievements would have been impossible without the telescope and the microscope, both of which were invented in about 1600 in the Netherlands. These enabling devices were decisive for the success of the Scientific Revolution because without them scholars would have simply remained "thinkers," as they had been since the time of the ancient Greeks. But with the telescope and the microscope they could penetrate deep into hitherto inaccessible areas—outer space and the inner workings of the human body. Henceforward, scholars with a scientific bent allied themselves with the crafts tradition, becoming in the process experimenters and empiricists.

Astronomy and Physics: From Copernicus to Newton

The intellectual shift from the earth-centered to the sun-centered universe was almost 150 years in the making and involved an international community of scholars. Heliocentrism, the new model of the world, was first broached in modern times by the Polish thinker Copernicus in 1543, and incontrovertible mathematical calculations to prove this view were published by the English scholar Newton in 1687. Between these dates, major steps in the revolution in science were taken by Brahe of Denmark, Kepler of Germany, and Galileo of Italy. Newton spoke the truth when he claimed that he "stood on the shoulders of giants" (Table 15.1).

Nicolas Copernicus When Nicolas Copernicus (1473–1543) published *Revolutions of the Heavenly Bodies* in 1543, he was reviving the discarded heliocentric theory of the third-century B.C. Greek thinker Aristarchus. In this highly technical work, Copernicus launched a head-on assault against Ptolemaic geocentrism. The main issue between Copernican astronomy and the older world view was not one of mathematical precision, for both were mathematically solid and thus equally able to predict planetary positions and solar and lunar eclipses. Rather, the basic question between the two systems was which one

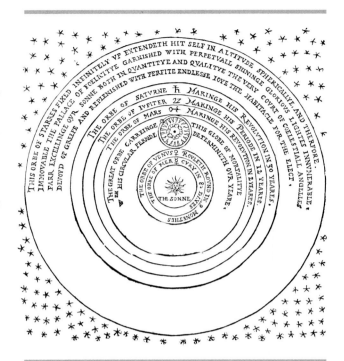

FIGURE 15.2 THOMAS DIGGES. The Sun-Centered Universe of Copernicus, from *A Perfit Description of the Celestiall Orbes.* 1576. The Huntington Library, San Marino, California. *This diagram drawn by the Englishman Thomas Digges agrees with the Copernican system except in one major way. Copernicus believed the universe was a finite, closed system, but Digges represents it as infinite. The infinitude is expressed in the stars scattered outside the orbit of fixed stars in the illustration.*

DATE	EVENT
1543	Copernicus publishes *Revolutions of the Heavenly Bodies*
1571–1601	Tycho Brahe makes his observations
Ca. 1600	Dutch lens grinders develop the telescope
1609	Kepler publishes his first and second planetary laws in *On the Motion of Mars*
1609	Galileo perfects his own telescope
1610	Galileo sights the four moons of Jupiter
1619	Kepler publishes his third planetary law in *The Harmonies of the World*
1620	Bacon publishes *New Organon*
1632	Galileo publishes *Dialogues on the Two Chief Systems of the World*
1633	Galileo humiliated by the Inquisition
1637	Descartes publishes *Discourse on Method*
1687	Newton publishes *Mathematical Principles of Natural Philosophy*

was simpler. Copernicus reasoned that a more convincing picture of the universe could be achieved by transposing the positions of the sun and the earth. Instead of the Ptolemaic notion of a finite world centered around a fixed earth, Copernicus envisioned a vastly expanded, but not infinite, universe with the planets orbiting the sun (Figure 15.2).

Recognizing the revolutionary nature of his hypothesis, Copernicus delayed printing his ideas until he was dying. In an attempt to mollify clerical critics, he dedicated his book to the pope, Paul III. At first, the pope and other religious leaders saw his views as ingenious speculation with no useful purpose, but later the religious establishment concluded that heliocentrism was dangerous and contrary to scripture; they therefore condemned it as a false system. What disturbed them was that when the earth was removed from the center of the universe, the place of human beings in the divine order was also reduced. In effect, human beings were no longer the leading actors in a cosmic drama, staged for them alone.

Catholics and Protestants alike denounced the ideas of Copernicus. Lutheran and Calvinist authorities condemned his views as unbiblical, and in 1610 the pope placed *Revolutions of the Heavenly Bodies* on the Index, the list of forbidden books created during the Counter-Reformation. Eventually the two religious groups came to a parting of the ways over this issue. For more than two hundred years, until 1822, the Roman Catholic church, with all of its considerable power and influence, opposed the sun-centered theory. In this policy the church reversed a centuries-old tradition of being open to innovative scientific thought. However, in Protestantism—where there was no focus of authority as there was in Roman Catholicism—some sects slowly accepted and adapted their beliefs to the new astronomy.

Johannes Kepler   The reception of Copernican astronomy by the scientific community was neither immediate nor enthusiastic. For example, the great Danish astronomer Tycho Brahe (1546–1601) rejected a thoroughgoing Copernicanism, believing that the other planets moved around the sun but that the earth did not. Brahe nevertheless made a major contribution to the ultimate triumph of heliocentrism because of his copious observations of planetary movement. So accurate were his sightings that they set a new standard for astronomical data.

Among Brahe's assistants was Johannes Kepler (1571–1630), a brilliant mathematician who dedicated his life to clarifying the theory of heliocentrism. When the Danish astronomer died, Kepler inherited his astronomical data. Inspired by Neo-Platonism to make sense of the regular and continuous sightings of Brahe, Kepler in 1609 published *On the Motion of Mars*, setting forth his solution to the problem of what kept the planets in their orbits. His findings were expressed in two scientific laws that were elegant in their simplicity. In the first planetary law, Kepler substituted the ellipse for the circle as the descriptive shape of planetary orbits. And his second planetary law, which was set forth in a precise mathematical formula, accounted for each planet's variable speed within its respective orbit by showing that nearness to the sun affected its behavior—the closer to the sun, the faster the speed, and the farther from the sun, the slower the speed. Together, these laws validated sun-centered astronomy, enabling Kepler to abolish the orbital deviations and the tangled calculations that had cluttered the Copernican system.

Kepler continued to manipulate Brahe's undigested data, convinced that other mathematical laws could be derived from observations of the heavens. In 1619, he arrived at a third planetary law, which, unlike his other two, had no equivalent in earlier astronomy. In the third law, he showed that the squares of the length of time for each planet's orbit are in the same ratios as the cubes of their respective mean distances from the sun. Through this formula, he affirmed that the solar system itself was regular and organized by mathematically determined relationships. This was the first expression of the notion that the universe operates with clocklike regularity, an idea that became an article of faith by the end of the Baroque age. Kepler took great pride in this discovery, because it confirmed his Neo-Platonist belief that there is a hidden mathematical harmony in the universe.

Galileo Galilei   While Kepler moved in the rarefied realm of theoretical, even mystical, science, one of his contemporaries was making major breakthroughs with experiments that relied on precise mathematics and careful logic. This patient experimenter was Galileo Galilei (1564–1642), whose most valuable contributions were his accurate celestial observations and his work in terrestial mechanics, the study of the action of forces on matter. Inspired by news that Dutch lens grinders had made a device for viewing distant objects, in 1609 Galileo made his own telescope, which enabled him to see stars invisible to the naked eye.

With these sightings Galileo demonstrated that the size of the universe was exponentially greater than that computed on Ptolemaic principles. Further, his observations of the moon's rough surface and the sun's shifting dark spots provided additional proofs against the ancient arguments that the heavenly bodies were perfectly formed and never changed. But his most telling discovery was that the planet Jupiter has moons, a fact that contradicted the Ptolemaic belief that all celestial bodies must move about a common center. Galileo's research affirmed that Jupiter's four satellites rotated around it in much the same way as the six planets orbited the sun. These telescopic sightings hastened the demise of the idea that the earth was the center of the universe.

Similarly, Galileo's research in terrestrial mechanics proved conclusively that both Aristotle and his fourteenth-century critics in Paris were wrong about one of the central questions of earthly motion, that is, the behavior of projectiles. Aristotle had claimed that projectiles stayed in flight because of the pushing motion of the air, and the Parisian scholars had countered with the theory of "impetus." Through experimentation, Galileo showed that a mass that is moving will go on moving until some force acts to stop it—the earliest expression of the modern law of inertia.

Galileo was probably the first scientist to make a clock a basic means for measuring time in his experiments. Like his contemporary Kepler, he reported his findings in the form of simple mathematical laws. Galileo's work was later validated by the conclusions

FIGURE 15.3 GODFREY KNELLER. *Sir Isaac Newton.* 1702. Oil on canvas, 29¾ × 24½". National Portrait Gallery, London. *As the most celebrated intellectual of his generation, the middle-class Newton was given star treatment in this portrait by the reigning society painter in England. Decked out fashionably in an elaborate Baroque wig, Newton peers somewhat uncomfortably at the viewer. The likeness tends to support Newton's reputation for vanity and ostentation.*

of Newton, who proved that the laws of mechanics on earth were the same as the laws of mechanics in the sky.

At the same time that Galileo was conducting the experiments that would make him a hero of modern science, he ran afoul of the religious authorities, who brought his career to a humiliating end. The church, as noted above, had by now abandoned its relative openness to ideas and was moving to stifle dissent. In 1633 Galileo was arrested by the Inquisition, the church court created in the thirteenth century to find and punish heretics. The great astronomer was charged with false teachings for his published support of the idea that the earth moves, a notion central to Copernicanism but untrue according to Aristotle and the church. Threatened with torture, Galileo recanted his views and was released. Despite living on for several years, he died a broken man. This episode abruptly ended Italy's role in the burgeoning revolution in science.

Isaac Newton Building on the research of the heirs to Copernicus, including Kepler's laws of planetary motion and Galileo's law of inertia, the English mathematician Isaac Newton (1642–1727) conceived a model of the universe that decisively overturned the Ptolemaic scheme and finished the revolution in astronomy begun by Copernicus (Figure 15.3). In Newton's world picture, there is uniform motion on earth and in the heavens. More significantly, Newton presented a satisfactory explanation for what held the planets in their orbits. Newton's solution was the force of gravity, and this topic formed the heart of his theory of the universe.

In a precise mathematical formula, Newton computed the law of universal gravitation, the formula whereby every object in the world exerts an attraction to a greater or a lesser degree on all other objects. By this law, the sun held in its grip each of the six planets, and each, in turn, lightly influenced the sun and the other planets. The earth and its single moon as well as Jupiter and its four satellites similarly interacted. In effect, because of gravity, the heavenly bodies formed a harmonious system in which each attracted the others.

Having described gravity and asserted its universal nature, Newton declined to speculate about what caused it to operate. For him, the universe behaved precisely as a machine, and his law was nothing but a description of its operation. Because Newton refused to speculate beyond what mathematics could prove, he has been called a "mind without metaphysics." Modern scientists have followed Newton's lead, preferring to ignore the *why* of things and to concentrate on the *how* and *what*.

Newton's views were set forth in his magisterial work, *Mathematical Principles of Natural Philosophy*. Known more familiarly as the *Principia* (the first word of its Latin title), this book quickly gained an authority that made Newton the modern world's equivalent of Aristotle. By the eighteenth century the English poet Alexander Pope could justifiably write:

Nature and Nature's Laws lay hid in Night;
God said, *Let Newton be!* and All was *Light*.

Even though Newton's work was the culmination of the revolution that brought modern science into being, he was not fully free of older attitudes. True, he believed that scientific truth was simply a matter of using methodical principles. He made mathematics his guiding ideal and used patient and careful observation. But Newton cared little for his own scientific achievement, believing that his lasting monument was his religious writings. A pious Christian, he devoted his last years to demonstrating that the prophecies in the Bible were coming true.

Newton also invented a form of calculus, a mathematical method of analysis that uses a symbolic notation. This breakthrough had huge potential for solving problems in physics and mechanics by providing a tool for computing quantities that had nonlinear variations. Newton's development of calculus, in contrast to his work in gravitation, was not a solo effort. He had to share this triumph with Gottfried Wilhelm von Leibniz (1646–1716), a German thinker who, simultaneously and independently of Newton, invented another version of calculus. Indeed, Leibniz's notation proved more useful than Newton's cumbersome technique, so that by 1800 Leibniz's symbols had become the universally accepted language of calculus.

Medicine and Chemistry

At the same time that Western understanding of the universe at its outer limits was being radically altered, another revolution was taking place in knowledge of the workings of the human body. This revolution in anatomical knowledge involved the discovery of the true circulation of the human blood. Unlike developments in astronomy, this breakthrough in medical science happened largely without the aid of technology. Only during the last step in the solving of the

mystery of the blood's circulation did early modern scientists use the newly invented microscope.

In 1600 knowledge of the workings of the human body was cloaked in darkness. There were many reasons for this, but the most powerful was that the church forbade the violation of corpses because of the teaching that the body would be resurrected. Biological research had been based on the dissection of animals with generalizations then applied, whether justified or not, to the human body. This practice had led to a great deal of misinformation and many half-truths.

Besides, in biology as in astronomy and physics, the authority of ancient Greek thinkers reigned supreme—Aristotle since the fourth century B.C. and Galen since the second century A.D. Though offering rival theories, Aristotle and Galen shared many false ideas, namely the notions that air ran directly from the lungs into the heart, that blood flowed from the veins to the outer part of the body, and that different types of blood coursed in the arteries and veins. The birth of modern medical science had to await the dispelling of these myths.

The problem of the circulation of the blood was eventually resolved by scientists at the University of Padua in Italy, the most prominent of whom was Andreas Vesalius (1514–1564). His painstaking observations led him to deny Galen's theory that blood passed from one side of the heart to the other through the septum, an impermeable membrane. At the same time his work proved the need for further careful study of human anatomy (Figure 15.4).

The research of Vesalius and his successors set the stage for William Harvey, an English scientist who studied and taught at the University of Padua. In 1628 Harvey (1578–1657) published his ground-breaking work, based on years of careful research, which overthrew the ancient theories and produced the correct view of circulation, including the role of the heart, the lungs, the arteries, and the veins. Mathematical calculation played a decisive role in this scientific triumph, just as it had in Newton's gravitation theory. Using arithmetic, Harvey proved that a stable quantity of blood constantly circulated throughout the body, thereby destroying Galen's ebb-and-flow theory. Harvey lacked knowledge of the capillaries, the connectors between the arteries and the veins, but in 1661 the Italian scientist Marcello Malpighi (1628–1694) identified these tiny vessels with the aid of the microscope, and with this critical piece of information an essentially correct, modern description of the blood's circulation was complete.

Chemistry did not become a separate discipline in the Baroque age, but it was during this time that the English physicist Robert Boyle (1627–1691) laid the

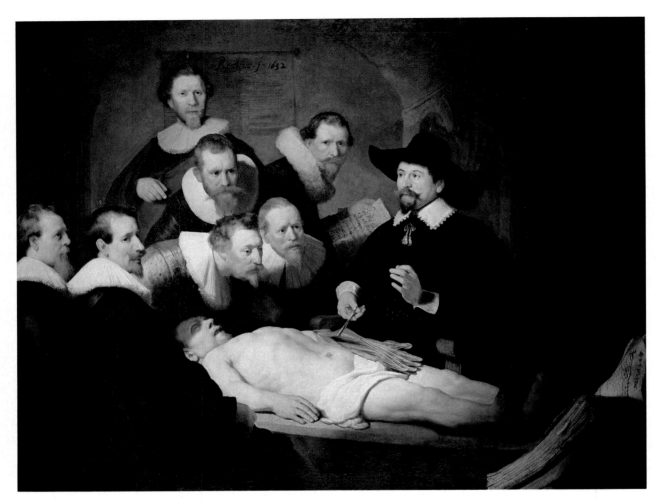

FIGURE 15.4 REMBRANDT VAN RIJN. *The Anatomy Lesson of Dr. Tulp.* 1632. Oil on canvas, 66¾ × 85¼". Mauritshuis, The Hague. *The pioneering work of Vesalius made the study of anatomy a central concern of medical science in the seventeenth century. In this painting, Rembrandt depicts Dr. Nicolas Tulp of Amsterdam as he demonstrates the dissection of the left arm. Rembrandt's use of Baroque effects, such as the dramatic light on the corpse, the contrast between Dr. Tulp's calm demeanor and the inquisitive faces of his pupils, and the flayed arm of the corpse, make this an arresting image.*

groundwork for modern chemistry. A major aspect of Boyle's thought linked him to Newton, for both believed that the universe is a machine. Boyle believed that the workings of nature could be revealed only through experimental study—the inductive method. Boyle's zeal for experimentation led him to study the behavior of gases and to formulate the famous law that bears his name. Boyle's law, which is still used in modern chemistry, is a method for computing the weight of compressed air in a tube.

Boyle was also one of the first to distinguish chemistry from alchemy, a set of magical practices that had been allied with chemistry since the time of the ancient Greeks. In medieval Europe, alchemy had led scholars to search vainly for the "philosopher's stone" that would miraculously turn a base metal like lead into gold. Rejecting alchemy's assumptions and methodology, Boyle sought to understand only those chemical reactions that happened naturally and could be analyzed in mathematical terms.

The Impact of Science on Philosophy

The Scientific Revolution had a profound influence on Western thought and also gave rise to a type of literature that reflected the impact of science on the wider culture. Three prominent contributors to this literature were the English jurist and statesman Francis Bacon and two brilliant French mathematicians, René Descartes and Blaise Pascal, whose speculative writings continued the French rationalist tradition begun by Montaigne in the 1500s (see Chapter 13).

Francis Bacon Francis Bacon (1561–1626) owes his fame to his ability to write lucid prose about science and its methodology. In a field that was dominated by scholars whose writings were accessible only to those learned in mathematics, Bacon's clear and eminently quotable prose opened the door to a curious and educated public. In the process of clarifying the techniques and the aims of the new science, he became the spokesman for the "experimenters," those who believed that the future of science lay in discarding Aristotle and seeing the world with fresh eyes. Condemning Aristotle for relying on deductive reason and unproven axioms, Bacon advocated the inductive method, the procedure that embraced the conducting of experiments, the drawing of conclusions, and the testing of results in other experiments. His claims were not new, but they were forcibly and memorably expressed; few scholars exhibited Bacon's optimism about the usefulness of science. He sincerely believed that the march of science inevitably led to mastery over the natural world, a view summarized in the famous phrase attributed to him, "knowledge is power." Bacon's slogan became the watchword of the forces of progress in the next century and remains so until the present day.

René Descartes An outstanding critic of the belief that the experimental method was the correct path to knowledge was René Descartes (1596–1650), a philosopher who urged a purely mathematical approach in science (Figure 15.5). His love of numbers came from a mystic side of his personality, as illustrated by his confession that a dream had inspired his belief that mathematics holds the key to nature. Descartes was the founder of analytic geometry, that branch of mathematics that describes geometrical figures by the formulas of algebra, and the author of a widely influential philosophical treatise, *Discourse on Method*, published in 1637.

In the *Discourse*, Descartes outlined four steps in his approach to knowledge: to accept nothing as true unless it is self-evident; to split problems into manageable parts; to solve problems starting with the simplest and moving to the most complex; and to review and reexamine the solutions. He used deductive logic in his method, only making inferences from general statements. But more important than his stress on deductive reasoning was his insistence on mathematical clarity. He refused to accept anything as true unless it had the persuasiveness of a proof in geometry.

Descartes's most influential gifts to Western philosophy were skepticism and a dualistic theory of knowledge. He rejected the authoritarian method of medieval scholasticism and began with universal doubt in order to determine what was absolutely certain in the universe. Step by step, he questioned the existence of God, of the world, and of his own body. But he soon established that he could not doubt the existence of his own doubting self. He reached this absolute conclusion in the famous phrase "*Cogito ergo sum*"—I think, therefore I am. This datum became

FIGURE 15.5 FRANS HALS. *René Descartes.* After 1649. Oil on canvas, 30¾ × 26¾". Louvre. *Descartes had the good fortune to be memorialized in paint by a great Dutch portrait artist and contemporary of Rembrandt, Frans Hals. In this likeness, Hals has captured the complex personality of the great French philosopher and mathematician. Descartes's piercing gaze shows his skeptical spirit, and his disdainful presence and rough features reveal his early background as a soldier. Hals apparently felt no need to flatter his sitter in this compelling portrait.*

both Descartes's conclusion to his doubting and the starting point from which he erected his view of the world. Having first destroyed the age-old certainties, he then, through deduction, reestablished the existence of his own body, the world, and finally, God.

Descartes's speculations were aimed at identifying clear and distinct ideas that were certain for everyone, but his efforts had a deeply ironic result. In the long run his thought fostered the growing awareness among the educated elite that absolute truth was not possible. Many who read his *Discourse* were unimpressed by his rational arguments, but they nevertheless accepted his radical doubt, and some even became atheists. That his work contributed to the rise of atheism would have horrified Descartes, since, to his own way of thinking, he had proven the existence of God. He had used skepticism merely as a means of achieving certainty.

God's plan. The bishop believed that the age's conflicts made autocratic rule a political necessity. Bossuet's belief in autocracy was also shared by the Englishman Thomas Hobbes who, however, explained absolute rule in different terms.

Absolutism and Liberalism: Hobbes and Locke   Thomas Hobbes (1588–1679) grew up in an England increasingly torn by religious, social, and political discord. A trained Classicist, Hobbes translated into English the work of the Greek historian Thucydides, whose reservations about Athenian democracy deeply impressed him (see Chapter 3). His study of the Greek geometer Euclid convinced Hobbes that certainty could be achieved only through geometrical reasoning, which in turn could be applied to topics such as human behavior and politics. The final stage of his intellectual initiation fell into place when he visited Galileo in Italy. Hobbes came away from this meeting certain that everything, including human beings and their social acts, could be explained by using mechanistic, natural laws to describe various states of motion or movement.

Hobbes's efforts to synthesize a universal philosophy founded on a geometric design and activated by some form of energy culminated in his best-known work, *The Leviathan*, published in 1651 (Figure 15.6). *The Leviathan* sets forth a theory of government based on the pessimistic view that individuals are driven by two basic forces, the fear of death and the quest for power. Hobbes imagined what life would be like if these two natural inclinations were allowed free rein and there were no supreme power to control them. Hobbes described human life under these circumstances as "solitary, poor, nasty, brutish, and short."

Hobbes thought that human beings, recognizing the awfulness of their situation, would decide to give up such an existence and form a civil society under the rule of one man. This first step in the evolution of government was achieved by means of a *social contract* drawn up between the ruler and his subjects. By the terms of this covenant the subjects surrendered all their claims to sovereignty and bestowed absolute power on the ruler. The sovereign's commands were then to be carried out by all under him, including the religious and civic leaders. Armed with the sword, the sovereign would keep peace at home and protect the land from its enemies abroad.

Hobbes made no distinction between the ruler of a monarchy and the head of a commonwealth, for he was less concerned with the form of government than with the need to hold in check destructive human impulses. In the next generation, Hobbes's pessimistic philosophy provoked a reaction from John

FIGURE 15.6   Frontispiece of *The Leviathan*. 1651. The Bancroft Library, University of California, Berkeley. *The original illustration for Hobbes's Leviathan conveys the political message of this controversial work in symbolic terms. Towering over the landscape is the mythical ruler, whose body is a composite of all of his subjects and in whose hands are the sword and scepter, symbols of his absolute power. Below this awesome figure is a well-ordered and peaceful village and countryside—Hobbes's political dream come true.*

Locke, who repudiated absolutism and advocated a theory of government by the people.

Despite their contradictory messages, Hobbes and John Locke (1632–1704) had been subjected to similar influences. Both adapted ideas from the new science, witnessed the English Civil War, and sought safety on the Continent because of their political views. But Locke rejected Hobbes's gloomy view of humanity and his theory of absolutism; he taught instead that human nature was potentially good and that human beings were capable of governing themselves. The two thinkers originated opposing schools of modern political thought: From Hobbes stems the absolutist, authoritarian tradition, and from Locke descends the school of liberalism. Their works represent two of the most significant legacies of the Baroque age to the modern world.

Locke set forth his political theories in his *Two Treatises of Government,* which he published anonymously in 1690. In the *First Treatise* he refuted the divine right of kings, and in the *Second Treatise* he laid out the model for rule by the people. The latter work has become the classic expression of early *liberalism.* In it Locke described the origins, characteristics, and purpose of the ideal political system—a government limited by laws, subject to the will of its citizens, and existing to protect life and property.

Locke shared some of Hobbes's ideas, such as the view that human life is violent and disorderly in the state of nature, that human beings must form civil governments to protect themselves, and that a social contract is the necessary basis of civil society. But Locke believed that basic rights, including life and property, exist in the state of nature. He also believed that human beings possess reason, are fundamentally decent and law abiding, and are slow to want change. From these principles he concluded that human beings would contract together to create a limited government that had no other purpose than the protection of the basic natural rights of life and property.

Locke rejected the idea that by making a social contract citizens surrender their sovereignty to a ruler. He argued instead that the people choose rulers who protect their rights in a fiduciary trust; that is, they expect their rulers to obey the social contract and govern equitably. If the rulers break the agreement, then the people have the right to revolt, overthrow the government, and reclaim their natural rights. Unlike Hobbes, Locke asserted that rulers possess only limited authority and that their control must be held in check by a balanced governmental system and a separation of powers. In later years, Locke's tract greatly influenced political thinkers and patriots who used its ideas to support both the American and the French revolutions.

Locke was not only a political theorist but the preeminent English philosopher of his day. He grappled with many of the same problems as Descartes, although his conclusions were radically different from the French thinker's. In his important philosophical work *An Essay Concerning Human Understanding,* published in 1690 (the same year he published *Two Treatises of Government*), Locke addressed the question, How is knowledge acquired? Descartes had proposed that the germs of ideas were inborn and that people were born knowing certain truths; education required nothing more than the strenuous use of the intellect without concern for new information from the senses.

Locke rejected these views and described the mind at birth as a **tabula rasa** (erased tablet) on which all human experiences were recorded. Locke maintained that all that human beings can know must first be received through their senses (a basically Aristotelian viewpoint) and then registered on their minds. The raw sensory data are manipulated by the mental faculties, such as comparing, contrasting, and so on, so that abstract concepts and generalizations are formed in the mind. According to Locke, individuals come to understand the world and to have ideas through a series of mental steps. As a result, reason and experience are united in human thought and together determine what is real for each person. Locke's explanation of the origin of ideas is the basis of modern empiricism—the theory that all knowledge is derived from or originates in human experience. His influence has been so great that many of his ideas seem to the modern reader to be just "common sense."

EUROPEAN EXPLORATION AND EXPANSION

The exploration begun in the late fifteenth century had led to a series of encounters with new peoples that slowly eroded the isolation and self-absorption of Europe. In the sixteenth century the pace of exploration quickened, and the globe was circumnavigated—events that intensified rivalries among the European states, increased the Continent's economic power, and diffused European culture and customs around the world.

The greatest success of European expansion was achieved through a series of permanent settlements in North and South America and by the opening of new trade routes to the Far East (Map 15.1). Expansion and colonization affected Europe in numerous ways: the introduction of new foodstuffs and other products, the establishment of innovative business methods, the disruption of old economic and social patterns, the introduction of novel ways of looking at the world, and the adoption of new symbols and themes in the arts. Whatever may have been the beneficial or harmful effects of these changes on European life, the negative impact on non-Europeans tended to outweigh the good that came with the introduction of Western culture. In Africa, the Europeans expanded the slave trade; in North, Central, and South America and the Caribbean, they annihilated many native tribes; and everywhere they forced trade agreements favorable to themselves on the local people.

Map 15.1

Expansion of Europe, 1715

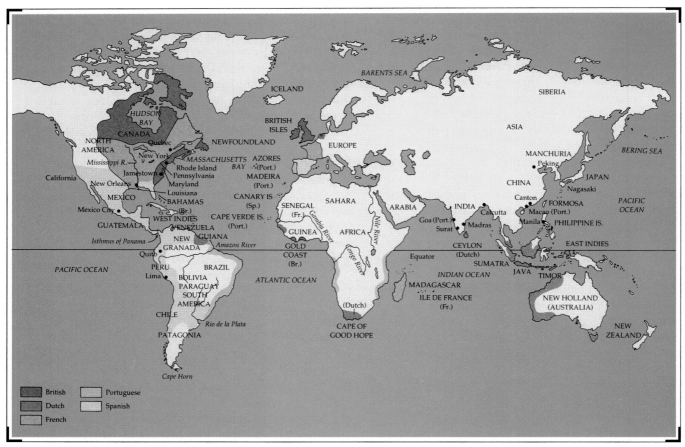

TABLE 15.2 SETTLEMENTS IN THE NEW WORLD DURING THE BAROQUE AGE

LOCATION	DATE OF FOUNDING	SETTLERS
Jamestown (Virginia)	1607	English
Quebec (Canada)	1608	French
Plymouth (Massachusetts)	1620	English
St. Kitts (West Indies)	1623	English
New Amsterdam (New York)	1624	Dutch
Barbados	1627	English
Brazil	1632–1654	Dutch
Curaçao (West Indies)	1634	Dutch
Honduras (Belize)	1638	English
Bahamas (West Indies)	1648	English
Jamaica (West Indies) (Captured from Spain)	1655	English

The earliest leaders in the European penetration of the Western Hemisphere were Spain and Portugal. Since the 1500s these two states had claimed South and Central America and the southern reaches of North America. Where possible, they mined the rich gold and silver veins, flooding Europe with the new wealth and gaining power and influence for themselves. But during the seventeenth century the mines were nearing exhaustion, and the glory days were a thing of the past.

While Spain's and Portugal's ties with the New World languished during the Baroque age, England, France, and the Netherlands were accelerating theirs, especially with North America. In 1607 English farmers settled along the Atlantic seaboard in Virginia, ready to exploit the land, and in 1620 English Puritans emigrated to New England in search of religious freedom. To the north, French explorers, missionaries, and fur traders founded Quebec in 1608 and then spread along the St. Lawrence river valley and southward into the Great Lakes region. At the same time, the French moved into the Caribbean basin, occupying many islands in the West Indies. After 1655 the English worked their way into the southern part of the Atlantic coast and the West Indies. These newly arrived colonists eventually either drove out the Spaniards or drastically reduced their influence. Meanwhile, the Dutch set up their own colonies in North America on the banks of the Hudson River and in scattered areas of the mid-Atlantic region (Table 15.2).

The English, French, and Dutch recognized the economic advantages of sending more explorers and families abroad and encouraged the founding of colonies. Relying chiefly on state or royal charters, they created large overseas settlements that soon led to a brisk trade in which raw products from the New World were exchanged for finished goods from the Old World. A typical example of the use of charters to encourage overseas growth was the governmental charter granted by England to William Penn (1644–1718) for the founding of Pennsylvania in 1681.

In the Far East, colonial developments relied less on charters than on joint stock companies, a private enterprise technique exploited by both England and the Netherlands. The English East India Company and the Dutch East India Company were the means whereby England and the Netherlands, respectively, opened trade routes and secured markets in the Far East. The two companies made lucrative contracts with Indian princes and Japanese and Chinese state officials.

RESPONSES TO THE REVOLUTIONS IN THOUGHT

The scientific discoveries, the growth of skepticism, the new political theories, and the overseas explorations provoked a variety of responses among the artists, intellectuals, and educated public of the 1600s. In the aristocracy, for example, a new social type appeared—the *virtuoso*, a person who dabbled in the latest science and gave it respectability. A new type of literature also appeared, in which the scientific concepts and discoveries were popularized for the consumption of educated elite. Overall, the innovations and changes of the seventeenth century found ample creative expression in the attitudes and images of the period.

The Spread of Ideas

In the exciting dawn of the Scientific Revolution, some scientists and intellectuals realized that new scientific findings needed to be given the widest dissemination possible, since the information would be of inestimable value to others who were engaged in their own research. Their enthusiasm for this task led them to share ideas in a variety of ways. At first, they exchanged information informally through personal contacts or by chance encounters in the universities. But by midcentury, the scientific society became the usual method for communicating new knowledge. The first one was in England, where King Charles II gave a charter to the Royal Society in 1662. Only a few years later, in 1666, Louis XIV supported the creation of the French *Académie des Sciences*, and in 1700 German scientists instituted the Berlin Academy of Science (Figure 15.7).

At the same time, many intellectually curious men and women, who wanted to learn more about the changes taking place in science and mathematics but who lacked specialized training, turned to writers who could demystify the new discoveries and explain them in popular language. One who responded to this interest was the French thinker Fontenelle (1657–1757), the long-lived secretary of the *Académie des Sciences*. His *Conversations on the Plurality of Worlds* set the early standard for this type of popular literature (Figure 15.8). With learning and wit, Fontenelle created a dialogue between himself and an inquiring countess in which Newtonian physics and the new astronomy were explained in an informative and entertaining way. Through publicists like Fontenelle the new theories and ideas became available to a general public and entered the broader culture.

Another French publicist, Pierre Bayle (1647–1706), created a famous work that launched the intellectual fashion for arranging ideas in systematic form, as in dictionaries and encyclopedias. Bayle's great popularizing work was called the *Historical and Critical Dictionary,* and it was probably the most controversial book of the Baroque age. For this encyclopedic work, Bayle wrote articles on biblical heroes, Classical and medieval thinkers, and contemporary scholars, many of which touched on and challenged Christian beliefs. Each article was a little essay with a text and lengthy footnotes. He approached the work with the aim of setting forth rival and contradictory opinions on each topic; if the result proved to be offensive to the pious, he pointed out that he himself was only following the Bible and the teachings of the Christian faith. Many readers responded to the essays by becoming skeptical about the subjects, as Bayle clearly was. Others

FIGURE 15.7   J. GOYTON after a painting by S. Leclerc. *Louis XIV at the* Académie des Sciences. 1671. Engraving. Bibliothèque Nationale, Paris. *Science became fashionable during the Baroque age, and rulers provided funds to advance the new discoveries. Louis XIV, king of France, is shown here visiting the French Royal Academy of Science, the premier organization of scientists in France. From this period dates the close alliance between science and government, a linkage based on mutual self-interest and a prominent feature of modern Western life.*

questioned Bayle's motives and accused him of atheism. The controversy over his works did not cease with his death. By 1750 his *Dictionary* had been reprinted many times and had spawned many imitations.

Bayle's *Dictionary* marked a new stage in the history of literature for two reasons. First, the work was sold to an audience of subscribers, for almost the first time anywhere. This step meant a turning away from the usual publishing method, which had prevailed since the dawn of printing, of issuing books under royal, aristocratic, or ecclesiastical patronage. Second, the extravagant success of his venture showed that a literate public now existed that would buy books if they appealed to its interests. Both of these facts were understood very well by authors in the next generation, who freed writing from the patronage system

and inaugurated the world of modern literature with its specialized audiences.

Impact on the Arts

The innovations in science and philosophy coincided with and fostered a changed consciousness not only in the educated public but in artists and writers as well. New attitudes, values, and tastes reflecting these ideas are evident in the creative works of the Baroque period, many of which are discussed and illustrated in Chapter 14. First and foremost among the new ideas is the belief that there is a hidden harmony in nature that may be expressed in mathematical laws. This belief led to the guiding principle of order and wholeness beneath wild profusion, such as the geometric order that controls the gardens and grounds of Versailles or the theme of redemption that unifies Milton's sprawling epic, *Paradise Lost*.

A second reflection of the Scientific Revolution and particularly of the discoveries in astronomy is the feeling of infinite space, of limitless boundaries, that pervades Baroque art. The love of curving lines, elliptical shapes, and flowing contours may be related to the new, expansive views of the planets and the universe. The ultimate expression of these interests and feelings, of course, is the illusionistic ceiling painting.

A final effect of the Scientific Revolution was the elevation of analytic reasoning skills to a position of high esteem in the arts. Just as Newton's genius led him to grasp concepts and laws that had eluded others down through the ages, so artists and humanists were inspired to use their powers of analysis to look below the surface of human life and search out its hidden truth. Racine's plays, for example, reveal acute insight into human psychology, and Rembrandt's cycle of self-portraits shows his ability and his desire to reveal his innermost feelings. Baroque art and literature demonstrate that although the Scientific Revolution may have displaced men and women from the center of the universe, an optimistic and even glorious view of the human predicament was still possible.

FIGURE 15.8 Frontispiece of *Conversations on the Plurality of Worlds.* 1686. *In this original frontispiece of Fontenelle's classic work, the narrator and his young pupil sit in a formal Baroque garden. He points to the sky, where the new Copernican model of the universe can be seen. Wealth, leisure, and the new scientific knowledge are brought together in this idyllic setting, indicating how the Scientific Revolution was beginning to affect upper-class life.*

The Legacy of the Revolutions in Scientific and Political Thought

One historian of science claims that the Scientific Revolution "outshines everything since the rise of Christianity and reduces the Renaissance and Reformation to the rank of mere episodes . . . within the system of medieval Christendom." Although others hesitate to go that far in praise of this singular event, enough evidence exists to show that the revolution in science speeded up the onset of modern times and caused a dramatic shift in the way human beings viewed themselves and their world. The Newtonian system became the accepted view of the universe until the twentieth century. Likewise, the new methodology—collecting raw data, reasoning inductively to hypotheses, and verifying results with mathematics—remains the standard in modern science. Out of the gradual spread of this method of reasoning to other areas of thought have emerged the modern social sciences. Even certain disciplines in the humanities—such as linguistics, the study of language—have adopted scientific methods to the extent that is possible.

At the same time that science held out the promise that its methods could unlock the secrets of nature, it was also leading to a dramatic upsurge in skepticism. Since the end of the Baroque age virtually everything in Western culture has been subjected to systematic doubt, including religious beliefs, artistic theories, and social mores. Although many causes besides science lie behind this trend to question all existing standards, the Scientific Revolution created a highly visible model and ready tools for universal doubt. In effect, because Aristotle's and other ancient thinkers' ideas were proven false, modern scholars were inclined to question all other beliefs received from the past. This trend has encouraged the intellectual restlessness that is perhaps the most prominent feature of modern life.

The legacies left by the innovations in Baroque political thought and the expansion of European culture cannot compare with the effects of the rise of modern science. Nevertheless, the changes in political theory and in the relations of Europe with the rest of the world did have strong consequences for modern life. In general, the new political theories gave rise to two rival heritages, the authoritarian tradition, which claims that a strong centralized government is the best way to ensure justice for all citizens, and the liberal tradition, which holds that the citizens are capable of ruling themselves. From this time forward, politics in the West has been organized around the conflicting claims of these two points of view. In the twentieth century, until relatively recently, the symbol of this development was the division of the world between the supporters of the authoritarian Soviet Union and the supporters of the libertarian United States.

As for the colonizing efforts in the New World during the 1600s, this early step meant that these regions would later be dominated by Western peoples and values and thus served to extend the geographic limits of the West. As a result, Western ideas and technology may be found today even in the most far-flung reaches of the globe. A negative consequence of the opening of the New World was that slavery, an institution that had virtually died in Europe in the early Middle Ages, was reintroduced with all its destructive consequences for the non-Western people who became enslaved. We in the modern age are reaping the bitter harvest of this development.

KEY CULTURAL TERMS

geocentrism

empiricism

inductive reasoning

deductive reasoning

heliocentrism

Scientific Revolution

social contract

liberalism

tabula rasa

virtuoso

SUGGESTIONS FOR FURTHER READING

PRIMARY SOURCES

BACON, F. *The Essays*. New York: Penguin, 1985. Judicious editing of Bacon's highly readable text, dating from 1625, which contributed significantly to the rise of modern scientific thinking.

BAYLE, P. *Historical and Critical Dictionary: Selections*. Translated by R. H. Popkin and C. Brush. Indianapolis, Ind.: Bobbs-Merrill, 1965. Typical and controversial excerpts from one of the first modern dictionaries; a work originally published in 1697.

LOCKE, J. *An Essay Concerning Human Understanding*. New York: Collier Books, 1965. A good edition, introduced by M. Cranston, of Locke's essay arguing that the mind is shaped by the environment, an assertion that made the progressive theories of the modern world possible; first published in 1690.

————. *Two Treatises of Government*. Cambridge: Cambridge University Press, 1967. An excellent edition with introduction and notes by the distinguished scholar P. Laslett; Locke's *Second Treatise*, making the case for the doctrine of government by consent of the governed, has become the bible of modern liberalism.

HOBBES, T. *The Leviathan*. Buffalo, N.Y.: Prometheus Books, 1988. A recent edition of Hobbes' most important work—first issued in 1651—advocating absolutist government without any restraint by the people; this work has inspired many modern forms of authoritarian rule.

SECONDARY SOURCES

BRONOWSKI, J., and MAZLISH, B. *The Western Intellectual Tradition*. New York: Harper, 1960. A classic work of cultural history with especially good chapters on changes in science.

BUTTERFIELD, H. *The Origins of Modern Science: 1300–1800*. New York: Macmillan, 1949. Since its first publication in 1949, this work has been recognized as the standard history of modern science.

HALL, A. R. *The Scientific Revolution, 1500–1800: The Formation of the Modern Scientific Attitude*. Boston: Beacon Press, 1956. A good guide for the beginning student.

HAZARD, P. *The European Mind, 1680–1715*. Translated by J. L. May. New York: New American Library, 1963. A groundbreaking work that first established the importance of this transitional period; the French original dates from 1935.

KOESTLER, A. *The Sleepwalkers*. New York: Macmillan, 1968. A popular account of the Scientific Revolution, focusing on its mystical aspects.

KOYRE, A. *From the Closed World to the Infinite Universe*. Baltimore: Johns Hopkins University Press, 1968. A challenging work on a difficult topic; well written.

KUHN, T. S. *The Copernican Revolution*. New York: Vintage, 1959. A study showing that the Copernican Revolution embraced cosmology, physics, philosophy, and religion as well as mathematical astronomy; for the serious student.

MANUEL, F. *A Portrait of Isaac Newton*. Cambridge: Harvard University Press, Belknap Press, 1968. A controversial study in psychohistory.

MERTON, R. K. *Science, Technology, and Society in Seventeenth Century England*. Rev. ed. New York: Harper & Row, 1970. A clear discussion of the social impact of the Scientific Revolution in England, the home of Isaac Newton.

NUSSBAUM, F. L. *The Triumph of Science and Reason, 1660–1685*. New York: Harper & Row, 1953. European thought and events are set in the context of changing attitudes toward the universe, the arts, and political systems.

TREVOR-ROPER, H., ed. *The Age of Expansion: Europe and the World, 1559–1660*. London: Thames and Hudson, 1968. Uneven collection of essays but with marvelous illustrations integrating history and culture.

WESTFALL, R. S. *Never at Rest: A Biography of Isaac Newton*. New York: Cambridge University Press, 1980. An up-to-date biography of the genius of the Scientific Revolution.

WILLEY, B. *The Seventeenth Century Background*. New York: Columbia University Press, 1982. Reprint of a standard work dealing with topics and individuals in intellectual history.

16

THE AGE OF REASON
1700—1789

The scientific discoveries and philosophic ideas that made the seventeenth century such an intellectually exciting time bore fruit in the eighteenth century, a period often referred to as the Age of Reason. The work of the giants of the 1600s—Isaac Newton, Francis Bacon, René Descartes, and John Locke—led thinkers in the 1700s to believe they were living in a time of illumination and enlightenment. Committed to scientific methodology, mathematical reasoning, and a healthy skepticism toward traditional habits of thought, they fervently believed their ideas and proposals could lead to the improvement of both the individual and society.

The Age of Reason was marked by four different trends. The first was the growing concentration of political power in the great states, each of which was controlled by a ruling dynasty—a development that had begun during the Baroque era. France was the most powerful of these states, followed by Great Britain (the new name of a unified England and Scotland), Prussia, Austria, Russia, and the Netherlands (Map 16.1). The second was the return of the aristocracy to prominence after a century or more of decline. The ostentatious culture spawned by the resurgent aristocrats proved to be their swan song.

The third trend was the achievement of political and cultural eminence by the middle class after a centuries-long rise from their origins in medieval times (Figure 16.1). The middle class supported those progressive thinkers who advocated social equality, social justice, and a thorough revamping of society. The

intellectual and cultural movement spawned by these thinkers is called the *Enlightenment*, and it constitutes the fourth and most important trend that helped to reshape Western life in the 1700s.

At the same time that these trends were occurring, a reaction was setting in against the excesses of the Baroque style in art, architecture, and music. In the early years of the eighteenth century a new style was emerging in France that was lighter, more informal and graceful, less ponderous and oppressive than the Baroque. Known as Rococo, it suited the light-hearted pursuits of the reinvigorated French aristocracy. After about 1750, in reaction to both the Rococo and the Baroque, a very different style developed, known as Neoclassical. Unlike the Rococo, the Neoclassical style in art and architecture spread widely throughout Europe and to the United States. In music, the second half of the eighteenth century saw the development of a refined and elegant new style known as Classical; the period was graced by the incomparable presence of Mozart, arguably the greatest musical genius who ever lived.

THE ENLIGHTENMENT

Eighteenth-century thinkers derived their ideals and goals from a variety of sources. Following the example of ancient Greece and Rome, they rejected super-

MAP 16.1

Europe 1763—1789

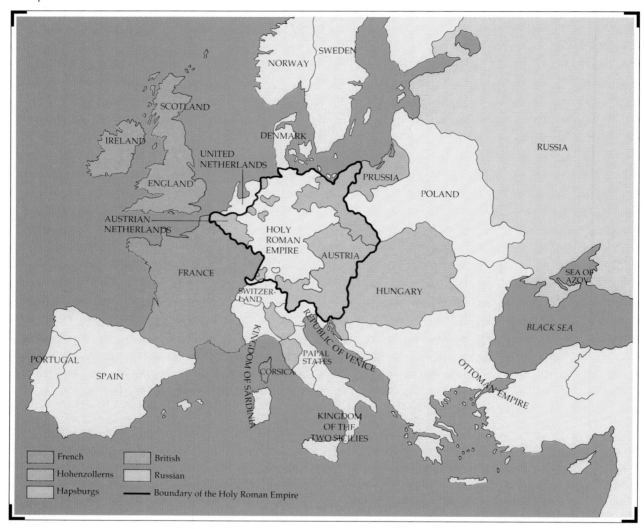

stition, sought truth through the use of reason, and viewed the world from a secular, human-centered perspective. Drawing on the Renaissance, they embraced humanism—the belief that a human being becomes a better person through the study and practice of literature, philosophy, music, and the arts. And from the seventeenth-century revolutions in science and philosophy, particularly the works of Newton, Bacon, Descartes, and Locke, they derived a reverence for rationalism, empiricism, skepticism, and the experimental method, along with a belief in the perfectibility of the individual through education and unlimited progress for humanity and society.

Despite the power of these ideas, the impact of the Enlightenment was limited to a relatively small percentage of Europe's population. It had its greatest effect in the major cultural capitals of France and Great Britain—Paris, London, and Edinburgh. Many

aristocrats read the works of Enlightenment writers, as did many members of the middle class, particularly educators, lawyers, journalists, and clergymen. Ultimately, enough literate and influential people were converted to the goals of the Enlightenment to have an effect on the revolutionary events that occurred later in the eighteenth century (Time Line 16.1).

The *Philosophes* and Their Program

The central figures of the Enlightenment were a small band of writers known as **philosophes**, the French word for philosophers. Not philosophers in a formal sense, the *philosophes* were more likely to be popularizers who wanted to transform the prevailing climate of opinion to make it accord with their point of view.

FIGURE 16.1 JEAN-BAPTISTE-SIMÉON CHARDIN. *Little Girl Playing Shuttlecock.* 1737. Oil on canvas, 31⅞ × 25⅝". Uffizi Gallery, Florence. *This painting by Chardin serves as a symbol of the middle class, whose rise to cultural prominence in the Age of Reason was a foretaste of their political power in the nineteenth century. The young subject is dressed as a small adult, the typical way that children were treated at every social level in this century. On the other hand, Chardin's portrayal of the young girl as quietly absorbed in her thoughts, oblivious of everything else, reflects the home-loving values of the middle class.*

TIME LINE 16.1   THE AGE OF REASON

1700	1714		1740	1748	1756	1763		1776		1783	1789
War of Spanish Succession			**War of Austrian Succession**		**Seven Years' War**			**American Revolution**			
			Richardson's *Pamela* 1740	First volume of the *Encyclopédie* 1750	Voltaire's *Candide* 1759	Frago-nard's *The Swing* 1766		Smith's *Wealth of Nations* 1776		Mozart's *Marriage of Figaro* 1786	
						Rousseau's *Social Contract* 1762				David's *Oath of the Horatii* 1785	

They avoided the methods of academic scholars, such as engaging in philosophical debates or writing only for colleagues, and tried to reach large audiences through popular means such as novels, essays, tracts, plays, poems, and histories. In this they were following the lead of Fontenelle, who popularized the new astronomy in his *Conversations on the Plurality of the Worlds* (see Chapter 15). When possible, they openly attacked what they deemed to be the evils of society and supported those rulers who favored change, the so-called enlightened despots. When the censors threatened, however, they disguised their radical messages or else published their criticisms in the Netherlands—the most liberal state in Europe at the time.

The Enlightenment was essentially a product of French cultural life, and Paris was its capital. The principal *philosophes* were Voltaire, Diderot, Montesquieu—all French—and by adoption the French-speaking Swiss writer Rousseau. But the Enlightenment was much more than a French phenomenon. Major *philosophes* appeared all over Europe, in Great Britain, and in Britain's North American colonies. The most influential of these voices were the English historian Edward Gibbon, the American writer Benjamin Franklin, and two Scottish thinkers, the economist Adam Smith and the philosopher David Hume.

The *philosophes*, though never in complete agreement and often at great odds, shared certain assumptions. They had full confidence in reason; they were convinced that nature was orderly, fundamentally good, and could be understood through the empirical method; they believed that change and progress would improve society since human beings were open to perfectibility. Faith in reason led them to reject religious doctrine, in particular Roman Catholic dogma, to denounce bigotry and intolerance, and to advocate freedom of religious choice. Maintaining that education liberated humanity from ignorance and superstition, the *philosophes* called for an expanded educational system independent of ecclesiastical control.

The *philosophes* thought that the political, economic, and religious institutions should be reformed to bring "the greatest happiness for the greatest numbers"—a phrase that expresses a key Enlightenment ideal and that, in the nineteenth century, became the battle cry of the English thinker and reformer Jeremy Bentham (see Chapter 18). These theorists anticipated a general overhaul of society, leading to universal peace and a golden age for humanity. Few *philosophes* thought that they would witness these radical changes, but all passionately believed that the future would bring unlimited improvements in the human race. In effect, these eighteenth-century thinkers preached a secular gospel that happiness need not be delayed until after death but could be enjoyed here on earth.

Envisioning a rejuvenated society that guaranteed natural rights to its citizens, the *philosophes* were almost unanimous in thinking exclusively in terms of men and not of women. They still considered women their intellectual and physical inferiors and thus in need of male protection or guidance. Not until the next period were voices raised in the name of women's rights and only then under the inspiration of the French Revolution.

One of those moved by the revolutionary winds blowing from France was the English writer Mary Wollstonecraft (1759–1797) who, in *A Vindication of the Rights of Woman* (1792), used Enlightenment ideals to urge the liberation of her own sex. The heart of this latter-day *philosophe's* argument was that women should abandon feminine artifice and guile, especially the all-consuming need to be socially pleasing, and, through education, become equal partners with educated men. Starting in the nineteenth century, reformers gradually began to take up Wollstonecraft's challenge, particularly her call for female education and women's suffrage.

Deism

Newtonian science implied that God had set the universe in motion and then left it to run by its own natural laws. The *philosophes* accepted this metaphor of God as a clockmaker, and in place of traditional Christianity some thinkers now offered a version of Christianity called *Deism*. Deists focused on the worship of a Supreme Being, a God who created the universe and set the laws of nature in motion but who never again interfered in natural or human matters. Believing in this idea of a clockmaker God, the Deists rejected the efficacy of prayer and reduced the role of Jesus from that of savior to that of a good moral example.

Deism was espoused by only a relatively small percentage of Westerners, however, such as Benjamin Franklin in the British colony of Pennsylvania. Religions that ran counter to the Enlightenment's ideas—including the new sect of Methodists founded by John Wesley (1703–1791) in England—continued to attract most of the populace. Although it did not find wide acceptance, Deism's appeal marked another shift in religious attitudes and was added evidence of the growing secularization of European consciousness in the 1700s.

FIGURE 16.2 Illustration from the *Encyclopédie*: Hand Manufacture of a Coach. 1751–1765. *As principal editor of the* Encyclopédie, *Diderot adopted Francis Bacon's notion that all knowledge is useful. Thus, the articles and the illustrations for this reference work focused on practical data such as soapmaking, human anatomy, and military drill. In this drawing, for example, the readers could peruse the interior of a shop in which horse-drawn coaches were made by hand.*

The *Encyclopédie*

The message of the *philosophes* was communicated by a variety of written and oral means, through pamphlets, essays, and books, through private and public discussions and debates, through the new journalistic press, and, especially in France, through the salon—the half-social, half-serious gatherings where the fashionable elite met to discuss ideas. But the outstanding voice of the *philosophes* was the *Encyclopédie*—the monumental project that remains the summation of the Enlightenment. Two earlier works, Chambers's *Cyclopedia* in England (1728) and Bayle's *Dictionary* in France (1697) paved the way for the *Encyclopédie*, which surpassed its predecessors in size and impact. Begun in 1750 and completed in 1772, the original work comprised seventeen text volumes and eleven books of plates and illustrations (Figure 16.2). More than 161 writers wrote articles for this educational venture, which was intended as a compendium of existing knowledge in the arts, crafts, and sciences.

The editorship of the *Encyclopédie* was in the capable hands of Denis Diderot (1713–1784), one of the giants of the Enlightenment. Diderot was constantly in trouble with the authorities because of the work's controversial essays, which he asserted were meant "to change the general way of thinking." Publication was halted in 1759 by the state censor but resumed secretly with the collusion of other government officials. Unlike many previous publications, the project was funded by its readers, not by the crown or the church. Even though there were only four thousand subscribers, the actual reading audience far exceeded that figure, for each paying household constituted many potential readers, and private circulating libraries rented the volumes to untold numbers of customers.

The Physiocrats

Under the broad umbrella of Enlightenment ideas, the *philosophes* were joined by a group of French writers who were concerned with economic matters—the **Physiocrats**, as they called themselves. (The term is a coined word, from Greek, meaning "rule of (or from) the earth.") The Physiocrats examined the general nature of the economy and, in particular, the strengths and weaknesses of mercantilism, the eighteenth century's prevailing economic system by which trade and production were regulated by the state for its own benefit. In the eyes of the Physiocrats, this state-run system had hindered, not helped, the growth of the economies of the various European countries. Contrary to its goals, mercantilism had lowered the productivity of workers, especially farmers, and had led to labor unrest and riots.

Guided by Enlightenment doctrine regarding the "natural laws" of society, the Physiocrats assumed that similar "laws" also applied to both economic growth and decline. After a thorough analysis of the

French economy, they concluded that some fundamental principles did exist, such as the law of supply and demand, and that these laws operated best when free from governmental interference. Accordingly, they recommended the dismantling of mercantilism and the adoption of *laissez faire*, French for "to let alone"—in other words, an economy where the self-regulating laws of free trade were in effect. In addition, they argued that unrestricted enjoyment of private property was necessary for individual freedom. These French thinkers concluded that both the individual and the entire society automatically benefited from allowing all people to serve their own self-interests instead of working for the good of the state.

At about the same time, the Scottish economist Adam Smith (1723–1790) was developing ideas similar to those of the Physiocrats. He reported his conclusions in *An Inquiry into the Nature and Causes of the Wealth of Nations* (1776), a book that became the bible of industrial capitalism for the next two centuries. In this work, Smith blamed mercantilism for the economic woes of his time, identified the central role played by labor in manufacturing, and called for open and competitive trade so that the "invisible hand" of a free-market economy could operate. Smith's ideas were quickly absorbed by budding entrepreneurs and had an immediate impact on the changes being generated by the Industrial Revolution (see Chapter 17).

THE GREAT POWERS DURING THE AGE OF REASON

In comparison to the seventeenth century, the period between 1715 and 1789 was less turbulent. What wars occurred were usually fought for practical motives such as territorial gain rather than for ideological or religious reasons. National rivalries did trigger a few major conflicts on the Continent and in the overseas colonies, but they were usually brief due to changes in military strategies, tactics, and organization; they were also less destructive to civilian populations, particularly in Europe. In addition, Europe experienced a slow but sound and steady economic expansion that was supported by a continuing increase in population. The prosperity fueled the rise of the middle classes, who now surged ahead, especially in Great Britain and Holland. In France, however, they made only modest gains, while in central and eastern Europe they constituted just a small fraction of the population.

Society: Continuity and Change

A major consequence of the century's modest economic growth was the growing urbanization of society. Although most Europeans still followed traditional lives on farms and in villages, cities and towns offered increasing opportunities for ambitious rural folk. The rural-to-urban shift originated in England, the home of the Industrial Revolution, and to a lesser extent in France. Only in the next century did it spread, and then slowly, to a few areas in central Europe and finally to the eastern countries.

The traditional hierarchical social structure that had originated in medieval times continued to keep each class in its place. The aristocracy constituted only about 3 percent of the total population, but they possessed tremendous political, economic, and social power (Figure 16.3). Below them, the upper middle class—made up of rich merchants, bankers, and professionals—normally resided in the rapidly expanding cities and towns and exercised their influence in business and governmental affairs. In the broad middle class were the smaller merchants, shopkeepers, skilled artisans, and bureaucrats. Beneath the middle ranks came the lesser artisans and craftspeople, and below them, the metropolitan poor, who did the menial labor and were often unemployed.

In the countryside, the nobility and the more prosperous farmers owned large sections of the land and controlled the rural populace. The small cultivators, tenant farmers, landless workers, and indentured laborers made up a complex group whose legal, social, and personal rights varied widely across Europe. Next were the peasants, whose status ranged from freedom in western Europe to serfdom in Russia. (Serfs were bound to the land they worked, but they had customary rights, and strictly speaking they were not slaves.) These impoverished people often bore the brunt of the taxes and the contempt of the other classes.

With few exceptions, such as the upper-middle-class women who played influential roles in the salons, women remained subordinate to men. As mentioned earlier, the *philosophes*, who made such a thorough critique of society, failed to recognize women's contributions or champion their rights. Even Rousseau, who was often at odds with his fellow writers, agreed with the *philosophes* that women were inferior to men and should be submissive to them.

Another group who gained little from the Enlightenment were the black slaves in Europe's overseas colonies. During the eighteenth century, ships from England, France, and Holland carried about six mil-

FIGURE 16.3 FRANÇOIS DE CUVILLIÉS. Hall of Mirrors, Amalienburg. 1734–1739. Munich. *Despite the growing size and power of the middle class in the 1700s, the aristocracy still set the tone of life and dictated styles in the arts. In their royal courts, their town houses, and their country estates, they reigned supreme, surrounding themselves with luxury. This grandiloquent room is in the Amalienburg, a hunting lodge built for the Elector of Bavaria. Inspired by its namesake, the Hall of Mirrors at Versailles, the room reflects the delicate Rococo sensibility that dominated aristocratic European taste in the first half of the eighteenth century.*

lion Africans to the New World and enslavement. Efforts to improve their conditions or abolish the slave trade proved futile despite the moral disapproval of the *philosophes* and the pleas of English Christians for the abolition of slavery.

Absolutism, Limited Monarchy, and Enlightened Despotism

The eighteenth century was the last great age of kings in the West. With a few exceptions, monarchs were everywhere the focus of the political system. In most countries the royal rulers followed proven policies even in the face of criticism or occasional opposition. Supported by inefficient bureaucracies and costly standing armies, they controlled the masses through heavy taxes and threats of brutality, while at the same time holding in check the aristocrats and other privileged groups that survived from the Middle Ages. Although a few monarchs attempted reforms in order to solve domestic problems, regardless of their strategies nothing finally seemed to work for these rulers. By the end of this period, most of the monarchies were showing signs of stress, as democratic sentiments continued to rise.

In France, the kings struggled to uphold the power and prestige they inherited from Louis XIV. In Great Britain, the kings fought a losing battle against Parliament and the restrictions of constitutional monarchy. In Prussia and Austria, so-called enlightened despots experimented with reforms to strengthen

TABLE 16.1 WARS OF THE EIGHTEENTH CENTURY

War of the Austrian Succession	1740–1748
Seven Years' War (Known in North America as the French and Indian War)	1756–1763
American Revolution	1775–1783

their states, while in Russia the czars found new ways to expand absolutism.

By mid-century the dynastic ambitions and rival territorial claims of these monarchs plunged the continent into a series of brief wars that ended the several relatively peaceful decades Europe had enjoyed (Table 16.1). These continental conflicts soon escalated into commercial and colonial rivalries on a world scale that ended only with the termination of the American Revolutionary War (1775–1783).

France: The Successors to the Sun King No French ruler was ever able to recapture the splendor that France had enjoyed under Louis XIV (Table 16.2). Louis XV (1715–1774), who succeeded to full political control at the age of thirteen, only compounded the problems of the French state. A charming man, Louis XV lacked a strong will to rule. He did not always pick talented, loyal subordinates, and he permitted his mistresses, who were not trained in government, to interfere in official matters. Even the king and his court seemed to sense that things were out of control. It is reported that when Louis XV, despairing over a military defeat, expressed his misgivings about the future of France to his royal favorite, Madame de Pompadour, she replied with the prophetic words, "Après-nous le déluge" ("After us, the flood").

Life at Louis XV's court could not be sustained in the grand manner of the late Sun King. The nobles began to leave Versailles for Paris, where they exchanged their cramped quarters at the royal court for spacious town houses, called *hôtels*, in the capital.

TABLE 16.2 FRENCH KINGS DURING THE AGE OF REASON

Louis XV (Regency under Duke of Orleans 1715–1723)	1715–1774
Louis XVI	1774–1792

Whether at Versailles or elsewhere, educated aristocrats became enamored of Enlightenment ideas. A large segment of top-ranked officials and their wives read the *Encyclopédie* and studied the writings of the *philosophes*. Upper-class women played influential roles in presiding over salons, where the enlightened thinkers and their admirers gathered to dine, gossip, and discuss the newest ideas, the latest literary works, and the current scandals. Even though the French elite debated the merits of reform and the more controversial topics raised by the *philosophes*, Louis XV clearly did not accept the movement's call for change. It is ironic that the country where the Enlightenment began failed to undertake any of its progressive reform. Indeed, when changes were introduced under Louis XVI (1774–1792), they were too little and too late.

Handicapped with a weak monarch, France found its preeminent position in foreign affairs threatened by challenges from Great Britain on the high seas and from Austria and Prussia on the Continent. Until 1756 France was at peace most of the time and the economy grew, but in that year the Seven Years' War began in which France suffered defeats in Europe and lost its holdings in both North America and India. During the American Revolution France sided with the colonists against Great Britain, her foe at home and overseas. France's aid to the American rebels further drained the diminishing financial resources and forced the nation deeper into debt.

While France's power declined abroad, at home the kings seemed unable to solve their domestic problems. This failure was the consequence of poor leadership, both at the top and among the royal officials, called *intendants*, who had the duty of coordinating the loose federation of provinces into a functioning French state. Similarly, the tax farmers (men empowered by the government to collect taxes, on which they made a profit) failed to provide adequate revenues for the state because of the corrupt tax system. And, most important of all, the crown was faced with a resurgent aristocracy determined to recover the feudal privileges taken from them by Louis XIV. Rather than joining in the reform efforts of the king, the nobility blocked the crown at every step. It was at this juncture that the middle class, who also wanted political power, joined forces with some sympathetic aristocrats and transformed what had been a feudal issue into a struggle for freedom in the name of the people. In 1789, during the reign of Louis XVI, the grandson of Louis XV, France started on a revolutionary course that united the nobility, the middle classes, and most of French society against the crown.

Great Britain and the Hanoverian Kings Great Britain under the Hanoverian kings was the nation that the French *philosophes* praised as the ideal model. To them, Britain seemed more stable and prosperous than the states on the continent, a success they attributed to the limited powers of the English monarchy imposed by Parliament during the Glorious Revolution of 1688. Furthermore, Britain's laws guaranteed to every Englishman certain political and civil rights, such as free speech and fair and speedy trials. Under the unwritten British constitution, new and often unpopular ideas could be openly debated and printed without fear of government censorship or church condemnation. Britain's economy, spurred on by enterprising merchants and progressive landowners, took the lead in an expanding global market and raised the standard of living for its steadily growing population.

After the death of Queen Anne in 1714, George, the Protestant ruler of the German principality of Hanover and a great-grandson of James I, succeeded to the English throne as George I. The Hanoverians inherited an English crown with certain rights and privileges, but they eventually lost most of them. This decline in royal powers happened because the first two of these kings seemed more interested in events in Hanover than in England (Table 16.3). The power vacuum left by the kings was quickly filled by factions who further eroded the crown's influence. In the end, the kings reigned in splendid isolation at the royal court, but the real power was in the hands of a coalition of London society and country landowners.

The first of the Hanoverian kings, George I (1714–1727), allowed Parliament to run the country. Under George II (1727–1760), Britain was drawn into the Seven Years' War but emerged victorious, the dominant presence in world trade. From this pinnacle of international power, Great Britain occupied center stage until the outbreak of World War I in 1914.

Nevertheless, Great Britain faced serious domestic problems once George III (1760–1820) was crowned because he set out to restore to the throne the powers lost to Parliament by his predecessors. This internal struggle affected foreign policy when the king and Parliament offered differing proposals to control the American colonies' economic development through export and import quotas, duties, and taxes. The differences between George III's and Parliament's plans hastened the onset of the American Revolution and probably contributed to Britain's eventual defeat. After the American struggle was settled in 1783, Great Britain had to face its most serious foreign crisis since the Hundred Years' War of the Late Middle Ages—the French Revolution.

Enlightened Despotism in Central and Eastern Europe The system of European states underwent some modifications during the Age of Reason. Great Britain and France now dominated western Europe because of their size, economic power, and military strength, and the less populous countries of Holland and Sweden declined from the powerful roles that they had played in the seventeenth century. Spain, whose glory years had been in the 1500s, turned more and more inward and all but disappeared from continental affairs. "Italy" was hardly more than a geographical expression, as it lay under Austrian and papal control and remained an economic backwater. Meanwhile, three states—Prussia, Austria, and Russia—jockeyed for control of central and eastern Europe. Under their absolutist rulers, these states pursued aggressive policies, seizing territories from one another and their weaker neighbors whenever they could. Even though these rulers played at being enlightened despots, their planned reforms bore little fruit, and their regimes remained entrenched in oppressive and authoritarian ways.

The kingdom of Prussia by 1740 had a solid economic base, a hardworking bureaucracy, and an efficient army—the necessary ingredients for a nation-state to succeed in the eighteenth century. Capitalizing on these advantages, Frederick II, known as Frederick the Great (1740–1786), turned Prussia into a leading European power. His pragmatic diplomacy, his brilliant military tactics, and above all his successful efforts to expand his territories added to his state's increasing authority and prestige. An admirer of French culture and a student of the Enlightenment, Frederick was an enlightened despot of the type so beloved by the *philosophes*. He even made an attempt (though it failed) to reform his state's agrarian economy and social system in accordance with the rational principle that all individuals have the natural right to choose personally the best way to live.

Prussia's chief rival in central Europe was Austria. In an age of states with relatively homogeneous ethnic populations, Austria was a relic from another time. Throughout the 1700s Austria's rulers struggled

TABLE 16.3 HANOVERIAN KINGS IN GREAT BRITAIN DURING THE AGE OF REASON

George I	1714–1727
George II	1727–1760
George III	1760–1820

to govern a population that included large numbers of Germans, Hungarians, Czechs, and Slovaks along with generous sprinklings of Poles, Italians, and various Slavic minorities. At the same time, the emperors tried, with mixed success, to assert Austria's role as a great power. Two rulers stand out from the rest, shoring up the faltering Austrian presence in central Europe and thus serving to entrench their dynasty—the Hapsburg—over their multiethnic peoples. These Hapsburg emperors were Maria Theresa and Joseph, her son, who reigned between 1740 and 1790.

Unlike Frederick II of Prussia, Maria Theresa (1740–1780) was not attracted to the ideas of the *philosophes.* More important in her psychological outlook was her simple Roman Catholic faith, which led her to portray herself to her subjects as their universal mother. She was perhaps the most beloved monarch in this age of kings. Maria Theresa's reforming zeal sprang not from philosophic principle but from a reaction against Austria's territorial losses during military defeats. She used all of her royal prerogatives to overhaul the political and military machinery of the state. Along with universal military conscription, increased revenues, and more equitable distribution of taxes, she wanted a general reorganization of society that gave more uniform treatment to all citizens. Her efforts were not wasted, for her son Joseph II took up her uncompleted task and became the ultimate personification of enlightened despotism.

During a brief reign Joseph II (1780–1790) attempted the most complete reform program of any of the age's monarchs. Convinced that his country's economic and social institutions had to be fully modernized if Austria were to survive, he launched far-reaching changes to raise farm production and to provide more economic opportunities for the peasants. He abolished serfdom and passed decrees guaranteeing religious toleration and free speech. Although these reforms brought about some striking improvements, he alienated many nobles and religious leaders. In the 1790s much of what he had accomplished was undone by his successors who, fearing the excesses of the French Revolution, acted to restore aristocratic and ecclesiastic control and privileges.

Russia was the newest member of the family of great powers, having achieved this stature during the reign of Peter the Great (1682–1725). Abroad, Peter had made Russia's presence known, and at home he had begun to reform political, economic, and social institutions along Western lines. For the most part his eighteenth-century successors were ineffective, if not incompetent, until Catherine the Great (1762–1796) became empress. She pursued the unifying policies of Peter, but unlike him she was able to win the powerful support of the large landowners. A devotee

of the Enlightenment, Catherine sought the advice of a few *philosophes,* including Diderot. She also made some efforts to improve the low farm productivity and the nearly enslaved condition of the peasants, but the vastness of Russia's problems and the reactionary autocratic government defeated any genuine reforms.

CULTURAL TRENDS IN THE EIGHTEENTH CENTURY: FROM ROCOCO TO NEOCLASSICAL

Even though the eighteenth century was dominated by the Enlightenment, other cultural trends also held sway. The Rococo style in the arts mirrored the taste of the French nobility; the succeeding Neoclassical style was adopted and supported by the progressive writers, artists, intellectuals, and ambitious members of the middle class. Meanwhile, innovations in literature were pointing the way toward the modern world.

The Rococo Style in the Arts

Conceived on a more intimate scale than the Baroque and committed to frivolous subjects and themes, *Rococo* taste arose in France in the waning years of the Sun King's reign. With his death in 1715 and the succession of his five-year-old heir, Louis XV, the nobility were released both from Versailles and from the ponderous Baroque style. Their exodus from Versailles made Paris once again the capital of art, ideas, and fashion in the Western world. There, the Rococo style was created for the French elite almost singlehandedly by the Flemish painter and decorator Jean-Antoine Watteau.

The Rococo gradually spread to most of Europe, but its acceptance was tied to religion and class. It was embraced by the aristocracy in Germany, Italy, and Austria; Roman Catholic nobles in Austria developed a version of Rococo that was second in importance only to that of France. The English, on the other hand, rejected the Rococo, possibly because its erotic undercurrent and sexual themes offended the Protestant middle-class sensibility. Consequently, Rococo style is a purely continental phenomenon; there is no English Rococo.

Rococo Painting Jean-Antoine Watteau (1684–1721) specialized in paintings that depict **fêtes galantes,** or aristocratic entertainments. In these works Watteau portrays the intimate world of the aristocracy,

FIGURE 16.4 Jean-Antoine Watteau. *Departure from Cythera.* 1717. Oil on canvas, 4'3" × 6'4½". Louvre. *Watteau's aristocratic lovers, mesmerized by a brief moment of pleasure, represent the idealized image that the eighteenth-century elite wanted to present to the world. No hint of the age's problems is allowed to disturb this idyllic scene. From the court costumes to the hovering cupids, this painting transforms reality into a stage set—the ideal of Rococo art.*

dressed in sumptuous clothing and grouped in parks and gardens often accompanied by costumed actors, another of Watteau's favorite subjects. He filled these bucolic settings with air and lightness and grace—all of which were a contrast to the occasionally heavy-handed Baroque. Mythological allusions kept Watteau's works from being mistaken for scenes of ordinary life.

In 1717 Watteau became the first Rococo painter to be elected to membership in the Royal Academy of Painting and Sculpture in Paris. As required by the terms of election, he submitted as his diploma piece *Departure from Cythera* (Figure 16.4). The setting is Cythera, the legendary island of Venus, whose bust on the right is garlanded with her devotees' roses. Forming a wavering line, the lovers express hesitation as they make their farewells: The couple under the statue are lost in reverie as a clothed cupid tugs at the woman's skirt; beside this group a suitor assists his lady to her feet; and next to them a gentleman accompanies his companion to the waiting boat as

she longingly gazes backward. This melancholy scene, signified by the setting sun and the departing lovers, represents Watteau's homage to the brevity of human passion.

In *Departure from Cythera,* many of the new values of the Rococo style can be seen. Where the Baroque loved tumultuous scenes depicting the passions and ecstasies of the saints, the Rococo focused on smaller, gentler moments, usually involving love of one variety or another, whether erotic, romantic, or sentimental. Where the Baroque used intense colors to convey feelings of power and grandeur, the Rococo used soft pastels to evoke nostalgia and melancholy. The monumentality and sweeping movement of Baroque art were brought down to a human scale in the Rococo, making it more suited to interiors, furniture, and architectural details than to architecture itself. *Departure from Cythera* shows the Rococo to be a refined, sensual style, perfect for providing a charming backdrop to the private social life of the eighteenth-century aristocracy.

FIGURE 16.5 Jean-Antoine Watteau. *The Sign for Gersaint's Shop.* Ca. 1720. Oil on canvas, 5'11⅝" × 10'1⅛". Schloss Charlottenburg, Berlin. *This painting of a shop interior illustrates the social dynamics of the emerging art market in the eighteenth century. The aristocratic customers act as if they own the place, turning it into a genteel lounge. The shop employees, on the other hand, have clearly inferior social roles; one brings forward a heavy painting for inspection, another holds a miniature work up to view, and a third stands downcast at the left. By using such clinical details, Watteau reveals the social gulf between classes that was implicit in the Rococo style.*

In one of his last works, *The Sign for Gersaint's Shop,* Watteau removed all mythological and idyllic references (Figure 16.5). His subject, a shop where paintings are sold, indicates the importance of the new commercial art market that was soon to replace the aristocratic patronage system. Within the store's interior, elegantly dressed customers browse, flirt, and study the shopkeeper's wares. The sexual motifs in the pictures on the walls and in the oval canvas on the right reinforce the sensuous atmosphere of this painting. But Watteau made this Parisian scene quite dignified by giving equal focus to the human figures and the role each plays in the overall composition.

Watteau's paintings convey a dreamy eroticism, but those of François Boucher (1703–1770) are characterized by outspoken sexuality. Boucher was the supreme exponent of the graceful Louis XV style, becoming official painter to the French crown in 1765. His voluptuous nudes, which were made more titil-

lating by their realistic portrayal without Classical trappings, appealed to the king and to the decadent court nobility. Boucher's *Nude on a Sofa* is probably a study of one of Louis XV's mistresses (Figure 16.6). The casually suggestive pose, the rumpled bed clothes, and the delicate pastel shades are all designed to charm and to seduce. Boucher's art, though masterful, epitomizes the lax morals of French noble life that were becoming increasingly offensive even to other Rococo artists.

A different focus is evident in the Rococo portraits of Louise-Elizabeth Vigée-Lebrun (1755–1842), who became the leading society painter of the later eighteenth century and one of the relatively few women to gain independent fame as an artist. In 1783 she painted a famous portrait of Louis XVI's queen, Marie Antoinette, whom she served as court painter (Figure 16.7). Elements of the Rococo style can be seen in this elegant portrait in the soft colors, the graceful ges-

FIGURE 16.6 FRANÇOIS BOUCHER. *Nude on a Sofa.* 1752. Oil on canvas, 23⅜ × 25⅜". Alte Pinakothek, Munich. *The trend toward the secularization of consciousness that had been building since the Late Middle Ages reached a high point in this nude by Boucher. Boucher's frank enjoyment of sensual pleasure and his desire to convey that feeling to the viewer represented a new stage in the relationship between artists and the public. By portraying his subject without any justification except eroticism, Boucher embodied a new artistic sensibility.*

FIGURE 16.7 ELISABETH-LOUISE VIGÉE-LEBRUN. *Queen Marie Antoinette.* 1783. Oil on canvas, 35⅜ × 28⅜". Schlossmuseum, Darmstadt, Germany. *Vigée-Lebrun's royal portrait shows the change toward fashionable simplicity that characterized the era of Louis XVI. In contrast to the shiny satins and stiff brocades of an earlier time, the young queen's muslin gown and straw hat are more informal. Marie Antoinette promoted this trend by having built at Versailles a rustic hideaway known as* Le Hameau, *where all rules of court etiquette were set aside.*

tures, and the feeling of intimacy and informality. Many members of the court found it too informal, however, and demanded that it be withdrawn from public view. The queen had a well-known fondness for simplicity, and Vigée-Lebrun's depiction of her in a white muslin dress suggested that the queen was really just an ordinary woman—a notion that shocked and outraged the aristocrats. Despite the scandal it created at the time, the painting today is regarded as a masterpiece of Rococo portraiture.

The last great French Rococo painter, Jean-Honoré Fragonard (1732–1806), continued the style into the nineteenth century. Fragonard revived Watteau's graceful, debonair themes, as in *The Swing* (Figure 16.8). A lounging suitor motions to a young woman as a servant pulls her in a swing. The lady coyly kicks her dainty slipper toward the young man, who is strategically positioned to study her legs and underclothing. What is fresh in Fragonard's art and prefigures Romanticism is his treatment of the natural setting, which, although resembling the idealized, parklike backgrounds of Watteau, has a vivid, luxuriant life of its own. In Fragonard's painting nature seems almost ready to overwhelm the couple. Despite his interest in landscape, however, Fragonard remained faithful to the Rococo style even after it fell out of fashion. His paintings continued to focus on the playful themes of dalliance and pursuit in a frivolous, timeless world.

entertainments, the hostess is having her hair curled while the would-be suitor lounges on a sofa, charming her with conversation. Nearby, guests, servants, and musicians play their complicitous roles in this sad tale. Hogarth, never willing to let the viewers draw their own conclusions, provides the moral lesson. In the right foreground, a black child-servant points to a small horned creature—a symbol of the cuckold, or the deceived husband—thus alluding to the wife's planned infidelity. Even the paintings on the walls echo Hogarth's theme of sexual abandon.

The Challenge of Neoclassicism

Soon after the middle of the eighteenth century the Rococo began to be supplanted by a new style, known as *Neoclassical*. With its backward glance to the restrained style of antiquity, the Neoclassical had its origins both in a rejection of the Rococo and in a fascination with the new archaeological discoveries made at mid-century. Excavations of Pompeii and Herculaneum—Roman cities buried by Mt. Vesuvius in A.D. 79 and only recently rediscovered—had greatly heightened the curiosity of educated Euro-

FIGURE 16.11   WILLIAM HOGARTH. *The Countess' Levée,* or *Morning Party,* from *Marriage à la Mode.* 1743–1745. Oil on canvas, 27 × 35". The National Gallery, London. *Hogarth's painterly techniques—learned in France—have transformed a potentially banal topic into a glittering social satire. On the left, a pig-snouted musician is used to ridicule the popular* castrati—*men who were emasculated as youths in order to preserve their boyish tenor voices. Hovering over the* castrati *is a flutist—his coarse features demonstrating the artist's loathing for this social type. Other rich details, such as the tea-sipping dandy in hair curlers and the female guest who is gesticulating wildly, confirm Hogarth's contempt for the entire gathering.*

FIGURE 16.12 JACQUES-LOUIS DAVID. *The Oath of the Horatii.* 1784. Oil on canvas, 10′10″ × 14′. Louvre. *David achieved a Classical effect in his works by arranging the figures so they could be read from left to right as in a sculptural frieze and by giving them the idealized bodies of Classical art. By omitting distracting details from the corners of his paintings, he further enhanced the sense that his central figures had been sculpted instead of painted.*

peans about the ancient world. At the same time, scholars began to publish books that showed Greek art to be the original source of ancient Classicism. The English authorities James Stuart and Nicholas Revett pointed out the differences between Greek and Roman art in *The Antiquities of Athens,* published in 1762. In 1764 the German Johann Joachim Winckelmann (1717–1768) distinguished Greek sculpture from the Roman in his *History of Art*—a study that led to the founding of the academic discipline of art history. The importance of Neoclassicism is indicated by the decision made in 1775 by the Paris Salon—the biennial exhibition that introduced the latest paintings to the public—to rebuff works with Rococo subjects and to encourage those with Classical themes.

Neoclassical Painting   In 1775, the first year of Louis XVI's reign and the same year the Salon began to promote Neoclassicism, the king appointed Joseph-Marie Vien to head the *Académie de France* in Rome, a leading art school. A strict disciplinarian, Vien returned the study of art to the basics by instructing his students to focus on perspective, anatomy, and life drawing, efforts that resulted in the purified style of Jacques-Louis David (1748–1825), the principal exponent of the Neoclassical style.

David's response to a commission from Louis XVI for a historical painting was the *Oath of the Horatii,* a work that electrified the Salon of 1785 (Figure 16.12). Taking a page from the history of the early Roman Republic, this painting depicts the Horatii brothers

FIGURE 16.13 JACQUES-LOUIS DAVID. *The Death of Socrates.* 1787. Oil on canvas,
4′11″ × 6′6″. Metropolitan Museum of Art, New York. Wolf Fund, 1931.
*Neoclassicism usually relied on ancient literature and traditions for inspiration, as in this
painting by David. The general setting rests on Plato's dialogue* Phaedo, *though David has
chosen to depict Plato present (at the foot of the bed), contrary to the literary account. Many
of the domestic details are based on artifacts uncovered at Pompeii, such as the shoes, the
lamp, and the bed.*

vowing to protect the state, even though their stand
means killing a sister who loves one of Rome's enemies. The patriotic subject with its tension between
civic duty and family loyalty appealed to the *philosophes,* who thereafter preferred Neoclassicism with
its implicitly revolutionary morality to the Rococo
with its frivolous themes.

David's *Oath of the Horatii* established the techniques and ideals that soon became typical of Neoclassical painting. His inspirational model was the
seventeenth-century French artist Poussin, with his
Classical themes and assured mastery of linear perspective. Rejecting the weightless, floating images of
Rococo painting, David portrayed his figures as frozen sculptures, painted in bold primary colors. The
Classical ideals of balance, simplicity, and restraint
served as a basis for many of David's artistic choices.

David showed his mastery of these techniques and
ideals in *The Death of Socrates,* which was exhibited in
the Salon of 1787 (Figure 16.13). Like Jesus in scenes
of the Last Supper, Socrates is portrayed shortly before his death, encircled by those men who will later
spread his message. Just as in the *Oath of the Horatii,*
David's arrangement of the figures reflected the Classical ideal of balance. Surrounded by grieving followers, the white-haired Socrates reaches for the cup of
poison and gestures toward his heavenly goal—serene in his willingness to die for intellectual freedom.

Neoclassical Architecture   No other painter could
compare with David, but the Scotsman Robert Adam
(1728–1792) developed a Neoclassical style in interior
decor that was the reigning favorite from 1760 until
1800. Classicism had dominated British architecture
since the 1600s, and Adam reinvigorated this tradition with forms and motifs gathered during his archaeological investigations. Kenwood House in London shows his application of Roman design to the
exterior of a domestic dwelling, combining Ionic columns, a running frieze, and a triangular pediment to

form a graceful portico, or porch, in the manner of a Roman temple (Figure 16.14). In the library Adam mixed Classical elements with the pastel colors of the Rococo to produce an eclectic harmony (Figure 16.15). To continue this theme, he borrowed from Roman buildings with his barrel-vaulted ceiling and adjoining apse.

French architects too began to embrace the Neoclassical style in the late 1700s. The leader of this movement was Jacques Germain Soufflot (1713–1780), who designed buildings based on Roman temples. Soufflot's severe Neoclassicism is characterized by its reliance on architectural detail rather than on sculptural decoration. Avoiding Adam's occasional intermingling of Rococo and Classical effects, Soufflot preferred pure Roman forms. The most perfect expression of Soufflot's style is the Pantheon in Paris. Soufflot's Classical ideal is mirrored in the Pantheon's basic plan, with its enormous portico supported by huge Corinthian columns (Figure 16.16). Except for the statues in the pediment, the building's surface is almost devoid of sculptural detail. The only other decoration on the stark exterior is a frieze of stone garlands around the upper walls. For the dome, Soufflot turned away from Roman models and found his inspiration in London—a sign that English architecture had come of age: The Pantheon's spectacular dome, with its surrounding Corinthian colonnade, was based on the dome of St. Paul's Cathedral in London.

FIGURE 16.14   ROBERT ADAM. Kenwood House, Exterior, the North Front. 1764. London. *English architecture had been tinged with Classicism since the seventeenth century. Even St. Paul's Cathedral, the grandest Baroque English structure of the period, was deeply imbued with a Classical spirit. Adam's restrained style in the late eighteenth century represented a strong reinfusion of Classical principles into the English tradition. His style, with its reliance on the Classical orders and the Classical principles of balance and proportion, appealed to all classes but especially to the sober-minded middle class.*

◄ **FIGURE 16.15** ROBERT ADAM. Library, Kenwood House. Begun in 1767. London. *Adam designed the library of Kenwood House with several basic elements of Classical architecture: columns, pilasters, and apses. By and large, he followed the Renaissance dictum of letting the architectural elements determine the chamber's decorative details. Nonetheless, he achieved a dazzling effect by his daring addition of mirrors and color.*

FIGURE 16.16 GERMAIN SOUFFLOT. The Pantheon. 1755–1792. Paris. *By 1789 advanced thinkers in France had begun to appropriate Classical images for their movement, with David's Neoclassical paintings leading the way. When the revolution began, its leaders determined to build a suitable monument to house the remains of those* philosophes *whose works had furthered the cause of reform. Hence, it was natural that the revolutionary government turn Soufflot's Classical church—with its portico modeled from Roman styles—into a patriotic shrine.*

Political Philosophy

Modern political theory continued to evolve after its founding in the seventeenth century. Absolutism, the reigning form of government in the eighteenth century, still had many staunch defenders. Voltaire, convinced that the people lacked political wisdom, advocated enlightened despotism. But with this outstanding exception, the other leading *philosophes* of the Age of Reason rejected absolutism and supported alternative forms of government.

The Enlightenment's chief political theorists were Baron de Montesquieu and Jean-Jacques Rousseau, whose contrasting social origins probably to some extent account for their radically different definitions of the ideal state. Montesquieu, a titled Frenchman and a provincial judge, believed that rule by an enlightened aristocracy would ensure justice and tranquility. Rousseau, an impoverished citizen of the Swiss city-

17

REVOLUTION, REACTION, AND CULTURAL RESPONSE
1760—1830

The Age of Reason was a time of radical talk and little action, but before the eighteenth century was over, three revolutions had changed the face of the Western world forever. So turbulent was the period between 1760 and 1830 that today it is considered a historical watershed. The Industrial Revolution created new ways of producing wealth; with this event, industrialism replaced agriculture as the soundest basis for the economic well-being of a state. The American Revolution demonstrated that government for and by the people was a viable alternative to monarchy. And the French Revolution showed that the time was ripe for sweeping changes in the distribution of political power in Europe.

These changes were not welcomed by all. Many groups attempted to hold on to old ways and tried in particular to prevent the spread of revolutionary political ideas. The middle class, known as the bourgeoisie, benefited the most from these revolutions, in some cases challenging aristocrats in wealth and power. Emboldened by their newly acquired status, the middle classes asserted themselves as the new standard bearers of culture, embracing Neoclassicism at first and then shifting their allegiance to the powerful new spirit and style of the age—Romanticism.

THE INDUSTRIAL REVOLUTION

Even before the birth of the Industrial Revolution, changes in agriculture had occurred in England that made industrialization possible. One of these was the

change in land use called enclosure, whereby common lands were fenced off by their wealthy owner and consolidated into one large estate. This practice brought hardship to smaller farmers but ultimately resulted in increased farm productivity. There were also improvements in farming techniques that increased crop yields and farm income, such as growing cash crops that replenished the soil instead of letting fields lie fallow to replenish themselves. Finally, better technology was leading to improved tools and farm implements, such as the iron plow and the reaper.

Industrialization in England

By the middle of the eighteenth century, changes both at home and abroad had created conditions that made England ripe for industrialization. An increase in population provided both a labor force and a market of consumers. Money to invest was available because of surplus capital generated by sound private and public fiscal practices. Several decades of peace had created an atmosphere conducive to economic growth, and the government's policies promoted further expansion. Free of internal tariffs or duties, goods moved with ease from one area of Britain to another, and canals and waterways offered cheap and convenient transportation. Britain's naval victories had resulted in the acquisition of colonies and trade rights that allowed its merchants access to raw materials and new overseas markets.

FIGURE 17.1 MICHAEL ANGELO ROOKER. *The Cast Iron Bridge at Coalbrookdale.* 1782. Aberdeen Art Gallery, Aberdeen, Scotland. *The earliest iron bridges, made from the superior grade of iron that was being produced in the new factories, were molded and cast to look like wooden bridges. The first iron bridge, located at Coalbrookdale, became a favorite subject for many artists. Architects did not begin to use iron in building construction until the early 1800s.*

Three economic changes were necessary before these conditions could combine to produce industrialism: the substitution of machines for manual labor; the replacement of animal and human power with new sources of energy such as water and steam; and the introduction of new and large amounts of raw materials. By 1800 these changes had taken place.

An abundance of domestic iron ore and coal at home made it possible to launch new industries, and the changes in the iron and coal industries contributed to innovations in other areas. Better grades of iron, processed in more efficient furnaces, allowed manufacturers to produce stronger tools and building materials that soon began to replace wood (Figure 17.1). The demand for more coal led to new mining techniques, and a redesigned steam engine enabled miners to pump water out of the pits, thus opening unexplored deposits and making working conditions safer. Indeed, the steam engine, which James Watt patented in 1769, transformed the way power was generated.

The changes in the cotton cloth industry dramatically illustrate the impact of the Industrial Revolution in England. Local woolen producers, feeling threatened by the competition of cotton, persuaded Parliament to prohibit the importation of inexpensive cotton goods from India; but still the demand grew. The English industry tried to meet the mounting demand for cotton cloth at home and abroad through the putting-out system—a method of hand manufacture in which workers wove the fabric in their homes—but this medieval technique proved hopelessly out-of-date. As a result, mechanics and entrepreneurs started tinkering with the manual looms and spinning machines in order to find ways to speed up manufacturing. The end result was the invention of the factory system: bringing together flying shuttles and

power looms under one roof, and locating this building near a swiftly flowing stream that supplied the water for the steam engines that drove this massive equipment.

The laborers had to adjust their sense of time, their work habits, and their entire lives to the demands of the factory system. No longer could rural workers stay at home to work looms or spinning wheels at their own pace (although the domestic weaving industry did not cease to exist). Towns near the factory rapidly expanded and new ones sprang up in the countryside next to the mill. In both cases, employees were crowded into miserable living quarters that were usually assembled haphazardly with little thought given to even the basic amenities of human existence.

With the factories came the "working class," as they were known in England. A realigned class system—with the capitalists and workers at either extreme—transformed the social order, created new indicators of wealth and success, and established different patterns of class behavior. The earlier cooperation between the gentry and small farmers was replaced by increasingly strained relations between the factory owners and the working class.

Classical Economics: The Rationale for Industrialization

Although the process of industrialization did not produce anything resembling a school of philosophy, it did generate serious thinking about the kind of new economic system that was coming into being. Much of this thought could be interpreted as a rationale for industrialization and a justification for profit-seeking. The French Physiocrats and the Scotsman Adam

Smith both advocated the abolition of mercantilism—the economy at the service of the state—and its replacement with a laissez-faire system—the economy at the service of the individual entrepreneur. In England, where Smith's views had the greatest influence, his ideas attracted a band of followers who carefully monitored the unfolding Industrial Revolution. What these observers wrote seemed to justify the economic changes that were transforming England from an agrarian country into an industrial power. Known as the Classical economists, this band of thinkers included Thomas Malthus and David Ricardo, along with Smith himself.

Smith's most significant contribution to Classical economics was his advocacy of a free-market system based on private property that would automatically regulate prices and profits to the benefit of all. He focused his *Wealth of Nations* (1776) on agriculture and commerce, while only glancing at manufacturing. As manufacturing started to loom larger in the English economy, however, businessmen read into his work a rationale for their activities. Smith was an optimist, a believer in the inevitability of progress—a man very much in the Enlightenment tradition. He argued that entrepreneurs acting mutually in enlightened self-interest would not only raise the standard of living for all but also get rich at the same time *if* the government left them alone. Such an argument was welcome news to the factory owners and other capitalists.

The ideas of Thomas Malthus (1766–1834) and David Ricardo (1772–1823) also tended to support the changes wrought by the Industrial Revolution. In his *Essay on the Principle of Population* (1788), Malthus forecast a world burdened with misery that would worsen if the human population continued to increase. Since the population grew at a geometric rate and the food supply advanced at an arithmetical rate, the number of human beings would soon far exceed the amount of food. Malthus's "law" of population led him to conclude that starvation could be prevented only by natural causes such as famines, plagues, and wars. Malthus's gloomy prediction persuaded most of the middle classes that laborers in the factories and mines were victims of their own thoughtless habits, including unrestrained sexuality, and could not be helped.

David Ricardo believed that he had identified a law that governed wages in an industrial society. In *Principles of Political Economy and Taxation* (1821) he maintained that wages for laborers would always hover around the subsistence level and workers would never be able to improve their standard of living beyond that level—his "iron law of wages." Tying Malthus's conclusion to his own, he argued that the

working class was inevitably mired in poverty. Each new generation of workers would share the same plight—receiving barely enough remuneration to eke out a living. The theories of the Classical economists provided ammunition for the business classes as they sought to justify the methods of industrialization and the degradation it brought to workers.

POLITICAL REVOLUTIONS, 1760–1815

During the approximately fifty years between the Treaty of Paris (1763) and the Battle of Waterloo (1815), Europe saw monarchies fall and old societies swept away. By 1830 Europe was divided into two camps—a conservative eastern Europe and a progressive western Europe that included the former colonies in the New World. In western Europe economic liberalism was on the rise, and limited monarchies prevailed except in the former British and Spanish colonies, where republics had been established. In contrast, eastern Europe was dominated by reactionary regimes that feared the power of liberal and nationalistic ideas to move their masses to revolt. This twofold division of the West persisted well into the twentieth century (Time Line 17.1).

The American Revolution

Great Britain in the 1760s was suffering from an outmoded tax structure, and the nation's fiscal soundness had been strained by debts contracted in the Seven Years' War. The royal ministers, aware that the American colonists paid few taxes except local ones, tried numerous schemes to make the overseas lands share in the burden of empire. The colonists, calling the British government's new taxes on sugar, stamps, and tea unconstitutional, claimed immunity from imperial taxation because, they asserted, they were not represented in the British parliament.

Protests, demonstrations, and violence succeeded in nullifying the parliamentary taxes and also contributed to uniting the colonies in a common cause. The colonists came of age in 1774 with the convening in Philadelphia of a Continental Congress. Even though this convention possessed no legal authority, it spoke for the American people against the "foreign power" of Great Britain. In April 1775 conflict between British troops and colonists in Massachusetts triggered a war. The congress in Philadelphia proclaimed the American goals in the Declaration of Independence, signed on July 4, 1776: government by

FIGURE 17.5 JACQUES-LOUIS DAVID. *The Coronation of Napoleon and Josephine.* 1805–1808. Oil on canvas, 20′ × 30′6½″. Louvre. *Napoleon orchestrated his own coronation and then guided David in painting it. For instance, Napoleon's mother did not attend, probably because of her disapproval of her son's grandiose ambitions, but Napoleon insisted that David depict her seated prominently at the center of the festivities. David also shows the pope's hand raised in benediction, contrary to the report of eyewitnesses who described him sitting with both hands resting on his knees.*

ing his empire in the eyes of Europe's older monarchs, who regarded him as an upstart. Napoleon's family members, who had been made kings, princes, princesses, and so on, are depicted in elaborate court dress. In addition, David's treatment of the coronation reveals the modern conception of political power. Instead of being crowned by the pope, Napoleon placed the crown on his own head. This painting shows Napoleon preparing to crown his empress, who is kneeling. Virtually ignored in this splendid moment for the Bonaparte family is the pope, who is seated at the right.

The only Neoclassical painter comparable to David is his pupil Jean-Auguste-Dominique Ingres (1780–1867). Ingres inherited the mantle of Neoclassicism from David, but he lacked his teacher's moral enthusiasm. As a result, Ingres's Classicism is almost cold-blooded and stark in its simple images. The finest expressions of Ingres's art are his portraits. With clean lines drawn with a sure and steady hand he created almost photographic images of his subjects.

Of Ingres's numerous portraits, one of the most exquisite is that of Madame Leblanc, a member of the new social order of Napoleonic France (Figure 17.6). Ingres's portrait may not probe deeply into the subject's psychology, but he does convey the sitter's high social position, stressing her poise and alluding to her wealth through the rich details of the marble-topped table, the floral still life, and the dangling watch and chain. In his own way, Ingres gives this member of the new bourgeois aristocracy the same glamorous treatment that had been accorded prerevolutionary nobles in Rococo portraits.

FIGURE 17.6 JEAN-AUGUSTE-DOMINIQUE INGRES. *Madame* ▶ *Jacques Louis Leblanc.* 1823. Oil on canvas, 47 × 36½″. Metropolitan Museum of Art, New York. Wolfe Fund, 1918. *Ingres was the last great painter of portraits in a field that was to be taken over by the camera after 1840. Claiming that drawing was superior to painting, he was able to render intense likenesses, as in this portrait of Madame Leblanc. Ingres stands alone in his ability to convey a subject's physical presence.*

FIGURE 17.13 JOSEPH MALLORD WILLIAM TURNER. *Snowstorm: Hannibal and His Army Crossing the Alps.* 1810–1812. Oil on canvas, 4'9½" × 7'9½". Tate Gallery, London. *Like so many Romantic painters, Turner borrowed subjects from literary sources. This scene of Hannibal crossing the Alps was based on an episode in a Gothic novel of the time. But Turner also had contemporary events in mind, since the titanic struggle between Hannibal and Rome mirrored the generation of warfare between Napoleon and England in the early 1800s.*

The Sublime appeared in German painting at about the same time that it developed in England. It was launched by Caspar David Friedrich (1774–1840), a painter who specialized in brooding landscapes, usually with a few human figures to give it a spiritual scale. A lifelong resident of Pomerania in northern Europe on the Baltic coast, he drew artistic inspiration from his homeland's deserted beaches, dense forests, and chalky cliffs. What sets his landscapes apart from those of earlier artists on the same subject is his desire to turn natural scenes into glimpses of the divine mystery. Avoiding traditional Christian subjects, Friedrich invented his own symbols for conveying God's presence in the world.

In *The Chalk Cliffs of Rugen* (Figure 17.14) the setting is the stark Baltic seacost as viewed from a cliff. Friedrich's intention is to convey how weak humans are when confronted by nature's power. By showing the figures from the back or the side—he never painted faces—Friedrich is encouraging the viewer to see what they see and to feel what they feel. What they are experiencing may be inferred from their gestures.

The woman on the left is feeling a fascinated horror as she holds to a bush and points to the yawning abyss before her. The male figure in the middle (probably Friedrich himself) is transfixed with terror; having thrown down his hat and cane, he kneels, hardly daring to peer over the cliff's edge. Lost in meditation is the third figure, who boldly stands on a scrub tree and gazes into space. The three figures together represent a common Romantic theme and a favorite of Friedrich's—the wonderful moment in friendship when a shared spiritual intimacy occurs.

In Spain, Romanticism flourished in the anti-Classical paintings of Francisco Goya (1746–1828), a major figure in Spanish culture. Reflecting a nightmarish vision of the world, his art ranges from Rococo fantasies, to sensual portraits, to grim studies of human folly, to spiritual evil, and finally to scenes of utter hopelessness. Various reasons have been suggested for Goya's descent into despair, but certainly his dashed hopes for the regeneration of Spain's political and social order were central to his advancing pessimism, as was his slow decline into deafness.

FIGURE 17.14 CASPAR DAVID FRIEDRICH. *The Chalk Cliffs of Rugen*. 1818. Oil on canvas, 90 × 70 cm. Museum Stiftung Oskar Reinhart, Winterthur, Switzerland. *In his seascapes Friedrich often included sailing ships approaching the land. These ships, as depicted here, became symbolic messengers, bringing tidings from some infinite realm to those human figures watching from shore. Friedrich thus reveals the underlying spiritual order of the world—a favorite theme of the Romantics.*

In the 1790s Goya was serving as court painter to King Charles IV, and signs of the artist's political disaffection can be detected in his revealing portrait of the royal family (Figure 17.15). He depicts the queen (center) as a vain, foolish woman and the king (left, front) as a royal simpleton. History has judged Goya's interpretations to be accurate, for this was a corrupt and stupid court. Perhaps the diaphanous gowns, the glittering medals, and the general elegance of the ensemble allowed him to get away with such unflattering portraits and survive within this dangerous environment.

In 1797 Goya published a collection of etchings that set forth his savage indictment of the age's social evils and established him as an outstanding humanitarian artist. The title of this series was *Caprichos,* or *Caprices,* a Romantic genre that allowed artists to express their personal feelings on any subject. One of the eighty *caprichos, The Sleep of Reason* was intended as the series' frontispiece and is the key to Goya's artistic purpose (Figure 17.16). The inscription on the desk reads, "The sleep of reason brings forth monsters," a statement that conveys the need for eternal vigilance against cruelty and superstition. The nocturnal creatures—bats, owls, and cats—symbolize the dark forces that continually threaten rationality.

Napoleon's conquest of Spain and the subsequent Spanish war of liberation form the background to Goya's masterpiece, *The Execution of the Third of May, 1808* (Figure 17.17). This protest against French imperialism is one of the world's most compelling de-

FIGURE 17.15 FRANCISCO GOYA. *The Family of Charles IV*. 1800. Oil on canvas, 9'2" × 11'. Prado. *Following a well-established Spanish tradition, Goya has painted himself into the canvas on the left, from which vantage point in the shadows he observes the royal family. Velásquez had followed this tradition 150 years earlier in* The Maids of Honor, *which this painting echoes. Goya portrayed the ravaged face of the king's sister on the left as a reminder of the fleeting nature of human beauty.*

FIGURE 17.16 FRANCISCO GOYA. *The Sleep of Reason.* 1797. Etching and aquatint, 215 × 150 mm. Museum of Fine Arts, Boston. Gift of Mr. and Mrs. Burton S. Stern, Mr. and Mrs. Bernard Shapiro, and the M. and M. Karolik Fund. *Goya's artistic technique in the* Caprichos *series is aquatint, a process that uses acid on a metal plate to create subtle shades of light and dark. The absence of color in the resulting engravings heightens the moral message of these works.*

pictions of the horrors of war. It shows Spanish captives being executed by a French firing squad. The French troops are a faceless line of disciplined automatons, and the Spanish soldiers a band of ill-assorted irregulars. The Spanish patriots are arranged in three groups: Those covered with blood and lying on the ground are already dead, those facing the firing squad will be dead in an instant, and those marching

FIGURE 17.17 FRANCISCO GOYA. *The Execution of the Third of May, 1808.* 1814–1815. Oil on canvas, 8′9″ × 13′4″. Prado. *A comparison of this painting by Goya with David's portrait of the assassinated Marat shows the difference in tone between Romantic and Neoclassical art. David makes Marat's death a heroic sacrifice in spite of its tragic circumstances. In contrast, Goya's passionate portrayal of the Spanish martyrs shows that there is nothing heroic about their deaths; their cause may be just, but the manner of their death is pitiless and squalid.*

FIGURE 17.18 THÉODORE GÉRICAULT. *The Raft of the* Medusa. 1818. Oil on canvas, 16'1" × 23'6". Louvre. *The devastated humanity on the raft underscored the breakdown in civilization that the entire* Medusa *incident came to represent. The painting itself became a rallying point for the critics of the restored Bourbon monarchy, who saw in the portrayal of a crew cast adrift a metaphor for the French nation.*

forward with faces covered are scheduled for the next round. The emotional center of this otherwise somber-hued painting is the whiteshirted man bathed in brilliant light. With his arms outstretched, he becomes a Christ figure, symbolizing Goya's compassion for all victims who die for a "good cause."

Romantic painting arrived in France in 1819 with the appearance of *The Raft of the* Medusa, a work by Théodore Géricault (1791–1824) that was based on an actual incident (Figure 17.18). The *Medusa*, a sailing ship, had foundered in the South Atlantic, and it was believed that all aboard were lost. Then after almost two months, a handful of survivors were rescued from a makeshift raft. From their story came shocking details of mutiny, crimes by officers, murder, cannibalism, and a government cover-up.

Géricault was attracted to this incident in which a few men outwitted death against all odds. Focusing on the precise moment of their rescue, he depicts these ordinary humans as noble heroes nearly overwhelmed by the terrible forces of nature. The nude

and partially clad bodies in the foreground convey a powerful sense of dignity and suffering. From here, the figures surge upward toward the black youth who is hoisted aloft and waving a flag at the unseen rescue ship. Géricault wanted his painting to be as realistic as possible—he interviewed survivors and had a replica of the raft constructed—but at the same time he imbued it with expression and pathos. The result was a highly emotional work that embodied the spirit of Romanticism.

Many of Géricault's ideas were taken up by Eugène Delacroix (1798–1863), who became the leader of a school of Romantic painting that was in open rivalry with Ingres and the Neoclassicists. Like Géricault, Delacroix was a humanitarian who drew artistic inspiration from his violent times. In the 1820s he identified with the Greeks in their war of independence against the Turks, expressing his support in the allegorical painting *Greece Expiring on the Ruins of Missolonghi* (Figure 17.19). Lord Byron had died at Missolonghi while trying to bring warring Greek fac-

Figure 17.19 Eugène Delacroix. *Greece Expiring on the Ruins of Missolonghi.* 1826. Oil on canvas, 6′11½″ × 4′8¼″. Musée des Beaux-Arts, Bordeaux. *Delacroix's representation of Greece as a woman was part of the Romantic convention of using female figures as national symbols. This trend climaxed in the writings of the French historian Jules Michelet, who concluded in 1846 that "France is a woman herself."*

tions together, an event the painting commemorates. Delacroix portrays Greece as a grieving woman kneeling on a group of blasted stones from which a dead hand protrudes. Behind her stands a turbaned Turk, the symbol of Greece's oppressors.

Delacroix's *Liberty Leading the People* was also inspired by a political incident, the July Revolution of 1830 (Figure 17.20). The painting combines realism and allegory, depicting revolutionaries on the barricades led by an idealized, bare-breasted goddess of Liberty. Surrounding Liberty are three central figures who symbolize the various classes that constitute

"the People": The man in the tall hat represents the middle classes, the chief beneficiaries of the revolution; the kneeling figure in the cap stands for the working-class rebels; and the boy brandishing the twin pistols is an image of the street urchin, among the lowest social groups.

The focal point of the painting is the tricolor, the revolutionary flag adopted in the revolution of 1789, outlawed from 1815 until 1830, and now restored as France's unifying symbol. The flag's red, white, and blue determine the harmony of color in the rest of this painting. Completed soon after the 1830 revolu-

FIGURE 17.20 EUGÈNE DELACROIX. *Liberty Leading the People*. 1831. Oil on canvas, 8′6″ × 10′8″. Louvre. *Delacroix's canvas bears some meaningful resemblances to Géricault's* Raft of the Medusa. *Each painting takes a contemporary event as its subject and transforms it into a symbol of France. Moreover, Delacroix's placement of two dead male figures, one partially nude and the other clothed, echoes similar figures in Géricault's work. Delacroix's portrayal of the people triumphant thus seems to be an optimistic response to Géricault's image of France adrift.*

tion, this work was purchased by the new king as a fitting tribute to the struggle that brought him to power. It was quickly hidden away, however, for the bourgeois establishment found the revolutionary heritage an embarrassment. Only later, with the creation of the Second Republic in 1848, did the French public see the painting.

Despite paying homage to radical forces, Delacroix was no true revolutionary. Even before painting *Liberty Leading the People,* Delacroix had been turning toward a more sensual art, an art that relied on gorgeous colors, as in *The Death of Sardanapalus* (Figure

17.21). Taking an anecdote from ancient history that had been dramatized by Lord Byron, he converted it into an image of Romantic destruction. In Delacroix's version, the doomed tyrant Sardanapalus, preparing to immolate himself, gazes unemotionally on the chaos caused by his order to kill everything—harem women, horses, and dogs—that he has ever loved. Much of the success of this haunting image depends on dramatic juxtapositions: passivity and passion, love and death, black and white, male and female. In paintings like this, Delacroix embodied the Romantic fascination with exotic, sensual, and violent subjects.

FIGURE 17.21 EUGÈNE DELACROIX. *The Death of Sardanapalus.* 1828. Oil on canvas, 12'10¼" × 16'¼". Louvre. *Delacroix's opulent painting caused a scandal when it was exhibited in the Paris Salon of 1827, but it also raised Delacroix to a position of leadership in the Romantic school. Its subject reflected the interest in the exotic Orient, which was a strong feature of French Romanticism. The subject allowed Delacroix's genius to run wild, imbuing the scene with confusion and surging colors.*

German Idealism

In philosophy the Romantic spirit led to idealism, a system of thought that flourished mainly in Germany and that espoused a spiritual view of life. From Kant through Hegel, the Germans constructed idealism as a philosophic alternative to conventional religion. In the 1790s Immanuel Kant (1724–1804) began the revolution in thought when he distinguished the world of phenomena (appearance) from the world of noumena (spirit). In Kantian terms, the phenomenal world may be understood by science, but the noumenal world may be studied, if at all, only by intuitive means.

Kant's followers, nonetheless, tried the impossible when they began to map out the spiritual realm. Johann Gottlieb Fichte (1762–1814) found reality in the World Spirit, a force having consciousness and seeking self-awareness. Friedrich Wilhelm Joseph von Schelling (1775–1854) equated nature with the Absolute, his name for ultimate reality. He also was the first to espouse the romantic belief in the religion of art by claiming that artists reveal divine truths in inspired works. Schelling's teaching on art influenced the English poet Coleridge and through him English Romanticism in general.

The climax of idealism occurred with Georg Wilhelm Friedrich Hegel (1770–1831) who explained human history as the record of the World Spirit seeking to know its true nature. Self-knowledge for the World Spirit arose only through a dialectical struggle. In the first stage, the Spirit developed a thesis that, in turn, produced an antithesis; in the second stage, a conflict then ensued between these two ideas that led to a synthesis, or a new thesis, which in turn gradually provoked new strife—a third stage, and so on *ad infinitum*. Hegel's theory of history ignored individuals because humans in the mass became tools of the World Spirit in its quest for freedom. In this view, wars, riots, and revolts were merely evidence of spiritual growth. For this reason, Hegel characterized Napoleon and his wars as embodiments of the World Spirit.

Hegelianism had a tremendous impact on later Western thought. Revolutionaries like Karl Marx borrowed his dialectical approach to history. Conservatives, especially in Germany, used Hegel's thought as a justification for a strong centralized state, and nationalists everywhere drew inspiration from his thought. Other thinkers rejected his denial of human responsibility and founded existentialist philosophies that glorified the individual.

The Birth of Romantic Music

As the middle class gained political power between 1789 and 1830, they converted the musical scene into a marketplace. Replacing elite forms of patronage, the bourgeoisie now attended programs that required admission fees and paid performers. Salaries and the demand for performances freed musicians from the patronage system. With their newly won independence, they became eccentric and individualistic—attitudes that were encouraged by the Romantic cult of the artist. Music grew more accessible as democracy progressed, and new industrial techniques and

production allowed more people to own inexpensive musical instruments.

The most gifted composer of this period, and one of the greatest musical geniuses of all time, was Ludwig van Beethoven (1770–1827), a German who spent most of his life in Vienna. He personified the new breed of musician, supporting himself through concerts, lessons, and the sales of his music (Figure 17.22). His works represent both the culmination of Classical music and the introduction of Romantic music. Working with the standard Classical forms—the sonata, the symphony, and the string quartet—he created longer works, doubling and even tripling their length. He also wrote music that was increasingly expressive and that showed more warmth and variety of feeling. He made several other significant musical innovations, including the use of choral voices within the symphonic form and the introduction of *program music*, that is, music that portrays a particular setting or tells a story.

Beethoven's career may be divided into three phases, but his extreme individualism left his unique stamp on everything that he composed. In the first phase, from the 1790s until 1803, he was under the shadow of Haydn, with whom he studied in Vienna. His First Symphony (1800) may be termed a Classical work, but in it he reveals a new spirit by lengthening the first and third movements and making the middle movement more lively than usual.

In the second phase, from 1803 until 1816, Beethoven's genius gave birth to Romantic music. He began to find his own voice, enriching and deepening the older forms. The Third Symphony (1803), which Beethoven called the "Eroica" ("Heroic"), is the most characteristic work from this second stage. The composer originally dedicated this symphony to Napoleon, whom he admired as a champion of democracy. But when the French ruler declared himself emperor in 1804, Beethoven angrily tore up the page and dedicated it instead "to the memory of a great man." In the Third Symphony, Beethoven substantially expands the musical material beyond the limits characteristic of earlier symphonies, making it longer and more complex. The music is grand, serious, and dignified, a truly heroic work.

In the third phase, from 1816 until 1827, Beethoven's music becomes freer and more contemplative, reaching its culmination in the Ninth Symphony (1822–1824). In the last movement of this work, Beethoven included a choral finale in which he set to music the poem "Ode to Joy" by the German Romantic poet Friedrich Schiller. Despite a life of personal adversities that included deafness from the age of thirty, Beethoven affirmed in this piece his faith in both humanity and God—"Millions, be you embraced! For the universe, this kiss!" The magnificent music and the idealistic text have led to the virtual canonization of this inspirational work.

Vienna also contributed another outstanding composer in Franz Schubert (1797–1828), who was famous for the beauty of his melodies and the simple grace of his songs. He lived a rather bohemian life, supporting himself, like Beethoven, by giving lessons and concerts. But unlike Beethoven, Schubert wrote mainly for the living rooms of Vienna rather than for the concert hall and is most famous for perfecting the *art song*, called in German **lied** (plural, *lieder*). The emergence of this musical form in the Romantic period was tied to the revival of lyric poetry. Schubert composed the music for over six hundred *lieder*, with texts by Goethe, Shakespeare, and other poets. His efforts raised the song to the level of great art.

A final composer of significance in this first period of Romanticism was the Frenchman Hector Berlioz (1803–1869). His most famous work is the *Symphonie fantastique (Fantastic Symphony)* (1830), a superb example of program music. Subtitled "Episode of an Artist's Life," this symphonic work illustrates musically a story that Berlioz described in accompanying written notes. In the tale, which takes the form of an opium dream, an artist-hero hopelessly adores an unfaithful woman and eventually dies for her. Relatively conventional in form, the symphony is most original in its use of a recurring musical theme, called an **idée fixe,** or "fixed idea," that becomes an image of the hero's beloved. Because every section contains the *idée fixe* in a modified form, it unifies the symphony in an innovative way. The success of Berlioz's symphony helped to strengthen the fashion for program music in the Romantic period.

FIGURE 17.22 FERDINAND GEORG WALDMÜLLER. *Ludwig van Beethoven.* 1823. Oil on canvas, 72 × 58 cm. Archiv Breitkopf and Härtel, Leipzig, Germany. Original destroyed in World War II. *Beethoven in his later years was the embodiment of the Romantic genius, disheveled in dress, singing to himself as he strolled Vienna's streets, mocked by street urchins; on one occasion, he was even arrested by the police as a tramp. In this 1823 portrait Waldmüller suggests Beethoven's unkempt appearance, but through the strong expression, fixed jaw, and broad forehead he also conveys the great composer's fierce determination and intelligence.*

The Legacy of the Age of Revolution and Reaction

During this period of revolution and reaction the West turned away from the past, with its monarchical forms of governments, its hierarchical society dominated by aristocratic landowners, its glacial rate of change, and its patronage system ruled by social, ecclesiastical, and political elites. Three events in particular—the Industrial Revolution and the American and the French revolutions—have left an indelible stamp on the modern world. The Industrial Revolution, which continues today, has gradually made humanity master of the earth and its resources, while at the same time accelerating the pace of life and creating the two leading modern social groups, the middle class and the working class. The Industrial Revolution also spawned Classical economics, the school of economists who justifed the doctrine of laissez faire that is still held to be the best argument for capitalism and continuous industrial growth. It is this same doctrine that has altered the patronage system, subjecting the creative works of modern artists, writers, musicians, and humanists to the law of the marketplace.

The American Revolution produced the first successful modern democracy, one that today stands as a beacon of hope for those oppressed by authoritarian regimes. The French Revolution contributed the idea of an all-encompassing upheaval that would sweep away the past and create a new secular order characterized by social justice and fairness. Although viewed with skepticism by some, for multitudes of others the notion of such a revolution became a sustaining belief. From the French Revolution also arises the idea that race and religion should not be used to exclude people from the right to vote—a reflection of its emphasis on the "brotherhood of man." Another outgrowth of the French Revolution is the Napoleonic Code, the law code that is used in the French-speaking world today.

Both the French and the American revolutions contributed certain beliefs that have become basic statements of Western political life, such as the idea that constitutions should be written down and that basic human liberties should be identified. Indeed, the progressive expansion of natural and civil rights to embrace all of society is an outgrowth of these two revolutions.

Other enduring legacies of this late eighteenth- and early nineteenth-century period are the Neoclassical buildings in Washington, D.C., and in most of the state capitals of the United States, the body of music of the Romantic composers, and the paintings of the Neoclassical and early Romantic schools. An ambiguous legacy of this period has been nationalism, the belief in one's own country and its people. At its best, nationalism is a noble concept, for it encourages people to get in touch with their roots and preserve their collective identity and heritage. At its worst, it has led to cutthroat behavior, dividing the people of a country against each other and leading to the disintegration of nations. Both forms of nationalism remain potent forces in the world today.

On a more personal level, this period saw the development of the Romantic view of life, an attitude that stresses informality, identification with the common people, the importance of feeling and imagination, and enjoyment of simple pleasures. Perhaps more than any other legacy of this period, the Romantic outlook has helped to shape the way that most men and women live in today's world.

KEY CULTURAL TERMS

Romanticism	*program music*
Sublime	*art song* (lied)
Sturm und Drang	idée fixe
Faustian	

SUGGESTIONS FOR FURTHER READING

PRIMARY SOURCES

AUSTEN, J. *Pride and Prejudice. Sense and Sensibility.* Introduction by D. Daiches. New York: Modern Library, 1950. Both novels deal with English provincial life. *Pride and Prejudice* (1813) focuses on the proud Mr. Darcy, who must be humbled before the "prejudiced" Elizabeth Bennet can take seriously his marriage proposal; *Sense and Sensibility* (1811) uses practical-mindedness ("sense") to expose the self-indulgence of the "picturesque" spirit ("sensibility"), an aspect of genteel taste in the late eighteenth century.

BYRON, G. G., LORD. *Don Juan.* Edited by T. G. Steffan, E. Steffan, and W. W. Pratt. New York: Penguin, 1973. One of Byron's most admired works, full of autobiographical references; dates from 1819–1824.

FICHTE, J. G. *Addresses to the German Nation.* Translated by R. F. Jones and G. H. Turnbull. Chicago: Open Court, 1923. The work that helped to launch German nationalism when first published in the early 1800s.

GOETHE, J. W. v. *Faust.* Part I. Translated and with an introduction by D. Luke. New York: Oxford University Press, 1987. A good modern English version of Goethe's drama of a man prepared to sacrifice his soul for the sake of knowledge based on feeling; originally published in 1808.

———. *The Sorrows of Young Werther.* Translated by E. Mayer and L. Bogan. Foreword by W. H. Auden. New York: Vintage, 1990. The 1774 Romantic novel that brought Goethe his earliest European-wide fame, translated by modern poets.

HEGEL, G. W. F. *Reason in History.* Translated and with an introduction by R. S. Hartman. New York: Liberal Arts Press, 1953. The best source for Hegel's theory that history moves through a dialectical process; first published in 1837.

KANT, I. *Critique of Pure Reason.* Introduction and glossary by W. Schwarz. Aalen, Germany: Scientia, 1982. A good recent version of Kant's difficult work that tried to establish what human reason can know apart from experience; dates from 1781.

MALTHUS, T. *On Population.* Edited and with an introduction by G. Himmelfarb. New York: Random House, 1960. One of the more recent editions of the influential essay, first published in 1788, that identified the modern dilemma of keeping population growth in equilibrium with food production.

RICARDO, D. *On the Principles of Political Economy and Taxation.* New York: Penguin, 1971. Ricardo's "iron law of wages"—that wages tend to hover around the subsistence level—became a central tenet of nineteenth-century laissez-faire theory.

SCHELLING, F. W. J. v. *Ideas for a Philosophy of Nature.* Translated by E. E. Harris. New York: Cambridge University Press, 1988. An excellent translation of Schelling's 1799 work that helped shape Romantic thinking by claiming to find God both in nature and in the human intellect.

WORDSWORTH, W. *Lyrical Ballads.* Edited by R. L. Braett and A. R. Jones. London: Routledge and Kegan Paul, 1988. A new edition of the original volume by Wordsworth and Coleridge that initiated the age of Romantic poetry in England; contains good introductory material.

SECONDARY SOURCES

ASHTON, T. S. *The Industrial Revolution, 1760–1830.* New York: Oxford University Press, 1964. A short but inclusive survey of the first stages of the Industrial Revolution.

BREUNIG, C. *The Age of Revolution and Reaction, 1789–1848.* 2d ed. New York: Norton, 1977. Excellent narrative history dealing with the French Revolution and its aftermath.

BRINTON, C. *The Anatomy of a Revolution.* New York: Vintage, 1960. A controversial study that attempts to establish a pattern in modern revolutions, including the French and American.

———. *A Decade of Revolution, 1789–1799.* New York: Harper Torchbooks, 1963. For the more serious student, this study has held up over the years for its summary of the major phases of the French Revolution and their impact on society, politics, and thought.

BRUUN, G. *Europe and the French Imperium, 1799–1814.* New York: Harper, 1938. Still a good guide to Napoleonic Europe; a volume in the Rise of Modern Europe series.

CANADAY, J. *Mainstreams of Modern Art.* 2d ed. New York: Holt, Rinehart, and Winston, 1981. An authoritative discussion by one of the leading scholars of modern art.

DOYLE, W. *Origins of the French Revolution.* Oxford: Oxford University Press, 1980. A survey of the varied interpretations of the causes of the French Revolution.

GIPSON, L. H. *The Coming of the Revolution.* New York: Harper & Row, 1954. On the American Revolution, especially good regarding Great Britain's view of events; excellent use of contemporary quotations.

HAMPSON, N. *The First European Revolution, 1776–1815.* New York: Harcourt, Brace, & World, 1979. Fully illustrated with many examples of high and popular art and a readable account of the major phases of the era.

HITCHCOCK, H. R. *Architecture: Nineteenth and Twentieth Centuries.* New York: Penguin, 1977. Thorough coverage with excellent illustrations and documents from the period.

HOLTMAN, R. *The Napoleonic Revolution.* Philadelphia: Lippincott, 1967. More on the institutions and reforms of the emperor than on the man himself.

JAMES, C. L. R. *The Black Jacobins.* 2d ed. New York: Vintage, 1963. A ground-breaking history of the black uprising in Santo Domingo from a Marxist perspective; a reprint of the 1938 classic.

LANDES, D. S. *The Unbound Prometheus: Technological Change and Industrial Development in Western Europe from 1750 to the Present*. London: Cambridge University Press, 1969. An excellent overview that analyzes all the phases of the Industrial Revolution.

LeBRIS, M. *Romantics and Romanticism*. New York: Skira, Rizzoli, 1981. A brilliant though idiosyncratic interpretation of the Romantic movement; beautifully illustrated.

LEFEBVRE, G. *The Coming of the French Revolution*. Translated by R. R. Palmer. New York: Vintage, 1961. An insightful summary of the causes of the revolution by an outstanding French scholar.

MARKHAM, F. *Napoleon*. New York: New American Library, 1963. Of the many biographies, this one is brief and well balanced.

MILLER, J. C. *Origins of the American Revolution*. Rev. ed. Palo Alto, Ca.: Stanford University Press, 1959. A study of the events leading up to the Declaration of Independence, focusing on economic factors.

MORGAN, E. S. *The Birth of the Republic, 1763–1789*. Chicago: University of Chicago Press, 1977. A brief narrative and sound interpretation of the revolutionary era, focusing on the struggle for political freedom.

MORRIS, R. B. *The Forging of the Union*. New York: Harper & Row, 1987. A fine study that explores how the U.S. Constitution was finally created.

PALMER, R. R. *The Age of Democratic Revolution: A Political History of Europe and America, 1760–1800*. 2 vols. Princeton: Princeton University Press, 1959, 1964. An excellent analysis that places the American and French revolutions in a wider context.

STROMBERG, R. *An Intellectual History of Modern Europe*. 3d ed. Englewood Cliffs, N.J.: Prentice-Hall, 1975. A thorough survey of the leading thinkers and intellectual movements.

WRIGLEY, E. A. *Continuity, Chance and Change: The Character of the Industrial Revolution in England*. Cambridge: Cambridge University Press, 1988. A provocative work that challenges traditional views of the English Industrial Revolution.

SUGGESTIONS FOR LISTENING

BEETHOVEN, LUDWIG VAN (1770–1827).

Composing mainly in Classical forms, notably the symphony and the string quartet, Beethoven moved from a Classical style in the manner of Haydn and Mozart to a Romantic style that was his own. The First Symphony (1800) shows his Classical approach; the Third Symphony, the "Eroica" (1803), inaugurated his Romantic style with its intense emotionalism and rich thematic variations. Of special note is the Ninth Symphony (1822–1826), a semimystical work whose final section blends full orchestra with a massed chorus. The emotional nature of the Violin Sonata No. 9 ("Kreutzer Sonata") inspired the Russian writer Leo Tolstoy to use the piece as a catalyst for murder in his story "The Kreutzer Sonata." Beethoven's stylistic development can also be traced in his sixteen string quartets: The first six quartets, dating from 1800, reflect the grace of Haydn and Mozart, and the last five, Nos. 12 through 16 (1823–1826), are technically difficult to play, enormously long, and characterized by mood shifts from light to tragic and unusual harmonic juxtapositions. The familiar piano piece, *Für Elise*, is a fine example of the rondo form.

BERLIOZ, HECTOR (1803–1869).

Berlioz was typically Romantic in going beyond the forms of Classicism and stressing the emotional possibilities of his music. For example, his *Requiem* (1837) is less a religious work than a dramatic symphony for orchestra and voices; its inspiration was the tradition of patriotic festivals originated during the French Revolution. Similarly, his opera *Damnation of Faust* (1846) is not an opera in a conventional sense but a series of episodes based on Goethe's play, a form that allowed the composer to focus on those scenes that seemed full of theatrical potential. Finally, the *Symphonie fantastique* (1830) is more than a symphony; it has been called "a musical drama without words"—the prototype of Romantic program music.

SCHUBERT, FRANZ (1797–1828).

Though a prolific composer of symphonies, operas, and piano sonatas, Schubert is most famous for perfecting the art song, or *lied*. Two of his best-known songs, with texts by Goethe, are *Gretchen am Spinnrade* ("Gretchen at the Spinning Wheel," 1814) and *Erlkonig* ("The Erlking," 1815). One of Schubert's most frequently played songs is *Die Forelle* ("The Trout," 1821), in which the lively, fluid music suggests the energetic movements of a swimming fish.

THE TRIUMPH
OF THE BOURGEOISIE
1830—1871

The revolutions of the late eighteenth century broke the monopoly on power that the aristocracy had held since the Early Middle Ages. The French and American revolutions offered the hope of political power to all disenfranchised groups, and the Industrial Revolution promised material gains to the impoverished. These expectations remained largely unfulfilled in Europe, however, as the nineteenth century unfolded. Benefits were reaped mainly by one group— the middle class, especially its wealthiest sector. Prosperous and successful, these businessmen, commercial property owners, and politicians dominated governments and enjoyed the fruits of the Industrial Revolution.

Left behind by the victory of the middle class was a new group created by industrialization—the proletariat, or working class. These urban workers remained dissatisfied and expressed their frustrations through political uprisings and social movements. The less prosperous segment of the middle class joined them in demanding universal suffrage and a fairer distribution of power and wealth. Against the liberalism of the bourgeoisie some of them set forth the ideals of socialism. But reform was limited at best, and successive waves of revolutionary uprisings failed to win significant improvements.

These dramatic changes were echoed in the cultural realm. From its brief peak in the 1820s, Romanticism began a long decline until it finally became exhausted toward the end of the century. Embraced by the middle class, it gained respectability and lost much of its creative fire. By midcentury a new style

was emerging that reflected changing political and social conditions. Known as Realism, it focused on ordinary people and attempted to depict in objective terms "the heroism of everyday life." At the same time, industrialization continued to spread, and people's ideas about themselves and the world were being challenged by everything from the theories of Charles Darwin to the invention of the camera (Time Line 18.1).

THE POLITICAL AND
ECONOMIC SCENE:
LIBERALISM AND NATIONALISM

Two powerful forces drove many events in Europe during the nineteenth century—liberalism and nationalism. The basic premise of liberalism was that the individual should be free from external control, a notion that resonated with the need of the bourgeoisie to liberate themselves from aristocratic society. The liberal political agenda included constitutionally guaranteed political and civil rights such as free speech, religious toleration, and voting rights for the propertied classes. Liberals themselves wanted to be left alone by the government, but they wanted the government to hold in check the aristocracy, the military, and organized religion. Perhaps most important, liberalism embraced the laissez-faire ideals in economics that allowed the wealthy middle class to maximize their profits in the business world.

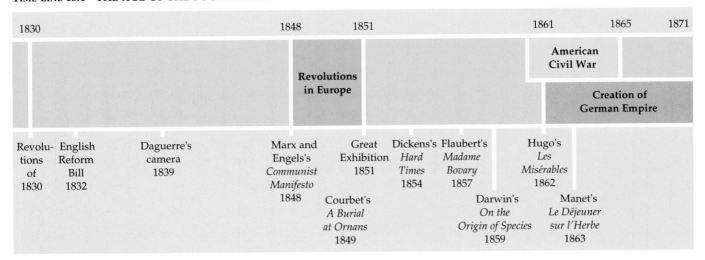

| 1830 | | | 1848 | 1851 | | | 1861 | 1865 | 1871 |

Revolutions in Europe

American Civil War

Creation of German Empire

Revolutions of 1830

English Reform Bill 1832

Daguerre's camera 1839

Marx and Engels's *Communist Manifesto* 1848

Great Exhibition 1851

Dickens's *Hard Times* 1854

Flaubert's *Madame Bovary* 1857

Hugo's *Les Misérables* 1862

Courbet's *A Burial at Ornans* 1849

Darwin's *On the Origin of Species* 1859

Manet's *Le Déjeuner sur l'Herbe* 1863

MAP 18.1

Europe after the Congress of Vienna, 1815

Liberal ideals had been at the heart of the American and French revolutions in the eighteenth century, and now a new generation of liberals carried forward the goals embraced by their predecessors. The spread of liberalism across Europe was uneven, however. It was most successful in England, France, and Belgium; it failed to take root in Italy and central and eastern Europe; and Russia remained reactionary throughout this whole period.

The other driving force of this era, nationalism, emphasized cooperation among all of a country's people who shared a common language and heritage. Overlooking class divisions, nationalists advocated humanitarian values, stressing the concept that all members of a nation are brothers and sisters. As nationalism proliferated, these basic ideas were often expanded to include other notions, particularly liberalism, republican principles, and even democratic beliefs. Nationalism became a driving force in central, southern, and eastern Europe, where the states of Germany and Italy, in particular, were still little more than "geographical expressions" (Map 18.1). After 1848 nationalism took on an increasingly militant aspect.

The Revolutions of 1830 and Their Aftermath

The repressive policies that had been imposed by the Congress of Vienna in 1815 were challenged in 1830 by a series of uprisings across Europe. The chain of revolutionary events started in July 1830 when the French overthrew their Bourbon ruler and put on the throne the so-called bourgeois monarch Louis Philippe (1830–1848), who pledged to uphold a liberal constitution (Figure 18.1). Liberal revolutions quickly followed elsewhere, including Belgium and areas of central and southern Europe.

In France, Louis Philippe established a liberal regime, but it increasingly became the tool of the newly rich middle class at the expense of the workers. Voting was limited to wealthy male property owners, and laws favored economic growth. Having gained political dominance and fulfilled their liberal agenda, the middle class intended to keep the benefits for themselves.

In central Europe, liberalism was stamped out. Local conservatives backed by Austrian troops quickly crushed the uprisings of 1830. Restored to power, they punished rebels, imposed martial law, reinstituted censorship, and took control of the school systems. Although liberals continued to hope for moderate reforms, conservatives kept their ideas in check through threats or direct suppression. Across central

FIGURE 18.1 FRANÇOIS RUDE. *The Departure of the Volunteers.* 1833–1836. Ca. 42 × 26'. Paris. *Under the "citizen king" Louis Philippe, bourgeois leaders were nervous about the revolutionary events that had brought them to power. Nevertheless, this group sculpture depicting the people on the march was hailed by all social ranks as an acceptable image of France's revolutionary past, including the revolution of 1830. Designed for the Arch of Triumph in Paris, the work came to be known affectionately as* La Marseillaise, *the name of the French national anthem.*

and eastern Europe, the one force emerging as a rallying point was nationalism, focusing as it did on ethnic identity and common cultural heritages.

The Revolutions of 1848

Accumulated dissatisfactions and frustrations erupted in another series of uprisings across Europe in 1848 (Table 18.1). Liberal ideals and nationalistic goals were driving forces behind these revolutions, but

MAP 18.2

Europe in 1871

ing liberal protests and the Prussian assembly and its laws. Nationalism replaced liberalism as the rallying cry of the Prussians, and Bismarck took advantage of this shift in attitudes to carry out his plans to unite the Germans around the Prussian state at the expense of Austria and France.

Bismarck achieved his goal by neutralizing potential enemies through deft diplomacy and fighting those who opposed him when diplomacy failed. By 1866 he had united the German states into the North German Confederation, a union that excluded Austria. In 1870 he engineered a diplomatic crisis that forced France to declare war on Prussia. Costly French defeats brought the ensuing Franco-Prussian War to an abrupt end later that year, toppled the Second Empire of Napoleon III, and resulted in France's humiliation in 1871 at Versailles, where the German Empire was proclaimed. The seeds of World War I were sown by this dramatic turn of events (Map 18.2).

Liberalism and nationalism were also at work in disruptions on the Italian peninsula, most of which

was ruled by Austrian princes. In the 1830s, Italian liberals inspired by the revolutionary writings of Giuseppe Mazzini (1805–1872) had banded together to form Young Italy, a nationalistic movement, and the small northern Italian state of Sardinia emerged as the hope of liberals and Young Italy. One of the few Italian states ruled by a native son, Sardinia was a constitutional monarchy that honored its subjects' civil and political rights. Its economy was well balanced between farming and trade, and in the 1840s it began to be industrialized. Under Prime Minister Count Camillo Benso di Cavour (1810–1861) Sardinia raised the standard of living for many of its citizens, in particular the middle-class merchants and manufacturers. In the 1850s Cavour made Sardinia a player in European affairs and thus set the stage for a move against Austria.

Between 1859 and 1871 Sardinia expelled most of the Austrians and became the center of an emerging state. As part of his grand strategy to unite Italy, Cavour allied himself with the sometimes unreliable Napoleon III of France, whose support encouraged

FIGURE 18.3 JOSEPH MALLORD WILLIAM TURNER. *The Slave Ship (Slavers Throwing Overboard the Dead and Dying, Typhoon Coming On).* Ca. 1840. Oil on canvas, 35¾ × 48¼". The Museum of Fine Arts, Boston. Henry Lillie Pierce Fund. *Growing revulsion against slavery led Parliament to abolish it in the British colonies in the 1830s, but the slaves in the United States were not freed until 1863. Turner's terrifying image of natural calamity and human cruelty reflected the humanitarian values that had surfaced during the parliamentary and national debates about slavery. The ghoulish scene, painted in Turner's unique Romantic style, depicts the castaway bodies of the dead and dying, encircled by hungry fish, as they sink into the stormy sea.*

Cavour to annex parts of central and southern Italy. Further assistance came from the fiercely patriotic soldier Giuseppe Garibaldi (1807–1882), who, with his personal army of a thousand "Red Shirts," invaded and liberated the Kingdom of the Two Sicilies from its Spanish Bourbon ruler. In 1860 the citizens of this now free region voted overwhelmingly to join Sardinia in a Kingdom of Italy, and soon thereafter the rest of the pieces of the Italian mosaic fell into place. In 1866 Austria yielded Venezia, its last Italian holding, to the new kingdom, and in 1870 Rome fell to nationalist troops and became Italy's capital.

Civil War in the United States

Paralleling the unification of Italy and Germany were the expansion and centralization of the United States, a vigorous and dynamic process that carried within it the seeds of conflict. The United States' economy was mixed and sharply divided between regions. On one side stood the Northeast, the national leader in commerce, trade, and banking and the site of a growing factory system; on the other side was America's South, a land dominated by huge plantations raising cotton plants cultivated by thousands of black slaves. The unsettled western lands and the ever-changing western frontiers formed a third element.

After 1830 the economic issues that divided the northern and the southern states became intensified over the question of slavery (Figure 18.3). As settlers moved into the central parts of the country, the debate over the spread of slavery into these areas aggravated sectional interests. Tempers were temporarily cooled through a series of compromises over ownership of slaves in the new territories and states, but by the late 1850s these compromises had failed, and in 1861 the southern states seceded from the union and provoked a civil war.

Unlike Europe's contemporaneous wars, which were short and resulted in relatively few deaths, the American Civil War lasted four years with huge losses on both sides. The northern victory in 1865, engineered by President Abraham Lincoln (1861–1865), saved the union and guaranteed freedom for the slaves. But animosity between the American north and south continued to smolder during the war's aftermath, called Reconstruction (1865–1876). Relations between these two sections have remained strained, especially over racial matters.

The Spread of Industrialism

Serving as a backdrop for all the political events of the nineteenth century was the growing industrialization of the Western world. Industrialism started to take root in France in the 1830s, and a short time later Belgium entered the industrial age. For the next forty years Belgium and France were the chief economic powers on the Continent. From France and Belgium industrialism spread, and by 1871 the factory and the railway systems radiated from Paris and Brussels to Vienna and Milan.

In the meantime, Great Britain passed into the second phase of the Industrial Revolution. England continued to build ships, to construct factories, and to lay rail lines; by 1850 all its major cities were linked (Figure 18.4). In 1846 Britain abolished tariffs on foreign wheat to usher in a free-trade era. The principles of free trade seemed to be justified by the results. Lower bread prices benefited workers and allowed employers to cut wages, and the fears that additional imports of grain would destroy the agrarian economy proved to be false because agriculture had to expand to meet the demands of a mushrooming urban population.

Prior to 1848 European mining and manufacturing were localized near ore deposits or clustered around urban areas, and railway construction was uncoordinated. But after 1848 rail lines expanded rapidly, and by 1870 a network of 65,000 miles covered Europe. Inventions in communications such as the telegraph brought Europeans closer together, and in 1866 engineers laid a transatlantic telegraph cable, making

FIGURE 18.4   W. P. FRITH. *The Railway Station*. Ca. 1862. Oil on canvas, 3'10" × 8'5". Royal Holloway College and Bedford New College, Surrey, England. *London was the hub of England's economy long before the Industrial Revolution, and with the coming of the railroads its position was enhanced. The massive new railway stations, often constructed of glass and iron, symbolized the changing business and leisure habits of life. In this painting of one of London's new rail stations, Frith's well-dressed middle-class citizens convey the excitement of travel as well as its novelty and uncertainty.*

FIGURE 18.5 JOSEPH NASH. Detail of *The Crystal Palace*. 1851. Color lithograph with watercolor. Ca. 21½ × 29⅝". Victoria and Albert Museum, London. *This detail from an 1851 lithograph illustrates the splendor and pageantry surrounding the moment when Queen Victoria opened the Great Exhibition of that year. After the fair closed, the Crystal Palace was disassembled, moved, and rebuilt in a suburb in south London, where it stood as an arts and entertainment center until it was destroyed by fire in 1936. Nevertheless, the "pre-fab" construction principles of the Crystal Palace foreshadowed modern building methods.*

communication easier between Europe and America. The opening of new coal and iron deposits in Europe and the rise of imports in raw materials for textiles and other goods kept the machines of industry humming. British financiers, joined by continental bankers, made loans to fledgling companies for new factories, warehouses, ships, and railways, thereby generating more wealth for capitalists who had surplus funds to invest.

As Europe's economy grew, two marvels of the industrial age—the Crystal Palace in London and the Suez Canal in Egypt—captured the world's imagination. The iron and glass Crystal Palace housed the Great Exhibition of 1851—in effect, the first world's fair. In a structure that used the most recent building materials and employed some of the most advanced architectural methods, the newest inventions and the latest machine-made goods were put on display for everyone—rich and poor—to see. Although other nations displayed products and inventions, Britain's exhibits were the most impressive and proved that it was the world's leading industrial and agricultural power (Figure 18.5).

The second marvel to attract the world's attention was the digging of the Suez Canal to link the Gulf of Suez and the Red Sea with the Mediterranean Sea. Funded by a French company and opened in 1869, the canal shortened the distance between Europe and India, thus enabling steamships to ferry passengers and goods around the globe more quickly and comfortably (Figure 18.6).

The Crystal Palace and the Suez Canal and all of the other wonders of the age were made possible by the labor of millions of workers—men, women, and

FIGURE 18.6 ANONYMOUS. *Suez Canal Opening*. 1869. Colored engraving. British Library, London. *Just as Great Britain showed the world what it could achieve through industry and agriculture, so France demonstrated its technological and engineering genius in digging the Suez Canal. The Suez Canal Company, headed by the French entrepreneur Ferdinand de Lesseps (1805–1894), began its work in 1859 and finally completed the canal ten years later after overcoming many financial and building problems.*

of years of divine activity, Protestant Christians were able to weather this particular intellectual storm. Not so easily overcome, however, was biology's threat to biblical authority.

Following the Bible, the church was clear in its explanation of humanity's origin: Adam and Eve were the first parents, having been created by God after he had fashioned the rest of the animate world. Paralleling this divine account was a secular argument for evolution. Based on Greek thought, but without solid proofs, it remained a theory and nothing more for centuries. In 1859, however, the theory of *evolution* gained dramatic support when the Englishman Charles Darwin (1809–1882) published *On the Origin of Species*. Marshalling data to prove that evolution was a principle of biological growth rather than a mere hypothesis, Darwin showed that over the course of millennia modern plants and animals had evolved from simpler forms through a process of natural selection.

In 1871, in *Descent of Man*, Darwin applied his findings to human beings, portraying them as the outcome of millions of years of evolution. Outraged clergy attacked Darwin for his atheism, and equally zealous Darwinians heaped ridicule on the creationists for their credulity. Today, the theory of evolution is one of the cornerstones of biological science, despite some continuing criticism.

Other advances in science were helping to lay the groundwork for the modern world. In the 1850s French scientist Louis Pasteur (1822–1895) proposed the germ theory of disease, the notion that many diseases are caused by microorganisms. This seminal idea led him to important discoveries and proposals for change. Claiming that germs were responsible for the spread of disease, he campaigned for improved sanitation and sterilization and thus paved the way for antiseptic surgery. He demonstrated that food spoilage could be prevented by killing microorganisms through heating, a discovery that led to the "pasteurization" of milk. His studies of rabies and anthrax led to the first use of vaccines against these diseases. As the founder of bacteriology and an important figure in the development of modern medicine, Pasteur is the embodiment of Francis Bacon's seventeenth-century assertion, "knowledge is power."

In chemistry a fruitful way of thinking about atoms was finally formulated, moving beyond the simplistic notions that had been in vogue since fifth-century B.C. Greece. In about 1808 the Englishman John Dalton (1766–1844) invented an effective atomic theory and, in 1869, the Russian Dmitri Mendeleev (1834–1907) worked out a periodic table of elements, based on atomic weights, a system that, with modifications, is still in use. By 1871 other chemists had moved from regarding molecules as clusters of atoms to conceiving of them as structured into stable patterns. Nevertheless, without means and equipment for studying the actual atoms, atomism remained merely a useful theory until the twentieth century.

Advances in chemistry also led to changes in anesthetics and surgery. In the 1840s chemists introduced nitrous oxide, chloroform, and other compounds that could block pain in human beings. Use of these new pain killers in obstetrics increased after Queen Victoria was given chloroform to assist her in childbirth in 1853. These desensitizers revolutionized the treatment of many diseases and wounds and made modern surgery possible.

CULTURAL TRENDS: FROM ROMANTICISM TO REALISM

In its triumph, the middle class embraced both Neoclassical and Romantic styles in the arts. In Neoclassicism, the bourgeoisie found a devotion to order that appealed to their belief that the seemingly chaotic marketplace was actually regulated by economic laws. In Romanticism, they found escape from the sordid and ugly side of industrialism.

But both styles slowly grew routinized and pretentious under the patronage of the middle class (Figure 18.7). One reason for this development was the inevitable loss of creative energy that sets in when any style becomes established. Another reason was the conversion of the cultural arena into a marketplace. Lacking the deep learning that had guided many aristocratic patrons in the past, the new bourgeois audiences demanded art and literature that mirrored their less refined values. Catering to this need, artists and writers produced works that were spectacular, sentimental, and moralistic. Simply put, successful art did not offend respectable public taste.

Adding to this bourgeois influence was the growing ability of state institutions to control what was expressed in art and literature. The most powerful of these was France's Royal Academy of Painting and Sculpture, founded in 1648 for the purpose of honoring the nation's best painters. After 1830 its leaders became obsessed with rigid rules, thus creating what was called "official art." Those artists who could not obtain the academy's approval for exhibiting their works in the annual government-sponsored Salons, or art shows, were virtually condemned to poverty

FIGURE 18.7 ÉDOUARD MANET. *Concert in the Tuileries.* 1862. Oil on canvas, 30 × 46". National Gallery, London. *The values of the well-to-do middle class influenced artistic standards in the mid-nineteenth century. Here, Manet depicts a carefree crowd of top-hatted artists and writers, along with their families and friends, at a musical entertainment in a popular Paris park. Such public spectacles were favorite activities of the middle class at this time. Painted in the post-1848 Realist style, the* Concert in the Tuileries *is a straightforward portrayal of an actual event and thus provides a sense of the times.*

unless they had other means of financial support. Rejected artists soon identified the Royal Academy as a defender of the status quo and an enemy of innovation. No other western state had a national academy with as much power as France's Royal Academy, although in other European countries similar bodies tried to regulate both art and literature.

In reaction to the empty, overblown qualities of official art, a new style began to appear in the 1840s. Known as *Realism*, this style focused on the everyday lives of the middle and lower classes. The Realists depicted ordinary people without idealizing or romanticizing them, although a moral point of view was always implied. Condemning Neoclassicism as cold and Romanticism as exaggerated, the Realists sought to convey what they saw around them in a serious, accurate, and unsentimental way. Merchants, housewives, workers, peasants, and even prostitutes replaced kings, aristocrats, goddesses, saints, and heroes as the subjects of paintings and novels.

Many forces contributed to the rise of Realism. In diplomacy this was the era of Bismarck's *Realpolitik*, the hard-nosed style that replaced more cautious and civilized negotiation. In science Darwin demystified earthly existence by rejecting the biblical view of creation and concluding that the various species, including human beings, evolved from simpler organisms. The spread of democracy encouraged the Realists to take an interest in ordinary people, and the camera, invented in the 1830s, probably inspired the Realists in their goal of truthful accuracy. All these influences combined to make Realism a style intent on scientific objectivity in its depiction of the world as it is.

Literature

In literature the Romantic style continued to dominate both poetry and novels until midcentury, when it began to be displaced by Realism. The Romantic authors were concerned with the depth of their characters' emotions and had great faith in the power of the individual to transform his or her own life and the lives of others. The Realists, by contrast, tended to be determinists who preferred to let the facts speak for themselves. They rejected the bourgeois world as flawed by hypocrisy and materialism and denounced the machine age for its mechanization of human relationships. Realism in literature flourished between 1848 and 1871, chiefly in France, England, and Russia.

The Height of French Romanticism: Victor Hugo   In France the leading exponent of Romanticism was the poet, dramatist, and novelist Victor Hugo (1802–1885). His poetry established his fame, and the performance of his tragedy *Hernani* in February 1830 solidified his position as the leader of the Romantic movement. Enlivened with scenes of rousing action and by characters with limitless ambition, this play seemed with one stroke to sweep away the artificialities of Classicism. Its premiere created a huge scandal. When the bourgeois revolution erupted in July 1830, many French people believed that Hugo's *Hernani* had been a literary prophecy of the political upheaval.

Hugo became something of a national institution, noted as much for his humane values as his writing. Because of his opposition to the regime of Napoleon III, he was exiled from France for eighteen years, beginning in 1851. While in exile he published his most celebrated novel, the epic-length *Les Misérables* (*The Wretched*) (1862), which expresses his revulsion at the morally bankrupt society he believed France had become after Napoleon I.

The hero and moral center of the book is the pauper Jean Valjean, who is imprisoned for seventeen years for stealing a loaf of bread. He escapes and becomes a prosperous, respectable merchant, but the law is implacable in its pursuit of him, and he is forced into a life of hiding and subterfuge. Hugo makes Valjean a symbol of the rising masses' will to freedom, and his bourgeois readers were fascinated and horrified at the same time by Valjean's ultimate triumph.

Romanticism in the English Novel   In England, Romanticism found its most expressive voices in the novels of the Brontë sisters, Charlotte (1816–1855) and Emily (1818–1848). Reared in the Yorkshire countryside far from the mainstream of cultured life, they created two of the most beloved novels in the English language. Their circumscribed lives seemed to uphold the Romantic dictum that true artistic genius springs from the imagination alone.

Emily's *Wuthering Heights* (1847) creates a Romantic atmosphere through mysterious events, ghostly apparitions, and graveyard scenes, but it rises above the typical Gothic romance. The work is suffused by a mystical radiance that invests the characters and the natural world with spiritual meanings beyond the visible. A tale of love and redemption, the story focuses on a mismatched couple, the genteel Catherine and the outcast Heathcliff, who are nevertheless soulmates. In the uncouth and passionate Heathcliff, Brontë creates a Byronic hero who lives apart from conventional morality. Her portrayal of him as a man made vengeful by cruel circumstances has led some to label this work the first sociorevolutionary novel.

Charlotte Brontë published *Jane Eyre* in the same year *Wuthering Heights* appeared. A dark and melancholy novel, the work tells the story of a governess's love for her brooding and mysterious employer. Her hopes for happiness are crushed by the discovery that the cause of his despair is his deranged wife, kept hidden in the attic. Narrated in the first person, the novel reveals the heroine's deep longings and passions as well as her ultimate willingness to sacrifice her feelings for moral values. Recognized at the time as a revolutionary work that dispensed with the conventions of sentimental novels, *Jane Eyre* was attacked by critics but welcomed by the reading public, who made it a best seller.

Realism in French and English Novels   Realism began in France in the 1830s with the novels of Honoré de Balzac (1799–1850). Balzac foreshadowed the major traits of Realism in the nearly one hundred novels that make up the series he called *The Human Comedy*. Set in France in the Napoleonic era and the early industrial age, this voluminous series deals with the lives of over two thousand characters, both in Paris and in the provinces. Balzac condemns the hollowness of middle-class society, pointing out how industrialism has caused many people to value material things more than friendship and family, although there are virtuous and sympathetic characters as well.

France's outstanding Realist is Gustave Flaubert (1821–1880), who advocated a novel free from conventional, accepted moral or philosophical views. His masterpiece is *Madame Bovary* (1857), which caused a scandal with its unvarnished tale of adultery. In contrast to Balzac's broad sweep, Flaubert focused on one small town and the daily comings and goings of a family, concentrating his greatest attention on a single person, the unhappy and misguided Emma Bovary. Objectively and clinically, he sets forth the inner turmoil of a frustrated middle-class woman trapped by her dull marriage and her social standing. By stressing objectivity and withholding judgment, Flaubert believed he was following in the footsteps of modern science. As a social critic he portrays with meticulous detail everyday life among the smug members of this small-town, bourgeois society. Notwithstanding the scandal it caused, *Madame Bovary* became an instant success and established the new style of Realism. For most readers, Emma Bovary became a poignant symbol of people whose unrealistic dreams and aspirations doom their lives to failure.

English novelists also wrote in the new Realist style. Like their French counterparts, they railed against the vulgarity, selfishness, and hypocrisy of the middle class, but unlike the French they chose mundane rather than sensational subjects, avoided sexual matters, and spoke out for social justice. England's most popular writer of Realist fiction was Charles Dickens (1812–1870), who favored stories dealing with the harsh realities of urban and industrial life. Forced to meet strict deadlines for his works, which first appeared as serialized magazine stories, Dickens poured out a torrent of words over a long literary career that began when he was in his twenties.

In his early works such as *Oliver Twist* (1837–1839) and *David Copperfield* (1849–1850) Dickens was optimistic, holding out hope for his characters and, by implication, for society in general. But in later novels like *Bleak House* and *Hard Times*, both published between 1851 and 1854, he was pessimistic about social reform or correcting the excesses of industrialism. Dickens's rich descriptions, convoluted plots with unexpected coincidences, and topical satire were much admired by Victorian readers, and his finely developed and very British characters, such as Mr. Pickwick, Oliver Twist, and Ebenezer Scrooge, have survived as a memorable gift to literature.

Realist fiction in England was also represented by important female writers. The two most successful were Elizabeth Gaskell (1810–1865) and Mary Ann Evans (1819–1880), better known by her pen name, George Eliot. Both wrote novels about the hardships imposed on the less fortunate by England's industrial economy. Gaskell's *North and South* (1855) underscores the widening gap between the rich, particu-larly in England's urban north, and the poor, concentrated in the rural south, within the context of the rise of the labor unions. Typically, her themes involve contrasts, contradictions, and conflicts, such as the helplessness of human beings in the face of impersonal forces and the simultaneous need to affirm the human spirit against the inequalities of the factory system. Similarly, in novels like *Middlemarch* (1872) George Eliot explores the ways human beings are trapped in social systems that shape and mold their lives, for good or ill. Eliot's outlook is less deterministic, however, stressing the possibility of individual fulfillment despite social constraints as well as the freedom of human beings to make moral choices.

The Russian Realists   During the Realist period, Russia for the first time produced writers whose works received international acclaim: Leo Tolstoy (1828–1910) and Feodor Dostoevsky (1821–1881). Like English and French Realists, these Russians depicted the grim face of early industrialism and dealt with social problems, notably the plight of the newly liberated serfs. Their realism is tempered by a typically Russian concern: Should Russia embrace Western values or should it follow its own traditions, relying on its Slavic and Oriental past? And, most significantly, Tolstoy and Dostoevsky transcend Western Realism by stressing religious and spiritual themes.

In his early works Tolstoy wrote with a clinical eye, free of moralizing. The novel *Anna Karenina* (1875–1877) describes the unhappy consequences of adultery in a sophisticated but unforgiving society. *War and Peace* (1865–1869), his greatest work, is a monumental survey of Russia during the Napoleonic era, portraying a huge cast of characters caught up in the surging tides of history. Although Tolstoy focuses on the upper class in this Russian epic, he places them in realistic situations without romanticizing them. In these early works he was a determinist, convinced that human beings were at the mercy of forces acting independently of their own will. But in 1876, after he had a religious conversion to a simple form of Christianity that stressed pacifism, plain living, and radical social reform, he repudiated all art that lacked a moral vision, including his own. Tolstoy devoted the rest of his life to a simple faith, following what he believed to be Jesus' teachings and working for a Christian anarchist society.

Feodor Dostoevsky was a powerful innovator who introduced literary devices that have become standard in Western letters. For example, *Crime and Punishment* (1866), long before the work of Sigmund Freud, analyzes the inner life of a severely disturbed personality. In *Notes from Underground* (1864) the unnamed narrator is hopelessly neurotic—the first appearance of a modern literary type, the anti-hero, the character who lacks the virtues conventionally associated with heroism, but who is not a villain.

In *The Brothers Karamazov* (1879–1880) Dostoevsky reaches the height of his powers. Like Flaubert in *Madame Bovary*, Dostoevsky sets his story in a small town and builds the narrative around a single family. Each of the Karamazov brothers personifies certain traits of human behavior, though none is a one-dimensional figure. Using the novel to address one of life's most vexing questions—If God exists, why is there suffering and evil in the world?—Dostoevsky offers no easy solution. Indeed, he reaches the radical conclusion that the question is insoluble, that suffering is an essential part of earthly existence and without it human beings could have no moral life.

Art and Architecture

Realism in art grew up alongside an inflated and overstated version of Romanticism that persisted well beyond midcentury. Even Neoclassicism was represented in the official art of France throughout this period. Both styles found favor with the wealthy bourgeoisie.

Neoclassicism and Romanticism after 1830 Jean-Auguste-Dominique Ingres, who had inherited the position of Neoclassical master painter from David, now held virtually complete power over French academic art until his death in 1867. He understood the mentality of the Salon crowds, and his works catered to their tastes. What particularly pleased this audience—composed almost exclusively of the wealthy, educated middle class—were chaste nudes on mythological or exotic themes, as in *The Turkish Bath* (Figure 18.8). The women's tactile flesh and the abandoned poses, though superbly realized, are depicted in a cold, Classical style and lack the immediacy of Ingres's great portraits.

Delacroix, Ingres's chief rival, remained a significant force in French culture with almost comparable artistic power. Delacroix perfected a Romantic style filled with gorgeous colors and fiery action. One of his finest works from this period is *The Abduction of Rebecca*, based on an incident in the novel *Ivanhoe* by the Scottish writer Sir Walter Scott (Figure 18.9). This literary subject inspired Delacroix to create a painting that is a feast for the eyes. In the foreground, the swooning Rebecca is kidnapped by knights and placed on the back of a spirited horse; in the background, flames pour through the openings in a burn-

FIGURE 18.8 JEAN-AUGUSTE-DOMINIQUE INGRES. *The Turkish Bath.* Ca. 1852–1863. Oil on canvas, diameter, 42½". Louvre. *Paintings of harem scenes reflected interest in Oriental themes, a continuous thread in France's nineteenth-century bourgeois culture. In his rendering of a Turkish bath, Ingres used a harem setting in which to depict more than twenty nudes in various erotic and nonerotic poses. The nudes nevertheless are portrayed in his typical Classical manner, suggesting studio models rather than sensual human beings.*

FIGURE 18.9 EUGÈNE DELACROIX. *The Abduction of Rebecca.* 1846. Oil on canvas, 39½ × 32¼". Metropolitan Museum of Art, New York. Wolfe Fund, 1903. *Romantic themes abound in Delacroix's painting of the abduction of Rebecca, such as its medieval subject, its literary source, and its use of bold colors to accentuate the violence. In addition, the struggling horse was a favorite symbol of Romantic artists, representing the untamable energy of nature.*

ing castle and lick the sky. In this and later paintings Delacroix tried to work out the secret laws governing colors—especially the effects that they have on the viewer. The results in *The Abduction of Rebecca* are seductive hues and the almost total absence of black. Later, the Impressionists based some of their color theories on Delacroix's experiments.

Like Romantic painting, nineteenth-century architecture tended to be romantically nostalgic, intrigued by times and places far removed from the industrial present. Particularly appealing were medieval times, which were considered exotic and even ethically superior to the present. Patriotism also contributed to the trend among Romantic architects to adapt medieval building styles, notably the Gothic, to nineteenth-century conditions, since the Middle Ages were a time when the national character of many states was being formed.

In London, when the old Houses of Parliament burned to the ground in 1834, a decision had to be made about the style of their replacement. Since English rights and liberties traditionally dated from the Magna Carta in 1215, during the Middle Ages, a parliamentary commission chose a Gothic style for the new building (see Figure 18.2). Designed by Charles Barry (1795–1860) and A. W. N. Pugin (1812–1852), the Houses of Parliament show a true understanding of the essential features of the Gothic style, using pointed arches and picturesque towers. Despite these features, this building is not genuinely Gothic, for it adheres to Classical principles in the regularity of its decorations and its emphasis on the horizontal.

The Rise of Realism in Art Dissatisfied with the emotional, exotic, and escapist tendencies of Romanticism, a new breed of painters who wanted to depict the real-life events they saw around them brought their vision to public attention after 1848. In that year the jury of the Salon, influenced by the democratic sentiments unleashed by the 1848 revolutions, allowed a new kind of painting to be shown. The artist most identified with this event was Gustave Courbet (1819–1877), a painter renowned for his refusal to prettify his works in the name of an aesthetic theory. His provocative canvases outraged middle-class audiences and made him the guiding spirit of militant Realism. Until about 1900, most painters in one way or another followed in Courbet's footsteps. A man of the people, a largely self-taught painter, and a combative individual, Courbet began to attract notice in 1849 by painting common people engaged in their day-to-day activities. Above all, he strove for an art that reflected the conditions of ordinary life.

In *A Burial at Ornans* Courbet shows a funeral party of provincials around an open grave in the stark

FIGURE 18.10 GUSTAVE COURBET. *A Burial at Ornans.* 1849. Oil on canvas, ca. 10′ × 22′. Louvre. *Courbet's realistic burial scene reveals a modern, secular outlook. Previously in such scenes, artists had focused on religious values, either suggesting that death is a preparation for heaven or stressing that the body is mortal. Courbet does neither; instead he portrays the final rites as a community affair, making no distinctions between clerical participants and lay mourners. For him this funeral is simply a social ritual, nothing more.*

FIGURE 18.11 GUSTAVE COURBET. *Interior of My Studio: A Real Allegory Summing Up Seven Years of My Life as an Artist.* 1855. Oil on canvas, 11'9¾" × 19'6⅝". Louvre. *Romanticism and Realism are joined in this allegorical work. The subjects—the artist and artistic genius—were major preoccupations of the Romantic era, as was the use of allegory. But undeniably Realist is Courbet's mocking attitude toward academic art and society.*

countryside near his home (Figure 18.10). Exhibited in the Salon of 1850, this huge painting caused an outcry from critics because it depicted people of no importance or interest to the wealthy bourgeoisie, and the mourners' realistic portrayal offended what was considered good taste. Instead of idealizing or romanticizing the peasants, Courbet portrayed them as flesh and blood, showing the same degrees of public sorrow as their so-called social betters. In the middle of the nineteenth century such humane treatment of the "lower orders" smacked of socialism. Courbet relished the controversy, claiming that this work represented the burial of Romanticism.

Courbet's art was not readily accepted under France's Second Empire. Typical of his neglect was an episode in 1855 when the Salon jury refused to accept for exhibit the monumental work that is today regarded as his masterpiece, *Interior of My Studio* (Figure 18.11). An intensely personal painting that visually summarizes his approach to art until this time, this work uses realistic contemporary figures to convey allegorical meaning. Its subtitle suggests Courbet's intent: *A Real Allegory Summing Up Seven Years of My Life as an Artist.* At the center of this canvas is the artist himself, in full light and painting a land-

scape while he is watched by a naked model and a small boy. The model and the fabric may be ironic references to the Salon's predilection for nudes and still lifes. To the left of this central group, in shadow, are depicted those who have to work for a living, the usual subjects of Courbet's paintings, including peasants (the hunter and his dog) and a laborer. To the right, also in shadow, are grouped those for whom he paints, including his friends and mentors, each representing a specific idea. For example, the man reading a book is the poet Charles Baudelaire, a personification of lyricism in art. As a total work, *Interior of My Studio* shows Courbet as the craftsman who mediates between the ordinary people pursuing everyday lives and the world of art and culture, bringing both to life in the process.

Although Courbet is considered the principal founder of the Realist style in art, he had a worthy predecessor in Honoré Daumier (1808–1879), a painter of realistic scenes before Realism emerged as a recognized style. Daumier chronicled the life of Paris with a dispassionate, clinical eye. In thousands of satirical lithographs, from which he earned his living, and hundreds of paintings, he depicted its mean streets, corrupt law courts, squalid rented

FIGURE 18.12 HONORÉ DAUMIER. *Le Ventre Législatif (The Legislative Belly).* 1834. Lithograph, 431 × 280 mm. Museum of Fine Arts, Boston. Bequest of William P. Babcock. *Daumier's career as a caricaturist was made possible by technological advances associated with the industrial era. After drawing a cartoon, he reproduced it for the mass market by the lithographic process, the first application of industrial methods to art. In early lithography the artist rendered an image on a flat stone surface and treated it so the nonimage areas would repel ink. Today's lithography makes use of zinc or aluminum surfaces instead of stone.*

rooms, ignorant art connoisseurs, bored musicians, cowardly bourgeoisie, and countless other urban characters and scenes. His works not only conjure up Paris in the middle of the century, but also symbolize the city as a living hell where daily existence could be a form of punishment.

No one and nothing were safe from Daumier's gaze. For example, in *Le Ventre Législatif (The Legislative Belly)* he depicts the legislators of the bourgeois monarchy of Louis Philippe as fat politicians feeding at the public trough (Figure 18.12). His razor-sharp wit was reflected in the politicians' bloated stomachs, cruel frowns, whispered asides, and general air of smug self-satisfaction. For such satire Daumier was awarded a six-month prison term in 1832, but to his adoring audience he was a hero.

One of the most famous of Daumier's images is the painting entitled *The Third-Class Carriage* (Figure 18.13). In Paris third-class coach was the cheapest sort of rail travel, and the resulting accommodations were cramped and plain. In Daumier's scene the foreground is dominated by three figures—a mother and her sleeping child, an old woman, and a sleeping boy. Behind them are crowded other peasants and middle-class businessmen, the latter recognizable by their tall hats. Although caricature is hinted at in this work, the painting is a realistic portrayal of the growing democratization of society brought on by the railway.

In contrast to Daumier with his urban scenes, Jean-François Millet (1814–1875) painted the countryside near Barbizon, a French village south of Paris where an artists' colony was located in the 1840s. Millet and the Barbizon school were influenced by the English Romantic Constable, whose painting *The Hay Wain* had been admired in the Paris Salon of 1824 (see Figure 17.11). Unlike Constable, who treated human beings only incidentally in his landscapes, Millet made the rural folk and their labors his primary subject.

One of Millet's early Barbizon paintings was *The Sower*, which he exhibited in the Salon of 1850 (Figure 18.14). This work depicts a youth casting seeds into a freshly plowed field; dimly visible in the back-

FIGURE 18.14 JEAN-FRANÇOIS MILLET. *The Sower.* 1850. Oil on canvas, 40 × 32½". Museum of Fine Arts, Boston. Gift of Quincy Adams Shaw through Quincy A. Shaw, Jr. and Mrs. Marian Shaw Haughton. *Like Daumier's peasant travelers, Millet's farm hand is depicted as a social type rather than as an individual. But Millet's Realist vision of peasant life is less forgiving than that of Daumier. He portrays the sower as little more than an animal and places him in a dark, nearly monochromatic landscape. Whereas Daumier's caricatures had provoked laughter or anger, Millet's painting produced fear.*

ground are a flock of birds and two oxen with a plowman. Ordinarily such a pastoral scene would have been a romantic idyll symbolizing the dignity of human work, but in Millet's canvas the toil degrades the laborer. Millet forces attention on the solitary peasant, isolated from the world in a desolate landscape. The resulting image is that of a hulking presence, powerfully muscled and striding boldly across the canvas. Salon critics reacted by calling the picture "savage" and "violent."

In *The Gleaners* Millet turned to another type of farm worker, the women laborers whose daily bread depended on scavenging the grain left from the regular harvest (Figure 18.15). These women were part of a depressed class that had fallen hopelessly behind in France's rush into industrialism. Millet's portrayal

FIGURE 18.13 HONORÉ DAUMIER. *The Third-Class Carriage.* Ca. 1862. Oil on canvas, 25¾ × 35½". Metropolitan Museum of Art, New York. Bequest of Mrs. H. O. Havemeyer, 1929. *Close study of this oil painting reveals Daumier's genius for social observation: the mother's doting expression, the old woman's stoicism, and the melancholy profile of the top-hatted man seen in profile. None of the figures is individualized, however, for all represent social types. Despite the cramped quarters, Daumier stresses the isolation of individual travelers by the jumbled heads in the back and the staring eyes that do not see.*

FIGURE 18.15 JEAN-FRANÇOIS MILLET. *The Gleaners.* 1857. Oil on canvas, 33 × 44".
Louvre, Paris. *Millet's realistic scenes of peasants were inspired in part by the biblical
quotation, "In the sweat of thy face shalt thou eat bread . . ." (Genesis 3:19). In The
Gleaners he expresses this idea with controlled beauty, depicting the women with simple
dignity despite their hard lot. The painting's earth tones reinforce the somber nature of the
subject.*

of stoop labor outraged some bourgeois critics, who
called him a "socialist." From today's perspective,
however, this painting is a sympathetic and truthful
record of a way of life that was rapidly disappearing.

If the Parisian art world was disturbed by the
paintings of Courbet and Millet, it was outraged by
the work of Édouard Manet (1832–1883), a painter
whose style is difficult to classify. He contributed to
the events which gradually discredited the Salon and
the Academy, encouraging painters to express themselves as they pleased, and thus was a bridge between the Realists of the 1860s and the group that
became known in the 1870s as the Impressionists. His
notoriety arose in 1863 when Emperor Napoleon III
authorized a *Salon des Refusés* (Salon of the Rejects)
for the hundreds of artists excluded from the official
exhibit. An audacious painting by Manet in this first

of the counter-Salons made him the talk of Paris and
the recognized leader of new painting.

Manet's "scandalous" painting is called *Le Déjeuner
sur l'Herbe*, which is usually translated as *Luncheon on
the Grass*, a title that the hostile audience attached to
the work in place of its actual name, *Le Bain* (The
Bath) (Figure 18.16). The woodland scene—two properly dressed young men accompanied by a seated
nude female and a second woman bathing in the
background—offended public decency. It seemed to
depict living French citizens in an erotic setting. In
actuality, however, the subject had roots deep in art
history. Two clothed males and two nude females
had been the subject of a painting by the sixteenth-
century Venetian painter Giorgione, and the pose of
the three central figures was borrowed from a work
by the Renaissance master Raphael.

More important than these historical connections, however, are Manet's artistic theories and practices, which strained against the boundaries of Realism. Unlike the other Realists, whose moral or ideological feelings were reflected in the subjects they painted, Manet moved toward a dispassionate art in which the subject and the artist have no necessary connection. What had confused bourgeois critics and audiences about *Le Déjeuner sur l'Herbe* was that they had tried to impose a little story onto what was simply the portrayal of four figures in a landscape with a still life (the picnic on the left). Manet's achievement was revolutionary, for he had discarded the intellectual themes of virtually all western art: reliance on anecdote, the Bible, Christian saints, politics, nostalgia, Greece and Rome, the Middle Ages, and sentimental topics. With his work, he opened the door to an art that had no other purpose than to depict what the artist chose to paint. In sum, Manet was the first truly modern painter.

FIGURE 18.16 ÉDOUARD MANET. *Le Déjeuner sur l'Herbe (Luncheon on the Grass).* 1863. Oil on canvas, 7' × 8'10". Louvre. *The bourgeoisie adopted many of the pleasures that had previously been the exclusive privilege of nobility. A leisure activity that particularly attracted the middle-class public was the public outing, and the holiday picnic was established as a suitable subject for painting by the mid–nineteenth century. One of the reasons for the furor surrounding Manet's painting was that he seemed to suggest that such picnics furnished opportunities for immoral behavior. To outraged bourgeois critics, Manet's picnic seemed a lewd joke.*

FIGURE 18.17 MATHEW BRADY. President Abraham Lincoln and General George B. McClellan. 1861. Library of Congress. *This hastily arranged photograph underscores the tension between the president and his general. The impression is confirmed by the men's isolation in the tent, their awkward composure, and their lack of sympathy for one another. Brady stresses a moral difference between the two subjects by portraying Lincoln in sunlight and McClellan in shadow. Brady's intuitive genius turned what could have been a routine double portrait into an incisive psychological study.*

Photography

One of the forces impelling painting toward a more realistic and detached style of expression was the invention of the camera. Two types of camera techniques were perfected in 1839. In France, Louis-Jacques-Mandé Daguerre (1787–1851) discovered a chemical method for implanting images on silvered copper plates to produce photographs called daguerrotypes. In England, William Henry Fox Talbot (1800–1877) was pioneering the negative-positive process of photographic images, which he called "the pencil of nature." Not only did the camera undermine the reality of the painted image, but it quickly created a new art form, photography. From the beginning, many photographers began to experiment with the camera's artistic potential, though only recently has photography received wide acceptance as serious art.

Among these early photographers was the American Mathew Brady (about 1823–1896), who abandoned his spacious Broadway studio in New York to create a pictorial record of the American Civil War. Brady was able to transform banal scenes into haunting images of psychological insight, as in his photograph of President Abraham Lincoln visiting General George B. McClellan on the battlefield. Their meeting arose because Lincoln, disappointed in the progress of the war, wanted to have a personal word with his general. Brady's photograph subtly conveys the tension between the two men. Lincoln's grim face shows his moral determination, while McClellan stares quizzically at the Commander-in-Chief. A few days after this photograph was taken, McClellan was relieved of his command (Figure 18.17).

Music

Originating shortly after 1800, Romantic music reigned supreme from 1830 until 1871. Romantic works grew longer and more expressive as composers forged styles reflecting their individual feelings. To achieve unique voices, Romantic composers adopted varied techniques such as shifting rhythms, complex musical structures, discordant passages, and minor keys. In addition, with the spread of nationalistic feelings across Europe, especially after 1850, composers began to incorporate folk songs, national anthems, and indigenous dance rhythms into their music. Nonetheless, throughout this era Romantic composers stayed true to the established forms of Classical music composition—the opera, the sonata, and the symphony.

Although a Baroque creation, opera rose to splendid heights under Romanticism. Partly accountable for this striking development was that the bourgeois public, bedazzled by opera's spectacle and virtuoso singers, eagerly embraced this art form. Operatic composers sometimes wrote works specifically to show off the vocal wizardry of the performers. So prolific were these musicians that they wrote over half of the operas still performed today.

Romanticism had an important impact on opera. The orchestras for operas became larger, inspiring composers to write long, elaborate works requiring many performers. Composers also began to integrate the entire musical drama, creating orchestral music that accentuated the actions and thoughts of the characters on stage. Most importantly, the form of opera itself was transformed. At first composers imitated the form that they had inherited, writing operas in which a series of independent musical numbers, that is, *arias* (melodious songs), alternated with *recitatives* (text either declaimed in the rhythms of natural speech with slight musical variations or sung with fuller musical support). The Italian composer Verdi brought this type of opera to its peak, advancing beyond the mechanical aria-recitative alternation. But even as Verdi was being lionized for his operatic achievements, a new style of opera was arising in Germany in the works of Wagner, which were written not as independent musical sections, but as continuous musical scenes.

Giuseppe Verdi (1813–1901), Italy's greatest composer of opera, followed the practice of the time and borrowed many of his plots from the works of Romantic writers. He was particularly attracted to complicated plots filled with passion and full-blooded emotionalism.

One of the operas that brought him international fame was *Rigoletto* (1851), based on a play by Victor Hugo. What makes this opera such a favorite with audiences are its strong characters, its beautiful melodies, and its dramatic unity—features that typify Verdi's mature works. A study in Romantic opposites, this work tells of a crippled court jester, Rigoletto, deformed physically but emotionally sensitive, coarse in public but a devoted parent in private. The jester's daughter Gilda is also a study in contrasts, torn between love for her father and attraction to a corrupt noble.

In *Rigoletto* Verdi continues to alternate arias with sung recitatives, but overall his music for the orchestra skillfully underscores the events taking place on stage. In addition, he employs musical passages to illustrate the characters' psychology, using convoluted orchestral backgrounds to accompany Rigoletto's monologues, for example, or shifts from simple to showy musical settings to demonstrate Gilda's conflicted nature. Other operas followed, enhancing Verdi's mounting celebrity: *La Traviata* in 1853, based on a play written by the French Romantic writer Alexander Dumas the younger, and *Aida* in 1871, commissioned by Egypt's ruler and first performed in the Cairo opera house.

Romantic opera reached its climax in the works of Richard Wagner (1813–1883), who sought a union of music and drama. A political revolutionary in his youth and a visionary thinker, Wagner was deeply impressed by the Romantic idea that the supreme expression of artistic genius occurred only when the arts were fused together. To this end he not only composed his own scores, but wrote the **librettos**, or texts, frequently conducted the music, and even planned the opera house in Bayreuth, Germany, where his later works were staged.

Wagner's major musical achievement was the monumental project entitled *The Ring of the Nibelung* (1853–1874), a cycle of four operas—or **music dramas**, as Wagner called them—that fulfilled his ideal of fusing music, verse, and staging. In these works the distinction between arias and recitatives was nearly erased, giving a continuously flowing melodic line. This unified sound was marked by the appearance of recurring themes associated with particular characters, things, or ideas, known as **leitmotifs**. Based on a popular Romantic source—medieval Norse myths—the *Ring* also reflected Wagner's belief that opera should be moral. In its totality the *Ring* cycle warns against overweening ambition, its plot relating a titantic struggle for world mastery in which both human beings and gods are destroyed because of their lust for power. Wagner may have been addressing this warning to the Faustian spirit that dominated capitalism in the industrial age—a message that went unheeded.

Another German, Johannes Brahms (1833–1897), dominated orchestral and chamber music after 1850 in much the same way that Wagner did opera. Unlike Wagner, Brahms was no musical innovator. A classical Romanticist, he took up the mantle vacated by Beethoven, and he admired the Baroque works of Bach. In Vienna, his adopted home, Brahms became the hero of the traditionalists who opposed the new music of Wagner. Neglecting the characteristic Romantic works of operas and program music, he won fame with his symphonies and chamber music. His individual sound is mellow, always harmonic, delighting equally in joy and melancholy.

Despite his conservative musicianship, Brahms's work incorporates many Romantic elements. Continuing the art-song tradition established by Schubert, he introduced folk melodies into his pieces. In his instrumental works he often aimed for the expressiveness of the human voice, the "singing" style preferred in Romanticism. He was also indebted to the Romantic style for the length of his symphonies, the use of rhythmic variations in all of his works, and, above all, the rich lyricism and songfulness of his music.

The Legacy of the Bourgeois Age

We in the modern world still live in the shadow of the bourgeois age. From this period come the political consequences caused by the unification of Germany in 1871, which upset the balance of power on the Continent, unleashed German militarism, and led to smoldering French resentment at Germany. The two world wars of the twentieth century had their seeds in these events. On the intellectual front this period gave birth to Marx's analysis of history, Darwin's theory of evolution, and Pasteur's work in immunology and microbiology. With liberalism in the ascendant, the middle-class values of hard work, thrift, ambition, and respectability became paramount, as did the notion that the individual should take precedence over the group.

On the artistic level this period introduced the camera and the art of photography, revived Gothic architecture, made Realism the reigning style, and inaugurated the high-tech tradition in art and architecture with London's Crystal Palace. Perhaps the most far-reaching development during this time was Manet's adoption of the artistic credo of "art for art's sake," a bold move followed by other artists in the post-1871 period.

KEY CULTURAL TERMS

Utilitarianism	*aria*
socialism	*recitative*
higher criticism	*libretto*
evolution	*music drama*
Realism	leitmotif

SUGGESTIONS FOR FURTHER READING

PRIMARY SOURCES

BALZAC, H. DE. *Cousin Bette*. Translated by M. A. Crawford. New York: Penguin, 1972. A representative novel from the *Human Comedy* series, Balzac's monumental commentary on French bourgeois society in the post-Napoleonic era.

————. *Père Goriot*. Translated by J. M. Sedgwick. New York: Dodd, Mead, 1954. Another of the best-known of Balzac's almost one hundred novels in the Human Comedy series.

BRONTË, C. *Jane Eyre*. Edited and with an introduction by M. Smith. London: Oxford University Press, 1973. A classic of Romanticism, this novel deals with a theme dear to the hearts of nineteenth-century women readers, the life and tribulations of a governess.

BRONTË, E. *Wuthering Heights*. Edited and with an introduction by I. Jack. New York: Oxford University Press, 1983. A classic of Romanticism, this novel recounts the doomed affair of the socially mismatched but passionate soulmates, Heathcliff and Catherine.

DICKENS, C. *Hard Times*. London: Methuen, 1987. A depiction of life in the new industrialized cities, this grim tale of forced marriage and its consequences reveals what happens when practical, utilitarian thinking replaces human values.

————. *Oliver Twist*. London: Longman, 1984. Dickens's moving tale of the orphan Oliver and his experiences among London's poor in the sordid conditions of the 1830s.

DOSTOEVSKY, F. *Crime and Punishment*. Translated by S. Monas. New York: New American Library, 1980. A masterpiece of psychological insight, this gripping tale of murder explores the themes of suffering, guilt, redemption, and the limits of individual freedom.

————. *The Brothers Karamazov*. Translated by D. Magarshack. New York: Penguin, 1982. In his novel Dostoevsky deals with broad metaphysical and psychological themes, such as the right of human beings to reject the world made by God because it contains so much evil and suffering, as dramatized through the actions and personalities of the brothers and their father.

ELIOT, G. *Middlemarch*. New York: Penguin, 1965. This classic of Realist fiction explores the psychology and growth in self-understanding of the principal characters.

FLAUBERT, G. *Madame Bovary*. Translated by A. Russell. New York: Penguin, 1961. One of the first Realist novels, and possibly the finest, Flaubert's work details the heroine's futile attempts to find happiness in a stifling bourgeois environment.

GASKELL, E. C. *North and South*. New York: Dutton, 1975. A portrait of economic and social disparities in mid-nineteenth-century England.

HUGO, V. *Les Misérables*. Translated by L. Wraxall. New York: Heritage Press, 1938. A good English version of Hugo's epic-length novel of social injustice in early nineteenth-century France.

MARX, K., and ENGELS, F. *Basic Writings on Politics and Philosophy*. Edited by L. Feuer. Boston: Peter Smith, 1975. A representative selection of their prodigious writings, which challenged industrial capitalism in the mid–nineteenth century and provided the theoretical basis for socialism and communism.

MILL, J. S. *On Liberty*. New York: Norton, 1975. Mill's examination of the relationship between the individual and society.

————. *Utilitarianism*. Indianapolis, Ind.: Hackett, 1978. A defense of the belief that the proper goal of government is to provide the greatest happiness for the greatest number.

TOLSTOY, L. *War and Peace*. Translated by L. and A. Maude. London: Oxford University Press, 1984. Tolstoy's epic novel traces the impact of the Napoleonic wars on the lives of his Russian characters and explores such themes as the role of individual human beings in the flow of history.

RICH, N. *The Age of Nationalism and Reform, 1850–1890*. New York: Norton, 1976. A country-by-country survey assessing the impact of nationalism.

SCHUMPETER, J. A. *Capitalism, Socialism, and Democracy*. 6th ed. London: Unwin, 1987. Sets complex debates in a broad political and cultural framework.

STEARNS, P. *European Society in Upheaval: Social History Since 1800*. New York: Macmillan, 1967. A history of the consequences of industrialization by a leading scholar sympathetic to industrialized life.

SECONDARY SOURCES

BAUMER, F. L. *Modern European Thought: Continuity and Change in Ideas, 1600–1950*. New York: Macmillan, 1977. Covers the major schools of thought over the course of four centuries and shows how they address the perennial questions of philosophy.

BINKLEY, R. C. *Realism and Nationalism, 1852–1871*. New York: Harper & Row, 1935. A solid cultural history that has held up over the decades.

BRIDENTHAL, R., and KOONZ, C., eds. *Becoming Visible: Women in European History*. Boston: Houghton-Mifflin, 1977. A collection of twenty essays by scholars with the common aim of uncovering the hitherto neglected role of women in European history, ranging from ancient Crete and Sumer to Nazi Germany.

BRION, M. *Romantic Art*. New York: McGraw-Hill, 1960. A comprehensive survey covering European and American Romantic art; readable and well illustrated.

CLARK, T. J. *The Absolute Bourgeois: Artists and Politics in France, 1848–1851*. London: Thames and Hudson, 1973. An indispensable analysis of artistic developments in this period; the text stresses the intersection of economics, politics, and art.

HEILBRONNER, R. L. *The Worldly Philosophers*. New York: Touchstone, 1980. This informative and entertaining collection of short biographies of the leading minds in early economic thought is practically a classic.

HENDERSON, W. O. *The Industrialization of Europe, 1780–1914*. London: Thames and Hudson, 1969. Shows in text and illustrations how industrialization spread across the Continent.

HOBSBAWM, E. J. *Industry and Empire: From 1750 to the Present Day*. New York: Penguin, 1969. Traces the origins and impact of the Industrial Revolution in England.

HOUGHTON, W. E. *The Victorian Frame of Mind, 1830–1870*. New Haven: Yale University Press, 1963. A penetrating analysis of Victorian emotional, moral, and intellectual attitudes as based on the public and private writings of the era's major figures.

LICHTHEIM, G. *A Short History of Socialism*. New York: Praeger, 1969. This brief work focuses on the ideas favoring collectivism that were compatible with the attitudes of the industrial working class; for the beginning student.

SUGGESTIONS FOR LISTENING

JOHANNES BRAHMS (1833–1897).

Brahms's four symphonies (1876, 1877, 1883, and 1885) demonstrate the disciplined style and majestic lyricism that made him the leader of the anti-Wagner school. Brahms also excelled in chamber music, a genre usually ignored by Romantic composers. His chamber works show him to be a worthy successor to Beethoven, especially in the Piano Quartet in G minor, Op. 25 (late 1850s), the Clarinet Quintet in B minor, Op. 115 (1891), and three string quartets, composed between 1873 and 1876.

GIUSEPPE VERDI (1813–1901).

Primarily a composer of opera, Verdi worked exclusively in the Romantic tradition, bringing to perfection the style of opera that alternated arias and recitatives. His operatic subjects are based mainly on works by Romantic authors, such as *Il Corsaro* (*The Corsair*) (1848), adapted from Lord Byron, and *La Traviata* (*The Lost One*) (1853), adapted from Alexandre Dumas the younger. Shakespeare, whom the Romantics revered as a consummate genius, inspired the librettos for *Otello* (1887) and *Falstaff* (1893). Like the Romantics generally, Verdi had strong nationalistic feelings that he expressed in, for example, *Les Vêpres Siciliennes* (*The Sicilian Vespers*) (1855) and *La Battaglia di Legnano* (*The Battle of Legnano*) (1849).

RICHARD WAGNER (1813–1883).

Wagner created a new form, music drama, that fused all the arts—a development that reflected his theory that music should serve the theater. His early style may be heard in *Der Fliegende Holländer* (*The Flying Dutchman*) (1842), which alternates arias and recitatives in the traditional way. By 1850, in *Lohengrin*, he was moving toward a more comprehensive operatic style, using continuously flowing music and the technique of recurring themes, called *leitmotifs*. He reached his maturity with *Der Ring des Nibelungen* (*The Ring of the Nibelung*), written between 1853 and 1874; in this cycle of four operas he focuses on the orchestral web with the arias being simply one factor in the constantly shifting sounds. His works composed after 1853 pushed the limits of Classical tonality and became the starting point for modern music.

19

THE AGE OF
EARLY MODERNISM
1871—1914

Between 1871 and 1914, the European continent enjoyed an almost unprecedented period of tranquility, completely free of military conflict. Many people thought that Europe had entered the new age predicted by the optimistic Enlightenment thinkers—a halcyon period in which war was no longer used as an instrument of national policy. But hindsight allows us to see this period as an age of rampant nationalism, aggressive imperialism, and burgeoning militarism, culminating with the outbreak of World War I in 1914. The prolonged and violent nature of that global struggle put to rest forever the unclouded optimism of prewar Europe.

At the same time the phenomenon known as "modern life" was emerging—the comfortable existence shared by an ever-growing proportion of society. Modern life evolved as people shared in the fruits of the Second Industrial Revolution and in the benefits of citizenship in strong nation-states. And in the cultural realm the period witnessed the birth of *Modernism*, a movement that rejected both the Greco-Roman and the Judeo-Christian legacies and tried to forge a new perspective, a vision of life true to modern secular experience. Modernism lasted for about one hundred years, going through three distinct stages. During its first phase (1871–1914), which is treated in this chapter, artists, writers, and thinkers established the movement's principles. The second phase, the zenith of Modernism (1914–1945), is the subject of Chapter 20; and the exhaustion and decline

of the movement, the third phase (1945–1970), is covered in Chapter 21.

EUROPE'S RISE TO WORLD LEADERSHIP

The period between 1871 and 1914 was an age of stupendous change and stress stimulated by imperialism, nationalism, and militarism. Acting as a catalyst was the middle class, which controlled the states of central and western Europe (Figure 19.1). Less affected by these forces were the relatively unindustrialized countries of eastern Europe, still dominated by landed gentry, agrarian economies, and weak centralized governments.

Imperialism—the quest for colonies—began as a search for new markets and increased wealth. Success over less developed areas was virtually assured by the superiority of European technology, military might, and management skills. In short order, Europe became a world power encircling the globe with a network of interlocking political and economic interests. Ironically, the competitive spirit that world-power status produced divided Europe against itself, transforming most countries into massed armed camps. Combined with ever-growing feelings of nationalism, imperialistic and militaristic impulses created an atmosphere in which rival states seemed incapable of stopping the headlong rush to war.

FIGURE 19.1 CLAUDE MONET. *Rue Montorgueil, Decked Out With Flags, 1878. 1878. Oil on canvas, 30 × 20½". Musée des Beaux Arts, Rouen, France. This colorful depiction of a street festival by Monet, a founder of Impressionism, is a fitting symbol of the first stage of Modernism. Such public spectacles were now flourishing across Europe, as the masses rose from obscurity to high visibility in urban life. The French flags lining the streets, represented by Monet as bright spots of color, give evidence of the importance of nationalistic feelings during this period.*

The Second Industrial Revolution and the Making of Modern Life

The Second Industrial Revolution differed in several major ways from its predecessor. For one thing, Great Britain, the world's industrial leader since 1760, now faced strong competition from Germany and the United States; factories even began to spring up in Russia and central and southern Europe. For another, science and research had a stronger influence than in the basically pragmatic first revolution. For example, scientific research into chemicals led to many new and improved industrial products, including fertilizers, synthetic dyes, soap, and paper. Scientific experimentation also led to a better, less expensive grade of steel, which began to replace iron in basic construction. Finally, steam and water power gave way to newer forms of industrial energy. Electricity ran machines in factories, offices, and homes, and electric trains began to displace horse-drawn streetcars in the cities. The internal combustion engine replaced the steam engine in ships and in the early 1900s gave birth to the automobile and the airplane. Oil began to be used as an energy source, though only later did it overcome coal's supremacy.

Technology, the practical offspring of science, was also busily reshaping the world. In communications, the wireless superseded the telegraph, the telephone made its debut, and national and international postal services were set up. Typewriters and tabulators made office and business practices more efficient. The rotary press enabled newspaper owners to print and sell thousands of copies of their papers per day to an increasingly literate public.

The Second Industrial Revolution affected almost every aspect of the economy. In transportation, more efficient steam engines meant lower transportation costs and cheaper products. Refrigeration techniques permitted perishable foods to be carried great distances without spoilage. Advertising became a significant source of revenue for publishers and at the same time a powerful force in the consumer economy. As a result of advertising, consumers were stimulated to buy household furnishings, ready-to-wear clothing, and prepared foods. Increased wealth meant more leisure, and new recreations cropped up, such as seaside resorts, music halls, movies, and bicycles—all contributing to the phenomenon known as modern life.

Industrialized cities with their promises of well-paying jobs, comfortable lives, and noisy entertainments were like magnets to the residents of small towns and farms, who flocked to the urban centers and cast off their rural ways. By 1900 nearly 30 percent of the people in the West lived in cities. New York and London were approaching four million, Berlin and Paris had at least two million, and Madrid, Brussels, and Birmingham numbered one million inhabitants each (Figure 19.2).

FIGURE 19.2 CAMILLE PISSARRO. *The Great Bridge to Rouen.* 1896. Oil on canvas, 29³⁄₁₆ × 36½". Carnegie Museum of Art, Pittsburgh. Purchase. *Pissarro's painting captures the energy of Rouen and transforms this French river town into a symbol of the new industrial age. Contributing to the sense of vitality are the belching smokestack, the bridge crowded with hurrying people, and the dock workers busy with their machinery. The fast pace is underscored by the Impressionist technique of "broken color," giving an immediacy to the scene.*

FIGURE 19.3   CLEMENT FLOWER. *The Empire Promenade.* 1902. Radio Times Hulton Picture Gallery, London. *Early twentieth-century England was a time of elegant sophistication and glittering social gatherings for the upper classes. Evening performances at the theater were events where it was important to be seen with the right people, dressed in the latest fashions. This style of life was swept away by the Great War in 1914, though its memory survived as a reminder of a brilliant bygone age.*

As cities grew in industrialized countries, the standard of living improved, especially for the middle class. Much of this prosperity was attributable to a general decline in prices and to steady—albeit low—wages and salaries. Within this period of general prosperity, however, were two quite distinct phases. The first (1873–1894) was characterized by a protracted depression. Manufacturers shifted to consumer goods, transportation costs declined, and international trade, notably in farm produce, soared. As a result, prices dropped sharply, causing hardship to farmers but benefiting consumers. The second phase (1895–1914) was a period of boom years as both prices and profits rose and unemployment went down (Figure 19.3).

While the middle classes enjoyed unprecedented prosperity, misery mounted among urban workers despite the creation of state-funded social welfare programs. As urban slums grew more crowded, living conditions worsened. The presence of squalor in the midst of plenty pricked the conscience of many citizens, who began to work for better housing and less dangerous working conditions for laborers. When these reforming efforts proved inadequate, the

FIGURE 19.4   EYRE CROWE. *The Dinner Hour at Wigan.* 1874. Oil on canvas, 30 × 42¼". Manchester City Art Gallery, Manchester, England. *Social possibilities for English women opened up to some degree during this era. This painting depicts a factory scene in which the young female workers gain a brief respite from their tasks. A few talk together quietly, while others remain apart or finish a chore. They all seem dwarfed by the huge mill in the background, a towering symbol of industrial power.*

stage was set for the birth of labor unions and their best weapon, the strike.

One of the reforms directed to the working class did succeed in a spectacular fashion: the founding of secular public education. Inspired by the liberal belief that religion was a private matter, reformers wanted to take education out of the hands of the church. They argued that public schools, financed by taxes and supervised by state agencies, would prepare workers for jobs in industrialized society and create an informed citizenry—two basic needs of modern life. Although the pattern was uneven, every Western country made some effort to spread literacy to the masses. An unanticipated result of the establishment of public school systems was that age-old ties between children and parents were loosened. Families were still expected to foster social and moral values, but in certain areas of their lives children became wards of the state.

The position of women also changed dramatically. New employment opportunities opened up for them in teaching, nursing, business offices, and retailing. Since some of these jobs required special skills, colleges and degree programs were developed to teach them to women. Many young females still turned to domestic service, but new household appliances reduced the need for servants. Woman labor in factories was now regulated by state laws, but the wives of small shopkeepers continued to work long hours in family businesses (Figure 19.4).

A small number of women reformers, primarily from the middle class, advocated more freedom for females, continuing a tradition that had begun on a limited scale prior to 1871. They launched successful campaigns to revise property and divorce laws, giving women greater control over their wealth and their lives. In several countries they founded suffrage movements, using protests and marches to dramatize their situation. After a vigorous, occasionally violent, campaign, women won the right to vote in Great Britain in 1918 and in the United States in 1920.

Response to Industrialism: Politics and Crises

After 1871 liberalism was in retreat in industrialized countries, its assumptions challenged from many quarters. Except in Britain and the United States, liberals were under siege in national legislatures both by socialists—who wanted more central planning and more state services for the workers—and by conservatives—who feared the masses and supported militant nationalism as a way to unify their societies. After 1900 political parties representing workers and

trade unionists further threatened the liberals' hold on power. Although never actually ruling, these workingmen's parties were strong enough to pass laws aimed at correcting the worst social problems of industrialism.

Most embarrassing of all—to liberals, at any rate—events seemed to discredit liberal theory. Theoretically, under free trade the population ought to decline or at least remain stable, and the economy ought to operate harmoniously, but neither happened. Population was surging and industrial capitalism was plagued by repeated uncertainty. Many observers therefore concluded that the so-called laws of liberal economics did not work.

Domestic Policies in the Heavily Industrialized West Whether they relied on liberal principles or not, Germany, France, Great Britain, and the United States all faced serious domestic crises during this period. Founded in 1871, the German Reich, or Empire, moved toward unity under the astute leadership of its first chancellor, Otto von Bismarck, and the new kaiser, or emperor, William I (1871–1888), former King of Prussia (Figure 19.5). Despite the illusion of parliamentary rule, foreign affairs and military policy were under the control of the chancellor, his ministers, and the kaiser. Many of the ruling elite were Prussian *Junkers*, owners of vast estates who clung to the old ways, and they set the tone of the imperial reich: conservative, militaristic, and nationalistic.

In France, the Third Republic was founded after the Second Empire's humiliating defeat by Germany in 1871. The government had made a remarkable recovery by 1875, although it remained hopelessly divided. The ceaseless struggle between republicans and monarchists was reflected in the regime's many prime ministers and coalition cabinets. Regardless of their politics, however, the republic's leaders initiated laws to correct the most glaring social injustices in order to counteract the rise of workers' political parties, the spread of socialism, and the threat of syndicalism—a movement whose central belief was that a general strike would bring down the capitalist state and lead to a more just form of government. Yet the workers' complaints, as well as other groups' demands, never seemed to be adequately addressed, and the specter of Napoleon or some other "man on horseback" haunted the Third Republic throughout its days. The nation's liberal center gradually evaporated, creating bitter deadlocks between socialists and conservatives that no government could resolve.

After 1895, the divisiveness in France intensified as a result of the Dreyfus Affair. The only Jewish member on the French general staff, Captain Alfred Dreyfus (1859–1935) was accused of treason by his

FIGURE 19.5 ANTON VON WERNER. *The Proclamation of the King of Prussia as German Emperor at Versailles.* 1871. Oil on canvas. London. *This painting commemorates the moment when the German Empire was proclaimed and King William of Prussia became its first emperor. Von Werner uses reflections from Versailles' famed Hall of Mirrors to make the stirring scene more theatrical, and added drama comes from the raised swords of the officers. The strong presence of the army was prophetic of the dominant role the military was destined to play in the German Empire.*

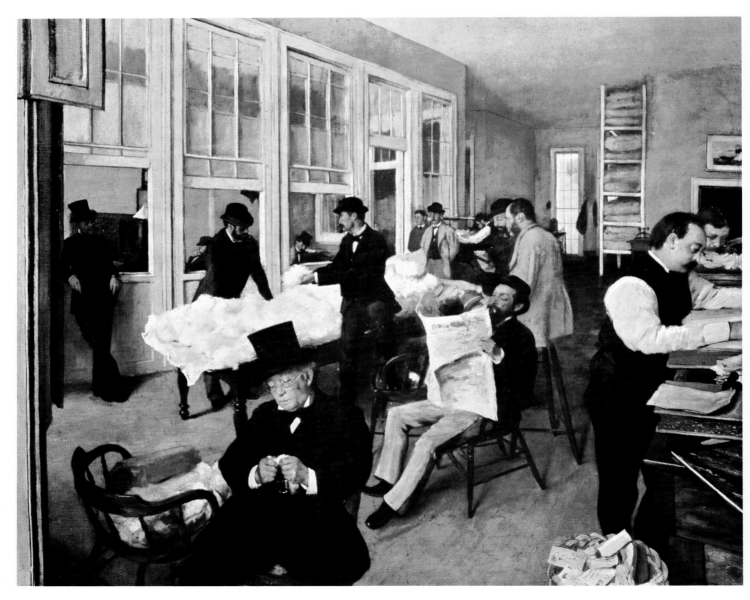

fellow army officers. Supported by intellectuals like Emile Zola, Dreyfus was later exonerated when it was shown that the charge has been fabricated. This case splintered the nation along political, religious, and social lines.

In contrast to the relative failures of the German Reich and France's Third Republic, Great Britain was remarkably successful in solving its domestic problems during this period. Controlled by political parties that represented the upper and middle classes, the British government passed social legislation that improved the working and living conditions of many poor families and created opportunities for mobility through a state secondary-school system. As in Germany and France, these reform efforts did not prevent workers from forming their own political party. British workers joined with the Fabians, a group of intellectuals who believed in evolutionary socialism, to found the Labour party. Not until after World War I, however, did Britain see its first Labour government.

Across the Atlantic, the United States began to challenge British industrial supremacy. America's rapidly expanding economy allowed big business to dominate politics at all levels until the reform movements of the early 1900s (Figure 19.6). These movements, spurred by America's democratic tradition, temporarily derailed the power of the large business conglomerations called trusts.

The geographical split that had characterized America's economy at midcentury now grew wider. The Northeast was the country's most prosperous region and the site of the most productive industries. Coming up rapidly in second place was the West, fueled by a railroad boom and agriculture. Having never fully recovered from the Civil War, the South lagged behind and remained an economic backwater.

Another major development in America at this time was an enormous increase in population from overseas. In the last decades of the nineteenth century, Europeans came to America in the largest migration of human population ever recorded. These newcomers—after painful adjustments, particularly in the crowded slums of the eastern cities—gradually entered the mainstream of American life. Largely

FIGURE 19.6   EDGAR DEGAS. *The Cotton Bureau in New Orleans.* 1873. Oil on canvas, 29⅛ × 36¼". Musée des Beaux-Arts, Pau, France. *By the third quarter of the nineteenth century the United States was offering challenges to English supremacy in world trade. The French painter Degas must have observed this scene—the interior of a cotton exchange in New Orleans—while visiting relatives in Louisiana. Whether consciously or not, Degas accurately depicted the social realities of this bourgeois work space: the capitalist idlers reading a newspaper, examining a cotton tuft, and lounging against a wall and, in contrast, the paid employees intent on their work.*

from eastern and central Europe, they transformed the United States into a much richer ethnic society than it had been before, making powerful contributions to the culture both as groups and individuals.

Domestic Policies in Central and Eastern Europe   The less industrialized states of central, southern, and eastern Europe faced problems even more difficult than those arising in Germany, France, and England. As the factory system made inroads into the region, these countries had no well-developed political and economic traditions for solving the resulting problems. Italy's response to industrialism was dictated by powerful regional interests that proved stronger than the unity the Italian kingdom had achieved at its founding in 1871. Led by weak prime ministers, the government allowed the northern areas to become industrialized, while the southern parts, including Sicily, remained in a semifeudal condition. As a result, the north, driven by an expanding middle class, moved far ahead of the agrarian south, with its vast estates worked by peasant labor.

In the Austro-Hungarian Empire the government's major problem was ethnic unrest, a direct outgrowth of the denial of political freedom to Slavic minorities, notably the Czechs and the Slovaks. In 1867 in the compromise that had created the Dual Monarchy, the Austrian Germans had given political parity to the Hungarians, allowing them free rein within their land. But nothing was done to address the simmering discontent among the Slavs. Even while the Dual Monarchy seethed with ethnic violence, however, its capital, Vienna, became a glittering symbol of Modernism. From *fin-de-siècle* ("end-of-the-century") Vienna came such familiar features of today's world as the cultural style called Expressionism and the psychology of Sigmund Freud.

Farther east, the Russian Empire slowly entered the industrial age, hampered by its vast size and its sluggish agrarian economy. Adding to Russia's woes were violent revolutionaries who despaired of any reform in this autocratic society. In 1881 an anarchist assassinated the liberal Czar Alexander II; his successor, Alexander III (1881–1894), was a tyrant who dismantled his predecessor's reforms. Under Nicholas II (1894–1917) the economy worsened and the imperial ministers grew more reactionary. Political parties were banned, and budding representative institutions ceased to exist. Disaster struck in 1905 when Japan defeated Russia in the brief Russo-Japanese War (1904–1905), setting off a short-lived revolution led by underpaid factory workers and starving peasants. By promising relief the czar weathered the storm, but few of his pledges were fulfilled. Tensions mounted as the state violently repressed dissent, and the imperial court grew dangerously isolated.

turned a corner, that a golden era was about to ~~~~ o This sanguine outlook was fueled by the spread of self-government, new technology, and advances in science that held the promise of unlimited moral and

pects to Nietzsche's thought. He believed in a new morality that glorified human life, creativity, and personal heroism. He forecast the appearance of a few

rights around the world. In order to maintain a high

FIGURE 19.9 EDVARD MUNCH. *The Scream.* 1893. *Oil on canvas, 36 × 29". Nasjonalgalleriet, Oslo. The Expressionists, whether writers, artists, or musicians, responded to the uncertainty of the modern world with images of despair, anxiety, and helplessness. The work of the Norwegian painter Edvard Munch provides a visual counterpart to the bleak and brooding plays of Strindberg and the terrifying stories of Kafka. Munch, whose paintings reflect a nightmarish vision of life as a tormented existence never free from pain, once said, "I hear the scream in nature."*

pages of his novels the aristocratic salons, the vulgar bourgeois world, and the riffraff of mistresses, prostitutes, and rich homosexuals. Today Proust's novels may be read in contradictory ways, as the supreme expression of a life lived for art or as the exemplification of a life empty of spiritual meaning.

Expressionist Literature Expressionism, the third of these styles, was the only one that did not originate in France, arising instead in Scandinavia in the works of the Swedish playwright August Strindberg and in central Europe in the fiction of Franz Kafka. Strindberg (1849–1912), having first achieved fame through Naturalistic drama, shifted to an Expressionist style in the 1890s. *The Dream Play* (first produced in 1907) is typical of his Expressionist dramas in employing generic figures with symbolic, all-purpose names ("Daughter," "Father," and so on), shadowy plots, and absurd fancies. In *The Dream Play* time and place became meaningless, as, for instance, when a love-sick soldier suddenly becomes old and shabby and his bouquet of flowers withers before the audience's eyes. Strindberg's innovative techniques were not meant to obscure his meaning but rather to initiate the public into new ways of seeing and understanding life.

The ultimate pioneer of Expressionism was Franz Kafka (1883–1924), whose strange, boldly symbolic stories invite the reader to question traditional concepts of reality. One of Kafka's most striking achievements is the short story *Metamorphosis* (1919), in which the hero awakens to discover that while asleep he has been transformed into a giant insect—a vivid image of an identity crisis and a gripping parable of what happens to a person who is suddenly perceived to be totally different from other people.

The Trial, a novel completed in 1914 and published in 1925, features a doomed main character with the generic name of Joseph K. An obscure minor government official, Joseph K. has his well-ordered world shattered when he is accused of a nameless crime. Unable to identify either his accusers or his misdeed and denied justice by the authorities, Joseph K. is finally executed by two bureaucrats in top hats. Kafka's faceless, powerless hero has become one of the most widely discussed figures of Modernism. In effect, Kafka has transformed his own alienation—as a German-speaking Jew from the Czech-speaking and Protestant section of predominantly Roman Catholic Austria—into a modern Everyman victimized by forces beyond human control (Figure 19.9).

The Advance of Science

The advance of science around the turn of the century was particularly strong in biology and chemistry. In biology, the Austrian monk Gregor Johann Mendel (1822–1884) had done groundbreaking research in 1865, but it was not until around 1900 that his discoveries were published, thus founding the new science of genetics. By applying mathematics to biological theory, Mendel proved the existence of dominant and recessive characters, and using the laws of probability he worked out the pattern for offspring over the generations. Mendelian laws were quickly applied to every kind of animal and plant.

In chemistry, the outstanding development was radiochemistry, the study of radioactive materials. The founder of this new discipline was Marie Sklodowska Curie (1867–1934), a Polish physicist and the first scientist to be awarded two Nobel prizes. Working with her French husband, Pierre Curie (1859–1906), in 1908 Madame Curie identified two new radioactive elements, polonium and radium. The isolation of radium stimulated research in atomic physics. Another contributor to radiochemistry was the German physicist Wilhelm Conrad Roentgen (1845–1923) whose 1895 discovery of X-rays led to their use in diagnostic medicine.

The discoveries in genetics and radiochemistry boosted the optimism and faith in progress that characterized this period, but developments in physics had the opposite effect, adding to the undercurrent of uncertainty and doubt that also existed. Three brilliant scientists—Max Planck, Niels Bohr, and Albert Einstein—launched a revolution that led other scientists to discard the previously accepted belief that Newton's laws of motion were universal and applied everywhere.

Max Planck (1858–1947) laid the foundation for modern physics in 1900 with research in quantum theory. His research called into question the wave theory of radiation, which dated from the 1700s. Working with hot objects, Planck observed that the radiative energy that emanated from a heat source did not issue in a smooth wave but in discrete bursts.

He measured each burst of radiation and computed a mathematical formula for expressing the released energy, a unit that he called a *quantum*—a word meaning a specified amount, derived from the Latin *quantus*, or "how much." When Planck could not fit his quantum formula into wave-theory physics, he realized the revolutionary nature of his discovery. Planck's quantum theory became a primary building block in the speculation of the second of the trio, Danish physicist Niels Bohr.

Bohr (1885–1962) was the prime mover in solving the mystery of the structure of the atom. When he began his research, the ancient Greek idea of the indivisible atom had already been laid to rest. Scientists in the early 1900s had proved that each atom is a neutral body containing a positive nucleus with negatively charged particles called electrons. And one researcher had speculated that electrons orbit a nucleus in much the same way that the planets move around the sun—suggesting a correspondence with Newtonian theory.

Until Bohr's theory of atomic structure was set forth in 1912, however, no one could explain how these miniature solar systems actually worked. Bohr's solution was based on bold assumptions: that an electron could revolve about a nucleus only in certain privileged orbits and that when it was in these orbits it did not emit radiation. Moving from these assumptions, he concluded that an electron radiated only when it leaped from orbit to orbit. Using Planck's quantum theory, he called these leaps quantum jumps, referring to the amount of radiative energy released. Bohr's discovery had tremendous consequences, leading eventually to the development of nuclear energy for weaponry and electrical generation.

German-born Albert Einstein (1879–1955) also did important theoretical work in atomic physics, but his most significant research in the early twentieth century involved the relationship between time and space. Newton had maintained that there existed absolute rest and absolute velocity, absolute space and absolute time. Einstein asserted that the only absolute in the universe is the speed of light, which is the same for all observers. He concluded that all motion is relative and that concepts of absolute space and absolute time are meaningless. If two systems move with relatively uniform motion toward each other, there exist two different spaces and two different times. He called this finding the special theory of relativity. This theory replaces Newtonian absolute space with a grid of light beams that in effect determines the meaning of space in each situation. Einstein's special theory was the first step in a reformulation of scientific concepts of space and time.

The Modernist Revolution in Art

After 1871 a revolution began in the arts and architecture whose aim was to discredit Renaissance ideals and replace them with Modernist principles. Although there were many trends within this revolution, in painting and sculpture it generally meant a shift from an art that reflected the natural world to one rooted in the artist's inner vision, from an art based on representational or naturalistic images to one devoted to nonrepresentational or nonobjective forms, and from an art focused on content to one dedicated to the process of creation itself. By the time the revolution in painting and sculpture was complete, artists had given up realism and made **abstraction** their ideal. In architecture, the Modernist revolution was less radical, though architects slowly turned away from the forms of the Greco-Roman and Gothic styles and created functional buildings devoid of decoration.

Impressionism The stylistic innovation in painting known as *Impressionism* began in the 1870s. In spite of owing much to Realism and even to Romanticism, this new style marked a genuine break with the realistic tradition that had dominated Western art since the fourteenth century. The Impressionists wanted to depict what they saw in nature, but they were inspired by the increasingly fast pace of modern life to portray fragmentary moments. They concentrated on the play of light over objects, people, and nature, breaking up seemingly solid surfaces, stressing vivid contrasts between colors in sunlight and shade, and depicting reflected light in all of its possibilities. Unlike earlier artists they did not want to observe the world from indoors. They abandoned the studio, painting in the open air and recording spontaneous impressions of their subjects instead of making outside sketches and then moving indoors to complete the work from memory.

Some of the Impressionists' painting methods were affected or made possible by technological advances. For example, the shift from the studio to the open air was made possible in part by the advent of cheap rail travel, which permitted easy and quick access to the countryside or seashore, and second by newly discovered chemical dyes and oils that led to collapsible paint tubes, which enabled artists to finish their paintings on the spot.

Although Impressionism was both a reflection and an outgrowth of industrial society, it was at the same time indebted to the past. From Realism the Impressionist painters learned to find beauty in the everyday world. From the Barbizon painters (a group of French landscape painters active in the mid–nineteenth century) they took the practice of painting in the open air. From the Romantics they borrowed the techniques of "broken color"—splitting up complex colors into their basic hues—and of using subtle color shadings to create a shimmering surface effect.

Impressionism acquired its name not from supporters but from angry art lovers who felt threatened by the new painting. The term *Impressionism* was born in 1874, when a group of artists who had been meeting and working together for some time organized an exhibition of their paintings in order to draw public attention to their work. Reaction from the public and press was immediate, and derisive. Among the 165 paintings exhibited was one called *Impression: Sunrise,* by Claude Monet (1840–1926). Viewed through hostile eyes, Monet's painting of a rising sun over a misty, watery scene seemed messy, slapdash, and an affront to good taste. Borrowing Monet's title, art critics extended the term *Impressionism* to the entire exhibit. In response, Monet and his twenty-nine fellow artists in the exhibit adopted the name as a badge of their unity, despite individual differences. From then until 1886 Impressionism had all the zeal of a "church," as the painter Renoir put it. The Impressionists gave eight separate art shows. Monet was faithful to the Impressionist creed until his death, although many of the others moved on to new styles.

Argenteuil, a Seine river town west of Paris, was important in the development of this style. Monet lived there from 1871 to 1878, and two other Impressionists, Auguste Renoir and Alfred Sisley, spent time nearby. Originally a sleepy backwater, Argenteuil in these years was undergoing radical changes. Not only were factories being thrown up—twenty in the 1870s alone—but crowds of pleasure seekers found the town a convenient half-hour train ride from Paris. With few exceptions, Monet's Argenteuil canvases present a carefree world of river vistas, rocking sailboats, and idle gaiety. His *Red Boats at Argenteuil* is typical of this period (Figure 19.10). Streaks of broken color in the water simulate dancing light, and the varied red shadings applied to the hulls convey the sun's weathering effect on the wood. That these techniques succeed so well shows the harmony between his scientific eye and painterly hand. His studies of changing light and atmosphere, whether depicting haystacks, Rouen cathedral, or water lilies (Figure 19.11), demonstrate his lifelong devotion to Impressionism.

Unlike Monet, Auguste Renoir (1841–1919) did not remain faithful to the Impressionist movement. In the early 1880s personal and aesthetic motives led him to move away from Impressionism and exhibit in the official Salon (when he could get his work accepted). In his modified style he shifted from a soft-focus image to a concentration on form, a move that brought quick support from art critics and wealthy patrons.

FIGURE 19.10 CLAUDE MONET. *Red Boats at Argenteuil.* 1875. Oil on canvas, 5' × 6'9". Louvre, Paris. *Monet's* Red Boats *illustrates the immediacy of Impressionism. With fresh eyes, the artist has transformed the substantial world of nature and its weighty human inhabitants into a constantly shifting, fragmented collection of daubs of broken color. As a result, everything in the painting, including the weathering boats, seems to be reduced to external appearances.*

FIGURE 19.11 CLAUDE MONET. *Water Lilies.* Ca. 1920. Oil on canvas, 16′ × 5′¹⁵⁄₁₆″. Carnegie Museum of Art, Pittsburgh. Acquired through the generosity of Mrs. Alan M. Scaife. *Knowledgeable about the art market and determined to escape a life of poverty, Monet produced nonthreatening works that appealed to conservative middle-class collectors. For these patrons he painted natural scenes, such as water lilies, that evoked pleasant memories of simple rural values. Begun in 1899, the water lily series occupied him for the rest of his life. Setting up his easel in his splendid garden at Giverny and working at different times of the day, Monet captured the effect of changing sunlight on this beloved subject.*

Painted around the time of his break with Impressionism, *The Luncheon of the Boating Party* demonstrates Renoir's splendid mastery of form (Figure 19.12). Its subject is a carefree summer outing on a restaurant terrace on an island in the Seine, the company being composed of the painter's friends, including fellow artists, a journalist, the cafe owner, and an actress. *The Boating Party* shows that Renoir had not given up—nor would he ever—his Impressionist ties, for his stress in this work on the fleeting, pleasure-filled moment was basic to the style, as was his use of broken color in a natural background. Nevertheless, what remained central to Renoir's creed were the foreground figures, treated clearly and with substance.

FIGURE 19.12 AUGUSTE RENOIR. *The Luncheon of the Boating Party.* 1881. Oil on canvas, 51 × 68″. Phillips Collection, Washington, D.C. *Renoir's return to traditional values is reflected in this vivid painting. He uses the restaurant's terrace to establish conventional perspective, the left railing forming a diagonal line that runs into the distance. He balances the composition, weaving the young men and women into a harmonious ensemble, painting some standing and others sitting. He also employs colors effectively, using orange, blue, and black to offset the vast expanses of white in the tablecloth and the men's shirts and women's blouses.*

FIGURE 19.13 BERTHE MORISOT. *Girl in a Boat with Geese.* Ca. 1889. Oil on canvas, 25¾ × 21½". National Gallery of Art, Washington, D.C. Ailsa Mellon Bruce Collection. *A dedicated Impressionist, Morisot exhibited in most of the school's shows. Her canvases typically emphasize the flatness of the picture's plane, in contrast to the three-dimensionality of paintings like Renoir's* Luncheon of the Boating Party. *Lack of depth was a prime characteristic of the Modernist revolution in painting.*

In contrast to Monet and Renoir, whose careers bloomed in poverty, Berthe Morisot (1841–1895) was a member of the upper middle class. Her wealth and artistic connections—Fragonard was her grandfather and Manet her brother-in-law—allowed her to apply herself to painting and play an important role in the founding of the Impressionist school. In her work she focused on atmosphere and the play of light on the human form, although she never sacrificed her subjects to the cause of color alone. Her trademark became sensitive and warm scenes of middle-class mothers and daughters in gardens or close friends relaxing at the seashore (Figure 19.13).

A few Americans also made significant contributions to this style. The most important of them was Mary Cassatt (1845–1926), a young woman who joined the Impressionist circle while studying painting in Paris. She was closest in artistic spirit to Renoir with her precise and intimate art. Like him, she often placed well-drawn figures in the foreground against an impressionistically rendered background. She preferred genre scenes, usually of mothers and children, as in *Mother about to Wash Her Sleepy Child* (Figure 19.14). The tender handling of this domestic scene was typical of her art.

Cassatt was from a prosperous, well-connected Philadelphia family, and it is largely through her social ties that Impressionist painting was introduced to America. She suggested to her wealthy friends that this art was worth collecting, and some of the most notable Impressionist works in American museums are there because of her influence.

Post-Impressionism The rebellious, experimental spirit instilled by the Impressionists had freed art from the tyranny of a single style. Artists now moved

FIGURE 19.14 MARY CASSATT. *Mother about to Wash Her Sleepy Child.* 1880. Oil on canvas, 39½ × 25¾". Los Angeles County Museum of Art. Bequest of Mrs. Fred Hathaway Bixby. *Cassatt's painting shows her allegiance to the Impressionist creed: the sense of a moment frozen in time, the vigorous brush work in the draperies, and the flat pictorial surface. Her subject also reflects the Impressionist interest in portraying the conditions of modern life.*

FIGURE 19.15 GEORGES SEURAT. *A Sunday Afternoon on the Island of La Grande Jatte.*
1884–1886. Oil on canvas, 6'9" × 10'1". Art Institute of Chicago. Helen Birch Bartlett
Memorial Collection, 1926. *Unlike most Impressionists, Seurat worked slowly and
methodically. In the case of* La Grande Jatte, *he spent years organizing the canvas and then
painting the thousands of dots required by the Pointillist technique. Such painstaking
attention to detail was necessary to achieve the harmonious effect his finished paintings
demonstrate.*

in many directions, united only by a common desire to extend the boundaries of Impressionism. This ambition signified the triumph of the Modernist notion that art must constantly change in order to reflect new historical conditions—the opposite of the Classical ideal of eternal truths. Impressionism was succeeded by *Post-Impressionism* (1886–1900), whose four most important artists are Georges Seurat, Paul Cézanne, Paul Gauguin, and Vincent van Gogh.

Like the Impressionists, Georges Seurat (1859–1891) painted the ordinary pleasures of Parisian life in a sunlit atmosphere, but his way of doing so was formulaic and theoretical, markedly different from the approach of, say, Monet. After studying scientific color theory, Seurat developed a technique known as *Pointillism* (or Divisionism), which meant applying to the canvas thousands of tiny dots of pure color juxtaposed in such a way that, when viewed from the proper distance, they merged to form a natural, harmonious effect of color, light, and shade. His most

famous Pointillist work is *A Sunday Afternoon on the Island of La Grande Jatte* (Figure 19.15), an affectionate, good-humored look at Parisians enjoying themselves. The technique may be novel and "scientific," but the composition is Classical and serene, with carefully placed and balanced figures and repeated curved shapes, visible in the umbrellas, hats, and other objects. Seurat's style led to a minor school of painters, but his influence was overshadowed by that of Cézanne.

Paul Cézanne (1839–1906), one of the pivotal figures in the history of Western art, was the prophet of abstraction in Post-Impressionism and a precursor of Cubism. With Édouard Manet, he is one of the founders of modern painting. He had exhibited with the original Impressionist group in 1874, but he had rejected the movement by 1878. He came to see the style as flawed because its depiction of nature lacked substance and weight, and he began a quest for a new way to portray nature so as to reveal its underlying solidity and order. After many experiments, Cézanne concluded that nature was composed of such geometric forms as cylinders, spheres, cubes, and cones. By trying to reveal this idea in his works, he opened up a new way of painting that has influenced art to the present day.

Cézanne's greatest works came after 1886, when he left Paris for his home in Aix-en-Provence in southern France in order to work in isolation. Among his favorite subjects was the nearby mountain, Mont Sainte-Victoire (Figure 19.16), which he painted many times. Like many of his later works, this painting points toward abstraction but never quite gives up representation. Amid the dense geometric forms in the picture's lower half, house shapes peek through daubs of green foliage, reminding the viewer that this is a realistic landscape. Later artists, like Kandinsky and Malevich, took up Cézanne's challenge of

FIGURE 19.16   PAUL CÉZANNE. *Mont Sainte-Victoire.* 1904–1906. Oil on canvas, 28⅞ × 36¼". Philadelphia Museum of Art. George W. Elkins Collection. *Although Cézanne was the founder of the Post-Impressionist movement that culminated in abstraction, he had a conservative approach to art. He claimed that he wanted to create paintings that had the solidity of the art in the museums, especially the works of the seventeenth-century painter Nicolas Poussin. Hence Cézanne continued to rely on line and geometric arrangement as well as on color and light, simplifying his paintings into austere images of order and peaceful color.*

telescoping the two-dimensional and the three-dimensional and created the first truly abstract paintings, the most visible signs of twentieth-century art (see Chapter 20).

The Post-Impressionist Paul Gauguin (1848–1903) began the movement known as primitivism—the term used to describe the West's fascination with non-Western culture as well as pre-Renaissance art. Gauguin's eccentric personal life also made him a legendary figure of Modernism. Rejecting the comforts of Parisian bourgeois life, he abandoned his career and his family and exiled himself to the French colony of Tahiti, living a decadent, bohemian existence.

Before moving to the South Pacific, Gauguin lived and painted among Breton peasants. He developed a personal style that favored flattened shapes and bright colors and avoided conventional perspective and modeling. He also became interested in non-Western, "primitive" religions, and many of his Tahitian works refer to indigenous beliefs and practices, as in *Manao Tupapau—The Spirit of the Dead Watching* (Figure 19.17). When exhibited in Paris, this painting created an uproar, for Western audiences were not accustomed to seeing dark-skinned nudes in art, and certainly not presented reclining on a bed as had been a custom for white-skinned subjects since the Renaissance (see Figure 16.6). Furthermore, the seated ghost at the right was a direct challenge to a secular world view. Today the shock caused by this and other paintings by Gauguin has subsided, and his role in art has been reevaluated. He is now honored for his introduction of other cultural traditions into Western art, which enriched its vocabulary, and for his expressive use of color.

With the Post-Impressionist Vincent van Gogh (1853–1890) the tradition of Expressionism begins to emerge in Western art, although he was not part of any of the various Expressionist schools of painters to be discussed later. "Expressionism" in his case meant that the work of art served as a vehicle for his private emotions to an unprecedented degree. Van Gogh sometimes allowed his moods to determine what colors to use and how to apply paint to canvas, a principle that led to a highly idiosyncratic style. Van

Gogh's life was filled with misfortune. Everything that this tormented Dutchman touched seemed to turn out badly except his painting, and even that had little recognition in his lifetime. In his early years he was rebuffed in his efforts to do missionary work among poverty-stricken Belgian coal miners. His attempts at friendship ended in failure, including a celebrated episode in the south of France with the painter Gauguin. Throughout his life overtures to women resulted in utter humiliation. In the end he became mentally unstable and committed suicide.

From his personal pain he created a memorably expressive style, however. Rejecting the smooth look of traditional painting and stirred by the colorful canvases of the Impressionists, he sometimes applied raw pigments with his palette knife or fingers instead of with a brush. His slashing strokes and brilliant colors often mirrored his mental states, giving the viewer a glimpse into his volatile personality. For instance, his *Self-Portrait with a Gray Hat* is dominated by shades of blue, suggesting his profound melancholy (Figure 19.18). The anguish in his eyes is reinforced by the vortex of color framing the head and the deep facial lines. In a sense, van Gogh's works constitute his psychological signature, and his style is perhaps the most easily recognizable one in Western art.

Fauvism, Cubism, and Expressionism   The preeminence of Paris as the fulcrum of Western culture was enhanced by the arrival of Henri Matisse and Pablo Picasso in about 1900. These innovative and prolific artists emerged as the leaders of the pre–World War I generation, later dominating the art world of the twentieth century in much the same way as Ingres and Delacroix had in the nineteenth century.

Henri Matisse (1869–1954) rose to fame in 1905 as a leader of ***Fauvism***. The *Fauves*—French for "wild beasts," a name their detractors gave to them—were a group of loosely aligned painters who exhibited together. Matisse's work, like that of his colleagues,

FIGURE 19.18   VINCENT VAN GOGH. *Self-Portrait with a Gray Hat.* 1887. Oil on canvas, 17¼ × 14¾". Vincent van Gogh Foundation/National Museum Vincent van Gogh, Amsterdam. *Van Gogh's self-absorption is reflected in the thirty-six self-portraits he painted during his eleven-year-long artistic career. Anguished and prone to mental breakdown, he must have found a measure of reassurance in recording the subtle changes in his own countenance. A constant in all of his likenesses is the haunted eyes, showing the inner torment from which he could never quite escape.*

◀ **FIGURE 19.17**   PAUL GAUGUIN. *Manao Tupapau—The Spirit of the Dead Watching.* 1892. Oil on burlap mounted on canvas, 28½ × 36⅜". Albright-Knox Art Gallery, Buffalo. A. Conger Goodyear Collection, 1965. *Until recently, Gauguin's life was viewed as one of the supreme archetypes of Modernism: the artist who abandons family duty and middle-class morality in his quest for aesthetic and sexual freedom. But this version of Gauguin's experience has been revealed as a myth. According to the latest research, Tahiti was no hedonistic paradise; the islanders were severely puritanical about sex; and contacts with the West had transformed the local culture, beginning more than a century before the painter's arrival. Even Gauguin's years in the South Pacific were less than idyllic: He died a lingering death from syphilis, contracted from an island prostitute.*

stemmed from the tradition of van Gogh, with color as its overriding concern. In *Open Window, Collioure* Matisse paints a kaleidoscope of colors—pinks, mauves, bluish greens, bright reds, oranges, and purples—that do not derive from the direct observation of nature but from the artist's belief that color harmonies can control the composition (Figure 19.19). The colors are "arbitrary" in the sense that they bear little reference to what one would actually see from the window, but they are far from arbitrary in their relation to one another—which is what interests Matisse.

Pablo Picasso (1881–1973), a talented young Spanish painter, was attracted to Paris's *avant-garde* art community about 1900. In 1907 he proved his genius with *Les Demoiselles d'Avignon* (*The Young Ladies of Avignon*), perhaps the most influential painting of the

FIGURE 19.19 HENRI MATISSE. *Open Window, Collioure.* 1905. Oil on canvas, 21¾ × 18⅛". Courtesy Mrs. John Hay Whitney, New York. *Like van Gogh, Matisse resisted quiet surface effects, preferring the look of paint applied in thick daubs and strips of varying length. His dazzling optical art was created by his use and placement of vibrant colors. In this painting Matisse interprets the glorious view from his studio overlooking the Mediterranean.*

twentieth century. This revolutionary work moved painting close to abstraction—the realization of Cézanne's dream. An unfinished work, *Les Demoiselles* reflects the multiple influences operating on Picasso at the time—the primitivism of African masks, the geometric forms of Cézanne, and the ancient sculpture of pre-Roman Spain. Despite its radical methods, this painting still has a conventional composition: five figures with a still life in the foreground. Nevertheless, with this painting Picasso redirected objective art into channels that would ultimately move beyond abstraction and into the development of nonobjective painting—although not in the work of Picasso himself—thus overturning a standard founded in the Renaissance (Figure 19.20).

Les Demoiselles was the prelude to **Cubism**, one of the early twentieth-century styles leading Western art toward abstraction. With his French colleague Georges Braque (1882–1963), Picasso developed Cubism. This style of painting, which went through different phases at the hands of different artists, basically fragments three-dimensional objects and reassembles them in a pattern that stresses their geometric structure and the relationships of these basic geometric forms. Braque and Picasso worked so closely together that their paintings could sometimes not be separately identified, even, it is said, by the artists themselves. An example of Picasso's Cubist style is *Pigeon with Baby Peas* (Figure 19.21). With Cubism, Picasso gave up Renaissance space completely, representing the subject from multiple angles simultaneously and shaping the figures into geometric designs. He also added a new feature to Cubism when he applied bits and pieces of other objects to the canvas, a technique called **collage** (French for "pasting"). Collage nudged Cubism closer to pure abstraction; the flat plane of the painting's surface was now simply a two-dimensional showcase for objects.

FIGURE 19.20 PABLO PICASSO. *Les Demoiselles d'Avignon. (The Young Ladies of Avignon.)* 1906-1907. Oil on canvas, 8' × 7'8". Collection, The Museum of Modern Art, New York. Acquired through the Lillie P. Bliss Bequest. *This painting's title derives from Picasso's native Barcelona, where Avignon Street ran through the red-light district. First intended as a moral work warning of the dangers of venereal disease (the figures still show provocative poses), the painting evolved over the months, changing as Picasso's horizons expanded. That he left the painting unfinished—like a scientist's record of a failed laboratory experiment—illustrates a leading trait of Modernism, the belief that truth is best expressed in the artistic process itself.*

FIGURE 19.21 PABLO PICASSO. *Pigeon with Baby Peas.* 1912. Oil on canvas, 25⅝ × 21¼". Musée d'Art Moderne de la Ville de Paris. Bequest of Dr. Maurice Girardin. *This painting's title, along with the undistorted word "cafe," suggest that Picasso's subject was his dinner. But content mattered little to him in this Cubist exercise with form. From now on in works by Picasso, as well as other artists, the battle between form and content became a central theme of Modernism.*

Although Paris remained the capital of Western art, other cities were also the scene of aesthetic experiment. Oslo, Munich, Vienna, and Dresden became artistic meccas, especially for Expressionist painters who followed the path opened by van Gogh and the *Fauves.*

In Munich, for example, Expressionism led to the formation of an international school of artists known as *Der Blaue Reiter* (The Blue Rider), named after a frequently used image. Rejecting the importance of artistic content and refusing to paint "safe" objects, this group of painters concentrated on basics such as color and line, which were meant to express inner feelings. Founded by the Russian exile Wassily Kandinsky (1866–1944) in 1911, this school made the first breakthrough to abstract art—nonrepresentational or nonobjective paintings that defy any sense of reality or connection to nature and are, as the artist himself put it, "largely unconscious, spontaneous expressions of inner character, non-material in nature." Kandinsky's "improvisations," as he labeled them, were free forms, possessing no objective content, consisting only of meandering lines and amorphous blobs of color (Figure 19.22). For all their seeming randomness, however, his paintings were planned to look that way. He consciously worked out the placement of the lines and the choices of color, leaving nothing to chance.

New Directions in Sculpture and Architecture Few sculptors of any consequence appeared in the 1871–1914 period and only one genius: Auguste Rodin (1840–1917). Rejecting the lifeless Classicism of the mid–nineteenth century, Rodin forged an eclectic style that blended Romantic subject matter, Renaissance simplicity, and Gothic angularity with the radical changes underway in painting. In the sculptural group *The Burghers of Calais* (Figure 19.23), he created a spiky Gothic effect using modern means, gouging, twisting, and otherwise torturing the surface of the human figures. The end result was both impressionistic (the play of light on the convoluted surfaces) and expressionistic (the traces of Rodin's fingers on the

FIGURE 19.22 WASSILY KANDINSKY. *Improvisation 33 for "Orient."* 1913. Oil on canvas, 34¾ × 39¼". Stedelijk Museum, Amsterdam. *Kandinsky's radical Expressionism rested on the Romantic idea that serious art can function as a substitute for religion. In 1912 he published his aesthetic beliefs in the treatise* Concerning the Spiritual in Art, *a work that became a fundamental text for modern artists. He also linked the fluidity of painting with the lyricism of music, a connection suggested in this work by the meandering lines.*

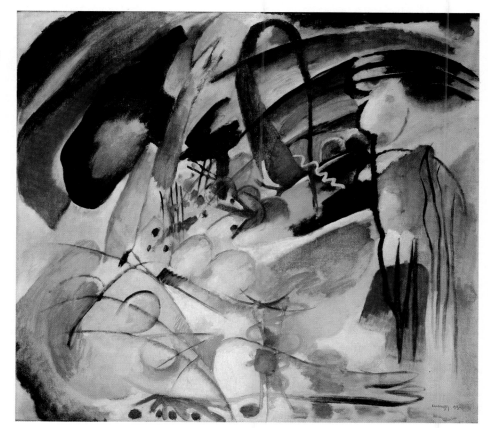

FIGURE 19.23 AUGUSTE RODIN. *The Burghers of Calais.*
1884–1895. Bronze, 6'10½" × 7'10" × 6'3". Rodin Museum,
Philadelphia Museum of Art. Gift of Jules E. Mastbaum.
The surface of Rodin's sculpture is Modernist, but its soul—the
artistic form—remains firmly rooted in the Classical ideals of the
Renaissance. In this sculptural group, which depicts six medieval
citizens who were prepared to sacrifice their lives for their city's
freedom, he drew on the tradition of Michelangelo. First modeling
the individual figures in the nude, he then prepared clothed versions
that he cast in bronze. In their finished state, the sculptures are
distinctively Michelangelesque, with powerful muscularity, quiet
dignity, and a general air of nobility under duress.

bronze medium, which so dramatically suggest the intensity of the artist's involvement).

Having lagged behind the other arts for most of the century, architecture began to catch up in the 1880s. The United States led the way, notably in the works of the Chicago School. The skyscraper, perfected by Chicago-based architects, became synonymous with Modernism and modern life. Unlike Modernist painting and sculpture, the new architecture arose for practical reasons: dense populations and soaring real estate values.

Using the aesthetic dictum that "form follows function," the Chicago School solved design problems without relying on past techniques and traditions. The author of this dictum, Louis Sullivan (1856–1924), produced a masterly example of the Chicago School's style in the Guaranty Building in Buffalo, New York, a structure whose steel frame is covered by a skin of stone and glass (Figure 19.24).

Sullivan's imprint can be seen in the way he allows the building to speak for itself: The plan of the exterior skin reflects the internal steel skeleton in the thin, continuous piers between the windows that rise from the base to the rounded arches at the top. The effect of this organization is to turn the building's exterior into a grid, a visual expression of the structural frame underneath. Although Sullivan rejected the rich ornamentation of the nineteenth-century Gothic as well as the balanced decorations of Classicism, he nevertheless developed his own decorative scheme, which may be seen in the vertical and horizontal elements, for example, and the spaces (blocks) between the windows.

Sullivan defined the public building for the twentieth century, and his disciple Frank Lloyd Wright (1869–1959) did the same for domestic architecture around 1910. In the Victorian era architects had discovered that the middle-class demand for comforta-

FIGURE 19.24 LOUIS SULLIVAN. Guaranty Building, Buffalo. 1895. *Purity became an identifying characteristic of Modernist style. It was apparent in Matisse's color experiments, Picasso's abstract Cubist forms, and even in the Expressionist's goal of unvarnished truth. In architecture, Louis Sullivan introduced the purity principal with his artistic credo that "form follows function."*

The Legacy of Early Modernism

From the unsettled period of 1871–1914 come many of the trends that have made the twentieth century such an exciting—and dangerous—era. The legacy of militant nationalism has given birth to the two great world wars that devastated our century. Even today, nationalism remains a potent force, threatening to overturn state boundaries and governments. Imperialism, another legacy, has had radically contradictory consequences. On the one hand it has exported Western peoples, values, and technology around the globe, bringing a higher standard of living and greater expectations for the future. On the other hand it has disturbed if not destroyed older ways of life and led to a series of wars as colonial peoples have struggled to cast off the yoke of Western oppression. And militarism, a third legacy, has made rivalry among states a perpetual source of anxiety and destruction.

On the cultural scene, the era of Early Modernism set the stage for our century. The rise of the masses has led to a growing proletarization of culture. As a result, the middle classes have been subjected to a cultural assault from urban workers in much the same way that aristocrats were attacked and displaced by the middle classes. Technology has fueled the rise of mass culture. A second legacy of this era has been the *avant-garde*, whose leaders have systematically tried to destroy the last vestiges of Judeo-Christian and Greco-Roman tradition. And finally, Early Modernism established the emotional and aesthetic climate of this century—its addiction to experimentalism, its love-hate relationship with uncertainty and restlessness, its obsession with abstraction, its belief in the hidden depths of the human personality, and its willingness to think the unthinkable.

KEY CULTURAL TERMS

Modernism
avant-garde
Naturalism
Decadence
Expressionism
abstraction
Impressionism
Post-Impressionism

Pointillism
Fauvism
Cubism
collage
atonality
syncopation
ragtime
blues

SUGGESTIONS FOR FURTHER READING

PRIMARY SOURCES

CHEKHOV, A. P. *Plays*. Translated and edited by E. K. Bristow. New York: Norton, 1977. Excellent versions of Chekhov's most memorable plays: *The Sea Gull, Uncle Vanya, The Three Sisters,* and *The Cherry Orchard.*

FREUD, S. *Civilization and Its Discontents*. Translated and edited by J. Strachey. New York: Norton, 1962. Freud's ideas about history and civilization, based on his psychological findings and theories; Strachey is the editor of the Standard Edition of Freud's complete works.

———. *The Interpretation of Dreams*. Translated and edited by J. Strachey. New York: Basic Books, 1955. Freud's seminal work about the role of the unconscious in human psychology and his new theory of psychoanalysis; considered by many his most important work.

HUYSMANS, J.-K. *Against Nature*. Translated by R. Baldick. New York: Penguin, 1966. A superb English version of this curious work, first published in 1884.

IBSEN, H. *A Doll's House*. Translated by C. Hampton. New York: S. French, 1972. An excellent English version of Ibsen's most often performed play, the story of a woman's awakening to the facts of her oppressive marriage.

JUNG, C. G. *Basic Writings*. Edited with an introduction by V. S. de Laszlo. New York: Modern Library, 1959. A good selection of the most important works of the Swiss psychiatrist who explored the importance of myths and symbols in human psychology.

———. *Memories, Dreams, Reflections*. Edited by A. Jaffé. New York: Vintage, 1963. Jung's highly readable autobiography in which he describes the origins of his theories.

KAFKA, F. *The Trial*. Translated by W. and E. Muir. New York: Schocken Books, 1968. A definitive edition of Kafka's nightmare novel in which the lead character is tried and convicted of a crime whose nature he cannot discover.

———. *The Metamorphosis, The Penal Colony, and Other Stories*. Translated by W. and E. Muir. New York: Schocken Books, 1988. This volume contains the best of Kafka's brilliant short prose works, all concerned with anxiety and alienation in a hostile and incomprehensible world.

NIETZSCHE, F. W. *The Portable Nietzsche*. Selected and Translated by W. Kaufmann. New York: Penguin, 1976. A collection of the most important writings of the German philosopher, compiled by the foremost Nietzschean scholar.

PROUST, M. *Remembrance of Things Past*. Translated by C. K. Scott Moncrieff, T. Kilmartin, and A. Mayor. London:

Chatto & Windus, 1981. Contains all seven volumes of Proust's monumental work, which portrays the early twentieth century as a transitional period with the old aristocracy in decline and the middle class on the rise.

WILDE, O. *The Portrait of Dorian Gray.* New York: Oxford University Press, 1981. Wilde's only novel recounts the story of a man whose portrait ages and decays while he remains young and handsome despite a dissolute life; the most enduring work of the Decadent school of late-nineteenth-century English literature.

ZOLA, E. *Germinal.* Translated and with an introduction by L. Tancock. New York: Penguin, 1954. A Realist novel that exposes the sordid conditions in the French mining industry.

SECONDARY SOURCES

BARRACLOUGH, G. *An Introduction to Contemporary History.* New York: Penguin, 1967. An interpretative synthesis that offers insights for the serious reader.

BIDDISS, M. D. *The Age of the Masses: Ideas and Society in Europe Since 1870.* New York: Penguin, 1977. A balanced account examining the influence of the masses both on society and on leading thinkers and writers.

BULLOCK, A. *The Twentieth Century: A Promethean Age.* London: Thames and Hudson, 1971. Excellent integration of cultural and political history; handsomely illustrated.

CLARK, T. J. *The Painting of Modern Life: Paris in the Art of Manet and His Followers.* Princeton: Princeton University Press, 1986. A superb analysis of key artists and their work that is rooted in economic developments.

FERRISS, T. *Coming of Age in the Milky Way.* New York: William Morrow, 1988. A brilliant presentation and discussion of the discoveries and developments that have created modern science.

HALE, O. J. *The Great Illusion, 1900–1914.* New York: Harper and Row, 1971. Weaves together the steps leading to World War I with prewar culture.

HAYES, C. J. H. *A Generation of Materialism.* New York: Harper and Row, 1963. Of all the books in the Rise of Modern Europe series, this one ranks at the top with its analysis of late nineteenth-century culture and its meaning for the next century.

HEADRICK, D. *Tools of Empire.* New York: Oxford University Press, 1981. A study of the interconnection of imperialism and technology, especially guns, medicine, and steam engines.

HOBSON, J. A. *Imperialism: A Study.* London: Unwin Hyman, 1988. First published in 1905, this modern classic identified most of the issues that are still debated about imperialism.

HUGHES, H. S. *Consciousness and Society: The Reorientation of European Social Thought, 1890–1930.* New York: Vintage, 1958. An illuminating study of the ideas and thinkers that helped shape the attitudes of early-twentieth-century governing elites.

JOLL, J. *The Origins of the First World War.* London: Longman, 1984. A brief look at the diplomatic, military, and economic causes of World War I; for the beginning student.

PASCAL, R. *From Naturalism to Expressionism: German Literature and Society, 1880–1918.* London: Weidenfeld and Nicolson, 1973. An insightful analysis of German writing as a reflection of the social values of the period.

SCHORSKE, C. *Fin de Siécle Vienna: Politics and Culture.* New York: Knopf, 1980. An interesting study claiming that Vienna produced political and cultural styles that have dominated the twentieth century.

STONE, N. *Europe Transformed, 1878–1919.* London: Fontana, 1984. A sound country-by-country survey of the five major European powers and how World War I changed them.

TUCHMAN, B. *The Guns of August.* New York: Dell, 1962. A popular but serious and well-written account of the events leading to World War I.

———. *The Proud Tower.* New York: Macmillan, 1966. An engrossing account of European society from 1890 to 1914, focusing on the leading personalities.

SUGGESTIONS FOR LISTENING

DEBUSSY, CLAUDE (1862–1918).
Debussy's veiled and subtly shifting harmonies helped to found Impressionist music. Excellent examples of his style may be heard in the orchestral works *Prélude à l'après-midi d'un faune* (*Prelude to the Afternoon of a Faun*) (1894) and *Nocturnes* (1899); in the collections for piano called *Estampes* (*Prints*) (1913) and *Préludes* (1910–1913); and in the opera *Pelléas et Mélisande* (1902). Not all of his music was Impressionistic, however; for example, in the piano music called *Children's Corner* (1908) he blended Classical values with his typical harmonic structures.

SCHOENBERG, ARNOLD (1874–1951).
By the end of this period, in 1914, Schoenberg was recognized as the leader of Expressionist music, particularly with the atonal work *Pierrot lunaire* (*Moonstruck Pierrot*) (1912), scored for chamber quintet and voice. In earlier works, he was less radical, as in the Second String Quartet (1908), which fused Classical forms and fragmentary melodies. Only after 1923 did Schoenberg make a breakthrough to serial composition, the type of music with which he is most identified (see Chapter 20).

STRAVINSKY, IGOR (1882–1971).
Stravinsky, who along with Schoenberg has dominated twentieth-century music, also began writing music during this period, principally as a composer of ballet scores based on Russian folk tales and traditions. These were *The Fire Bird* (1910), *Petrushka* (1911), and *Le Sacre du Printemps* (*The Rite of Spring*) (1913). With *Le Sacre* he established his originality as a composer, especially in his innovative rhythms and his handling of folk themes.

JOPLIN, SCOTT (1868–1917).
Typical of Joplin's ragtime compositions with a syncopated beat are *Maple Leaf Rag* (1899), *Sugar Cane Rag* (1908), and *Magnetic Rag* (1914). He also wrote a ragtime opera *Treemonisha* (1911), a failure in his lifetime but a modest success in recent revivals.

20

THE AGE OF THE MASSES AND THE ZENITH OF MODERNISM

1914—1945

The years between 1914 and 1945 were dominated by wars, depression, and totalitarian movements. Below the surface of these chaotic events even more potent forces were at work, including the rise of the masses at the expense of the bourgeoisie and the debate over the rival ideologies of democracy, capitalism, socialism, and communism. Old ideas, one after the other, were challenged and overturned, leading scholars to describe this turbulent period as an era of illusions.

The events of the first half of the twentieth century are seen differently today than they were seen at the time. Historians are beginning to see World War I (1914–1918) and World War II (1939–1945) not as two separate conflicts but as a single struggle divided by a twenty-year peace. They believe that the Great Depression of the 1930s was not a signal that the capitalist system didn't work but was simply an episode of economic downturn. And they know that the making of the masses into a historically powerful force was the most significant event of this time and of greater consequence than the wars, the economic hardships, or the political upheavals. The rise of the masses heralded the onset of a new phase of culture in which ordinary men and women from the lower middle class and working class challenged bourgeois dominance in much the same way as the bourgeoisie had earlier threatened and eventually overcome the aristocracy.

The appearance of the masses on the world stage was also instrumental in shaping cultural events. The needs of this public led to the birth of mass culture, resulting in fresh forms of popular expression. Mass culture triggered negative responses in most serious artists, writers, and musicians, who preferred the difficult and somewhat remote style of Modernism that had arisen after 1870 and who had been nurtured in an environment hostile to bourgeois, industrialized society. The leaders of Modernism, partly under pressure from the extreme popularity of mass culture, now fashioned works that grew more and more revolutionary in form, constantly testing the limits of the arts. The period between 1914 and 1945 saw both the rise of mass culture and the zenith of Modernism.

THE COLLAPSE OF OLD CERTAINTIES AND THE SEARCH FOR NEW VALUES

Before World War I, liberal values guided the expectations that most people had for their personal lives and their societies. During the period between the outbreak of World War I and the ending of World War II, however, the values of liberalism were sorely tried and in some cases overthrown. Wars, revolutions, and social upheavals often dominated both domestic and foreign affairs. Even the brief breathing spaces during the rare months of peace were fraught with tensions as some states prepared for new rounds of conflict. To those who clung to liberalism, the world seemed to have gone mad (Figure 20.1). Civility appeared outmoded because war now seemed a

Figure 20.1 Pablo Picasso. *Guernica.* 1937. Oil on canvas, 11′5½″ × 25′5¾″. Prado. Guernica *is a vivid symbol of the violent twenty years between World War I and World War II. Depicting the bombing of the unarmed town of Guernica by Nazi planes during the Spanish Civil War, the painting transforms the local struggle into an international battle between totalitarianism and human freedom—the issue that also dominated the age's ideological debates.*

more normal condition than peace, and other key liberal ideas were assaulted by the period's events. The ideal that government should represent the desires of the people was rendered meaningless in Russia, Italy, Germany, and Spain, where totalitarian forms of government were established. In these states individual rights became secondary to the needs of the total society or often simply to the wishes of the ruling party. The doctrine of laissez faire also fell into discredit during the Depression of the 1930s, bringing capitalism itself into question and leading to the rise of state-controlled economies.

When World War II ended in 1945, little vitality remained in the liberal tradition among Europeans. Europe—shattered by the war, its major cities devastated, its population diminished, its transportation system destroyed, its economy in ruins—was at a crossroads, uncertain whether to stay on the liberal path or move in the direction of socialism. Though disillusioned, one group of Europeans, chiefly those in the western countries who voted for their ruling parties, held fast to liberalism and refused to see that its values had been damaged by the irrationality of historic events. Another group, composed chiefly of those central and eastern Europeans who were attracted to totalitarian solutions, was enthralled by the socialist vision and believed that collectivist action was the only way to achieve a just society. And a third group, composed of people who scorned all political solutions—such as the alienated youth of the

1950s known as Beatniks in the United States and Angry Young Men in Britain—seemed not to care one way or the other and retreated into pleasure-seeking or sank into bitterness, cynicism, and despair.

Most Americans in 1945, however, still held to the liberal vision. Not having been subjected to a land war at home in either of the two worldwide conflicts, Americans were less pessimistic than Europeans. Moreover, Europe's devastation meant that the United States was the world's leading military, industrial, and financial power. The country emerged at the end of World War II as the liberal leader of the West, committed to human rights, political freedom, and free enterprise. A symbol of the new U.S. role in world affairs was the founding in New York City of the headquarters of the United Nations—the international organization dedicated to keeping the peace and protecting human rights.

World War I and Its Aftermath

In 1914 came the war that nobody expected, and, despite predictions to the contrary, it dragged on for four years and took the lives of an estimated ten million soldiers and civilians. On one side were Germany, Austria-Hungary, Turkey, and Bulgaria—the Central Powers. The principal war aim of these countries was to assert the power of their central European region, which had been eclipsed by western Europe for almost two hundred years. The most dramatic cause of central Europe's new feeling of importance was the unification of Germany in 1871, which made the German Empire the most powerful industrial and military state on the continent. Austria-Hungary, though little industrialized, wanted to spread its imperial power into southeastern Europe, replacing the Turkish influence and also countering the Russians, who had been trying to dominate this region.

Opposed to the Central Powers were the Allied Powers of France, Russia, and Great Britain. In 1915 Italy, blaming its former friends Germany and Austria-Hungary for starting the war, joined the Allied Powers. The Allies refused to allow the Central Powers to revise the balance of power and, in particular, were determined to keep Germany from gaining new lands. Both sides, hopeful of swift victory, found themselves bogged down in seige warfare that led to huge losses on the battlefield and appalling hardships at home (Figure 20.2).

In the spring of 1917 the stalemate between the Allies and the Central Powers was upset by two dramatic events. First, the United States entered the war on the side of the exhausted Allies, promising fresh troops and supplies. Second, revolution broke out in Russia, interrupting its war effort and eventually causing the newly formed Communist regime to make peace with the Central Powers in early 1918. Freed from fighting the Russians in the east and determined to strike before American troops could reach Europe in great numbers, the Germans launched a massive attack on the western front, but the Allies, supported by thousands of American troops, foiled the Germans, forcing them to sue for peace in November 1918.

The armistice that ended the war was based in part on a plan outlined by the U.S. president, Woodrow Wilson (1913–1921). Wilson believed that his plan—calling for self-determination of nations, democratic governments, and an international agency to maintain the peace, known as the League of Nations—would keep Europe safe from war. The president's proposals were modified by the victorious Allies and became the basis for the 1919 Treaty of Versailles.

Despite the optimism surrounding its signing, the Versailles Treaty sowed the seeds of discord that contributed to World War II (Map 20.1). The German diplomats who signed the treaty were representatives of a hastily thrown together civilian government and not the officials and army officers who had suffered defeat. Later these defeated officials and officers rallied nationalist feelings by denouncing the treaty as a humiliation for their country, especially those provisions that were meant to keep Germany industrially and militarily weak and the requirement that Germany pay war claims—called reparations—to the victorious Allies.

Peace brought boom times to the economies of the victorious Allied Powers. Britain and France returned to business as usual, as political parties shifted in and out of office. The United States reverted to its prewar isolationism, turning its back on Europe. Between 1924 and 1929 the United States also exhibited the

FIGURE 20.2 PAUL NASH. *"We Are Making a New World."* 1918. Oil on canvas, 28 × 36". Imperial War Museum, London. *Paul Nash, one of Britain's official artists during World War I, made the reality of the war's destructive power evident to civilians at home. In his battle scenes farmlands were turned into quagmires and forests into "no man's lands." The artist's choice of the title for this painting mocks the politicians' promises that tomorrow will be better.*

MAP 20.1

Europe after World War I

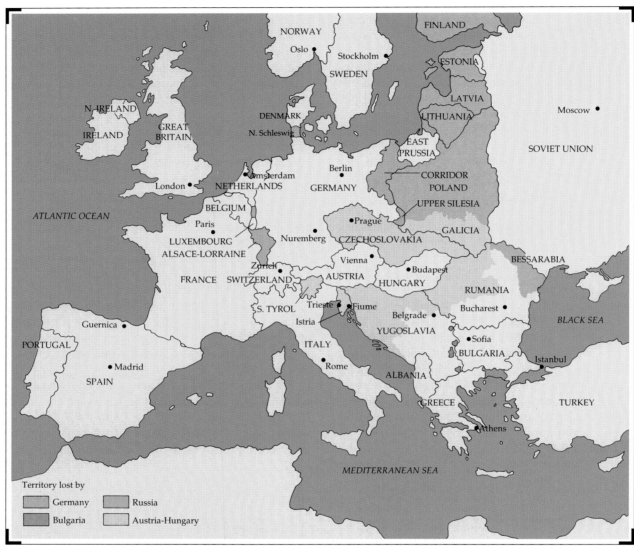

Territory lost by

Germany

Bulgaria

Russia

Austria-Hungary

best and the worst of free enterprise—unprecedented prosperity and rampant greed.

The Central Powers also rebuilt their economies in the 1920s. After a shaky start, Germany survived near bankruptcy to become once again the leading industrial state on the Continent. Germany was now known as the Weimar Republic, after the city where its postwar constitution was drafted; Weimar had once been Goethe's home, and for many it symbolized a new era. Once again, Germany became a center for European culture, providing key leaders in *avant-garde* painting and literature. Conversely, Austria was reduced to a shadow of its former self, its imperial lands stripped away and reorganized into democratic nations and its Slavic population dispersed among several states. The Austro-Hungarian

monarchy ceased to exist. Austria, lacking a sound economic base, never fully recovered from its defeat.

As the 1920s drew to a close a warning signal sounded: the crash of the New York stock market in October 1929. After the market crash the buoyant atmosphere of the twenties lingered for a few months until the early 1930s. Then economic depression in the United States, now a central cog in the world's economy, brought down Europe's financial house.

The Great Depression of the 1930s

The Depression wiped out prosperity, and the order of the day became mass unemployment, street demonstrations, and near starvation conditions for many people. As a result, severe strains were placed on Europe and the United States, forcing governments to try various experiments in order to restore their economies. Great Britain and France were compelled to discard some cherished ideas, such as free trade and the gold standard, and move toward government-controlled economies and paper money systems. Under President Franklin Delano Roosevelt (1933–1945) and his New Deal program, the United States followed a policy of state intervention as the answer to its economic plight (Figure 20.3). Roosevelt

started public projects—dams, roads, and conservation programs—"priming the pump," as he called it. He also sponsored programs to benefit working people, including social security and unemployment insurance. To prevent another panic, he introduced legislation regulating Wall Street and the banks. Depressed conditions, notably high unemployment, hung on until World War II, however.

Germany suffered the most of any country in Europe from the Great Depression. Domestic problems, brought on in part by bank failures and rising un-

FIGURE 20.3 WALKER EVANS. *Elizabeth Tengle in the Kitchen, Hale County, Alabama.* 1936. Photography Collection, Harry Ransom Humanities Research Center, the University of Texas at Austin. *Tenant farmers in the southern United States, who had been victimized by low cotton prices and high interest rates for decades, were reduced to subsistence levels or worse by the Great Depression. This photograph shows the misery of one of the farm women in her kitchen with little food, few utensils, and no labor-saving appliances. Walker Evans's shocking photographs, which accompanied James Agee's book* Let Us Now Praise Famous Men, *provided the supporters of Roosevelt's New Deal with visual documentation of the wretched living conditions of tenant families.*

The landed aristocrats, the Roman Catholic Church, and some generals plotted to restore monarchical rule and the church's influence. In 1936 civil war broke out. General Francisco Franco (1939–1975) led the conservative forces to victory in 1939, defeating an alliance of republicans, socialists, anarchists, and communists. During hostilities, Hitler and Mussolini supplied Franco's fascist army with troops and equipment, while Stalin backed the losing faction. For the Germans and the Italians, Spain's civil war was a practice run for World War II. For example, the bombing of unarmed towns like Guernica foreshadowed the indiscriminate bombing and killing of civilians that characterized the later war.

FIGURE 20.5 MARGARET BOURKE-WHITE. Russian Tank Driver. 1941. *Photojournalism, a popular form in which the photograph rather than the text dominates the story, reached new heights during World War II, particularly in illustrated magazines like* Life. *Margaret Bourke-White, one of the first women war journalists, was the only foreign correspondent-photographer present in the Soviet Union when the Germans invaded in June 1941. In this photograph she shows a Russian tank driver peering through his window with the cannon jutting out over his head—a vivid image of the integration of human beings into mechanized warfare.*

World War II: Origins and Outcome

The origins of World War II lay in the Versailles Treaty, the Great Depression, and nationalistic feelings. Hardly was the ink dry on the Versailles Treaty before many Germans were denouncing it as a "dictated" peace. Especially infuriating to nationalistic Germans was the loss of lands to Poland and France. The worldwide economic breakdown in the 1930s further fanned the fires of German resentment against the treaty, causing the lost territories to become burning political issues. Once the Nazis had secured their position, they turned their attention to recovering the former territories as well as annexing other areas with large German populations.

After less than a year in office, Hitler began a campaign to revise the Versailles Treaty while at the same time engaging in a propaganda crusade that focused on Germany's glorious past. His regime, he boasted, was the Third Reich, or empire, which would last for a thousand years—like the centuries-long Holy Roman Empire (1000–1806) rather than the short-lived German Empire (1871–1918). Hitler withdrew Germany from the League of Nations, to which it had been admitted in the 1920s, and renounced the provision of the Versailles Treaty that forbade Germany to rearm. In 1936 he marched troops into the Rhineland, the industrial heartland of Germany, which had been demilitarized by the treaty. When the world failed to respond to this challenge, Hitler concluded that Germany's former enemies were weak and proceeded to initiate a plan to conquer Europe.

In the next two years, Europe watched as Hitler took Austria and Czechoslovakia and began to threaten Poland. France and Great Britain followed a policy of appeasement, believing that if Hitler's demands were met, war could be averted, but they promised to come to Poland's aid if Germany attacked. World War II began on September 1, 1939, when Germany invaded Poland; France and Britain responded with declarations of war.

Within nine months the Nazis occupied most of western Europe. By the fall of 1940 Britain stood alone, taking the brunt of the German air raids. The British, under their wartime leader Winston Churchill, bravely held on. Hitler, unable to defeat England by air, now turned eastward and initiated a land invasion against the Soviet Union in June 1941, breaking a mutual nonaggression pact he had signed with Stalin in August 1939 (Figure 20.5). Shortly thereafter the Soviet Union and Great Britain became allies against Nazi Germany. Then in December 1941 Japan attacked American bases in the Pacific, and a few days later Germany and Italy joined Japan by declaring war on the United States.

FIGURE 20.6 Nazi Death Camp in Belsen, Germany. 1945. *When the Nazis came to power in Germany in 1933 they secretly began to imprison their political enemies in concentration camps, where they were tortured or executed. By 1942 the Nazis had extended this secret policy across Europe to include foreign civilians, particularly Jews. Photographs such as this one revealed to the world the horrible atrocities committed by the Nazi regime.*

At first the European Axis powers—Germany and Italy—were victorious, but in the fall of 1942 the Allies—Britain, the Soviet Union, and the United States—began to turn the tide. By December 1943 the Russians were rolling the Germans back, Italy had broken ranks with the Nazis, and American and British bombers were pounding Germany. In June 1944 a combined army of Allied troops invaded the Continent, and the Germans surrendered in May 1945.

In the Pacific the war against the Asian Axis power, Japan, intensified as American troops fought their way toward Japan, island by island. In August 1945 America brought the war to an abrupt end by dropping atomic bombs on the Japanese cities of Hiroshima and Nagasaki. The over 200,000 Japanese killed in these two raids climaxed the bloody six years of World War II, adding to its estimated thirty to fifty million deaths.

By 1945 the world had witnessed some of the most brutal examples of human behavior in history. Few were prepared for the shock of the Nazi death camps, however. Gradually it became known that the Nazis had rounded up the Jews of Germany and eastern Europe and transported them in cattle cars to the extermination camps, where they were killed in gas chambers. The Nazis referred to their plan to eliminate the Jewish people as the Final Solution, but the rest of the world called it the Holocaust. This genocidal policy involved the murder of six million Jews out of a population of nine million, along with millions of other people the Nazis deemed undesirable, such as gypsies and homosexuals (Figure 20.6).

In 1945, after six years of war waged across the globe, Germany and Japan lay in ruins. Italy escaped with less damage. France, partly occupied by the Germans for most of the war, was readmitted to the councils of the Allies. England, though victorious, emerged exhausted and in the shadow of her former allies, the United States and the Soviet Union. The old European order had passed away. The Soviet Union and the United States were now the two most powerful states in the world.

THE ZENITH OF MODERNISM

Modernism had originated in the latter part of the nineteenth century as a reflection of the fast-paced modern world whose foundations and boundaries seemed to be constantly shifting. The Modernist sensibility, with its underlying spirit of skepticism and experimentation, continued to guide artistic and literary expression in the twentieth century. But this style was limited in its appeal, and an ever-growing general public was isolated from *avant-garde* developments in art, music, and literature. If and when this wider audience bestirred themselves about high culture, they usually responded negatively to Modernist works, which they often considered incomprehensible, obscene, or decidedly provocative in some way. They turned instead to the increasingly available and affordable pleasures offered by *mass culture*.

Like Modernism, mass culture was a direct outgrowth of industrialized society. Its roots reached back to the late nineteenth century, when skilled workers began to enjoy a better standard of living than had previously been possible for members of the lower classes. This new generation of consumers demanded products and amusements that appealed to their tastes: inexpensive, energetic, and easily accessible.

In response to their desires, entrepreneurs using new technologies flooded the market with consumer goods and developed new entertainments. Unlike the folk culture or popular culture of earlier times, modern mass culture was also mass-produced culture. The untapped consumers' market led to the creation or expansion of new industries, in particular automobiles, household products, and domestic appliances. Most forms of mass culture—the radio, newspaper comic strips and cartoons, professional sports, picture magazines, recordings, movies, and musical comedies—had originated before World War I, but now, between the wars, they came into their own. The 1920s was the golden age of Broadway's musical comedies, and radio reached its peak in the years after 1935.

The spread of mass culture heightened the prestige of the United States as it became known as the source of the most vigorous and imaginative popular works. The outstanding symbol of America's dominance of popular culture is Walt Disney (1901–1966), the creator of the cartoon figures of Mickey Mouse (1928) and other characters. By 1945 in the more advanced societies, mass culture was playing an ever-growing role in the public and the private lives of most citizens. A handful of creative people began to incorporate elements of mass culture into their works, using jazz in "serious" music or film in theatrical performances, for example, but in the main most artists, writers, and musicians stood apart from mass culture. Their isolation reflected an almost sacred commitment to the Modernist ideals of experimentation, newness, and deliberate difficulty. And some Modernists, especially among the visual artists, imbued these ideals with spiritual meaning.

Experimentation in Literature

Modernist writers between 1914 and 1945 maintained Early Modernism's dedication to experimentation, a stance that reflected their despair over the instability of their era. By challenging the traditional norms and methods of literature through their carefully composed experimental works, the Modernists were convinced that they could impose an order on the seeming randomness and meaninglessness of human existence.

The Novel Depiction of the narrator's subjective consciousness was a principal concern of the Modernist novelists, who otherwise differed markedly from one another. The most famous method that arose from this concern was *stream-of-consciousness* writing, a method in which the narrative consists of the unedited thoughts of one of the characters, through whose mind readers experience the story. Stream-of-consciousness fiction differs from a story told in the first person—the grammatical "I"—by one of the characters (for example, Dickens's *David Copperfield*) in that it is an attempt to emulate the actual experience of thinking and feeling, even to the point of sounding fragmented, random, and arbitrary.

The Irish author James Joyce and the English writer Virginia Woolf were important innovators with the stream-of-consciousness technique. In his novel *Ulysses*, James Joyce (1882–1941) uses this device as a way of making the novel's characters speak directly to readers. For instance, no narrator's voice intrudes in the novel's final forty-five pages, which are the scattered thoughts of the character Molly Bloom as she sinks into sleep. This long monologue is a single run-on sentence without any punctuation except for a final period.

Despite the experimental style of *Ulysses*, Joyce aspired to more than technical virtuosity in this monumental work. He planned it as a modern version of the *Odyssey*, contrasting Homer's twenty-four books of heroic exploits with an ordinary day in the lives of three Dubliners. Joyce's sexual language, while natural to his characters, offended bourgeois morals. *Ulysses*, first published in France in 1922, became the era's test case for artistic freedom, not appearing in America or England until the 1930s.

Rejecting traditional narrative techniques, Virginia Woolf (1882–1941) experimented with innovative ways to explore time, space, and reality. In her early novel *Jacob's Room* (1922), for example, she develops the title character through fragments of other people's comments about him. In *Mrs. Dalloway* (1925) she uses interior monologues to trace a woman's experiences over the course of a day in London. Like her contemporaries Joyce and Freud, Woolf was interested in examining the realities that lie below surface consciousness. Many consider *To the Lighthouse* (1927) Woolf's finest novel. In it she uses stream-of-consciousness to strip the story of fixed realism and capture the differing senses of reality experienced by the characters—in much the same way as the Cubist painters aimed at representing multiple views. To this end she focuses on the characters' inner selves, creating diverse effects through interior monologues. For instance, one character's narrow, matter-of-fact mentality differs from his wife's emotional, free-ranging consciousness. A distinguished literary critic and the author of well-known feminist works such as *A Room of One's Own*, Woolf gathered around her the *avant-garde* writers, artists, and intellectuals known as the Bloomsbury Group and founded, with her husband Leonard, the Hogarth Press.

American writers also contributed experimental fiction to the Modernist revolution. By and large these Americans made their first contacts with Europe during World War I and stayed on until the Great Depression drove them home (Figure 20.7). Ernest Hemingway (1899–1961) was the first of the Americans living abroad to emerge as a major literary star. His severely disciplined prose style relied heavily on dialogue, and he often omitted details of setting and background. His writing owed a debt to popular culture: From the era's hardboiled detective fiction he borrowed a terse, world-weary voice to narrate his works, as in his 1926 novel, *The Sun Also Rises*. In this novel he portrays his fellow American exiles as a "lost

FIGURE 20.7 PABLO PICASSO. *Gertrude Stein*. 1906. Oil on canvas, 39¼ × 32". Metropolitan Museum of Art, New York. Bequest of Gertrude Stein, 1946. *Talented Americans were introduced to Paris by American writer and expatriate Gertrude Stein, who made her studio a gathering place for the Parisian avant-garde. There she entertained Matisse and Picasso, composer Igor Stravinsky, writers Ernest Hemingway and F. Scott Fitzgerald, and many other brilliant exponents of Modernism. Stein was shocked at first by the starkness and brooding presence of Picasso's portrait of her, but she came to regard it as an accurate likeness, saying, "For me it is I, and it is the only reproduction of me which is always I."*

generation" whose future was blighted by World War I—a Modernist message. In Hemingway's cynical vision, politics was of no importance; all that mattered were drinking bouts with male friends and casual sex with beautiful women.

William Faulkner (1897–1962) was another American who became one of the giants of twentieth-century literature. The stream-of-consciousness technique is central to his 1929 masterpiece, *The Sound and the Fury*. With a story line repeated several times but from different perspectives, this novel is especially audacious in its opening section, which narrates events through the eyes of a mentally defective character. More important than his use of such Modernist devices was his lifelong identification with his home state of Mississippi, where, after a brief sojourn in Europe, he began to explore themes about extended families bound together by sexual secrets. Faulkner's universe became the fictional county of Yoknapatawpha, which he peopled with decaying gentry, ambitious poor whites, and exploited blacks. His artistic power lay in his ability not only to relate these characters to their region but to turn them into universal symbols.

While experimentalism was a highly visible aspect of Modernist fiction, not all Modernist writers were preoccupied with innovative methods. Other writers were identified with the Modernists because of their pessimistic viewpoints or their explosive themes. The Modernism of the British writer D. H. Lawrence (1885–1930), for example, was expressed in novels of sexual liberation. Frustrated by the coldness of sexual relations in bourgeois culture, Lawrence, the son of a miner, concluded that the machine age emasculated men. As an antidote, he preached a religion of erotic passion. He set forth his doctrine of sexual freedom most clearly in the 1928 novel *Lady Chatterley's Lover*, issued privately and quickly banned for its explicit language and scenes. Not until the 1960s, and only after bitter court battles, was this novel allowed to circulate freely. In the novel the love-making episodes between Lady Chatterley, wed to an impotent aristocrat, and the lower-class gamekeeper Mellors were presented as models of sexual fulfillment with their mix of erotic candor and moral fervor.

Falling outside the Modernist classification is the English novelist and essayist George Orwell (1903–1950), who nevertheless is one of the major figures of the interwar period. Born Eric Blair to an established middle-class family, Orwell changed his name, rejected his background, lived and worked among the poor and downtrodden, and became a writer. He also became the conscience of his generation because he remained skeptical of all of the political ideologies of his day. In the allegorical novel *Animal Farm* (1945) he satirized Stalinist Russia. In the anti-utopian novel *1984* (1948) he made totalitarianism the enemy, especially as practiced in the Soviet Union, but he also warned of the dangers of repression in capitalist society. What made Orwell remarkable in this age torn by ideological excess was his claim to be merely an ordinary, decent man. It is perhaps for this reason that today Orwell is claimed by socialists, liberals, and conservatives alike.

Poetry Modern poetry found its first great master in William Butler Yeats (1865–1939). His early poems are filled with Romantic mysticism, drawing on the myths of his native Ireland. By 1910 he had stripped his verses of Romantic allusions, and yet in his later works, he never gave up entirely his belief in the occult or the importance of myth. As Irish patriots grew more hostile to their country's continued submersion in the United Kingdom, climaxing in the Easter Rebellion of 1916, Yeats's poems took on a political cast. His best verses came in the 1920s, when his primary sources were Irish history and Greco-Roman myth. Perhaps his finest lyric is "Sailing to Byzantium," a poem that conjures up the Classical past in order to reaffirm ancient wisdom and redeem the tawdry industrialized world.

T. S. Eliot (1888–1965) was another founder of Modern poetry. Reared in St. Louis and educated at Harvard, Eliot moved to London in 1915, becoming an English citizen in 1927. He and Ezra Pound (1885–1972), another American exile, established a school of poetry that reflected the crisis of confidence that seized Europe's intellectuals after World War I. Like those of the late Roman poets, Eliot's verses relied heavily on literary references and quotations.

"The Waste Land," published in 1922, showed Eliot's difficult, eclectic style; in 403 irregular lines, he quotes from or imitates thirty-five separate authors, including several citations from Shakespeare and Dante, adapts snatches from popular songs, and uses phrases in six foreign languages. Form matches content because the "waste land" itself represents a sterile, godless region without a future, a symbol drawn from medieval legend but changed by Eliot into a symbol of the hollowness of modern life. In 1927 he moved beyond such atheistic pessimism, finding solace by being received in the Church of England—a step he celebrated in the poem "Ash Wednesday," published in 1930.

The black American poet Langston Hughes (1902–1967) also belongs with the outstanding Modernists. Hughes drew inspiration from many sources, including Africa, Europe, and Mexico, but the ultimate power of his poetry came from the American experience: jazz, spirituals, and his anguish as a black man in a white world. Hughes's emergence, like that of many black writers, occurred during a population shift that began in 1914 when thousands of blacks from the American South settled in northern cities like New York, Chicago, and Detroit in hopes of a better life.

At the same time that America's ethnographic map was being redrawn, a craze for Negro culture sprang up that was fueled by jazz and the *avant-garde* cult of primitivism. This craze sparked the Harlem Renaissance, a 1920s cultural revival in the predominantly black area of New York City called Harlem. Hughes was a major figure in this black literary movement. His earliest book of verses, *The Weary Blues* (1926), contains his most famous poem, "The Negro Speaks of Rivers." Dedicated to W. E. B. DuBois (1868–1963), the founder of the National Association for the Advancement of Colored People, Hughes's verse memorializes the deathless spirit of his race by linking black history to the rivers of the world.

Drama During the interwar years drama moved in new directions in both Europe and America. An Expressionist in aesthetics and a Marxist in politics, the German Bertolt Brecht (1898–1956) blended a discordant style learned from the Berlin streets with his hatred of bourgeois society into what he called *"epic theater."* Rebelling against traditional theater, which he thought merely reinforced class prejudices, he devised a radical theater centered on a technique called

the "alienation effect," whose purpose was to make the bourgeois audience uncomfortable (Figure 20.8). Alienation effects could take any form, such as outlandish props, inappropriate accents, or ludicrous dialogue. By breaking the magic spell of the stage, Brecht's epic theater challenged the viewers' expectations and prepared them for his moral and political message. A victim of Nazi oppression, Brecht fled first to Scandinavia and then to America, where he lived for fifteen years before moving to East Berlin in 1952 to found a highly influential theater company.

A year before he officially embraced Marxism, Brecht teamed with the German-born composer Kurt Weill (1900–1950) to create one of the best-known musicals in modern theater, *The Threepenny Opera* (1928). Loosely based on an eighteenth-century Eng-

FIGURE 20.8 GEORGE GROSZ. *Life Model (Akt).* Ca. 1919. Watercolor, India ink, and collage, 42 × 29 cm. Thyssen-Bornemisza Foundation Collection, Lugano, Switzerland. *The works of German artist George Grosz provide a visual counterpart to the dramas of Brecht. Grosz portrays bourgeois society as morally bankrupt, as in this painting of a brothel scene that shows a prostitute as a willing victim. Brecht makes the same point in the drama* Mother Courage *by presenting a businesswoman heroine interested only in making money even though it means sacrificing her sons in war.*

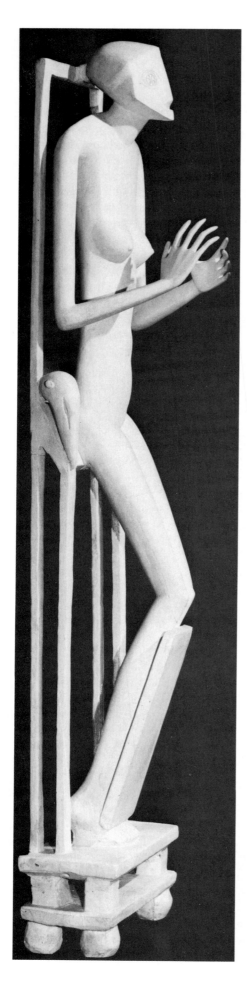

lish opera, Brecht and Weill's Expressionist version was raucous, discordant, violent, and hostile to bourgeois values. The playwright, believing that bourgeois audiences wanted goodness to triumph over evil, made the hero a small-time hoodlum ("Mack the Knife") and then saved him at the last moment from a hanging that he richly deserved.

Besides such pathfinders as Brecht, this period also produced two major Modernist playwrights. The first of these was Jean Cocteau (1889–1963), a French dramatist who helped to launch the French trend for modernizing the Greek classics. For example, Cocteau's *The Infernal Machine* (1934) updates Sophocles' *Oedipus*. In this modern retelling, the story is filled with Freudian overtones—Oedipus is portrayed as a "mother's boy"—and film clips are introduced for flashbacks. A second major Modernist was Eugene O'Neill (1888–1953), America's first dramatist to earn worldwide fame. Like Cocteau, O'Neill sometimes wrote new versions of Greek tragedies, as in *Mourning Becomes Electra* (1931), which was modeled on Aeschylus's *Oresteia*. But O'Neill's best plays are his tense family dramas in which generations battle one another, as in *Long Day's Journey into Night*, staged posthumously in 1956.

Philosophy and Science: The End of Certainty

During this period the Idealist philosophy that had dominated continental speculation since the early 1800s was replaced by two new schools of thought. First, in Austria and England Ludwig Wittgenstein developed ideas that helped establish the logical positivist school, which became known after World War II as the analytical school. Second, in Germany Martin Heidegger founded the existentialist school. Both schools tried to create new philosophies that were in harmony with Modernist developments.

The Austrian Ludwig Wittgenstein (1889–1951) believed that the West was in a moral and intellectual decline that he attributed to faulty language, for which he surmised that current philosophical meth-

▶ **FIGURE 20.9** ALBERTO GIACOMETTI. *Hands Holding the Void.* 1934. Plaster sculpture, original cast, ht. 61½". Yale University Art Gallery, New Haven, Connecticut. Anonymous gift. *The uncertainty of the modern world—as demonstrated both by physics and by the economic and social realities of everyday life—is poignantly symbolized in Giacometti's sculpture. Despite the problems they faced, human beings could no longer expect answers to their questions from traditional sources, such as science and philosophy. Giacometti's melancholy figure clutching an invisible object evokes the anguish of this predicament.*

ods were to blame. Wittgenstein asserted that traditional philosophical speculation was senseless because, of necessity, it relied on language that could not rise above simple truisms.

Wittgenstein's solution to this intellectual impasse dethroned philosophy from the summit from which it had looked down on the rest of culture since the time of the Greeks and made philosophy simply the servant of science. He set forth his conclusion in his *Tractatus Logico-Philosophicus* in 1922. In this treatise he reasoned that, although language might be faulty, there still were tools for comprehending the world, namely mathematical computation and scientific empiricism. He proposed that thinkers give up the study of values and morals and assist scientists in a quest for truth. This conclusion led to *logical positivism*, a school of philosophy dedicated to defining terms and clarifying statements.

Wittgenstein later rejected the idea that language is a flawed instrument and substituted a theory of language as games, in the manner of children's play. Nevertheless, it was the point of view set forth in the *Tractatus* that made Wittgenstein so influential in the universities in England between 1930 and 1960 and in America after World War II.

While Wittgenstein was challenging philosophy's ancient role, Martin Heidegger (1889–1976) was assaulting traditional philosophy from another angle by founding modern *existentialism*, although the result of Heidegger's massive criticism was to restore philosophy to its central position as the definer of values for culture. Heidegger's major work, *Being and Time,* was published in 1927. The focal point of his thinking was the peculiar nature of human existence (the source of the term "existentialism") as compared with other objects in the world. In his view human existence leads to anxiety, a condition that arises because of the consciousness that there is a future that includes choices and death. He noted that most people try to avoid facing their inevitable fate by immersing themselves in trivial activities. For a few, however, Heidegger thought that the existential moment offered an opportunity in which they could seize the initiative and make themselves into authentic human beings. "Authenticity" became the ultimate human goal: to confront death and to strive for genuine creativity—a typical German philosophical attitude shared with Goethe and Nietzsche.

Heidegger is among the twentieth century's foremost philosophers, but his politics have made him a controversial figure. He used his post as a German university professor to support the rise of Nazism in the 1930s. To hostile eyes, Heidegger's existential views—which acknowledged that individuals, powerless to reshape the world, could only accept it—

seemed to support his political position. Indeed, some commentators have condemned existentialism for this reason.

Heidegger's best-known disciple, though one who rejected Nazism, was the French thinker Jean-Paul Sartre (1905–1980). Sartre's major philosophical work, *Being and Nothingness* (1943), was heavily indebted to his mentor's concepts. From Heidegger came his definition of existentialism as an attitude characterized by concern for human freedom, personal responsibility, and individual choices. Sartre used these ideas to frame his guiding rule: Because human beings are condemned to freedom, that is, not free *not* to choose, they must take responsibility for their actions and live "without excuses." After 1945 Sartre rejected existentialism as overly individualistic and thereafter tended to support Marxist collectivist action.

In the sciences, physics remained the field of dynamic activity. The breakthroughs made before World War I were now corroborated by new research that compelled scientists to discard the Newtonian model of the universe as a simple machine. They replaced it with a complex, sense-defying structure based on the discoveries of Albert Einstein and Werner Heisenberg (Figure 20.9).

Einstein was the leading scientist in the West, comparable to Newton in the eighteenth century. His special relativity theory, dating from 1905, was accepted by most physicists. By this theory the Newtonian concept of fixed dimensions to time and space was overthrown because, in Einstein's view, absolute space and time are meaningless categories since they vary with the situation. In 1915 he expanded this earlier finding into a general theory of relativity, a universal law based on complex equations that applied throughout the cosmos.

The heart of the general theory was that space is curved as a result of the acceleration of objects (planets, stars, moons, meteors, and so on) as they move through undulating trajectories. The earth's orbit about the sun is caused not by a gravitational "force" but by the curvature of space-time around the sun. In 1919 a team of scientists confirmed his theory by observing the curvature of space in the vicinity of the sun. They found that space curved to the degree that Einstein's theory had forecast. Since then his general theory has survived many tests of its validity and has opened new paths of theoretical speculation.

Despite his commanding role in twentieth-century science, Einstein ignored the other great breakthrough of modern physics, the establishment of quantum physics. Prior to 1914 the German physicist Max Planck had discovered the quantum nature of radiation in the subatomic realm. Ignoring the classical theory that energy is radiated continuously, he proved that energy is emitted in separate units that he called *quanta*, after the Latin for "how much" (as in *quantity*), and he symbolized these units by the letter *h*.

Working with Planck's *h* in 1927, which by now was accepted as a fundamental constant of nature, the German physicist Werner Heisenberg (1901–1976) arrived at the uncertainty principle, a step that encompassed a decisive break with classical physics. Heisenberg showed that a scientist could identify an electronic particle's exact location or its path, but not both. This dilemma led to the conclusion that absolute certitude in subatomic science is impossible because scientists with their instruments inevitably interfere with the accuracy of their own work—the uncertainty principle. The incertitude involved in quantum theory caused Einstein to remark, "God does not throw dice." Nevertheless, quantum theory joined relativity theory as a founding principle of modern physics.

A practical result of the revolution in physics was the opening of the nuclear age in August 1945. The American physicist J. Robert Oppenheimer (1904–1967), having made basic contributions to quantum theory, was the logical choice to head the team that built the first atomic bomb. Oppenheimer's other role as a member of the panel that advised that the atomic bombs be dropped on Japan raised ethical questions that divided the scientific community then and continues to do so.

Art, Architecture, and Film

The art, architecture, and film of the interwar period were driven by the same forces that were transforming literature and philosophy. Modernism reached its zenith in painting and architecture, and the movies became established as the world's most popular form of mass culture (Time Line 20.1).

Painting   Painting dominated the visual arts in the interwar period. Painters launched new art movements every two or three years, although certain prevailing themes and interests could be discerned underneath the shifting styles: abstraction, primitivism and fantasy, and Expressionism. This era's most explosive art was produced within these stylistic categories. Picasso and Matisse, the two giants of twentieth-century art, continued to exercise their influence, yet they too worked within these three categories, all of which had arisen in the Post-Impressionist period.

ABSTRACTION   The history of modern painting has been rewritten in the last twenty-five years to accommodate the contributions of Soviet painters to abstract art. No one questions the primary role played by Picasso and Braque in Cubist paintings prior to World War I, but Soviet painters, beginning in 1917, moved beyond Cubism and toward full abstraction, thus staking out claims as early founders of modern abstract art. The most influential of these Soviet artists was Kasimir Malevich (1878–1935).

Influenced by the Cubists and the Futurists—an Italian school of artists who depicted forms in surging, violent motion—Malevich was already working

FIGURE 20.10   KASIMIR MALEVICH. *Suprematist Composition, Black Trapezium and Red Square.* After 1915. Oil on canvas, 101.5 × 62 cm. Stedelijk Museum, Amsterdam. *Malevich's geometric style reflected his belief that abstract images had a spiritual quality comparable to religious icons. In other words, an abstract form could become a meditation device. His belief was typical of thinking among the German and Russian avant-garde in the early 1900s. In the interwar period the principle of the spirituality of abstract art became widely accepted by Modernist painters throughout Europe and, after World War II, by Abstract Expressionist artists in America.*

TIME LINE 20.1   HIGH MODERNISM, 1914–1945

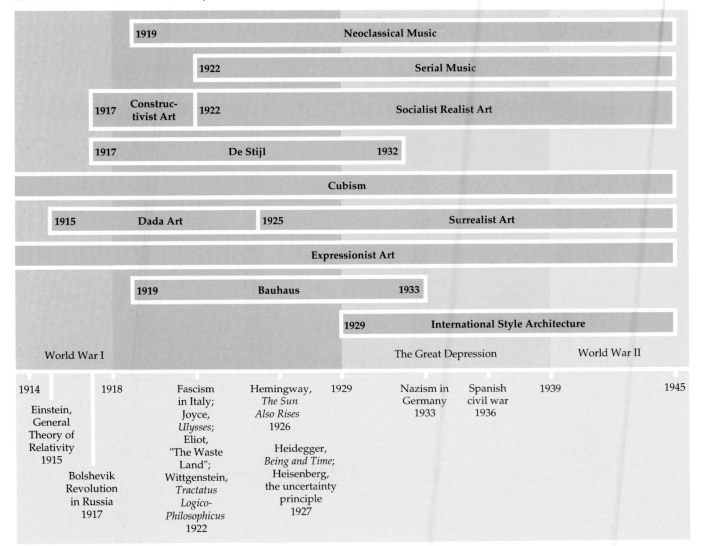

in an abstract style when World War I began in 1914. Four years later he was painting completely nonobjective canvases. Believing that art should convey ethical and philosophical values, he created a style of painting devoted to purity, in which he made line, color, and shape the only purposes in his art. He called this style *Suprematism,* named for his belief that the feelings are "supreme" over every other element of life—"feelings," that is, expressed in a purely rational way.

Searching for a way to visualize emotions on canvas, Malevich adopted geometric shapes as nonobjective symbols, as in *Suprematist Composition, Black Trapezium and Red Square* (Figure 20.10). In this painting design has triumphed over representation. There are only geometric shapes of different sizes, dominated by the trapezium and the square, along with lines of varying length. The choice of the geometric shapes reflects their role as basic elements of com-

position with no relation to nature. The qualities shown in Malevich's painting—flatness, coolness, and severe rationality—remain central to one branch of abstract art today.

Malevich's Suprematism helped to shape *Constructivism,* the first art style launched by Lenin's regime in 1917 and the last modern art movement in Russia. Malevich's philosophical views, which were rooted in Christian mysticism, ran counter to the materialism of the Marxist government, however, and the flowering of abstraction in the Soviet Union was abruptly snuffed out in 1922. In that year Lenin pronounced it a decadent form of bourgeois expression, and its leaders were imprisoned or exiled. In place of Constructivism the Soviet leaders proclaimed the doctrine of *Socialist Realism,* which demanded the use of traditional techniques and styles and the glorification of the communist ideal. This type of realistic art also had greater appeal to the Soviet masses,

◀ **FIGURE 20.11** PIET MONDRIAN. *Composition in Red, Yellow, and Blue.* 1921. Oil on canvas, 80 × 50 cm. Collection Haags Gemeentemuseum, The Hague. *Allied with those artists who identified abstract forms with spiritual values, Mondrian originated "the grid" as the ideal way to approach the canvas, allowing the verticals and horizontals to establish the painting area. Mondrian's devotion to "the grid," along with his spare use of color, gave rise to many of the dominant trends in art after World War II: two-dimensional images, geometric shapes, and "all over" paintings without a specific up or down.*

who had been alienated by the abstract style of Constructivism.

A movement similar to Suprematism and Constructivism, called **De Stijl** (The Style), originated in the Netherlands during this period, lasting from 1917 to 1932. *De Stijl* artists shared the belief that art should have spiritual values and that if artists were to revamp society along rational lines, from town planning to eating utensils, a more harmonious vision of life would result.

The *De Stijl* movement was led by the painter Piet Mondrian (1872–1944), who after 1919 worked successively in Paris, London, and New York. He developed an elaborate theory to give a metaphysical meaning to his abstract paintings. A member of the Theosophists—a mystical cult that flourished around 1900—he adapted some of their beliefs to arrive at a grid format for his later paintings, notably using the Theosophists' stress on cosmic duality in which the vertical represented the male and the horizontal the female. His paintings took the form of a rectangle divided by heavy black lines against a white background. Into this highly charged field he introduced rectangular patches of the primary colors, blue, yellow, and red, which in his mystic vision stood as symbols of the sky, the sun, and dynamic union, respectively (Figure 20.11).

Despite the pioneering work of Suprematism and the *De Stijl* school, Cubism remained the leading art movement of this period, and Pablo Picasso was still the reigning Cubist. Picasso's protean genius revealed itself in multiple styles after 1920, but he continually reverted to his Cubist roots, as in *The Three Musicians* (Figure 20.12). Like the rest of his works, this painting is based on a realistic source, in this case a group of masked musicians playing their instruments. The forms appear flattened, as if they were shapes that had been cut out and then pasted to the pictorial surface—the ideal of flatness so prized by Modern art.

The most famous work of Picasso's long career also dates from this period: the protest canvas *Guernica*, painted in a modified Cubist style. Picasso named this painting for an unarmed town that had been bombed by the Nazi air force (in the service of Franco) during the Spanish Civil War. Picasso used every element in the work to register his rage against this senseless destruction of human life (see Figure 20.1). The black, white, and grey tones conjure up newspaper images, suggesting the casual way that newspapers report daily disasters. An all-seeing eye looks down on a scene of horror made visible to the world through the modern media—as symbolized by the electric bulb that acts as a retina in the cosmic eye. Images of death and destruction—the mother cradling a child's body, the stabbed horse, the enraged bull, the fallen man, and the screaming woman—are made even more terrifying by their angular forms. In retrospect, *Guernica* was a watershed painting both topically and stylistically. The blending of Cubism with social protest was new—as was Franco's type of unbridled warfare. *Guernica* forecast even more horrifying events to come.

FIGURE 20.12 PABLO PICASSO. *The Three Musicians.* 1921. Oil on canvas, 6'8" × 6'2". Philadelphia Museum of Art. The A. E. Gallatin Collection. *This Cubist painting captures the energy of a musical performance. Here and there among the flattened shapes can be seen hints of musical instruments being fingered by disembodied hands. Only a little imagination is needed to bring this masked trio to life. The brilliant colors coupled with the broken and resynthesized forms evoke the jagged rhythms the musicians must have been playing.*

◄ **FIGURE 20.13** MARCEL DUCHAMP. *The Bride Stripped Bare by Her Bachelors, Even (or, The Large Glass). 1915–1923. Oil and lead wire on glass, 9'1¼" × 5'9⅛". Philadelphia Museum of Art. Bequest of Katherine M. Dreier. Shortly after this legendary assemblage was built, the glass shattered. Duchamp repaired the work, replacing the glass with heavier panes and installing a reinforced frame. But effects of the accident are still apparent. Duchamp claimed to be delighted by these chance additions to his original design. In making this claim, he was the forerunner of the Modernist idea that chance should play a guiding role in art. After World War II many artists began to incorporate random effects into their works.*

PRIMITIVISM AND FANTASY The Modernists' admiration for Primitivism led to **Dada**, the most unusual art movement of the twentieth century. Named for a nonsense word chosen for its ridiculous sound, Dada flourished in Zurich and Paris between 1915 and 1925, chiefly as unruly pranks by disaffected artists who wanted to "hurl gobs of spit in the faces of the bourgeoisie." They staged exhibits in public lavatories, planned meetings in cemeteries, and arranged lectures where the speaker was drowned out by a bell. Slowly it became evident that these outrageous acts conveyed the message that World War I had made all values meaningless. These artists could no longer support the spiritual claims and traditional beliefs of Western humanism. The Dada group embraced anti-art as the only ethical position possible for an artist in the modern era.

The most influential exponent of Dada was the French artist Marcel Duchamp (1887–1968), who abandoned Cubism in about 1915. His best-known Dada piece is the "definitely incomplete" work called

The Bride Stripped Bare by Her Bachelors, Even, a mixture of oil, wire, and lead foil on two glass panels made between 1915 and 1923, sometimes called *The Large Glass* (Figure 20.13). Although it is certainly enigmatic, and in the eyes of many viewers it looked like a giant swindle, much is clear about *The Large Glass*. It has an erotic theme, as indicated by the bride's "apartment" in the upper half, the bachelors' "chamber" below, and the thin tubes filled with oil linking the two segments. Duchamp's point seems to be similar to that of the novelist D. H. Lawrence: Sex in the machine age has become boring and mechanized.

Dada led to **Surrealism**, an art movement that began in the 1920s. Unlike Dada, Surrealism was basically a pictorial art. Inspired by Freud's teaching that the human mind conceals hidden depths, the Surrealists wanted to create a vision of reality that also included the truths harbored in the unconscious. They portrayed dream imagery, fantasies, and hallucinations in a direct fashion that made their paintings more startling than Dada. Among the leading Surrealists were Salvador Dali and Paul Klee.

The Spanish painter Salvador Dali (1904–1989) concentrated on subjects that surfaced from his lively imagination and often contained thinly disguised sexual symbols. Probably his most famous work is the poetically named painting *The Persistence of Memory*, which depicts soft, melting watches in a desert-like setting (Figure 20.14). Sexual themes may be read in the limp images of watches—perhaps a reference to sexual impotence. Regardless of its meaning, the painting gives a strange twist to ordinary things,

FIGURE 20.14 SALVADOR DALI. *The Persistence of Memory. 1931. Oil on canvas, 9½ × 13". Collection, The Museum of Modern Art, New York. Given anonymously. Dali liked to paint images that were actually optical illusions. In this painting, the watch depicted on the right is draped over an amorphous shape that, on inspection, appears to be that of a man. Dali's use of such optical effects reflected his often-stated belief that life itself is irrational.*

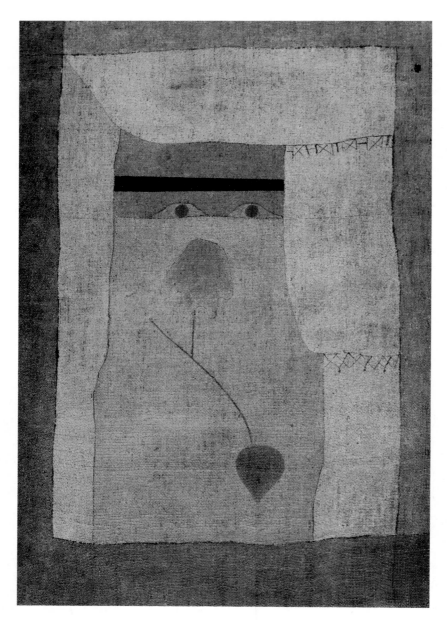

FIGURE 20.15 PAUL KLEE. *Arab Song.* 1932. Gouache on unprimed burlap, 35⅞ × 25½". Phillips Collection, Washington, D.C. *Klee's enigmatic art is difficult to classify. Because he preferred small images, he is sometimes classed as a minor artist. And unlike most European artists of his generation, who made spiritual claims for art, Klee had modest, earthbound goals for his whimsical works. Yet Klee's playful images remain in the mind long after the stark abstract designs of Malevich and Mondrian have faded.*

evoking the sense of a half-remembered dream—the goal of Surrealist art. Despite obvious painterly skills, Dali cultivated a controversial, even scandalous personal image. His escapades earned him the public's ridicule, and the Surrealists even disowned him. From today's vantage point, however, Dali is admired for two reasons: for having created some of Modernism's most fantastic images and for being a link with the Pop artists of the 1960s.

The Swiss painter Paul Klee (1879–1940) may be grouped with the Surrealists, but he was too mercurial to be restricted to a single style. He is best known for an innocent approach to art, which was triggered by his fondness for children's uninhibited scrawls. The childlike wonder portrayed in his whimsical works have made him a favorite with collectors and viewers. A professor from 1920 until 1930 at the Bauhaus, Germany's leading art institute between the wars, Klee created poetic images, rich in color and gentle wit, as in *Arab Song* (Figure 20.15). The draperies, painted on burlap, evoke an Arabic mood with their twin references to tents and to a veiled woman. The leaf and bud, floating in space, contribute an unexpected, lyrical note. Other traits of Klee's style may be seen in *Arab Song*'s small scale, radiant colors, and playfulness.

EXPRESSIONISM The chief Expressionist painters in this era were Henri Matisse, a founder of Fauvism before World War I, and Max Beckmann, the heir to German Expressionism. In the 1930s Matisse's art was distinguished by its decorative quality, a tendency since his Fauvist days. *Large Reclining Nude* shows his new style, which is characterized by a fresh approach to the human figure: enlarged, simplified, though clearly recognizable (Figure 20.16). The nude figure is depicted completely flat, without modeling or shading, so that it looks as if it has been cut out and glued to the gridded surface. He has also abandoned the highly saturated colors of Fauvism and replaced them with cooler tones, in this case a cotton-candy pink. Nevertheless, Matisse stayed true to the Expressionist principle of distortion, as demonstrated by the nude figure's elongated body and dangling limbs.

Matisse has been rebuked for concentrating on pretty subjects while the world slipped into anarchy.

No such charge can be made against the German painter Max Beckmann (1884–1950), whose Expressionist paintings register horror at the era's turbulent events. *The Temptation of St. Anthony* is typical of his paintings, being concerned with both personal and spiritual issues (Figure 20.17). The structure of the painting—divided into three panels like a medieval altarpiece—suggests that it has religious meaning. In the central panel Beckmann depicts an artist, bound at the wrists and ankles and musing before a nude model, perhaps a symbol of Beckmann himself, whose art the Nazis condemned as degenerate. The side panels, with themes of temptation and cruelty, reinforce the connection between the artist-sufferer and a medieval saint. In the same year this painting

FIGURE 20.16 HENRI MATISSE. *Large Reclining Nude*. 1935. Oil on canvas, 66 × 92 cm. Baltimore Museum of Art. The Cone Collection. Large Reclining Nude *established the archetypal images—a still life and a model in an interior—that Matisse painted for the rest of his life. It was also the first expression of his later style, which was characterized by the human figure being simply another element in an overall design.*

FIGURE 20.17 MAX BECKMANN. *The Temptation of St. Anthony*. 1937. Oil on canvas, triptych, center panel, 6′6¾″ × 5′7″; side panels each 7′1″ × 3′3⅜″. Bayerische Staatsgalerie Moderner Kunst, Munich. *Beckmann often adopted Christian symbols as his paintings became more overtly spiritual in their content. In paintings like* Temptation *he identified twentieth-century artists with medieval saints, drawing the parallel that both had to go against the common wisdom of their times in order to reach seemingly impossible goals.*

was completed, pressure from the Nazis forced Beckmann to seek refuge in Amsterdam, where he managed to survive World War II.

Architecture In the 1920s and 1930s, architects continued their search for a pure style, free of decoration and totally functional. Their search resembled a mystical quest, stemming from the belief that new architecture could solve social problems by creating a new physical environment—a recurrent theme in European Modernism.

This visionary conception of architecture was best expressed in Germany's Bauhaus, an educational institution whose aim was to bring about social reform through a new visual environment, especially in the design of everyday objects. To this end, the school brought together artists, craftspeople, and architects. During its brief lifetime, which lasted from its founding in 1919 until 1933 when it was closed by the Nazis, the Bauhaus, under Walter Gropius (1883–1969), was the center of abstract art in Germany. The Bauhaus affected later culture in two ways. First, it developed a spartan type of interior decoration characterized by all-white rooms and wooden floors, streamlined furniture, and lighting supplied by banks of windows by day and recessed lamps at night. Sec-

ond, it introduced the ***International Style*** in architecture, which is sleek, geometrical, and devoid of ornament.

The International Style's most distinguished representative in the period between the wars was the Swiss architect Charles-Edouard Jeanneret, better known as Le Corbusier (1887–1965). Le Corbusier's artistic credo was expressed in the dictum, "a house is a machine for living." In pursuit of this ideal, he pioneered building methods like prefabricated housing and reinforced concrete as ways to eliminate ordinary walls. His Savoye House became the prototype of private houses for the wealthy after World War II (Figure 20.18). The Savoye House was painted white and raised on columns; its ground floor had a curved wall; and its windows were slits. A painter before becoming an architect, Le Corbusier designed architecture that combined Cubism's abstractness (the raised box) with Constructivism's purity (whiteness).

Film Motion pictures—the movies—were immediately popular when they were introduced early in the twentieth century, and by the mid–1920s they had become the most popular mass entertainment, drawing larger audiences than the theater, vaudeville, and the music halls. The American film director D. W. Griffith (1875–1948) showed in such pioneering works as *The Birth of a Nation* (1915) and *Intolerance* (1916) that it was possible to make movies that were serious, sustained works of art. His technical innovations, such as cross-cutting and the close-up, made more complex film narratives possible, but such attempts to develop the medium were rare. Although other directors quickly appropriated Griffith's techniques, few went beyond them, and the movies remained resolutely lowbrow. The present-day distinction between "movies" (the widest possible audience) and "film" (appealing to more educated, intellectual audiences) had not yet arisen.

One of the era's most inventive directors was the Russian Sergei Eisenstein (1898–1948), who introduced directorial techniques that had an enormous influence on the rise of art films. In *The Battleship Potemkin* (1925) he pioneered the montage technique, which consisted of highly elaborate editing patterns and rhythms. He developed the montage because he believed that the key element in films was the way the scenes were arranged, how they faded out and faded in, and how they looked in juxtaposition to one another. By focusing on the material of the film itself instead of highlighting the plot or the characters' psychology, Eisenstein showed his allegiance to the artistic aspect of movie making.

The United States (which eventually meant Hollywood, California) had dominated the motion picture industry since World War I, and the industry underwent important changes during the interwar years. Sound movies became technically feasible in the late 1920s, and in the early 1930s three-color cinematography processes were developed. Both these technical developments became basic to the movies throughout the world, but other experiments, such as wide-screen and three-dimensional photography, were less successful. Another important development in this period was the descent on Hollywood of many German filmmakers in flight from the Nazis. In the Hollywood of the 1930s these exiles helped to create some of the outstanding achievements in world cinema.

A sign of the excellence of Hollywood movies in these years is Orson Welles's *Citizen Kane* (1941), often called America's best film. An American, Welles (1915–1985) had learned from the German exiles and their Expressionist methods. From them he borrowed such devices as theatrical lighting and multiple nar-

FIGURE 20.18 LE CORBUSIER. Savoye House. 1929–1931. Poissy, near Paris.
Le Corbusier wanted to make a break with previous styles of architecture and create a new style in tune with the machine age. His design for the Savoye House realizes this ambition completely through its severe geometrical form, its absence of decoration except for architectural details, and its sparkling white walls. When finished, the Savoye House had the streamlined look associated with industrial machinery, an achievement much admired in the 1930s.

rative voices. Welles's own commanding presence in the lead role also contributed to making this an unforgettable movie. But one of the hallmarks of the movie—its dark look, which underscores the brooding theme of unbridled lust for power—was in actuality a money-saving device to disguise the absence of studio sets. Is *Citizen Kane* a "film" or a "movie"? It is a measure of Welles's success that it is triumphantly both: The frequency of its showing both on television and in theaters attests to its popularity, yet it has probably been discussed and analyzed in film journals and books as much as any film ever made.

Music: Atonality, Neoclassicism, and American Idiom

During the 1920s and 1930s Western music was fragmented into two rival camps as a result of developments that had begun in the period before World War I. On one side was the Austro-German school headed by Arnold Schoenberg, who had introduced atonality before 1914 and in the 1920s pioneered serial music. On the other side was the French school led by Igor Stravinsky, who had experimented with primitive rhythms and harsh dissonances in the early 1900s but after World War I adopted a stern Neoclassical style.

Having abandoned tonality in 1909, Schoenberg in the 1920s introduced **serial music**, a method of composing with a **twelve-tone scale**—twelve tones that are related not to a tonal center in a major or minor key but only to each other. Lacking harmonious structure, serial music sounded dissonant and random and tended to create anxiety in listeners. As a result, serial music appealed to cult rather than mass audiences. Lack of a huge responsive public did not halt Schoenberg's pursuit of atonality. His serial system culminated in *Variations for Orchestra* (1928), a composition that uses the Classical form of theme with variations. In 1933 he emigrated to America, where his devotion to atonality mellowed. Some of Schoenberg's later works mix twelve-tone writing with tonality.

Stravinsky, in exile from the Soviet Union after 1917, was now living in Paris, where he became the dominant figure of *Neoclassicism* in music, borrowing features from seventeenth- and eighteenth-century music (Figure 20.19). In his Neoclassical works, he abandoned many of the techniques that had become common to music since the Baroque period, such as Romantic emotionalism and programmatic composition as well as Impressionism's use of dense orchestral sounds. Austere and cool, his Neoclassical compositions used simple instrumental combinations and sounded harmonious. Stravinsky's

works from this period made him the outstanding composer of the twentieth century.

Stravinsky originated Neoclassicism in 1919 with the ballet *Pulcinella* and brought the style to a close in 1951 with the opera *The Rake's Progress*. Between these two major works is one of his most admired compositions, the *Symphony of Psalms*, dating from 1930. *Pulcinella* and *The Rake's Progress* owe much to the music and comic operas of the Classical composers Pergolesi and Mozart, respectively, and the *Symphony of Psalms* follows a Baroque model in its small orchestra and musical structure. Despite borrowing forms and ideas, Stravinsky made them his own, introducing occasional dissonances and continuing to experiment with complex rhythmic patterns.

American music, meanwhile, was discovering its own idiom. Charles Ives (1874–1954) focused on American melodies, including folk songs, hymns, marches, patriotic songs, ragtime tunes, and music of his beloved New England. Working without

FIGURE 20.19 PABLO PICASSO. *Stravinsky*. 1920. Pencil on gray paper, 24⅜″ × 19⅛″. Musée Picasso, Paris. *Picasso's pencil sketch of Stravinsky is a perceptive character study. Long before Stravinsky became almost unapproachable, Picasso portrayed him as an aloof, self-absorbed young man. Stravinsky's cold demeanor is obvious in the tense posture, the harsh stare, and the clasped hands and crossed legs. Picasso's sketch also hints at Stravinsky's genius by exaggerating the size of his hands, perhaps to emphasize their role in the composer's creative life.*

models, Ives experimented with tonality and rhythm in similar ways to the European *avant-garde*. Typical of his work is the *Concord Sonata* for piano (1909–1915). Another American composer, Aaron Copland (1900–1990), had achieved some success by imitating European styles, but in the 1930s he began to develop a distinctive American style. His ballet scores *Billy the Kid* (1938), *Rodeo* (1942), and *Appalachian Spring* (1944) draw on hymns, ballads, folk tunes, and popular songs of the period. His delightful melodies, brilliant sound, jazzy experimentation, and upbeat rhythms ensured the popularity of these pieces.

During this period jazz began to reach larger audiences, in part because of the development of the radio and phonograph. Many jazz greats created their reputations in these years. The fame of the finest jazz composer, Duke Ellington (born Edward Kennedy Ellington, 1899–1974), dated from 1927 at Harlem's Cotton Club. Ellington's songs balanced superb or-chestration with improvisation and ranged from popular melodies, like *Sophisticated Lady,* to major suites, like *Such Sweet Thunder,* based on Shakespeare. Jazz's premiere female vocalist also appeared now, Billie Holiday (1915–1959), whose style was marked by innovative phrasing and a bittersweet sound.

Two jazz performers whose careers extended well beyond this period are Louis Armstrong (1900–1971) and Ella Fitzgerald (1918–). Armstrong, better known as "Satchmo," became a goodwill ambassador for the United States with his loud and relaxed New Orleans-style trumpet playing. Ella Fitzgerald, a vocalist noted for her bell-like voice and elegant phrasing, became the peerless interpreter of jazz standards as well as pop tunes. In the next period, jazz fragmented into a host of styles and was a vital ingredient in the explosive birth of rock-and-roll, the popular music form originating in the 1960s that has since dominated popular music.

The Legacy of the Age of the Masses and Modernism

The Age of the Masses has transformed material civilization in the West in both good and bad ways. It has given us the most destructive wars of history, the greatest economic depression since the fourteenth century, the most absolute forms of government since the late Roman Empire, the first modern attempt to eliminate an entire people, and a weapon capable of destroying the planet. At the same time, it has brought a better standard of living to most people in the West and given millions of Westerners their first taste of democracy.

This age has also had a contradictory impact on cultural developments. On the one hand, it saw the growth of a worldwide mass culture, led by American ingenuity, which began to dominate public and private life for most people. On the other hand, it inspired a revolt by Modernist artists, writers, and musicians to create works free of mass culture's influence. Their Modernist creations were experimental, perplexing, and often committed to what they defined as spiritual values. A few Modernists refused to become mass culture's adversaries, and these moderating voices pointed toward a healthier relationship between mass culture and the elitist tradition after World War II.

Besides the polarization between mass and high culture, this period left other cultural legacies. During this time films became accepted as a serious art form, and they remain the greatest legacy of mass culture to the twentieth century. It was also during this period that America emerged as a significant cultural force in the West, partly because of the tide of intellectuals flowing from Europe, partly because of America's growing political, economic, and military power, and partly because of excellent native schools of writers, musicians, and artists. And finally, a questioning mood became the normative way of looking at the world, replacing the certainty of previous centuries.

The Modernists had pioneered a questioning spirit around 1900, and in this period the revolution in physics seemed to reinforce it. Einstein's conclusion that space and time are interchangeable was echoed by artists, writers, and musicians who focused on form to define content in their work. And Heisenberg's uncertainty principle seemed to reverberate everywhere—from Wittgenstein's toying with language, to the highly personal narrative voices that dominated the novel, to the constantly shrinking set of basic beliefs that characterized the period's religious thought, and ultimately to the widespread belief that Western civilization had lost its course.

KEY CULTURAL TERMS

mass culture

stream-of-consciousness

epic theater

logical positivism

existentialism

Suprematism

Constructivism

Socialist Realism

De Stijl

Dada

Surrealism

International Style

serial music

twelve-tone scale

Neoclassicism

SUGGESTIONS FOR FURTHER READING

PRIMARY SOURCES

BRECHT, B. *The Threepenny Opera*. English version by D. Vesey and English lyrics by E. Bentley. New York: Limited Editions Club, 1982. An excellent adaptation of Brecht's biting drama about the underworld in Victorian England; Bentley's lyrics capture the slangy flavor of the German play first staged in 1928.

COCTEAU, J. *The Infernal Machine and Other Plays*. Norfolk, Conn.: New Directions, 1964. Cocteau fuses Classicism with experimental methods in his Modernist plays; he updates the Oedipus legend, for example, by introducing Freudian ideas and using film clips to present flashbacks.

ELIOT, T. S. *Collected Poems, 1909–1962*. New York: Harcourt, Brace & World, 1963. Eliot's early portrayal of his times as an exhausted era abandoned by God made him a pillar of Modernism.

FAULKNER, W. *The Sound and the Fury*. New York: Modern Library, 1946. The most admired novel from the Yoknapatawpha series, Faulkner's monumental study of post–Civil War Mississippi society.

HEIDEGGER, M. *Being and Time*. Translated by J. Macquarrie and E. Robinson. New York: Harper, 1962. First published in 1927, this work helped launch the existentialist movement by portraying the universe as a meaningless place and human existence as a never-ending quest for authenticity.

HEMINGWAY, E. *The Sun Also Rises*. New York: Scribner, 1970. Hemingway's semiautobiographical first novel, set in France and Spain in 1925.

HUGHES, L. *Selected Poems of Langston Hughes*. London: Pluto, 1986. Poetry by one of the twentieth century's outstanding black writers.

JOYCE, J. *Ulysses*. New York: Penguin, 1986. This classic of Modernism uses a tapestry of narrative styles to portray a day in the lives of three middle-class citizens of Dublin.

LAWRENCE, D. H. *Lady Chatterley's Lover*. New York: Modern Library, 1983. A controversial work that poses sex as a panacea for the ills of contemporary industrialized life.

O'NEILL, E. *Three Plays: Desire Under the Elms, Strange Interlude, Mourning Becomes Electra*. New York: Vintage, 1961. O'Neill's trilogy of plays based on Aeschylus' *Oresteia* and involving a contemporary New England family.

ORWELL, G. *Animal Farm; Burmese Days; A Clergyman's Daughter; Coming Up for Air; Keep the Aspidistra Flying; Nineteen Eighty-four*. New York: Octopus/Heinemann, 1980. This volume contains Orwell's most significant writings, most of which convey the author's hatred of tyranny and his skepticism about the future of humanity.

SARTRE, J.-P. *Being and Nothingness: An Essay in Phenomenological Ontology*. Translated and with an introduction by H. E. Barnes. Abridged. New York: Citadel Press, 1956. Sartre sets forth his existentialist philosophy, focusing on such key ideas as individual freedom and personal responsibility.

WOOLF, V. *To the Lighthouse*. London: Hogarth Press, 1974. A typical Woolf novel in its stream-of-consciousness technique and its exquisitely detailed observations of contemporary thinking.

WITTGENSTEIN, L. *Tractatus Logico-philosophicus*. Translated by D. F. Pears and B. F. McGuiness, with an introduction by B. Russell. London: Routledge and Kegan Paul, 1974. An excellent English-language version of the treatise that led to logical positivism in philosophy.

YEATS, W. B. *The Collected Poems of W. B. Yeats*. Edited by R. J. Finneran. New York: Collier Books, 1989. One of Modernism's leading voices, Yeats wrote poetry devoted to such themes as Celtic myth, the tragic violence of Irish history, and the mystical nature of human existence.

SECONDARY SOURCES

ARENDT, H. *The Origins of Totalitarianism*. New York: Meridian Books, 1964. In this important work, Arendt traces the roots of totalitarianism to late-nineteenth-century anti-Semitism, imperialism, and racism.

BARRETT, W. *Time of Need: Forms of Imagination in the Twentieth Century*. New York: Harper & Row, 1972. Excellent analysis of key literary works, chiefly from an existentialist perspective.

BAUMONT, M. *The Origins of the Second World War*. Translated by S. D. Ferguson. New Haven: Yale University Press, 1978. An overview that looks for the causes of World War II in the failed peace after World War I.

CANTOR, N. F. *Twentieth Century Culture: Modernism to Deconstruction*. New York: Peter Lang, 1988. An engaging account with an invaluable section on Post-Modernism, despite the author's hostility to many of its features.

CARSTEN, F. L. *The Rise of Fascism*. 2d ed. London: Batsford, 1980. An overview of the origins of fascism in different countries; for the beginning student.

HAMILTON, G. H. *Painting and Sculpture in Europe, 1880–1940*. New York: Penguin, 1967. A well-organized history of the rise of Modern painting and sculpture; illustrated in black and white.

JOHNSON, P. *Modern Times: The World from the Twenties to the Eighties*. New York: Harper & Row, 1983. A lively and argumentative review of twentieth-century politics and culture by a leading conservative analyst.

LIDDELL HART, B. H. *History of the Second World War*. New York: Putnam, 1971. A first-rate study by a leading military historian.

———. *The Real War, 1914–1918*. Rev. ed. London: Cassell, 1970. A military history admired for its thoroughness and impartial treatment of major battles.

MARWICK, A. *War and Social Change in the Twentieth Century: A Comparative Study of Britain, France, Germany, Russia and the United States.* London: Macmillan, 1975. A survey of the impact of two world wars on each country.

SHIRER, W. L. *The Rise and Fall of the Third Reich.* New York: Simon and Schuster, 1960. Written by a witness to the rise of Hitler and the Nazis in Germany, this is a monumental yet very readable work.

SONTAG, R. J. *A Broken World, 1919–1939.* New York: Harper & Row, 1971. Records the upheavals of the interwar years, along with the changes in science, technology, and the arts.

THOMAS, H. *The Spanish Civil War.* New York: Harper & Row, 1977. Perhaps the most thorough and accurate account in English of the war that preceded World War II.

WRIGHT, G. *The Ordeal of Total War, 1939–1945.* New York: Harper & Row, 1968. For the more serious student interested in the phases of the war and its impact on all aspects of society.

SUGGESTIONS FOR LISTENING

COPLAND, AARON (1900–1990).

Copland's most popular works incorporate folk melodies and pay homage to the American way of life. Copland used cowboy songs in the ballet scores *Billy the Kid* (1938) and *Rodeo* (1942); he incorporated variations on the Shaker hymn *The Gift to Be Simple* in *Appalachian Spring* (1944), originally a ballet score that was later rearranged as a suite for sym-phony orchestra. His faith in the future of democracy is expressed most fully in the short, often-performed work, *Fanfare for the Common Man.*

ELLINGTON, EDWARD KENNEDY ("DUKE") (1899–1974).

Ellington's jazz style blended careful orchestration with ample opportunity for improvisation. Many of his songs have become standards in the popular music repertory, such as *Creole Love Call* (1928), *Mood Indigo* (1934), *Don't Get Around Much Anymore* (1940), and *Sophisticated Lady.* Less well known are his serious compositions, like *Such Sweet Thunder* and *In the Beginning God* (1965), a religious work.

IVES, CHARLES (1909–1951).

America's first great composer, Ives experimented with atonality, clashing rhythms, and dissonant harmony long before these became a standard part of twentieth-century music. He frequently drew on American themes, as in the *Concord Sonata* for piano (1909–1915) and the orchestral *Three Places in New England* (1903–1914, first performed in 1931), works that evoked the landscape of his native region. A good example of one of his atonal works is *The Unanswered Question* (1908), a small work for trumpet, four flutes, and strings.

SCHOENBERG, ARNOLD (1874–1951).

During this period Schoenberg, the leader of the school of atonality, originated serialism as a method of composing, as may be heard in *Variations for Orchestra* (1928), the unfinished opera *Moses and Aaron* (1932), and *Violin Concerto* (1936).

STRAVINSKY, IGOR (1882–1971).

Schoenberg's rival Stravinsky became the leader of Neoclassicism in music with the ballet *Pulcinella* (1919) and continued this musical style in such works as the *Symphony of Psalms* (1930), the opera-oratoria *Oedipus Rex* (*Oedipus the King*) (1927), the *Symphony in C* (1940), and the opera *The Rake's Progress* (1951).

21

THE AGE OF ANXIETY AND BEYOND

1945–

Fear of nuclear war had a profound and chilling effect on attitudes and events after 1945. It led to a massive buildup of weapons by the United States and the Soviet Union, since the conventional wisdom was that the specter of mutually assured destruction—MAD—was the best deterrent to war. The arms race in turn contributed to out-of-control national budgets devoted to military spending at the expense of needed domestic programs. Anxiety about nuclear war led many people to work for disarmament, but for others it produced a sense of absurdity and a mood of despair. Against the backdrop of these realities, the cultural style known as Late Modernism captured the feelings of anguish experienced by many artists, writers, and intellectuals.

Starting in about 1970, however, some of the gloom lifted as threats of nuclear war showed signs of subsiding and international tensions relaxed. In the arts, a more upbeat style referred to as Post-Modernism began to emerge. Characterized by a cautious optimism and an interest in reinterpreting past styles, Post-Modernism reflects a search for more positive ways of responding to the world.

Dramatic events in recent years have further altered the shape of the modern world and influenced its direction for the future. Changes in the political and economic structures of the Soviet Union and the countries of eastern Europe, a broadening of international influence beyond the traditional Western powers, and pressing environmental concerns have all contributed to the emergence of a global perspective on world events. The growth of a global culture is reflected in Post-Modernism, which is democratic and embraces diversity. At this point, the trend for the future seems to be toward a world civilization that recognizes common human concerns and honors the creative impulse in all people (Time Line 21.1).

FROM A EUROPEAN TO A WORLD CIVILIZATION

The end of World War II, instead of bringing peace, brought the Cold War, an era of international tensions and conflicting ideologies. World relations were governed by a bipolar balance of power. The United States stood for free enterprise and individual freedom and the Union of Soviet Socialist Republics (USSR) symbolized state planning and collectivist values. The American bloc came to include western Europe, the British Commonwealth, and the states defeated in World War II—Japan, West Germany, and Italy—and the Soviet bloc embraced virtually all of eastern Europe and, after 1949 when the Communists took power, China.

The chance that the Cold War could become a hot war seemed to increase daily for two reasons. First, the superpowers extended their confrontations to the Third World, rushing in to fill the vacuum as the West's colonial empires fell and were replaced by struggling independent states. Second, the development of ballistic missiles capable of hurtling nuclear

TIME LINE 21.1   CULTURAL STYLES, 1945–PRESENT

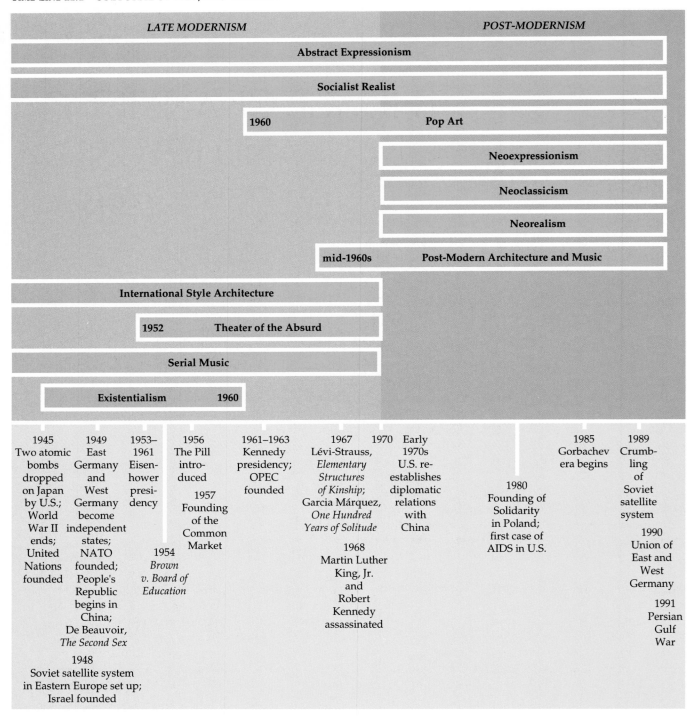

LATE MODERNISM	*POST-MODERNISM*

Abstract Expressionism

Socialist Realist

1960   **Pop Art**

Neoexpressionism

Neoclassicism

Neorealism

mid-1960s   **Post-Modern Architecture and Music**

International Style Architecture

1952   **Theater of the Absurd**

Serial Music

Existentialism   1960

1945	1949	1953–	1956	1961–1963	1967	1970	Early		1985	1989
Two atomic	East	1961	The Pill	Kennedy	Lévi-Strauss,		1970s		Gorbachev	Crumb-
bombs	Germany	Eisen-	intro-	presidency;	*Elementary*		U.S. re-		era begins	ling
dropped	and	hower	duced	OPEC	*Structures*		establishes			of
on Japan	West	presi-		founded	*of Kinship;*		diplomatic	1980		Soviet
by U.S.;	Germany	dency	1957		Garcia Márquez,		relations	Founding of		satellite
World	become		Founding		*One Hundred*		with	Solidarity		system
War II	independent		of the		*Years of Solitude*		China	in Poland;		
ends;	states;		Common					first case of		1990
United	NATO	1954	Market		1968			AIDS in U.S.		Union of
Nations	founded;	*Brown*			Martin Luther					East and
founded	People's	*v. Board of*			King, Jr.					West
	Republic	*Education*			and					Germany
	begins in				Robert					
	China;				Kennedy					1991
	De Beauvoir,				assassinated					Persian
	The Second Sex									Gulf
										War

1948
Soviet satellite system
in Eastern Europe set up;
Israel founded

weapons across inter-continental distances raised the possibility of sudden strikes and mass destruction without warning.

Other dramatic changes intensified the postwar period's growing mood of uncertainty. These included an international population explosion that raised the specter of food shortages and famines, new technological breakthroughs that seemed to entail employment crises, and mounting environmental calamities that threatened the earth's ecosystem. By the 1970s these issues were being recognized as world problems and not simply Western dilemmas, and thus they contributed to the rise of a global culture (Figure 21.1).

FIGURE 21.1 ANSELM KIEFER. *The High Priestess/The Land Between the Rivers.*
1985–1989. 5 × 8 × 1 meters. Astrop Collection, Oslo. Courtesy Anthony D'Offay
Gallery, London. *Kiefer's monumental work stands as a judgment on five thousand years of
history that began in Mesopotamia, the land between the Tigris and Euphrates rivers and the
cradle of civilization. Weighing several tons, the twin bookcases contain some two hundred
books made of lead. They are angled to suggest the two rivers, and, more specifically, the
accumulated wisdom of world culture. The books are linked by copper threads, Kiefer's image
of destructive technology, which he identifies with a pagan goddess—the high priestess of the
work's title. Though the books embrace all human knowledge, their pages are stuffed with
odds and ends of dried peas, human hair, and photographs of polluted earth, sky, and water,
and thus they are symbols of civilization in ruins. A powerful representative of the Age of
Anxiety, Kiefer is a Late Modernist in his pessimism and a Post-Modernist in his global
thinking.*

The Era of the Superpowers, 1945–1970

Between 1945 and 1970, the West was divided into
two patterns of civilization. For the American bloc of
states, democracy was the rule, social welfare expanded without becoming comprehensive, and the
economies were booming. For the Soviet bloc countries, collectivist regimes prevailed, social welfare was
fully comprehensive, and the economies either stag-
nated or grew slowly. The two systems emerged as
seemingly inevitable consequences of World War II.

Postwar Recovery and the New World Order The
chief Allied powers—the United States led by
Franklin D. Roosevelt, Great Britain led by Winston
Churchill, the Soviet Union led by Joseph Stalin—

began to plan for the postwar era well before World
War II ended. They agreed to occupy Germany and
Japan, giving those nations representative forms of
government and wiping out their military systems.
They also joined with forty-eight other countries in
1945 to found the United Nations, a peace-keeping
and human rights organization set up to deal with
international disputes and problems (Figure 21.2). Finally, the Allies laid the groundwork for worldwide
economic recovery by establishing a transnational
monetary fund to help nations devastated by the war.

When peace came in September 1945, the victorious Allies began to rethink their options and to tai-
lor their recovery plans to address conditions on a
continent whose cities, factories, and railroads were
in ruins. In order to restore this ravaged society, they
had to cooperate, and, most importantly, they had to

FIGURE 21.2 WALLACE K. HARRISON INTERNATIONAL COMMITTEE OF ARCHITECTS. United Nations Headquarters. 1949–1951. New York. *The decision to locate the United Nations in New York made that city the unofficial capital of the world, and the choice of a "glass box" skyscraper for the United Nations Secretariat, on the left, helped to ensure that the International Style would be the reigning style of architecture in the postwar period. Although this type of structure had been used in Europe before the war, the U.N. Secretariat was the first instance of it in New York.*

find visionary leaders who could inspire the people, whose hopes for orderly lives had been wrecked by war. The most troubling problem was that the key to the full recovery of Europe was a rejuvenated Germany—the state that provoked the war.

Convinced that Germany should be demilitarized and denazified, the Allies split the country into four occupied zones—British, French, American, and Soviet. In 1949 Britain, France, and the United States united their zones into the Federal Republic of Germany (West Germany), and the USSR set up its sector as the German Democratic Republic (East Germany). East and West Germany gradually became separate and distinct societies. By 1969 West Germany, led by moderates devoted to capitalism, was transformed into Europe's chief industrial power, and East Germany, under a collectivist regime, lagged far behind. This contrast mirrored changes that were occurring within the American and Soviet blocs.

Even more spectacular than West Germany's rise from the ashes of defeat was Japan's postwar success. The American victors imposed on Japan a democratic constitution that kept the emperor as a figurehead, introduced a parliamentary system, gave the vote to women, workers, and farmers, and virtually eliminated the military. Between 1950 and 1973, under this renovated system, Japan's domestic product grew at the amazing average of more than 10 percent a year, surpassing that of any other industrialized nation.

While West Germany and Japan were undergoing their economic miracles, Great Britain and France were moving along a more rocky path to recovery. By the early 1950s both countries were enjoying a moderate economic boom, although each was beset with continuing labor unrest. To deal with worker discontent, left-wing governments in both states nationalized major industries and founded national health-care systems, although periodically conservative leaders came along and returned some businesses to private hands. France survived its most severe postwar crisis in 1958 when a government resigned in disgrace because of the domestic turmoil set off by a war with its North African colony Algeria. Turning to the World War II hero, Charles de Gaulle (1958–1970), the French people elected him president and approved a new constitution. Under de Gaulle, France continued its economic boom and regained much of the influence in international affairs that had been lost after World War II.

France and West Germany were the first to recognize that in the age of the superpowers the era of the small state was over. In order to guarantee peace and economic stability, they had to join economic forces, and in 1957 France and West Germany became the nucleus for a free-trade zone that also included Belgium, the Netherlands, Luxembourg, and Italy. Called the European Economic Community, or the Common Market, this organization became the driving force in Europe's prosperity over the next decade.

Part of the reason for the formation of the Common Market was that the Soviet Union, as it established its superpower status, threatened to dominate Europe. When World War II ended, Soviet troops remained in neighboring countries in eastern Europe as an occupying force, ostensibly to provide a military shield for the U.S.S.R. By 1948 the Soviets had converted these countries into Communist satellites, their industrial and agricultural systems tied to the

Soviet economy. Thus, the Soviet Union loomed more as a menace than an ally to western Europe.

The architect of the Soviet Union's rise to superpower status was Joseph Stalin, who from 1945 until his death in 1953 rebuilt the USSR's war-shattered economy. A tyrant and a devout communist, he was determined to keep the collectivist system free of the taint of capitalism and the Western idea of freedom. He demanded extreme sacrifices from Soviet citizenry as they were forced to keep up with the pace set by the advanced industrialized states.

Stalin's successors, Nikita Khrushchev (1956–1964) and Leonid Brezhnev (1964–1982), were more moderate, but both continued the policies of censorship and repression. Without detracting from the primary goal of building a nuclear arsenal, they also tried to broaden their priorities to include greater availability of consumer goods and the elimination of chronic food shortages, but with little success. Despite a mixed record, the Soviet Union did have one momentous accomplishment during these years: In 1957 it launched the first artificial satellite into orbit around the earth, thus becoming the leader in space exploration—a feat that appealed to the world's imagination and preoccupied both superpowers during the 1960s and beyond.

The United States, the other superpower, took up the torch of free world leadership in 1945, claiming to have earned this status because of crucial contributions to Allied victory. It further believed that the war had been a moral crusade for human freedom and thus had given the country a blank check to protect the rights of people everywhere. Armed with these beliefs, the United States abandoned its old isolationist foreign policy and took on the role of the world's watchdog.

Between 1945 and 1970 the United States was probably the wealthiest and most powerful state that ever existed. Its heyday was under President Dwight Eisenhower (1953–1961), a former general who had served as Supreme Commander of the Allied forces in Europe during the war. He was succeeded by John F. Kennedy (1961–1963), a charismatic and popular figure whose assassination stunned a country unused to political violence. Kennedy pushed America to the forefront of space exploration, a challenge to Soviet domination that climaxed in 1969 with the landing of two astronauts on the moon.

American domestic life in this era was marked by a radical shift in mood from the 1950s to the 1960s. The 1950s was a decade of complacency and blandness symbolized by the "man in the gray flannel suit." The 1960s, in contrast, was a turbulent decade around the world, of which the American experience was only a part. A cultural event in itself, the 1960s was one of the most unruly periods in modern history, involving radical protests by millions of people against the War in Vietnam, racism, and old ways of thinking. Hippies cultivated a bohemian lifestyle and contributed to the emergence of a "counterculture" that rejected mainstream values. These protests showed that many Americans, along with much of the world's population, distrusted authority and were skeptical of traditional beliefs.

Of the domestic problems faced by the United States at this time, racial prejudice was the most pressing because it was so embedded in the country's history. In 1954 the Supreme Court declared segregation in public schools—"separate but equal" facilities—unconstitutional. In the next year, Rosa Parks (1913–   ), a black Alabaman, refused to move to the back of a bus as required by state law and was jailed. The social protest that erupted around the jailing of Parks marked a watershed in race relations in America. Rejecting a historically passive role, black citizens began to use civil disobedience as a weapon in their crusade to win equal rights.

Nevertheless, the civil rights movement did not begin on a national scale until the Kennedy presidency. After some foot dragging, the federal government threw its weight behind the movement to bring about changes in education, living conditions, and voting rights. What Kennedy started, President Lyndon Johnson (1963–1969) tried to complete with his War on Poverty and Great Society plans. In 1968 the civil rights struggle temporarily lost direction and momentum when its leader, Martin Luther King, Jr., was assassinated, but fresh faces arose in America's black community who have continued the struggle against racism.

The Cold War The hopes for peace and cooperation among the victorious powers disappeared after 1945 as the Soviet Union and the United States squared off and defined their respective spheres of influence. By 1949 an "iron curtain," to use Winston Churchill's phrase, had descended in Europe, dividing the West (France, England, Belgium, the Netherlands, Luxembourg, Italy, West Germany, and, later, Austria) from the East (Poland, Hungary, Rumania, Bulgaria, Czechoslovakia, East Germany, and Russia) (Map 21.1).

Events soon caused the Cold War to heat up. In 1949 fear of a Russian invasion led the western democracies to form a military alliance called the North Atlantic Treaty Organization (NATO) with the United States as its leader. The eastern bloc countered with the Warsaw Pact, an alliance headed by the Soviet Union. A race to stockpile weapons ensued, dividing the industrial world into armed camps. By 1955 a

MAP 21.1
Europe in 1955

ICELAND

ATLANTIC
OCEAN

NORWAY

SWEDEN

FINLAND

NORTH
SEA

BALTIC
SEA

SOVIET UNION

IRELAND

DENMARK

UNITED
KINGDOM

NETHERLANDS

EAST
GERMANY

POLAND

BELGIUM

LUXEMBOURG

WEST
GERMANY

CZECHOSLOVAKIA

FRANCE

AUSTRIA

HUNGARY

SWITZERLAND

RUMANIA

YUGOSLAVIA

BLACK
SEA

PORTUGAL

ITALY

BULGARIA

SPAIN

ALBANIA

MEDITERRANEAN
SEA

GREECE

TURKEY

ALGERIA

▨ Original NATO Alliance

▨ Communist Bloc (Members of Warsaw Pact)

balance of terror seemed to have been reached because both the United States and the USSR now possessed the atomic bomb and the even more deadly hydrogen bomb. Nevertheless, the urge for more weapons continued to mount.

Although the East-West conflict originated in Europe, the contest spread to other regions of the world, where it threatened to become a three-sided struggle. In 1949 Chinese Communists defeated General Chiang Kai-shek (1928–1949) and his Kuomintang party and commenced to build a socialist system under the leadership of Mao Zedong (1949–1976) (Figure 21.3).

The triumph of Communism in China shifted the struggle between the superpowers to the Far East, where a limited type of warfare now emerged in Korea—divided after World War II into two independent states reflecting the influence of the United

States and the Soviet Union. In 1950 Soviet-dominated North Korea invaded South Korea to reunite the two states. Alarmed at this expansion of Communism, the United States, under the auspices of the United Nations, sent troops in support of the South Koreans. Later in the year, China sent soldiers to help the North Koreans. After months of bloody fighting, a stalemate resulted along the old borders, which were guaranteed in 1953 by an armistice. The Korean War ended in a draw, but it established one of the guiding principles of the nuclear age—that wars would be fought with conventional weapons rather than with nuclear arms.

The early 1960s witnessed worsening relations between the United States and the Soviet Union over the Berlin Wall and the Cuban missile crisis. The Berlin Wall was built in 1961 by East Germany, with the permission of the Soviet Union, to prevent its citizens

FIGURE 21.3   ANDY WARHOL. *Mao.* 1973. Acrylic and silkscreen on canvas, 14′ 6⅞″ × 11′ 4½″. The Art Institute of Chicago. Mr. and Mrs. Frank G. Logan Purchase Prize and Wilson L. Mead Funds. *A feature of totalitarian societies in this century has been the personality cult, the practice of giving a political leader heroic dimensions. In Communist China the cult of Mao Zedong established Mao as a secular god. American pop artist Andy Warhol turned Mao's official photograph into a pop culture icon, suggesting that there is no difference between propaganda in a totalitarian state and media stardom in a free society.*

from going to West Berlin. Conceived as a way of saving Communism, this armed boundary only intensified divisions between the two Europes. Then in 1962 the Soviet plan to base missiles in Cuba brought the superpowers to the brink of war, but in the end both states backed away from armed conflict.

The severest strain on the superpower system was the Vietnam War, which erupted in the early 1960s. Originating as a civil war, it became a Cold War contest when the United States joined South Vietnam to repel the troops invading from the Communist north. For American soldiers the war was doubly difficult to wage because it was fought in unfamiliar jungle terrain using conventional arms against a guerrilla army and because it became so violently unpopular at home. At the peak of the war in May 1970, protests spread across the United States, culminating in incidents at universities in Ohio and Mississippi, when six students were killed in clashes with public authorities (Figure 21.4).

FIGURE 21.4   The National Guard at Kent State, Ohio. 1970. *This photograph bears a striking resemblance to Goya's* Execution of the Third of May, 1808, *a painting that protested the killing of Spanish civilians by French soldiers. In the tense days after the Kent State deaths, this photograph served a similar function in American society as many people began to think of the dead students as martyrs to the anti–Vietnam War cause.*

The Vietnam War proved to be a turning point in world affairs. The United States withdrew from South Vietnam in 1973, thereby allowing its eventual conquest by North Vietnam. Certain conclusions were quickly drawn from this setback to American might. First, because the Vietnam War weakened the United States internally by dividing the citizens about the war and its goals, it cast doubt on the country's superpower status and made the leaders reluctant to exercise military power abroad except in the Western Hemisphere, an area historically subject to American intervention. Second, the Vietnam War illustrated a new principle of foreign relations—namely, that even superpowers could not conquer minor states by conventional forces alone. Taken together, these post–Vietnam era principles suggested that the international influence of the United States was in decline and opened the door to new forms of global cooperation in the 1970s.

Emergence of the Third World After 1945 Europe's overseas territories began to struggle for freedom and self-government, and by 1964 most of the empires had been replaced by independent countries. Independence for the former colonies came at different times and in diverse ways. In the Far East, the United States led the way in 1946 when it let go of its former colony, the Philippines. Great Britain, the West's largest imperial power, followed in 1947 by agreeing to divide India into a Hindu-dominated state—India—and a separate Muslim state—Pakistan. A year later the British withdrew from Burma, thus ensuring its free status. The Dutch gave up the East Indies, which in 1950 became Indonesia. France tried to hold on to Indochina, having reclaimed it from Japan, but in 1954 the French were driven out by a bloody uprising, and the former colony was divided into two separate countries, North and South Vietnam. In 1975 these two countries were finally unified as a single state at the conclusion of the Vietnam War.

In the Middle East, the small, mainly Arab states were freed by France and Britain, who had dominated them since 1919. After 1945 the region was kept in turmoil because its rich oil fields were needed by the industrialized states, its geopolitical position in the eastern Mediterranean attracted the superpowers, and Islamic fundamentalism gave birth to militant Arab nationalism. But the founding of Israel as a Jewish state following World War II and the Holocaust contributed the most to an unstable Middle East. Israel's founding in 1948—pushing the British out—resulted in the expulsion of more than a half million Arabs from Palestine, and the fate of these refugees has kept the region in turmoil. With the refugee problem unresolved, Israel, backed by the

United States, has had to fight constantly against its Arab neighbors to remain an independent nation. Further instability in the region has been caused by a change in the balance of power—the decline of Iran and the rise of Iraq as an aggressive state.

In Africa nearly all of the colonies became free, but the transition was usually painful and often costly. In 1962 France concluded a bloody war in Algeria, releasing its ties to this once prized possession. Having learned her lesson, France freed most of her colonies in West Africa during the 1960s. In East Africa, the British, at the same time, withdrew slowly, leaving behind bureaucracies that could serve the new states. Rhodesia became Zimbabwe in 1980, achieving independence under black majority rule.

A major exception to this move by the African peoples to throw off their colonialist past is the Union of South Africa. Unlike its neighbors, South Africa remained a country ruled by a white minority, descendants of early settlers. Moreover, after 1948 South Africa's black majority was subjected to apartheid—a segregation program that denied them the vote, restricted them to certain areas, limited their work opportunities, and, in general, treated them as second-class citizens. After the world's media began to reveal the cruelties of apartheid in the 1960s, the white government found itself increasingly isolated. By 1991 South Africa still had a segregated society, but a global economic boycott, coupled with well-orchestrated black protest, caused white leaders to make tentative gestures of reform.

Toward a New Global Order, 1970–1991

The year 1970 marked a turning point in history, not only for Western civilization but also for the world. The balance of political power began to shift from the bipolar, superpower model to a multipolar system embracing the superpowers along with Japan, China, and western Europe. This reshuffling of global influence began when the superpowers moved toward *detente*, a French term meaning a waning of hostility. By the early 1970s *detente* produced several arms limitations treaties between the Soviet Union and the United States and thus created a favorable climate for a reappraisal of Cold War attitudes. *Detente* soon led to a reduction of ideological battles in Europe and around the world. In addition, the industrialized nations began to experience energy shortages that showed how dependent they were on the oil-producing states—countries that heretofore had exerted little influence on world events.

National Issues and International Realignment The general rise in the standard of living for most citizens in western Europe and the United States suffered a sharp setback with the Arab oil embargo of the early 1970s. In 1960 the oil-rich states of the Middle East had founded the Organization of Petroleum Exporting Countries (OPEC), a cartel that initiated an energy-price revolution whose consequences are still being felt. As a result, most western nations went into a recession that resulted in both rising unemployment and inflation—two economic events that most experts believed could not occur at the same time. The Soviet Union was also experiencing economic problems as it became increasingly clear that the regimented system was no longer able to produce both arms and consumer goods.

Politically, the 1970s were a time of drift in the United States. President Richard Nixon (1969–1974) began to wind down the Vietnam War in 1970, thus defusing domestic discontent. When South Vietnam fell to the Communists in 1975, most American units were already back home. He also made a historic opening to China, a step that eventually led to a realignment of the world's powers. But Nixon disgraced himself through the Watergate scandal of 1973–1974, which turned on the question of his knowledge of illegal wiretaps and attempted obstruction of justice. As a result, several high government officials were imprisoned, and he resigned from the presidency—a first in American history.

The 1980s brought dramatic changes both nationally and internationally. The United States experienced an economic turnaround under President Ronald Reagan (1981–1989), whose advisers prescribed a dose of "Reaganomics," or laissez-faire policies, to treat inflation and recession. The economy responded with the longest run of uninterrupted prosperity since World War II. The nation paid dearly for its prosperity, however, with increased military spending, an astronomical national debt, and, in foreign trade, a shift from creditor to debtor status. And for those trapped in poverty, homelessness, and urban violence, reduced government spending under Reagan and his successor, George Bush, turned the American dream into a nightmare.

Reagan also launched a massive military spending campaign to strengthen the American presence around the world. This was partly in response to two events that had clouded the international scene—a Soviet invasion of Afghanistan in 1979 in support of local Communist leaders and the founding in 1980 of Solidarity in Poland, a labor movement that used strikes to push for economic reform. When Solidarity brought the country to the edge of revolution, the government, supported by the Soviet Union, ruthlessly suppressed the movement. In a hostile international atmosphere, Cold War sentiments revived, ongoing disarmament talks between the superpowers broke down, and an intensified arms race seemed imminent.

All this changed in 1985 with the appearance of Mikhail Gorbachev as leader of the Soviet Union. Using a moderate approach, partly because the Soviet economy was in shambles, he introduced a new era of *detente* and appeared to bring the Cold War to a peaceful close. His overtures to the United States resulted in limited arms reductions and, more importantly, opened up lines of communication between the two superpowers.

At home, Gorbachev made changes in the state bureaucracy and the Communist party designed to raise the standard of living. His plans—restructuring the economy's production and distribution system (*perestroika*) and allowing public criticism of the Communist party (*glasnost*)—have changed the course of events in the Soviet Union, eastern Europe, and the world. In the Soviet Union, Gorbachev's reforms have cast in doubt the future of the centralized structure of the U.S.S.R., as some member states—Latvia, Estonia, and Lithuania, for example—have taken steps toward independence while other member states want more local control of their affairs.

Since 1989 Gorbachev's policies toward the satellite states, whether intentional or not, have destroyed the Communist bloc in eastern Europe (Figure 21.5). The Communist parties in those nations have either resigned or been turned out of office, and coalition cabinets, often led by intellectuals and outspoken critics of past governments, have come to power. While many of these former Communist states want to keep their social welfare programs and to protect the workers in other ways, some of them are rapidly moving toward democratic governments and market economies. Nearly all of these countries are restructuring their production and distribution systems, dismantling the secret police apparatus, and rewriting their constitutions to ensure civil rights, a multiparty political system, and freedom of expression and thought.

Friendly ties between the superpowers and other changes in international affairs reflect, to some extent, a decline in influence of both the Soviet Union and the United States. Neither world power has the will to wipe out the other and neither has the wealth and resources to dominate the world. The superpowers must now accept a multipolar arrangement that includes China and Japan, both rising in international influence, as well as the growing economic might of the other new economic powers in the Pacific Rim, such as South Korea, Taiwan, Singapore, and Thai-

FIGURE 21.5 Fall of the Berlin Wall. 1989. *Given the Soviet Union's previous use of force in Eastern Europe, no one had predicted that the collapse of the Communist states would be so quick and bloodless. The most symbolic event of this extraordinary period has been the dismantling of the wall that separated East Berlin from West Berlin.*

land. Likewise, the superpowers must respond to the challenge of western Europe, which will be the most powerful economic region in the world after 1992, when it becomes a free-trade zone with a single currency. In the emerging global economic order, all countries, including those in Africa, the Middle East, eastern Europe, and Latin America, seem to recognize that if they are to share in the wealth and goods of the planet, they must develop market economies and become competitive.

The Persian Gulf Crisis and Its Impact Despite the promising developments of 1989, a new crisis arose in 1990. The world was shocked when Iraq, under the leadership of Saddam Hussein (1979–), invaded and annexed Kuwait, its small, wealthy neighbor on the Persian Gulf, and appeared ready to move on into Saudi Arabia. Concerned about both the already precarious balance of power in the Middle East and the world's oil supply, U.S. President Bush declared the aggression unacceptable. Under the auspices of the United Nations, the United States put together a broad diplomatic and military coalition of nearly fifty countries dedicated to freeing Kuwait. In a historic first, the Soviet Union joined in condemning its

former ally Iraq in the United Nations. By mid-January 1991, the United States and its allies had gathered a military force of about 500,000 troops in Saudi Arabia, where they faced about the same number of Iraqi soldiers—the largest massing of troops since World War II. Following an all-out air campaign against Iraq and a brief ground assault, the allied coalition achieved its major war aim with the liberation of Kuwait (Figure 21.6).

Although some hoped that the Gulf crisis would create an opportunity to settle the Palestinian refugee problem, another refugee population was created by the war. Fleeing from Iraqi vengeance in the wake of the failure of their civil uprising against Hussein, millions of Iraqi Kurds were forced to abandon their homes and seek refuge in the harsh mountains of northern and eastern Iraq. The Kurds are a Muslim people scattered across the Middle East, with millions of others in Syria, Iran, Turkey, and the Soviet Union. Since the 1920s they have pushed unsuccessfully for an independent Kurdish state. Their plight creates another thorny problem in a region divided by volatile issues.

The Persian Gulf crisis brought into clearer focus the broader trends underway in the world since 1970.

FIGURE 21.6 Kuwaitis Celebrate their Country's Liberation, March 1991. *Parading in front of the U.S. embassy in Kuwait City, these Kuwaiti citizens celebrate their country's liberation from Iraq. They wave small Kuwaiti flags and a large American flag emblazoned with a picture of the late Hollywood star Marilyn Monroe. The juxtaposition of Monroe's face and the stars and stripes is a vivid reminder of the way American political power and American mass culture are intertwined in many minds. This image, flashed around the world by satellite and news wire services, also exemplifies how this "TV war" was presented to the global village.*

It dramatically validated the perception that the Cold War is over; at the same time, it reasserted the image of the United States as a superpower and signaled a decline in the Soviet Union. The crisis also underscored the nature of the global economy and its dependency on oil, as evidenced by the complex coalition against Iraq. Included in the coalition were heretofore neutral countries, Third World nations, Pacific Rim states, countries defeated in World War II, former Iron Curtain states, moderate Arab states, and the highly industrialized nation-states of NATO along with Australia and New Zealand. They were motivated in part by the belief that stopping Iraq would benefit their economies by keeping oil flowing from the Middle East.

Problems with a Global Dimension A positive result of the nuclear age was that it taught the West and the rest of the world to think globally. As the threat of nuclear war has subsided since 1970, other menacing problems have surfaced that transcend national borders and affect all people all over the planet. The ur-

gency of these issues makes them seem more relevant to people's lives than events that occur on a local or national level. Of the international problems facing the world, the two most pressing are the population explosion and the deteriorating environment, neither of which appears to have a simple solution.

The world's population is in danger of becoming an unbearable burden on the globe's limited resources. In the 1980s there were devastating famines in Ethiopia and elsewhere (Figure 21.7). In 1990 the earth's population was estimated to be 5.23 billion and projected to reach 6.2 billion by 2000. Many international groups have called for ways to limit the birth rate, ranging from abortion to contraceptives. But because all birth control proposals affect moral and religious beliefs, they have touched off heated debates and, in the case of abortion, have led to violence. The abortion question is further complicated by being in conflict with the women's movement, for there seems to be no way to reconcile the claims of a fetus with a woman's right to control her own body.

The environmental problem turns on the issue of

FIGURE 21.7 JOHN ISAAC. *Famine in Ethiopia. 1984. In the early 1980s the nightly television news brought images of famine and death in Ethiopia into living rooms around the world, just as it had earlier brought images of the War in Vietnam. The Ethiopians were the victims of drought and other natural disasters, of civil war, and of short-sighted economic policies that had replaced local agriculture with export crops. Although food was sent by international relief agencies, partisan soldiers often prevented it from reaching the people. The agony of Ethiopia taught the world that solving environmental problems also means dealing with tough political and economic issues.*

preserving the natural world for future generations. Even though assaults on the planet's ecosystem occurred earlier, the period of greatest destruction to the earth began after 1945, especially with the advent of nuclear power, of a huge rise in the earth's population, and of the growing industrialization of the world. Today few parts of the globe are free from diseases caused by industrial pollution and waste from factories. Two glaring examples of environmental disasters are the Chernobyl nuclear power plant fire in the Soviet Union in 1986 and the mammoth oil spill in Alaska in 1989. There are many other environmental hazards, such as acid rain, which threatens the world's flora and fauna, the warming of the

earth, which might melt the polar ice caps, the depletion of the ozone layer, which would destroy the planet's protective shield, and the poisoning of rivers and oceans, which would eliminate fish and pollute much of humanity's water supply.

One concrete result of the rise of environmental concerns is the forming of political parties devoted to environmental issues, most notably in Europe. Because these problems are not limited by national frontiers or geographical barriers, international agencies such as the United Nations have led the movement to bring potential environmental calamities under control. What makes protection of the earth such a dilemma today is that it flies in the face of an almost equal demand for economic growth to sustain the world's current style of life. Although many people are prepared to sacrifice material needs to preserve the earth, millions of others are complacent and do not want to give up their creature comforts.

THE END OF MODERNISM AND THE BIRTH OF POST-MODERNISM

In 1947 the British-American author W. H. Auden published a poem entitled "The Age of Anxiety" that expresses the melancholy spirit of his times. He describes a period caught between a frantic quest for certainty and a recognition of the futility of that search. Responding to the unparalleled violence of World War II, Auden's anxious age is characterized by a sense of death and destruction, fueled by memories of the Holocaust in Europe and the two atomic bombs dropped on Japan. As relations between the Soviet Union and the United States deteriorated and made World War III seem inevitable, melancholy could and often did turn into despair. In this gloomy setting Modernism entered its final phase.

Late Modernism, flourishing from 1945 until 1970, expressed the vision of a group of artists, writers, and thinkers who seemed almost overwhelmed by this despairing age. Existentialism—with its advice to forget the past and the future and to live passionately for the present—appeared to be the only thinking that made sense. Paradoxically, diminished faith in humanity kept the Modernists at their creative tasks and prevented them from falling into hopeless silence.

Like earlier Modernists, Late Modernists thought of themselves as an elite. They were committed to saving what they considered worth saving in Western culture while destroying all in the past that was irrelevant, ignoring mass culture, and borrowing insights from depth psychology and non-Western sources. Armed with a sense of mission, they stripped their works down to the most basic components, abandoning strict rationality and making randomness the rule. They threw subject matter out the window and pressed experimentation to the extreme, reducing painting to lines and colors, sculpture to textures and shapes, and music to random collections of sound. Like earlier Modernists, they then invested these works with spiritual or metaphysical purposes by claiming that abstract paintings and sculptures were meditation devices and that music that mixed noise and harmony echoed the natural world.

In the early 1970s Late Modernism was challenged by a new movement that became known as *Post-Modernism.* Having grown to maturity after World War II and feeling that Late Modernism's anxiety was outdated, the Post-Modernists turned from existentialism to *structuralism,* a type of thinking that affirmed the uniformity of the human mind in all places and times. Unlike the Late Modernists, this new generation embraced mass culture and preferred a more playful approach to creativity (Figure 21.8). Because the United States is a microcosm of global society, its artists and scholars have played a key role in establishing the culture of Post-Modernism.

The Post-Modernists' cultural vision caused them to look in two directions at the same time—forward to an emerging global civilization that was many-voiced and democratic and backward to the roots of the Western tradition. This vision embraced the works of women, minority group members, and representatives of the Third World at the same time that it reexamined both Classical and pre-Classical civilizations. Only time will tell if Post-Modernism is merely a period of fragmentation prior to regrouping or the beginning of a cultural revolution.

Philosophical, Political, and Social Thought

Existentialism, born between the two world wars, dominated Western thought from 1945 until the 1960s, when it was eclipsed by structuralism and other intellectual movements, notably feminism and black consciousness. Unlike existentialism, with its focus on freedom and choice, structuralism asserts that human freedom is limited. Structuralists maintain that innate mental patterns cause human beings to interact with nature and each other in recurring ways, regardless of the historical period or the social setting. It follows that civilization (as represented in governments, social relations, and language, for

FIGURE 21.8   KEITH HARING. *Andy Mouse 2.* 1986. Silkscreen print, 38 × 38″. Courtesy George C. Mulder, New York. *Post-Modernist Keith Haring embraced the emblems and vocabulary of mass culture as Andy Warhol had done earlier. In this silkscreen print he pays homage to Warhol and celebrates his lifelong love affair with mass culture. Haring emblazoned Mickey Mouse's face on a cartoon dollar bill held aloft by two jubilant figures—presumably, Warhol and himself. The dancing figures, surrounded with radiant lines, were Haring's trademark.*

example) and ideas (such as freedom, health, and beauty) arise from deep-seated modes of thought instead of from the environment or progressive enlightenment. Structuralists reason that not only is all knowledge conditioned by the mind but civilization itself reflects the mind's inborn nature. By defining and analyzing the substrata of culture, they attempt to garner some understanding of the elemental nature of the human mind.

The two leading structuralists are Noam Chomsky (1928–), an American linguist, and Claude Lévi-Strauss (1908–), a French anthropologist. Chomsky's *Syntactic Structures* (1957) prompted a revolution in linguistics, the scientific study of languages. He argues that below the surface form of sentences (that is, the grammar) lies a deeper linguistic structure that is intuitively grasped by the mind and is common to all languages. Similarly, Lévi-Strauss made war on empirical thinking with his 1967 study, *The Elementary Structures of Kinship.* He claimed that beneath the varied relations among clans in different societies exist certain kinship archetypes with such common themes as the incest taboo and marriage patterns. Chomsky and Lévi-Strauss imply the existence of common universal structures running through all minds and all societies that can be expressed as a general code. This conclusion gives a strong psychoanalytic cast to structuralist thought, because it leads researchers to focus on the subconscious mind.

Following Chomsky and Lévi-Strauss, other scholars have studied subsurface patterns in such disciplines as history, child development, and literature. No thinker has yet unified the various structuralisms into a coherent theory of mind. It is an intriguing coincidence, however, that the trend of thought that points to a universally shared mind set parallels the rise of a global culture under Post-Modernism.

The revival of feminist thought has been another significant development in philosophy since World War II. The French thinker and novelist Simone de Beauvoir (1908–1986) sparked this revival, following the dry spell that set in after many Western women won the right to vote in the 1920s. In her 1949 treatise *The Second Sex*, de Beauvoir argued that women were treated as "the Other," an anthropological term meaning that men accord women a different and lower existence than themselves. Drawing on personal anecdote and existentialist thought, she advised women who wanted independence to avoid marriage and, like men, create their own immortality (Figure 21.9).

De Beauvoir's message was heard around the world, but it was especially in the United States that women heeded her. America's outstanding feminist in the 1960s was Betty Friedan (1921–). She awakened the dormant women's movement with *The Fem-*

FIGURE 21.9 JUDY CHICAGO. *The Dinner Party.* 1979. Installation view. Multimedia, china painting on porcelain, needlework, 48 × 48 × 48' installed. © Judy Chicago. *The rebirth of feminism led some women artists to adopt explicit feminist themes in their art, as in the works of Judy Chicago (born Gerowitz, 1939–). Chicago abandoned Abstract Expressionism in the late 1960s at about the same time she changed her name, thereafter devoting her art to the feminist cause.* The Dinner Party, *her most ambitious project to date, is dedicated to leading historical and mythological women of Western civilization. In this work she arranges a triangular-shaped dining table with thirty-nine places decorated in individual styles, honoring such famous women as Sappho and Eleanor of Aquitaine.*

FIGURE 21.10 ROMARE BEARDEN. *The Prevalence of Ritual: Baptism.* 1964. Collage on board, 9 × 12″. The Hirshhorn Museum and Sculpture Garden, Smithsonian Institution, Washington, D.C. *Romare Bearden (1914–1988), the United States' most honored post–World War II black painter, blended Modernism with elements from his cultural heritage. In the 1960s he developed a style reminiscent of Cubism that used collage and flattened, angular figures and that drew on his personal experiences, as in this painting of a baptismal scene—an allusion to the important role played by churches in the black American tradition. Bearden places the person to be baptized in the center of the composition, a large hand over his head. The references to African masks suggest that this ritual unites an ancient way of life with the present.*

inine *Mystique* (1963), arguing that society conspired to idealize women and thus discourage them from competing with men. In 1966 she founded the National Organization for Women (NOW), a pressure group that has attracted millions of members. According to its founding manifesto, NOW supports "equal partnership with men" and is committed to "integrating women into the power, privileges, and responsibilities of the public arena." Friedan did not always agree with the more radical feminists of the 1970s, and in 1982 she showed that she was still a moderate in *The Second Stage*, a book that advocated men's liberation as a condition for women's equality.

Like feminism, the black consciousness movement has flourished since 1945 (Figure 21.10). The earliest significant theorist of black identity was Frantz Fanon (1925–1961), a psychiatrist from French Martinique who practiced medicine among the Arabs of Algeria. An eyewitness to French oppression, Fanon became convinced that the West had doomed itself by abandoning its own moral ideals. By the late 1950s Fanon began to justify black revolution against white society on the basis of existential choice and Marxism. In 1961 in *The Wretched of the Earth* he issued an angry call to arms, urging nonwhites to build a separate culture. Some black leaders in America welcomed Fanon's message in the 1960s, as did Third World thinkers who turned their backs on Western ideologies in the 1970s.

America in the 1960s produced a radical black voice in Malcolm X (1925–1965), the pseudonym of Malcolm Little. A fiery personality, he made sharp ideological shifts, moving from advocacy of black separatism to a call for an interracial civil war and, after his conversion to orthodox Islam, to support of racial harmony. Assassinated allegedly by former colleagues, he remains today a prophetic voice for many African-Americans who want a clearer sense of their history, culture, and accomplishments in a predominantly white society.

In the turbulent 1960s Malcolm X's voice was overpowered by that of Martin Luther King, Jr. (1929–1968), a visionary who dreamed of a world free from racial discord. Probably the most famous black figure in Western history, King was an advocate of civil disobedience—based on Christian teachings, the writings of the New England philosopher and abolitionist Henry David Thoreau, and the example of India's liberator, Gandhi. An inspirational leader and a superb orator, King galvanized blacks, along with many whites, into the Southern Christian Leadership Conference, a mass movement to end segregation in American life, notably in schools and universities. Though King was assassinated before his dream was fully realized, his vision of an integrated society lived on, and he left a cadre of able leaders.

Science and Technology

Although important developments occurred in biology and physics during the postwar period and after, for most people more important were the spectacular advances in applied science. Ordinary life and manners have been irretrievably altered by an unending stream of inventions and discoveries, notably the birth control pill, communication satellites, and the computer. The invention of a safe birth control pill in 1956 triggered a sexual revolution that slowed down only in the 1980s with the advent of AIDS (acquired immune deficiency syndrome) and a dramatic rise in the incidence of other sexually transmissible diseases. The introduction of communication satellites, a byproduct of the United States space program of the 1960s, has made a global culture possible. Multinational corporations are linked by these satellites, and individuals all over the world watch televised events at the same time thanks to satellite communication.

Perhaps most important, the computer has revolutionized life on every level, making previously unimaginable quantities of data immediately accessible, simplifying complex tasks, and contributing to "cocooning," a mode of living in which people center their lives in their private homes surrounded by electronic devices and venture out into the public domain for amusement and social contact less and less.

Breakthroughs in medicine also changed the nature of human life for millions. In the 1950s polio was eradicated through vaccines developed by the American physicians Jonas Salk (1914–) and Albert Sabin (1906–). Innovative surgical methods, radiation treatment, and chemotherapy drastically reduced cancer mortality. Organ transplants and the use of artificial organs have prolonged life for many otherwise without hope, although these practices have embroiled the medical profession in ethical controversy because of charges that only a few or the wealthy benefit from these costly procedures. Likewise, new methods in human reproduction, such as test-tube fertilization and surrogate parenting, while helping a few, have also raised moral dilemmas and led to court cases.

The Literature of Late Modernism: Fiction, Poetry, and Drama

France's leading postwar thinkers, Jean-Paul Sartre and Albert Camus, were among Late Modernism's outstanding voices. In a trio of novels called *Roads to Freedom*, published between 1945 and 1950, Sartre interwove Marxist collectivist beliefs with existentialism's focus on the individual. While accepting the existentialist view that life is cruel and must be confronted, he portrayed his characters as cooperating for a new and better world, presumably one in which they would be able to live in harmony. Sartre also wrote a series of plays on current issues that are infrequently performed today. His most successful drama, and perhaps his most enduring literary work, was *No Exit*, which showed how three characters turned their lives into living hells because of their unfortunate choices in desperate situations.

Like Sartre, the Algerian-born writer and thinker Albert Camus (1913–1960) wrote novels, plays, and philosophical works that mirrored his political thinking and personal values. His finest literary work was *The Fall* (1956), a novel published at the height of his reputation as one of the West's main moral voices. In 1957 he was awarded the Nobel Prize in literature, an honor that Sartre declined in 1964. Written as a single rambling monologue, *The Fall* portrays an anguished, self-doubting central character who accuses himself of moral fraud. When admirers recognized Camus himself in the narrator's voice, they were shocked because they were unwilling to accept this harsh self-judgment. Whether this self-mocking confession heralded Camus's move toward God—as some critics have maintained—can never be known, for an auto accident prematurely ended his life.

Existentialism's rejection of bourgeois values and its affirmation of identity through action appealed to black writers in the United States. As outsiders in a white-dominated society, these writers identified with the French thinkers' call to rebellion. The first black author to adopt an existential perspective was Richard Wright (1908–1960), whose outlook was shaped by his birth on a Mississippi plantation. His works, such as his novel *Native Son* (1940) and his autobiography *Black Boy* (1945), were filled with too much rage at racism to be accepted by white literary critics in the 1940s. His later years were spent in Paris, where he further developed his interest in existentialism.

The most successful black American author of this time was James Baldwin (1924–1987), who began to write during a self-imposed exile in France (1948–1957), where he had fled from racial discrimination. In a series of novels and essays, he explored the consequences of growing up black in a predominantly white world. In the novel *Go Tell It on the Mountain* (1953), he drew on his Christian beliefs to mute his anger against the injustices that he believed blacks daily endured. This novel, which held out hope for an integrated society, established the literary theme that he pursued until Martin Luther King, Jr.'s assassination caused his vision to darken. In later novels, such as *No Name in the Street* (1972), he regretfully accepted violence as the only path to racial justice for black Americans.

In postwar fiction existentialism sometimes took second place to a realistic literary style that concentrated on exposing society's failings. Three major writers who blended existential despair with Realism's moral outrage were Norman Mailer (1923–), Doris Lessing (1919–), and Alexander Solzhenitsyn (1918–). Their goal was to uncover the hypocrisy of their age.

Mailer, an American, drew on his experience as a soldier in World War II to capture the horror of modern war in his first and finest novel, *The Naked and the Dead* (1948). This work portrays a handful of enlisted men, a microcosm of America, as victims of their leaders' bad choices. He describes their officers as pursuing fantasies of glory, inspired by a notion that the world is godless and without lasting values. In the late 1960s Mailer began to write journalism, eventually achieving so much fame that today his essays overshadow his novels. His best journalism is the book-length essay *The Armies of the Night* (1968), an account of the October 1967 peace march on Washington, D.C., in which he participated. This book won Mailer a Pulitzer Prize.

Doris Lessing, a British writer, used Realism to show the contradictions at work in her homeland, Rhodesia (modern Zimbabwe), between blacks and whites, British and Dutch, British and colonials, capitalists and Marxists, and, always, women and men.

In the *Children of Violence* series (1950–1969), consisting of five novels, she presents the story of the rise of black freedom fighters and the diminishing of white control in what was then a British colony. This disintegrating world serves as a backdrop to the existential struggle for self-knowledge and independence by the main character, Martha Quest. In her best-known novel, *The Golden Notebook* (1962), Lessing addresses, among other issues, the socialization process that stifles women's creativity. Her concerns, however, are not just female identity but the moral and intellectual fragmentation and confusion she sees in the modern world. In recent years she has turned to science fiction to address these issues.

The Russian Solzhenitsyn writes realistic novels that praise the Russian people while damning Marxism, which he regards as a "Western heresy," opposed to Orthodox Christianity. His short novel *One Day in the Life of Ivan Denisovich* (1962) reflects his own rage at being unjustly imprisoned under Stalin. This novel, published during Khrushchev's de-Stalinization drive, offers an indelible image of the tedium, harrassment, and cruelty of life in a forced labor camp. And yet Ivan Denisovich remains a Soviet John Doe, dedicated to Marxism, his work, and his comrades (Figure 21.11).

When Solzhenitsyn's later books, which only now have begun to appear in the Soviet Union, revealed his hatred for communism, he was deported in 1974. Despite choosing exile in America, he has expressed disgust with the West for its atheistic materialism and softness toward the Soviets. His values—Christian fundamentalism and Slavophilism, or advocacy of Russia's cultural supremacy—resemble those of Russia's great nineteenth-century pre-existentialist novelist, Dostoevsky.

Many late Modernist poets used a private language to such a degree that their verses were often unintelligible to ordinary people. A few who used more conventional verse styles, however, earned a large readership. Of this latter group the Welsh poet Dylan Thomas (1914–1953) was the most famous and remains so today. Thomas's poems mirror the obscurity favored by the times, but what makes his works so memorable is their glorious sound. With their strong emotional content, jaunty rhythms, and melodious words, they are perfect to read aloud.

Better known than Thomas's poems, though, is his verse play *Under Milk Wood* (1954), arguably the best-loved poetic work of Late Modernism. Unlike the poems, this verse play is direct and imbued with simple emotions. Originally a play for radio, it presents a typical day in a Welsh village, a world he knew well, having grown up in such a place. His portrait of the colorful speech and intertwined lives of the

FIGURE 21.11 VITALY KOMAR AND ALEKSANDER MELAMID. *Stroke (About March 3, 1953).* 1982–1983. Oil on canvas, 6′ × 3′11″. Collection Evander D. Schley. Courtesy Ronald Feldman Fine Arts, New York. *The two Russian emigré painters Komar and Melamid—who work as a team—have devoted their artistic efforts to trying to understand the Russian Revolution and the reign of Stalin. In* Stroke *they depict the lonely death of Stalin and the discovery of his body by a member of his inner circle. The artists subtly criticize both Stalin and the Soviet system in the way the official stares unmoved at the dead tyrant. Komar and Melamid show their Post-Modernist tendencies in their use of elements from earlier styles of art, such as the theatrical lighting and unusual perspective typical of Caravaggio.*

eccentric villagers has moved millions of listeners, evoking for them bittersweet memories of their own youth.

A Late Modernist poet who is able to be experimental and yet win a large audience for his verses is the American writer Allen Ginsberg (1926–), the most significant poet produced by the Beat Generation of the 1950s. Like Dylan Thomas, he has an ear for colloquial speech, and his ability to construct new forms to convey iconoclastic views is unequaled by any other poet of his time. His outstanding poem is "Howl" (1956), a work of homage to rebel youth and illicit drugs and sex. Overcoming censorship, this poem of Ginsberg's opposed capitalist, heterosexual, bourgeois society and became the anthem of the Beat Generation.

During Late Modernism the most radical changes in literature took place in drama. Sharing existentialism's bleak vision and determined to find new ways to express that outlook, a group of dramatists emerged called the *"theater of the absurd."* The absurdists shifted the focus of their plays away from the study of the characters' psychology to stress poetic language and abandoned realistic plots in order to concentrate on outrageous situations. A typical absurdist play mixed tragedy with comedy, as if the playwright thought that the pain of existence could be tolerated only if blended with humor.

Samuel Beckett (1906–1989), an Irish writer who lived in Paris, is the best-known dramatist of absurdist theater. His *Waiting for Godot* (1952) is a play in which almost nothing "happens" in the conventional sense of that word. Combining elements of tragedy and farce, *Waiting for Godot* broke new ground with its repetitive structure (the second act is almost a replica of the first); its lack of scenery (the stage is bare except for a single tree); and its meager action (the characters engage in futile exchanges based on British music hall routines). What plot there is also reinforces the idea of futility, as the characters wait for the mysterious Godot, who never appears.

In later years Beckett's works began to explore the dramatic possibilities of silence, as in the one-act drama *Not I* (1973). In this play, a voice—seen only as a mouth illuminated in a spotlight—tries to, but cannot, stop talking. Beckett's plays portray human consciousness as a curse; yet at the same time his works affirm the human spirit's survival in the face of despair.

The Literature of Post-Modernism

Post-Modernist literature is notable for the rise of new literary voices in Latin America and in central and eastern Europe, a shift that was part of the general decline of the dominance of the Paris-New York cultural axis and the rise of a more broadly based civilization. For the first time, Latin American authors put the Spanish-American novel on the international map. Most of these writers were distinguished by left-wing political opinions and devotion to a literary style called *"magic realism,"* which mixed realistic and supernatural elements. The ground had been prepared for the magic realists by the Argentinian author Jorge Luis Borges (1899–1986), whose brief, enigmatic stories gave this movement its stress on fantasy and linguistic experimentation.

The outstanding representative of the magic realist school is Gabriel Garcia Márquez (1928–) of Colombia, who received the 1982 Nobel Prize for literature—the first Latin American novelist to be so honored. His *One Hundred Years of Solitude* (1967) is among the most highly acclaimed novels of the postwar era. Inspired by William Faulkner's fictional county of Yoknapatawpha, Mississippi, Garcia Márquez invented the town of Macondo to serve as a symbol of his Colombian birthplace. Through the eyes of an omniscient narrator—probably an unnamed peasant—who sees Macondo as moving toward a predestined doom, he produced a hallucinatory novel that blends details from Latin American history with magical events, such as a character's ascent into heaven.

While Latin America's authors were enjoying international renown for the first time, the writers of central and eastern Europe—the other new center of Post-Modernism—were simply renewing an old tradition. From the early 1800s until communist regimes were installed in this century, the finest writers of central and eastern Europe had often been honored in the West. The revival of the literature of this region was heralded by the 1950s cultural thaw initiated by Soviet leader Khrushchev, but this thaw proved premature as controversial writers were either silenced or forced to seek refuge in the West.

Exile was the choice of the novelist Milan Kundera (1929–) of Czechoslovakia, who moved to France after his first novel, *The Joke* (1969), put him in disfavor with Czech authorities. Kundera's style has affinities with magic realism, notably the blending of fantasy with national history, but unlike the authors of Latin America, he uses fantasy to emphasize moral themes, never for its own sake. He is also more optimistic than the magic realists, hinting that the power of love can lead its devotees to a different and better life. Indeed, Kundera tends to identify sexual freedom with political freedom.

The equation of sexual and political freedom is certainly the message of Kundera's finest novel to date, *The Unbearable Lightness of Being* (1984). He made the center of this work two historic events—the coming of Communism to Czechoslovakia in 1948 and its reimposition after the 1968 uprising. He describes the obsessive and ultimately destructive behavior of his main characters as they try to define their sexual natures in the repressive Czech state. Although his novel shows how insignificant human existence is in the face of political repression, he refuses to despair. That his characters struggle for sexual fulfillment, even when faced by overpowering odds, is his way of affirming the strength of human nature. Ultimately, Kundera endorsed the belief of humanism that the human spirit can be diminished but never broken.

A similar belief is apparent in the work of the American writer Alice Walker (1944–). In her poetry, essays, and fiction she brings a positive tone to her exploration of the African-American experience. Her most engaging novel to date is *The Color Purple* (1982), the story of a black woman abused by black men and victimized by white society. The literary device she uses to express this woman's anguish is an old one, a story told through an exchange of letters. What is unique is that in some letters the suffering woman simply pours out her heart to God—an unexpected but moving twist in the skeptical atmosphere of the postwar world. *The Color Purple* also drew on Walker's feminist consciousness, showing that the heroine's survival depended on her solidarity with other black women.

Late Modernism and the Arts

In the postwar art world, leadership shifted from Paris to New York. The end of Parisian dominance had been predicted since the swift fall of France to the Nazis in 1940, and the economic and military superiority of the United States at the war's end ensured that America's largest city would be the new hub of Western culture. New York's cultural leaders were divided in 1945, however. On one side stood those who wanted to build on the native school of American art, which was realistic and provincial, while on the other side was a group ready to take up the mantle of leadership of the West's *avant-garde*. The chief institutional ally of this latter group, which soon dominated the field, was the Museum of Modern Art (MOMA) in New York City, founded principally by the Rockefeller family in 1929.

In determining the direction of Modern art, the New York artists had to contend with the domination of painting by Picasso, whose restless experimentation seemed to define art's leading edge (Figure 21.12); the prevalence of psychological theories that encouraged artists to experiment with spontaneous gestures and to seek insights from primitive peoples and from religious experience; and the cardinal need for constant newness. Although these had all been elements in Modernism since 1900, what made the postwar scene different was that the need to dispel illusions was greater and the level of despair higher, based on the destructive war, the Holocaust, and the postwar arms race.

FIGURE 21.12 PABLO PICASSO. *La Joie de Vivre (The Joy of Life)*. 1946. Oil on fiber-cement panel, 3'11¼" × 8'2½". Picasso Museum, Antibes, France. *Picasso remained the leading painter in the world almost until his death in 1973. His style at the time he painted this work, in the first year after World War II, was a semiabstract, semirepresentational approach that had grown out of Cubism. Another force driving his art was a love of whimsy, as may be seen in the figures dancing and playing musical instruments. Jackson Pollock and the New York School of painters had to contend with Picasso's immense authority in order to establish themselves as authentic voices of Modernism in the late 1940s.*

Painting Shortly after 1945 an energetic style of painting arose that dominated Late Modernism and still plays a major role: *Abstract Expressionism*, sometimes called Action Painting. Like earlier Modernists, the Abstract Expressionists made spiritual claims for their work, identifying their spontaneous methods as liberating the human spirit. One of the founders of Abstract Expressionism was the American Jackson Pollock (1912–1956) who launched this style with his "drip paintings," created between 1947 and 1950. Influenced by Jungian therapy to experiment with spontaneous gestures, Pollock nailed his canvases to the floor of his studio and dripped loops of house paint onto them from buckets with holes punched in

FIGURE 21.14 MARK ROTHKO. *Ochre and Red on Red.* 1954. Oil on canvas, 7'8⅝" × 5'3¾". Phillips Collection, Washington, D.C. *In his paintings Rothko aims to create secular icons for a nonreligious age, a spiritual theory inherited from the Russian Constructivist tradition. Accordingly, he banishes all references to nature from his art and focuses on fields of color floating in space—timeless, universal images.*

their bottoms (Figure 21.13). The drip canvases led to a new way of looking at art in terms of randomness, spontaneity, "all overness," and stress on the actual physical process of painting. Pollock's tendency to move around the canvas during its execution also introduced the idea of the artist interacting with the artwork.

◀ **FIGURE 21.13** JACKSON POLLOCK. *Blue Poles.* 1952. Oil, enamel, and aluminum paint, 210.4 × 486.8 cm. Collection, Australian National Gallery, Canberra. *This painting is virtually unique among Pollock's drip canvases by having a recognizable image, the blue poles. He achieved this effect by first swirling paint onto the canvas and then applying a stick covered in blue pigment onto its surface. His refusal to use traditional methods reflects both his belief that rational approaches to art are flawed and his faith that subconscious feelings, when released, reveal hidden truths—an attitude typical of the Abstract Expressionists.*

The first generation of Abstract Expressionists was attracted by the movement's energy, rawness, and seriousness. An outstanding recruit to the new art was Mark Rothko (1903–1970), a Russian émigré who painted in a style very different from Pollock's. A mystic, Rothko envisioned eliminating pigment and canvas and suspending clouds of shimmering colors in the air. After 1950 he settled for creating huge paintings that focused on no more than two or three fields of color (Figure 21.14).

By the mid-1950s a new generation of Abstract Expressionists emerged, the most important of whom were Helen Frankenthaler (1928–), Jasper Johns (1930–), and Robert Rauschenberg (1925–). Following in Pollock's footsteps, Frankenthaler adopted a method of spilling pigment onto canvas from coffee cans. By guiding the paint's flowing trajectory, she stained the canvas into exquisite, amorphous shapes

◀ **FIGURE 21.15** HELEN FRANKENTHALER. *Jacob's Ladder*. 1957. Oil on unprimed canvas, 9'5⅜" × 5'9⅞". Collection, The Museum of Modern Art, New York. Gift of Hyman N. Glickstein. *Frankenthaler's staining method—pouring paint onto a canvas—illustrates the tension between spontaneity and control typical of Abstract Expressionism. On the one hand, this technique leads naturally to surprises because of the unpredictable flow of the paint. On the other hand, the artist exercises control over the process, ranging from choosing the colors and thickness of the paint to manipulating the canvas during the staining. In effect, she becomes both a participant in and the creator of the final work of art.*

that, though completely flat, seem to suggest a third dimension (Figure 21.15).

Johns and Rauschenberg found Abstract Expressionism too confining and overly serious, however. Although he did not abandon Expressionism, Johns added ordinary objects to his works, as in *Target with Plaster Casts* (1955) (Figure 21.16). In this work he

paints a banal image below a row of wooden boxes enclosing molds of body parts. A basic feature of his art is the contrast between the precisely rendered human organs (above) and the painterly target (below). Johns's fascination with such tensions paved the way for the self-contradicting style of Post-Modernism. Similarly, Rauschenberg abandoned pure painting to become an **assemblage** artist, mixing found objects with junk and adding a dash of paint. In *Monogram*, he encircles a stuffed goat with a rubber tire and splashes the whole thing with color, thus turning ready-made objects into an abstract image (Figure 21.16).

Johns and Rauschenberg, with their playful attack on serious art, opened the door to the *Pop Art* movement. Rejecting the Modernist belief that spiritual values may be expressed in nonrealistic works, the Pop artists frankly admitted that they had no spirit-

FIGURE 21.16 JASPER JOHNS. *Target with Plaster Casts*. 1955. Encaustic on canvas with plaster cast objects, 51 × 44 × 3½". Courtesy Leo Castelli Gallery, New York. *Johns was a key figure in the transitional generation of painters between the Abstract Expressionists and the Pop Artists. He rebelled against the pure abstraction of the older movement, yet he shied away from embracing mass culture images as directly as did the younger school of painters. His* Target with Plaster Casts *is typical of his playful, witty style. In this work he makes a visual play on words, juxtaposing a bull's-eye with plaster casts of body parts, each of which has been a "target," that is, a subject, for artists to represent throughout history.*

FIGURE 21.17 ROBERT RAUSCHENBERG. *Monogram.* 1959. Multimedia construction, 4' × 6' × 6'. Moderna Museet, Stockholm. *In his glorification of junk, Rauschenberg helped to open the door to Post-Modernism. In works such as* Monogram *he showed that anything, no matter how forlorn, even a stuffed goat and a discarded automobile tire, could be used to make art. Such irreverence reflected a democratic vision in which no object is seen as having greater artistic merit than any other.*

ual, metaphysical, or philosophic purpose—they simply created two-dimensional images. Even though a kind of Pop Art began in London in the 1950s, it was not until a new generation of New York artists began to explore commercial images in the early 1960s that the movement took off.

The most highly visible Pop artist was Andy Warhol (1927–1987), a former commercial artist who was fascinated by the vulgarity and energy of popular culture. Warhol's deadpan treatment of mass culture icons became legendary, whether they were Campbell's Soup cans, Coca Cola bottles, or Marilyn Monroe (Figure 21.18). By treating these icons in series, much in the same way as advertisers blanket the media with multiple images, he conveyed the ideas of repetitiveness, banality, and boredom. An artist who courted fame, Warhol recognized America's obsession with celebrity in his often-quoted line, "In the future everyone will be famous for fifteen minutes."

FIGURE 21.18 ANDY WARHOL. *Marilyn Monroe.* 1962. Oil, acrylic, and silkscreen enamel on canvas, 20 × 16". Collection, Jasper Johns. Courtesy Leo Castelli Gallery, New York. *Warhol's portrait of Marilyn Monroe, America's most famous postwar sex symbol, was typical of his style, which placed little value on originality. Working from a photograph supplied by her Hollywood studio, he merely used his brushes and paint to heighten the image that studio hairdressers and cosmetologists had already perfected. In effect, Warhol's art was a gilding of the lily. His commercial approach to portraiture made him the most celebrated society artist of his generation.*

◀ **FIGURE 21.19**   DAVID SMITH. *Cubi XIX.* 1964. Stainless steel, 9′5⅛″ × 21¾″ × 20¾″. Tate Gallery, London. *Smith's ability as a sculptor of enormous and rather destructive energies shines through in the monumental* **Cubi** *series, the last artworks he made before his accidental death. A machinist by training, Smith liked to work with industrial metals, welding and bending them into geometric units to meet his expressive needs. His desire to shape mechanical images into expressive forms related him to the Abstract Expressionist movement in painting.*

FIGURE 21.20   LOUISE NEVELSON. *Atmosphere and Environment, I.* 1966. Construction of enameled aluminum, 6′6¼″ × 12′3⅜″ × 4′1½″. Collection, The Museum of Modern Art, New York. Mrs. Simon Guggenheim Fund. *Though a Modernist, Nevelson anticipated Post-Modernism by combining genres, as in this free-standing wall that integrates architecture, sculpture, and painting. Typical of her art of this time, she divided the wall into a grid, stuffed found objects into the wall's compartments, and painted the finished work black. In the Post-Modern period Nevelson's decorative walls have had more influence on architects, such as Venturi, than on sculptors, who have tended to favor realistic styles.*

Sculpture   Styles in sculpture were similar to those in painting. Abstract Expressionist painting had its equivalent in the works of several American sculptors, notably David Smith (1906–1965) and Louise Nevelson (1899–1988), a Russian émigrée. Smith's point of departure, however, differed from that of the painters in that he drew inspiration from the symbols of primitive cultures, as in *Cubi XIX,* a geometric work that, according to the artist, represents an altar with a sacrificial figure (Figure 21.19). If the viewer is unaware of this intended meaning, however, this stainless steel work has the inaccessible look of a Pollock drip canvas. In contrast, the wooden sculptures of Louise Nevelson are not about representation at all but are simple compositions fashioned from old furniture and wooden odds and ends (Figure 21.20).

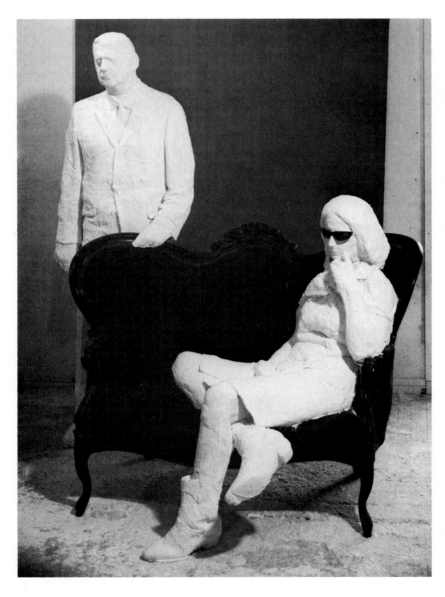

FIGURE 21.21 GEORGE SEGAL. *Robert and Ethel Scull.* 1965. Plaster, canvas, wood, and cloth, 8' × 6' × 6'. Private Collection. Courtesy Sidney Janis Gallery, New York. *Segal distances himself from fellow Pop artists by looking at the world through existential eyes. Where Warhol glamorizes his celebrity subjects, Segal portrays his wealthy patrons, the Sculls, as beset by anxiety. He conveys their anguish though fixed facial expressions and heavy limbs, while keeping their appearances generalized. His modeling technique, which requires subjects not to move any muscles until the plaster dried, reinforces the melancholy image.*

FIGURE 21.22 LUDWIG MIËS VAN DER ▶ ROHE AND PHILIP JOHNSON. *Seagram Building.* 1954–1958. New York City. *Miës's decision to use bronze-tinted windows as virtually the only decorative feature of the Seagram Building's simple geometrical design had a profound impact on his contemporaries. Following his lead, other architects made the high-rise skeleton-frame building with tinted windows the most recognizable symbol of Late Modernism.*

The use of found objects allowed Nevelson to realize the Abstract Expressionist's goal of spontaneous art devoid of references to the artist's life.

Pop Art was an influence in the works of George Segal (1924–). Segal's ghostly sculptures are made by applying a plaster mixture to his living subjects to produce generic figures, as in his dual portrait of Robert and Ethel Scull, leading patrons of the Pop Art movement (Figure 21.21). Segal himself rejects the Pop Art label—pointing out that his sculptures have expressionistic surfaces, like Rodin's works (see Chapter 19)—but his method reduces the body to a cartoon form and thus relates it to popular culture.

Architecture In Late Modernist architecture the most influential architect was the German-born Ludwig Miës van der Rohe (1886–1969). The last head of the Bauhaus, Germany's premier design school before World War II, Miës closed its doors in 1933 and moved to the United States in 1938. In the 1950s he captured the world's attention with a glass skyscraper, New York's Seagram Building (Figure 21.22). Based on the artistic creed, "less is more," this building's design is simple, a bronze skeletal frame on which are hung tinted windows. The implementation of his ideals of simplicity and restraint also led him to geometrize the building, planning its structural relationships according to mathematical ratios. So successful was Miës van der Rohe's "glass box" building that today skyscrapers built according to similar designs dominate the skylines of cities around the world.

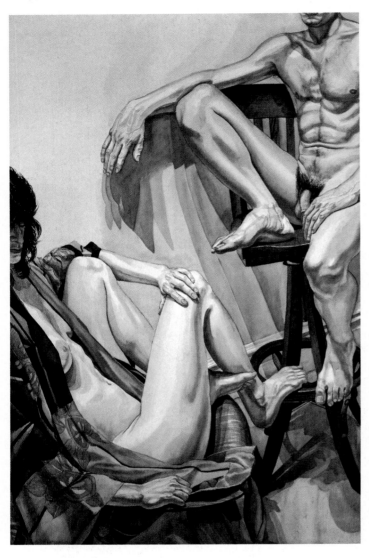

Figure 21.23   Philip Pearlstein. *Female on Eames Chair, Male on Swivel Stool.* 1981. Watercolor, 60 × 40″. Collection of Eleanor and Leonard Bellinson. Courtesy Donald Morris Gallery, Birmingham, Mich. *Pearlstein's refusal to glamorize his nude subjects is part of a democratizing tendency in Post-Modernism. Just as some Post-Modernist authors borrow freely from mass-circulation genres such as Sherlock Holmes and science fiction, so Pearlstein focuses attention on bodily features like sagging breasts and bulging veins that had been overlooked by realistic painters.*

Post-Modernism and the Arts

The arts began to change around 1970 as artists and architects struggled to move beyond Late Modernism, which seemed to have dissolved into weak minimalist schools. In Post-Modernism, the shock of the new gave way to the shock of the old. Seeking a way out of Late Modernism's chaotic pessimism and its focus on abstraction that seemed to have led to a dead end, Post-Modern artists were more optimistic and

revived earlier styles, although always with added layers of meaning, nuance, or irony. Realism made a triumphant return to art, flourishing as *Neorealism*, a style based on photographic clarity of detail; as *Neoexpressionism*, a style that offers social criticism and focuses on nontraditional painting methods; and as *Neoclassicism* (not to be confused with the Neoclassicism of the late eighteenth century), which had been dormant since the early twentieth century and pronounced dead by the Late Modernists. Neoclassicism is the most striking style within Post-Modernism, in both painting and architecture, perhaps because it looks so fresh to modern eyes. In addition to these various forms of realism, Modernist abstraction remains a significant facet of Post-Modernism. In their openness to artistic possibilities and their refusal to adopt a uniform style, the Post-Modernists resembled the Post-Impressionists of the late nineteenth century.

Painting   An outstanding Neorealist painter is the American Philip Pearlstein (1924–   ), who specializes in nonidealized nudes. Starting in the 1960s he made his chief subject human bodies beyond their prime, perhaps as a way of reflecting the melancholy of the age. His nudes are rendered in stark close-up, the bodies at rest like hanging meat, and with cropped heads and limbs as in a photograph (Figure 21.23). His works seem to parody the "centerfold sexuality" that accompanied the sexual revolution brought on in part by the birth control pill.

Whereas Neorealism tends to neutrality or moral subtlety, Neoexpressionism uses realism to create paintings that are overtly socially critical. The outstanding Neoexpressionist and the most highly regarded painter among the Post-Modernists is the German artist Anselm Kiefer (1945–   ). Kiefer's works have blazed new trails with nontraditional painting materials, including dirt, tar, and copper threads. Existential anguish is alive in his works, which tend to focus on apocalyptic images of a blasted earth—a chilling reference to the threat of nuclear destruction (Figure 21.24). Post-Modern optimism may nevertheless be read in his borrowings from Mesopotamia and Egypt, which affirm the continuity of Western culture from its earliest stages to the present. In his use of personal references and historical allusions, Kiefer is perhaps the contemporary artist closest to the German Expressionists of the early twentieth century.

A painter who uses Neoclassicism to make a subtle commentary on modern life is the American Stone Roberts (1951–   ). In *The Conversation* he blends Classical features of Renaissance space, Baroque lighting, and Dutch genre precision (Figure 21.25). A repre-

FIGURE 21.24 ANSELM KIEFER. *Osiris and Isis.* 1985–1987. Diptych, mixed media on canvas, 12′6″ × 18′4½″ × 6½″. The San Francisco Museum of Modern Art. Courtesy Marian Goodman Gallery, New York. *Kiefer drew on an ancient Egyptian myth to give shape to his fears of modern technology. He represents Isis, the goddess who restored her husband-brother Osiris to life, as an electronic keyboard at the top of a pyramid. He adds actual copper wires to connect the circuit board to broken bits of ceramics, his symbol of Osiris's fragmented body. In Kiefer's Post-Modern imagination, technology has become a deity with the capacity to destroy or create.*

FIGURE 21.25 STONE ROBERTS. *The Conversation.* 1985. Oil on canvas, 6′ × 7′6″. Private Collection. Courtesy Robert Schoelkopf Gallery, New York. *In* The Conversation *Roberts brings Classicism up-to-date by applying its features and principles to a contemporary American context. He fills the setting with Classical references, including fluted columns, a Greek-style marble fireplace, a rounded arch, and vases after Greek models. The figures are grave and self-contained, and the symmetry of the fireplace and columns reflects the Classical ideal of harmony.*

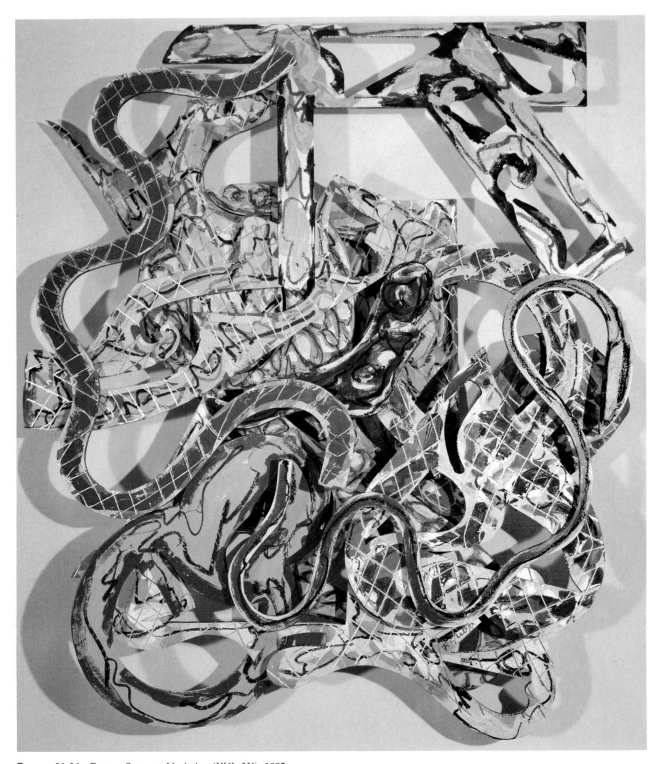

FIGURE 21.26 FRANK STELLA. *Norisring (XVI, 3X)*. 1983.
Mixed media on etched aluminum, 6'7" × 5'7" × 1'3".
Private Collection. Courtesy M. Knoedler & Co., New York.
*Largely because of his lively intelligence, Stella has stayed on the
cutting edge of Post-Modernism. He has kept abstraction alive
almost singlehandedly at a time when realist styles are dominant.
His 1960s innovation, the shaped canvas, allowed him to replace the
rectilinear canvas with an abstract form. By the early 1980s he had
transformed the shaped canvas into a blend of sculpture and
painting, as in the Shard series.*

FIGURE 21.27 JOHN DE ANDREA. *Seated Man and Woman.* 1981. Polyvinyl, polychromed in oil, life-size. Courtesy ACA Galleries, New York. *Unlike Pearlstein, who uses nudity to register his disgust, De Andrea designs his polyvinyl nudes to celebrate the glossy lives of the upper middle class. The bodies of his nude subjects convey what today's consumer culture urges everyone to be: healthy, sleek, athletic, and sexy.*

sentation of a bittersweet moment in middle-class life, it evokes the feeling of a social gathering when guests are reluctant to depart. The darkening background reinforces the air of melancholy and hints that this way of life is passing.

Modernist abstraction continues to have a powerful impact on Post-Modernism. The most brilliant current disciple of abstraction is Frank Stella (1936–), a painter who has produced an immense and varied body of work. A minimalist in the 1950s, painting black-striped canvases, he became a forerunner of Neoexpressionism in the 1970s, using gaudy color and decorative effects. He has remained true to abstract ideals, as in *Norisring*, one of the *Shard* series that uses the scraps left over from other works (Figure 21.26). Fully abstract and nonrepresentational, this work is nevertheless Post-Modernist since it combines the genres of painting and sculpture—an ambition of many Post-Modernists.

Sculpture Like painters, Post-Modernist sculptors began to work with realistic forms. For example, serving as complements to the Neorealist paintings of Philip Pearlstein are the sculptures of the American John De Andrea (1941–). Typically, De Andrea uses traditional poses, as in *Seated Man and Woman* (Figure 21.27), a work inspired by Rodin. But De Andrea's human figures are fully contemporary, suggestive of two young upwardly mobile professionals ("yuppies") who have taken off their clothes. Whether or not his works are satirical, he manages to capture in sculptural form the erotic quality considered so desirable by modern advertising, movies, and mass media.

Architecture The chief exponent of Post-Modern architecture is the American Robert Venturi (1925–), whose ideas are summarized in his book *Complexity and Contradiction in Architecture* (1966). Rejecting Modernist architecture, which he thinks inhuman because of its starkness, he attempts to create buildings that express the energy and ever-changing quality of contemporary life. Fascinated by mass culture, he is inspired by popular styles of architecture, such as Las Vegas casinos and motels in the form of Indian tepees—a kitsch style sometimes called "vernacular." A work that enshrines his love of the ordinary is his Guild House, a retirement home in a lower-middle-class section of Philadelphia (Figure 21.28). Faceless and seemingly artless, this building is indebted to popular culture for its aesthetic appeal—for instance, the wire sculpture on the roof looks like a television antenna, and the recessed entrance and sign evoke memories of old-time movie houses. Venturi's playful assault on Modernism opened the door to the diversity of Post-Modernism.

One of the strains in Post-Modernism is called *high tech*, a style that revives industrial techniques whose roots stretch back to the Crystal Palace and the Eiffel Tower. Richard Rogers (1933–) of England and Renzo Piano (1937–) of Italy launched this revival with the Pompidou Center in Paris, which boldly displays its factory-made metal parts and transparent walls (Figure 21.29). Commissioned by France to restore Paris's cultural position over New York, the Pompidou Center has spawned many imitations as well as a style of interior decoration.

The most controversial building in Post-Modern architecture is the thirty-seven-story, pink granite headquarters building of American Telephone and Telegraph, executed in a Neoclassical style (Figure 21.30). Designed by Philip C. Johnson (1906–), an American disciple of Miës van der Rohe, this building was a slap in the face to the Modernist ideal because it used Classical forms. The AT&T Building has a base, a middle, and a top, corresponding to the foot, shaft, and capital of a Greek column—the basic element of Greco-Roman building style. As a final blow to Modernist purity, Johnson topped his building with a split pediment crown, causing a hostile critic to compare it to an eighteenth-century Chippendale highboy. Notwithstanding the furor surrounding its creation, this building heralded the resurgence of Neoclassicism in the Post-Modernist age.

Late Modern and Post-Modern Music

The major musical styles that were dominant prior to World War II persisted in Late Modernism. New York was the world's musical capital, and styles were still polarized into tonal and atonal camps, led by Stravinsky and Schoenberg, respectively. After Schoenberg's death in 1951, however, Stravinsky abandoned tonality and adopted his rival's serial method. Stravinsky's conversion made serialism the most respected type of atonal music, though other approaches to atonality sprang up, notably in the United States. Under Late Modernism, this dissonant style became the musical equivalent of the spontaneous canvases painted by Pollock and the Abstract Expressionist school.

Despite embracing the dissonance and abstraction of serialism, Stravinsky filled his Late Modernist works with energy and feeling, the touchstones of his musical style. Two of his finest serial works were *Agon* (1957), a score for a ballet with no other plot than a competition among the dancers, and *Requiem Canticles* (1968), a religious service for the dead marked by austere solemnity.

An important American composer indebted to Schoenberg is John Cage (1912–), whose unusual, even playful, approach to music opened the door to Post-Modernism. Briefly Schoenberg's student, Cage gained most of his controversial notions—in particular, his goal of integrating noise into music—from the enigmatic teachings of Zen Buddhism. A work that demonstrates this goal is called *4'33"* (*Four Minutes and Thirty-three Seconds*). The title describes the time period that the performer is to sit immobile before a piano keyboard so that the music, in effect, becomes the concert hall sounds during the silence. Cage's spirited experiments made him the darling of the *avant-garde*. Along with assemblage artists, choreographers, and sculptors, he has helped to break down the divisions among the art forms—an anticipation of a Post-Modernist development.

In the 1960s innovative composers appeared who rejected atonality for its overintellectuality and its apparent devotion to harsh sounds. In place of atonal-

FIGURE 21.28 ROBERT VENTURI. Guild House. 1965. Philadelphia. *Venturi's aesthetic aim is to transform the ordinary into the extraordinary. He followed this democratic ideal in Guild House, where he took a "dumb and ordinary" (his term) concept and tried to give it a monumental look. Whether he succeeds in achieving his goal is a matter of taste. Nevertheless, his ironic intelligence and his perverse delight in mass culture have made him a guiding spirit of Post-Modernism.*

ity, these composers founded a Post-Modern style devoted to making music more emotionally appealing, though they remained committed to experimental methods. Among the most notable composers working within this style is the American Philip Glass (1937–), who has made it his mission to return exuberance to music. He has pursued this goal while working in a minimalist tradition, although he draws on varied sources, including classical Indian music, African drumming, and rock-and-roll. Much of Glass's music is written for **synthesizer,** a machine with a simple keyboard that can duplicate the sounds of up to twelve instruments simultaneously. He composes with simple tonal harmonies, pulsating rhythms, unadorned scales, and, above all, lilting arpeggios, the cascading sounds produced by playing the notes of a chord in rapid sequences. A Glass piece is instantly recognizable for its repetitiveness and obsessive quality.

A composer of chamber works, film scores, and dance pieces, Glass has gained the widest celebrity for his operas. His first opera, *Einstein on the Beach* (1976), produced in collaboration with the equally controversial American director Robert Wilson (1941–), was staged at New York's Metropolitan Opera, a rarity for a living composer in this century. In their kaleidoscopic work, Glass and Wilson redefined the operatic form, staging a production lasting four and one-half hours without intermission and with Glass's driving music set to Wilson's texts with no recognizable plot, no formal arias, and no massed choruses. So successful was this venture that Glass followed it with operas based on other remarkable

FIGURE 21.29 RICHARD ROGERS AND RENZO PIANO. The Georges Pompidou Center for Art and Culture. 1971–1977. Paris. *Designed in a gaudy industrial style and erected in the heart of a quiet section of Paris called Beaubourg, the Pompidou Center was controversial from the start, as it was planned to be. Its showy appearance sharply contrasted with the historic styles of neighboring structures—a contrast that has become a guiding ideal of Post-Modernist architects. The furor that greeted the Pompidou Center on its opening has occurred in other places where city governments have placed colorful and brash high-tech temples amid their more traditional buildings.*

◀ **FIGURE 21.30** PHILIP C. JOHNSON AND JOHN BURGEE.
American Telephone and Telegraph Headquarters.
1979–1984. New York. *Although Classical rules were followed in
the planning of Johnson and Burgee's AT&T Headquarters, it was
built using Modernist methods. Like Modernist structures, the
building has a steel frame to which exterior panels are clipped.
Despite its Modernist soul, the physical presence of this Post-
Modernist building conveys the gravity and harmony customarily
associated with Classical architecture.*

figures, *Satyagraha* (1978) dealing with the life of Gandhi, India's liberator, and *Akhnaten* (1984) focusing on
the Egyptian pharaoh who is sometimes called the
first monotheist.

Mass Culture

In the postwar era American mass culture began to
serve as the common denominator of an emerging
world civilization. Because of its democratic and energetic qualities, sexual content, and commitment to
free expression, this culture has attracted people
around the globe. Scenes of American life—conveyed
through television, movies, and advertising—have
mesmerized millions, who imitate these images as far
as they are able. The popularity of the clothing (jeans,
T-shirt, and running shoes), the food (hamburgers,
fries, and cola), and the music (rock-and-roll) of the
American teenager has influenced behavior even in

eastern Europe, the Soviet Union, and the Third
World.

The information boom has been the explosive force
Americanizing the world and transforming it into a
global village, with television providing the means of
transformation. As the earth has shrunk, more electronic gear—the video cassette recorder, the compact-
disc player, the digital recorder, the video camera
recorder, the computer—has reduced the individual's
world even more, turning each home into a communications center.

The rise of a worldwide mass culture has produced
an insatiable demand for popular entertainment. It
has led to the replacement of old types of amusements with new forms, such as the rock concert and
the rock video, along with the creation of innovative
means of media coverage, including cable television
with MTV and all-sports channels. This demand has
given birth to extravagantly popular figures—like El-
vis Presley (1935–1977), America's first postwar music idol, Michael Jackson (1958–   ), America's super-
star of the mid-1980s, and Madonna (1959–   ),
America's queen of popular songs in the early
1990s—who are role models for teenagers and young
adults across the world. Except for the Beatles, the
British rock quartet that was the most popular rock
group of the 1960s, few superstars are non-American.
Only time will tell if Post-Modernist mass culture can
produce a civilization that is truly pluralistic and
global.

A Summing Up

We stand on the threshhold of a new era. The
division of the world into rival armed camps
after World War II seems to be at an end, and
many voices have proclaimed the death of the
Cold War. Winds of freedom are blowing everywhere. After forty-five divided years, Germany is
reunited. *Glasnost* has opened up the societies of
the satellite countries of the Soviet system, and
the Soviet Union is caught in turbulent events
whose outcome is unpredictable. South Africa,
where a white minority has always denied rights
to the black majority, shows signs of a change
to a more just society.

Future shifts in economic power among the
world's great states promise more changes in the
old political order. As of 1992 western Europe
will be the most powerful trading and financial
area of the world. The unification of Germany
will have incalculable ramifications on global

events. And growing debt among the Third
World states makes them perennial trouble spots
because of their vulnerability to internal unrest
and external aggression.

A new world order may already be seen, struggling to be born, in our Post-Modernist era. It is
global and democratic and embraces the contributions, tastes, and ideas of many groups of
people, men and women, people of all races,
and people of all countries. It is also open-ended,
freely borrowing from high culture and mass
culture. Nevertheless, the driving force for the
emerging global culture in the foreseeable future
is Western civilization, largely because of its immense capacity to adapt and bend and yet ultimately to survive—something Western artists,
writers, and peoples have been doing since the
first cities were founded in Sumer and Egypt five
thousand years ago.

KEY CULTURAL TERMS

Late Modernism
Post-Modernism
structuralism
theater of the absurd
magic realism
Abstract Expressionism
assemblage art

Pop Art
Neorealism
Neoexpressionism
Neoclassicism
high tech
synthesizer

SUGGESTIONS FOR FURTHER READING

PRIMARY SOURCES

The Autobiography of Malcolm X. With the assistance of A. Haley. Secaucus, N.J.: Castle Books, 1967. In his own words Malcolm X describes his rise from obscurity to become a powerful figure posing radical solutions to racial problems.

BALDWIN, J. *Go Tell It On the Mountain.* New York: Grossett and Dunlap, 1953. A novel representative of Baldwin's early optimism about reconciliation of the black and white races.

———. *No Name in the Street.* New York: Dial Press, 1972. A novel representative of Baldwin's bitterness after the murder of Martin Luther King, Jr.

BECKETT, S. *Waiting for Godot.* Edited and with an introduction by H. Bloom. New York: Chelsea House Publishers, 1987. The central image of Beckett's absurdist play—pointless waiting—has become a metaphor for the disappointed hopes of Late Modernism.

CAMUS, A. *The Fall.* Translated by J. O'Brien. New York: Knopf, 1957. Camus's most autobiographical novel, dealing with self-deceit and spiritual yearning.

CHOMSKY, N. *Syntactic Structures.* The Hague: Mouton, 1957. The work that revolutionized linguistics by claiming that there is a structure that lies hidden beneath the surface of language.

DE BEAUVOIR, S. *The Second Sex.* Translated and edited by H. M. Parshley. New York: Vintage, 1974. One of the books that helped launch the feminist revival by arguing that women must abandon "femininity" and create their own immortality just as men do.

FANON, F. *The Wretched of the Earth.* Translated by C. Farrington. New York: Grove Press, 1968. Fanon's ground-breaking study of racism and colonial liberation; a classic of modern revolutionary theory.

FRIEDAN, B. *The Feminine Mystique.* New York: Norton, 1963. Denouncing men for conspiring to keep women in second place, this work was a milestone in the rebirth of feminism in the United States.

GARCIA MÁRQUEZ, G. *One Hundred Years of Solitude.* New York: Cambridge University Press, 1990. A classic of Post-Modernism that mixes magical happenings with realistic events in the mythical Columbian town of Macondo.

GINSBERG, A. *Collected Poems, 1947–1980.* New York: Harper & Row, 1984. A Late Modernist, Ginsberg writes poetry that reflects his openness to diversity and his passion for freedom.

KING, M. L., JR. *A Testament of Hope: The Essential Writings of Martin Luther King, Jr.* New York: Harper & Row, 1986. A good introduction to the thought of the most powerful black American in history.

KUNDERA, M. *The Unbearable Lightness of Being.* Translated by M. H. Heim. New York: Harper & Row, 1984. A novel that explores the anguish of life under Communism in eastern Europe.

LESSING, D. *Children of Violence.* (Includes *Martha Quest, A Proper Marriage, A Ripple from the Storm, Landlocked.*) New York: Simon and Schuster, 1964–1966. *The Four-gated City.* New York: Knopf, 1969. Together, these five books make up the *Children of Violence* series. Covering the period between the 1930s and 1960s, this series is Lessing's literary meditation on the transformation of her colonial homeland, Rhodesia, into the black state of Zimbabwe. Martha Quest, the focal point of this quintet of novels, is the author's surrogate witness to these turbulent events.

LÉVI-STRAUSS, C. *The Elementary Structures of Kinship.* Translated by J. H. Bell and others. Boston: Beacon Press, 1969. A classic of social anthropology, this work established that there are only a few basic patterns of kinship relationships in all societies.

MAILER, N. *The Naked and the Dead.* New York: Rinehart, 1948. Mailer's novel of World War II, his first and best work.

SARTRE, J.-P. *The Age of Reason and The Reprieve.* Translated by E. Sutton. *Troubled Sleep.* Translated by G. Hopkins. New York: Knopf, 1947, 1947, and 1950. Sartre's trilogy of novels called *The Roads to Freedom* demonstrates existentialism in action.

———. *No Exit and Three Other Plays.* Translated by L. Abel and S. Gilbert. New York: Vintage, 1976. *No Exit* is Sartre's most famous drama illustrating his idea that "Hell is other people" because they strive to define us and see us as objects; also includes *Dirty Hands, The Respectful Prostitute,* and *The Flies.*

SOLZHENITSYN, A. *One Day in the Life of Ivan Denisovich.* Translated by R. Parker. New York: Dutton, 1963. Published with permission of the Soviet authorities, this novel revealed the existence of Stalin's slave labor camps.

THOMAS, D. *The Collected Poems of Dylan Thomas.* New York: New Directions, 1953. The finest lyric poet of the Late Modern period, Thomas wrote on such themes as sex, love, and death.

———. *Under Milk Wood, A Play for Voices.* New York: New Directions, 1954. A verse play set in a mythical Welsh village that comes to symbolize a lost world in an urbanized age.

WALKER, A. *The Color Purple.* New York: Harcourt Brace Jovanovich, 1982. An uplifting novel that describes the central black female character's rise from degradation to modest dignity. The heroine's use in her letters of awkward but poignantly moving black English underscores the difficulty and the ultimate heroism of her victory.

WRIGHT, R. *Native Son.* New York: Grossett and Dunlap, 1940. Wright's most celebrated novel, the powerful story of the violent consequences of racism in the life of the black hero.

———. *Black Boy: A Record of Childhood and Youth.* New York: Harper, 1945. Wright's description of his rise from sharecropper status to international renown.

SECONDARY SOURCES

ASHTON, D. *The New York School: A Cultural Reckoning.* New York: Viking, 1973. Outstanding discussion of the generation that founded Abstract Expressionism; superbly illustrated.

BANKS, O. *Faces of Feminism: A Study of Feminism as a Social Movement.* New York: St. Martin's Press, 1982. One of the first histories of feminism as a popular movement, extending from 1840 to 1980.

BLACKBURN, G. *The West and the World Since 1945.* New York: St. Martin's Press, 1985. This short survey is a useful introduction to the complex problems of the modern world; weak on cultural developments.

CROUZET, M. *The European Renaissance Since 1945.* Translated by S. Baron. London: Thames and Hudson, 1970. Full of relevant paintings, photographs, and examples of popular culture to illustrate Europe's recovery and rebirth.

FEIS, H. *From Trust to Terror: The Onset of the Cold War, 1945–1950.* New York: Norton, 1970. A close examination by a leading scholar of the origins of the Cold War.

GARDNER, H. *The Quest for Mind.* New York: Vintage, 1974. A superb, succinct treatment of structuralism and its varieties.

GUILBAUT, S. *How New York Stole the Idea of Modern Art: Abstract Expressionism, Freedom and the Cold War.* Translated by A. Goldhammer. Chicago: University of Chicago Press, 1983. A brilliant study that blends artistic developments with political events.

JENCKS, C. *Post-Modernism: The New Classicism in Art and Architecture.* New York: Rizzoli, 1987. The most thorough attempt to understand this new cultural style.

KENNEDY, P. *The Rise and Fall of the Great Powers.* New York: Random House, 1987. For the serious student, a provocative analysis that explains changes in the great powers' fortunes in terms of the competing demands of economic growth and military needs.

LAQUER, W. *A Continent Astray: Europe 1970–1978.* New York: Oxford University Press, 1979. A pessimistic analysis of the 1970s, perhaps outdated by recent events.

———. *Europe Since Hitler.* New York: Penguin, 1982. A first-rate study of postwar Europe to 1970.

LUCIE-SMITH, E. *Movements in Art Since 1945.* London: Thames and Hudson, 1984. The best survey available of developments in art since 1945.

MEADOWS, D. H. *The Limits of Growth: A Report for the Club of Rome's Project on the Predicament of Mankind.* New York: New American Library, 1972. One of the first works that helped to change attitudes toward industrial growth and population trends.

MORLEY, J. W., ED. *The Pacific Basin: New Challenges for the United States.* New York: Academy of Political Science, 1986. An up-to-date collection of essays focusing on the potential for growth in the Pacific Basin countries.

ROSECRANCE, R. N. *The Rise of the Trading State: Commerce and Conquest in the Modern World.* New York: Basic Books, 1986. Presents the provocative thesis that a new international order is emerging based on cooperation among trading states.

SCHELL, J. *The Fate of the Earth.* New York: Knopf, 1982. One of the most influential studies of the past decade on what humans are doing to their environment.

SUGGESTIONS FOR LISTENING

CAGE, JOHN (1912–).
Since the late 1950s Cage's music has come to be characterized by wholly random methods that he calls *aleatory* (from the Latin *alea* for dice), as represented by *4'33"* (*Four Minutes and Thirty-three Seconds*) (1952), *Variations IV* (1963), and *Aria with Fonatana Mix* (1958).

STRAVINSKY, IGOR (1882–1971).
After 1951 Stravinsky replaced his Neoclassical style with the techniques of serial music, as in the song *In Memoriam Dylan Thomas* (1954), the ballet *Agon* (1954–1957), and the orchestral works *Movements* (1959) and *Orchestral Variations* (1964).

GLASS, PHILIP (1937–).
Glass's pulsating rhythms and cascading sounds have made him a popular and successful figure in Post-Modern music. He is best known for his operas, including *Einstein on the Beach* (1976), *Satyagraha* (1978), and *Akhnaten* (1984), and for his film scores, such as *Koyaanisqatsi* (1983) and *Mishima* (1985).

APPENDIX

Writing for the Humanities:
Research Papers and Essay Examinations

The most important part of a man's education is the ability to discuss poetry intelligently.
— PROTAGORAS, FIFTH CENTURY B.C.

I would have the ideal courtier accomplished in those studies that are called the humanities.
— CASTIGLIONE, SIXTEENTH CENTURY A.D.

The idea of "writing for the humanities" has a long history, extending back over twenty-five centuries to ancient Greece. There, in fifth-century-B.C. Athens, the Sophists invented what we today call a "liberal education." These philosophers, who could be termed the first humanists, taught literature, the arts, music, and philosophy, along with what we call political science, anthropology, psychology, and history, to young Athenians, particularly those who hoped to play a leading role in politics. Not only did the Sophists demand that their students master a specific body of knowledge, but they also took care to instruct them in putting the humanistic disciplines into practice. They believed that individuals who had honed their analytical skills in the study of the humanities would be able to make wise judgments in private and public matters and to contribute to the community's political affairs.

The Sophists' educational ideal—training for good citizenship—was later adopted by the Romans, who transmitted it to the medieval West where it became a guiding principle of university education down to the present. Today, college humanities professors give writing assignments because of their belief in the liberal education ideal as well as because of their con-

viction that writing, despite the spread of mass media technology, remains an essential tool of private and public communication and the hallmark of the truly educated person.

AN INTEGRATIVE APPROACH TO WRITING ABOUT THE HUMANITIES

In your study of the humanities, you will probably be given writing assignments that reflect the integrative approach of *The Western Humanities* (see the Introduction). This means that your papers and examinations will not be limited to a single humanistic discipline. Instead, you will be expected to draw information from all of the humanities as well as other disciplines that help illuminate the historical setting, such as political science, economics, and psychology. For example, if you were assigned a term paper on some aspect of nineteenth-century Europe, you would have to consider the civilization as a whole, both its material and cultural developments, and at the same time bring into clearer focus such specific factors as the impact of the ruling middle class on stylistic changes in the arts and literature or the influence of the rise of nationalism on cultural developments. This integrative approach to writing reinforces the message of the textbook—that the humanities are best understood when studied holistically in their historical setting.

A-1

GENERAL RULES FOR WRITING

Typically, writing assignments for a college-level humanities course are out-of-class research or term papers and in-class essay examinations. Regardless of the writing format, keep in mind three general rules. First, think of writing as an exercise in persuasion. Assume the teacher is unfamiliar with the topic, and write to demonstrate your mastery of the material. Second, follow basic principles of good grammar and punctuation. Some teachers will penalize you for mistakes in grammar and punctuation. Even if this is not the case, instructors cannot help but be skeptical of your learning if your writing is riddled with errors. Third, accept criticism and learn from past mistakes. Few individuals are born with a gift for writing; most have to struggle to reach a writing level that is personally satisfying. Even many authors, including famous ones, still find the writing process itself deeply frustrating. Like swimming, writing cannot be learned by talking about it; it is a skill you acquire through experience. Writing well requires patience, practice, and the willingness to learn from mistakes.

RESEARCH AND TERM PAPERS

Learning to write well starts with good work habits. Establish a quiet and comfortable work space, such as a table at a library, a desk in a dormitory room, a computer station, or a desk in an empty classroom. A typewriter or computer is useful, as is access to references, such as dictionaries and biographical books. Develop an orderly schedule of study; plan ahead so things are not left until the last minute. Balancing work and play is a prelude to writing well, since you need brief respites from intense study to rest and refresh your mind. If you arm yourself with good work habits, you will be ready to face the challenge of writing a research or term paper.

Steps in Writing a Paper

The first step in writing a research or term paper is to pick a topic. Choose a topic that is interdisciplinary, involving at least two humanistic fields of study, like the arts and literature of a specific historical period. Make sure your topic is manageable, neither too narrowly nor too broadly focused for your paper's length. Above all, select a topic that sparks some intellectual interest in you. Otherwise, your finished paper, even if it is carefully researched, may turn out to be uninspired and pedestrian. If you cannot find something that appeals to you on a list of suggested topics, consult with your instructor about a new subject satisfactory to both of you. As part of choosing a topic, you should also decide what approach to use in your paper, such as analytical, impressionistic, overview, or other. These approaches are described in detail in the next section.

The next step is to establish a basic bibliography. Scan your school library's holdings, either through the card catalogue system or by computer, to identify books and articles relevant to your topic. Once you have accumulated a bibliography of perhaps twenty to thirty sources, check the library stacks for additional books with appropriate call numbers that you may have overlooked in your search thus far. Then survey all these sources, treating them as background reading. At this preparatory level, take some notes on file cards and draw up a fuller list of secondary and, if needed, primary sources, such as diaries or documents, from the bibliographies in the books you are examining. After completing this survey, you are ready to make an outline.

The outline—whether for a five-page paper or a major research project—is mandatory. The outline is a memory device that serves several functions: It forces you to stick to the main topics, keep an accurate perspective, incorporate relevant information, follow the framing narrative, and proceed in an orderly fashion from the opening to the conclusion. Rework your outline until it includes all relevant points and ideas. Think of it as the framework on which you raise your final piece of writing, molded into a coherent shape.

With the outline set, you are ready to make a first draft of your paper. One approach is to expand each section of the outline into a paragraph, incorporating your ideas, the facts, your examples, and your references into a narrative. Be sure to relate each paragraph to both the preceding and the succeeding paragraphs, keeping in mind the overall organization of the paper. Each paragraph should begin with a topic sentence, include examples and references to support the topic, and conclude with a summary sentence or an idea that leads into the next paragraph. Strive to remain invisible in the narrative except where a personal observation might be helpful, and try to write in the active rather than the passive voice. At times you will have to search for the word or phrase that best expresses your thought, perhaps with the help of a dictionary or a thesaurus.

The next step is to edit and re-edit your work until it sounds right. When you reread a first draft, it usually sounds like a first draft, tentative and filled with half-finished thoughts. A good test of your first draft is to read it aloud, either to yourself or to a fellow student. You will be more likely to notice gaps in logic, infelicitous words or phrases, and obvious errors in fact when you hear them out loud. At this point your good work habits will pay off, because you should now have time to polish and improve the text. Don't forget to proof the paper for misspelled words, typographical errors, and misstatements. Attention to literary style and correctness makes the difference between a satisfactory and an excellent paper.

Especially critical in writing a research paper is the citation of sources, or footnotes. Instructors have their varying policies about the use of footnotes, but the following rules apply in most situations. Short quotations (that is, a phrase or one or two sentences) may be cited in the text if the proper recognition is given. Sources for longer quotations (that is, three or more sentences) should be placed in a footnote. A full bibliography listing all books consulted, whether cited directly in the paper or not, should be included at the end of the paper. Regardless of the style you use, make sure the citation forms for footnotes are consistent throughout the paper. You should purchase a writing and style manual; often the instructor will tell you which one to buy. Three of the most frequently used manuals are the following:

Bailey, E. P., and P. A. Powell. *Writing Research Papers*. 2d ed. New York: Holt, Rinehart and Winston, 1986.

Gibaldi, J., and W. S. Achtert. *MLA Handbook for Writers of Research Papers*. 3d ed. New York: Modern Language Association of America, 1988.

Turabian, K. *Student's Guide to Writing College Papers*. 3d ed. Chicago: University of Chicago Press, 1976.

Types of Term Papers Assigned in the Humanities

In your humanities course you may be assigned any one of various types of research or term papers, reflecting the breadth of the disciplines that are covered under the humanities rubric. The most common types are the impressionistic paper, the analytical paper, the historical overview, and the integrative paper. Each type requires a different approach, even though the basic writing techniques described above are valid for all.

The Impressionistic Paper   In this type of paper you offer a personal, though informed, reaction to some aspect of culture, such as the Gothic style or Post-Modernist art and architecture. Despite its focus on subjective feelings, the impressionistic paper nevertheless has to be documented with specific information, such as key historical events, biographical data, and details about particular works of art, literature, and music.

The Analytical Paper   Here, you compare and contrast two creative works. More strictly scholarly than an impressionistic paper, the analytical research paper usually requires that you study both the original works and the leading secondary sources that provide critical commentaries. Using this approach, you might examine two works within the same historical period, such as Aeschylus's tragedy *Agamemnon* and Sophocles' tragedy *Oedipus Rex*; or works across historical periods, such as Aeschylus's tragedy *Agamemnon* and Shakespeare's tragedy *Hamlet*; or works across genres, such as Aeschylus's tragedy *Agamemnon* and Verdi's opera *Rigoletto*.

The Historical Overview   In this type of paper you survey a specific time period in order to establish or explain a particular outcome, such as the prevailing world view, or the leading cultural characteristics, or the impact of a particular social class. For example, if your topic were the role of aristocratic courts on the arts of the Italian Renaissance, you would have to survey fifteenth- and sixteenth-century Italian history and culture as well as the history of specific courts, such as that of the Medici in Florence and the Sforza in Milan.

The Integrative Paper   This type of paper offers a versatile approach, since it allows for a combination of many topics. For example, if you wanted to write on Freudian theory and its application to culture, you would have to research the principles of Freudian theory and discuss Freudian interpretations of specific examples of art and literature. Or, if your topic were the Classical ideal of restraint in the late eighteenth century, you would have to research the period's music, art, literature, economic theory, and political theory.

ESSAY EXAMINATIONS

Besides research papers, you will also have to write essay tests in most college-level humanities courses. The purpose of such tests is to allow you to demonstrate how well you comprehend the course lectures and readings. To succeed on essay tests, you must learn to take notes efficiently during class and while reading out-of-class assignments and to analyze the assigned material in study sessions.

The following steps will help you write better essays on examinations:

1. Before the exam, master the assigned material through sound and productive work habits. This means keeping up with daily assignments, rereading and studying lecture notes, and reviewing study materials over a four- to five-day period prior to the test.

2. During the exam, read the entire test carefully before beginning to write. This will ensure that you understand all the questions and allow you to set a time frame for completing each section of the exam. If you are unsure about the meaning of a question, do not hesitate to ask the instructor for a clarification.

3. If there are choices, answer those questions first that seem the easiest. This rule simply reflects common sense; it is always best to lead with your strength.

4. Briefly outline the answer to each question. The outline should include an introduction, a section for each part of the question, and a conclusion. If time permits, it is also helpful to include the major points you want to cover, specific examples or illustrations, and ideas for topic sentences and conclusions of paragraphs. The outline will help you stick to the main topics and finish the exam on time. It can also trigger more ideas while you are writing it.

5. Follow sound writing rules in composing each essay. Begin each paragraph with a topic sentence; then give examples from a wide range of sources in the humanities to support the opening statement; and conclude with a paragraph that pulls the main arguments together. Take nothing for granted. Be concise but specific. Unless they are asked for, keep your own opinions to a bare minimum.

6. Review the exam. Prior to turning in the exam to the monitor, review your test to correct errors, give added examples, and clarify arguments, where needed. Always allow time to proofread an essay exam.

If you score poorly on the first essay exam in a course, consult with the instructor about how to improve your performance. But remember that improvement is seldom instantaneous and good writing is achieved only after practice. Old habits die hard; the only way to do better on papers and essay exams is to keep on writing.

GLOSSARY

Italicized words within definitions are defined in their own glossary entries.

Abstract Expressionism Also known as Action Painting, a nonrepresentational artistic style that flourished after World War II and was typified by randomness, spontaneity, and an attempt by the artist to interact emotionally with the work as it was created.

abstraction In Modern art, nonrepresentational or nonobjective forms in sculpture and painting that emphasize shapes, lines, and colors independent of the natural world.

a capella [ah kuh-PEL-uh] From the Italian, "in chapel style"; music sung without instrumental accompaniment.

aisles The side passages in a church on either side of the central *nave*.

Alexandrianism [al-ig-ZAN-dri-an-ism] A literary style developed in the Hellenistic period, typically formal, artificial, and imitative of earlier Greek writing.

ambulatory [AM-bue-la-tor-e] A passageway for walking found in many religious structures, such as outdoors in a cloister or indoors around the *apse* or *choir* of a church.

Anglicanism The doctrines and practices of the Church of England, which was established in the early sixteenth century under Henry VIII.

anthropomorphism [an-thro-po-MOR-fizm] The attributing of humanlike characteristics and traits to nonhuman things or powers, such as a deity.

apocalypse [uh-POK-uh-lips] In Jewish and early Christian thought, the expectation and hope of the coming of God and his final judgment; also closely identified with the last book of the New Testament, Revelation, in which many events are foretold, often in highly symbolic and imaginative terms.

apse In architecture, a large projection, usually rounded or semicircular, found in a *basilica*, usually in the east end; in Christian basilicas the altar stood in this space.

arabesque [air-uh-BESK] Literally, "Arabian-like"; decorative lines, patterns, and designs, often floral, in Islamic works of art.

arcade A series of arches supported by *piers* or columns, usually serving as a passageway along a street or between buildings.

Archaic style The style in Greek sculpture, dating from the seventh century to 480 B.C., that was characterized by heavy Egyptian influence; dominated by the *kouros* and *kore* sculptural forms.

architrave [AHR-kuh-trayv] The part of the *entablature* that rests on the *capital* or column in Classical *post-beam-triangle construction*.

aria [AH-ree-uh] In music, an elaborate melody sung as a solo or sometimes a duet, usually in an *opera* or an *oratorio*, with an orchestral accompaniment.

art song (*lied*) In music, a lyric song with melody performed by a singer and instrumental accompaniment usually provided by piano; made popular by Schubert in the nineteenth century.

ashlar [ASH-luhr]   A massive hewn or squared stone used in constructing a fortress, palace, or large building.

assemblage art   An art form in which the artist mixes and/or assembles "found objects," such as scraps of paper, cloth, or junk, into a three-dimensional work and then adds paint or other decorations to it.

ataraxia [at-uh-RAK-see-uh]   Greek, "calmness"; in *Hellenistic* philosophy, the state of desiring nothing.

atonality [a-toe-NAL-uh-tee]   In music, the absence of a key note or tonal center and the use of the tones of the chromatic scale impartially.

atrium [A-tree-uhm]   In Roman architecture, an open courtyard at the front of a house; in Christian *Romanesque* churches, an open court, usually colonnaded, in front of the main doors of the structure.

attic   The topmost section or crown of an arch.

autarky [AW-tar-kee]   Greek, "self-sufficient"; in *Hellenistic* thought, the state of being isolated and free from the demands of society.

avant-garde [a-vahn-GARD]   French, "advanced guard"; writers, artists, and intellectuals who push their works and ideas ahead of more traditional groups and movements.

baldacchino [ball-duh-KEE-no]   An ornamental structure in the shape of a canopy, supported by four columns, built over a church altar, and usually decorated with statues and other ornaments.

baptistery   A small, often octagonal structure, separated from the main church, where baptisms were performed.

bard   A tribal poet-singer who composes and recites works, often of the *epic poetry* genre.

Baroque [buh-ROKE]   The prevailing seventeenth-century artistic and cultural style, characterized by an emphasis on grandeur, opulence, expansiveness, and complexity.

barrel vault   A ceiling or *vault* made of sets of arches placed side by side and joined together.

basilica [buh-SILL-ih-kuh]   A rectangular structure that included an *apse* at one or both ends; originally a Roman building used for public purposes, later taken over by the Christians for worship. The floor plan became the basis of nearly all early Christian churches.

bay   A four-cornered unit of architectural space, often used to identify a section of the *nave* in a *Romanesque* or *Gothic* church.

bel canto [bell KAHN-toe]   Italian, "beautiful singing"; a style of singing characteristic of seventeenth-century Italian *opera* stressing ease, purity, and evenness of tone along with precise vocal technique.

blind arcade   A decorative architectural design that gives the appearance of an open *arcade* or window but is filled in with some type of building material such as stone or brick.

blues   A type of music that emerged around 1900 from the rural African-American culture, was originally based on work songs and religious spirituals, and expressed feelings of loneliness and hopelessness.

Byzantine style [BIZ-uhn-teen]   In painting, decoration, and architecture, a style blending Greco-Roman and Oriental components into a highly stylized art form that glorified Christianity, notably in domed churches adorned with *mosaics* and polished marble; associated with the culture of the Eastern Roman Empire from about 500 until 1453.

calligraphy   Penmanship or handwriting, usually done with flowing lines, used as a decoration or as an enhancement of a written work; found in Islamic and Christian writings.

Calvinism   The theological beliefs and rituals set forth in and derived from John Calvin's writings, placing emphasis on the power of God and the weakness of human beings.

canon   A set of principles or rules that are accepted as true and authoritative for the various arts or fields of study; in architecture, it refers to the standards of proportion; in painting, the prescribed ways of painting certain objects; in sculpture, the ideal proportions of the human body; in literature, the authentic lists of an author's works; in religion, the approved and authoritative writings that are accepted as divinely inspired, as for Jews and Christians the *Scriptures*; and in religious and in other contexts, certain prescribed rituals or official rules and laws. In music, a **canon** is a composition in which a melody sung by one voice is repeated exactly by successive voices as they enter.

canzone [kan-ZOH-nee]   Latin, "chant"; a type of love poem popular in southern France during the twelfth and thirteenth centuries.

capital   In architecture, the upper or crowning part of a column, on which the *entablature* rests.

cathedral   The church of a bishop that houses a *cathedra*, or throne, symbolizing the seat of power in his administrative district, known as a diocese.

cella [SELL-uh]   The inner sanctum or walled room of a *Classical* temple where sacred statues were housed.

chanson de geste [shan-SAWN duh zhest]   A poem of brave deeds in the *epic* form developed in France during the eleventh century, usually to be sung.

chiaroscuro [key-ahr-uh-SKOOR-oh]   In painting, the use of dark and light contrast to create the effect of modeling of a figure or object.

chivalric code The rules of conduct, probably idealized, that governed the social roles and duties of aristocrats in the Middle Ages.

choir In architecture, that part of a *Gothic* church in which the service was sung by singers or clergy, located in the east end beyond the *transept*; also, the group of trained singers who sat in the choir area.

chorus In Greek drama, a group of performers who sang and danced in both tragedies and comedies, often commenting on the action; in later times, a group of singers who performed with or without instrumental accompaniment.

Christian humanism An intellectual movement in sixteenth-century northern Europe that sought to use the ideals of the *Classical* world, the tools of ancient learning, and the morals of the Christian *Scriptures* to rid the church of worldliness and scandal.

chthonian deities [THO-nee-uhn] In Greek religion, earth gods and goddesses who lived underground and were usually associated with peasants and their religious beliefs.

civilization The way humans live in a complex political, economic, and social structure, usually in an urban environment, with some development in technology, literature, and art.

Classic, or **Classical** Having the forms, values, or standards embodied in the art and literature of Greek and Roman *civilization*; in music, an eighteenth-century style characterized by simplicity, proportion, and an emphasis on structure.

Classicism A set of aesthetic principles found in Greek and Roman art and literature emphasizing the search for perfection or ideal forms.

clerestory windows [KLEER-stor-ee] A row of windows set along the upper part of a wall, especially in a church.

collage [koh-LAHZH] From the French *coller*, "to glue"; a type of art, introduced by Picasso, in which bits and pieces of materials such as paper or cloth are glued to a painted surface.

comedy of manners A humorous play that focuses on the way people in a particular social group or class interact with one another, especially regarding fashions and manners.

concerto [kuhn-CHER-toe] In music, a composition for one or more soloists and *orchestra*, usually in a symphonic form with three contrasting movements.

consort A set of musical instruments in the same family, ranging from bass to soprano; also, a group of musicians who entertain by singing or playing instruments.

Constructivism A movement in nonobjective art, originating in the Soviet Union and flourishing from 1917 to 1922 and concerned with planes and volumes as expressed in modern industrial materials such as glass and plastic.

contrapposto [kon-truh-POH-stoh] In sculpture and painting, the placement of the human figure so the weight is more on one leg than the other and the shoulders and chest are turned in the opposite direction from the hips and legs.

Corinthian The third Greek architectural order, in which temple columns are slender and *fluted*, sit on a base, and have *capitals* shaped like inverted bells and decorated with carvings representing the leaves of the acanthus bush; this style was popular in *Hellenistic* times and widely adopted by the Romans.

cornice In architecture, the crowning, projecting part of the *entablature*.

Counter-Reformation A late sixteenth-century movement in the Catholic church aimed at reestablishing its basic beliefs, reforming its organizational structure, and reasserting itself as the authoritative voice of Christianity.

covenant In Judaism and Christianity, a solemn and binding agreement or contract between God and his followers.

cruciform [KROO-suh-form] Cross-shaped; used to describe the standard floor plan of a church.

Cubism A style of painting introduced by Picasso and Braque in which objects are broken up into fragments and patterns of geometric structures and depicted on the flat canvas as if from several points of view.

culture The sum of human endeavors, including the basic political, economic, and social institutions and the values, beliefs, and arts of those who share them.

cuneiform [kue-NEE-uh-form] Wedge-shaped characters used in writing on tablets found in Mesopotamia and other ancient *civilizations*.

Cynicism A *Hellenistic* philosophy that denounced society and its institutions as artificial and called on the individual to strive for *autarky*.

Dada [DAH-dah] An early-twentieth-century artistic movement, named after a nonsense word, that was rooted in a love of play, encouraged deliberately irrational acts, and exhibited contempt for all traditions.

Decadence A late-nineteenth-century literary style concerned with morbid and artificial subjects and themes.

Deism [DEE-iz-uhm] A religion based on the idea that the universe was created by God and then left to run according to *natural laws*, without divine interference; formulated and practiced in the eighteenth century.

deductive reasoning The process of reasoning from the general to the particular, that is, beginning with an accepted premise or first statement and, by steps of logical reasoning or inference, reaching a conclusion that necessarily follows from the premise.

De Stijl [duh STILE] Dutch, "the style"; an artistic movement associated with a group of early-twentieth-century Dutch painters who used rectangular forms and primary colors in their works and who believed that art should have spiritual values and a social purpose.

devotio moderna [de-VO-tee-oh mo-DER-nuh] The "new devotion" of late medieval Christianity that emphasized piety and discipline as practiced by lay religious communities located primarily in northern Europe.

Diaspora [dye-AS-puhr-uh] From the Greek, "to scatter"; the dispersion of the Jews from their homeland in ancient Palestine, a process that began with the Babylonian Captivity in the sixth century B.C. and continued over the centuries.

Doric The simplest and oldest of the Greek architectural orders, in which temple columns have undecorated *capitals* and rest directly on the *stylobate*.

Early Renaissance style A style inspired by *Classical* rather than *Gothic* models that arose among Florentine architects, sculptors, and painters in the late fourteenth and early fifteenth century.

empiricism The process of collecting data, making observations, carrying out experiments based on the collected data and observations, and reaching a conclusion.

Enlightenment The eighteenth-century philosophical and cultural movement marked by the application of reason to human problems and affairs, a questioning of traditional beliefs and ideas, and an optimistic faith in unlimited progress for humanity, particularly through education.

entablature [en-TAB-luh-choor] In architecture, the part of the temple above the columns and below the roof, which, in *Classical* temples, included the *architrave*, *frieze*, and *pediment*.

entasis [EN-ta-sis] In architecture, convex curving or enlarging of the central part of a column to correct the optical illusion that the column is too thin.

epic poetry Narrative poetry, usually told or written in an elevated style, that recounts the life of a hero.

epic theater A type of theater, invented by Brecht, in which major social issues are dramatized with outlandish props and jarring dialogue and effects, all designed to alienate middle-class audiences and force them to think seriously about the problems raised in the plays.

Epicureanism [ep-i-kyoo-REE-uh-niz-uhm] A *Hellenistic* philosophy, founded by Epicurus and later expounded by the Roman Lucretius, that made its highest goals the development of the mind and an existence free from the demands of everyday life.

eschatology [es-kuh-TOL-uh-jee] The concern with final events or the end of the world, a belief popular in Jewish and early Christian communities and linked to the concept of the coming of a *Messiah*.

evangelists From the Greek *evangelion*, a term generally used for those who preach the Christian religion; more specifically, the four evangelists, Matthew, Mark, Luke, and John, who wrote about Jesus Christ soon after his death in the first four books of the New Testament.

evolution The theory, set forth in the nineteenth century by Charles Darwin, that plants and animals, including humans, evolved over millions of years from simpler forms through a process of natural selection.

existentialism [eg-zi-STEN-shuh-liz-uhm] A twentieth-century philosophy focusing on the precarious nature of human existence, with its uncertainty, anxiety, and ultimate death, as well as on individual freedom and responsibility and the possibilities for human creativity and authenticity.

Expressionism A late-nineteenth-century literary and artistic movement characterized by the expression of highly personal feelings rather than of objective reality.

fan vault A decorative pattern of *vault* ribs that arch or radiate out from a central point on the ceiling; popular in English *Perpendicular* architecture.

Faustian [FOW-stee-uhn] Resembling the character Faust in Goethe's most famous work, in being spiritually tormented, insatiable for knowledge and experience, or willing to pay any price, including personal and spiritual integrity, to gain a desired end.

Fauvism [FOH-viz-uhm] From the French *fauve*, "wild beast"; an early-twentieth-century art movement led by Matisse and favoring exotic colors and disjointed shapes.

Fête galante [fet gah-LAHNN] In *Rococo* painting, the theme or scene of aristocrats being entertained or simply enjoying their leisure and other worldly pleasures.

Flamboyant style [flam-BOY-uhnt] A Late French *Gothic* architectural style of elaborate decorations and ornamentation that produce a flamelike effect.

Florid Baroque style A variation of the *Baroque* style specifically identified with the Catholic church's patronage of the arts and used to glorify its beliefs.

fluting   Decorative vertical grooves carved in a column.

flying buttress   An external masonry support, found primarily in *Gothic* churches, that carries the thrust of the ceiling or *vault* away from the upper walls of the building to an external vertical column.

forum   In Rome and many Roman towns, the public place, located in the center of the town, where people gathered to socialize, transact business, and administer the government.

Fourth Century style   The sculptural style characteristic of the last phase of the *Hellenic* period, when new interpretations of beauty and movement were adopted.

French Baroque style   A secular variation of the *Baroque* style that was identified with French kings and artists, was rooted in *Classical* ideals, and was used mainly to emphasize the power and grandeur of the monarchy.

fresco   A painting done on wet or dry plaster that becomes part of the plastered wall.

friars   Members of a thirteenth-century mendicant (begging) monastic order.

frieze   [FREEZ]   A band of painted designs or sculpted figures placed on walls; also, the central portion of a temple's *entablature* just above the *architrave*.

gallery   In architecture, a long, narrow passageway or corridor, usually found in churches and located above the *aisles*, and often with openings that permit viewing from above into the *nave*.

gargoyle   [GAHR-goil]   In architecture, a water spout in the form of a grotesque animal or human, carved from stone, placed on the edge of a roof.

genre subject   In art, a scene or person from everyday life, depicted realistically and without religious or symbolic significance.

geocentrism   The belief that the earth is the center of the universe and that the sun, planets, and stars revolve around it.

goliards   [GOAL-yuhrds]   Medieval roaming poets or scholars who traveled about reciting poems on topics ranging from moral lessons to the pains of love.

Gospels   The first four books of the New Testament (Matthew, Mark, Luke, and John) that record the life and sayings of Jesus Christ; the word itself, from Old English, means good news or good tales.

Gothic style   A style of architecture, usually associated with churches, that originated in northern France and whose three phases—Early, High, and Late—lasted from the twelfth to the sixteenth centuries. Emerging from the *Romanesque* style, Gothic is identified by pointed arches, *ribbed vaults*, *stained glass* windows, *flying buttresses*, and carvings on the exterior.

Greek cross   A cross in which all the arms are of equal length; the shape used as a floor plan in many Greek or Eastern Orthodox churches.

Gregorian chant   A style of *monophonic* church music sung in unison and without instrumental accompaniment and used in the *liturgy*; named for Pope Gregory I (590–604).

groined vault, or **cross vault**   A ceiling or *vault* created when two *barrel vaults*, set at right angles, intersect.

heliocentrism   The belief that the sun is the center of the universe and that the earth and other planets revolve around it.

Hellenic   [hell-LENN-ik]   Relating to the time period in Greek civilization from 480 to 323 B.C., when the most influential Greek artists, playwrights, and philosophers, such as Praxitiles, Sophocles, and Plato, created their greatest works; associated with the *Classical* style.

Hellenistic   [hell-uh-NIS-tik]   Relating to the time period from about 323 to 31 B.C., when Greek and Oriental or Middle Eastern cultures and institutions intermingled to create a heterogeneous and cosmopolitan *civilization*.

hieroglyphs   [HI-uhr-uh-glifs]   Pictorial characters used in Egyptian writing, which is known as hieroglyphics.

High Classical style   The style in Greek sculpture associated with the ideal physical form and perfected during the zenith of the Athenian Empire, about 450–400 B.C.

higher criticism   A rational approach to Bible study, developed in German Protestant circles in the nineteenth century, that treated the biblical *Scriptures* as literature and subjected them to close scrutiny, testing their literary history, authorship, and meaning.

High Renaissance   The period from about 1495 to 1520, often associated with the patronage of the popes in Rome, when the most influential artists and writers of the *Renaissance*, including Michelangelo, Raphael, Leonardo da Vinci, and Machiavelli, were producing their greatest works.

high tech   In architecture, a style that uses obvious industrial design elements with exposed parts serving as decorations.

Homeric epithet   A recurring nickname, such as "Ox-eyed Hera," used in Homer's *Iliad* or *Odyssey*.

hubris   [HYOO-bris]   In Greek thought, human pride or arrogance that leads an individual to challenge the gods, usually provoking divine retribution.

humanism   An attitude that is concerned with

humanity, its achievements, and its potential; also, the study of the *humanities*; in the *Renaissance*, identified with *studia humanitatis.*

humanities In the nineteenth century, the study of Greek and Roman languages and literature; later set off from the sciences and expanded to include the works of all Western peoples in the arts, literature, music, philosophy, and sometimes history and religion; in *Post-Modernism* extended to a global dimension.

idealism In Plato's philosophy, the theory that reality and ultimate truth are to be found not in the material world but in the spiritual realm.

idée fixe [ee-DAY FIX] French, "fixed idea"; in music, a recurring musical theme that is associated with a person or concept.

ideogram [ID-e-uh-gram] A picture drawn to represent an idea or a concept.

idyll A relatively short poem that focuses on events and themes of everyday life, such as family, love, and religion; popular in the *Hellenistic* Age and a standard form that has been periodically revived in Western literature throughout the centuries.

illuminated manuscript A richly decorated book, painted with brilliant colors and gold leaf, usually of sacred writings; popular in the West in the Middle Ages.

illusionism The use of painting techniques in *Florid Baroque* art to create the appearance that decorated areas are part of the surrounding architecture, usually employed in ceiling decorations.

impasto [ihm-PAHS-toe] In painting, the application of thick layers of pigment.

Impressionism In painting, a style introduced in the 1870s, marked by an attempt to catch spontaneous impressions, often involving the play of sunlight on ordinary events and scenes observed outdoors; in music, a style of composition designed to create a vague and dreamy mood through gliding melodies and shimmering tone colors.

impressionistic In art, relating to the representation of a scene using the simplest details in order to create an illusion of reality by evoking subjective impressions rather than aiming for a totally realistic effect; characterized by images that are insubstantial and barely sketched in.

inductive reasoning The process of reasoning from particulars to the general or from single parts to the whole and/or final conclusion.

International style In twentieth-century architecture, a style and method of construction that capitalized on modern materials, such as ferro-concrete, glass, and steel, and that produced the popular "glass box" skyscrapers and variously shaped private houses.

Ionic The Greek architectural order, developed in Ionia, in which columns are slender, sit on a base, and have *capitals* decorated with scrolls.

Italo-Byzantine style [ih-TAL-o-BIZ-uhn-teen] The style of Italian *Gothic* painting that reflected the influence of *Byzantine* paintings, *mosaics*, and icons.

Jesuits [JEZH-oo-its] Members of the Society of Jesus, the best organized and most effective monastic order founded during the *Counter-Reformation* to combat Protestantism and spread Roman Catholicism around the world.

keystone The central stone at the top of an arch that locks the other stones in place.

koine [KOI-nay] A colloquial Greek language spoken in the *Hellenistic* world that helped tie together that *civilization.*

kore [KOH-ray] An *Archaic* Greek standing statue of a young draped female.

kouros [KOO-rus] An *Archaic* Greek standing statue of a young naked male.

Late Gothic style A style characterized in architecture by ornate decoration and taller cathedral windows and spires and in painting and sculpture by increased refinement of details and a trend toward naturalism; popular in the fourteenth and fifteenth centuries in central and western Europe.

Late Mannerism The last stage of the *Mannerist* movement, characterized by exaggeration and distortion, especially in painting.

Late Modernism The last stage of *Modernism*, characterized by an increasing sense of existential despair, an attraction to non-Western cultures, and extreme experimentalism.

leitmotif [LITE-mo-teef] In music, and especially in Wagner's *operas*, the use of recurring themes associated with particular characters, objects, or ideas.

liberalism In political thought, a set of beliefs advocating certain personal, economic, and natural rights based on assumptions about the perfectibility and autonomy of human beings and the notion of progress, as first expressed in the writings of John Locke.

libretto [lih-BRET-oh] In Italian, "little book"; the text or words of an *opera*, *oratorio*, or musical work of a similar dramatic nature involving a written text.

liturgical drama Religious dramas, popular between the twelfth and sixteenth centuries, based on biblical stories with musical accompaniment that were staged in the area in front of the church, performed at first in Latin but later in the *vernacular languages*; the mystery plays ("mystery" is derived from the Latin for "action") are the most famous type of liturgical drama.

liturgy A rite or ritual, such as prayers or ceremonies, practiced by a religious group in public worship.

logical positivism A school of modern philosophy that seeks truth by defining terms and clarifying statements and asserts that metaphysical theories are meaningless.

logos [LOWG-os] In *Stoicism*, the name for the supreme being or for reason—the controlling principle of the universe—believed to be present both in nature and in each human being.

Lutheranism The doctrine, liturgy, and institutional structure of the church founded in the sixteenth century by Martin Luther, who stressed the authority of the Bible, the faith of the individual, and the worshiper's direct communication with God as the bases of his new religion.

lyric poetry In Greece, verses sung and accompanied by the lyre, a stringed instrument; today, intensely personal poetry.

machiavellianism [mahk-ih-uh-VEL-ih-uhn-iz-uhm] The view that politics should be separated from morals and dedicated to the achievement of desired ends through any means necessary ("the end justifies the means"); derived from the political writings of Machiavelli.

madrigal [MAD-rih-guhl] A *polyphonic* song performed without accompaniment and based on a secular text, often a love lyric; especially popular in the sixteenth century.

maenad [MEE-nad] A woman who worshiped Dionysus, often in a state of frenzy.

magic realism A literary and artistic style identified with Latin American *Post-Modernism* that mixes realistic and supernatural elements to create imaginary or fantastic scenes.

Mannerism A cultural movement between 1520 and 1600 that grew out of a rebellion against the *Renaissance* artistic norms of symmetry and balance; characterized in art by distortion and incongruity and in thought and literature by the belief that human nature is depraved.

mass culture The tastes, values, and interests of the classes that dominate modern industralized society, especially the consumer-oriented American middle class.

medallion In Roman architecture, a circular decoration often found on triumphal arches enclosing a scene or portrait; in more general architectural use, a tablet or panel in a wall or window containing a figure or an ornament.

Messiah A Hebrew word meaning "the anointed one," or one chosen by God to be his representative on earth; in Judaism, a savior who will come bringing peace and justice; in Christianity, Jesus Christ (*Christ* is derived from a Greek word meaning "the anointed one").

metope [MET-uh-pee] In architecture, a panel, often decorated, between two *triglyphs* on the *entablature* of a *Doric* Greek temple.

minaret In Islamic architecture, a tall, slender tower with a pointed top, from which the daily calls to prayer are delivered; located near a *mosque*.

miniature A small painting, usually of a religious nature, found in *illuminated manuscripts*; also, a small portrait.

Modernism A late-nineteenth- and twentieth-century cultural, artistic, and literary movement that rejected much of the past and focused on the current, the secular, and the revolutionary in search of new forms of expression; the dominant style of the twentieth century until 1970.

modes A series of musical scales devised by the Greeks and believed by them to create certain emotional or ethical effects on the listener.

monophony [muh-NOF-uh-nee] A style of music in which there is only a single line of melody.

mosaic An art form or decoration, usually on a wall or floor, created by inlaying small pieces of glass, shell, or stone in cement or plaster to create pictures or patterns.

mosque A Muslim place of worship, often distinguished by a dome-shaped central building placed in an open space surrounded by a wall.

motet A multivoiced song with words of a sacred or secular text, usually sung without accompanying instruments; developed in the thirteenth century.

mural A wall painting, usually quite large, used to decorate a private or public structure.

muse In Greek religion, any one of the nine sister goddesses who preside over the creative arts and sciences.

music drama An *opera* in which the action and music are continuous, not broken up into separate *arias* and *recitatives*, and the music is determined by its dramatic appropriateness, producing a work in which music, words, and staging are fused together; the term was coined by Wagner.

narthex The porch or vestibule of a church, usually enclosed, through which worshipers walk before entering the *nave*.

Naturalism In literature, a late-nineteenth-century movement inspired by the methods of science and the insights of sociology, concerned with an objective depiction of the ugly side of industrial society.

natural law In *Stoicism* and later in other philosophies, a body of laws or principles that are believed to be derived from nature and binding on human society and that constitute a higher form of justice than civil or judicial law.

nave The central longitudinal area of a church, extending from the entrance to the *apse* and flanked by *aisles*.

Neoclassical style In the late eighteenth century, an artistic and literary movement that emerged as a reaction to the *Rococo* style and that sought inspiration from ancient *Classicism*. In the twentieth century, between 1919 and 1951, *Neoclassicism* in music was a style that rejected the emotionalism favored by Romantic composers as well as the dense orchestral sounds of the Impressionists; instead, it borrowed features from seventeenth- and eighteenth-century music and practiced the ideals of balance, clarity of texture, and non-programmatic works. Also, since 1970, **Neoclassicism** is a highly visible submovement in *Post-Modernism*, particularly prominent in painting and architecture, that restates the principles of *Classical* art—balance, harmony, idealism.

Neoexpressionism A submovement in *Post-Modernism*, associated primarily with painting, that offers social criticism and is concerned with the expression of the artist's feelings.

Neorealism A submovement in *Post-Modernism* that is based on a photographic sense of detail and harks back to many of the qualities of nineteenth-century *Realism*.

Neolithic Literally, "new stone"; used to define the New Stone Age, when human *cultures* evolved into agrarian systems and settled communities; dating from about 10,000 or 8000 B.C. to about 3000 B.C.

Neo-Platonism A philosophy based on Plato's ideas that was developed during the Roman period in an attempt to reconcile the dichotomy between Plato's concept of an eternal World of Ideas and the ever-changing physical world; in the fifteenth-century *Renaissance*, it served as a philosophical guide for Italian humanists who sought to reconcile late medieval Christian beliefs with *Classical* thinking.

New Comedy The style of comedy favored by *Hellenistic* playwrights, concentrating on gentle satirical themes, in particular romantic plots with stock characters and predictable endings.

Nominalism [NOM-uh-nuhl-iz-uhm] In medieval thought, the school that held that objects were separate unto themselves but could, for convenience, be treated in a collective sense because they shared certain characteristics; opposed to *Realism*.

octave In music, usually the eight-tone interval between a note and a second note of the same name, as in C to C.

oculus [OK-yuh-lus] The circular opening at the top of a dome; derived from the Latin word for eye.

Old Comedy The style of comedy established by Aristophanes in the fifth century B.C., distinguished by a strong element of political and social satire.

Olympian deities In Greek religion, sky gods and goddesses who lived on mountain tops and were worshiped mainly by the Greek aristocracy.

opera A drama or play set to music and consisting of vocal pieces with *orchestral* accompaniment; acting, scenery, and sometimes *choruses* and dancing are used to heighten the dramatic values of opera.

oratorio A choral work based on religious events or *scripture* employing singers, *choruses*, and *orchestra* but without scenery or staging and performed usually in a church or concert hall.

orchestra In Greek theaters, the circular area where the *chorus* performed in front of the audience; in music, a group of instrumentalists, including string players, who play together.

organum [OR-guh-nuhm] In the ninth through the thirteenth centuries, a simple and early form of *polyphonic* music consisting of a main melody sung along with a *Gregorian chant*; by the thirteenth century it had developed into a complex multivoiced song.

Paleolithic Literally, "old stone"; used to define the Old Stone Age, when crude stones and tools were used; dating from about 2,000,000 B.C. to about 10,000 B.C.

pantheism The doctrine of or belief in multitudes of deities found in nature.

pantomime In Roman times, enormous dramatic productions featuring instrumental music and dances, favored by the masses; later, a type of dramatic or dancing performance in which the story is told with expressive or even exaggerated bodily and facial movements.

pastoral A type of *Hellenistic* poetry that idealized rural customs and farming, especially the simple life of shepherds, and deprecated urban living.

pediment In *Classical*-style architecture, the triangular-shaped area or gable at the end of the building formed by the sloping roof and the *cornice*.

pendentive [pen-DEN-tiv] In architecture, a triangular, concave-shaped section of *vaulting* between the rim of a dome and the pair of arches that support it; used in Byzantine and Islamic architecture.

peristyle [PER-uh-stile] A colonnade around an open courtyard or a building.

Perpendicular style The highly decorative style of *Late Gothic* architecture that developed in England at the same time as the *Late Gothic* on the European continent.

perspective A technique or formula for creating the illusion or appearance of depth and distance on a two-dimensional surface. **Atmospheric perspective** is achieved in many ways: by diminishing color intensity, by omitting detail, and by blurring the lines of an object. **Linear perspective,** based on mathematical calculations, is achieved by having parallel lines or lines of projection appearing to converge at a single point, known as the *vanishing point*, on the horizon of the flat surface and by diminishing distant objects in size according to scale to make them appear to recede from the viewer.

philosophes [FIL-uh-sawfs] A group of European thinkers and writers who popularized the ideas of the *Enlightenment* through essays, novels, plays, and other works, hoping to change the climate of opinion and bring about social and political reform.

phonogram A symbol used to represent a syllable, word, or sound.

Physiocrats [FIZ-ih-uh-kratz] A group of writers, primarily French, who dealt with economic issues during the *Enlightenment,* in particular calling for improved agricultural productivity and questioning the state's role in economic affairs.

pianoforte [pee-an-o-FOR-tay] A piano; derived from the Italian for "soft/loud," terms used to describe the two types of sound emitted by a stringed instrument whose wires are struck with felt-covered hammers operated from a keyboard.

pictogram A carefully drawn, often stylized, picture that represents a particular object.

pier In architecture, a vertical masonry structure that may support a *vault*, an arch, or a roof; in *Gothic* churches, piers were often clustered together to form massive supports.

Pietà [pee-ay-TAH] A painting or sculpture depicting the mourning Virgin and the dead Christ.

pilaster [pih-LAS-tuhr] In architecture, a vertical, rectangular decorative device projected from a wall that gives the appearance of a column with a base and *capital*; sometimes called an applied column.

Platonism The collective beliefs and arguments presented in Plato's writings stressing especially that actual things are copies of ideas.

Pointillism [PWANT-il-iz-uhm] Also known as Divisionism, a style of painting, perfected by Seurat, in which tiny dots of paint are applied to the canvas in such a way that when they are viewed from a distance they merge and blend to form recognizable objects with natural effects of color, light, and shade.

polyphony [puh-LIF-uh-nee] A style of musical composition in which two or more voices or melodic lines are woven together.

polytheism [POL-e-the-iz-uhm] The doctrine of or belief in more than one deity.

Pop Art An artistic style popular between 1960 and 1970 in which commonplace commercial objects drawn from *mass culture*, such as soup cans, fast foods, and comic strips, became the subjects of art.

post-and-lintel construction A basic architectural form in which upright posts, or columns, support a horizontal lintel, or beam.

post-beam-triangle construction The generic name given to Greek architecture that includes the post, or column, the beam, or lintel, and the triangular-shaped area, or *pediment*.

Post-Impressionism A late-nineteenth-century artistic movement that extended the boundaries of *Impressionism* in new directions to focus on structure, composition, fantasy, and subjective expression.

Post-Modernism An artistic, cultural, and intellectual movement, originating in about 1970, that is more optimistic than *Modernism*, embraces an open-ended and democratic global civilization, freely adapts elements of high culture and *mass culture*, and manifests itself chiefly through revivals of earlier styles, giving rise to *Neoclassicism*, *Neoexpressionism*, and *Neorealism*.

Praxitelean curve [prak-sit-i-LEE-an] The graceful line of the sculpted body in the *contrapposto* stance, perfected by the *Fourth Century style* sculptor Praxiteles.

program music Instrumental music that depicts a narrative, portrays a setting, or suggests a sequence of events; often based on other sources, such as a poem or a play.

Protestant Baroque style A variation of the *Baroque* style identified with Dutch and English architects and painters who wanted to reduce Baroque grandeur and exuberance to a more human scale.

Puritanism The beliefs and practices of the Puritans, a small but influential religious group devoted to the teachings of John Calvin; they stressed strict rules of personal and public behavior and practiced their beliefs in England and the New World during the seventeenth century.

putti [POOH-tee] Italian, plural of *putto*; in painting and sculpture, figures of babies, children, or sometimes angels.

ragtime A type of instrumental music, popularized by African-Americans in the late nineteenth and early twentieth centuries, with a strongly syncopated rhythm and a lively melody.

Rayonnant [ray-yo-NAHNN] A decorative style in French architecture associated with the *High Gothic* period, in which walls were replaced by sheets of *stained glass* framed by elegant stone *traceries*.

Realism In medieval philosophy, the school that asserted that objects contained common or universal qualities that were not always apparent to the human senses but that were more real or true than the objects' physical attributes; opposed to *Nominalism*. In art and literature, a mid- to late-nineteenth-century style that focused on the everyday lives of the middle and lower classes, portraying their world in a serious, accurate, and unsentimental way; opposed to *Romanticism*.

recitative [ress-uh-tuh-TEEV] In music, a rhythmically free but often stylized declamation, midway between singing and ordinary speech, that serves as a transition between *arias* or as a narrative device in an *opera*.

Reformation The sixteenth-century religious movement that looked back to the ideals of early Christianity, called for moral and structural changes in the church, and led ultimately to the founding of the various Protestant churches.

relief In sculpture, figures or forms that are carved so they project from the flat surface of a stone or metal background. **High relief** projects sharply from the surface; **low relief** or **bas relief** is more shallow.

Renaissance [ren-uh-SAHNS] From the French for "rebirth"; the artistic, cultural, and intellectual movement marked by a revival of *Classical* and *humanistic* values that began in Italy in the mid–fourteenth century and had spread across Europe by the mid–sixteenth century.

revenge tragedy A type of play popular in sixteenth-century England, probably rooted in Roman tragedies and concerned with the need for a family to seek revenge for the murder of a relative.

ribbed vault A masonry roof with a framework of arches or ribs that reinforce and decorate the *vault* ceiling.

rocaille [roh-KYE] In *Rococo* design, the stucco ornaments shaped like leaves, flowers, and ribbons that decorate walls and ceilings.

Rococo style [ruh-KOH-koh] An artistic and cultural style that grew out of the *Baroque* style but that was more intimate and personal and that emphasized the frivolous and superficial side of aristocratic life.

romance A story derived from legends associated with Troy or Celtic culture but often set in feudal times and centered on themes of licit and illicit love between noble lords and ladies.

Romanesque style [roh-muhn-ESK] A style of architecture, usually associated with churches built in the eleventh and twelfth centuries, that was inspired by Roman architecture such as the *basilica* and was thus Roman-like. Romanesque buildings were massive, with round arches and *barrel* or *groined vaulted* ceilings, and had less exterior decoration than *Gothic* churches.

Romanticism An intellectual, artistic, and literary movement that began in the late eighteenth century as a reaction to *Neoclassicism* and that stressed the emotional, mysterious, and imaginative side of human behavior and the unruly side of nature.

rose window A large circular window, made of *stained glass* and held together with lead and carved stones set in patterns, or *tracery*, and located over an entrance in a *Gothic* cathedral.

sarcophagus [sahr-KOF-uh-guhs] From the Greek meaning "flesh-eating stone"; a marble or stone coffin or tomb, usually decorated with carvings, used first by Romans and later by Christians for burial of the dead.

satyr-play [SAT-uhr] A comic play, often featuring sexual themes, performed at the Greek drama festivals along with the *tragedies*.

scenographic [see-nuh-GRAF-ik] In Renaissance architecture, a building style that envisioned buildings as separate units; in the painting of stage scenery, the art of *perspective* representation.

scherzo [SKER-tso] From the Italian for "joke"; a quick and lively instrumental composition or movement found in *sonatas* and *symphonies*.

scholasticism In medieval times, the body or collection of knowledge that tried to harmonize Aristotle's writings with Christian doctrine; also, a way of thinking and establishing sets of arguments.

Scientific Revolution The seventeenth-century intellectual movement, based originally on discoveries in astronomy and physics, that challenged and overturned medieval views about the order of the universe and the theories used to explain motion.

scripture The sacred writings of any religion, as the Bible in Judaism and Christianity.

serial music A type of musical composition based on a *twelve-tone scale* arranged any way the composer chooses; the absence of a tonal center in serial music leads to *atonality*.

Severe style The first sculptural style of the *Classical* period in Greece, which retained stylistic elements from the *Archaic* style.

sfumato [sfoo-MAH-toh] In painting, the blending of one tone into another to blur the outline of a form and give the canvas a smokelike appearance; a technique perfected by Leonardo da Vinci.

shaft graves Deep pit burial sites; the dead are usually placed at the bottom of the shafts.

skene [SKEE-nee] A small building behind the *or-*

chestra in a Greek theater, used as a prop and as a storehouse for theatrical materials.

Skepticism A *Hellenistic* philosophy that questioned whether anything could be known for certain, argued that all beliefs were relative, and concluded that *autarky* could be achieved only by recognizing that inquiry was fruitless.

social contract In political thought, an agreement or contract between the people and their rulers defining the rights and duties of each so that a civil society might be created.

socialism An economic and political system in which goods and property are owned collectively or by the state; the socialist movement began as a reaction to the excesses of the factory system in the nineteenth century and ultimately called for either reforming or abolishing industrial capitalism.

Socialist Realism A Marxist artistic theory that calls for the use of literature, music, and the arts in the service of the ideals and goals of socialism and/or communism, with an emphasis in painting on the realistic portrayal of objects.

sonata [soh-NAH-tah] In music, an instrumental composition, usually in three or four movements.

sonata form A musical form or structure consisting of three (or sometimes four) sections that vary in key, tempo, and mood.

stained glass An art form characterized by many small pieces of tinted glass bound together by strips of lead, usually to produce a pictorial scene of a religious theme; developed by *Romanesque* artists and a central feature of *Gothic* churches.

stele [STEE-lee] A carved or inscribed vertical stone pillar or slab, often used for commemorative purposes.

Stoicism [STO-ih-sihz-uhm] The most popular and influential *Hellenistic* philosophy, advocating a restrained way of life, a toleration for others, a resignation to disappointments, and a resolution to carry out one's responsibilities; Stoicism appealed to many Romans and had an impact on early Christian thought.

stream-of-consciousness A writing technique used by some modern authors in which the narration consists of a character's continuous interior monologue of thoughts and feelings.

structuralism In *Post-Modernism*, an approach to knowledge based on the belief that human behavior and institutions can be explained by reference to a few underlying structures that themselves are reflections of hidden patterns in the human mind.

Sturm und Drang [STOORM-oont-drahng] German, "Storm and Stress"; a German literary movement of the 1770s that focused on themes of action, emotionalism, and the individual's revolt against the conventions of society.

studia humanitatis [STU-di-ah hu-man-ih-TAH-tis] (**humanistic studies**) The Latin term given by Renaissance scholars to new intellectual pursuits that were based on recently discovered ancient texts, including moral philosophy, history, grammar, rhetoric, and poetry. This new learning stood in sharp contrast to medieval *scholasticism*.

style galant [STEEL gah-LAHNN] In *Rococo* music, a style of music developed by French composers and characterized by graceful and simple melodies.

stylobate [STY-luh-bate] In Greek temples, the upper step of the base that forms a platform on which the columns stand.

Sublime [suh-BLIME] In *Romanticism,* the term used to describe nature as a terrifying and awesome force full of violence and power.

Suprematism [suh-PRIM-uh-tiz-uhm] A variation of abstract art, originating in Russia in the early twentieth century, characterized by the use of geometric shapes as the basic elements of the composition.

Surrealism [suh-REE-uhl-iz-uhm] An early-twentieth-century movement in art, literature, and theater, in which incongruous juxtapositions and fantastic images produce an irrational and dreamlike effect.

symbolic realism In art, a style that is realistic and true to life but uses the portrayed object or person to represent or symbolize something else.

symphony A long and complex *sonata*, usually written in three or four movements, for large *orchestras;* the first movement is traditional fast, the second slow, and the third or fourth movement fast.

syncopation [sin-ko-PAY-shun] In music, the technique of accenting the weak beat when a strong beat is expected.

syncretism [SIN-kruh-tiz-uhm] The combining of different forms of religious beliefs or practices.

synthesizer [SIN-thuh-size-uhr] An electronic apparatus with a keyboard capable of duplicating the sounds of many musical instruments, popular among *Post-Modernist* composers and musicians.

tabula rasa [TAB-yuh-luh RAH-zuh] "Erased tablet," the Latin term John Locke used to describe the mind at birth, empty of inborn ideas and ready to receive sense impressions, which Locke believed were the sole source of knowledge.

terza rima [TER-tsuh REE-muh] A three-line stanza with an interlocking rhyme scheme (aba bcb cdc ded, and so on), used by Dante in his *Divine Comedy.*

theater of the absurd A type of theater that has come to reflect the despair, anxieties, and absurdities of modern life and in which the characters seldom make sense, the plot is nearly nonexistent, bizarre and fantastic events occur on stage, and tragedy and comedy are mixed in unconventional ways; associated with *Late Modernism*.

theology The application of philosophy to the study of religious truth, focusing especially on the nature of the deity and the origin and teachings of an organized religious community.

tracery Ornamental architectural work with lines that branch out to form designs, often found as stone carvings in *rose windows*.

tragedy A serious and deeply moral drama, typically involving a noble protagonist and describing a conflict between seemingly irreconcilable values or forces; in Greece, tragedies were performed at the festivals associated with the worship of Dionysus.

transept In church architecture, the crossing arm that bisects the *nave* near the *apse* and gives the characteristic *cruciform* shape to the floor plan.

triglyph [TRY-glif] In Greek architecture, a three-grooved rectangular panel on the frieze of a *Doric* temple; triglyphs alternated with *metopes*.

trope [TROHP] In *Gregorian chants*, a new phrase or melody inserted into an existing chant to make it more musically appealing; also called a turn; in literature, a figure of speech.

troubador [TROO-buh-door] A composer and/or singer, usually an aristocrat, who performed secular love songs at the feudal courts in southern France.

twelve-tone scale In music, a fixed scale or series in which there is an arbitrary arrangement of the twelve tones (counting every half-tone) of an *octave*; devised by Arnold Schoenberg.

tympanum [TIM-puh-num] In medieval architecture, the arch over a doorway set above the lintel, usually decorated with carvings depicting biblical themes; in *Classical*-style architecture, the recessed face of a *pediment*.

Utilitarianism [yoo-til-uh-TARE-e-uh-niz-uhm] The doctrine set forth in the social theory of Jeremy Bentham in the nineteenth century that the final goal of society and humans was "the greatest good for the greatest number."

vanishing point In linear *perspective*, the point on the horizon at which the receding parallel lines appear to converge and then vanish.

vault A ceiling or roof made from a series of arches placed next to each other.

vernacular language [vuhr-NAK-yuh-luhr] The language or dialect of a region usually spoken by the general population as opposed to the wealthy or educated elite.

vernacular literature Literature written in the language of the populace, such as English, French, or Italian, as opposed to the language of the educated elite, usually Latin.

via antiqua [VIH-uh ahn-TEE-kwah] The "old way," the term used in late medieval thought by the opponents of St. Thomas Aquinas to describe his *via media*, which they considered outdated.

via media [VIH-uh MAY-dee-ah] The "middle way" that St. Thomas Aquinas sought in reconciling Aristotle's works to Christian beliefs.

via moderna [VIH-uh moh-DEHR-nah] The "new way," the term used in late medieval thought by those thinkers who opposed the school of Aquinas.

virtuoso [vehr-choo-O-so] An aristocratic person who experimented in science, usually as an amateur, in the seventeenth century, giving science respectability and a wider audience; later, in music, a person with great technical skill.

voussoir [voo-SWAR] A carved, wedge-shaped stone or block in an arch.

ziggurat [ZIG-oo-rat] A Mesopotamian stepped pyramid, usually built with external staircases and a shrine at the top.

For readers using the two-volume set of *The Western Humanities*, page numbers 1–327 refer to material in Volume I: *Beginnings Through the Renaissance* and 273–591 refer to material in Volume II: *The Renaissance to the Present*.

Chapter One   1.2, Ampliaciones y Reproducciones MAS, Barcelona; 1.3, Archiv für Kunst und Geschichte, Berlin; 1.4, From *The Sumerians* by Samuel Kramer. ©1963 University of Chicago Press; 1.6, Erich Lessing/Archiv für Kunst und Geschichte, Berlin; 1.7, Scala/Art Resource, New York; 1.8, Hirmer Fotoarchiv, Munich; 1.9, Hirmer Fotoarchiv, Munich; 1.10, PHOTRI Inc.; 1.11, From *People of the Earth* by Brian Fagan. Reprinted by permission of Harper Collins publishers; 1.12, ©Tim Schermerhorn; 1.13, Erich Lessing/Magnum; 1.14, Archiv für Kunst und Geschichte, Berlin; 1.17, Bildarchiv Preussischer Kulturbesitz, Berlin; 1.18, Hirmer Fotoarchiv, Munich; 1.20 © Lee Boltin.

Chapter Two   2.1, Hirmer Fotoarchiv, Munich; 2.2, The Ancient Art and Architecture Collection, London; 2.3, Scala/Art Resource, New York; 2.4, Erich Lessing/Magnum; 2.5, Hirmer Fotoarchiv, Munich; 2.6, Hirmer Fotoarchiv, Munich; 2.7, Hirmer Fotoarchiv, Munich; 2.8, Erich Lessing/Magnum; 2.12, SEF/Art Resource, New York; 2.13, Art Resource, New York; 2.15, C. M. Dixon, Canterbury; 2.16, Hirmer Fotoarchiv, Munich; 2.17, C. M. Dixon, Canterbury; 2.18, Hirmer Fotoarchiv, Munich; 2.19, Hirmer Fotoarchiv, Munich.

Chapter Three   3.1, Photo Nimatallah/Art Resource, New York; 3.2, Marburg/Art Resource, New York; 3.3, Hirmer Fotoarchiv, Munich; 3.5, Hirmer Fotoarchiv, Munich; 3.6, Erich Lessing/Magnum; 3.7, Photo Nimatallah/Art Resource, New York; 3.8, The Ancient Art and Architecture Collection, London; 3.12, The Granger Collection, New York; 3.13, C. M. Dixon, Canterbury; 3.14, The Ancient Art and Architecture Collection, London; 3.15, Scala/Art Resource, New York; 3.16, Hirmer Fotoarchiv, Munich; 3.17, Hirmer Fotoarchiv, Munich; 3.18, Hirmer Fotoarchiv, Munich; 3.19, Marburg/Art Resource, New York; 3.20 Erich Lessing/Archiv für Kunst und Geschichte, Berlin; 3.21, Hirmer Fotoarchiv, Munich; 3.22, From *Greek Architecture* by Roland Martin. ©1980 Electa/Rizzoli New York. Drawing by Pepi Merisio; 3.24, Photo Nimatallah/Art Resource, New York; 3.25, Hirmer Fotoarchiv, Munich.

Chapter Four   4.3, From *Greek Society* by Frank Frost. ©1987, D C Heath and Company; 4.5, Alinari/Art Resource, New York; 4.7, Hirmer Fotoarchiv, Munich; 4.8, C. M. Dixon, Canterbury; 4.9, Marburg/Art Resource, New York; 4.10 Erich Lessing/Magnum; 4.12, Archiv für Kunst und Geschichte, Berlin; 4.13, The Bridgeman Art Library, London; 4.14, Photo Nimatallah/Art Resource, New York; 4.15, Hirmer Fotoarchiv, Munich; 4.16, Scala/Art Resource, New York; 4.17, Archiv für Kunst und Geschichte, Berlin.

Chapter Five   5.1, Scala/Art Resource, New York; 5.2, Alinari/Art Resource, New York; 5.3, Alinari/Art Resource, New York; 5.4, Alinari/Art Resource, New York; 5.5, Leonard von Matt, Buochs, Switzerland; 5.6, Hirmer Fotoarchiv, Munich; 5.7, Fototeca Unione, Rome; 5.8, Scala/Art Resource, New York; 5.9, Archiv für Kunst und Geschichte, Berlin; 5.10 The Ancient Art and Architecture Collection, London; 5.12, Giraudon/Art Resource, New York; 5.13, Alinari/Art Resource, New York; 5.14, Leonard von Matt, Buochs, Switzerland; 5.15, Fototeca Unione, Rome; 5.16, Scala/Art Resource, New York; 5.17, Scala/Art Resource, New York; 5.18, Fototeca Unione, Rome; 5.19, Fototeca Unione, Rome; 5.20 Lionel Isy-Schwart/The Image Bank; 5.21, C. M. Dixon, Canterbury; 5.23, Archiv für Kunst und Geschichte, Berlin; 5.24, Alinari/Art Resource, New York; 5.25, The Ancient Art and Architecture Collection, London; 5.26, Scala/Art Resource, New York; 5.27, Scala/Art Resource, New York; 5.28, Scala/Art Resource, New York; 5.29, Archiv für Kunst und Geschichte, Berlin; 5.30 Erich Lessing/Magnum.

Chapter Six   6.2, The Bettmann Archive; 6.3, Erich Lessing/Magnum; 6.4, ©Richard Nowitz; 6.7, ©Paul W. Lapp; 6.8, Zev Radovan, Jerusalem; 6.9, Zev Radovan, Jerusalem; 6.10 ©Carl Purcell; 6.11, Scala/Art Resource, New York; 6.12, Hirmer Fotoarchiv, Munich; 6.13, Scala/Art Resource, New York; 6.14, Erich Lessing/Magnum.

Chapter Seven   7.1, Hirmer Fotoarchiv, Munich; 7.2, Scala/Art Resource, New York; 7.3, Erich Lessing/Archiv für Kunst und Geschichte; 7.4, C. M. Dixon, Canterbury; 7.5, Scala/Art Resource, New York; 7.7, From *Roman Imperial Architecture* by J. B. Ward-Perkins. The Pelican History of Art, 1981. ©J. B. Ward-Perkins, 1970, 1981; 7.8, ©E. Michael Fisher; 7.9, -Archiv für Kunst und Geschichte, Berlin; 7.10 From *Drawings of Great Buildings* by W. Blaser and 0. Hannaford. Reprinted with the permission of Birkhäuser Verlag, Basel; 7.11, Archiv für Kunst und Geschichte, Berlin; 7.12, Alinari/Art Resource, New York; 7.13, Scala/Art Resource, New York; 7.14, ©1991 ARS New York/SPADEM; 7.15, Gabinetto Fotografico Nazionale, Rome; 7.16, C. M. Dixon, Canterbury; 7.17, German Archaeological Institute, Rome; 7.18, Alinari/Art Resource, New York; 7.20 Erich Lessing/Magnum; 7.21, Hirmer Fotoarchiv, Munich.

Chapter Eight   8.1, C. M. Dixon, Canterbury; 8.2, Archiv für Kunst und Geschichte, Berlin; 8.3, Centre d'Etudes Gabriel Millet, Ecole Pratique des Hautes Etudes, Paris; 8.4, Costa Manos/Magnum; 8.5, Erich Lessing/Magnum; 8.6, Scala/Art Resource, New York; 8.7, Scala/Art Resource, New York; 8.8, Archiv für Kunst und Geschichte, Berlin; 8.9, Foto Hinz, Allschwil, Switzerland; 8.10 Werner Forman Archives, London; 8.11, Ampliaciones y Reproducciones MAS, Barcelona; 8.13, C. M. Dixon, Canterbury; 8.14, The Ancient Art and Architecture Collection, London; 8.15, Courtesy Uitgeverij Het Spectrum BV 1974; 8.16, Courtesy Marian Moffett; 8.18, Rheinisches Bildarchiv/Museen der Stadt Koln; 8.21, Marburg/Art Resource, New York.

Chapter Nine   9.1, Archiv für Kunst und Geschichte, Berlin; 9.2, Hirmer Fotoarchiv, Munich; 9.4, The Bridgeman Art Library, London; 9.5, The Bettmann Archive; 9.6, Scala/Art Resource, New York; 9.7, Giraudon/Art Resource, New York; 9.8, Giraudon/Art Resource, New York; 9.9, From *Drawings of Great Buildings* by W. Blaser and O. Hannaford. Reprinted with the permission of Birkhäuser Verlag, Basel; 9.10 Giraudon/Art Resource, New York; 9.11, Courtesy Lawrence Wodehouse; 9.12, ©1991 ARS New York/SPADEM; 9.13, Hirmer Fotoarchiv, Munich; 9.16, Hirmer Fotoarchiv, Munich; 9.17, From *Gardner's Art Through the Ages*, sixth edition, by Horst de la Croix and Richard G. Tansey, ©1975 by Harcourt Brace Jovanovich, Inc. reprinted by permission of the publisher; 9.18, From *Drawings of Great Buildings* by W. Blaser and O. Hannaford. Reprinted with the permission of Birkhäuser Verlag, Basel; 9.19, Hirmer Fotoarchiv, Munich; 9.20 The Ancient Art and Architecture Collection, London; 9.21, The Ancient Art and Architecture Collection, London; 9.22, Hirmer Fotoarchiv, Munich; 9.23, Hirmer Fotoarchiv, Munich; 9.24, ©1991 ARS New York/SPADEM; 9.25, Giraudon/Art Resource, New York; 9.26, From *Drawings of Great Buildings* by W. Blaser and O. Hannaford. Reprinted with the permission of Birkhäuser Verlag, Basel; 9.27, Hirmer Fotoarchiv, Munich; 9.28, Hirmer Fotoarchiv, Munich.

Chapter Ten   10.1, Giraudon/Art Resource, New York; 10.2, Ampliaciones y Reproducciones MAS, Barcelona; 10.3, Giraudon/Art Resource, New York; 10.5, Archiv für Kunst und Geschichte, Berlin; 10.7, ©1991 ARS New York/SPADEM; l0.8, Scala/Art Resource, New York; 10.9, Scala/Art Resource, New York; 10.10 Scala/Art Resource, New York; 10.11, The Ancient Art and Architecture Collection, London; 10.12, Scala/Art Resource, New York; 10.13, Scala/Art Resource, New York; 10.14, Kavaler/Art Resource, New York; 10.15, Archiv für Kunst und Geschichte, Berlin; 10.16, Art Resource, New York; 10.17, Archiv für Kunst und Geschichte, Berlin; 10.18, Scala/Art Resource, New York; 10.19, Scala/Art Resource, New York; 10.20 The Bridgeman Art Library, London.